PERFORMANCE IMPROVEMENT INTERVENTIONS: ENHANCING PEOPLE, PROCESSES, AND ORGANIZATIONS THROUGH PERFORMANCE TECHNOLOGY

Darlene M. Van Tiem
University of Michigan - Dearborn

James L. Moseley
Wayne State University

Joan Conway Dessinger
The Lake Group

International Society for Performance Improvement
Silver Spring, MD, 2001

Performance Improvement Interventions
Enhancing People, Processes, and Organizations through Performance Technology

© 2001, by the International Society for Performance Improvement

ISBN: 1-890289-12-4

Published by
International Society for Performance Improvement
1400 Spring Street
Suite 260
Silver Spring, MD 20910
301.587.8570
Fax: 301.587.8573

Visit our website at www.ispi.org. To order books, log on to www.ispi.org/bookstore.

About ISPI

Founded in 1962, the International Society for Performance Improvement (ISPI) is the leading international association dedicated to improving productivity and performance in the workplace. ISPI represents more than 10,000 international and chapter members throughout the United States, Canada, and 40 other countries. ISPI's mission is to develop and recognize the proficiency of our members and advocate the use of Human Performance Technology (HPT). Assembling an Annual Conference & Expo and other educational events—including the award-winning HPT Institutes—publishing several periodicals, supporting research, and producing a full line of publications and resources are some of the ways ISPI works toward achieving this mission. For more information, please write ISPI, 1400 Spring Street, Suite 260, Silver Spring, MD 20910; phone: 301.587.8570; fax: 301.587.8573; email: info@ispi.org; web: www.ispi.org.

*"Writing a book is an adventure; to begin with,
it is a toy and an amusement, then it becomes a master,
and then it becomes a tyrant; and the last phase
is just as you are about to be reconciled to your servitude—
you kill the monster and fling it— to the public."*

—Sir Winston Churchill

This book is dedicated to:

Phillip Van Tiem
DVT

Raelene and Mark Bugaj and the memory of my parents
JLM

Gary Dessinger and Joy Wilkins
JCD

TABLE OF CONTENTS

TABLE OF CONTENTS

TABLE OF CONTENTS

TABLE OF CONTENTS

TABLES

TABLES

TABLES

FIGURES

JOB AIDS

JOB AIDS

FOREWORD

Performance Improvement Interventions: Enhancing People, Processes, and Organizations through Performance Technology may just be the only book you will ever need about putting a Human Performance Technology (HPT) organization into action. It covers just about everything. It not only tells in great detail what to do, but it also explains how to do it, then goes on to provide the tools to accomplish it.

The first thing that has to impress you when you begin to delve into this book is the amazing synthesis of information. The authors list all of the sources they used to develop their concept of the HPT Model—from B.F. Skinner's theory of human behavior to Douglas McGregor's Theory X and Theory Y. I'm quite certain that when most of these writers contributed to their disciplines, they never imagined that one day they would be adding to the field of HPT.

I was gratified to see that Darlene, Jim, and Joan took the time to explain how all of their sources contributed to HPT theory! Not many books take the time to fully explain the grounding of the discipline. Some of the theories included in their model include human resources, training, organizational development, career development, psychology, quality management, ergonomics, and financial systems. A lot of readers will skip over the theory sections of most books because they are "too esoteric." They "just want the facts." Most publishers won't publish books with "too much theory" for fear readers will not buy them. I congratulate both the authors and ISPI for being so perceptive. As W. Edwards Deming, one of the listed theorists, said, "You must understand theory. It is the only thing that allows you to ask the right questions." Not understanding theory is the reason, in my estimation, that HPT efforts often fall short of expectation. Practitioners often miss asking that one important question that leads to a deeper level of understanding of the business issue. Understanding theory would have intuitively led them to ask that question.

The authors draw attention to the fact that the HPT Model is a return to the craftsman era when businessmen were experts in their field, took pride in their work, and maintained quality by limiting the number of people who entered the craft. A silver smith and apprentice of the 1700s in America would never have had to take a course in customer service. It was hammered into the silver with the pride of having produced it. Why did corporations ever desert that model? Oh, yes, the Industrial Revolution! Assembly line mass production has probably had the greatest impact on the deterioration in workmanship in products and deterioration of customer service. I think of the factory worker in a major automobile assembly plant who, upon retirement, was asked what the first thing he was going to do after retirement. He responded, "I'm going to walk down to the other end of this assembly line and see what comes out the other end."

This book is important because most of the world is no longer in a manufacturing environment where lack of knowledge of the part-to-whole relationship is acceptable. Only 100 years ago, 80% of all work was mechanical and 20% intellectual. Today, the exact opposite is true. That means employees cannot work in isolation. They have to have a broader picture of what is happening in their organization and how what they do impacts everyone else. As organizations become more complex, so is the task of making certain everyone knows and appreciates the organizational goals of the company.

The complexity of engineering worthy performance should come through these pages along with the realization that an organization will probably never find the "superman" who embodies all of these areas of specialized knowledge. Moving from a training department to an HPT function sounds the death knell for the one-person training department. This book will help organizations determine the areas of expertise they need to find and/or develop.

The book also addresses why HPT is so complex. With training all you have to think about are the "activities." HPT requires thinking "systemically." The HPT professional must be integrated at the strategic level of a corporation, not just be an "order-taker" serving up management's decisions.

The HPT Model from analysis through evaluation forms the foundation of the book but what's in between is filled with such topics as the importance of communication, the structure of the HPT organization, knowledge management, employee selection, financial systems, recognition, and technology. You can expect this book to help readers recognize the impact of almost any workplace activity and it is designed to be a "desk reference" of performance solution opportunities, even containing discussions of such topics as hiring, retirement, compensation, and the cost of turnover.

The treatment of knowledge management is very impressive and comprehensive. It is good to have the valuable resource companies lose when experienced employees leave pointed out. The coverage of technology as the receptacle and delivery mechanism for knowledge, information, and communication is very pointed and contains a lot of common sense.

The numerous case studies interspersed throughout the book demonstrate how the various tools can be used within each phase of the process. They show the practical application of the concepts the authors put forth.

William W. Lee

Director of Performance Technology
American Airlines Corporate FlagShip University

ACKNOWLEDGMENTS

As the companion book to *Fundamentals of Performance Technology: A Guide to Improving People, Process, and Performance*, this book is a continuation of an effort that began in the fall of 1998. At that time, it was apparent that graduate students and people entering the field needed a book to help them understand the scope and practice of performance technology. Clearly, the Rosenberg and Deterline HPT Model was useful and credible. Many students and practitioners also appreciated the International Society for Performance Technology flyer, "What is HPT?" However, they needed more detail to use the model, some information on theory, how-to examples, and steps to implement performance technology and practice in the field.

Jim, Joan, and I realized that we could not do justice to the complexity of interventions and the inter-relationship among interventions in a book focused on the HPT Model. As a result, we wrote this companion book, *Performance Improvement Interventions: Enhancing People, Processes, and Organizations through Performance Technology*, to focus on solutions to performance problems. As lead author, I realize that it is rare for a writing team to stick together for over two years. We live near each other and have been colleagues and friends for many years. We all received our doctoral degrees from Wayne State University. With great respect for each other and extraordinary appreciation for the uniqueness of each individual, we have remained friends.

Fortunately, the Detroit area has many companies, governmental organizations, universities, and vendors active in the performance technology field. There is significant support for the International Society for Performance Improvement (ISPI) and its performance improvement leadership. Three major Detroit area organizations have corporate memberships in ISPI. In addition, the Michigan Chapter of ISPI has won numerous national awards for leadership and excellence. Two universities, University of Michigan-Dearborn and Wayne State University, have major coursework in performance technology. In other words, this energy and enthusiasm for performance improvement generates willingness to help develop case studies, provide cartoons, and write rough drafts of chapters.

TABLE i-1: ISPI Corporate Memberships in the Detroit Area

Maritz Performance Improvement	Advocate	Regional Office
GP (General Physics)	Patron	Regional Office
Triad Performance Technologies	Patron	Headquarters

Student and Graphics Contributions

Students provide new energy by challenging assumptions, providing examples, and figuring out new professional applications of performance technology. University of Michigan-Dearborn students wrote the initial drafts of six sections of the book. Wayne State University students created specific case studies. In addition, another University of Michigan-Dearborn student developed a helpful job aid on team effectiveness. Their academic research and independent study helped create a framework for writing the chapters.

TABLE i-2: Student Authorship Support

Student	Topic
Joyce Katona	HPT Model
Judy Gohl	Individual Growth
Judy Gohl	Personal Growth
Judy Gohl	Empowerment
Margaret Korosec	Organizational Values

Humor helps us take a second look and avoid rigid assumptions. A University of Michigan-Dearborn student, Jed Vier, and his associate, Buck Jones, design and publish daily cartoons for the American Greetings web site. Jed and Buck provided cartoons for each chapter to lighten the cognitive complexity of this interventions book.

Triad Performance Technologies, Inc. designed the cover to be a companion cover to the first book, *Fundamentals of Performance Technology*. Paul Burry and Antonio Drommi provided informational resources. Finally, we thank Annetta Ellis for typing sections of the original manuscript.

Case Studies

The concept of blending multiple interventions to solve performance improvement problems is relatively unexplored. However, performance technology integrates interventions from distinct areas such as human resources, engineering and human factors, accounting and finance, organizational development, and many other areas of study. As a result, the scope and involvement of colleagues is much wider for this book.

Case studies illustrate the intervention concepts and processes. They were selected as successful applications. Case study writing is challenging because it is difficult to describe a situation with objectivity and to attain agreement that the description is honest and accurate. Many colleagues helped write the cases from a wide range of organizations. In addition, there is a mega-case study designed to illustrate application of the job aids. This megastudy involved a primary writer, Mim Munzel, with many others in the Arbor Consulting Group adding information and suggestions.

TABLE i-3: Case Studies by Chapter

Chapter Title	Intervention/Focus	Work Site	Source
HPT Model	HPT Model Application	Anonymous	Joyce Katona
Instructional Systems	Knowledge Management	Atlantic Richfield Company (ARCO)/BP Amoco	Joan Dessinger
Non-Instructional Systems	Standards	Anonymous home building company	Joan Dessinger
Job Analysis	Job Description/Specification	Proprietary School	James Moseley
Work Design	Job Design	Injection Molding	David A. Grant
Human Factors	Safety Engineering	Ford Motor Company	UAW-Ford Joint Comm. on Health and Safety with Moseley and Dessinger
Quality Improvement	TQM	Mt. Clemens General Hospital	Lee Holmberg
Personal Development	Mentoring	Ford Motor Company Engineering	Judy Gohl
HR Systems	Employee Development	Opus One Restaurant	Maria and James Kokas
Individual Growth	Performance Appraisal	Flint Ink	Tom Emerson
Organizational Growth	Management/Supervisor Development	Frank's Nursery and Crafts	Maria Kokas
Organizational Communication	Information System	Anonymous urban cancer institute	David Maier
Empowerment	Decision Making	Mott Community College	Kelly Banks
Organizational Pro-Action	Restructuring	Mann+Hummel	Margaret Korosec
Organizational Values	Culture	Interior Systems Contract Group	Billie Jo Wanink
Financial Systems	Cash Flow Analysis	Stratford Tool and Die	Alan P. Witucki
Overall Interventions	Mega Case Study	Arbor Consulting Group	Mim Munzel

Advisors

Paul deSousa (Bellisle Company), Ben St. Clair (St. Clair and Associates), Jerry Kaminski (Independent Consultant), and Sunny Gillett (Sunny Gillett Training Services, Inc.) provided critiques and advice regarding the assessment tool. They focused on making the tool right for their own consulting needs, which should translate to "right for PT practitioners' needs." Rosalie Rishavy, coordinator of mediation for the Equal Employment Opportunity Commission, helped secure information regarding diversity. Due to Rosalie's efforts there is extensive information on audits and programs to improve situations in the workplace.

Mary Beth Kinsel read our first chapters and provided advice. Mary Beth is pursuing her graduate degree in secondary English education. She provided insight into the response of people unfamiliar with the field, but familiar with related fields.

ISPI Support

We are indebted to Matthew Davis, former Director of Publications for ISPI, for not recognizing the folly of having three authors for a second time. In short, he encouraged us to enhance the performance technology field with a companion book, complete with an assessment tool. When Matt left to become a senior editor at Jossey-Bass/Pfeiffer, April Syring Davis helped us move the book from manuscript to published work. Finally, we appreciate the efforts of our editor, Kate Kuhn, for her flexibility, insight, and exactness.

Darlene Van Tiem
January 2001

CHAPTER

SYSTEMATIC AND REPRODUCIBLE SOLUTIONS

THE WORLD'S TOP SCIENTISTS GET TOGETHER
TO DETERMINE <u>EXACTLY</u> WHY THE CHICKEN
CROSSED THE ROAD.

INTERVENTIONS AS SOLUTIONS

"America is a nation where creative approaches yield real solutions to our problems… It's clear to me that performance technology is just such an approach."

—President George Bush[1]

Work and the workplace have changed dramatically in the past 200 years. As the Industrial Era emerged in the 1800s, people began working in large groups and living in large communities. The isolation, independence, and importance of farming diminished, as did the role of craftspeople in small towns who supported agriculture. Industry brought large-scale machinery operated by large work forces. The industrial workplace emphasized work design and quality.

Work Design

Work, work processes, and job design took on great importance as people began working together in factories. Efficiency was the goal. The ability to coordinate and control hundreds of employees in one location led to product dominance and business success. For example, many small companies could build automobiles; but only Henry Ford, with his assembly line, could create vehicles that were affordable by the "common man."[2] Maximizing the capability of a large work force was a significant competitive advantage.

Quality

As time went on, the ability to coordinate and control workers was not enough. Competitive advantage now moved to the quality of the product. Employers measured value by the ability to provide customers with timely, innovative, defect-free merchandise at a reasonable cost. The quality movement flourished and helped unify work practices globally. For 30 years, American quality guru W. Edwards Deming helped Japan improve its product quality, and he spearheaded efforts to produce items with little variation and extraordinary reliability.[3] American companies also learned how to maximize quality from Deming and others.

Information

Optimizing information became the next competitive edge. Data became readily available for analysis, problem solving, and decision making. Developers wrote software to integrate work, thereby increasing accuracy, reducing time and cost, and extending predictions and planning. For example, Thomas Watson at IBM envisioned the value of computers and helped incorporate them universally in organizations.[4] Bill Gates enabled information to be readily available and usable throughout the world.[5]

The Information Era has ushered in changes of similar magnitude to the Industrial Revolution. The workplace now focuses on information and the people who add value to information. Just as industrial machinery was automated to improve its functionality, much has been done to automate information through software, hardware, and Internet innovation. The Information Era brings increasing recognition of the value of people as integrators and users of information.

People

It is now apparent that truly great organizations realize the value of people and maximize their potential.[6] All the efficient machinery operation, quality control, and information access in the world does not make an organization outstanding. People, with their skills, knowledge, motivation, values, and dreams, make organizations thrive and prosper. For instance, Jack Welsh, CEO of General Electric, harnessed the value of people to make a world-renowned, competitive, innovative, energized organization.[7] He accomplished this through personal involvement in management training, product and strategy review "workouts," and communication.

Performance Technology

Just as work design, quality, and information require continuous commitment to achieve maximum competitiveness, integrating performance solutions needs unwavering attention, as well. Performance technology (PT) is the science and art of improving people, process, and performance. "…Performance technology is a set of methods and procedures, and a strategy for solving

TABLE 1-1: Gilbert's Behavior Engineering Model

Information	Instrumentation	Motivation	
Data	**Instruments**	**Incentives**	
• Relevant and frequent feedback • Performance descriptions • Clear and relevant guides to performance	• Tools and materials of work to match human factors	• Financial incentives • Nonmonetary incentives • Career development opportunities	**→ Rooted in the Environment**
Knowledge	**Capacity**	**Motives**	
• Scientifically designed training • Placement	• Flexible scheduling of performance • Prosthesis • Physical shaping • Adaptation • Selection	• Assessment of motives to work • Recruitment of the right people	**→ Rooted in the Individual Worker**

Based on Gilbert, 1978.

problems, or realizing opportunities related to the performance of people. It can be applied to individuals, small groups, and large organizations."[8] According to *Webster's Dictionary*, technology refers to standardized methods or processes used to handle problems.[9] PT is based on widely accepted, common practices using quantitative and qualitative analytical methods for decisions.

Thomas Gilbert, the founder of performance technology,[10] described people's behavior in terms of "worthy [or worthwhile] performance." His Behavior Engineering Model (see Table 1-1) focuses on environmental support and the employee's repertory of behavior, and it establishes the framework for performance improvement outcomes and PT.[11]

Integrating Science and Art

PT is a science because analytical processes and methods are the bases for selecting and implementing solutions, known as interventions. Yet, it is also an art because it requires intuition and creativity regarding people, with all of their values, emotions, idiosyncrasies, and variability.

Most readers have varying experience with people-related disciplines, such as human resources, training, organizational development, career development, psychology, quality, or ergonomics. Many readers suspect or believe that any of the previously listed disciplines, applied singularly, rarely solves performance problems, especially complex problems. PT meshes ideas and theories from many disciplines and is a comprehensive approach.[12] Table 1-2 illustrates the disciplines that are most influential to PT.

PT Leading Contributors

Many experts have shaped the field of PT (see Table 1-3). Although each expert focused and refined a particular knowledge area, PT practitioners need to integrate their contributions to provide a background for the field. PT applies the knowledge and models of many experts by fitting their ideas, as subsets, into the human performance technology (HPT) model. Although Table 1-3 is extensive, it is only a selected list of the contributions of experts.

Interventions

Interventions are planned measures designed and developed to alleviate or solve problems in the workplace, thus affecting job performance. They cause change, small or large, due to improved performance. Interventions influence individuals, groups, or organizations. The number of possible interventions is almost infinite, because any number of organizational, environmental, and people factors affect performance.

PT applies the HPT Model (see Figure 1-1) to solve job-related problems. Following analysis of the performance problem and its cause, sufficient data should be available to select and design solutions, known as interventions. Solutions facilitate change by interrupting poor behaviors, preventing errors, reducing conflict, or providing vision for the future. This book covers an overview of the HPT Model. However, it is explained in detail in the companion book, *Fundamentals of Performance Technology: A Guide to Improving People, Process, and Performance.*[13]

Strategic Partner

PT practitioners, like all human resources professionals, need to partner with operational and staff units.[14] The PT practitioner's role needs to be strategic, not as an employee champion. PT practitioners help solve critical business issues. They design interventions that are aligned to business objectives. They consult as a member of the management team, contributing to business decisions. They participate on business task forces and lead change efforts. Using systems thinking, they redesign organizations and processes and reengineer workplaces.

TABLE 1-2: Theoretical Foundation of Performance Technology

Discipline	Focus	Contribution
Behaviorism	Predicting behavior	• Small steps of instruction and feedback • Learn to manipulate and control the environment by the individual's responses to it
Diagnostic and Analytical Systems	Data as basis for understanding behavior	• Practitioners use comprehensive analytical tools • Diagnosis is based on gap (difference between desired and actual situation) • Causes of situation are defined before intervention is selected and implemented
Instructional Systems Design and Organizational Learning	ADDIE (analysis, design, development, implementation, and evaluation) model, forerunner of HPT model	• Developed in 1940s and 1950s, responding to need to train thousands of military personnel during World War II • Various instructional methods were found to be valuable, such as role play, video, case study, and lecture
Organizational Design (OD) and Change Management	Changing performance at organizational and individual levels	• OD interventions improve culture, group dynamics, and structure of the organization • Change management helps individuals and groups adapt to change through timely information, appropriate resources, and strategies for resistance, and turmoil that accompanies change • Theoretical basis includes systems dynamics, human motivation, group and team dynamics, competency modeling, organizational learning systems, and feedback systems
Evaluation	Determining value and impact of interventions	• Produces credibility that practitioners need • Real costs against real savings attained by organization, return on investment (ROI)
Management Sciences	Dividing "thinkers" and "doers" and analyzing and describing jobs and tasks	• Theories led to standardized production system, such as Henry Ford's assembly line • Emphasis evolved to physical and psychological issues, such as motivation, job satisfaction, professional growth, and empowerment

Based on Sanders and Ruggles, 2000, pp. 26–36.

TABLE 1-3: Leading Contributors in Performance Technology

Leader	Field	Focus	Contribution
Chris Argyris	Action Science	Reflection and inquiry on the reasoning that underlies people's actions	• Developed concepts of learning organization, double-loop learning, and feedback systems • "Coined the term *skilled incompetence* to explain how defensive behavior and the fear of collective inquiry by management may protect us from threat or embarrassment but also may block learning" (p. 31) • Pioneered team building with upper management
Benjamin Bloom	Educational Technology	Hierarchical taxonomy of intellectual objectives based on what learners are supposed to do	• Vary instruction according to learner requirements and difficulty of cognitive domain level
W. Edwards Deming	Total Quality Management (TQM)	Emphasized quality rather than production targets	• "14 points" model of quality • Statistician who helped turn around Japanese economy after World War II
Peter Drucker	Management Sciences	Businesses are human centers as well as economic centers; work must have social meaning	• Developed concepts of decentralized large organizations, management by objectives, and role of the knowledge worker • Coined phased *self-governing plant community* proposing that many managerial responsibilities should be undertaken by individual employees or work teams

Robert Gagné	Instructional Systems Design	Task analysis and sequencing tasks	• Created Information Processing Model and Nine Events of Instruction
			• "Learners need to receive feedback on individualized tasks in order to correct isolated problems" (p. 32)
			• HPT needs to deal with multiple rather than serial objectives
			• Five types of learning:
			  1. Psychomotor skills
			  2. Verbal information
			  3. Intellectual skills
			  4. Cognitive strategies
			  5. Attitudes

Thomas Gilbert	Behavioral Engineering	Founded the field of human performance technology	• Behavioral Engineering Model focuses on changing work environment aspects such as information, resources, incentives, knowledge, capacity, and motives to improve performance • "Absence of performance support (not skills and knowledge) is the greatest block to exemplary work performance" (p. 32)
Joe Harless	Front-End Analysis	Diagnose problem early because problem cause often dictates solution	• Coined the phase *front-end analysis* to describe the rigorous diagnostic framework applied prior to addressing solutions • Analysis can be conducted by employee teams

TABLE 1-3: Leading Contributors in Performance Technology *Continued*

Leader	Field	Focus	Contribution
Roger Kaufman	Strategic Planning	Addresses mega (societal), macro (organizational), and micro (individual) levels	• Enchanced Kirkpatrick's four-level evaluation model to include intervention strategies
Donald Kirkpatrick	Evaluation	Four-levels of evaluation criteria (reaction, learning, behavior, and results)	• Clarified role of evaluation relative to HPT and training
Malcolm Knowles	Androgogy	Adult learning needs to be "lifelong" and ideally should involve "learning contracts"	Adults need to: 1. Self-direct their own learning 2. Know the purpose of what they're learning 3. Apply their relevant experiences to learning 4. Require a problem-centered approach
Kurt Lewin	Force Field Analysis	Force field assesses human behavior in terms of opposing forces (driving and restraining) that motivate action	• Performance improvement occurs when restraining forces are reduced • "Participative management" linked Taylor's scientific thinking with democratic values • Three-stage organizational change process: 1. Unfreezing old behavior 2. Moving to new level of behavior 3. Refreezing the new behavior
Robert Mager	Instructional Objectives	Instructional objectives should describe what learners will be able to do and represent improved performance	• Created performance analysis flowchart with Peter Pipe
Douglas McGregor	Theory X & Y	'X management style' is repressive, authoritarian, fearful 'Y management style' is optimistic, creative, and independent	• Metaphors for master and servant polarity • Pioneered industrial relations
Susan Markle	Programmed Instruction	Developed concept of programmed instruction following experiments with Skinner's "teaching box"	• Three types of learning necessary for programmed instruction: discriminations, generalizations, and chains (series of simple responses to form a sequence) • Programmed Learning Model combines operant conditioning, cognitive learning, with information gathering (developed with Philip Tiemann)
Geary Rummler	Three Levels of Organizational Performance	Three levels: organizational, process, and individual job or performer	• Emphasized the importance of improving process, which he called the "white spaces"

TABLE 1-3: Leading Contributors in Performance Technology *Continued*

Leader	Field	Focus	Contribution
Peter Senge	Learning Organization	Five critical practices for creating a learning organization: 1. Personal mastery 2. Mental models 3. Shared vision 4. Team learning 5. Systems thinking	• Pioneered systems-oriented approach to achieving high performance
B. F. Skinner	Behaviorism	Small-step instruction, followed by extensive feedback, enhances learning	• Behavioral theories fundamental to human performance technology and instructional design
Frederick Taylor	Scientific Management	Integration of methods, policies, planning, and people	• Scientific management principles include: 1. Authority based on knowledge instead of position 2. The first wage incentive system 3. Breaking down tasks into smaller components 4. Creation of a productivity expert • Laid the foundation for the modern assembly line
Sivasailam (Thiagi) Thiagarajan	Games and Playfulness	Integrated playfulness, person-to-person interaction, and experiential learning	• Elevated serious play, games, and fun as performance interventions
Donald Tosti	Feedback	Critical characteristics of feedback are tied to who gives it, the content, where and when it is given	• Specialized in applying human performance technology to organizational change culture
Marvin Weisbord	Six Boxes	Organizational diagnostic framework composed of six critical areas: 1. Purpose 2. Structure 3. Leadership 4. Relationships 5. Rewards 6. Helpful Mechanisms	• Widely used in organizational development

Based on Sanders and Ruggles, 2000, pp. 26–36.

What to Expect in This Book

Performance Improvement Interventions: Enhancing People, Processes, and Organizations through Performance Technology is a compendium of interventions based on the HPT Model. It is designed as a desk reference of performance solution opportunities. Like a Sears or J.C. Penney's catalog, there is something for almost any need and nearly every occasion. The intent is to identify and explain common interventions. Each intervention has at least two headings, "definition and scope" and "implementation," plus one job aid to assist the reader in applying the intervention. Each section or cluster of interventions contains one case study to help the reader visualize implementation and its impact on the workplace.

One goal of this book is to help readers recognize and anticipate the performance impact of almost any workplace activity. Some interventions may be common concepts but are unfamiliar as interventions, such as strategic planning, globalization, profit-versus-cost centers, or value engineering. At times, activities are carried out or innovations are adopted without thinking through the impact on the organizational culture, group dynamics, or worker's behavior. For example, senior officers complete a strategic plan and convey this vision only to executives. However, if the strategic plan is communicated throughout the work force, it can affect job performance and decisions within the entire organization. Likewise, globalization is often a high-level strategy. Yet, each employee can use this global frame of reference consistently when making decisions and taking actions.

Finally, the book also contains a tool called Intervention Selection Process. Due to the enormity of intervention options and the complexity of interfaces between the interventions, the tool contains individual and group stages. Successful implementation requires consensus among (at least leaders and representatives of) affected parties. Therefore, the group phase is essential. However, due to the complexity of intervention options, each group member needs to prepare independently. Each group member should individually measure options against his or her own personal values and the organization's values, goals, mission, processes, plus the group's dynamics.

HUMAN PERFORMANCE TECHNOLOGY (HPT) MODEL

Have you ever pondered, "What is happening that I wish wouldn't?" or "What isn't occurring that I wish would occur?" If you have ever uttered these words, you may well be on your way to understanding the need for PT.

What Is Performance Technology?

PT improves performance in the workplace, making the organization and the workplace better. The HPT Model provides the map. In simple terms, if PT practitioners follow the model, they will arrive at their desired performance improvement destination. The results achieved will be an effective organization with a skilled and competent work force.

PT is "the systematic process of linking business goals and strategies with the work force responsible for achieving the goals."[1] It involves, ideally, a "marriage" between an organization's decision makers (upper management or executives) and the performance improvement staff, such as PT practitioner, organizational development professional, internal consultant, or training and development specialist. To link business goals and strategies with the work force responsible for achieving the goals, manage-ment must set forth clear performance expectations. Once expectations are conveyed, all parties must make a conscious, shared decision that using the PT concepts will be a top priority. Otherwise, it is likely that the half-hearted organizational attempt to improve will ultimately fail.

Why the HPT Model?

PT practitioners use the HPT Model as a diagnostic and strategic tool for improving workplace performance. Following the HPT Model has several advantages. It provides insight into gaps in an organization's performance, such as revenue loss, delivery delays, or staffing mismatches. By using the HPT Model, organizations can fine-tune internal systems and processes and maximize their human capital. HPT enables optimal employee performance by ensuring that appropriate individuals are assigned to and fulfill specific organizational roles by matching employee skill sets to functional job titles.

When a mismatch occurs between employees and their jobs, employees become discouraged and, all too often, they perform their job tasks incorrectly or at substandard levels. Employees are then more likely to leave an organization if they experience job dissatisfaction. "When a key person leaves, businesses experience tremendous hurt and dislocation, resulting in lost business and lower margins."[2] Often senior management underestimates the impact and consequences of employee turnover, which can "cost as much as three to five times the annual salary of the individual involved."[3]

HPT Model Overview

The companion book, *Fundamentals of Performance Technology: A Guide to Improving People, Process, and Performance*, fully discusses the HPT Model (see Figure 1-1). The remainder of this chapter is an overview of the

HPT Model with a case study used to illustrate application of each of the five phases in the model. Each of the five phases is illustrated by analyzing how a nationally known training company applied the model to improve organizational effectiveness.

Phases of the HPT Model

1. Performance Analysis
2. Cause Analysis
3. Intervention Selection and Design
4. Intervention Implementation and Change
5. Evaluation

Phases should be followed sequentially and no phase should be omitted. Just as a medical doctor diagnoses a

FIGURE 1-1: Human Performance Technology (HPT) Model

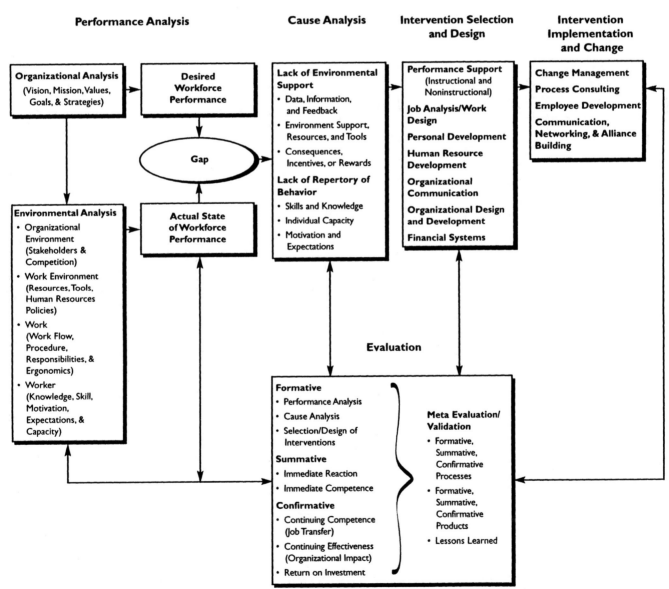

Based on Van Tiem, Moseley, and Dessinger, 2000.

condition and then prescribes treatment based on the patient's symptoms, physical exams, and diagnostic tests, PT practitioners should not prescribe an intervention without first observing and analyzing the situation. In PT, practitioners make recommendations after analyzing the current organizational state and determining its ideal situation. Only then can they select valid interventions.

Phase 1: Performance Analysis

"Performance analysis is the process of identifying the organization's performance requirements and comparing them to its objectives and capabilities."[4] Performance analysis is important because it identifies the cause(s) of the problem. It is difficult to fix a problem if no one can agree on what the problem is. Without identifying the problem and its cause, it is easy to focus on

something totally unrelated, thus wasting time, money, and resources (see Figure 1-2).

Organizational Analysis, Environmental Analysis, and Gap Analysis

There are three types of performance analysis and each type contains different components.

- Organizational analysis looks into the heart of the organization—its vision, mission, values, goals, and strategies.
- Environmental analysis identifies and prioritizes the realities that support actual performance by examining:
  — Organizational environment (external performance support), which includes stakeholders and the competition

FIGURE 1-2: HPT Model: Performance Analysis Phase

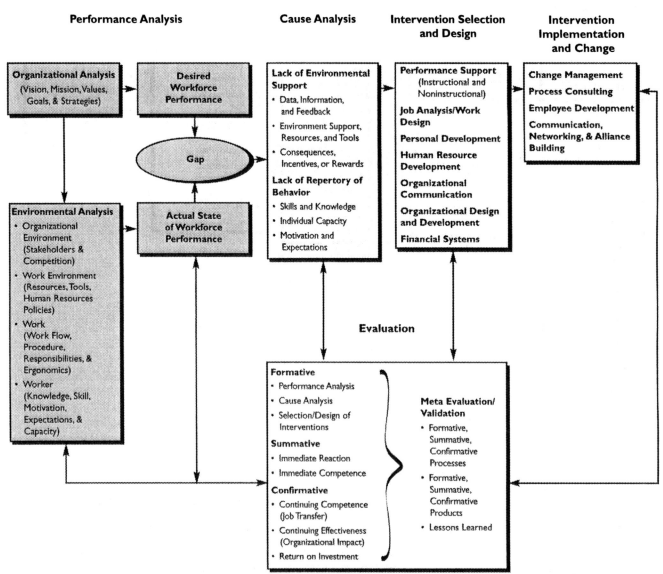

Based on Van Tiem, Moseley, and Dessinger, 2000.

— Work environment (internal performance support), meaning the available resources, tools, and policies of the organization

— Work itself (job design and performance support), including workflow, ergonomic issues, and procedures

— The worker, considering skill level, knowledge base, motivation, and expectations.

• Gap analysis focuses on the current state of an organization as compared to the desired (ideal) state. The difference between the two states is referred to as a "gap." A gap is a performance problem or what needs to be aligned.

PT Analysis Techniques and Methods

Performance analysis typically incorporates five techniques, which can be used to analyze both the organization and the environment within the organization.

1. *Extant data analysis:* Reviewing documents and various organizational records such as sales reports, customer surveys, safety reports, concentrating on accomplishments or performance outcomes.

2. *Needs analysis:* Gathering opinions from job incumbents, stakeholders, customers, management, subject matter experts, etc.

3. *Knowledge task analysis:* Defining in detail what the worker needs to know in order to complete a specific job or task successfully. This is done by examining reference literature regarding the job and speaking with subject matter experts and top performers.

4. *Procedural task analysis:* Observing and studying the visible details of current and optimal job performance. This means watching the "interaction between the performer and the objective or output of the performance" and also understanding thoroughly the future tasks.

5. *Systems task analysis:* Studying and describing the linkages between the job and other work interfaces, "focusing on the expertise workers must have to respond effectively to abnormal conditions."[5]

The methods used to conduct performance analysis cover a wide range of possibilities, including interviews, surveys, observation, and document analysis.

• *Interviews* are the most popular method; they are most effective for rapport building, especially when done face to face.[6]

• *Surveys/Questionnaires* are the most time efficient method because a large sample can be covered at one time.

• *Observation* has advantages when "directly observing the job performance as well as the job environment will often yield information not obtained through interviews or questionnaires."[7]

• *Document Analysis* involves reviewing organizational documents relative to the problem, such as human resource forms, project logs, and related items that may lend valuable insight into possibilities overlooked in the other methods.

Case Study 1-1: HPT Model—Performance Analysis

A nationally recognized training company's performance analysis indicated that it was accepting bids for project work and committing resources although there was uncertainty about the availability of professional and staff resources. This practice resulted in a shortage of resources and sometimes a mismatch between worker and task. The outcome was employee dissatisfaction, ultimately resulting in unnecessary employee turnover.

The company needed readily accessible and up-to-date information regarding the available employee resource pool. The company realized that without this information, it was difficult to bid on and allocate resources to new projects accurately. For instance, if a bid committed three instructional system designers, one editor, and one graphic artist, then management needed to know that these resources were indeed available to be assigned to the project.

Phase 2: Cause Analysis

Performance analysis identifies *what* is happening. It is also critical to determine *why* it is happening. Cause analysis (see Figure 1-3) determines why the performance gap exists. According to Gilbert, probable causes can usually be attributed to either the lack of environmental support or lack of repertory of behavior for the worker.[8]

Lack of environmental support refers to aspects that management provides, such as tools and resources, motivational factors such as incentives or rewards, and sufficient information and feedback to do the job well. Lack of repertory of behavior refers to the workers' own skills and knowledge of the job, their capacity to do the job, and the desire to do the job well.

Cause Analysis Steps

Cause analysis includes the following steps:

1. Identify the possible causes of the performance gap. To do this, apply appropriate analysis techniques, many of which are typically used in quality improvement activities. Common techniques include histograms, flowcharts, run charts, fishbone diagrams, interviews, focus groups, surveys, and observations.

FIGURE I-3: HPT Model: Cause Analysis Phase

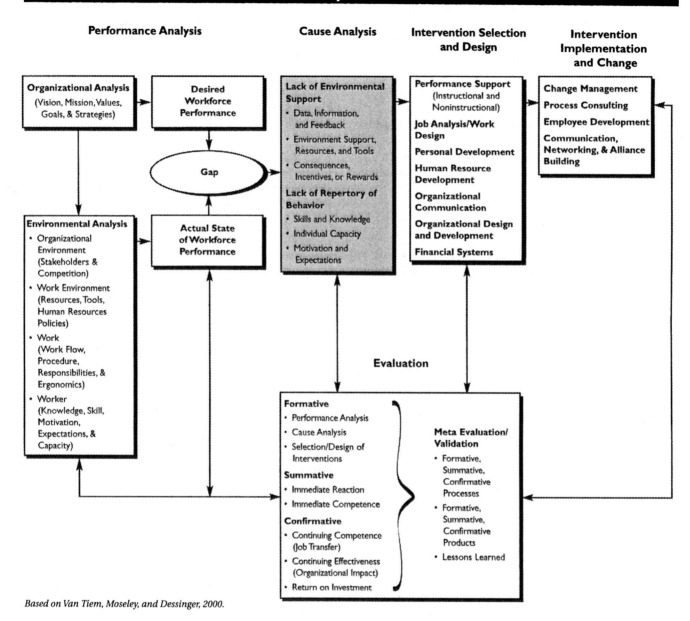

Based on Van Tiem, Moseley, and Dessinger, 2000.

2. Classify the cause by determining where it originated.
   - Organizational environment refers to culture, traditions, structure, processes, and procedures, etc.
   - Work environment refers to supervision, equipment, information, resources, and feedback, etc.
   - Work refers to tasks, ergonomics, and human factors, consequences, incentives, and rewards, and so on.
   - Worker refers to motivation, skills, knowledge, abilities, and individual capacities, and similar issues.

3. Prioritize the causes according to high or low impact on the performance environment.

4. Generate as many cause examples as possible.
   - Examples or scenarios help people visualize the situation and clarify nuances relative to impact and outcomes, and help determine if there is consensus. They promote good discussion.

5. Verify the selection of the kinds of causes and corresponding examples with someone not directly involved in the cause analysis, such as a PT practitioner colleague or the sanctioning person.
   - Ask "who, what, where, when, and why" questions.

Just as in performance analysis, methods used in cause analysis include observation, interviews, and surveys/questionnaires.

Case Study 1-2: HPT Model—Cause Analysis

As discussed earlier in performance analysis, the training company experienced trouble staffing projects with the appropriate people in a timely fashion. Cause analysis was the phase to figure out why.

Upper management conducted a cause analysis by interviewing managers and supervisors directly involved in the staffing situation. The cause analysis identified that there was neither an employee skill inventory that identified employees' competencies nor a tracking system for employee project assignments. As a result, the staffing section of proposals was based on an author's memory regarding which employee did what for the company as well as on speculation as to which employees were likely to have time to dedicate to the new project. The cause analysis results

identified a definite lack of work environment support: data, feedback, tools, information, and resources. "Environmental support includes those things that management provides and the performer needs in order to perform effectively and efficiently."[9]

Phase 3: Intervention Selection and Design

After performance and cause analyses are complete, PT practitioners can recommend interventions (see Figure 1-4). Simply put, interventions are proposed solutions to address the gaps identified in an organization. This book, *Performance Improvement Interventions: Enhancing People, Processes, and Organizations through Performance Technology,* covers most common or high-value PT interventions.

FIGURE 1-4: HPT Model: Intervention Selection and Design Phase

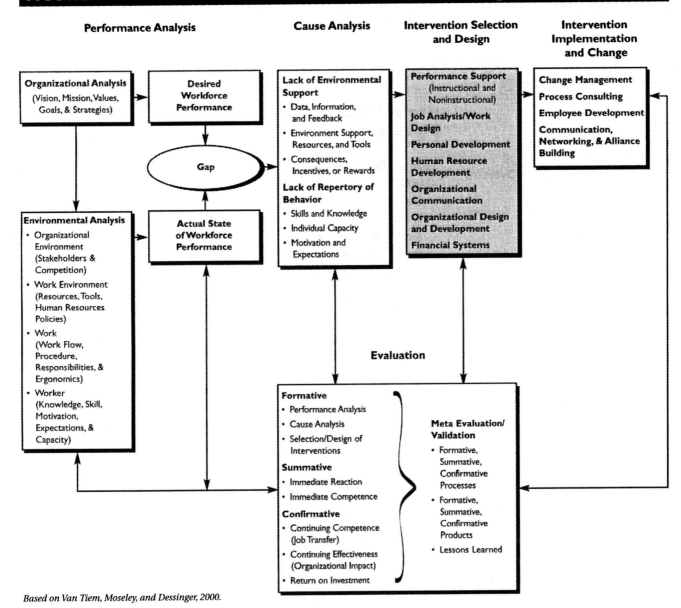

Based on Van Tiem, Moseley, and Dessinger, 2000.

TABLE 1-4: List of Interventions

Performance Support Systems

Instructional Performance Support Systems
Knowledge Management
Learning Organization
• Corporate Universities
Action Learning
Education and Training
• Self-Directed Learning
• Technical and Non-Technical Training
• Just-in-Time Training
• On-the-Job Training
Interactive Learning Technologies
• Enterprise Training
• Classroom Learning
• Distance/Distributed Learning
• Computer-Based Learning
• Online/e-learning
Games and Simulations

Non-Instructional Performance Support Systems
Job Aids
Electronic Performance Support Systems (EPSS)
Documentation and Standards

Job Analysis/ Work Design

Job Analysis
Job Descriptions
Job Specifications

Work Design
Job Design
Job Enlargement
Job Rotation
Job Enrichment

Human Factors
Ergonomics
Safety Engineering
Preventive Maintenance (PM)

Quality Improvement
Total Quality Management (TQM)
Continuous Improvement
Value Analysis/Value Engineering (VA/VE)

Personal Development

Feedback
Coaching
Mentoring
Emotional Intelligence
Career Development

Human Resource Development

Human Resource Management (HRM)
Staffing
Compensation
Retirement Planning
Health and Wellness
Employee Development

Individual Growth
Motivation (Incentives and Rewards)
Performance Appraisals
Competency Testing
Assessment Centers
Literacy

Organizational Growth
Succession Planning
Career Pathing
Leadership Development
Executive Development
Management Development
Supervisory Development

Organizational Communication

Communication Networks
Information Systems
Suggestion Systems
Grievance Systems
Conflict Resolution

Organizational Design and Development

Empowerment
Team Strategies
Problem Solving
Decision Making

Organizational Pro-Action
Strategic Planning
Operations Management
Environmental Scanning
Benchmarking
Reengineering, Realigning, Restructuring

Organizational Values
Culture
Diversity
Globalization
Ethics
Spirituality in the Workplace

Financial Systems

Open Book Management
Profit Versus Cost Center
Financial Forecasting
Capital Investment and Spending
Cash Flow Analysis/Cash Flow Forecast
Mergers, Acquisitions, and Joint Ventures

List of Interventions

Table 1-4 contains a list of interventions identified by PT experts. Consider the factors listed below to ensure a successful intervention.

- *Cost:* The intervention needs to be cost effective for the organization. "Although overused, the term 'bottom line' still captures the attention of management. A candid discussion of budgets, including overhead and additional expenses, if related to the expected results, will preclude later rejection of the program."[10]
- *Sustainability:* If the intervention is not one that is easily maintained, then it probably will have little support and will be discontinued soon after the PT practitioner leaves the project.
- *Accountability:* An intervention needs a sponsor, someone who will attempt to guarantee its maintenance. Sponsorship means ongoing commitment. "It should never be assumed that intervention sponsorship and support will be perpetual. Sponsorship must be nurtured."[11]

Because there are so many options, it is difficult to select the right interventions. Not all interventions are appropriate or applicable for all circumstances.

Case Study I-3: HPT Model—Intervention Selection and Design

In the national training company's situation, the business unit director and operations unit manager determined that a web-based, employee skill-inventory tool should be created as an intervention. The company had a tool that tracked employee labor hours, which served as the foundation for the new, comprehensive skill-inventory tool. The existing labor-hours tool was expanded to include functional titles, names of the employees who fit those descriptions, and employee profile sheets that provided more detailed information about employees. Additionally, a self-assessment skill sheet was created for employees to rate their own skills and competencies.

Tables 1-5, 1-6, and 1-7 illustrate the training company's web-based skill-inventory tools.

TABLE I-5: Functional Titles Chart

List employee name under the title which he or she fulfills in your organization.

Courseware Developer	Instructional Designer	Training Specialist	Technical Editor	Technical Writer	Desktop Publisher
Graphics Specialist	Media Design Specialist	Instructor/ Facilitator	Training Operations Administrator	Course Administrator	HR Coordinator
Project Manager	Program Manager	Account Manager	Client Manager	Quality Manager	Product Line Manager
Engineer	Quality Engineer	Senior Analyst	Computer Programmer Analyst	Controls Specialist	Account Executive

TABLE 1-6: Employee Profile Sheet

Employee Name _____

Employee Job Title _____

Home Address _____
_____

Home Phone _____
Cellular Phone _____

Work Preference (Highest priority = 1)
Rank according to preference
GM ___   Ford ___   Daimler-Chrysler ___   Other ___

Are you comfortable taking a "lead role" with the client? ____

Travel
Are you willing to travel? _____
Amount of notice required _____
Restrictions/accommodations needed: _____
_____
_____

Date _____

Work Location Address_____
_____

Work Phone _____
Pager _____

Instructor/Facilitator Data
Do you have a desire to instruct/facilitate? _____
Do you have any experience? _____
If you have taught classes before, are there any subject
areas that are your favorites? _____
If so, what are they?_____
_____

Normal Work Schedule
Mon.   _____
Tue.   _____
Wed.   _____
Thur. _____
Fri.   _____

Professional Interests and Goals

Comment on any professional interests you may have

Comment on your career goals

Background Information
Educational

Professional

Certifications

TABLE 1-6: Employee Profile Sheet *Continued*

Work History

Present project:

Name

Length of project

Size of budget

Project lead

Project co-workers

Previous projects:

Name

Length of project

Size of budget

Project lead

Project co-workers

Length of time in present position _____   Years of experience in training field _____

Area(s) of specialty/expertise:

Employee Comment Section

Evaluation/Feedback Section

Peer

Project Manager

Customer

TABLE I-7: Individual Skills Assessment Sheet

Assessment Scale: Beginner = B   Intermediate = I   Expert = E

Using the scale provided, rate yourself in the following areas:

Project Management	B	I	E	Comments
Statement of Work Development				
Proposal Writing				
Creating Timelines				
Pricing				
Managing Project Tasks				
Managing Project Resources				
Meeting Management				
Meeting Facilitator Skills				
Resource Planning				
Budgeting				
Analysis	**B**	**I**	**E**	**Comments**
Interviewing Individuals				
Conducting Focus Groups				
Survey/Questionnaire Development				
Report Writing				
Data Compilation and Analysis				
Front End Analysis				
Web-based Research Skills				
Paper-based Research Skills				
Database (Educational, Library)				
Design	**B**	**I**	**E**	**Comments**
Designing Curricula				
Designing Courseware				
Designing Modules				
Designing Activities				
Designing Quick Reference Cards				
Developing Terminal Objectives				
Developing Enabling Objectives				
CBT/Web-based Training				
Development	**B**	**I**	**E**	**Comments**
Instructor Led				
Computer/Web-based				
Self-study				
Presentation Script Writing				
Video Script Writing				
Script Writing				
Test Item Development				
Creative Writing				
Technical Writing				
Mentoring/OJT				
Interactive Distance Learning				
User Manuals				
Job Aids				
Quick Reference Cards				
Editing/Proofing				

TABLE 1-7: Individual Skills Assessment Sheet *continued*

Development (continued)	B	I	E	Comments
Simulation Activities				
Game Activities				
Case Study Scenarios				
Delivery	**B**	**I**	**E**	**Comments**
Coordination/Administration				
Classroom Instruction				
Interactive Distance Learning				
Other Deliverables				
Evaluation	**B**	**I**	**E**	**Comments**
Level 1 (Smile Sheet)				
Level 2 (Pretest/Post-test)				
Level 3 (Skills Applied in the Workplace)				
Level 4 (Return on Investment)				
Scantron (Optical Mark Reader)				
Automatic Response System Keypads				
Data Compilation and Analysis				
Evaluation Report Writing				
Business Area	**B**	**I**	**E**	**Comments**
Administrative				
Communications				
Customer Service				
Engineering				
Executive Development				
Finance				
Health and Safety				
Human Resources				
Leadership				
Management				
Manufacturing				
Marketing				
Quality				
Sales				
Other				
Technology Skills	**B**	**I**	**E**	**Comments**
MS Word				
Power Point				
ABC Flowchart				
Visio				
Excel				
Project				
Access				
Lotus Notes				
Other E-Mail Packages				
Pagemaker				
Internet				
Scantron				
Scanner				
Home Page, Web-based Training				

Phase 4: Intervention Implementation and Change

The fourth phase in the HPT Model (see Figure 1-5) requires the actual doing, the putting into motion of the selected intervention(s). Communication is critical to achieving this step. The entire organization must understand senior management's expectations. Furthermore, communication not only conveys expectations for change but also allays employees' fears and concerns about the intervention. Establishing collaboration between individuals or departments, often minimizes resistance and simplifies implementation. It is best to pay careful attention to resistance and fears because it helps contain problems.

Implementation can be gradual through planned change. This approach usually involves an implementation team working with senior management and the affected departments to schedule and evaluate the activities. However,

sometimes implementation needs to be extensive and requires major process changes. There may be organizational restructuring or realignment to implement the intervention. Normally, a strong team (often with outside consultants) makes extensive plans, prepares to implement the intervention gradually, evaluates each sub-step extensively, and takes corrective measures, as appropriate.

Dormant proposes five suggestions for optimizing intervention implementation and minimizing resistance to change and new ideas. The emphasis is on accentuating the positive and defusing the negative in the minds of those targeted to participate in the change. Careful preparation can have a dramatic impact on results.

1. *Relative advantage:* Highlight the advantages for the user and present a compensatory advantage for each disadvantage. Use cost-benefit information and focus on quick return.
2. *Simplicity:* Make changes seem doable and valuable through success stories, site visits to similar applications,

FIGURE 1-5: HPT Model: Intervention Implementation and Change Phase

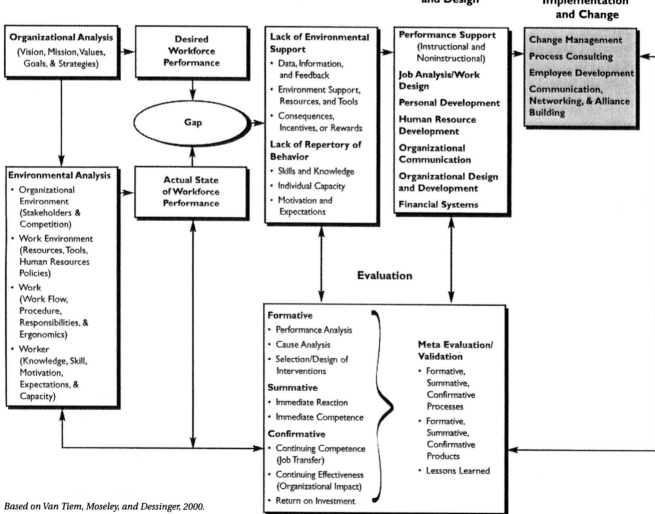

Based on Van Tiem, Moseley, and Dessinger, 2000.

20

FIGURE I-6: HPT Model: Evaluation Phase

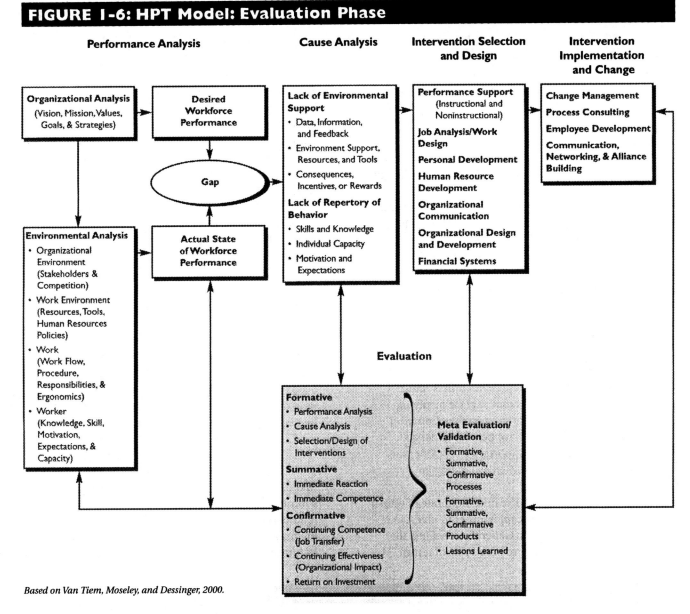

Based on Van Tiem, Moseley, and Dessinger, 2000.

and peer testimonials. Minimize hurdles through job aids, training, and other performance support.

3. *Compatibility:* Identify similarities in aspects, procedures, and results with current situations and acknowledge potential problem areas.

4. *Adaptability:* Highlight areas to be changed without loss of functioning. Identify all areas most likely to be changed.

5. *Social Impact:* Identify relationships with key people and key groups. Anticipate how changes will affect them. Use empathy when communicating workable solutions.[12]

Case Study I-4: HPT Model—Intervention Implementation and Change

To implement its proposed intervention, the training company conducted a management meeting to communicate the plans of the intervention—the web-based employee skill-inventory tool.

All managers learned how the tool would work, the function it would serve, and the benefits it offered. Once the managers were briefed on the intervention, they explained the tool and showed a paper-based sample to their teams. A rollout of the web-based tool took place within two months of the initial managerial decision.

Phase 5: Evaluation

The fifth and final phase in the PT process is evaluation (see Figure 1-6).

The purpose of evaluation is to generate information that will accomplish two outcomes:

- Help the organization to value or judge the results of a performance intervention
- "Trigger or support a decision regarding the performance, the performer, or, ultimately, the organization itself"[13]

The following evaluation methods are used to measure results:
- *Formative* is diagnostic and developmental. It is designed to shape the ongoing events in the HPT process.
- *Summative* focuses on the effectiveness of the HPT process and the intervention implemented. Effectiveness focuses on immediate reaction of employees and management.
- *Confirmative* looks at enduring and long-term effects through data analysis by placing value on the change resulting from the intervention.
- *Meta evaluation* ensures the accuracy and appropriateness of each phase of the evaluation process. That is, it evaluates the processes and products relative to formative, summative, and confirmative evaluation.

Evaluation Methods

Table 1-8 illustrates the different evaluation methods.

Financial Justification of Interventions

One component of confirmative evaluation is return on investment (ROI), which is essential for justifying projects and gaining adequate sponsorship. Common financial evaluation options have been provided as an evaluation example. It is important to consider the following financial concepts when evaluating an intervention for ROI:
- *Required Rate of Return:* "The minimum rate of return that an investor would accept in order to invest in a project of a particular risk. Generally speaking, the higher the risk, the higher required rate of return."[14]

As an example, for a company investing $850,000 to upgrade to a new computer software package when the software product has just been introduced into the market, the required rate of return would be substantially higher than if it only invested $25,000 for a new software package with less features from a reputable, well-known software manufacturer. There is less risk and a lower required rate of return with using the well-known product for less money.
- *Net Present Value (NPV):* "A capital budgeting model that compares the present value of the project's benefits with the present value of the project's costs. The difference between the benefits and costs is the net present value of the project."[15] The following formula illustrates this concept:

$$NPV = PV \text{ of Benefits} - PV \text{ of Costs}$$

For instance, if a company has outgrown its present facility and is looking to purchase a new building to accommodate its employees and the present value of benefits is calculated to be $500,000 annually and the present value of costs is calculated to be $750,000 annually, then it doesn't appear to be a wise move because the net present value would be negative.

$$-\$250,000.00 = \$500,000.00 - \$750,000.00$$

In other words, the present value of costs ($750,000) subtracted from the present value of benefits ($500,000) is a net present value of –$250,000. Numbers representing future values are converted to present value, such as future anticipated revenues or future costs.

TABLE 1-8: Evaluation Methods

What? (Type/Process of Evaluation)	Why? (Purpose)	When? (Timing)
Formative	Improve performance intervention package	During performance analysis, cause analysis, and selection or design of interventions
Summative	Determine immediate competence of user and effectiveness of package	During implementation and change management
Confirmative	Determine continuing competence of user and effectiveness of package	6–12 months after implementation
Meta	Evaluate formative, summative, and confirmative processes to provide insight to evaluator	After confirmative evaluation

Based on Van Tiem, Moseley, and Dessinger, 2000.

- *Payback:* "A capital budgeting model that answers the question: How long will it take to recoup the initial investment?"[16] This question can be answered with the help of Figure 1-7:

An organization initially invested $850,000 into a new project. In two years, there is an expected profit of $125,000. The payback in this example is three years. If an organization required a one-year payback, this situation would not be acceptable.

Case Study 1-5: HPT Model—Evaluation

Organizations evaluate situations and make decisions using numerical and other considerations. The training company's management faced some of the following ROI confirmative evaluation issues:

- Will additional resources need to be hired and trained in order to input and maintain the data, thus resulting in increased labor costs? Will the NPV be positive?
- Will the training company need to purchase new computer equipment to accommodate the web-based technology software necessary for the inventory tool? Will it be worth the expense? Will the payback be acceptable?
- Once the capital budgeting analysis calculations are complete, is the required rate of return acceptable to management?
- Do the benefits of the employee skill-inventory tool outweigh the costs? Again, the issue is NPV.
- Is the amount of time needed to recoup the initial investment acceptable? This is another payback decision.

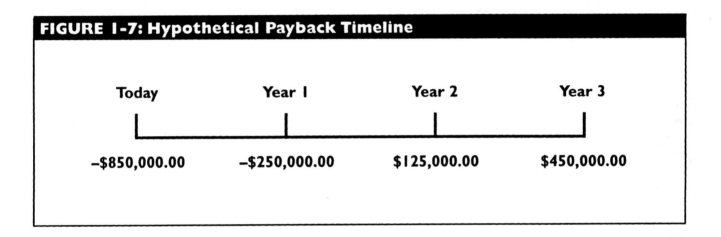

FIGURE 1-7: Hypothetical Payback Timeline

Today	Year 1	Year 2	Year 3
–$850,000.00	–$250,000.00	$125,000.00	$450,000.00

PERFORMANCE TECHNOLOGY AS A PROBLEM SOLVER

The HPT Model makes workplace challenges and problems more manageable because it offers direction for handling and possibly eliminating these problematic issues. The model provides organizations that lack problem solving ability with a five-step process. Organizations already possessing problem solving abilities are more likely to embrace PT concepts and will have an easier time dealing with performance problems, enabling them to operate to their full potential.

Main identified four criteria necessary for successfully understanding and using the HPT Model:
1. "HPT functions within a *systematic framework*.
2. HPT mandates a comprehensive *analytic process*.

3. Practitioners must use a *nonlinear perspective* to solve performance problems or take advantage of performance improvement opportunities.
4. HPT practitioners must develop a network of professionals to serve on *diverse teams* because no individual can possess all the required skills."[17]

When an organization runs at peak performance, employees are more satisfied and less likely to hunt for new jobs. P.J. Harkins says it best: "The most successful organizations hold onto their key resources."[18] PT gives organizations the tools necessary to do just that.

Chapter was written in collaboration with Joyce Katona, MA, General Physics Corporation. Used with permission.

CHAPTER

2

PERFORMANCE SUPPORT SYSTEMS

"DON'T YOU THINK IT'S TIME HE
LEARNED TO FLY ON HIS OWN?"

PERFORMANCE SUPPORT SYSTEMS (PSS)

The story of performance support systems (PSS) is a wondrous tale of times past and present; of low tech and high tech; of formal training and the informal "follow Harry around" style; of paper-based job aids and electronic performance support systems (EPSS).

At one time, many centuries ago, the entire learning process for everyone and everything was invisibly embedded in the processes of work (and play)...When, for example, the apprentice potter needed to know how to fire a glaze, she watched the master do it, asked any necessary questions, and tried to imitate the steps observed. The finish on the pot spoke for itself regarding her degree of success...Human culture did not abandon this model or learning...Now, however we have an opportunity to provide some of the support mechanisms from the master-apprentice relationship by way of computer...the computer can emulate the master... The performance support system allows learning and doing to be reintegrated, so learning can once again happen in our most natural and best way.[1]

In today's world of work, "There's too little time and too much knowledge to be shared for it to happen only in the classroom, in a traditional training environment."[2] The *new language* of PSS stresses the integration of learning and doing and technology:

- Integrated Performance Systems/Performance Systems—the use of technology-based, media-based, print-based, and human-based information, learning, and support components to develop the attitudes, behaviors, skills, knowledge, and abilities employees need to optimally perform their jobs.
- Performance-Centered Applications or Systems— environment integrating traditional business information processing with task or job structuring support and related business knowledge, reference, data, and tools (see Chapter 6, Information Systems).
- Electronic Performance Support System (EPSS)—the use of technology to provide on-demand access to integrated information, guidance, advice, assistance, training, and tools to enable high-level job performance with a minimum of support from other people.[3] (See EPSS section later in this chapter).

The goal of a PSS is to move individuals systematically: "Give performers what they need, when they need it, and in the form in which they need it so that they perform in a way that consistently meets organizational objectives."[4] To accomplish this goal, a PSS must include the following characteristics:

- *Intuitiveness*—provides guidance even if the user has minimal or no prior learning or experience
- Integration—presents a seamless union of people, process, and devices
- *Immediacy*—offers on-demand access to tools, information, advice, training, communication, etc.
- *Individualization*—supports needs of novices, competent performers, and experts at the individual, group, or organizational level
- *Interactivity*—opens a "dynamic dialogue" between user and PSS.[5]

Determining whether a PSS is the right intervention usually requires analysis of the organization, environment, and potential users. Figure 2-1 suggests that listening may be the best way to discover whether an organization needs a PSS.

The remainder of this chapter will describe the PSS interventions from the enhanced HPT Model (see Table 2-1) and discuss how the PT practitioner may help to implement these interventions in the workplace. Note that PSS, in the context of the HPT Model, is very broad based, ranging from knowledge management and learning organizations to training and education to "a doohickey that tells you just what you need to know, just when you need to know it."[6]

FIGURE 2-1: PSSt...Just Listen

We need to downsize, rightsize, save time/money, increase productivity/ efficiency, improve performance/quality, watch the competition, add value, roll out new...

We need knowledge/skills, just-in-time, on-the-job access to information and support resources, help with multitasking, fewer data dumps, more need-to-know information...

TABLE 2-1: Performance Support System (PSS) Interventions From Enhanced HPT Model

- **Instructional Performance Support Systems**
  - Knowledge Management
  - Learning Organization
    - Corporate Universities
  - Action Learning
  - Education and Training
    - Self-Directed Learning
    - Technical and Non-Technical Training
    - Just-in-Time Training
    - On-the-Job Training
  - Interactive Learning Technologies

  - Enterprise Training
  - Classroom Learning
  - Distance Learning/Distributed Learning
  - Computer-Based Learning
  - Online Learning/e-learning
  - Games and Simulations

- **Non-Instructional Performance Support Systems**
  - Job Aids
  - Electronic Performance Support Systems (EPSS)
  - Documentation and Standards

INSTRUCTIONAL PERFORMANCE SUPPORT SYSTEMS (PSS)

Instruction is "an effort to assist or to shape growth";[1] it is using teaching and learning strategies to help workers store information in memory for real-time, on-the-job access.[2] The purpose of instruction is to change knowledge, skills, or even attitudes. The PT practitioner may select or design an instructional PSS intervention when a gap exists between the current knowledge, skill, or attitude of a worker or group of workers and the job specifications. An instructional PSS helps workers change their actual performance until that performance becomes the same as or better than the desired performance.[3] It helps move the individual and the organization from idea or theory to competence.

A true instructional PSS reinforces the integration of workplace learning and performance (WLP):

WLP is the integrated use of learning and other interventions for the purpose of improving human performance, and addressing individual and organizational needs. It uses a systematic process of analyzing and responding to individual, group, and organizational performance issues. It creates positive, progressive change within organizations by balancing humanistic and ethical considerations.[4]

This section approaches knowledge management (KM), learning organization, education and training, and education as instructional PSS that links workplace learning to performance.

Knowledge Management

KM is a global phenomenon that aims at integrating workplace knowledge and performance improvement.

Knowledge management is an effort by organizations to manage some or all of the knowledge within them as a resource, much as they manage real estate, inventory, and human resources... This transformation has spawned new concepts and terminology, a strengthening of the relationship between information and technology, new processes and approaches to designing information resources, and new cultures. Most significantly, this transformation could herald significant changes for the training and performance improvement business.[1]

In addition to recognizing and managing knowledge as an organizational asset, "enterprises are realising how important it is to *know what they know* and be able to make maximum use of the knowledge."[2] The desired outcome is not knowledge but individual and business performance: "What companies are banking on is this: *If you know, you will do.* Thus knowledge also implies action."[3]

Definition and Scope

"There are a thousand definitions of knowledge management and companies that have begun to wrestle with the beast are attacking it from many different angles."[4]

From a procedural point of view, KM is a systematic and conscious effort to identify, capture, codify, store, transform, disseminate, and share knowledge so that people within the organization can use the organization's collective knowledge and experience to foster business innovation and competitive advantage.

KM is also "a way of thinking about your business."[5] From a business perspective, KM activities become integral to strategy, policy, and practice at all levels of the organization, and there is a direct connection between an organization's intellectual assets and positive business results.[6]

Perhaps the most useful definition is the following "60-second definition":

> [KM is] the systematic approach to helping the enterprise make money, save money, be competitive, and make better decisions by managing how information is gathered, stored, and shared across the enterprise. It's a business discipline whose currency is information, and it involves managing how new information assets are created and how existing assets are leveraged. It addresses the behavior of individuals and groups as well as specifying the most appropriate tools and repositories, with a goal of helping everyone achieve access to the right information at the right time, so they can turn that information into the knowledge needed to bring value to the organization.[7]

About Knowledge

KM systems contain data, information, and knowledge:
- Data are the fundamental building blocks.
- Information is data that has context and meaning.
- Knowledge is a body of information that has value.[8]

KM can transform basic data into information that "goes beyond facts and provides rich detail, commentary, and reflections…(for example, assessment tools, best practices, and lessons learned)."[9] KM can also leverage knowledge by transforming it into knowledge assets. Knowledge assets are "the knowledge regarding markets, products, technologies and organisations that a business owns or needs to own and which enable its business processes to generate profits."[10]

Two *types* of knowledge exist within organizations:
- Explicit knowledge is recorded and transmitted among individuals, for example, a written policy or procedure.
- Tacit knowledge (know-how) is not recorded and is rooted in personal experience, for example, rules of thumb or heuristics for solving a specific problem.[11]

Five *sources* of knowledge are present within organizations:
- *Acquired knowledge* comes from outside an organization and may be bought or leased.

- *Adapted knowledge* results from customizing new processes or technologies to fit the organization.
- *Dedicated knowledge* comes from individuals or groups within the organization who perform research and development activities.
- *Fused knowledge* is created by bringing together people with different perspectives to work on the same project.
- *Networked knowledge* is based on information that people formally or informally share with one another.[12]

When all is said and done, however, the definition, type, and source of knowledge are less important than the act of using systematic knowledge management to achieve a positive business result.

Evolution of KM: Generation Two

KM is now in its second generation:
- First generation KM emphasized using technology to share and integrate existing knowledge and enable individual learning.
- Second generation KM recognizes the importance of existing knowledge, technology, and individual learning but focuses on producing and sharing new knowledge through people sharing, with a focus on organizational learning to foster business innovation and competitive advantage.[13]

Both generations are "rooted in computer networks… because of the new opportunities they offer not just for storing and codifying information but for allowing people in global companies to communicate more easily…"[14] In fact, organizations may consciously decide to use either generation or both, depending on their business strategy and where they are on the KM continuum:

> At the efficiency end of the continuum, knowledge management is seen as an effort to build a repository of data and information that workers need, and provide them with efficient access to it… At the innovation end of the continuum, knowledge management is seen as an effort to spark new products, processes, and business opportunities that help an organization thrive.[15]

Figure 2-2 illustrates the KM continuum.

Components of a KM System

The three components of a KM system are people, technology, and content:
- "Knowledge lives in people's heads and is embedded in process through people."[16] The process of knowledge management begins and ends with people who select or design, use, and maintain the technology required to transform and share knowledge.[17]
- "Technology is an enabler, not an answer."[18] A KM system requires the same basic technology as

FIGURE 2-2: Knowledge Management Continuum

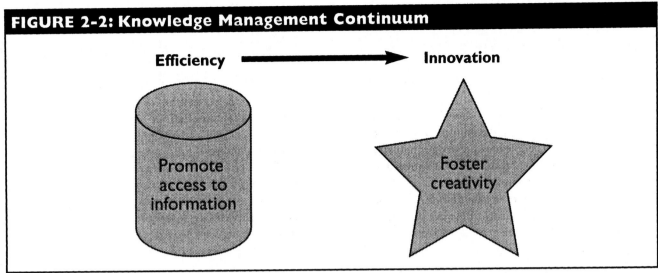

Efficiency ⟶ Innovation

Promote access to information

Foster creativity

Based on Eight Things That Training and Performance Improvement Professionals Must Know About Knowledge Management, *2000, p. 2.*

an information system (see Chapter 6), and usually includes an intranet and groupware.

- "The heart of a good knowledge management system is in the content itself. If the knowledge management system does not provide users with timely, accurate information, inform them of best practices, and link them to expertise, organizations will not realize the full value of their investment in the system."[19]

KM Activities
"KM is all about applying a strategy. It is a very active process, more like a verb than a noun."[20] Wherever an organization fits on the continuum, an effective KM system involves nine major activities:

1. Identifying the organization's knowledge assets, both explicit and tacit
2. Capturing and explicitly recording the tacit knowledge within an organization
3. Codifying (cataloging, mapping, linking) knowledge assets for easier retrieval
4. Storing knowledge assets in a central area where all members of an organization who need to know have access to it
5. Transforming knowledge by making connections among pieces of information
6. Generating new knowledge to help achieve competitive advantage
7. Disseminating knowledge to people when, where, and how they need it
8. Sharing best practices and technology to enable all of the activities listed above
9. Managing the processes, people, and technology that enable these activities

Each of the nine activities provides unique challenges and opportunities in terms of implementing an effective KM system.

Challenges
The major challenges involved in converting an organization to KM are common to most or all of the activities listed above. For example:

- Organizations must use a wide variety of tools and techniques to perform all of the activities listed above. The tools and techniques also must adapt to different types of hardware, software, and user requirements.
- Organizations need a common vocabulary to ensure that the knowledge is correctly understood. Selecting or developing this vocabulary can be a daunting task, especially for a global organization.
- There is the danger that making more knowledge available to more people will increase information overload. Sifting between nice-to-know and need-to-know information adds a layer of complexity that often has a negative effect on doing the job now.
- Another danger involves cultural change. For example, some organizations are infected with the silo syndrome. Information piles up vertically within departments or divisions and is not integrated into the KM system so people in other areas of the organization may use it.[21]

Opportunities
KM offers opportunities as well as challenges:

- A well-designed KM system minimizes information overload, focusing instead on how to get information into the right hands, at the right time, and in the right form. KM achieves this by giving information to those who can act on it and give it value, filtering out information that does not support an individual's immediate or long-term need or goal, and presenting information in the form appropriate for the context and the individual who needs the information.[22]
- Today's savvy organizations use buzzwords like "work smarter not harder," "manage intellectual capital,"

and "harness brainpower" to describe why they have embraced KM. However, the bottom line is that KM is a way to achieve "a harvest of efficiencies in operations and innovations in products and business practices (that) yields competitive advantages, which lead to tangible (and ideally, sizeable[sic]) profits."[23]

- "When you start talking about knowledge, it's really about people, relationships, communities, and a new way of sharing."[24] People are knowledge enablers; they are key to identifying and sharing tacit knowledge and creating and sharing new knowledge:

    At a time when key business assets reside in the heads of employees (tacit knowledge), the most basic steps in managing those assets are to find and keep the right heads. That's why the human resources department is central to a knowledge-savvy organization's strategic planning.[25]

Case Study 2-1 at the end of this section illustrates what happens when heads roll during a merger of two organizations that are committed to preserving tacit knowledge. In this case, the role of human resources was to provide incentives for knowledge sharing.

Evaluating KM
"Quantifying the benefits from KM projects has long been every practitioner's Achilles' heel." For example, "the benefits of computerization, especially of technology applied to knowledge management, have been notoriously difficult to quantify."[26] Very few organizations use metrics to verify the impact of KM on business and many do not measure at all "because they had executive-level sponsorship and could rely on anecdotes…"[27] However, respondents to a KM survey indicated that:

> *measuring the value and performance of knowledge assets ranked as the second most important challenge companies face today (43 percent), surpassed only by changing people's behavior (56 percent). But only four percent claimed to be good or excellent at measuring the value of knowledge assets or impact of knowledge management.*[28]

The ASTD Effective Knowledge Management Working Group has developed the *Intellectual Capital Measurement Model* to help organizations identify inputs (existing intellectual capital stocks such as number of patents); KM processes and enablers, and outputs (financial performance and changes in intellectual capital stocks). The coordinating factor is the business strategy: "Everything that occurs in a firm's system must be aligned with its primary strategic objectives."[29]

The ASTD group has also developed core and elective measures for four categories of intellectual capital stocks.

Table 2-2 presents some sample elective measures for the four categories.

Implementing KM in the Workplace

A PT practitioner is a natural for the role of a KM practitioner, a role that has a definite performance technology flavor.

> *A KM initiative must support the goals of the business and must be oriented toward performance….the KM practitioner needs to start with the performance goals (business and individual) and the business and performance context before proceeding to assessing and analyzing the knowledge domain….During the knowledge gathering stage it is also a good idea to begin to think about access to the KM system from the performer's perspective.*[30]

To strengthen his or her role in the implementation process, the PT practitioner should become a subject matter expert (SME) on KM and the various domains and disciplines that support KM (see Table 2-3). In addition, the PT practitioner needs to keep up to date on changes in the world of work that could affect how the organization copes with and manages knowledge.

Getting Started
If there are areas of the organization where KM is practiced, for example, specific work groups or teams are involved in knowledge creation and sharing, the PT practitioner should locate the pockets of activity and join in the action. One way to accomplish this is to model and encourage knowledge sharing.[31] If KM is not active within the organization, the PT practitioner could help design a KM system that is user friendly. User-friendly KM links collection, storage, and retrieval of knowledge to how people will use the knowledge and supports people when they capture and share knowledge.

Strategic Design
During strategic design, the PT practitioner can help explore how knowledge is used and valued in the organization (see Job Aid 2-1). The PT practitioner can also support integration of KM with other strategic initiatives. According to a Conference Board study, "less than one percent of companies (surveyed) fully integrate their organizational learning efforts with training and development programs, and nearly half have not integrated knowledge management and learning."[32]

Helping to integrate KM with human resources (HR), training and development, performance improvement, and finance can benefit the entire organization. For example:
- HR is uniquely positioned "to fill gaps in a company's knowledge by finding and retaining employees who

TABLE 2-2: Measuring Intellectual Capital Stocks

Intellectual Capital Stocks	Sample Elective Measures
Innovation Capital Knowledge, skills, and competencies of people in organization	• Organizational learning • Learning transfer • Management credibility • Employee wages and salaries • Educational levels
Innovation Capital Capability of an organization to innovate and create new products and services	• Copyrights, trademarks, patents • Planned obsolescence • New opportunities exploited • New markets developed • R&D productivity
Process Capital An organization's processes, techniques, systems, and tools	• Strategy execution • Quality of decisions • Percent of company effectively engaged with customers • IT access per employee • Strategy innovativeness
Customer Capital Value of an organization's relationships with customers	• Market growth • Customer needs met • Marketing effectiveness • Annual sales per customer • Market share

Suggested Criteria for Selecting Appropriate Measures:
1. Relevance to organization's KM objectives
2. Strategic importance to top executives and external stakeholders
3. Collectability or availability of information or data
4. Applicability to current/future situation

Based on VanBuren, 1999, pp. 5–7.

TABLE 2-3: Inputs to KM

Input	Contribution
Cognitive science Insights on how people learn	Tools and techniques for gathering and transferring knowledge
Expert systems, artificial intelligence (AI), and knowledge base management systems Lessons learned	Directly applicable to codifying, storing, transforming, and retrieving knowledge
Computer-supported collaborative work Integrated computer applications (groupware)	Supports collaborative work efforts and sharing of documents, databases, calendars, and other sources of knowledge
Library and information science Research and practice in classification and organization of knowledge	Tools for thesaurus construction and controlled vocabularies
Technical communication Body of theory and practice including help-desk technology	Directly relevant to effective representation and transfer of knowledge
Document management Professional processes and technologies for making knowledge accessible and re-usable	Full-text search and retrieval, electronic publishing technology
Decision support systems How knowledge workers perform cognitive tasks related to decision making	Supports use of knowledge for better and faster business decisions
Semantic networks Forming networks from ideas and the relationships among them; hypertext applications	Useful for representing and storing domain knowledge in an explicit way that can be shared.
Relational and object databases Models and tools for managing structured (relational) and unstructured (object) data	Useful for representing and managing knowledge
Organizational Science Science of managing organizations	Increasingly deals with the need to manage knowledge (for example, American Management Association sponsors KM events)

Based on Barclay and Murray, 1997, pp. 5–6.

not only have the skills and experience that the company needs, but are also capable of learning new skills and creating new knowledge."[33] (See also Chapters 5, Human Resource Interventions.)

- "Knowledge fuels learning," yet training and development and KM are often "like two trains going down parallel tracks."[34] The two initiatives should merge for maximum effectiveness.
- Taken collectively, performance improvement and KM stand for "learning, knowing, and doing."[35] After all, the goal of KM is to improve organizational performance.
- Finance should include knowledge capital investments in the planning and budgeting process. In fact, some US corporations have "four to eight times more knowledge assets than financial assets."[36]

Tactical design
"Tactical design provides a framework for preparing knowledge management systems and other interventions that support and enhance the use of knowledge."[37] The fact that the PT practitioner "typically profiles users, analyzes tasks, and determines business requirements as part of the performance consulting process"[38] makes him or her invaluable during tactical design of KM systems. For example, the PT practitioner can help the design team with the following:

- Developing a needs hierarchy
- Conducting feasibility studies
- Writing an implementation plan to meet the needs of the users
- Designing user-friendly PSS and online learning programs
- Designing single modules of content for many possible uses
- Fostering cultural change to promote sharing of knowledge[39]

The PT practitioner is also the expert when it comes to resolving issues involving the users.

Culture Change
Culture change is a major factor in successful implementation and maintenance of knowledge management: "Organizations are failing to grasp the fundamental changes to their day-to-day operations and culture that successful KM implementation requires."[40] One issue directly related to culture change is the issue of sharing knowledge.

> ...knowledge management is about sharing information, not owning it. As a result, some of the greatest challenges in capturing information for use in a knowledge management system stem from practices of hoarding it, practices that organizational cultures have nurtured and supported through the years. Changing that culture is one way that training and performance

improvement professionals can contribute to knowledge management efforts.[41]

The PT practitioner may begin by analyzing the current situation:
- How much do we share?
- What do we share?
- How well is it protected?
- With whom do we show it?[42]

Then the PT practitioner can suggest ways to control the risk. "Effective security is an ongoing process and offers a series of repeatable steps to ensure that a company keeps up with potential threats."[43] For example, the organization can implement access controls (Who gets the information?), authentification controls (Are you who you say you are?), and authorization controls (Who can access what?).[44]

Below are some additional contributions that the PT practitioner can make during tactical design to help organizations avoid culture shock when a KM system is implemented.
- Identify practices and incentives that promote knowledge hoarding.
- Work with senior management, line management, and human resources to develop an organizational culture that rewards the sharing of knowledge and frowns on hoarding.
- Suggest cross training to balance expertise so one person does not become the sole expert in a subject.
- Provide tools to capture expert knowledge. For example, design a template that guides experts through the process of sharing information. Many people don't share knowledge because they don't know what to share or how.[45]

Maintenance
Once KM is implemented, the PT practitioner can use his or her consulting skills to "nurture the communities in which knowledge is created and shared."[46] One way to help maintain the momentum of the KM initiative is to encourage and help foster the *making and mining* of intellectual capital: "If intellectual capital is the only appreciable asset a company has, then it needs to be nurtured methodically."[47]

Evaluation
The PT practitioner can help the organization focus the evaluation. For example, Sveiby suggests that in order to find out whether KM is working, the organization needs to focus on output, outcome, and impact: "It is not until you achieve the impact of changing a client's behavior that you have actually transferred knowledge."[48]

Focusing the evaluation up front during strategic planning increases chances for successfully evaluating the KM system, especially from the perspective of return on investment. The PT practitioner can also use knowledge of and experience with performance evaluation techniques and tools to help plan, design, develop the materials, implement, and analyze the results of the evaluation. (For potential measures of intellectual capital, see Table 2-3.) The basic heuristics for measuring KM are:

- If you don't measure, it's just practice.
- Always start with an existing objective important to the company's overall goals, then identify the KM initiatives that go toward its achievement.
- Modesty is preferable to bombastic claims.[49]

Measuring learning is part of the KM process. The PT practitioner can help with a learning audit. For example, one evaluation project plans to use Garvin's three stages of organizational learning to infer the current effect of the KM process:

1. Cognitive—people are exposed to new ideas, expand their knowledge, and begin to think differently
2. Behavioral—people begin to internalize new insights and alter their behavior
3. Performance improvement—changes in behavior lead to tangible, measurable improvements in results, for example superior quality, better delivery, or increased market share.[50]

Learning Organization

Flash! "Learning has become a new form of labor," and many organizations now believe that—

Competitive advantage comes from continuous incremental innovation and refinement of ideas that spread throughout the organization...the ability to learn faster than the competition may be the only sustainable competitive advantage.[1]

JOB AID 2-1: A KM Primer

Directions: Use the following activities and questions to guide the planning of a new or evaluating an existing KM intervention. Revise the questions as needed to meet existing or emerging organizational needs.

---

1. **Identify knowledge assets (explicit and tacit).**
   - Where is the knowledge asset?
   - What does it contain?
   - What is its use?
   - What form is it in?
   - How accessible is it?

2. **Analyze how each knowledge asset can add value.**
   - What are the opportunities for using the knowledge asset?
   - What would be the effect of its use?
   - What are the current obstacles to its use?
   - What would be its increased value to the company?

3. **Specify what actions are necessary to achieve maximum usability and added value for each knowledge asset.**
   - How to plan the actions to use the knowledge asset
   - How to enact actions
   - How to monitor actions

4. **Review (evaluate) use of each knowledge asset to ensure added value.**
   - Did its use produce the desired added value?
   - How can the knowledge asset be maintained for this use?
   - Did the use create new opportunities?

Developed by Joan Conway Dessinger. Adapted from Mcintosh, A. Position Paper on Knowledge Asset Management. Edinburgh, UK: Artificial Intelligence Applications Institute (AIAI). Available online: http://www.aiai.ed.ac.uk/~alm/kam.html. ISPI © 2001. Permission granted for unlimited duplication for non-commercial use.

The learning organization is a natural outcome of second-generation KM (see the previous section of this chapter). In fact, the most striking distinction between first- and second-generation KM is "the explicit connection now being drawn between knowledge management and organizational learning…Second generation KM is all about beefing up an organization's ability…to learn and to learn effectively (faster than competitors)."[2]

One distinction between KM and learning organizations is based on the difference between tacit and explicit knowledge. First-generation KM focused on identifying, cataloging, storing, and retrieving explicit knowledge; second-generation KM focuses on integrating both explicit and tacit knowledge, and the learning organization is more focused on tacit knowledge.

In traditional perceptions of the role of knowledge in business organizations, tacit knowledge *is often viewed as the real key to getting things done and creating new value. Not explicit knowledge. Thus we often encounter an emphasis on the* learning organization *and other approaches that stress internalization of information (through experience and action) and generation of new knowledge through managed interaction.*[3]

This section will focus on the learning organization as an instructional PSS and a performance improvement intervention.

Definition and Scope

A learning organization is much like a butterfly; it is an entity "that learns continuously and can transform itself."[4] Two doctoral candidates at Wayne State University offer this cut-through-the-clutter definition of a learning organization: a learning organization is person, process, and place. This definition is presented in Figure 2-3.

FIGURE 2-3: The Three Ps of the Learning Organization

Person—a learning organization cannot exist without people who are willing to learn and strive for continuous self-improvement (I have a vision)

Process—transform conversational and collective thinking skills so groups can reliably develop intelligence and ability greater than the sum of individual member's talents

Place—location (virtual/real) where the organization makes resources available to support people and process; infrastructure including physical environment, time, management support, money, information, and more

Based on Tracey and Solomon, 1999.

If systems thinking is the "fifth discipline" and driving force of a learning organization, then continuous improvement and continuous learning are the heart.

A learning organization is one which continuously improves its processes, products, and services, facilitates the learning of all of its members both individually and as a team, and expands its capacity to produce results and transform itself in order to meet its strategic goals.[5]

Background
Literature in the field dates back to the late 1980s and includes the work of Chris Argyris, David Garvin, Edgar Schein, and Peter Senge. Did learning organizations exist before the late 1980s? Any organization that exhibits the following characteristics is—in fact, if not in name—a learning organization:
- Individuals take ownership for their own development and learning on a self-directed basis (see the section on self-directed learning later in this chapter)
- The organization supports, recognizes, and rewards people for learning
- The organization has developed the capacity for capturing learning in its different parts and storing them in the corporate knowledge base to generate new capabilities.
- Senior management leads in creating the vision and the map for incorporating learning organization concepts into the overall strategic plan; middle managers are facilitators, coaches, and negotiators; and employees are empowered to work in teams to improve quality and customer satisfaction.[6]

Several factors created the need for learning organizations:
- Changes in the nature of organizations and work
- Rapid job restructuring
- Explosion of technology and technical innovation
- Use of continuous improvement processes
- Growing recognition that knowledge and the ability to acquire, disseminate, and use it provides competitive advantage.[7]

Most learning organizations are built on Peter Senge's five disciplines:
1. Systems thinking, a learnable, habitual thinking process that allows individuals and organizations to see the patterns of complex interrelationships.
2. Personal mastery, that continually clarifies and deepens an individual's personal vision of what could or should be and what is (reality).
3. Mental models or assumptions that influence how organizations and individuals understand and respond to various situations.
4. Shared vision or competency that is developed by a group, team, or organization and fosters commitment rather than compliance.

5. Team learning, which is conducted through dialogue, a process that involves suspending assumptions and thinking together for the collective good.[8]

Keys to Success
One key to success resides in the concepts of *continuous* improvement and *continuous* learning: "It involves the organization removing roadblocks to learning, building in the capability to learn, and continuously adjusting the infrastructure to always respond to deliver new capabilities."[9] Another key to success is moving the organization from individual to true organizational learning. "People learn, and people learn in organizations, but not all organizations learn from what their members learn."[10] The most successful learning organizations operate at three levels, and "each level provides a foundation for the next level."[11] Figure 2-4 describes the three levels.

In order for learning organizations to succeed they need to recognize that people learn without the help of their organization, but no organization can learn unless the people within it learn.[12] Learning organizations also need to accept their role as facilitators of learning at all three levels illustrated in Figure 2-4. Learning organizations also need to put into place mechanisms or systems that help them manage, interpret, and transfer learning throughout the organization and also deposit it into corporate memory repositories.[13]

Team learning is the layer that holds the learning organization together and filters learning from the individual to the organization and vice versa: "The basic premise has always been that when we are talking about organizational knowledge, skills, and capabilities, they are embedded in working teams. Otherwise, they don't exist."[14]

One other viewpoint on successful implementation of learning organizations focuses on the learner rather than on the organization.

The single most important element in training is to help people make the transition from performers *to* learners. *Indeed, with all the buzz about the concept of the* learning organization *I'm struck by how few people seem to have embraced the idea of becoming a true learning person…The link between learning and performance is self-evident, but for the true learning person (or organization for that matter) performance is not the ultimate why of learning.*[15]

Corporate Universities
As corporations began to realize that their most important asset is human capital and the tacit knowledge it represents, many corporations sought ways to maximize these resources, and discovered the corporate university. "Acting as the connective tissue of the organization, the

---

FIGURE 2-4: Three Levels of a Learning Organization

Organization
- Continuously builds the capability to regularly create market opportunities
- Quickly capitalizes on market opportunities by identifying existing organizational capabilities
- Defines emerging market demands to determine new capability requirements

Teams
- Teams work together to share assumption, learn through dialogue, build new mental maps, and actively transfer their learning to others
- Individual participants gain self-understanding and develop skills for thinking and acting more effectively
- The organization supports empowerment and gains problem solving and decision making capabilities

Individuals
- Individuals are willing to learn continuously (competencies, skills, knowledge)
- The organization rewards individuals for doing it (feedback)
- Key words are effective feedback
- Teams gain effective members

Based on Greenwood, Wasson, and Giles, 1993, p. 8.

corporate university links employee learning to overall company strategy and is beginning to drive business.[16]

The corporate university is a steadily growing phenomenon: "The number of corporate universities has quadrupled…from 400 in 1988 to 1,600 in 1999."[17] Table 2-4 illustrates how a corporate university differs from a corporate training department.

The American Productivity & Quality Center (APQC) and Motorola University joined together in 1998 to conduct a study of corporate universities. The purpose of the study was to:
- Identify and examine innovations, best practices, and key trends in the area of corporate learning initiatives
- Gain insight and new learnings about the processes involved[18]

Because the study was largely about benchmarking, the term *benchmarking* was defined for the study as "the process of identifying, learning, and adapting outstanding practices and processes from any organization, anywhere in the world, to help an organization improve its performance."[19] Five of 29 businesses that participated in the study were designated as *benchmarking partners* based on the quality of their corporate universities. The top best practices are listed in Job Aid 2-2 at the end of this section.

Future Trends
What does the future hold for the corporate university? This is how some experts answered that question.
- "Corporate universities must develop a mechanism for creating a cost-effective, continuous stream of problem-specific/solution-specific online training programs. By forming alliances with other corporate universities and T&D groups, needed programs can be developed and produced for significantly less money than would otherwise be required."[20]
- "The biggest trend is organizations (Sun Microsystems, Procter & Gamble, IBM, etc.) are going from offering isolated online courses to developing an enterprise-wide strategy for online learning. Companies with corporate universities are in the forefront of this movement."[21]
- "One of the most sobering things is that teams that really accomplish things within a larger organization are at the most risk…my advice is you can't go it alone…The biggest challenge, though, remains the diffusion process: getting ideas and information out on a large scale. These ideas are so threatening that diffusion is difficult. We're finding…that the guiding principle is that significant innovations must be diffused through informal, self-organizing networks, through horizontal communities of practice."[22]

TABLE 2-4: Training Department or Corporate University?

Training Department	Corporate University
Limited to training	Broadens the concept of training to include all aspects of performance improvement
Training director does not "sit at the table with the executives"	Chief learning officer is involved in strategic decision making
Responsible for training	Responsible for training, performance support, and knowledge management
Peopled with trainers	Peopled with performance consultants

Based on Regalbuto, cited in Gordon, 1999, pp. 30–31.

Evaluating Learning Organizations

When organizations commit to broad, long-term interventions to achieve continuous improvement they want to see results. However, Peter Senge warns:

You can never prove anything. You can do a million things right in an organization and then, through bad luck or due to conditions outside the organization, there is a business downturn…An organization is a complex system—and you never get to see what would have happened if you hadn't made the change…You can run a bunch of numbers on either investment (technology or people) but they are always based on a lot of assumptions. They prove little. What we do is work to build long-term relationships within organizations to keep the process alive over time. People aren't stupid. They won't keep doing things over a long period of time if they don't think they are getting something out of it.[23]

Senge provides an example of an ongoing intervention in the sales area of a large organization. The intervention started six years ago and combines elements of KM, action learning, and learning organization: "Nobody talks about return on investment on a project like that. It's just part of the way they do business."[24] What keeps the project going are anecdotal records on customer satisfaction, records that document savings in time and money, and increases in sales revenue.

Implementing Learning Organization Interventions in the Workplace

Helping an organization become a learning organization is to some extent the same as helping an organization manage knowledge. For example, the PT practitioner can help promote the following structures within a learning organization:

- Acquisition processes used to gain new data, information, and knowledge

- Distribution processes used to pass on data, information, and knowledge within the organization
- Interpretation and translation processes used to make meaning from data or information in order to transform it into useful knowledge
- Storage and retrieval processes used to record data, information, and knowledge and recall it on demand to benefit the organization.[25]

The PT practitioner may accomplish this task by helping to:
- Assess the organization's current structures for acquiring, interpreting, storing, retrieving, and distributing data, information, and knowledge (see the previous section on KM)
- Align goals for improving learning processes with strategic goals of the organization
- Build tools (performance analysis tools, group process tools, etc.) to help the organization improve processes that contribute to achievement of the organization's strategic goals.[26]

The PT practitioner may also recommend methods to improve the effectiveness of learning processes for individuals, teams and the organization as a whole. Sometimes the PT practitioner may need to help the organization decide whether to focus on individual learning, team learning, organizational learning, or all three.[27]

Since the early 1990s, there has been a shift in the reality of work and the workers' relationship to work. "Today's workers are being asked to *think*. Today's companies are full of *knowledge workers* much of whose most important *behavior* goes on inside their heads."[28] Some ways that PT practitioners can help develop knowledge workers include the following:
- Suggest knowledge task analysis as part of job or performance analysis[29, 30]
- Share information on learning and learning styles

- Encourage and support training and development efforts that focus on decision making, problem solving, and creativity.

In addition, the PT practitioner can help select or design techniques and tools that will support the learning organization as it develops and grows.

- Team building and group process techniques and tools to empower teams to perform at the highest possible level
- Change management techniques and tools to encourage and support *new thinking*
- Feedback techniques and tools to motivate, incentivize, and reward employees
- Focusing techniques and tools to keep the organization centered on a shared vision of continuous improvement and continuous learning as they relate to the business goals and objectives

Many of the interventions discussed in this book are also useful for developing and maintaining a learning organization, for example communication interventions (information technology), HR interventions (selection and staffing, incentives and rewards, motivation), and analysis interventions (job analysis, work design, job specifications). The PT practitioner consulting within today's learning organization must truly become a generalist when it comes to performance interventions.

Action Learning

Action learning, organizational learning, and creating a learning organization go hand in hand: "The most structured application of action learning is in a learning organization where there is an overt commitment to using learning as a strategy and a value placed on capturing and sharing learning."[1] In fact, according to Peter Senge,

---

JOB AID 2-2: Thought Starter: Corporate University Best Practices

Directions: This list of best practices is based on a benchmarking study conducted by the Institute for Education Best Practices (IEBP) and American Productivity and Quality Center (APQC). Use the following checklist to:

- Start a dialogue about corporate university best practices
- Begin to plan a corporate university
- Evaluate a corporate university

Corporate influence

☐ Corporate university fits the mission, values, and culture of the organization

☐ Senior management is strongly committed to develop and educate the work force

☐ Business units are consciously involved in all aspects of the learning process

Structural considerations

☐ Business strategy drives the structure of the university

☐ Learning process is distinct from traditional HR processes

☐ Corporate university operates as cost center

Learning process

☐ No universal process map exists for designing learning interventions; flexible and user friendly

☐ Radical movement toward the use of technology occurs only after close examination of the business process

☐ Corporate university identifies outcomes first, then determines training goals and related requirements

Managing information

☐ Benchmarking is a key driver of creation and innovation

☐ Corporate university is a powerful tool for creation and management of knowledge capital within the organization

Adapted from The Corporate University Best-in-Class Report. *(1998). Institute for Education Best Practices (IEBP) and American Productivity and Quality Center (APQC). Available online:* http://www.apqc.org. *ISPI © 2001. Permission granted for unlimited duplication for noncommercial use.*

"Knowledge generation primarily occurs in working teams. Individual learning is a by-product of what goes on in really innovative teams...What really matters is how the team thinks and acts together."[2]

The concept of action learning was developed some 60 years ago as a way to improve performance in an environment where "organizations are too busy fighting alligators to find time to drain the swamp."[3] Action learning allows learning and action to occur simultaneously so organizations can fight the alligators and drain the swamps at the same time. It is a way to integrate learning with doing that goes beyond case studies and simulations, a way to "create real results in real time."[4]

Action learning has its roots in the fields of education (Knowles, Dewey, Kolb), management (Drucker, Senge), psychology (Lewin, Jung, Maslow), and sociology (Weick, Hofstede, Kohls).[5] One of the major proponents of action learning is Reginald Revans, who has written and lectured on the topic since the late 1960s. Many consider Revans to be the father of action learning.[6] According to Revans, "What was (once) identified as evolution can now rightfully be referred to as action learning."[7]

Definition and Scope

Action learning is a small group process that integrates commitment, learning, and doing to solve real, relevant, and challenging organizational problems. Action learning is both a process and a program. Members of the group share, question, experience, reflect, make decisions, take action. Sivasailam Thiagarajan (Thiagi) provides a view of action learning as a process.

Action learning involves a combination of action and reflection by a team solving complex, strategic problems in a real-world organizational setting. Team members apply existing skills and knowledge and create new skills, knowledge and insight through continuously reflecting and questioning the problem definition, the collaborative behavior, and the ensuing results.[8]

There are two basic types of action learning programs:
- Single-project program—organization provides a single problem, everyone in the group works on it, and the group usually has a sponsor or champion to smooth the way; action learning may become the vehicle for resolving organizational challenges.
- Open-group program—each member brings a problem to the group and takes a turn as the action learning *client*.[9]

Elements of Action Learning
The elements of action learning are the same for both types of programs; the processes vary. Figure 2-5 presents the elements of action learning that set it apart from other problem solving and decision making activities: problem, people, process, and commitment.

What's the Problem?
Action learning groups deal with problems that are:
- Important to the organization
- Complex, systemic issues
- Not easily solved by experts or ready-made right answers.[10]

Some examples of problems suited to action learning interventions are systemic organizational issues such as "reducing turnover in the work force, improving information systems, increasing sales, resolving conflict between departments, handling a management issue, and developing a new performance appraisal system."[11]

Action Learning Is Active Learning
Action learning is definitely not a spectator sport.[12] Action learning group meetings involve reporting, clarifying, and resolving problems so that the group can understand the problem, develop alternatives, construct a solution, and take action.[13] Group participants ask questions, reflect on the problem and possible solutions, and take action, "while at the same time focusing on what they are learning and how their learning can benefit each group member and the organization as a whole."[14]

Many experts stress that action learning programs should not be confused with task forces or quality circles; experiential or outdoor learning; simulations, case studies, or business games. However, Sivasailam Thiagarajan (Thiagi) does include action learning in his list of 25 types of "games people play."[15]

One aspect of action learning that sets it aside from other activities is the fact that action learning takes group members outside their areas of expertise and asks them to work on unfamiliar problems. The results of this process are illustrated in Figure 2-6.

Achieving Success
One key to success, and the challenge of action learning, is "to practice it with discipline and consistency."[16] For example, regular meetings are important because they provide the opportunity for members to recognize changes occurring within themselves and/or the organization and to learn from these changes.

Concentration and distribution of time is also important to success. Action learning groups may solve problems and acquire learning in a few hours; however, to gain maximum benefit and resolve more complex problems the group may need from 3 to 12 months of part-time, full-time, or a combination of part- and full-time meetings.[17]

FIGURE 2-5: Action Learning Is PC...

People
- Group, team, or set of four–eight members (functional or cross-functional, internal or external to the organization) who are committed to learning while resolving the problem
- Facilitator or set advisor who helps members reflect on the problem and process and focus on the outputs and outcomes
- Sponsor or champion (for internal action learning groups) who provides visibility, acceptance, and access to resources

Problem
- Issue, project, challenge, or task
- Real, important, and relevant to client (individual, team, and/or organization)
- No easily identifiable solution; a challenge
- Within responsibility and power of the team to resolve
- Provides an opportunity for individual and organizational learning

Process
- Ask questions to clarify problem
- Reflect on answers and on problem solving process
- Identify possible solutions
- Take action

Commitment
- Commit to learning while doing
- Commit to take action

Based on Marquardt, 1999, pp. 5–8.

FIGURE 2-6: Action Learning Cascades New Knowledge

Action Learning starts here

Ask fresh questions

Reshape assumptions

Develop new mental models

Reassess current knowledge

Generate new knowledge

Based on Dilworth, 1998, pp. 37–38.

Another key to success is to perfect the element of reflection or meditation—"a *potent pause* (that) provides an opportunity for learning."[18] Individuals and groups frequently find themselves problem solving and making decisions on automatic pilot with little time for questioning and no time for reflection. Reflection is a pivotal component of critical thinking. The reflection element of action learning is the key that allows individuals and teams to learn new truths about their organization and to create fresh solutions based on those truths: "Wisdom arises unbidden when the mind is no longer driven to find answers."[19]

A final key to success is to SEDUCE the members of the action learning group. SEDUCE is an approach to discovery or experiential learning that may also be applied to action learning.

> *SEDUCE…creates an environment in which participants realize on their own what they need to know and/or do differently. The approach is seductive in that it can transform initial resistance into willing, even avid, interest. [Participants are] enticed into heightened levels of personal discovery which, in turn creates the dissonance necessary to facilitate individual (and organizational) change.*[20]

SEDUCE requires a facilitator and includes the following steps:
1. Start Up—set up the learning experience by stating the problem (if it is pre-established) and clarifying the objectives, process, participant roles and responsibilities, and any rules that may apply to the particular action learning session
2. Experience—involve participants consciously and actively in both the problem solving and the learning components of the action learning experience
3. Debrief—help participants discover and share their learning-related reactions and experiences; use learning logs (see Job Aid 2-3) and a structured discussion activity (see Implementing Games and Simulations)
4. Unveil concepts—help the participants identify and discuss broader concepts and principles discovered during the learning experience; one strategy is to *map* their thoughts, ideas, and lessons learned
5. Execute—help the participants identify what to do now (next steps or action steps).[21]

Applications of Action Learning
"Although action learning contains some essential principles and elements, it is flexible and adaptable enough to work magnificently in a multitude of settings and situations."[22] The five major applications of action learning are the same as the five most important needs facing organizations today: problem solving, organizational learning, team building, leadership development, and professional growth and career development. Table 2-5 describes the five applications of action learning.

Core Competencies for Action Learning
The effectiveness of action learning as a performance intervention is affected by the following core competencies for individuals, teams, and the organization:
- Individual competencies—critical reflection skills, inquiry skills, and the desire and ability to remain open to change and to create a personal vision.
- Team competencies—conversation (dialogue) skills, facilitation skills, and the desire and ability to create a shared vision.
- Organizational competencies—desire, knowledge, and ability to adopt a systems perspective, create a shared vision, design a learning infrastructure that supports action learning, create a learning culture, and cultivate new leaders (stewards).[23]

Benefits of Action Learning
Action learning as a performance improvement intervention has many benefits. "Ultimately, the most significant benefit of action learning…may be that it can prepare organizational members better to resolve future problems."[24] In addition, action learning can accomplish the following:
- Serve a dual purpose as a leading-edge component of core training for executives and managers and as an ongoing strategy for organizational problem solving and decision making: "Action learning provides a valuable *practice field* for innovative thinking."[25]
- Become "an important vehicle for transformation of organizational culture, increasing the learning capacity of the enterprise and empowering workers."[26]
- Promote positive changes such as:
  — Commitment to shared learning throughout various levels of the organization
  — Greater self-awareness and self-confidence due to new insights and feedback
  — Enhanced ability to ask *fresh* questions and be more reflective
  — Improved communications and teamwork[27]
  — Provide a vehicle for organizations to "solve complex problems in a systemic way so they stay solved."[28]
- Boost organizational performance and create a *dynamic equilibrium* (balance) between learning and change by building the learning capacity of the organization and breaking with well-established mindsets.[29]

In short, many large corporations like General Electric, Ameritech, Whirlpool, and Accenture, formerly Anderson Consulting, use action learning to adapt better in turbulent times, promote continuous learning, and accelerate change.[30]

TABLE 2-5: Applications of Action Learning

Problem solving applications

- Solving technical problems by knowing how to obtain and apply knowledge efficiently and rationally
- Solving adaptive problems by developing skill in dealing with people-related issues that involve attitudes, habits, and even beliefs

Organizational learning applications

- Promoting and enabling a learning organization that integrates self-directed learning and doing: "Action learning is the DNA of a learning organization."
- Fostering four key learning skills: systems thinking, mental models, commitment to personal mastery, and dialogue (listening and communication)

Team building applications

- Developing effective teams through cooperation and collaboration
- Teaching team building skills such as communication, commitment, and creativity
- Developing team leaders who can inspire and facilitate

Leadership development applications

- "Growing" individuals who become:

— Systems thinkers	— *Polychronic coordinators* (wear many hats; multitask)
— Change agents	— Instructors, coaches, and mentors
— Innovators and risk takers	— Visionaries
— Servants and stewards	

Personal and career development applications

- Helping individuals acquire the following skills and attributes:

— Critical reflection	— Active listening
— Inquiry and questioning	— Courage and frankness
— Openness and willingness to change	— Ability to advise and help others
— Clear personal vision	— Facilitation and presentation skills
— Personal mastery	— Wisdom and common sense
— Empathy	— Self-awareness

Based on Marquardt, 1999b, pp. 57–122.

One study also suggests that action learning enables transfer. In order for learning transfer to occur, "participants must engage other members of the workplace in resolving issues and must encounter and deal with policies, practices, or systems that otherwise make transfer of training difficult."[31] Action learning teams can enable learning transfer by making sure that the following elements are in place:

- Real and challenging workplace issues
- Focus on just-in-time problem solving
- Opportunity to reflect on new learnings and apply them in different contexts

Barriers to Action Learning

There are barriers that may interfere with accepting action learning as the performance improvement intervention of choice. The major problem is that action learning may not match established ways of doing business because it:

- May require the use of cross-functional or global teams
- Encourages learning *outside the box* of formal training and may threaten traditional training departments
- Requires people to problem solve in areas that are outside of their primary expertise
- May result in outcomes that are difficult (but not impossible) to measure.[32]

Cultural values and practices that exist in the non-Western world may create another barrier to action learning, or they may be treated as "a source of synergy that contributes to a variety of perspectives that can actually augment the power and success of action learning programs."[33] Each of the key elements of action learning—forming the action learning group, selecting the problem, questioning and reflecting, committing to action—contains Western assumptions, values, and practices that may cause a cultural reaction from participants in Latin America, Asia, the Middle East, Africa, or Southern Europe.[34] For example, Chinese participants may resist the reflection element of action learning because they find it difficult to openly discuss their feelings and observations; their culture supports private and informal feedback.[35]

Implementing Action Learning in the Workplace

The PT practitioner can play a major role in promoting, designing, implementing, and evaluating action learning as a performance improvement intervention:

- Develop organizational awareness of what action learning is and is not
- Develop organizational awareness of the individual, group, and organization-wide benefits of action learning
- Promote action learning as a means to achieve competitive advantage
- Suggest ways to "weave action learning into the very fabric of the organization."[36] For example, integrate action learning into other performance improvement interventions such as organizational development, individual growth, career development, "mentoring, and learning organization interventions."
- Promote the integration of action learning into other activities, for example, strategic planning, project management, and developing models for knowledge creation and capture.

JOB AID 2-3: Daily Action Learning Log

There is no assurance that there will be any residual capacity to solve the next problem that arises, whether it is similar or dissimilar, if participants in the process have not reflected on what, if anything, they have learned.
Willis, V. J. (1998). Action learning design features and outcomes at Georgia State University. *Performance Improvement Quarterly, 11*(2), p. 40.

Although things that go right may help us feel competent and successful, the things that go wrong are what teach us the most and are often the source of our greatest accomplishments.
Brooks, A. K. (1998). Educating HRD leaders at the University of Texas at Austin: The use of action learning to facilitate university-workplace collaboration. *Performance Improvement Quarterly, 11*(2), p. 52.

Directions: Use the template below as a learning log that individual members of an action learning group, team, or set may use to record daily *lessons learned*. The log is set up to reflect the concepts of critical incident analysis. At the end of the action learning experience, the individual members may decide to review and summarize their logs, and share the summaries with the action learning group or others in the organization.

Note: This activity may be culture sensitive and may not be appropriate for global application. For example, see Yiu, L. & Saner, R. (1998). Use of action learning as a vehicle for capacity building in China. *Performance Improvement Quarterly 11*(1), p. 145.

Daily Action Learning Log

Action Learning Group _____

Member _____ Date _____

| 1. When was I most engaged? |
| 2. When was I most disengaged? |
| 3. When was I most affirmed? |
| 4. When was I most puzzled? |
| 5. What was the single most important thing I learned today? Why? |
| 6. How will I capitalize on this most important lesson learned in the future? |

Adapted from Dilworth, R.L. (1998). Action learning in a nutshell. Performance Improvement Quarterly, 11*(1), p. 41.*
ISPI © 2001. Permission granted for unlimited duplication for noncommercial use.

- Design and develop an action learning core competency program for individuals, teams, and the organization.
- Facilitate and mentor action learning groups, teams, or sets, or support selected facilitators/mentors.
- Help select action learning set, group or team members. Dilworth suggests using a learning style questionnaire, for example, the questionnaire by Honey and Mumford, based on David Kolb's model, to make sure there are both active and reflective learning types in the group.[37]
- Develop training, job aids, or other performance support systems (PSS) to help action learning groups master the processes of questioning, reflection, and action, as well as basic group processes and skills such as establishing ground rules, communicating effectively, time management, resolving conflicts, and so forth (see Job Aid 2-3).
- Suggest criteria and methods for evaluating the process and outcomes of action learning by using the evaluation component of the HPT Model.[38]

Throughout the process, the PT practitioner should remain current in the field of action learning (theory and best practices) and knowledgeable about current and emerging organizational needs.

Education and Training

Education and training interventions are two sides of the same coin. They are both:

- Instructional PSS that organizations use to enhance and enable employee learning and development
- Reliant on (interactive) learning technologies to involve the learner and support the concepts of just-in-time and just-for-me learning.
- Important to employee retention—[It is the company's willingness to educate and train that turns new hires into long-term employees."[1]
- Important to achieving or maintaining competitive advantage.

Here is an example. One way to keep up with the competition is to change the design of an organization. Organization design is "a broad intervention that addresses strategy, structure, systems, and people."[2] The steps in the design process are assess and plan, begin education, then develop, implement, and maintain the organizational changes.[3] In this case, the step *begin education* includes both education and training:

Education is related to the first four stages of change— developing awareness, understanding, acceptance, and commitment. In addition, competence—knowledge and skills—is crucial to the (organization) design process because change cannot go farther than employees' ability to successfully develop, implement, and maintain change. Therefore, education and training constitute an extremely important step.[4]

Before discussing education and training as instructional performance support interventions, there are two components of both education and training systems that need a brief introduction—self-directed learning and free agent learners.

Self-Directed Learning

Self-direction, which is traditionally linked to adult education, is becoming a critical factor in the success of both education and training. Self-directed learning is the tendency of adult learners to prefer taking charge of their own learning. It is often touted as the distinguishing characteristic of the adult learner; however, it is necessary to insert a disclaimer here: "There are many individuals who are chronologically adults but who show a marked disinclination to behave in anything approaching a self-directed manner in any area of their lives."[5]

Self-directed learning is critical to the success of higher education as more and more working adults seek undergraduate or graduate degree programs that accommodate their work schedules.

Although many adults still prefer the traditional college classroom, time and cost pressures are causing them to look for more convenient and affordable means of education, including television, videotape, audiotape, independent study, and computer-guided tutorials.[6]

Self-directed learning is also becoming an important success factor as organizations turn more and more to just-in-time (real-time) training.

Workers and their natural environment are the key to successful real-time learning. Real time training assumes the workers are the best judges for determining what they need to know and when they need to know it.[7]

Finally, the growing need for enterprise-wide training is best met by hiring and retaining workers who are self-directed learners, because enterprise training requires adults to willingly interact with various computer-based, distance, and online learning technologies. (Read the discussion of enterprise training in the Interactive Learning Technologies section of this chapter.)

Free Agent Learners

A natural outcome of the emphasis on self-directed learning is the concept of the *free-agent learner*. Even education and training suppliers are getting excited about free-agent learners. According to the hype, the free-agent learner is:

...the newest consumer class to hit the training industry. They're motivated, they're mobile, and they want to control their own learning. They are independent and highly motivated adults who are taking responsibility for their own ongoing learning and development, as opposed to relying on employers to provide it for them. They're people who understand the need for lifelong learning and are doing something about it.[8]

Even the federal government is getting into the act. At the summit meeting *21st Century Skills for 21st Century Jobs,* attendees called for the following:

- More scholarships to secure the benefits of education and training for employees and employers, including tax-free benefits for undergraduate and graduate education
- New Internet services (learning portals) to search for education and training (see Learning Portals at the end of this section)
- Creation of a leadership group (CEOs, college presidents, labor union leaders, and others) to discuss how employers, institutions of higher learning, labor unions, and others can help the American worker by *investing in work force skills and training*[9]

There may be a downside to the rise of the self-directed or free-agent learner.

- Organizations will need to take a serious look at outsourcing training and development activities to take advantage of lower costs and greater accessibility
- Internal training departments will need to learn how to compete with external providers
- All training and education providers will need to focus on motivating adult learners to select a particular education or training program
- As learners become more competent and confident, they may challenge the status quo, expect to incorporate new ideas into the organization, and expect a reward for obtaining an education.[10]

However, education and training can meet the challenge by reinventing themselves within the context of the organization and the learners they serve.

Definition and Scope—Education

Despite the heavy emphasis on training, education is still an integral part of the way organizations develop the world's work force. For example, *ASTD's 2000 Annual Accounting of Worldwide Patterns in Employer-Provided Training* found that organizations across all six regions (Australia/New Zealand, Asia, Japan, Canada, United States, and Europe) almost universally supported attendance at conferences and tuition reimbursement.[11]

Defining education is a matter of perspective:

- The dictionary defines education as "the process of training and developing the knowledge, skill, mind, character, etc. especially by formal schooling, teaching, and training."[12]
- The definition from a systems perspective is "a deliberately constructed, complex human activity system ...designed to carry out the specific societal function of nurturing learning and human development."[13]
- The definition of education as a process is "the process by which human beings (alone, in groups, or in instructional settings) seek to improve themselves or their society by increasing their skill, their knowledge, or their sensitiveness. Any process by which individuals, groups, or institutions try to help human beings improve in these ways."[14]

Traditionally, the term *education* usually refers to learning that takes place within the K–12 or higher education systems. From this viewpoint, education includes:

- Classes in basic skills such as reading, writing, and math (literacy)
- High school completion classes or preparation sessions for the General Educational Development (GED) high school equivalency exam
- Undergraduate college courses leading to an associate or bachelor's degree or special certification
- Graduate courses that lead to an advanced degree at the specialist, master's, or doctoral level

However, there is a lifelong way to view education, which focuses on accepting five primary purposes for educating people of all ages:

- Encourage continuous growth and development, for example, continuing education programs, staff development programs, conferences, workshops
- Help people respond to practical problems and issues of adult life, for example, stress workshops, substance abuse support groups, pre-retirement seminars
- Prepare people for current and future work opportunities, for example formal apprenticeship programs, basic skills (literacy) programs, high school completion programs, higher education courses or degree programs
- Help organizations achieve desired results and adapt to change, for example, TQM program or technology transfer programs
- Provide opportunities to examine community and societal issues[15]

The two primary outcomes of educational programs are individual and organizational change.[16] In order for either or both changes to occur, "education should be seen as a fundamental and ongoing process...The education process should emphasize immediate application of learnings."[17] The employer or the employee can determine and act on the need for education, and the employer may reimburse education expenses for classes related to the employee's current or future job.

Definition and Scope—Training

Training in its broadest sense is instruction provided to employees by employers to establish, improve, maintain, or extinguish performance as it relates to business needs. Langdon views training as a four-part performance intervention:

- Objectives describe the outcomes (what the trainees are expected to know or do when the training ends)
- Content provides information to help the trainees learn
- Interaction gives the trainees a chance to demonstrate what they have learned
- Feedback provides the trainees (and the instructor) with information and data to compare the interaction to an *exemplary model.*[18]

Training develops employee knowledge, abilities, skills, and attitudes to "maximize the human resource contribution to an enterprise."[19] A variety of training occurs globally; however, regional differences exist in subject-area training offered to employees. For example:

- Managerial and supervisory skills training was the largest expenditure in Japan and Asia.
- Information technology skills training and technical processes and procedures training were well funded in all regions except Japan.
- Occupational safety and compliance training accounted for large expenditures in the United States, Canada, and Australia/New Zealand.
- Basic skills training expenditures were higher in Europe and Asia.
- Customer relations training expenditures were highest in Asia.[20]

On the Plus Side

Much has been written in praise of training in the new millennium, mainly in support of training's role in knowledge management and employee retention. Here are just three examples:

- "As companies seek to transform themselves into knowledge-centered organizations, training becomes ever more crucial to maintaining competitive advantage."[21]
- "Organizations need to attract and keep skilled workers in a tight labor market and to retrain their existing work forces fast."[22]
- Smart companies "recognize the attraction of training and development—and they're using it to win the (employee) retention game…"[23]

Training is big business. The 12 leading corporate training companies generated revenues of approximately $8 billion in 1998, with $4.9 billion going to information technology (IT) training and $3.2 billion to soft skills training.[24] A year later, US organizations budgeted $62.5 billion for training, with $15 billion going to outside providers.[25]

The Other Side of Training

Some paint a less-than-flattering picture of what they call *traditional* or *typical* training systems:

- "…Training—as it is set up in most organizations today—is an enemy of empowerment and continuous learning. In many cases, it decreases overall organizational performance by adding to information overload, stress, and cynicism. Traditional training policies and underlying assumptions are in direct contradiction with most contemporary organizational visions—even in those organizations embracing the notion of the learning organization."[26]

To Train or Not to Train

Training is the performance intervention of last resort.

Not every human performance problem lends itself to a training solution. Training should be used to solve human performance problems only when workers lack the competencies to perform. It should not be used when workers lack motivation, appropriate tools or equipment, appropriate supervision, or when other issues are affecting performance.[27]

Training *is* appropriate when:

- Alternative performance improvement interventions "will not address the underlying causes of human performance problems or capitalize on human performance enhancement opportunities."[28]
- Adequate resources exist to design, develop, implement, and evaluate the training. Training professionals traditionally use some form of the instructional system design (ISD) approach to training (assess needs, design, develop, implement, evaluate). ISD has evolved over the years to "keep pace with growing technologically oriented instructional support options, the declining half-life of knowledge, and the growing popularity of performance support systems."[29]

The best person to make this call is the PT practitioner, preferably working together with the stakeholders including HR and training professionals.

Training, KM, and EPSS

Training, KM, and EPSS are converging.

Training, electronic performance support (EPS), and knowledge management (KM) share the same fundamental goal: to reduce the cycle time to effective—hopefully expert—job performance. And the same computer systems that facilitate knowledge management are blurring the distinctions between KM, EPS, and training. In some ways the three are converging...[30]

An EPS tool can be viewed as an *ultimate example* of KM because it delivers useful information on demand via an easy and seamless interface. At the same time, *chunks* of stored information or *learning objects* (from a KM or EPS system) can be linked and reused to form modules for a training course.

From a broader perspective:

Companies need to quit thinking in terms of training and start thinking about knowledge creation and knowledge transfer as distinct business processes...The question is not, How do we deliver training to x number of people? It is, How do you make sure you have the right people in the right place with the right knowledge to execute your business plan?[31]

The convergence of KM and training is still in process. Only 42% of the respondents to a survey distributed at the 1999 Training Directors Forum on KM said they were *very involved* in their organization's KM activities. In addition, of the 35% who said KM has a *home* in their company, just 16% indicated that *home* is in the training function rather than in information systems (IS) or some other business function.[32]

Global Trends in Training

Training needs to transform itself "from resource to source of competitive advantage."[33] The need for change is complicated by an environment of constant and fast-paced change: "The way that technology is transforming the training and development field is like viewing a weather forecast. You have a vague idea of what's expected, but you don't know exactly how it will pan out."[34]

Dr. David Waugh, secretary general of the International Federation of Training and Development Organizations (IFTDO), suggests that there are 10 global trends in training and development. The 10 trends are outlined in Table 2-6 along with the major needs that are driving the trends. The list of trends supports three major training needs:

- Ongoing need for technical training and retraining triggered by the redefinition of work and by technology innovations
- Increased need for non-technical training in areas such as diversity, customer satisfaction, and creativity
- Increased need for just-in-time and on-the-job training to support rapid work force response to change.[35]

Technical and Non-Technical Training

Organizations are recognizing that training boosts competitive advantage by increasing work force capability and capacity. This means they will need to emphasize training or retraining in specific skill areas where they have or seek to have a competitive advantage.[36] The skill areas may be technical (hard) or non-technical (soft).

Technical Training

Technical training is all about *the hard stuff* that builds capability, capacity, and skill in the work force. Technical training includes five types of content:

- Facts—singular, unique objects or unique associations among concepts, for example, the specific purchase order form required for ordering office equipment, or the meaning of a specific numerical code on a credit form.[37]
- Concepts—groups of objects or ideas that are given a common name, for example, chair or continuous improvement.[38]
- Processes—description of the nature of a business or technical system task and how it works, for example, how a gasoline engine operates or how X company hires new employees.[39]
- Procedures—directives that guide the worker through a series of clearly defined steps, which result in achievement of a task, for example, logging on to a computer or taking a customer order.[40]
- Principles—rules or standards that support optimal job/task performance and the achievement of desired outcomes, and are influenced by specific work situations, for example, rules for closing a sale or tolerance standards for machine parts.[41]

The trainee must process or learn the content of technical training at two levels:

1. *Remember* key information, for example, recall or recognize the basic steps or stages in a process.
2. *Apply* the information to specific job tasks, for example, solve a problem or make an inference based on a process.[42]

The audience for technical training includes workers who are responsible for the following tasks:

- Producing, packing, or distributing tangible products (automobiles, electronic components, soap) or services (customer billing, hiring)
- Using equipment or technologies (fork lifts, computers applications, magnetic resonance imaging, total quality management, techniques and tools)
- Servicing or maintaining equipment, technologies, or processes
- Troubleshooting equipment, technologies, or processes.

Some tasks, like troubleshooting, require both hard (technical) and soft (non-technical) skills. "Technical

TABLE 2-6: Global Trends in Training and Development

Trend	Driver
1. Training will continue as a highly valued activity.	Need to build, enhance, or change skills required by organizations and individuals
2. Training in skill areas where nations or organizations have or seek to have competitive advantage will be emphasized.	Recognition that training boosts competitive advantage by increasing work force capability and capacity
3. Training in soft skills will gain ascendancy.	Specific needs for training in diversity issues, customer satisfaction, creativity, safety, quality, etc.
4. Training in working new ways and in new venues will gain importance.	Redefinition of work to accommodate environmental and social concerns, new forms of work organizations, new technologies, etc.
5. Training will take place in globe-spanning mega-corporations.	Decrease in the number of country-specific enterprises; work force development will become a global undertaking
6. Re-training rather than training will be the norm.	Technological innovation and other factors will cause skills to deteriorate and be re-constituted
7. Training systems will be fluid, flexible, responsive, and results driven, adaptive to needs of a global economy.	Global economy will demand rapid work force response to change; individuals will hold several jobs in different occupational structures over a lifetime
8. Training via distance learning technologies will be mainstreamed.	Global work force and changing lifestyles will require access to training 24 hours a day from all time zones
9. Learning organizations will be common and investment in people will outperform investment in technology.	Human capital investment and knowledge management will be key elements in strategic business plans
10. Training will focus on new categories of workers.	Aging of population will signal an aging work force; large number of disabled persons will join work force, enabled by technology

Based on Waugh, 1999, p. 3

troubleshooting involves the detection, diagnosis, and repair of faulty equipment…(and) requires the use of knowledge, skills and experience to interact effectively with a complex technical (or human) system that is behaving in some unusual way."[43]

Non-Technical Training

The report on global trends in training also suggested that training in *soft skills* will become more important because of specific needs such as training in diversity issues, customer satisfaction, creativity, safety, quality, etc.[44] Non-technical training is another term for *soft skills training.* Non-technical training often involves changing attitudes rather than knowledge or skills. One way to determine whether the skill or task is technical or non-technical is to

ask: Is there one right or wrong way to perform? If *yes,* then the skill or task is technical; if *no,* then the skill or task is soft; if *sometimes,* then the skill or task may be a hybrid with hard and soft components (for example, troubleshooting).

Just-in-Time Training

Future training systems need to be fluid, flexible, responsive, results oriented, and adaptive to the needs of a global economy that demands rapid work force response to change.[45] According to many major corporations, just-in-time training is "a paradigm shift for the year 2000."[46] In its broadest sense, just-in-time training is training that takes place just before or concurrent with the trainee's need to use a specific knowledge or skill.

In this form of flexible training, defined as access to integrated learning materials, information banks, communication channels, and tools, the learner can call up whatever amount and type of learning material is most necessary and most useful at the most opportune time.[47]

It is truly a learn-and-do intervention and focuses on need-to-know rather than nice-to-know content. "The logical extension of using just-in-time training is to use just the right amount of training…(for example) an EPSS that provides in-context support to perform a task."[48] (See the section on Non-Instructional PSS beginning on p. 67.)

Just-in-time training is considered an emerging trend in performance interventions: "Workers will use on-the-job information systems to access policies, procedures, and data on an as-needed basis. They also will engage in brief segments of technology-mediated or one-to-one coached learning on the job."[49] The challenge is to perform a thorough and systematic up-front analysis and to design the training using performance-based design techniques that will "ensure both the training's relevance and its effectiveness."[50]

The rush to just-in-time has also caused an increase in the use of online training and is changing the face of the internal training department from training provider to quality and career development assurance. For example, workers and line supervisors know what kind of training an employee needs, but the trainer can "differentiate between substantive education and people going off all willy-nilly…"[51]

On-the-Job Training

On-the-job training (OJT) is one way to meet the need for training and retraining due to technological innovation and rapid changes in the work force.[52] OJT is not a new concept and may be more prevalent than most training professionals care to admit. Respondents to ASTD's annual training surveys tend to report that up to 80% of all training is delivered using instructor-led classroom systems.[53] However, some sources suggest a different scenario:

A growing body of research has shown that employees receive substantially more training through on-the-job training (OJT) than through classroom programs. Furthermore, OJT has been reported as the most frequently used training method across most jobs and job levels, including skilled and semiskilled industrial, sales, and supervisory-managerial positions…
Perhaps the contradictory information about OJT demonstrates the adage that truth depends on the perspective of the respondent (training manager or front-line performer).[54]

OJT is a "real-time change strategy"[55] that is defined by time, place, and resources. It is individual or small-group training conducted at or on the worksite by one or more *expert* performers (peers or supervisors) during work hours. OJT focuses on developing novices into competent performers of a "discrete set of tasks."[56]

Structured and Unstructured OJT

OJT ranges from unstructured (informal) to structured (formal). Unstructured OJT is also known as *"follow Joe (or Jane) around the plant training, sink-or-swim training, sit by Nellie training, and learning by the ropes."*[57] OJT is considered unstructured if the primary way that the novice acquires knowledge and skill is through any of the following:

- Impromptu explanations or demonstrations by others
- Self-initiated trial-and-error
- Self-motivated reading, investigating, or questioning
- Imitation of others' behavior.[58]

There are risks involved in using unstructured OJT. For example, the novices may or may not achieve competency and training content may or may not be accurate, complete, clear, and unambiguous.

Structured OJT is planned and formal. It involves show-tell-do with elements of coaching and mentoring, and is preceded by job/task analysis and train-the-OJT trainer. During structured OJT the experienced employee:

- Demonstrates and discusses specific information associated with a task
- Provides opportunities for the novice employee to practice
- Provides feedback to the novice employee
- Repeats the process until the novice masters the task.[59]

Table 2-7 lists some of the strengths and weaknesses of OJT as a performance intervention.

Even at its best, traditional training can only teach the basic skills required on the job.

Real-time training emphasizes the average person's intrinsic interest in his or her work and the desire to be self-directed, to seek responsibility, and to develop the capacity to be creative with coworkers in solving work-related problems.[60]

Implementing Education and Training Interventions in the Workplace

In general, to help implement education and training as performance improvement interventions, the PT practitioner needs to think like a business leader, act like a strategist, and see like a systematist:

TABLE 2-7: Strengths and Weaknesses of OJT

Strengths	Weaknesses
Does not require special training facilities	May disrupt the workplace
Does not require large training organization	Experts may lack training skills
Training is presented by workers or supervisors on the worksite	Experts may not follow standard procedures (for example, experts tend to use heuristics or rules of thumb for troubleshooting based on their experience)
Takes less time to train on the job than in the classroom	May cause health and safety problems
Does not require duplication of equipment or costly simulations	Hands-on or practice time may vary due to worksite constraints
Does not require the expert to leave the worksite for an extended period of time	Gives the expert an extra workload
Cost effective for training an individual or small group	May lower productivity

Based on Rothwell and Kazanas, 1994; Rothwell, 1996, pp. 249–250.

- A business leader tries to identify and understand the strategic agenda driving the initiative, the work environment, the expectations and measures for successful accomplishment of the initiative, the current performance barriers, and the current enhancers of performance improvement *before* taking action.
- A strategist conducts a complete performance analysis to determine gaps and align the various elements (for example, corporate strategies and employee performance). Then the strategist plans a multifaceted intervention that drives and supports individual and organizational transformation; changes or maintains the intervention over time; measures and evaluates the results; and makes revisions as needed.
- A systematist takes the long view and considers *all* the success factors for integrating and enabling the intervention. For example, the systematist would convene a task force, enlist the support of top management, launch the intervention for maximum recognition and buy-in, and continually measure and communicate results.[61]

Changing Roles for HR and Training Professionals
Another implementation strategy is to encourage HR and training personnel to assume new roles. First, help HR and training professionals understand that the movement from training to performance improvement requires change. Then explain that the new role feels a lot like the role of a PT practitioner.

[The role of HR and training professionals] is now far broader and has deeper implications for shaping the future of the organization. The stakes have been raised in every component of your work. Because your role has shifted from managing employee training to shaping strategic direction, your work is viewed by top management as significantly more important than in the past. By the same token, accountability is more stringent. You have to demonstrate that your initiatives made a difference to the organization…to continuously link the alignment of individual performance with changing business results necessary for the organization to survive.[62]

Table 2-8 compares the old role and the new role of HR and training professionals.

Transforming Training
Another way that PT practitioners can implement training interventions is to help transform traditional training. If training is the key to effective knowledge management and employee retention, then organizations need to explore how to transform traditional training systems into learning and performance systems (see Figure 2-7).

PT practitioners have the competency to help organizations find their way through the transformation maze, and a vested interest in achieving the goal of a workplace where learning and performance are strategically linked (see Job Aid 2-4).

TABLE 2-8: Old/New Roles for HR and Training Professionals

Component	Old Role	New Role
Scope	Narrow, specific skills training	Long-term employability for employee retention
Deliverables	Programs and events	High-performance work systems
Work Environment	Static work environment	Dynamic work environment
Accountability	Delivering training	Organizational change
Delivery Method	Classroom	Multifaceted development activities and training
Results	Assumed behavior change	Results that demonstrate organizational value
Your Response	Assumes training alone will change behavior	Assumes there are multiple performance levers that affect behavior change

Based on Charchian and Cohen, 2000, p. 13.

FIGURE 2-7: Transforming Training

Traditional Training ➡ ➡ ➡ Integrated Performance and Learning

Traditional Training	Integrated Performance and Learning
• Event-based	• Continuous learning
• Top-down planning	• Collaborative learning
• Other directed	• Self-directed learning
• Knowledge-based	• Performance improvement based
• Creating and designing curriculum	• Creating and managing infrastructure for learning and collaboration to support business needs

Based on Gayeski, 1999, p. 8; Rothwell and Sanders, 1999.

Interactive Learning Technologies

Learning technologies are methods or media designed and used to present information to learners and to enhance learning. The two major delivery systems for learning technologies are instructor-led classrooms and distance learning. Both delivery systems use computer and wired or wireless telecommunication technologies to enable and enhance learning.

The *2000 ASTD International Comparisons Report* provides the following information on worldwide patterns in the use of learning technologies for classroom or distance training:

- Learning technologies account for 9% or less of the training conducted in 1999 in all six regions of the globe.
- Text-only and multimedia computer-based training (CBT) were the two learning technologies used by the largest percentage of respondents
- Groupware was third in terms of use
- Virtual reality was the least used learning technology[1]

Although the data showed little change in the use of learning technologies from 1997 to 1999, "most firms around the world continue to believe that learning technologies will play an increasingly important role in the future, but have discovered the difficulty of making their contribution a reality."[2]

JOB AID 2-4: Selecting Learning Portals

A learning portal is an Internet-based, on-demand point of entry into choices for learning. It is a relatively inexpensive way to jump-start both education and training interventions. Organizations and individuals can access a learning portal to:
- Find education and training resources
- Participate in education or training
- Find, register for, and buy training

Instructions: Use the following criteria to evaluate and select the most appropriate learning portal(s) for yourself or for a specific organization.

Choice	Yes	No	Not Sure
Provides corporation with an instant virtual university			
Provides individuals with one central place for courses on a variety of topics			
Offers education or training courseware on a variety of topics			
Offer opportunities for learning communities to share knowledge online			
Offers option to buy education or training resources on a variety of topics			
Convenience	**Yes**	**No**	**Not Sure**
Services available on a 24/7 basis			
Easy to access through work or home computer			
Ability to host custom content for corporations, without getting IT involved			
Speed	**Yes**	**No**	**Not Sure**
Adapts quickly to changing business needs			
Provides just-in-time training options			
Offers short-term education or training options			
Offers high-speed upload and download capabilities			

Adapted from Abernathy, D., and Ellis, R. (2000, May). An open-door discussion on learning portals. Training and Development, 54(5), 58; 60.
ISPI © 2001. Permission granted for unlimited duplication for noncommercial use.

All learning technologies possess some level of interactivity—they offer the learner an opportunity to become actively involved with the technology, the content, the instructor, other learners, and/or additional learning resources such as performance support tools. For example, Table 2-9 describes the interactivity level for computer-based, groupware, and virtual reality, the learning technologies reported in the ASTD survey.

The remainder of this section will discuss the following:
- Interactive learning technologies in general, including the concept of interactivity and the impact of enterprise training
- Classroom delivery and related interactive technologies such as electronic white boards
- Distance delivery and related interactive learning technologies, including a scenario using telecommunication and computer technologies
- Computer-based and online technologies to enable and enhance learning, including hybrid applications

- Ways to implement interactive technologies for both classroom and distance learning

Definition and Scope

Interactive learning technologies are more than software and hardware. They are any learning technology (method or media) that encourages and supports the active involvement of the learner with the content, the instructor, the technology, other learners, and the learning resources.

Interactivity Is...Is Not...
There are some misconceptions about interactivity that influence the design, evaluation, and ultimate success of interactive learning technologies.

Interactivity does not depend on the number of times a learner has to press the space bar to advance the program or on the number of key-strokes per minute, nor is it related to merely asking questions immediately after

TABLE 2-9: Interactivity Level of Learning Technologies Reported in ASTD Survey

Learning Technology	Interactivity Level
Text-only CBT	"Simple program for presentation support" (a page turner)
Multimedia CBT	"Interactivity is probably the essential component of a multimedia learning system"
Groupware	Highly interactive
Virtual reality	Allows for "complex interaction."

Based on Gayeski, 1999, pp. 591–603; See knowledge management (KM) section in this chapter.

presenting some information to the learner. Interactivity is the active participation of the learner in the learning process.[3]

Levels of Interactivity
Interactivity occurs at different levels. Computer-based learning and online learning all have the potential for high-level interactivity. Factors that limit both the use of learning technologies and the degree of interactivity include:
- Delivery systems—intrinsic or design limitations
- Technology—availability, intrinsic limitations, or design of hardware, software, electronics, and other components
- Content—intrinsic limitations, organization or user perceptions (don't play around with serious stuff)
- Instructional design—degree to which interactivity is planned
- User—motivation, comfort level, and sophistication in terms of technology use
- Instructor or facilitator—(if appropriate) comfort level and expertise
- Resources—time, money, human expertise, technology.

Benefits
Interactive learning technologies help learners "learn to learn" because they:
- Encourage participation and communication by providing learners with a means of engaging with one another, for example, to dialogue, share information, influence others, reach consensus, agree to conform
- Help learners to clarify performance expectations and new ideas, and judge the quality of their performance
- Provide a vehicle for defining the scope, depth, and breadth of a new idea
- Give learners alternative examples to explain new ideas and make new information more meaningful
- Provide learners with information needed to manage depth of study, range of content, media, and time

- Stimulate the acquisition of, and facilitate the use of, skills and abilities that enhance learning, for example, creativity, curiosity, higher order thinking skills, recognition and acceptance of individual differences, effective listening, respect for others, shared sense of responsibility
- Allow for the cross fertilization of ideas that comes from sharing.[4]

Interactive learning technologies are learner centered. They empower learners by encouraging users to:
- Select their own pace
- Choose the learning topics or sequence that meets their specific needs
- Tailor the learning experience to their particular thinking and learning style
- Sharpen their problem solving ability and high-level thinking skills
- Take responsibility for their own learning
- Develop their initiative and capacity to innovate.[5]

Enterprise Training
Enterprise training is both a driver and client of interactive learning technologies. It is largely defined by scope—and that scope is BIG. Enterprise training delivers instruction that is critical to the entire organization and must be disseminated to a large number of people dispersed over a wide geographic area. The logistics and time elements for enterprise training are daunting and the budget can be staggering.[6] There are some major issues waiting in the wings as enterprise training becomes more and more prevalent (see Job Aid 2-5 on p. 61).

Enterprise resource planning (ERP) drives the need for enterprise training. For example, many companies are faced with backing up process change with massive software implementation that *touches a lot of jobs* and requires enterprise-wide training.[7] Another driver of enterprise training is e-commerce—e-companies need to invent new ways to distribute information to customer reps and customers. In fact, "there's no guarantee that the name enterprise won't be jettisoned in favor of some sexier new term like *e-learning*."[8]

The major concept behind enterprise training is that "training delivered via the web has no boundaries, that it can reach anyone in any far-flung corner of a global business organization, 24 hours a day."[9] (See the discussion of online learning in this chapter.) Enterprise learning also uses distance learning technologies such as satellite broadcasting and could also change how classroom and computer-based training are designed and delivered to a global audience.

Classroom Learning Delivery Systems

Basically, classroom education or training is delivered by a live instructor to a group of learners at a location separated from the actual worksite. Approximately 80% of the respondents to a recent survey of worldwide patterns in training indicated that instructor-led classroom training predominates in their organizations.[10]

"The most interesting learning decision facing organizations is how to mix training delivered in a classroom with the new and exciting learning technologies hitting the market."[11] The benefits of classroom delivery systems include the following:
- Organizations (including learners) are familiar with it.
- Learners are separated from the distractions of the workplace.
- Learners have an opportunity to interact in real time with peers as well as the instructor and the instructional materials.[12]

Barriers to the use of classroom learning as a performance improvement intervention may include time, cost (especially the hidden cost of lost production), special equipment requirements, class size (too small or too big), lack of qualified instructors, and location of the classroom site (may involve travel time and costs).

From a training perspective, classroom-based learning is the best intervention if:
- Adequate and cost-effective facilities are available
- The content adapts to a classroom presentation
- Instructors are available to motivate the learners and explain the knowledge or skill to the learners
- The learners can practice the knowledge or skill in a classroom setting.[13]

Interactive Learning Technologies for the Classroom
Instructor-led classrooms have always had the potential for a high level of interactivity between instructor and student, between and among students, and between students and resource materials. Yet, research suggests that classroom instructors tend to talk too much. One research study found that classroom instructors talk approximately 86% of the time whether the class is held in a traditional classroom or conducted through teleconferencing.[14]

New interactive learning technologies have the potential to increase the interactivity level of typical classroom learning. For example, educators, trainers, and learners are now using electronic white boards. Electronic white boards make it possible for both instructors and learners to:
- Project computer-generated slides, overhead projector transparencies, videos, or real objects onto the whiteboard
- Use touch-screen technology to write, underline, circle, and erase directly on the whiteboard
- Write on an overhead projector transparency or type into a computer and project the written or typed information on the whiteboard
- Print and distribute information generated during class, included information written on the whiteboard.

Electronic whiteboard technology engages and motivates the learner and provides opportunities for interactivity beyond asking and answering questions or participating in traditional individual and group activities.

Additional technologies that enhance classroom learning and the potential for interactive learning include fax machines, telephones (one-to-one or group teleconferencing), computers, and online technologies (email, research databases, bulletin boards, or chat rooms).

Distance Learning Delivery Systems

Distance learning (also known as distance education, distance training, interactive distance learning, and tele-training[15]) is instruction delivered to learners who are separated by time and/or space. A June 2000 publication reported the following statistics about the increasing use of distance learning:

Community colleges and universities are offering more than 52,000 courses at a distance and many more are in the planning stage. Corporate universities have increased from 400 to 1,600 in the past decade, most of them using online or distance instruction as a means of training employees.[16]

The term *interactive distance learning* (IDL) is currently used to stress the fact that well-designed distance learning is truly an interactive learning technology because it encourages and supports interaction between instructor and learner, among and between learners, and between learners and a variety of learning resources.

Distance Learning Technologies
Distance learning uses a variety of print (yes, print), computer, Internet, and telecommunication technologies to reach a geographically dispersed work force.[17] Technically, electronic or telecommunication technologies are not required for distance learning, although they have become synonymous with the term. The term *distance learning* was reportedly used for the first time back in 1892 by the University of Wisconsin and refers to "any formal approach to learning in which a majority of the instruction occurs while educator (or trainer) and learner are at a distance from one another."[18] Since this definition was established, distance learning has evolved from correspondence-type courses to a one- or two-way, real-time exchange of video, audio, text, and graphic information.

Distance learning technologies include print, audioconferencing, audiographic teleconferencing, interactive compressed-video teleconferencing, computer-mediated conferencing, and video teleconferencing using satellite, broadcast, coaxial cable, and fiber optic transmission media.[19] The good news is that "the professional literature provides ample empirical evidence supporting the important role played by well-designed and well-implemented distance learning initiatives."[20]

Distributed Learning
The term *distributed learning* refers to "a methodologically distinct variation on distance learning that responds to calls for supporting the needs of individuals on terms they are increasingly defining for themselves."[21] (See the section on self-directed learning in this chapter.) While the terms distance learning and distributed learning are often used synonymously, there are *operational distinctions* between the two. Table 2-10 illustrates the similarities and differences between distance and distributive learning.

TABLE 2-10: Distance or Distributed Learning?

Similarities

Distance Learning and Distributed Learning

- Offer an alternative to classroom instruction
- Meet performance improvement needs of geographically dispersed learners
- Require special design and development to leverage their unique strengths
- Offer limited regular contact between instructors and learners
- Rely on a variety of technologies to deliver content
- Are learner-centered

Differences

Distance Learning	Distributed Learning
Extended classroom via technology	Just-in-time and just-for-me orientation
Learners usually participate in small groups or cohorts	Learners usually participate individually
Influenced by technologies that enable conferencing between and among learners and instructor to replicate classroom communication dynamics	Influenced by interactive connectivity linking learners with learning resources (information, performance support tools, and instructional opportunities)
Affected by deregulation and competition in cable television and telephone industries	Jump-started by developments in computer hardware, software, and networking industries (for example, increased desktop processing speed, new browser technology, platform-independent data transmission, and availability of Internet service providers)
Uses a variety of audio, text, and video modalities to connect people	Uses a digital pipeline to converge audio, video, and data-transmission media

Based on Wagner, 1999, pp. 627–630.

FIGURE 2-8: View from the Studio—DL via Satellite

Satellite-based one-way video means that the trainees can see the instructor or visual aids on a TV monitor; however, the instructor cannot see the trainees. The visual aids for this course include overhead transparencies, slides, and video clips. Internet-based two-way audio communication links the instructor and the trainees during and between classes. This allows both the instructor and the trainees to ask questions, provide feedback, make comments, and generally interact with each other.

Keypad technology enhances the interactivity and makes it possible to gather and capture learner responses for both instant and later analysis. For example, after the trainees answer a question using the keypad system the instructor projects a histogram showing the number of students who responded to each item. In this way both the instructor and the trainees receive immediate feedback.

The instructor uses a semi-scripted instructor guide and the trainees use a participant manual as a course guide and study aid. The participant manual includes copies of the slides, additional information, structured note taking, tests, forms, and other required material.

The studio is equipped with an instructor's podium that has a touch-screen computer, a computer tool that allows the instructor to annotate the on-screen graphics, and an overhead document camera. The instructor handles the equipment on the podium; a technician monitors the satellite link and controls the video and computer-generated slides. Learner sites are located in a classroom setting equipped with a television monitor (minimum 27 inches) and keypads. An on-site coordinator turns on the equipment and distributes course materials.

Based on Dessinger, Brown, Reesman, and Elliott, 1998, p. 336.

The need to accomplish any or all of the following goals may trigger the selection of distance learning as a performance intervention:

- Increase global competitiveness
- Ensure that the work force keeps current with and implements rapidly changing technology
- Cope with frequent skill updates, information glut, and rapidly changing business needs and priorities.[22]

Interactive Distance Learning Technologies
At the low end, IDL technology is composed of a multimedia CBT and one learner. A high-end distance learning experience is a satellite broadcast from a studio to multiple sites, which involves computer-based and telecommunication technologies. Figure 2-8 is an overview of an actual broadcast sent out from a Midwest studio to sites across the United States and Canada.

Computer-based Learning Technologies

Computer-based learning technologies, such as computer-based training (CBT) or computer-based education (CBE), are not inherently interactive learning technologies—pressing keys is not true interactive learning. It is tools such as hypermedia that enable computer-based learning technologies to become interactive learning technologies. Hypermedia offers a potentially high level of interactivity at a relatively low cost through the use of hardware, software, CD-ROMs, DVDs, servers, and integrated or stand-alone scanners and fax machines.

"Hypermedia is the nonlinear representation of text, graphics, sound, animation, and any other form of information randomly accessible with the aid of computer technology (hardware and software)."[23] It actually models good learning strategy because it links nodes of information by building relationships that make sense to the user. Hypermedia is actually a form of knowledge management that provides a high level of learner control and makes it easy for the learner to access large quantities of interrelated information using a variety of media. Learners can actually learn to learn by using hypermedia.[24]

Interactive Computer-based Learning Technologies
Two distinct types of interactions apply to computer-based learning technologies:

- *Baseline interactions,* such as using standard interface features such as menu bars, glossary buttons, or directional arrows
- *Content-specific interactions,* such as responding to questions or hypertext simulation steps.[25]

There are also four levels of interactivity (enriching, supportive, conveyance, and constructive) that are possible when designing computer-based learning technologies. Table 2-11 describes the possible levels of interactivity and shows how they relate to baseline and content-specific interactions.

As the hardware and software capabilities increase for PC desktops, the lines are beginning to blur between pure

TABLE 2-11: Levels of Interactivity for Computer-Based Interactions

Level of Interactivity	Baseline Interactions	Content-Specific Interactions
Enriching interactions enable learners to access information but do not convey information in and of themselves, for example, pop-ups, links, or forward and back buttons	X	X
Supportive interactions directly assist learner to understand material, for example, zoom features, calculator, or search and query functions	X	X
Conveyance interactions demonstrate concepts or enable learners to try out knowledge, for example, questions, simulations, or process decision points		X
Constructive interactions invite the learner to organize and map his or her own knowledge and understanding, for example, building knowledge trees or mental maps.		X

Based on Stroupe, 1998, pp. 19–20; Hannafin, 1992, pp. 49–63.

CBT and online learning. The PC now has the capability to plug into streaming video and audio. Add a camera and microphone and there is the potential for two-way audio and video. Put in a CD-ROM or DVD and learn with one-way audio and video and point-and-click interactivity. Meanwhile, the Internet, with its virtual learning environment, is just a click away, and enterprising organizations are mixing and matching technologies to reach a global work force. Each iteration will impact the type and level of interactivity that is possible and desirable from a design standpoint, and measurable (quantitative or qualitative) from an evaluation standpoint.

The important outcome of education or training is whether the knowledge and skills learned will apply to the real world. Application is enhanced by conveyance and constructive interactions "that demand the highest level of cognitive interaction."[26] It is certainly possible to *go by the numbers* when designing or evaluating computer-based learning technologies. The designer or evaluator can total the number of times a learner pushes a button or uses a hyperlink, count the number of total interactions for each learner or group of learners, and even use frequency counts to distinguish between baseline and content-specific interactions. However, designers and evaluators alike must focus on quality rather than quantity—on the level of the interaction rather than the type of interaction.

Online Learning Technologies

Online learning (also called web-based learning, web-based training [WBT], or e-learning) is defined as a system for delivering instruction to learners using Internet or intranet technology. In turn, e-learning has *redefined* how education and training is done and who will control it. Individuals are taking control of their own learning while training departments shift to quality assurance issues.[27]

"The new framework for e-learning, enabled by the web, is about online training and knowledge management interacting with each other."[28] This interaction enhances online learning in particular, and education and training in general, because KM adds the following to the learning equation:

- A broader audience—knowledge communities, learning communities, or communities of practice (these terms are used interchangeably)—built around content or disciplines
- Efficient access to a broad range of accurate and up-to-date information
- Broad range of performance support tools
- Collaborative features that help to engage learners in the learning process.[29]

Online learning, while it eliminates the need for virtual education and training infrastructures such as classrooms or buildings, requires an extensive *digital plant infrastructure* of its own:

- Personal communication tools and applications for teaching, learning, and research, such as browsers plus learning tools and applications, are evolving from the desktop to the palmtop.
- Network of local area networks, wide area networks, or global networks serve as a virtual campus and may

include hardware, software applications, middleware, licensing, and bandwidth services.

- Dedicated servers and software applications manage email, websites and applications, program- and course-management systems, and other systems.
- Software applications and services such as licensed library and research services, Internet services, or content resources, usually involve external providers.
- People with special skill sets design, implement, manage, and maintain the digital plant.[30]

The popularity of online learning is growing because of the need for just-in-time and just-for-me education and training: "That's the overriding need. The model is changing and we have to keep up with it. It's all about e-learning and that means completely altering the way education is delivered, valued, and measured."[31]

The basic requirement for online learning is access to the Internet. This may sound simplistic, however, even if an organization has Internet access, it may not provide the same access to staff members who are the potential learners. Some companies are developing their own intranet to act as a host for internal and external (vendor and customer) education and training. One international company used its intranet to replace 12 instructor-led certification courses with online learning courses.[32] Another corporation "internally developed courses on its intranet and also encouraged employees to register for online classes offered by outside providers. Within six months more than 400 employees logged on."[33]

Benefits of Online Learning
One major benefit of online learning is that it has the potential to improve the learning experience.

When you provide collaborative (and high-end interactive) educational experiences online, students are not only better able to learn the material for the course but they also learn how to interact in a virtual team environment. In many cases this could be more valuable than the specific course knowledge.[34]

Cost savings and flexibility are two other benefits of online learning. The cost of Internet delivery is going down due largely to hardware standardization, advances in data-streaming methods, the fact that developers are finding ways to avoid obsolescence and combine products from multiple vendors, and cost savings from cuts in travel, record keeping, and lost production.[35]

Flexibility may turn out to be more of a barrier than a benefit: "One of the greatest benefits of online learning—the fact that it allows anytime, anywhere instruction—also has been an ongoing problem…I wouldn't be surprised if

the completion rate is less than 50%."[36] Other barriers to participation include slow Internet connections and incompatibility between the website and local dial-up connections that make it impossible to download the courses.

Improving the Quality of Online Learning
Below are some suggestions for improving the quality (and hopefully the completion rate) of online learning while still maintaining flexibility:

- Apply ISD principles to online course design
- Use online learning to deliver just-in-time training
- Blend classroom and online components
- Add high-end interaction to engage the learner
- Use highly trained faculty to support the online components through video conferencing, chat rooms, electronic bulletin boards, or email followup.[37]

However, applying systematic design practices is not the complete answer to effective e-learning. "The question is no longer whether organizations will implement online learning, but whether they will do it well. Having the right technology and delivering good learning programs using that technology is essential but insufficient."[38] Critical success factors also include:

- Building a learning culture
- Marshalling true leadership support
- Deploying a nurturing business model
- Sustaining the change throughout the organization.[39]

Interactive Online Learning Technologies
Though the various transformations of online learning (for example, e-learning and telelearning):

…might differ in details, such as bandwidth, user interface, and interactivity, online learning technologies, which share the common strategy to deliver learning to audiences at disparate locations, have begun to converge around common technology standards and the delivery infrastructure known as the Internet.[40]

The most interactive learning technologies for online learning include multimedia CBT, video and audio conferencing, and live instructors, mentors, or coaches. Every day new technologies with interactive potential are migrating to the web, for example, two-way video and audio has migrated from the satellite to the Internet domain.[41]

Hybrid Interactive Learning Technologies
Hybrid interactive learning technologies integrate delivery and support modes—CBT, web-based training (WBT), and instructor led classroom training—into one product or training bundle.

However you define it, hybrid training gives both the student and the employer more flexibility. What customers are looking for is something that has some CBT, some course work, some skills assessment, and some web-based training; something that can be integrated so individuals can customize it to their own special needs.[42]

Hybrids may take many forms and use a variety of interactive technologies, from human to high tech:

- A *live* mentor supplements WBT; instructor, other students, or an expert provide email or teleconference feedback and followup.
- Learners take a web-based skills assessment test, the test is scored immediately, and the test site generates a learning map based on test results.
- Instructor meets with learners to test what they learned on a CBT and give the go-ahead to proceed. Learners who do poorly on CBT attend additional classroom sessions.
- Course materials are distributed on CD-ROM to accommodate learners who are unable to download course materials from the website due to the incompatibility of local dial-up connections.
- Once bandwidth increases the learner may begin with a CBT and then click on an icon that brings him or her to the actual site to practice a task.[43]

Issues Surrounding Hybrid Applications
A number of the biggest issues facing Internet education and training sponsors focus on hybrid applications:

- Will WBT and CBT supplement classroom training or vice versa? "Sure, many instructors will use CBT and WBT to supplement classroom time...but it's more likely the instructor will wind up supplementing the technology."[44]
- What about customer expectations that WBT design and development is as time efficient as plugging into the Internet?
- Does the instructor need to monitor student work more carefully when hybrid online learning is selected as the intervention?
- How do designers make sure they "don't get caught up chasing the technology elements...and not chasing the learning need"?[45]

In addition, issues surrounding the level of interactivity include the following:

- Is it enough to post questions on an electronic bulletin board or do learners need a virtual chat room?
- Is multimedia enough or should organizations invest in broadband capabilities with live video and audio and link learner and instructor in a virtual classroom?
- How do you combine learning content and interactivity on a PC desktop?
- How do you make sure that there is not more than 15 minutes between interactions?

- If we move too fast, will we lose control?
- Can we trust the new breed of provider who is lightning fast at harnessing new online delivery technologies?[46]

Implementing Interactive Learning Technologies in the Workplace

With large-scale drivers and clients in the picture, implementing interactive learning technologies could be a monumental task. Perhaps the best way for a PT practitioner to begin is to ignore the enterprise and begin at the department level. Implementing small interactive learning technology interventions will build confidence. Whether the intervention is big or small, the process is the same:

- Think goals and objectives, both from an organizational and a learning point of view
- Think careful planning and up-front analysis—interactive technologies, especially on a large scale, can be expensive and it will be essential to carefully document the process and the progress
- Think project management techniques and tools—because implementing interactive learning technologies is a project
- Think team effort—implementing interactive learning technologies is best approached as a team effort, and the team should include the users, the champion, the technical staff, the instructional designers and developers, and the instructor
- Think evaluation—formative, summative, even confirmative and meta evaluation—and plan it from the beginning of the project.

Integrating Enterprise Learning
The PT practitioner, as both a generalist and a synthesizer, can help organizations initiate and implement the three major steps for integrating enterprise learning technologies into the overall education and training strategy:

1. Select an infrastructure (learning management system) to support enterprise-wide learning
2. Decide how to populate the system with courses (for example, analyze learner and organizational needs, existing courses, available technology, and instructional standards)
3. Identify vendors to provide off-the-shelf or custom-designed courses.[47]

In addition, the PT practitioner will help the organization stay focused on integrating learning with the organization's business needs.

Motivating the Learner
Motivating learners is crucial to the success of online learning. The PT practitioner may want to suggest a model

like the ARCS model as one way to design and develop interactive learning technologies that motivate the learner to use the technology and complete the course work:

- Attention—use strategies to get and keep the learner's attention
- Relevance—clarify WIIFMs (what's in it for me?)
- Confidence—provide feedback on objectives, completion time, etc.
- Satisfaction—reward the learner.[48]

Experiencing Interactive Learning Technologies

It is important to feel comfortable with interactive learning technologies before trying to implement them. The classroom is a good place to start, especially because some of the new interactive learning and teaching technologies such as the interactive white board are also used for distance learning. Then, the PT practitioner could observe or participate in a satellite learning broadcast or get involved in a distance learning project.

Of course, opportunities abound to surf the web and find examples of interactive learning technologies. The PT practitioner could take a survey, join a professional chat room, participate in a teleconference, or join a bulletin board discussion. Even shopping on the web can generate ideas for interactivity!

Again, if time is not a factor, the PT practitioner could explore what the organization, and the competition, are currently offering in terms of classroom, computer-based, online, or distance learning. Some additional sources of information and updates include:

- Vendors send out many sample CD-ROMs to advertise their programs
- Professional organizations sponsor conferences specific to the various applications of interactive learning technology
- Professional publications and the Internet offer a plethora of books, articles, white papers, and links to technology-specific sites.

Listening to Lessons Learned

Implementation, especially at the enterprise level, takes time, commitment, and long-range planning. Ford Motor Company began in the early 1990s to plan and build a satellite-based distance training system for 50,000 dealership personnel in more than 6,000 locations—a system that would carry over into the millennium. Currently technology-based distance learning accounts for approximately 92% of the 700,499 courses completed annually by dealership personnel. Ford is a model for other organizations. Below are some of the lessons Ford learned about implementing and sustaining a highly interactive learning technology at the enterprise level.

- Leadership is vital for execution of a technical strategy that resists unnecessary change, gains maximum value

out of investments made, and assures that needed technology renewal is funded.
- The role of the champion is vital. At a minimum, it involves conception, sale, and implementation of the program. Care and maintenance of champions is crucial to success.
- It is necessary to constantly assess new technology, rationalize its reality with the training model, and guide the organization to embrace or resist change, whichever makes the most sense in terms of training and organizational needs.
- One strength is the close cooperation between the business and technical support organizations, which was enabled by co-location and shared reporting relationships.[49]

A Word of Warning

The problem with technology, in addition to the fact that it changes so rapidly, is the fact that new technology is not always the right answer. This is especially true when it comes to learning technologies. The PT practitioner is constantly bombarded with "new and improved" technologies that are "guaranteed to improve learning and performance." The siren call of new e-learning technologies is a good example.

Before jumping on the e-learning (or any learning technology) bandwagon, take the advice offered by ISPI Director Brenda Sugrue:

A blended approach is much more compatible with a human performance technology (HPT) mindset. HPT professionals are not comfortable recommending or working with only one solution and certainly not one delivery medium for one solution. Blending e-learning with e-performance support is an example of blending two solutions that are both delivered on line. We can also build online and offline elements. [PT practitioners] can play a significant role in the next wave of e-learning. We should develop generic blending models and rules for customizing blends for particular situations.[50]

Games and Simulations

Games and simulations are inherently interactive. They are experiential learning techniques that rely on interactive learning technologies for their existence. They are used frequently to help individuals or teams develop problem solving and decision making skills. "Experiential learning methods such as games and simulations are particularly appropriate for team learning."[1] Games tend to focus on rivalry and competition between individuals or groups, although neither games nor simulations take real action and there are no real consequences for actions. The level of reality (fidelity) in simulations is usually higher than the level of reality in games.

JOB AID 2-5: Are You Ready for Enterprise Training?

Directions: Use these questions to start a dialogue with the stakeholders. Respond to the questions individually, then start a group dialogue. When new questions occur add them to the list.

Issue	Response
Who will control such big ventures?	
How can organizations build a support structure to handle an immediate and immense new user base?	
What is the best virtual infrastructure to accommodate a wide variety of training and learning strategies?	
How will bandwidth affect global delivery?	
What is this thing called interactivity and how much is needed?	
Other:	

Adapted from Stamps, D. (1999a). Enterprise training: This changes everything. Training, 36 *(1), 40–48.*
ISPI © 2001. Permission granted for unlimited duplication for noncommercial use.

All games and simulations have a beginning (introduction), a middle (experience), and an end (debriefing). They range in complexity from highly technical, DVD- or computer-driven simulators to a live role play, a board game, or a one-page, print-based case study.

Definition and Scope—Games

Games are activities for two or more participants that contain elements of competition and fun. Games involve participants physically or psychologically and "when a game is matched appropriately to the training objectives, it provides a low-risk, highly successful learning experience."[2] For example, a game may help a learner memorize content, review a skill, or gain an *A-ha* (new insight).

Elements of Success

In 1980, Stolovitch and Thiagarajan (Thiagi) listed four *critical characteristics* that make a successful game; later Thiagi added a fifth characteristic:

1. Conflict—there are obstacles to achieving the goal and players (individuals or teams) compete with each other
2. Control—rules specify the process (how to play the game) and the consequences
3. Closure—rules specify how and when the game ends (target scores, elimination, time limits), usually in terms of winning or losing
4. Contrivance—built-in inefficiencies "prohibit the most efficient solution to the problem" (for example, a basketball player simply clutching the ball and running with it)
5. Competency—the specific skill areas that the game is designed to improve.[3,4]

In addition to containing all five characteristics, a successful game also meets these major criteria:

- Provides a simple, single-purpose activity that focuses the participants on a job-related concern
- Incorporates on-the-job application of the learning
- Provides just-in-time training

- Is carefully integrated into the total training session
- Uses a short and clear procedure (two to four steps are ideal).[5]

Definition and Scope—Simulations

Simulations are "interactive, dynamic learning experiences that mirror a real-life situation; through their decisions and actions, participants can effect changes or be affected by those changes."[6] They are useful when training requires a *show and do* approach and it's impossible to do it in the real world because of excessive costs or safety factors.[7] Simulations have the built-in capability to develop fully functional individuals who are "ready to hit the street running."[8]

Simulations are also a strategy for improving the impact of training: "Perhaps no other technology is capable of evoking such admiration in the eyes of military trainers, joy in the heart of computer game lovers, and dread among budget-minded training managers."[9] A recent survey of medical educators, conducted by the Association of American Medical Colleges (AAMC), predicts that by 2010:

- All procedural skills—from placing a simple IV line to removing a gallbladder through a laparascope—will be taught on digital simulators
- Patient simulations, or *virtual patients*, will be used to evaluate the clinical skills and decision making abilities of medical students.[10]

How Real Is Real?
The question is how real should a simulation be? The answer is not clear-cut. First, designers of simulations need to determine up front which elements of a job or task absolutely *must* be simulated accurately in order for workers to be able to perform successfully. This requires a strong grounding in job/task and performance analysis as well as the concepts of training transfer. Then, designers need to select the level of *fidelity* (degree of distortion or accuracy) required to assure transfer. Simulations come in many levels of *fidelity*. Table 2-12 gives some examples.

Until research supports the relationship between the level of fidelity and the success of learning transfer, companies will rely on cost-benefit analysis data to justify the cost of expensive, high-fidelity simulators. For example, Table 2-13 shows how a city transit system built a business case for using initially expensive driving simulators to train their bus drivers.

Under the right circumstances, return on investment from even high-fidelity simulators can more than cover the heavy initial costs of design and development.

You can imagine how complex it gets in multiple-step simulations, where you have large decision trees and you must create simulations for each scenario...But when you're talking about simulating complex equipment with heavy training requirements, the return on investment (ROI) over five years is pretty impressive.[11]

Barriers to Using Simulations
Even when simulations provide good return on investment there are other barriers that may hamper the widespread development and use of simulations:

- Lack of knowledge by training professionals of simulation capabilities and affordability
- Intensive and time-consuming development time
- Lack of authoring tools to build simulations
- Requirement for high-end computers because standard PCs lack power
- High cost of custom simulations.[12]

Well-trained designers can avoid some of these barriers by:

- Consistently asking whether simulation is the right tool for the learner and the business need
- Remaining focused on the educational components and avoiding getting too caught up with the bells and whistles
- Working closely with the simulator developers.[13]

The good news is that the cost of medium- and high-fidelity simulators is steadily declining. In addition, "the Simulation Interoperability Standards Organization (SISO),

TABLE 2-12: Levels of Fidelity

Low	Medium	High
Simple software simulation that mimics functions of a software application	Three-dimensional, cardboard and plastic model of the equipment involved in a new manufacturing process	Three-dimensional, immersive systems used to train pilots
CBT simulation with text, graphics, and hyperlinks	Video enactment of a typical meeting situation	Actors involving the audience in a true-to-life meeting scenario

Based on Barron, 1999, pp. 12–17.

TABLE 2-13: Building a Business Case for Virtual Driving

Sample baseline data	
Initial cost of simulators in 1994	$480,000
Current number of training and testing days	18 days
Current number of drivers trained per year	500

Sample data to build the business case	
Reduction in number of training and testing days since startup	1 day
% of participants who pass the training	95%
Annual savings (reduction in insurance, maintenance, and gas costs)	$375,000
Reduction in number of accidents per million miles	1994–42.6 1998–34.1
Revenue generation from using simulators to provide training to private carriers, utility systems, and other transit systems	Profits used to update simulators

Based on Wetzel, 2000, p. 31.

which turned 10 years old in 2000, is working to establish standards to provide simulation developers an object-oriented approach to simulation development…(that will) shorten development time."[14] The web address for the organization's newsletter is http://www.sisotds.org/webletter.

Types of Simulations
There are three types of simulations: simulation games, scenario-based training, and case study method. Each variation uses different levels of interaction and different technologies.

Simulation Games
Simulation games are activities that combine the characteristics of a game and a simulation (game-based simulations).[15] There is a direct or indirect similarity between components of the game and the real world.[16] The most well-known categories for simulation games are gamut running (resembles a board game like Chutes and Ladders™), allocation games (deal with allocation of resources, budget, or power and influence), group interactions (expose participants to a new point of view or way of thinking), and general system games (take the participants through a complex model of an organization or a process).[17]

Scenario-Based Training
Scenarios are a less high-tech version of a simulation. They are "open-ended, narrative descriptions of typical

and critical situations in which prospective users participate."[18] Scenario-based training uses real-life situations and formal role-playing by professionals (business theater facilitators or subject matter experts) who enact scripted, real-life situations to reinforce classroom learning. Trainees may answer questions based on lessons learned or actually participate in the scenario at specific points in the script, or coach the professionals when problems arise or the situation requires an action-based decision. For example:

> The FBI Academy has long used professional role players and scripted situations to engage trainees with the subject matter more effectively. The Academy recognizes that practical application injects realism and adds a decision making process that reinforces classroom lecture.[19]

Frequently the scenarios address only one training objective, module, or competency; however, there are times when an entire course is planned around a developing scenario. "This integrated approach identifies a need among the trainees for particular skills, offers the skills as a solution, and provides opportunities to practice the skills."[20]

When scenarios of human interaction are well designed they match the reality of the workplace and "enable human activity."[21] For example, scenarios are useful for identifying trends in organizations, formulating

63

organizational or group vision and strategy, and developing alternative courses of action.[22] The elements of a scenario include:

- *Driving forces*—elements that move the plot of the story and determine the outcome
- *Predetermined elements*—phenomena or constraints that do not depend on a particular chain of events for their existence
- *Critical uncertainties*—determined by questioning assumptions about predetermined elements.[23]

The best way to design a scenario is to use a systematic approach:

1. Identify and analyze key factors affecting the focal issue, pre-determined elements, and critical uncertainties (factors that are completely uncertain and affect the outcome)
2. Rank critical uncertainties by importance and degree of uncertainty
3. Select scenario logic (the plot that best captures the dynamics of the situation and communicates the point effectively)
4. Flesh out the scenario (how each factor *plays out*)
5. Develop implications
6. Select leading indicators and signposts.[24]

It is essential to pilot scenarios before implementation. Because of the real nature of scenarios and the fact that they mirror current human interactions, they also need to be "more or less continually redeveloped and reinterpreted."[25]

Case Study Method
If generating fresh ideas and solutions to current problems is important to an organization, then case studies are a relatively inexpensive intervention. Case studies are in-depth, written accounts of an event or situation presented in story form and designed to seek justifiable answers or solutions to problems. Case studies may vary from one to several pages in length. Traditionally, they are a learning tool rather than a tool for implementing performance improvement; however, they have become more and more popular in training environments over the past decade.

The case method traces back to the parables and questioning techniques of ancient Chinese, Hebrew, and Greek teachers. Harvard University is credited for the current name and form of the case method. By 1990, after almost a century of development, Harvard reportedly had "more than 4,000 active cases, supported by printed materials and, sometimes, software and videos."[26] Computer technology, such as email, bulletin boards, chat rooms, and online meeting software, is currently reinventing the case study method. However, the basic process remains the same:

- Analyze the case individually.

- Write a formal report (state the problem, identify the symptoms and causes, critique the actions of the parties involved, offer alternative solutions, and make and justify recommended actions [optional])
- Discuss and analyze the case as a group.

While case studies are traditionally associated with business and law curricula, there is also evidence of their usefulness in the training literature:

Training literature associates the case method with participants' practice and improvement of skills in analysis, communication (listening, questioning, and persuading), interpersonal relations, problem solving, and decision making.[27]

The case study method also helps participants sharpen their reflective thinking skills, develop heuristics (rules of thumb), and build knowledge across a range of subjects. The problem or beauty of case studies, depending on the point of view, is that, "whenever participants agree on a single answer quickly, chances are that the case is not well crafted. Case studies rarely have clear-cut answers, much less a single *right* answer."[28]

There are some other disadvantages to using the traditional case study method:

- Case studies provide a *snapshot* taken at one point in time while real business problems occur over time and may require action over time.
- Participants make decisions but do not go out and implement the decisions in the real world.
- The *reality* of case studies is constrained by time and format, for example, x number of printed pages and x minutes during a training session.

The best way to overcome these disadvantages is to *get real*:

- Use the case method to document a real problem.
- Attach real memos, emails, or other problem documentation to the narration.
- Aim at finding a real solution.

Advantages of Games and Simulations
Games and simulations can jump-start the transfer of knowledge, skills, and attitudes to the workplace by "combining real-life tasks with important information or insights connected with those tasks"[29] and by requiring participants to collaborate as they would in work teams. They can be fun and memorable: a real, live *mnemonic* (memory device) to trigger future application of learning.

Sivasailam Thiagarajan (Thiagi) notes that the advantage of using games is that they:

- Lend themselves to level four evaluation (does the training benefit the organization?)

- Are tightly linked to objectives
- Are tailored both to the audience and to the subject matter.[30]

The same advantages apply to well-designed simulations.

Resistance to Games and Simulations

The major disadvantage of games and simulations is that participants may view them as frivolous and resist their use in training programs. Some participants are accustomed to traditional training in which the learner is passive.

These participants often expect to leave a training session with a notebook crammed full of notes and a serious case of writer's cramp. When they have participated in games or simulations instead, they may leave feeling frustrated and even angry, believing they have not learned anything.[31]

On the flip side, the new generation of learners has experienced the fast pace and excitement of computer games and simulations: "You're now training the Nintendo generation and these learners have no patience for lecture. The most effective games are designed for cross-cultural and cross-functional groups that are capable of multitasking and don't withhold feedback."[32]

Finally, management may view games and simulations as budget line items with no value added. Games and simulations can require equipment, facilities, or both that are expensive or difficult and time consuming to design, develop, and set up. They may also require an experienced group facilitator to LEAD the game or simulation (see Job Aid 2-6 at the end of this section):

- Lead with a clear purpose
- Empower individuals to participate
- Aim to accomplish the goal
- Direct the process.[33]

Implementing Games and Simulations in the Workplace

Once more, the PT practitioner can come forward to promote a *better* way to high performance and performance improvement. First of all, the PT practitioner should become familiar with the various types of games and simulations that are available and possible in the current organizational environment.

The PT practitioner also needs to understand the concept of interactivity as it relates to education and training (see the sections on Interactive Learning Technologies and Self-Directed Learning). The PT practitioner may need to explain the importance of interactivity in training transfer and can stress how the use of interactivity stimulates

learning and enhances collaboration, both in education and training sessions and on the job.

The PT practitioner also needs to be a cheerleader for using games and simulations to help improve performance: "Games have come into their own as learning tools. They're no longer just a diversion. If employee empowerment is the movement of the nineties, then games are the tools that support it."[34] The PT practitioner should become a cheerleader for games and simulations and help organizations overcome resistance from trainers, trainees, and the organization itself. "Resistance can be diverted by emphasizing real-life applications."[35]

Once a game or simulation is selected as an intervention, the PT practitioner can also help link the goals of the game or simulation with training objectives, which in turn are linked to business needs and goals. Course design is critical to the success of games and simulations. The PT practitioner may also use knowledge and skill in instructional design to help:

- Write relevant terminal and enabling performance objectives.
- Determine how the chosen game or type of simulation will be conducted so the instructions are complete, accurate, and unambiguous and the segues into and out of the activities are seamless.
- Assess whether the game or simulation is designed to meet the stated goals and objectives, the business needs of the organization, and the needs of the participants, including requirements for transfer to the workplace.
- Develop processes and questions for debriefing the game or simulation.[36]

Debriefing

Debriefing is critical to the success of games or simulations. Thiagi defines debriefing as "the process of facilitating discussion to help participants reflect on their experiences, gain valuable insights, and share them with one another."[37] He suggests a process that includes generating seven lists (events, adjectives, objects, feelings, people, principles, and scenarios) and using the lists as a basis for generating questions on the following topics:

- How do you feel?
- What happened?
- What did you learn?
- How does this relate?
- What if?
- What next?[38]

A Final Warning

There is one more role for the PT practitioner to play—helping management and designers heed the following warnings issued by David Merrill during an interview about adapting computer games for training. Although Merrill was discussing games, his warnings apply to other types of interactive technologies as well: know your audience and avoid "gobs of frosting and precious little cake."[39]

how to transfer the archives that spanned 35 years of knowledge capture and storage at ARCO. This case study illustrates what happens when heads roll during a merger of two organizations that are committed to preserving both explicit or recorded knowledge and tacit knowledge—knowledge that resides in the heads of employees and is usually not documented.

Case Study 2-1: The Human Side of Knowledge Transfer

Situation

When Atlantic Richfield Company (ARCO) merged with BP Amoco in the spring of 2000, both companies struggled with

Intervention

ARCO combined input from employees and a customized KM technology from a vendor. The technology included special software to tie existing databases together and a web interface to help users search for information stored in different formats. The project involved three layers of data:

JOB AID 2-6: Game and Simulation Facilitator Checklist

Not everyone feels comfortable facilitating a game or simulation…or has the *right stuff* to be a successful facilitator. The following checklist contains a list of skills that are critical to high performance as a game or simulation facilitator. Use the checklist three different ways (or use all three processes for a 360° assessment):
   1. Self-assessment tool   2. Observation tool   3. Participant evaluation tool

Directions: Check the words, phrases, or statements that *definitely apply* to you (or the facilitator you are evaluating). Select next steps based on the total number of check marks.

☐   1. Sense of humor
☐   2. Extroverted (outgoing)
☐   3. Creative
☐   4. Casual and relaxed when facilitating a group
☐   5. Comfortable using games and simulations as an instructional strategy
☐   6. Able to put a group of people at ease
☐   7. Able to make people feel safe enough to take risks
☐   8. Able to develop trust with a group
☐   9. Excellent facilitator
☐ 10. Enjoys facilitating group activities
☐ 11. Flexible
☐ 12. Able to move people smoothly from one task to the next
☐ 13. Able to explain rules so people understand them
☐ 14. Able to keep groups focused on what they need to accomplish
☐ 15. Able to overcome individual or group resistance

_____   **Total number of check marks**

Total check marks	Next Steps
15-13	Ready, willing, and able
12-10	Could use coaching in some areas
9 or less	Needs training and practice

Adapted from Salopek, J.J., and Kesting, B. (February, 1999). Stop playing games. Training and Development, 53 (2), 28–38.
ISPI © 2001. Permission granted for unlimited duplication for noncommercial use.

- Knowledge assets—what you take to the shelter during a tornado
- Work-in-progress—documents employees generate and store on their computers
- Older documents—material that was never stored electronically.[a]

Fortunately, ARCO had begun a KM system in 1995 so it did not need to start from scratch. However, the project involved collecting, organizing, and storing approximately 100,000 boxes of archives plus huge digital databases.

Transferring tacit knowledge was even more daunting. Employees focused on the second layer of data—work in progress. "Employees were asked to cut out duplicate files, clean up their data, and submit information to a predetermined location on the server."[b] To complicate matters, several thousand people lost their jobs during the merger, so capturing and transferring tacit knowledge became a real issue.

> Getting employees to make a sudden switch (from knowledge hoarding) to openly sharing their expertise can be difficult, if not outright impossible. But if you think that's a tough sell, try convincing employees to hand over their hard-won knowledge to a company that just gave them a pink slip.[c]

ARCO looked to human resources to provide incentives for knowledge sharing. Employees who assisted in the knowledge capture and transfer received severance pay. "It was hard to convince people to sit down and transfer what was in their heads…You have to think about what enforcement tools you have…without using a big stick."[d] All in all, the project cost approximately $1,000,000 and took about one year to complete.

Results

The results of this project were worth the challenges. BP Amoco employees can access knowledge from both company repositories through a web interface and even "follow bread-crumbs of information on the digital trail to uncover related files."[e] In addition, the new system also has standardized the format so that documents look the same no matter what software program was originally used to process them.

Lessons Learned (on the Human Side)
- Despite the incentives, "Some people expressed a feeling of pain at having to do this. In the end, though, nearly all the 650 permanent employees from the technology center took part in the effort."[f]
- People are the major knowledge enablers. In this case, "They donated years of research and knowledge, in part just to ensure their hard work has a legacy at BP Amoco."[g]

This case study was based on Jossi, F. (2000). Under construction. Inside Technology Training, 4(7), 20-22.[a-g]

NON-INSTRUCTIONAL PERFORMANCE SUPPORT SYSTEMS (PSS)

The line between instructional and non-instructional performance support systems is thin. Support easily becomes instruction—humans learn from being led through a particular procedure or task. Many non-instructional PSS consciously build in interactivity or aspects of problem solving or decision making that involve the user and lead to a learning experience. As the technology of performance support evolves, the blurring of differences will increase. Now, however, non-instructional PSS is defined as PSS that integrates *doing and technology* but may inherently or consciously include elements of *learning and instruction.*

Non-instructional PSS provide workers with just-in-time and just-enough information to perform a task. They appear in many forms, including paper-based, computer-based, and video-based. The non-instructional PSS listed in the enhanced HPT Model are job aids, electronic performance support systems (EPSS), and documentation and standards.

Job Aids

Job aids have been around since "the details of fire tending, skinning, and cooking adorned cave walls."[1] The military has relied heavily on job aids since the 1950s and the manufacturing industry is also a heavy user of job aids. Job aids not only support performance but they also have the potential to support the performer by "providing feedback and giving visibility to an individual's success."[2]

Definition and Scope

Inside every fat training course there is a thin job performance aid screaming to get out. A job aid (also called job performance aid or ergonomic performance aid) is "a repository for information, processes, or perspectives that is external to the individual and that supports work and activity by directing, guiding, and enlightening performance."[3] It provides just-in-time, on-the-job, and just-enough information to enable a worker to perform a task efficiently and successfully without special training or reliance on memory.

There are three basic types of job aids:
- Job aids that inform—Who? What? Where? When? Which?
- Job Aids that support procedures—How? When? In what sequence?
- Job aids that support decisions—Why? If…then what?[4]

Job aids are most frequently used during performance, but they are also used before (to review performance) and after performance (to validate completion of a task). Job aids either replace or enhance training. They replace training when a task is simple and enhance training when a task is too complicated or is performed too infrequently to remember every step.

Formats
The five most familiar formats for job aids are numbered lists, checklists, decision tables, flowcharts, and hybrids.[5] Figure 2-9 presents an example of a hybrid job aid composed of a numbered list and a decision (If…Then…) table. Job Aid 2-7 at the end of this section is a checklist that can be used to select or evaluate the use of a job aid format.

Arrays (spreadsheets) and worksheets (forms that include instructions for filling in each field) are also popular formats for job aids. Computers have also made it possible to add touch-screen technology, animation, and other enhancements to traditional job aid formats.

Benefits and Drawbacks
The major benefit of job aids is that they "enrich the environment with information rather than storing data or perspectives in someone's memory."[6] In addition, job aids also:
- Reduce the need for special training, transfer from training to the job, and the amount of time required to recall steps in a task
- Ensure consistency of performance across time and space, despite barriers such as rapid employee turnover or the need to hire less-skilled employees
- Adapt to novices and experts
- Support decision making and critical thinking
- Support cross-training
- Signal when to begin a task, take action, choose an alternative action, and when the task is completed
- Encourage the worker (following the job aid should guarantee success and lessens uncertainty)
- Save money (mainly money spent on training or rework)[7]

FIGURE 2-9: Hybrid Job Performance Aid (Numbered List and Decision Table)

X-Ray Shutdown Procedure

1. Push black button OFF
2. Turn main switch to COOL DOWN
3. Turn power control button OFF
4. Wait 5 minutes
5. Remove main key
6. Put key in work table drawer
7. Push DOOR OPEN button
8. Close all shutters

	If…	Then…
9.	All shutters closed	Sweep the floor
10.	Sign on door says KEEP CASTINGS	Put ID tag on all castings
11.	All castings have ID tag	Put castings in scrap bin

12. Push DOOR CLOSE button
13. Cover controls
14. Cover video equipment
15. Turn A-1 air valve OFF
16. Pull main disconnect handle to OFF

Based on Dessinger and Moseley, 1992, p. 25.

From a PT perspective there is an additional benefit:

A less obvious, but very large benefit of opting to develop a job aid is that it forces the analyst and expert to grapple with the basic question that underlies all others in the field of performance technology: What do we want the performer to accomplish and do?[8]

One drawback to using job aids as a performance improvement intervention is the need for skilled analysts and designers.

Implementing Job Aids as Performance Interventions

In an ideal world, the PT practitioner is a member-in-good-standing of the job aid design team. In the real world, PT practitioners do not usually become involved in implementing job aids until after the fact:

...as things stand now, HPT becomes involved when the design of a system has already been agreed to, a task has been identified, and it has become apparent that the skills required to perform the task may exceed the skills currently available in those who must perform [it].[9]

The role of the PT practitioner is to assure that *form follows function.*

In effect, the technologists' role would be that of consumer advocates, and their concerns would be those of the ultimate users. They would dig for anything likely to confuse or frustrate users, either while learning or on the job, and they would also uncover places where there is little or no tolerance for failure and therefore a need for immaculate performance.[10]

The skilled PT practitioner should conduct an environmental analysis (organizational environment, work environment, work, and worker)[11] and help to design both the job and the job aid. In addition to strong analysis skills, designing job aids calls for creativity, problem solving skills, and knowledge of how new technologies can enhance job aid design and development.

A word of warning—the PT practitioner needs to know that there is a danger in *overanalyzing and paralyzing* the analysis and design process or oversimplifying the job aid itself. "The advice is...be as rigorous as possible until there is enough of an answer (then) stop looking for more answers and make sure that what one has is as effective as

---

JOB AID 2-7: When to Use Standard Job Aid Formats

Directions: Use the following checklist to select the most appropriate format for a job performance aid (JPA). The formats are useful for paper-based or computer-based job aids.

☐ **Numbered List**
    ☐ Performance requires a simple, linear action sequence
    ☐ Performance may become so repetitious that steps may be left out
    ☐ Task is performed infrequently.

☐ **Checklist**
    ☐ Performance involves inspecting, observing, or planning
    ☐ Performance requires documentation
    ☐ Performance requires user to calculate or record data

☐ **Matrix or Decision Table**
    ☐ Performance is simple but involves making a maximum of two decisions
    ☐ Performance requires identification of particular conditions to continue action

☐ **Flow Chart**
    ☐ Performance is complex; requires branching to explore alternatives
    ☐ Performance is enhanced by visualizing relationships between components

☐ **Hybrid** (mixture of two or more formats)
    ☐ Performance requires a complex set of instructions involving both sequence and decision making
    ☐ Users range from novice to advanced

---

one can make it."[10] Here is a suggestion for developing a procedural job aid by using expert performers to analyze tasks and develop the job aid simultaneously. With the PT practitioner as the facilitator, the experts will:

- Select a task that is appropriate for a job aid
- Write task steps on individual sticky notes
  — Write one step per note
  — Use a different shape or color to indicate decision points
- Arrange the notes in a list or a flowchart on a whiteboard or a wall
- Discuss and revise until consensus is reached on the content and sequence
- Document the finished product (take a picture, use a word processor).

If the technology is available, enhance and speed up this activity by using networked computers, meeting software, and/or electronic whiteboards. These technologies provide simultaneous documentation and the ability to include experts from different locations.

Electronic Performance Support Systems (EPSS)

Gloria Gery, a guru of EPSS, indicated a decade ago that the focus needed to change from traditional performance support such as classroom training to *automated performance support systems*: "We must develop new learning, information-access, problem-structuring, and decision support models based on new technological alternatives."[1] EPSS is fast becoming the model and the PSS intervention of choice for many organizations, especially large, learning organizations.

Definition and Scope

EPSS is a highly sophisticated job aid, offering access to large databases of information designed to coach users via a user-friendly question-and-answer format. It is "the electronic infrastructure that enables the learning organization."[1] More explicitly, EPSS is:

- "the computer system that is produced as a result of applying the concept of performance support. It integrates software tools, knowledge, and learning experiences to improve business performance by (a) bringing *individuals* up to speed in their work as quickly as possible and with the minimum of support from other people, and (b) providing an electronic infrastructure to enable organizational learning."[2]
- "software that provides integrated, on-demand access to information, advice, learning experiences, and tools to enable a high level of job performance with a minimum of training and support from others."[3]

EPSS is not an intelligent job aid or a type of computer-based training (CBT).

There is, of course, a very ill-defined dividing line between an EPSS (which focuses on performance but includes some implicit teaching) and a CBT system (which focuses on training and thus improves performance).[4]

Both job aids and CBT are considered *subsets of EPSS.*[5]

EPSS Levels

EPSS may select from three levels of computer-mediated performance support: intrinsic, extrinsic, and external.

- *Intrinsic support* is inherent to the system itself and cannot be differentiated from the system (transparent interface). Users receive support without taking any specific action; they feel as if they are just doing their work.
- *Extrinsic support* is integrated into the system but is not the primary workspace. Users access a support system that is contextual to the activities that are being performed but outside of the performance environment, such as "Wizards." The user can accept or reject the advice by turning it on or off.
- *External support* is outside of and not integrated into the computer-mediated workspace. The user performs the integration by completely leaving the workspace to access computer-mediated or other support, for example, use a printed manual, go to a website, or call a help desk.[6]

EPSS levels range from simple to complex:

At its simplest level, EPSS guides performers through a task, enabling them to learn a process while they use it—a virtual coach and an explicit task model. A more complex EPSS provides the performer with on-line help, a searchable reference database with live updates, and electronic access to expert users. It may even be possible to design an EPSS that combines elements of interactive learning, electronic communications, and expert systems...[7]

Characteristics of EPSS

EPSS is:

- Based on a diverse set of electronic support tools
- Delivered on a computer
- Designed to help workers complete job tasks
- Available to the worker on the job at the moment of need.[8]

Viewing EPSS as an infrastructure adds many characteristics of KM:

- Encompasses all the software needed to support individual performance
- Integrates knowledge assets rather than making them add-on components
- Considers the complete KM cycle including capture and distribution

- Includes the management of non-electronic as well as electronic assets.[9]

EPSS also needs to be dynamic. It must "be able to learn from users' experience, be updatable and adjustable by users, and augment the supports found in the users' community."[10] It must empower the user as performer and learner, enhance organizational learning, and enable KM.

Benefits of EPSS

EPSS offers major benefits to the user:
- Adapts to the learning pace and working style of diverse users
- Matches learning context to operational context
- Integrates with the work process so users get up to speed faster and work more efficiently

- Offers an engaging learning model in which the user actively seeks information
- Manages complexity and work flow for the user by structuring the activities necessary to complete tasks, representing knowledge with graphics, sound, or animation, providing data related to the task, and providing built-in tools such as calculating fields for carrying out tasks
- Enables users to share knowledge through email, chat rooms, video conferencing, or other tools.[11,12]

EPSS also benefits the organization and provides significant return on investment by:
- Enhancing productivity and work flow
- Reducing training costs
- Increasing worker autonomy
- Increasing quality due to uniform work practices
- Enabling knowledge capitalization.[13]

TABLE 2-14: EPSS: Some Assumptions and Issues Revisited

Assumptions	Issues
Learning is best accomplished during job performance	• Workers who must respond quickly to job demands may not have time to use EPSS • Workers in a *noisy* work environment may not be able to concentrate on EPSS
Learning is best accomplished by the provision of small task-oriented training *granules*	• Novices need a *big picture* overview—a unified view of the whole job and how the tasks fit together • Granules provide novices with a fragmented knowledge base
Workers are most qualified to take control of their learning processes—they know best what they need	• Novices may need guidance to determine what knowledge and skills they need, what sequence to use to tackle the information, and how much practice they need • Experienced workers can use learner-controlled EPSS effectively on their own
The decision to use EPSS is straightforward—analyze the task and pick a valid tool-task interface (for example, outlining tool for a writing task)	• EPSS use based on task analysis and a valid tool-task interface may or may not improve performance • Decision to use EPSS must also be based on: — Analysis of the user—user-task-tool-outcome interface — Analysis of the work environment—noise level, space for EPSS hardware, etc.
EPSS is a *cognitive replacement tool*—workers *do* instead of *think and do*	• EPSS could have a *de-skilling* effect on the worker by replacing cognitive processes • EPSS could limit workers' future contributions to the organization
Problems with *traditional* training are best resolved by replacing it with EPSS	• The solution is not to replace low-tech interventions with costly, complicated high-tech interventions • Use EPSS to support training rather than replace it • Base decision on how to support performance on practical experience and research on how people learn and think

Adapted from Clark, 1992, pp. 23–25.

Cultural and Other Roadblocks to EPSS

"No matter what technologies you're using or what activity you are trying to support, the main issues in system development are always more organizational than technical."[14] EPSS as an electronic infrastructure requires an organizational infrastructure of its own to succeed. The organizational infrastructure should include the following:

- A high-level organizational champion
- Coordinated support and resources from multiple departments, including domain experts and implementation specialists
- A large body of potential users
- Job tasks appropriate to the use of EPSS
- Support for thinking *outside the box* in terms of design and development
- Extensive training and re-training of cross-discipline design and development teams composed of performance technologists, instructional designers, systems developers, documentation designers, and support staff
- Technology (hardware and software) and technical support required to support all this activity.[15,16]

There are also a number of issues that arise from basic assumptions about EPSS. These assumptions and some related issues are presented in Table 2-14. The issues may need to be addressed before implementing EPSS as performance interventions.

Implementing EPSS in the Workplace

The PT practitioner needs a working knowledge of how EPSS works for individuals and organizations. The best way to acquire this knowledge is to personally participate in many different levels of EPSS, and read the literature from the late 1980s to the present.

The next step is to get involved with an EPSS project team that is working to develop a new system or improve an existing system. As with other performance improvement interventions, the PT practitioner can fill the roles of cheerleader, analyst, evaluator, facilitator, and, in some cases, designer. In addition, the roles and activities suggested for implementing job aids may also be appropriate for implementing EPSS.

JOB AID 2-8: Selecting EPSS as a Performance Intervention

Directions: Read each statement and decide whether you agree or disagree. If you agree, put a check in the box to the left of the statement. If you do not agree, leave the box blank.

All stakeholders and project team members should complete the checklist individually, then discuss the results. Try to reach consensus whenever possible. Note that items 3–5 in the left column may be negotiable if the need for EPSS is strong enough.

When Not to Use EPSS	When to Use EPSS
☐ 1. A computer is not practical for the task	☐ 1. A computer is fundamental to the task
☐ 2. Task is simple and repetitive	☐ 2. Task complexity is wide and deep with many paths and many variables
☐ 3. Task is constantly changing, which would increase maintenance costs and cancel out performance gains	☐ 3. After design and programming is complete, system maintenance can handle process and task changes
☐ 4. Adequate development funds are not available	☐ 4. System must support all levels of performers—novice to expert
☐ 5. Experts are not available to design, program, and maintain the EPSS	☐ 5. Inadequate performance has significant business consequences, even if number of performers is limited
	☐ 6. Turnover is high; there is a regular need to train new performers
	☐ 7. There is a need to redesign an old system or develop a new system
	☐ 8. There is a large performer population
	☐ 9. Performers must gather or create and share knowledge

Adapted from Gery, G. J. (1999). Electronic performance support system (EPSS). In D.G. Langdon, K.S. Whiteside, and M.M. McKenna. (Eds.), Intervention resource guide: 50 performance improvement tools *(pp. 144–145). San Francisco, CA: Jossey-Bass/Pfeiffer. ISPI © 2001. Permission granted for unlimited duplication for noncommercial use.*

FIGURE 2-10: Hale's Hierarchy of Interventions

Congruency and Clarity (how organization defines itself)

1. Vision and missions

2. Goals and objectives

3. Values, incentives, rewards, and policies

Efficiency (how organization operates in terms of efficiency and cost)

4. Organization and job structures

5. Work processes, procedures, and practices

6. Documentation and standards

7. Job aids, signage, and labels

Resiliency and Capability (extent to which organization invests in physical and human resources)

8. Physical facilities and space

9. Training and development

10. Resource capacity and sufficiency

Based on Hale, 1998, p. 126.

One of the skills a PT practitioner can bring to an EPSS project team is helping them decide when to select EPSS as a performance intervention. Job Aid 2-8 provides a checklist and a process for deciding when to use EPSS.

Documentation and Standards

Documentation and standards are part of the organizational culture and support the performance of both individuals and the organization as a whole. They are part of the human resource (HR) system and are closely connected to job analysis and work design, quality improvement, and human resource development (HRD) interventions (compensation and benefits and performance appraisals). Within Hale's Hierarchy of Interventions (see Figure 2-10), documentation and standards contribute to the efficiency of organizations.

Definition and Scope—Documentation

When workers want to know *how, when,* and *what* they usually turn to documentation.[1] Documentation codes information, preserves it, and makes it accessible to the current and future work force. "Interventions in this family make information continuously accessible…it is important that people be able to retrieve and reference information on an as-needed basis."[2] In addition to providing access to information, documentation has many uses:

- Codifies and records progress, accomplishments, failures, lessons learned, policies, procedures, job specifications, standards, problems, and decisions

- Provides feedback and data to analyze, validate, clarify, track, report, and record information for current and future (history) reference

- Helps institutionalize best practices and lessons learned.

For example, in order to institutionalize process management once process improvement projects are completed, organizations rely on documentation more than anecdotal feedback. They monitor and sustain progress through the use of some of the following documents:

- Process maps and procedures
- Customer-driven measures
- Process control charts, accident reports, and other documentary information about current and past performance
- Process management team meeting minutes
- Annual business plans
- Process improvement suggestions
- Procedures and vehicles for solving process problems and capitalizing on process opportunities.[3]

Legal Implications

Documentation has important legal implications: "One vital element of a defense is documentary evidence… training professionals may minimize their own and their employers' vulnerability in civil lawsuits by maintaining appropriate and accurate documentation."[4] Another example relates to performance appraisals:

> *…Employers must consistently document unsatisfactory performance…With evaluations employers can avoid the dual problems of lack of warning and lack of*

documentation. Moreover, when managers have a precise format for conducting an evaluation, they are less likely to discriminate.[5]

From Print to Video

Documentation may range from paper-based manuals to online help screens. Even video is used for documentation.

Video can also be used as a device for data collection or documentation. For example, if a training developer needs to conduct a task analysis, he or she can use video to capture the processes demonstrated by a master performer. Unusual events can also be taped so that they can be examined later by people who have not been exposed to them.[6]

For example, videotapes of firefighters in action during the massive brush fires in California were later used to:
- Develop lessons learned
- Validate existing policies and procedures
- Establish new policies and procedures
- Validate or improve existing performance standards
- Address issues of liability for death or injury
- Train new firefighters.

Structured Writing

Structured writing is a useful tool for preparing documentation and standards, both print-based and computer-based or on line.

Structured writing is a synthesis of tools and techniques for the analysis of complex subject matters and jobs. It consists of a group of standards and techniques for the management of large amounts of rapidly changing information and also procedures for planning, organizing, sequencing, and presenting communications, especially training courses and documentation in business.[7]

Structured writing also includes methodology for labeling information blocks, establishing document formats, handling document life cycle, and integrating graphics. It uses *information blocks* instead of paragraphs, and a grouping of one to nine information blocks is called an *information map*. Job Aid 2-9 provides a sample of structured writing and more information about how to produce a document using basic structured writing methodology.

Minimalist Documentation

Minimalist documentation is an example of user-based documentation that encourages people to *learn by doing*. The concept was first developed during the 1980s to "reduce the obstacles to self-directed discovery and achievement that can inhere [sic] in modern systems and documentation."[8] Proponents identified and examined "the most critical and typical usability problems people

have in getting started with computer interfaces"[9] and came to the conclusion that the systems approach to instructional documentation "more or less guarantees these sorts of problems."[10] Table 2-15 lists the usability problems that triggered the development of minimalist training documentation for new computer systems.

Purpose and Principles

Minimalist documentation attempts to accomplish three things:
- Provide an exploratory environment for the new user
- Encourage active involvement (interactivity) with the system
- Manage the consequences of error so greatest possible benefit is obtained.[11]

There are five principles to follow when developing minimalist documentation:
1. Allow the user to get started fast and focus on need-to-know functions.
2. Rely on the user to think and improvise, but avoid providing ambiguous information that may lead to faulty inferences.
3. Direct training toward real tasks.
4. Exploit what people already know to speed up the learning process.
5. Support error recognition and recovery.[12]

Examples

Development of minimalist documentation is based on thorough analysis of the user and the task. Emphasis is on what content to *eliminate* rather than what content to include. Examples of minimalist documentation include Guided Exploration Cards, Minimal Manual, and Training Wheels. They all stress brevity, error recovery, and learning by doing:
- *Guided Exploration Cards* are task oriented and stand alone. Each card deals with a specific function and relies in part on the user's experience (it encourages the user to *get involved*). There is a checkpoint (If…then…) to help users detect and diagnose and recover from errors.
- *Minimal Manual* helps users perform basic, real, familiar functions as quickly as possible. Users are encouraged to try "x" and *see what happens*. The manual does not contain repetition, summaries, reviews, practice exercises, or material not directly related to the task at hand.
- *Training Wheels* is an interface that blocks the consequences of major new-user errors. For example, if a user selects a function that will not work at this point in time, the computer displays a message indicating that the function is *disabled*. This keeps the user from getting tangled up in error consequences and reduces the amount of content needed to explain errors and help the user recover from errors.[13]

TABLE 2-15: Summary of Most Critical and Typical Usability Problems of New System Users

- Users tend to get used to a new system by *plunging in*, which can have disastrous effects if they lack appropriate knowledge and experience

- Users are not always careful planners and often become intrigued by functions that are irrelevant to what they need to know and do

- Users are not good at following procedures systematically, especially if the sequenced steps lack *clearly motivated prerequisite relationships*; for example, users rarely follow the instructions to *read everything before doing anything*

- Users' reasoning about situations is often subject to interference from what they know about superficially similar situations; for example, function keys may not have the same use in the new system

- Users are often poor at recognizing, diagnosing, and recovering from errors they make, especially when they are not taught the consequences of certain actions

Based on Carroll, 1992, pp. 332–334.

Application

Minimalist documentation principles can also be applied to other systems, for example, telecommunication systems and computer-aided design (CAD). However, the concept of minimalist documentation is not always easy to sell: "It conflicts fundamentally with the standard practices of providing thorough systems and documentation and remedying observed problems with the addition of further enhancements."[14] Another problem is directly related to *speed-of-lightning* changes in technology, applications, and interfaces. The nature of minimalist documentation makes it relatively easy for designers to respond to change, however:

> *...the vast majority of people in the work force remain uninitiated. They are losing ground in the race between more powerful function and greater ease of use. This is not merely because more powerful systems present more functions to master; it is also because functional innovations in computing systems quite often address existing usability problems while creating new ones (faster than user problems can be studied, understood, and addressed).[15]*

Transferring Print to Online Documentation

Whether documentation is designed as traditional prose, structured writing, or minimalist documentation, transferring it to the computer screen for online distribution is a real challenge. Here are some tips from the trenches that help bridge the gap between printed and online documentation:

- Avoid page turners that simply reproduce paper-based documentation. Use the potential of the media to enhance the documentation; for example, create hyperlinks that allow the user to easily access required or additional information as needed.

- Analyze the content. What information do users need and why do they need it? For example, if the users need *how to* information, format the index as a series of questions: *How do I access...? How do I troubleshoot...?*

- Analyze the users. How do they learn and think and what is their level of computer experience?

- Make the main menu structure fast, easily accessible, and understandable. For example, leave the menu in a secondary window for easy access.

- Use but don't abuse hyperlinks. Hyperlink menu items to related content or simple content statements to more detailed discussions, but don't hyperlink every word!

- Avoid full-text search. A searchable index that recognizes synonyms and related phrases is much more user friendly.

- When documentation is or includes a help system for novices, make it automatic and intuitive—for example, a human or animal character that sits in the lower right corner of the screen and makes suggestions on what to do next or explains what an object does on the screen when the user clicks on it.

- Before beginning an online documentation project, get as much training and advice as possible. If you build a well-organized document the first time, people will use it, and will recognize it as a valuable tool.[16]

Definition and Scope—Standards

The term *standards* may refer to principles or criteria for ethical conduct or for consistent, superior performance. In this section the topic is standards as they relate to performance.

Standards support TQM, performance improvement, continuous improvement, and process/job design or redesign initiatives as well as performance appraisal systems, and the establishment of equitable compensation and benefits systems. Standards also:

- Improve interfaces
- Allow for an appropriate type of flexibility
- Result in lower costs because they permit economies of scale.[17]

The goals of standards are to help achieve consistent performance, allow for interchangeability, and increase product flexibility and longevity.[18] Two examples of the impact of standards on modern organizations are ISO 9000 and beyond and the movement toward certification of professionals and workers at all organizational levels.

The following are examples of interventions that standardize because they support interfacing and consistency:

- Requiring all production runs to produce the same volume
- Requiring production workers to follow the same line setup procedures
- Adopting standard labels and icons
- Designing new technology to work with old technology
- Applying the same formatting rules to documents and training materials
- Using an automated answering system to handle customer calls
- Installing process controllers to monitor and run production lines.[19]

Implementing Documentation and Standards Interventions in the Workplace

Documentation and standards are two *organizational culture items* that PT practitioners "could have some impact on, and by doing so could help to shape the relationship between the organization and the employee."[20] The PT practitioner must understand when to select documentation or standards as a performance intervention and how to implement the interventions. Table 2-16 provides some guidance.

Implementing Interventions That Document

Helping to implement documentation interventions requires strong analytical, performance consulting, and design skills. The PT practitioner may be called upon to conduct a cost-benefit analysis as well as "clarify, gain consensus, and help make information available."[21]

If the decision to implement includes using a *non-traditional format*, such as structured writing or minimalist documentation, then the PT practitioner will need to put on his or her change agent hat until the new format

becomes institutionalized. Finding a high-level champion and producing documentation that is so user friendly it *sells itself* will ease the transition. It may also be necessary to suggest special training for the designers, developers, and subject matter experts.

Implementing Interventions That Standardize

Hale suggests that the performance consultant should develop a set of personal standards for efficiency, responsiveness, accuracy, effectiveness, and cost.[22] This is one way to begin to understand the impact of standardization on organizations and industries, and to model the use of standards for performance improvement. Implementing standards also calls for the PT practitioner to use his or her change-agent and facilitation skills. Knowledge of evaluation theory and practice and statistical measurement is also helpful, especially when standardization is mandated from sources external to the organization.

Case Study 2-2: Documentation and Standards: One Step at a Time

Situation

The mission of a small, forward-looking home construction company was to reach high levels of customer satisfaction, profitability, local market dominance, and employee stability. The company also envisioned itself as setting a standard for operational excellence among home builders. To achieve these goals the company sought individual accountability, results-oriented performance, and strict adherence to performance standards. The missing ingredient was solid operational guidelines to evaluate results, provide performance standards, and support continuous improvement.

Intervention

The president hired outside performance consultants to meet weekly with himself and a cross-functional team of supervisors and employees. The goal was to analyze and document the company's business system cycle and each cycle component. For example, the seventh phase in the cycle, pre-construction, included six major tasks:

1. Finalize buyer selections and changes
2. Prepare preliminary construction plans
3. Prepare for the pre-construction meeting
4. Acquire permits
5. Conduct pre-construction meeting
6. Finalize the construction plans

The consultants gathered input on pre-construction from a CAD designer, sales representative, buyers, building superintendent, management, administration, and the company controller. The consultants then produced documentation for the

TABLE 2-16: How to Select and Implement Documentation and Standards

If these conditions currently exist...	and you are certain that...	then implement documentation...
• Variance in behavior is undesirable • Variance exists • Variance is caused by operating inefficiency, waste, or unnecessary costs • Information can reduce variance • Information is not currently accessible over time • Information is very complex • Job aids, manuals, help screens are not available, inadequate, inaccurate, or not easy to access	• It is possible to document required information in a form that is accurate, user friendly, and easily accessible • Documentation will facilitate consistent interpretation or compliance • Documentation will contribute to efficiency • The cost of not doing anything or doing something else is greater than the cost of gathering, communicating, and maintaining documentation	• Form a project team of stakeholders (including experts and technical support staff as appropriate) • Identify what information is required to improve performance • Determine how to codify information for easy accessibility and user friendliness • Prepare standards for measuring effectiveness of documentation • Develop documentation • Pilot documentation • Manage (distribution) and maintain (update) documentation
If these conditions currently exist...	**and you are certain that...**	**then implement standards...**

• Deviation in equipment, materials, specifications, procedures, common practices, and so on
  — adds extra costs
  — results in lower yields
  — causes variance in the quality of work
• Industry, government, and/or customers mandate standardization
	• Stakeholders agree that lack of standardization is the cause of the problem
	• Stakeholders agree to standardize
	• Stakeholders agree that standardization will meet business needs
	• Stakeholders agree standardization will fit the organizational culture or the culture will adapt to it
	• Stakeholders agree standardization is essential for gaining or maintaining competitive advantage
		• Conduct a feasibility and/or cost-benefit analysis
		• Identify industry standards
		• Identify existing internal standards
		• Prepare measurement criteria
		• Develop appropriate standards for organization
		• Implement change management interventions
		• Pilot standards
		• Implement standards
		• Control and maintain standards

Adapted from Hale, 1998, pp. 136; 155–157; 161.

pre-construction phase using information mapping techniques. The documentation included flowcharts, matrices, lists, and an appendix of forms. It covered the following:
• Objective and overview
• Resource requirements
• Step-by-step procedures
• Roles and responsibilities
• Guidelines or standards for performance
• Products

The documentation was designed and developed to utilize the company's existing software and hardware capabilities, make it easy to print and update segments as needed, and ease an anticipated transition to online documentation.

All team members reviewed and approved the documentation before it was loaded onto the client's system. An administrator was assigned to monitor and maintain the documentation.

Future action items included establishing a system for using the documentation to evaluate performance and results.

Results

The user-friendly formats and accessibility of the documentation made it a useful tool for employees at all levels of the organization. The format also made it possible to use the documentation as an individual training tool supported by mentoring and coaching, and a video library.

Lessons Learned

• Good facilitation skills are essential in a situation involving team members from various levels of an organization. At first the president dominated the work sessions; however, over time team members became confident enough to provide *real* input on improving processes and procedures.

JOB AID 2-9: A Structured Guide to Structured Writing

Directions: Use the following sample to (a) learn more about structured writing and (b) guide you in developing documentation based on structured writing. Practice by writing an information block for the first task in a simple procedure.

Structured Writing	
Definition	Structured writing is a synthesis of tools and techniques for the analysis of complex subject matters and jobs.
	It consists of a group of standards and techniques for the management of large amounts of rapidly changing information and also procedures for planning, organizing, sequencing, and presenting communications, especially training courses and documentation in business.
When to Use Structured Writing	Structured writing is useful in the following circumstances: • Performance is primarily based on task and knowledge and does *not involve psychomotor functioning* • Workers do not need training in *soft or interpersonal skills* • Workers need large amounts of information • Workers need just-in-time learning • Need exists to develop computer-stored knowledge bases that are modular and easily accessed • Document must be user friendly • Simplified document updating and maintenance are a priority
	Structured writing is *not* appropriate to document performance involving psychomotor functioning or when training in soft (interpersonal) skills is required.
Information Blocks	Structured writing uses *information blocks* instead of paragraphs.
	Each information block contains one or more sentences and/or diagrams, tables, or other illustrations about a limited topic, not to exceed nine sentences.
	Each information block is labeled to clearly identify the content of the information block.
Seven Types of Information Blocks	There are approximately 40 different types of information blocks which can be sorted into seven basic classifications called *information types:* 1. Procedure 2. Process 3. Concept 4. Structure 5. Classification 6. Principle 7. Fact
Four Principles for Information Blocks	There are four principles or constraints that guide the generation of information blocks: 1. *Chunking:* Group all information into small, manageable units 2. *Relevance:* Each chunk should include information related to one main point only 3. *Consistency:* Use similar words, labels, formats, sequences, and organizations for similar subject matter 4. *Labeling:* Label each chunk or group of chunks according to specific criteria
Information Map	An information map is an intermediate level of documentation.
	It is composed of one to nine information blocks.
Purpose of Information Map	The information map enables systematic sequencing and formatting and helps the reader understand the structure of the subject matter and the document.

Adapted from Horn, R.E. (1999). Structured writing. In D.G. Langdon, K.S. Whiteside, and M.M. McKenna. (Eds.), Intervention resource guide: 50 performance improvement tools *(pp. 357–364). San Francisco, CA: Jossey-Bass/Pfeiffer. ISPI © 2001. Permission granted for unlimited duplication for noncommercial use.*

- The cross-functional nature of the team was helpful to the team members as well as to the consultants. For example, the team began to recognize the importance of *internal customers* and how individual roles and responsibilities impact other individuals and the entire process.
- Team members were very willing to take responsibility for implementing the processes and procedures that *they created* during the analysis process.

- It is important not to over-analyze processes and procedures. Team members assigned to an analysis project are busy people, and budget constraints also have an impact on the level of analysis. Consultants need to keep the analyze-document-review-approve process moving along at a steady pace and establish a solid, systematic *monitor-and-maintain* process to accommodate additional input, changes, or updates.

This case study was written by Dr. Joan Conway Dessinger based on a real-world experience. Used with permission.

CHAPTER

3

JOB ANALYSIS/ WORK DESIGN

"DARN IT."

JOB ANALYSIS/WORK DESIGN

Langdon[1] states that work is "one version of performance" or what the worker must do on the job. All organizations perform three different types of work:

- *Direct work* contributes directly to the fulfillment of an organization's mission and goals.
- *Management work* guides or administers personnel, material, and other organizational resources so that direct work can be accomplished; includes aligning the organization with its external environment.
- *Support work* provides products or services that

are vital to the accomplishment of direct or management work.[2]

Job analysis and work design are complementary interventions (see Table 3-1) that help all types of workers—direct, management, or support workers—maximize organizational efficiency and employee satisfaction. This chapter will explore the job analysis and work design interventions contained in the enhanced HPT Model (see Table 3-2).

JOB ANALYSIS

Job analysis is a formal way of evaluating job requirements by looking at the job itself and at the kind of person needed to fill each job. It provides valuable information for the preparation of both job descriptions and job specifications. A job description is a written account of what a job incumbent does and how he or she does it, and may include the environment, conditions of employment, and job tasks. Job specifications list the minimum qualifications that a person must possess in order to perform the job successfully. Figure 3-1 illustrates the relationship between job analysis, job description, and job specifications.

Definition and Scope

Job analysis is the systematic, technical process of collecting job information by identifying appropriate skills, duties, knowledge, and accountability issues.[1,2] Companies engage in job analysis because of changes and paradigm shifts inherent in jobs or job environments—organizational environment, work environment, work, or worker.[3] Job analysis is conducted when any or all of the following conditions occur:

- A new organization is established
- New jobs are created

TABLE 3-1: Job Analysis and Work Design as Complementary Interventions		
	Job Analysis	**Work Design**
Input	• Data on work, worker, and work environment • Organizational environment	• Job descriptions • Job specifications
Process	• Job/task analysis • Performance analysis	• Work design (enlargement, rotation, enrichment) • Human factors (ergonomics, safety engineering, PM) • Quality improvement (TQM, continuous improvement, value engineering)
Output	• Job descriptions (work) • Job specifications (worker)	• Blueprint of job performance requirements • Blueprint for maximizing organizational efficiency and worker satisfaction

---

TABLE 3-2: Job Analysis and Work Design Interventions From Enhanced HPT Model

Job Analysis
- Job Descriptions
- Job Specifications

Work Design
- Job Design
- Job Enlargement
- Job Rotation
- Job Enrichment

Human Factors
- Ergonomics
- Safety Engineering
- Preventive Maintenance (PM)

Quality Improvement
- TQM
- Continuous Improvement
- Value Analysis/Value Engineering (VA/VE)

FIGURE 3-1: Input-Output Relationship of Job Analysis, Job Descriptions, and Job Specifications

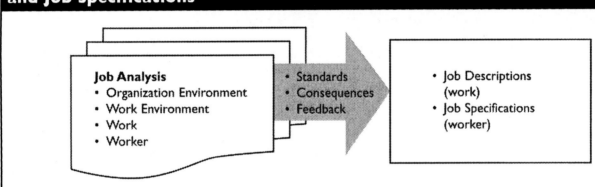

Job Analysis
- Organization Environment
- Work Environment
- Work
- Worker

- Standards
- Consequences
- Feedback

- Job Descriptions (work)
- Job Specifications (worker)

- Significant changes are needed because of new technologies, system changes, or new policies and procedures[4]

PT-Related Purposes

In the performance technology (PT) arena, job analysis is usually part of the up-front performance analysis, which takes place prior to gap analysis, cause analysis, and the design or selection of performance improvement interventions.[5] It may also be considered a *performance intervention* on its own merit. Frequently, in the course of job analysis, performance improvement issues are both identified and resolved without the need for further intervention. This occurs primarily when past or current job performers, supervisors, and customers actively participate in the job analysis process.

HRD-Related Purposes

For HRD purposes, "job analysis is necessary for legally validating the methods used in making employment decisions, such as selection, promotion, and performance appraisal."[6] It is also useful for other HRD functions such as the following:
- Recruiting quality job applicants
- Developing and maintaining a compensation system that considers the true value of job contributions
- Identifying knowledge or skill gaps for training and development planning

- Organizing jobs
- Human resource planning
- Career pathing
- Labor relations
- Engineering safety into work and equipment design
- Vocational guidance
- Rehabilitation counseling
- HRD research.[7,8]

Implementing Job Analysis in the Workplace

Gatewood and Feild suggest the following guidelines for conducting a proactive job analysis for the purpose of employee selection.[9] The guidelines are also applicable to job analysis in general, regardless of the purpose.

1. Select a job(s) that really needs to be analyzed, for example, a job that changes frequently or an entry-level job that has not been analyzed recently
2. Plan the job analysis—inputs, process, and outputs
3. Collect the appropriate job data using the appropriate job analysis techniques
4. Verify the accuracy of the data by checking with past and current performers, supervisors, customers, etc.
5. Develop a blueprint or roadmap of the job—where the job may lead, its prime purpose, job performance qualifications, etc.

6. Document the data and write a job description focusing on duties, responsibilities, and tasks.

Ideally, PT practitioners with an HRD background conduct job analysis. However, companies may also use HRD practitioners, outside consultants, business managers, industrial engineers, methods analysts, and even job incumbents, supervisors, and customers to conduct the analysis.[10]

Collecting Job Analysis Data

A variety of data-collection methodologies is used to gather job-related information, including those listed below.

- Questionnaires and surveys—employees respond to questions or comments about tasks, responsibilities, difficulty level, etc. (see Job Aid 3-1).
- Interviews—structured interviews secure data from employees, supervisors, or customers
- Observations—a trained PT or HRD practitioner observes employees actually performing the job and records key activities and features based on what is actually seen
- Diaries and logs—employees document their own activities, time requirements, etc.
- Focus groups—groups of 8–12 employees discuss specific job-related questions and their dialogue is transcribed and used for enhancing job descriptions.

Depending on the availability of qualified personnel to conduct job analysis, cost factors, job complexity issues, and organizational culture concerns, more formal methodologies may be used:

- Formal task inventory analysis to determine the appropriate knowledge, skills, and attitudes required for the job
- Critical incident techniques to focus on behavioral descriptions and dimensions of jobs
- Eclectic approaches using a variety of data-collection methodologies, for example, canned instruments (surveys or questionnaires) used with structured interviews and focus groups[11,12,13]

Implementation Inputs-Process-Outputs

Job analysis answers 11 important questions regarding the inputs, process, and outputs or outcomes of a specific job. These questions provide the framework for conducting a thorough job analysis for any purpose. Figure 3-2 lists the inputs-process-outputs of job analysis.

As a performance analysis tool, job analysis provides data on and an understanding of the inputs, process, and outputs of a given job for use in PT and HRD activities such as employee recruitment, selection, and compensation. Job analysis as an interactive intervention may clarify a performance problem and identify a solution without any further intervention. By taking job analysis two steps further, it is also possible to do the following:

- Link the job to the mission, vision, and strategic management plan in order to understand the job role within the value framework of the organization
- Interview employees and use the data to analyze and benchmark positions within the industry or the organization.[14]

FIGURE 3-2: Job Analysis Inputs-Process-Outputs

Inputs to Job Analysis

- Purpose—Why is the job performed?
- Location and environment—Where is the job performed?
- Frequency—How often is the job performed?
- Importance—How important is the job to the overall success of the process? the organization?
- Qualifications—What knowledge, skills, and attitudes are required to perform the job successfully?
- Tools—What tools are required to perform the job?

Job Analysis Process

- Procedures—How does the worker do the job?
- Difficulty—How hard is it to perform the job (physically? mentally?)?

Outputs of Job Analysis

- Standards—How does the worker know when the job is completed successfully?
- Consequences—What are the results of job performance? job non-performance?
- Feedback—What information (expectations, incentives, changes, etc.) is provided to or elicited from the worker to support and enhance performance?

Based on Langdon, 1995, pp. 71–93; Spitzer, 1989, p. 37.

TABLE 3-3: Government Acts Impact the Focus of Job Analysis

Government Act	Focus
Fair Labor Standards Act	Exempt and non-exempt workers
Equal Pay Act	Comparable pay for similar jobs for both men and women
Civil Rights Act	Unfair discrimination in selection and promotion
Occupational Safety and Health Act (OSHA)	On-the-job factors that endanger safety and health
Americans with Disabilities Act (ADA)	Granting reasonable accommodation for physically challenged workers

Legal Dimensions of Implementation

Job analysis is essential to solid, proactive, human resource management. Government legislation also has an effect on the focus of thorough job analysis. Table 3-3 describes the five major government acts that have an effect on job analysis.

Job Descriptions

One output of job analysis is job descriptions. Carefully researched and clearly written job descriptions help to improve performance. When no job description exists, or if the existing description is unclear, incomplete, inaccurate, or ambiguous, writing a job description may be the performance intervention of choice.

Definition and Scope

A job description is a written statement documenting the tasks and functions of a job. It includes what is done on the job, how it is done, and under what conditions it is done. The information generated through job analysis makes it possible to write job descriptions effectively. The variety of data that are collected before and during job analysis may be recorded as quantitative or qualitative measurements; verbal, visual, or written narrative descriptions; or graphic and written procedural documentation. Mondy, Noe, and Premeaux offer a practical and extremely useful summary of seven types of data that may be generated through job analysis and applied to developing job descriptions:

1. Work activities—processes, procedures, responsibility levels, and similar issues
2. Worker activities—human behaviors, personal and physical energy expenditures, etc.
3. Job resources—machines, tools, equipment, work aids
4. Job tangibles and intangibles—knowledge, management, products delivered, services performed
5. Work performance—documented job standards; records dealing with quantity, quality, time, or safety, and so on

6. Job context—setting, communication, culture
7. Special job requirements—previous education, training, and practical experience[1]

Implementing (Writing) Job Descriptions in the Workplace

Although there is no standard form used for the content of a job description, the writer should include sufficient detail so that the performers understand:
- What to do to complete the job successfully
- Products/services generated as a result of the job
- Standards applied to the job
- Conditions under which the job is performed
- Job design characteristics.[2]

Depending on the job and the organizational requirements, a job description may include the following information:
- Major tasks performed
- Percentage of time devoted to each task
- Performance standards
- Working conditions, including possible hazards to safety and health
- Reporting chain both internal and external
- Non-human resources used on the job.[3]

The job description also includes an identification section. This highly informative section may include the following:
- *Job:* Title, status, code, location, grade level, and pay range (depending upon the organization, the last two items may be "attached" to the job or the performer)
- *Job Description*: Date the job description was written, person(s) who wrote the description, person(s) who approved the description
- *Performer:* Person(s) or positions who perform the job and who supervise the job.[4]

Attention to detail and consistency of terms are critical. For example, job titles may be misleading. The person writing the job description should attempt to standardize

JOB AID 3-1: Job Analysis Survey

Directions: Use the following job analysis survey or adapt the survey to gather data about a specific job in your organization. It is helpful to use the same survey with *all* the internal and external stakeholders including performer, manager, supervisor, customer, supplier, etc.

---

1. Demographic Data

Name of organization _____

Name of performer(s)_____

Title/Position of performer(s)_____

Division/Department/Unit_____

---

2. Describe the job:

Work processes (action over time, e.g., completing a form, assembling a door) _____

_____

_____

Work activities (tasks performed to complete a process) _____

_____

_____

Work procedures (how processes/tasks are performed) _____

_____

_____

Work expectations:

    Performer _____

    Supervisor _____

    Customer _____

---

3. What are the results of the job?_____

_____

---

4. Describe specific task attributes related to the job:

What does the performer need to *know* to perform the job successfully? _____

_____

What *skills* does the performer need to perform the job successfully? _____

_____

What *abilities* does the performer need to perform the job successfully? _____

_____

What *attitudes* support successful completion of the job? _____

_____

JOB AID 3-1: Job Analysis Survey *Continued*

5. Identify the non-human resources required for the job (technology, machines, equipment, tools, etc.):

_____
_____

6. List any actions faced on the job that may endanger health and safety: _____

_____
_____

7. List the direct report chain from the performer to the person holding ultimate responsibility for the job (internal or external): _____

_____
_____

8. List the people who report to the job performer (internal or external): _____

_____
_____

9. Identify the support requirements for successful completion of the job:

Education _____

Training _____

Personality and Interests _____

Previous Work Experience _____

10. What are the consequences of job performance?

Good performance _____

_____

Poor performance _____

_____

11. What feedback is available to help the performer achieve success?

To the performer _____

From the performer _____

12. List other data/facts not included above that help to describe the job: _____

_____
_____
_____
_____

job titles by using the *Dictionary of Occupational Titles (DOT)*. This handy Department of Labor resource, located in the reference section of most libraries, lists job titles, duties, and related information for a myriad of jobs. The writing tone and style are also important:

- Be clear.
- Indicate the scope of authority and important relationships.
- Be specific—use action verbs such as analyze, gather, assemble, plan, devise, infer, deliver, transmit, maintain, supervise, recommend, etc.
- Be brief.
- Recheck by asking, "Will a new employee understand how to do this job if he or she reads this job description?"

Usefulness of Job Description Interventions

Schuler and Huber indicate that job descriptions serve many purposes and uses. In addition to helping the employee understand and perform the job, job descriptions may be useful for conducting the following activities:

- Job classification, compensation, design/redesign
- Employee recruitment, selection, staffing, training,

development, performance appraisal, and retention[5] (see Job Aid 3-2).

Job Specifications

While the job description focuses on the job, job specifications are performer focused.[1,2] Frequently, they are used to guide employee hiring or selection, compensation, classification, training, performance appraisal, and retention. (see Job Aid 3-3).

Definition and Scope

Job specifications list the minimum qualifications that a person must possess in order to perform the job successfully. The list should include knowledge, skills, abilities, aptitudes, previous experience, and capacity.[3] Table 3-4 defines the components of a job specification.

Implementing (Writing) Job Specifications in the Workplace

Job specifications focus on the performer. The specifications should answer the following questions:

JOB AID 3-2: Validating Existing Job Descriptions

Directions: Secure a copy of a job description from the Personnel Department and analyze it by focusing on and validating each of the components listed below based on the following criteria: Is the written description clear, complete, accurate, and unambiguous?

Key: Clear—Is the writing style easily understood by all who read the description?
Complete—Does the content describe all the major components of the job?
Accurate—Does the description document the current job tasks and standards correctly?
Unambiguous—Is there any question about what the description says/means?

Job Title								
Job Description Components	**Validation**							
	Clear		**Complete**		**Accurate**		**Unambiguous**	
	Yes	**No**	**Yes**	**No**	**Yes**	**No**	**Yes**	**No**
Job Identification								
Job Summary								
Relationships								
Responsibilities, duties								
Authority of incumbent								
Standards of performance								
Working conditions								
Job specifications								
Comments:								

TABLE 3-4: Definitions of Job Specification Components

Specifications	Definition
Knowledge	Cognitive mastery of some principles, guidelines, rules, or other content. Knowledge is invisible until it is applied.
Skills	Visible degree of proficiency or expertise in carrying out an applied task. The skill level may include such factors as knowledge of process, exercise of judgment, manual dexterity, responsibility for product and equipment, length of training period, etc.
Abilities	Powers possessed by an individual…that characterize his [sic] capacity to do. Can be physical, mental, or social; inherited or acquired; general or special. It implies that the task can be done now without further training.
Aptitudes	A natural disposition, tendency, capacity, or talent toward a particular action or effect.
Attitudes	Personal values and beliefs that pre-dispose a person to act in a certain way and may affect specific performance outcomes.
Experience	Total background an individual brings to the job.
Capacity	Ultimate limits to which an individual develops any function given appropriate training, tools, equipment, and environment.

Based on Hopke, 1968, pp. 3, 6, 331; Brinkerhoff, 1987, p. 126.

- What basic knowledge, skills, abilities, aptitude, attitude, and experience are required to perform this job successfully?
- Which of the requirements are nice to have? Which are "need to have"?
- What are the legal implications of the job specifications?

Job specifications may be translated easily into performance appraisal tools or job advertisements. For example, Otterbein College placed the classified advertisement shown in Figure 3-3 in the *Chronicle of Higher Education*.[4] The ad is composed of job specifications.

Case Study 3-1: Job Analysis at a Proprietary School

Situation

The setting for this case study is a proprietary school that trains and certifies medical technologists, medical assistants, and medical technicians. A valued employee with 16 years' seniority left employment for personal reasons. The employee was in charge of the school's testing program. The job involved planning, preparing, scoring, statistically analyzing, and re-posting examination data for 200 students. The employee was also responsible for supervising a clerk who typed and processed exams after they were received from the faculty. When the employee left,

FIGURE 3-3: Using Job Specifications to Advertise a Job

Help Wanted: Instructional Designer

- Master's degree in Instructional Technology or related field, Doctorate preferred
- Minimum two years' experience in instructional design and distance learning in traditional and non-traditional learning environments
- Proficiency in MS Windows web page design
- Experience designing courses for web-based/distance learning delivery and with interactive compressed video delivery
- Experience conducting workshops in instructional design
- Experience in educational multimedia production, storyboarding, digital development, test development, and graphic design
- Ability to think clearly, write concisely, and communicate effectively
- Ability to invent options in the learning environment

Based on Otterbein College—Instructional Design, 1999, p. B66

JOB AID 3-3: Job Specifications Template

Directions: Select a job and identify the job specifications using the following template. Include all the knowledge, skills, abilities, aptitudes, attitudes, and experience required to perform the job successfully. Use current, validated job analysis or job descriptions if available..

Job Title: _____

_____

Job Summary (statement of major duties and work conditions):

_____

_____

_____

_____

Knowledge: _____

_____

_____

Skills: _____

_____

_____

Abilities: _____

_____

_____

Aptitudes: _____

_____

_____

Attitudes: _____

_____

_____

Experience: _____

_____

_____

Capacity: _____

_____

_____

the Curricular Affairs Department decided to upgrade the position from a staff position to a professional/administrative position, and from a data coordinator title to a psychometrician.

Intervention

Many factors necessitated upgrading the position, including the following:

- A student body that was comfortable in challenging statistical data.
- The requirement to support curricular decisions with test data.
- A faculty development mandate from the dean of faculty and the academic dean to write quality, unchallenged exam questions.

A committee was formed to write a job description and support the description with job specifications. The school uses a commercial classification and compensation system for defining all jobs, and the committee began by answering questions in a position questionnaire. Areas addressed in the questionnaire included:

- Position purpose—purpose and scope of intended job and what the encumbent performed
- Department functions—mission and role of department in which position was housed
- Organizational structure—who answers to whom; relationships
- Quantitative data—measures of size, influence, effect
- Essential job functions—statements that describe major duties for which the position is accountable (what is done, how it is done, why it is done, and percentage of total time)
- Principal challenges—typical and complex job challenges
- Special projects—nature, role, expected results
- Functional guidance—guidance received in fulfilling duties
- Authority and responsibility
- Key contacts
- Performance measurement—employee appraisal
- Job knowledge and experience—minimum and desirable
- Additional information—creativity, generation of new ideas, externally imposed guidelines, and so on.

FIGURE 3-4: Job Description and Specifications for Psychometrician Position

Job Title: Psychometrician

Job Level: Psychometric Services Officer I

Job Description: Oversee and administer individual and group standardized testing by instructing exam proctors in proper testing methods and monitoring to ensure compliance with professional psychometric guidelines. Position duties require the application of specialized skills that can be acquired through appropriate educational background, job-related training, and on-the-job experience.

Job Specifications: Duties and Responsibilities
- Administer individual and group test programs
- Train proctors in testing procedures and maintain testing conditions
- Score and analyze test data
- Tally test results using electronic and optical scoring machines
- Manipulate scoring instruments to allow faculty to select weighting of test questions
- Prepare statistical interpretation of test results
- Ensure testing situations are in compliance with professional psychometric guidelines
- Administer special sessions for testing of the physically challenged

Job Description and Specifications
- Answer inquiries and resolve problems regarding test administration, methods, and procedures for students, faculty, counselors, and outside organizations
- Prepare, explain, and help apply test data to support curricular functions
- Assist faculty in writing quality, unchallenged examination questions

Job Specifications: Qualifications
- Graduation from an accredited institution in statistics and measurement at the master's and preferably at the doctoral level
- Background in educational evaluation and measurement
- Reasonable analytic and problem solving skills
- Familiarity with testing programs and packages
- Knowledge of a variety of computer programs
- Ability to communicate effectively with others

Based on Case Study 3-1.

The committee sought input from the school's Human Resource Department, the immediate supervisor for the position, academic dean, and the dean of faculty to answer these questions.

Results

After the Human Resource Department, the immediate supervisor, and deans reviewed the completed questionnaire and the committee responded to a series of requests for additional information, the position was authorized as outlined in Figure 3-4.

After a six-week posting period, the position was filled by an internal candidate. The candidate was completing a master's degree in educational measurement and evaluation.

Lessons Learned

- Writing a job description and job specifications is a tedious and time-consuming process requiring thorough familiarity with the nature and function of the job and knowledge of organizational culture.
- It is necessary and helpful to work cooperatively with the organization's classification and compensation department to make the position a reality.
- Adding a performance improvement specialist to the committee would have helped to keep all players on target, match job duties and functions with organizational goals, and keep the organizational communication channels fluid.

This case study was written by James L. Moseley, EdD, LPC, CHES, Wayne State University School of Medicine. Used with permission.

WORK DESIGN

Job Design

Jobs should not occur in organizations by accident or chance. Jobs will empower the worker,[1] create enthusiasm, and enhance worker and organizational performance[2] if they are designed or redesigned deliberately to reflect the following:
- Organization's vision, mission, strategic management plan, hard and soft technologies, and environmental context
- Workers' interests, capabilities, and aspirations

Three interventions fall under the umbrella of job design or redesign: job enlargement, job rotation, and job enrichment. Figure 3-5 describes how one government agency attempted to redesign a job to make it easier to recruit and retain employees.

Definition and Scope

Before discussing alternatives for designing or redesigning jobs it is necessary to set the stage by discussing the overall process of job design. Job design is the process of putting tasks together to form complete jobs.[3] The importance of job design as a performance intervention is twofold:
1. An employee's behavior and attitudes about the nature of work, the job to be performed, and the personal impact of the job are influenced by the way an organization chooses to construct its jobs.

2. In order to improve performance and productivity, it is often easier to alter the job rather than the employee.[4]

To design a new job or redesign an existing job, the PT practitioner must analyze a combination of elements including:
- Tasks to be performed
- Methodologies used to perform specific tasks
- Relationship of the job to other organizational work[5]
- Challenges and autonomy for employees.[6]

It is also extremely helpful for the PT practitioner to be familiar with industrial and organizational psychology and the psychology of work.

Implementing Job Design

Schuler and Huber provide the following step-by-step approach for planning and implementing a job design or redesign:
1. Recognize the need for change
2. Select the approach or focus for the change effort
3. Determine how, when, where, why to change the job
4. Determine whether job design or redesign is appropriate
5. Diagnose the organization, workflow, processes, etc.
6. Provide training and support to the performer(s)
7. Make the job changes
8. Evaluate the job changes.[7]

FIGURE 3-5: Example of Job Redesign

In early 2000, a Naturalization Service spokesperson, speaking on public radio, reported that the Service was having trouble recruiting and retaining employees in the San Diego area, long a hotbed of illegal entry activity. The number of illegal entries had dropped significantly due to the addition of 70 miles of new fencing and the use of electronic surveillance devices. Patrolling the border had become a routine job with little or no action. One employee stated that most evenings he drove to work, signed in, drove 20 miles to his post, and sat in his car for the entire shift.

The spokesperson for the Service stated that, because the new system was working so well, they had no intention of changing (job redesign) the tasks and responsibilities assigned to the job of the border patrol. However, they were encouraging employees to take short-term assignments in more active areas (job rotation), or to perform community service such as volunteering to coach sports teams of Mexican youth for local teen centers to enhance the image of the border patrol (job enrichment).

Approaches to Implementation

Based on the research in the field, job design can be approached from five different perspectives: scientific management, motivation, job characteristics, sociotechnical systems, and human factors/ergonomics.[8,9]

- *Scientific management* is the classical approach to job design and is highlighted in the work of Frederick Taylor. Work is analyzed using scientific methods to determine the very best strategies to complete a task. Tasks are routinely studied, workers are carefully selected and trained, and the goals include cooperation and collaboration between employees and management.[10]

- *Motivation theory* emphasizes how to make jobs satisfying, pleasurable, challenging, and motivating to the worker. This research is based essentially on Frederick Herzberg's motivation-hygiene theory[11] and Hackman and Oldham's job characteristics theory.[12] Motivation-hygiene theory focuses on two factors: hygiene (extrinsic rewards) and motivation (intrinsic rewards). Extrinsic rewards stem from work policies, work conditions, job supervision, job compensation, etc. Intrinsic rewards include opportunities for personal growth and career advancement, training, recognized achievement, and so on. The distinction between extrinsic rewards from hygiene factors and intrinsic rewards from motivators is well researched in job design and redesign literature.[13]

- *Job characteristics theory* indicates that five core job dimensions or intrinsic characteristics may be used to motivate workers:

  Skill variety: Job requires a variety of skills and abilities

  Task identity: Job includes complete tasks as opposed to parts of tasks

  Task significance: Job is important inside and outside the organization

  Autonomy: Job provides worker with freedom and independence in decision making

  Feedback: Supervisor or organization provides information to the employee about performance

The five core job dimensions are related to job meaningfulness, responsibility for outcomes of work, and knowledge of the results of work activities, which, in turn, facilitate personal and work outcomes such as worker motivation, quality of work performance, worker satisfaction level, and worker absenteeism and turnover levels.

- *Sociotechnical system approach* stresses the importance of the interaction of people (social system) with the tools and techniques required to do the job (technical system).[14]

Redesign of jobs in the system is based on a diagnosis of all aspects of the work operations by people who have a stake in the work outcomes...work is redesigned in a way that attempts simultaneously to meet the organization's technical requirements and employee requirements.[15]

- *Human factors/ergonomics* approach focuses on how to design and shape a job to fit the physical, mental, and affective characteristics of the worker. This approach recognizes that one performance standard does not fit all and that a variety of performers may succeed at a given job if the job is designed to accommodate individual differences.[16]

The decision on which design theory or approach to use is complex. All four schools of thought described above offer guidance in job design and redesign efforts; however, their approach is descriptive rather than prescriptive. Table 3-5 suggests how to determine which approach to use in the job design effort.

Job Enlargement

Both positive and negative aspects are associated with using job enlargement as a job design performance improvement intervention. Although research shows some merit to job enlargement efforts, it is not a popular workplace trend. Taken literally, job enlargement could result in small or no improvement, because workers are

TABLE 3-5: Focusing Job Design: Selecting the Appropriate Approach

If the purpose of the job design or redesign is to...	Then the approach should be based on...
• Set clear guidelines for performance • Set and maintain consistent performance standards • Set guidelines for efficient performance	Scientific Management
• Provide meaningful work • Provide sufficient feedback for accomplishing the work tasks • Provide employees with growth opportunities	Motivation
• Empower employees • Enhance interaction and support between employer and employee • Stress teamwork	Sociotechnical
• Accommodate the job to a variety of employees • Provide access for all employees	Human Factors/Ergonomics

Based on Scarpello and Ledvinka, 1988, pp. 202–206.

assigned additional job duties. Job enlargement may also be interpreted as a ruse by management to increase worker efforts and productivity while down sizing/right sizing occurs.[1]

Definition and Scope

Traditionally, job enlargement is a work design option that increases the job scope by expanding a performer's job duties.[2] In this context, job design efforts result in smaller and more specialized jobs. When jobs have a narrow scope and when they are highly specialized, performers find them tedious and become bored. Motivating employees is problematic in this type of job environment.[3] "Rather than encouraging an individual to concentrate on a fraction of the product or service, job enlargement requires workers to perform numerous, often unrelated job tasks."[4]

When job enlargement focuses only on task enlargement, it does not produce the desired effect. However, when knowledge enlargement activities are added to task requirements, workers experience more job satisfaction, fewer job errors, and enhanced customer satisfaction.[5]

Implementing Job Enlargement in the Workplace

The Internal Revenue Service (IRS) spends more than $1 billion yearly to improve its image, operations, processes, and products. In addition to extensive technological advances, the IRS favors job enlargement activities by providing workers with multiple tasks.[6] Some financial service companies use job enlargement to resolve

ergonomic/human factors issues. Figure 3-6 discusses an example of job enlargement.

The first step in implementing job enlargement is to focus on a specific family of jobs. Then perform the following steps:
1. Scope out the job family to determine the tasks required and the frequency of repetition for each task.
2. Focus the breadth of knowledge on direct work, management work, or support work.
3. Consult with a supervisor or work team to clarify specific job or political dimensions. This step may be particularly important when operating within a union shop.
4. Select one or two jobs for enlargement based on the job scope. Select the jobs that expand breadth of knowledge rather than those that only expand a task.
5. Monitor the scope and selection process. Ask the employee(s) for frequent and pointed feedback about the process.
6. Re-visit the job enlargement process on a quarterly basis (see Job Aid 3-4).[7]

Job Rotation

Job rotation is a job design alternative that exposes employees to a kaleidoscopic view of organizational life. It is a lateral transfer process often used to relieve boredom and burnout caused by stressful working environments. When companies establish job rotation policies, everyone wins. The employee is re-energized and the employer has a recommitted employee.

FIGURE 3-6: Job Enlargement Scenario

Darlene, Joan, and Jim are employed by XYZ Friendly, Inc. Their responsibilities are as follows: Darlene makes the product, Joan packages the product, and Jim distributes the product. All three workers are valued employees; however, their enthusiasm for their jobs is decreasing.

In an attempt to retain their interest and enthusiasm and challenge their potential, their immediate supervisor enlarged their jobs. Under the new arrangement the following occurs:
- Darlene continues to make the product but also takes over some of the packaging duties
- Joan is still the lead packager but also puts the finishing touches on the product prior to packaging
- Jim is still responsible for distribution, but also takes over two packaging tasks from Joan and four warehousing tasks that were formerly assigned to another worker.

JOB AID 3-4: Planning Job Enlargement

Directions: Involve job incumbents, co-workers, and supervisors in each of the following steps:
  1. Identify the job that has been selected for job enlargement and the primary task(s) assigned to that job
  2. List the job title and primary tasks in the left column.
  3. Identify alternative tasks for enlarging the selected job.
  4. List the alternatives in the right column.
  5. Prioritize the alternatives by writing 1–4 next to each alternative (1=top).
  6. Specify tasks for each alternative or for the top-priority alternative.

Job Selected for Enlargement	Alternatives for Job Enlargement
Example **Job Title:** Instructional Designer **Primary Task:** Develop instructional blueprint or map for new or revised training programs.	*Example* **Alternatives (prioritized):** 1. Add needs analysis tasks 2. Add product development tasks 3. Add implementation tasks 4. Add evaluation tasks **Selected Tasks for Top-Priority Alternative:** • Interview subject matter experts • Benchmark best practices • Attend weekly Analysis Team Meetings
Job Title: **Primary Task:**	**Alternatives** (prioritized): **Selected Tasks for Top-Priority Alternative:**

Definition and Scope

Job rotation is a form of job enlargement that occurs when employees do numerous and entirely different jobs on a flexible, revolving schedule without disrupting the workflow. Job rotation usually involves cross training. For example, a cook may be trained in salad, pastry, and soup preparation; an airline employee may be trained in reservations and sales, marketing, ramp service, and flight services.[1]

It is not uncommon for a worker to shift at two-hour intervals among three workstations.[2] "Organizations may allow employees to rotate between jobs on a daily, weekly, or monthly basis, depending on organizational needs or the seniority of the employee."[3] Assembly line job rotation provides a good example. On an assembly line, a worker whose job is to install tires that come off of a conveyor belt may be rotated to another station to install fenders. Later, she may rotate to a third workstation to inspect certain components of the cars once they leave the assembly line.

Strengths and Weaknesses of Job Rotation

Table 3-6 presents strengths and weaknesses associated with using job rotation as a performance intervention.

Implementing Job Rotation in the Workplace

The following guidelines will assist the PT practitioner in implementing a job rotation activity:

- Select the jobs that could be rotated based on a predetermined set of criteria, for example, the direct, management, or support jobs associated with a specific output or outcome.
- Select employees who are in the early phase of their career or are top performers in their job.

- Assign employees to a variety of jobs within different units of the organization.
- Monitor job skills through traditional means (surveys, interviews, observations).
- Record progress in a job log. Look for job satisfaction indicators.
- Provide feedback to employees regarding career opportunities, promotions, and salary adjustments (see Job Aid 3-5).[4]

Job Enrichment

Job enrichment is analogous to putting icing on a cake. Enrichment increases job depth and allows employees to control work factors. It is a motivating tool that empowers employees to become independent thinkers and responsible workers.

Definition and Scope

Job enrichment is a job-enhancing process that makes a job more rewarding and satisfying. It is an approach to job design (see Figure 3-7) that enhances the job horizontally by adding tasks and vertically by adding responsibilities.[1,2]

Herzberg's Five Factors

Job enrichment effects can be traced to Herzberg's extrinsic and intrinsic high-performance motivation factors: achievement, recognition, growth, responsibility, and performance of entire jobs rather than specialized parts of jobs.[3,4] PT practitioners may use Herzberg's five-factor approach to enrich employees' jobs by suggesting the following performance-improvement strategies:

- Extend the level of job difficulty and job responsibility
- Permit employees to retain authority and control over work demands and performance outcomes
- Create new tasks that require training
- Provide the employee with job performance reports

TABLE 3-6: Strengths and Weaknesses of Job Rotation

Strengths	Weaknesses
Proactive way of dealing with absenteeism and general worker dissatisfaction—workers perform a variety of tasks, which alleviates boredom and offers a challenge	May lead to increased work loads and decreased productivity for rotating workers
Supports career advancement—workers are trained to perform a variety of job-related functions	May cause disruption of workflow as employees learn new jobs
	May decrease the motivation of employees who are not selected for job rotation

Based on Gordon, 1999, p. 438.

FIGURE 3-7: Vertical and Horizontal Aspects of Job Enrichment

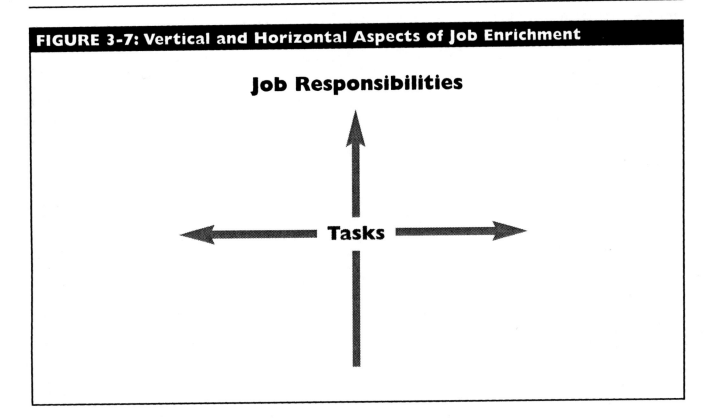

- Assign specific job tasks to individuals to move them from novice to expert.[5]

For example, an instructional designer may be responsible for analyzing, designing, developing, implementing, and evaluating a stress-management training module. At the same time, a PT practitioner may be responsible for context, gap, performance, and cause analysis. Additional tasks and responsibilities could enhance both jobs and make them more fruitful and challenging. For example, the instructional designer also could take on the analysis tasks and responsibilities of the PT practitioner, or the PT practitioner could add design and evaluation tasks as a natural followup to analysis and a way to gain personal closure.

Strengths and Limitations of Job Enrichment

The job enrichment process has both strengths and limitations. Job enrichment may provide more opportunities for autonomy, feedback, and decision making (work scheduling, methodology, quality, etc.);[6] however, it is probably not a solution to dissatisfaction with compensation, benefits, or employment insecurity. Furthermore, managers and supervisory personnel may be intimidated and challenged when employees receive increased decision making opportunities and more job responsibility.[7]

Implementing Job Enrichment in the Workplace

There are several ways to implement job enrichment, including the following:

- Form natural work groups. Alter the job so that each employee owns a unique body of work.
- Combine tasks. Empower the employee to perform the job from beginning to end instead of having different people perform different operations.
- Establish client relationships. Allow the employee and the client to confer about the product. This increases customer satisfaction and worker pride.
- Vertically load the job. Allow the employee to plan and control the job rather than allowing an external locus of control.
- Open feedback channels. Provide opportunities for efficient and timely sharing of information.[8]

The following process is one way to implement a job enrichment activity:

1. Based on performance and cause analysis, identify a family of jobs that could be enriched to improve current performance.
2. Ask internal and external stakeholders (managers, supervisors, job incumbents, customers, etc.) to select a job(s) that could be enriched to add value to the performer and the organization (see Job Aid 3-6).
3. Brainstorm the tasks and responsibilities that may be added to the job.
4. Prioritize which tasks and responsibilities would best enrich the job and could be implemented within the context of the work and organizational environments.[9]

JOB AID 3-5: Justifying Job Rotation

1. **List the jobs within your organization that may be improved by job rotation.**
2. **Benchmark best practices within or outside of your industry:** • What organizations have successfully implemented job rotation for the jobs you have listed? • How did these organizations justify their selection of job rotation as an intervention (time, cost, increased productivity, worker retention, etc.)? • What were the actual savings (be specific)? • What were the strengths and weaknesses of the job rotation process?
3. **Write a justification for job rotation using the following outline:**

3. **Write a justification for job rotation using the following outline:**

- *Background Information*
  - Establish historical or contextual information required to understand the feasibility report
  - Describe research and benchmarking process
  - Identify criteria for evaluating alternative interventions (cost, time, resource requirements, etc.)
- *Need*
  - Identify the performance improvement problem
  - Describe the performance improvement problem in terms of input, process, output outcomes
- *Idea*
  - Present an overview of the alternatives—job titles, analysis, descriptions, and specifications
  - Summarize research and benchmarking results

- *Assessment*
  - Assess alternatives based on evaluation criteria
  - List benefits to organization
- *Recommendation*
  - Suggest the best job rotation alternative
  - Review benefits of alternative
- *Implementation*
  - Suggest how to implement the recommended job rotation intervention (budget, schedule, cross-training requirements, etc.)
  - Provide an action plan
- *Conclusion*
  - Urge acceptance of job rotation alternative
  - Offer support for implementation (if appropriate)

Based on Ewald, H.R., and Burnett, R.E. (1997). Business communication. *Upper Saddle River, NJ: Prentice Hall. pp. 440–456.*

JOB AID 3-6: Selecting Jobs for Enrichment

Directions: This is an opportunity for each internal and external stakeholder to analyze the job itself, technology, the worker, and management to determine whether job enrichment is the most appropriate performance improvement intervention for a specific job. Ask each stakeholder to:
1. Check the number that indicates where the current job fits in the numerical continuum between two opposing statements.
2. If the statements contain the words *and/or*, then be prepared to discuss which part of the statement most influenced the stakeholder's rating.
3. Total the number of points assigned to statements 1–18.
Then you or the facilitator may:
4. Tabulate the total scores (frequency count).
5. Facilitate a group discussion of the results. Is enrichment a viable choice for this job performance intervention?

Job Title:						
The Job Itself						
	1	2	3	4	5	
1. Quality is important and attributable to the worker.						Quality is not too important and/or is not controllable by the worker.
2. Flexibility is a major contributor to job efficiency.						Flexibility is not a major consideration.
3. The job requires the coordination of tasks or activities among several workers.						One worker acting independently of others performs the job.
4. The benefits of job enrichment will compensate for the efficiencies of task specialization.						Job enrichment will eliminate substantial efficiencies realized from specialization.

JOB AID 3-6: Selecting Jobs for Enrichment *Continued*

	1	2	3	4	5	
5. The conversion and one-time setup costs involved in job enrichment can be recovered in a reasonable period of time.						Training and other costs associated with job enrichment are estimated to be much greater than the expected results.
6. The wage payment plan is not based solely on output.						Workers are under a straight piecework wage plan.
7. Due to the workers' ability to affect output, an increase in job satisfaction can be expected to increase productivity.						Due to the dominance of technology, an increase in job satisfaction is unlikely to significantly affect productivity.
Technology						
8. Changes in job content would not necessitate a large investment in equipment and technology.						The huge investment in equipment and technology over-rides all other considerations.
The Workers						
9. Employees are accustomed to change and respond favorably to it.						Employees are set in their ways and prefer the status quo.
10. Employees feel secure in the jobs. Employment has been stable.						Layoffs are frequent. Many employees are concerned about the permanency of employment.
11. Employees are dissatisfied with their jobs and would welcome changes in the job content and work relationships.						Employees are satisfied with their present jobs and general work situation.
12. Employees are highly skilled blue- and white-collar workers, professionals, and supervisors.						Employees are semi-skilled and unskilled blue- and white-collar workers.
13. Employees are well educated, with most having college degrees.						The average employee has less than a high school education.
14. Employees are from a small town and/or a rural environment.						The company is located in a large, highly industrialized metropolitan area.
15. The history of union-management (if no union, worker-management) relations has been one of cooperation and mutual support.						Union-management (worker-management) relations are strained and the two parties are antagonistic to one another.
Management						
16. Managers are committed to job enrichment and are anxious to participate in its implementation.						Managers show little interest in job enrichment and even less interest in having it implemented in their departments.
17. Managers have attended seminars, workshops, etc., are quite knowledgeable of the concepts, and have had experience in implementing it.						Managers lack the training and experience necessary to develop and implement job enrichment.
18. Management realizes that substantial payoffs from job enrichment usually take one to three years to materialize.						Management expects immediate results (within six months) from job enrichment projects.
Total score _____			**+18**			_____ **Job enrichment rating**

Case Study 3-2: An Injection Molding Company Implements Job Design

Situation

An injection molding company in the Midwest was expanding rapidly. In addition to gaining a larger share of its industry's market, the organization was expanding its facilities and increasing its employee base in a geographic area with low unemployment figures. A major issue that management needed to resolve was the fact that turnover was high due to increasingly higher wages at other companies. In an effort to reduce the turnover rate and to maintain a high level of technical employees, the company set business strategies to develop its technical work force as the company continued to grow:

- To select, develop, and retain a technical work force that would continually produce quality products at a competitive cost.
- To create a nurturing environment that would enable new and current employees to increase their job responsibilities and skills as they gained valuable experiences and knowledge in cross-functional, self-sufficient work centers.

The company worked to reduce employee turnover by creating an environment that would enable its employees to develop enriching and rewarding careers without leaving the company.

Intervention

To create an environment that would enable each employee to maximize his or her opportunity to progress to a desired level within the organization, the company chose job analysis and job design as the interventions. The intervention activities listed below included aspects of job enlargement and enrichment based on job analysis data.

1. Conduct a job/task analysis on the hourly positions within the organization and define the skills and knowledge required to perform the work. These positions included mold press operators, mold setters, forklift drivers, warehouse workers, quality control inspectors, materials handlers, etc.
2. Analyze data to identify similarities in job tasks across the hourly positions.
3. Form new job clusters and/or departments based on the analysis data and input from supervisors and Human Resources Department management personnel.
4. Rank tasks by complexity to establish career-path progression ladders for employees. (See the discussion of career pathing under Organizational Growth in Chapter 5.)
5. Identify training requirements for each step in the career path progression ladder.
6. Identify training methods, criteria, performance standards, assessment techniques, certification requirements, minimum hours required on the job, and link tasks to training.

To complete the work listed above, an analysis team conducted a series of interviews with a representative sample of employees in each of the job families. Both experienced and inexperienced employees were selected for the interviews to gain a better understanding of the job tasks, communication skills, environment, and basic skill requirements. Next, the team of analysts met with supervisors and ranked the importance, criticality, and frequency of each task within each job. This began to shape the hierarchy in which the progression levels were formed.

The analysts then compared the tasks that spanned similar jobs to determine whether there were tasks that were performed in more than one job. Jobs with a high number of similar tasks were combined. Once combined, the tasks were analyzed and ranked on the progression ladder within the newly formed job cluster. After the management team reviewed and approved the formation of the new job clusters, at least on paper, the analysts:

- Identified the acceptable levels of performance
- Linked tasks to new and/or existing training programs
- Identified performance indicators
- Recommended training techniques
- Targeted various assessment strategies for each training program.

Results

The analysis team recommendations were made to enlarge and/or change the current job families. In addition, the team recommended career progression ladders for each of the newly formed job clusters. The following components were recommended for each step in the progression ladder:

- Performance standards
- Hourly wages
- Minimum time required to perform job before moving to the next level
- Training programs required to enhance skill development
- Desired methods of training delivery
- Written and performance-based assessment techniques.

As a result of the recommendations, staff developed matrices containing the information listed above for each step in the progression ladder to illustrate employees' career choices and to begin to develop the career ladder components.

Lessons Learned

- Identify political ramifications early in the design and development stages of the program to achieve the desired organizational business requirements. Some groups may not agree with the direction in which the organization is heading, and you need to know this early on.
- Conduct program "self-checks" frequently to ensure that the business needs are being satisfied.
- Early in the program, begin to communicate the effects of change to the organization. This includes not only financial commitment and contribution but also commitment to cultural change.
- Address critical issues early with management and with the employees to ensure that they do not become constraints during program implementation.

This case study was written by David A. Grant, MEd, Performance Assessment Manager, Raytheon Training, LLC. Used with permission.

HUMAN FACTORS

Human factors is a field of inquiry and action that focuses on the design or redesign of machines and other equipment for human use in the workplace. It is an interdisciplinary approach in which work, work environments, machines, equipment, and processes are married to human physical and cognitive characteristics—in which machine and person are consciously and purposefully linked to produce results.[1]

Two areas of human factors that interface in a performance environment are ergonomics and safety engineering. Internal or external PT practitioners often provide expertise to managers who wish to improve, maintain, or establish workplace ergonomics or safety initiatives, and may be asked to coordinate and monitor ergonomics or safety programs.[2] They also may help organizations address the following issues:

- *Employee and Public Relations:* Organizations with good safety programs and sound ergonomic principles in place need to maintain their safety levels by retaining and recruiting safety-minded employees
- *Reduced liability:* Good safety and sound ergonomics reduce liability costs when people are injured
- *Marketing:* High marks on safety and ergonomics help companies win and maintain contracts
- *Productivity:* Morale and productivity increase with these programs in place[3]

In addition, PT practitioners help organizations create appropriate psychological environments and attitudes that foster a safe, healthy, and productive workplace.

Ergonomics

The term *ergonomics* is used interchangeably with *human factors*. Professional literature in the United States seems to favor *ergonomics*, while British literature speaks to *human factors*. The word *ergonomics* is derived from the Greek *ergon* meaning *work* and *nomos* meaning *laws*. Other terminology, such as human engineering and engineering psychology, is also used interchangeably with ergonomics and human factors.

Definition and Scope

Ergonomics involves the study and design of workstations, work practices, workflow, equipment, and tools to accommodate the physical and psychological capabilities and limitations of employees. Whatever it is called, ergonomics has the following purpose:

> *[Ergonomics] attempts to accommodate the human capabilities and deficiencies of those who are to perform a job. It is concerned with adapting the entire job system—the work environment, the machines, the equipment, and the processes—to match human characteristics. In short, it seeks to fit the machine to the person rather than the person to the machine... (and) to minimize the harmful effects of carelessness, negligence, and other human fallibilities that otherwise may cause product defects, damage to equipment, or even the injury or death of employees.[1]*

Through ergonomics, an appropriate fit is fashioned between machine and work environment including "all attempts to structure work conditions so they maximize energy conservation, promote good posture, and allow workers to function without pain or impairment."[2] Three key pillars of ergonomics are:

- Fit the task and workplace to the individual.
- Design the workplace for individuals with a range of body sizes.
- Design the workplace for individuals at the extremes of the body-sized range.[3]

Ergonomists focus on two major areas: physical and cognitive.

Physical Ergonomics

The primary focus of ergonomics is the design or redesign of machines and tools to match the physical ability of the employee. Physical ability includes the ability to use the machines or tools and the ability to "react through vision, hearing, and touch to the information that the machine (or tool) conveys."[4] Physical ergonomics goes beyond determining the strength required to pull a switch. It must also assess the "user friendliness" of the visual displays, auditory displays, or other indicators that trigger the need to pull the switch, given a range of users and any environmental considerations such as machine noise or poor lighting.

In recent years, a major trigger of physical ergonomics interventions is repetitive stress injury (RSI), which is a workplace curse. RSI affects nerves, tendons, muscles, and supporting structures of the body when parts of the body are exposed to forceful exertions, awkward positions, constant vibrations, and frequent manual handling of equipment.[5] Two specific results of RSI are carpal tunnel syndrome and lower back pain.

Repetitive flexing and extension of the wrist and hand cause carpal tunnel syndrome. It results in numbness, tingling, or pain. The person afflicted often lacks strength in the hand and is unable to make a fist, hold an object, or perform simple wrist-hand tasks. To prevent carpal tunnel syndrome, the ergonomist may suggest that the employee take the following actions:

- Keep wrists straight.
- Take exercise breaks from repetitive activities.
- Alternate tasks.
- Shift positions periodically.
- Adjust chair height.
- Work with feet flat on the floor.
- Be conscious of posture.
- Use padded wrist supports.[6]

It is estimated that nearly 50% of workers suffer from back injury. The disorder results from long-term injury to the back rather than from specific incidents. Manual handling tasks involving lifting, lowering, pushing, pulling, and carrying are responsible for nearly all lower back injuries. Lifting heavy objects, prolonged sitting, and prolonged standing are associated with lower back pain risks.[7] To help an employee prevent back injury the ergonomist may suggest the following actions:

- Analyze risks by discussing concerns with a supervisor.
- Formulate a plan that will limit repetitive and long-term activities.
- Develop a "safety first" motto on the job, for example, bend the knees when lifting heavy objects, neutralize awkward postures that cause strain and tension by keeping the body in a natural relaxed position, etc.
- Seek treatment when necessary—medications and physical therapy help relieve pressure, increase range of motion, and strengthen support structures.

Cognitive Ergonomics

Another area receiving attention in the ergonomics literature is rooted in performance rather than physical well-being. Performers receive, process, and act on information in order to produce a result. At times, stimuli, such as smells, pressure, texture, temperature, sounds, or surfaces against the skin, can interfere with performance. The interference caused by these stimuli limits a performer's ability to receive and process information and produces sensory overload and underload.[8]

Two types of work exist: mental and physical. Mental work addresses thinking skills and the performer's ability to process information. Mental work is essentially invisible

and the chief reason why cognitive ergonomics is neglected in the workplace. "Cognitive ergonomics refers to the impact of the physical/sensory (ergonomic) environment on our mental (cognitive) process."[9] Mental work is routine work with a focus on the linear, the repetitive, the familiar. Mental work is also complex work, with emphasis on the lateral, the exploratory, and the unfamiliar.[10] Table 3-7 highlights characteristics of both kinds of mental work.

Physical work or physical ergonomics is visible. Decisions are made about appropriate chair heights, proximity of equipment such as computer, printer, scanner, and telephone to the workspace, how to reach, lift, bend, flex, etc.

Implementing Ergonomics in the Workplace

An ergonomist's main job is to fit (or retrofit) the task to the worker and, like a balancing act in the circus, this task requires a great deal of sophistication. A knowledge of human anatomy and physiology, basic engineering principles, electronics, and mechanics, coupled with a thorough understanding of the psychology of work provide necessary technical expertise. Knowledge of basic risk management is also helpful. The ergonomist will need to balance the risk of injury or poor job performance against the cost of implementing an intervention.

The ergonomist may be called on to design major changes in the work environment such as:

- Work practices (revise assembly methods, redesign jobs or tasks)
- Workstation design (re-orient workstations to performers, design user-friendly workstation access, provide mechanical aids)
- Design tools (add anatomically correct components, suspend tools, reduce weight, provide fixture supports)

On a more individual note, the ergonomist at work may be asked to perform any of the following tasks:

- Choose ergonomically designed chairs for good posture and comfort to accommodate 90% of the population.
- Select properly sized tools to accommodate the hand sizes of both a 6'5" male and a 5'2" female.
- Adjust lifting capacities for employees at the extremes of body-size ranges.
- Design task components to require the minimum force necessary to complete a job.
- Eliminate distractions such as outside noise, glare, intense lighting.[11]

Solving ergonomic problems can be costly. For example, one ergonomically friendly store offers workstations ranging in cost from $875–$5,745. Accounting for part of the cost differential were the following items: adjustable

TABLE 3-7: Characteristics of Routine and Complex Mental Work

Routine Mental Work	Complex Mental Work
• Clearly stated goals, procedures, policies, practices	• Ambiguous and often unclear goals, procedures, policies, practices
• Distractions do not hinder thought processes	• To process information, new data must be combined with existing data
• Leftover attention capacity is available	• Intense work episodes demand full attention

Based on Kearney and Smith, 1999, pp. 12–13

JOB AID 3-7: : Physical Risk Factors and Suggested Modifications of Work Environment

Directions: Consider the job-based risk factors that are present in a work setting. Check the factors that impact the ergonomics of a given job, then suggest how you would modify the work environment to take each factor into account.

Job-Based Ergonomic Risk Factors	Suggested Modifications
• Force (amount of physical force exerted to complete job)	
• Repetition (number of manipulations per day)	
• Posture (extreme positions of body)	
• Static contraction (continuous exertion)	
• Compression (hard surface against soft surface)	
• Vibration (exposure to vibrating or power tools)	
• Temperature extremes (high or low extremes)	
• Light extremes (high or low extremes)	
• Other…	

ISPI © 2001. Permission granted for unlimited duplication for noncommercial use.

chairs @ $700, footrests @ $55, and wrist rests @ $78. However, not all ergonomic interventions are costly. The following interventions may improve performance without increasing the organization's expenditures:
- Lighten up! Facilitate adequate rest breaks and appropriate number of hours worked.
- Stretch. Take a structured stretch break with small groups of employees. Touch toes; flex arms, shoulders, and necks; do eye stretching exercises.
- Encourage eye exams for computer users. Eye exams can prevent poor performance before it happens. For example, special computer glasses may help the "aging" eye focus on the screen.
- Disconnect the bulbs. Florescent lighting may make it difficult to see the computer screen.
- Divert attention. Suggest that employees focus on something else besides the computer screen for a few minutes every hour. Provide a scenic company

calendar, fine art print, a place for family photos, etc.
- Introduce a novel approach! Reward employees for their suggestions on how to improve the ergonomics of a job (see Job Aid 3-7).[12]

Additionally, a PT practitioner or ergonomist can encourage the initiation of an organization-wide ergonomics program that includes some or all of the following:
- Employee complaint and concern (grievance) system
- Employee suggestion system
- Procedures for prompt and accurate reporting of ergonomic issues
- Safety and health committees
- Ergonomics team to identify stressors and offer solutions
- Ergonomic training
- Family spotlights (involve family members of workers in the planning process and in actual ergonomics programs).[13]

Safety Engineering

Occupational diseases, occupational stress, and low quality of work life may cause physiological/physical and sociopsychological conditions that are hazardous to employees' safety and health. Table 3-8 lists typical hazardous symptoms or conditions that may exist in a workplace.[1] The PT practitioner may also use Table 3-8 as a checklist to analyze a specific workplace.

Definition and Scope

Safety engineering is a planned process to reduce the symptoms and costs of poor safety and health and make the work environment safer and healthier for employees. Safety engineering has two goals:

1. Create a psychological context or environment— values, attitudes, and so on—that promotes safety.
2. Encourage a safe physical context or work environment that eliminates or reduces the occurrence of accidents.[2]

Organizations that make concerted efforts to address safe and healthy work environments show commitment to their work force. The benefits are well recorded in the literature of occupational health and safety:

- Greater productivity
- Lower absenteeism
- Increased efficiency for involved workers
- Lower medical and insurance costs
- Lower workers' compensation rates because fewer claims are filed
- Increased flexibility and adaptability in the work environment because of greater participation and ownership
- Favorable selection ratios because the organization offers an attractive place to work.[3]

OSHA's Impact on the Workplace

Prior to 1970, the nation's businesses were staggering due to lost productivity and wages, medical expenses, and disability compensations initiated by reported cases of occupational diseases.[4] These problems led Congress to pass the 1970 Occupational Safety and Health Act, "to assure so far as possible every working man and woman in the nation safe and healthful working conditions and to preserve our human resources."[5] The Act operates under the general standard that employers "shall furnish to… employees employment and a place of employment which are free from recognized hazards that are causing or are likely to cause death or serious physical harm…"[6] The federal agency responsible for enforcing the Occupational Safety and Health Act is the Occupational Safety and Health Administration (OSHA), an agency within the Department of Labor. The agency sets safety and health standards for workers. OSHA inspectors with warrants in hand ensure compliance. Inspection priorities are these:

- Imminent danger situation
- Catastrophes, fatalities, accidents
- Valid employee complaints of violations of standards
- Periodic, special-emphasis inspections aimed at high-hazard occupations and industries
- Random inspections and reinspections.[7]

Both employers and employees have responsibilities and rights under the Occupational Safety and Health Act. In January 2000, a respected trade newspaper in Detroit reported that the US Labor Department would begin holding employers liable for the health and safety of employees who work at home.[8] This policy was retracted by mid-week, as employers and employees alike cried out that OSHA was over-reaching its mandate and that the new policy would have serious negative effects on telecommuters and others who work at home.

TABLE 3-8: Typical Workplace Hazards

Hazardous Physiological/Physical Symptoms or Conditions	Hazardous Sociopsychological Symptoms or Conditions
• Loss of life or limb	• Dissatisfaction
• Cardiovascular diseases	• Apathy
• Lung cancer	• Withdrawal
• Emphysema	• Tunnel vision
• Arthritis	• Mistrust of others
• Chronic bronchitis	• Irritability
• Brown/black lung disease	• Procrastination
• Other	• Becoming distraught over trifles
	• Other

Employers must provide a hazard-free workplace and become totally familiar with OSHA standards. They may seek preliminary advice from OSHA and be advised about reasons for inspections. Employees must comply with OSHA standards; maintain the safety and health rules, regulations, and policies established by the employer; and report hazardous conditions to authorities. They have a right to expect a safe and healthy job experience without fear of reprisals, punishments, or punitive actions.[9] OSHA and the Administration have both been focal points for criticism because of nitpicking rules and regulations. As a result, the Comprehensive Occupational Safety and Health Reform Act was introduced to Congress in 1991. Although the Act did not become law, it remains high priority for labor organizations and many members of Congress. Among other things, it would require employers to maintain safety and health programs, provide worker safety training and education, and establish joint labor-management safety and health committees to inspect the workplace.[10]

Contemporary Safety and Health Issues

A variety of contemporary safety, health, and behavioral issues fall under the protective coat of safety engineering. Organizations today are sensitive to workplace concerns such as the following:
- An employee contracts acquired immunodeficiency syndrome (AIDS)
- An employee becomes a victim of workplace violence
- Management must restrict workplace smoking
- A pregnant employee is exposed to hazardous chemicals that might damage the fetus
- Chemical dependency prohibits work functioning
- Job stress and burnout cause an employee to become dysfunctional
- Occupational respiratory disease-causing substances such as asbestos, lead, or carbon dioxide are present in the workplace

Implementing Safety Engineering Interventions in the Workplace

OSHA requires organizations to maintain adequate records of the incidences of injuries and illness. After conducting a performance analysis, the PT practitioner should be conversant with three simple formulae[11] (see Table 3-9) in order to:
- Verify that a "real" problem exists
- Determine the nature of the problem
- Justify the need for a safety engineering intervention
- Select or design an intervention targeted at the high-risk area(s).

Once a safety- or health-related problem has been discovered, a number of possible interventions can be used, depending on the general problem area. Table 3-10

TABLE 3-9: Formula for Analyzing Injury and Illness

To determine:	Multiply:	Then divide the results by:
Incidence Rate	# of injuries and illness x 200,000	Number of employee hours worked
Severity Rate	Total hours charged x 1,000,000	Number of employee hours worked
Frequency	# of injuries & illness x 1,000,000	Number of employee hours worked

Based on Schuler and Huber, 1993, pp. 669–670.

TABLE 3-10: Suggestions for Selecting Safety Engineering Interventions

If the problem is...	You may want to suggest...
Accidents	• Redesigning the work environment • Setting goals and objectives for accident prevention • Establishing safety committees • Training in health and safety • Encouraging financial incentives for good health and safety practices
Diseases	• Discussing the work environment • Setting goals and objectives for preventing occupational diseases • Analyzing incidence, severity, and frequency of illness and accidents
Stress	• Establishing organizational stress programs • Establishing individual stress strategies • Monitoring employees' progress toward stress reduction

may serve as a guide to selecting appropriate safety engineering interventions (see Job Aid 3-8).

Preventive Maintenance (PM)

Preventive maintenance (PM) and safety engineering are cousins in manufacturing responsibilities. They are related activities that follow a similar proactive approach to preventing accidents in the workplace. PM occurs before a problem happens. The key words here are "before a problem happens."[1] Traditionally, PM is a manufacturing-related process that focuses on repair and adjustment issues within a production system. However, with the new emphasis on the systems approach, the concept of PM may be applied to any operating system including management systems, human resource development systems, information systems, etc.

Definition and Scope

Prevention-based thinking has its origins in the total quality literature. Van Tiem, Moseley, and Dessinger call PM "a proactive approach to equipment maintenance involving such things as oiling and greasing gears, checking parts for flaws, cracks, etc., calibrating precision tools, labeling fixtures...etc."[2] This is the traditional, manufacturing-based definition. Changing the organization's climate through analysis and diagnosis of the context in which activities occur, and through employee involvement in all areas of production, are foundational elements in prevention-based thinking on a broader spectrum.[3] PM thus becomes everyone's business, but essentially it is performer-centered, whether the performer is the equipment operator or the salesman. In manufacturing, PM is integrated into production schedules and into

JOB AID 3-8: Justifying Safety and Health Practices in an Organization

Directions: Rules and regulations concerning safety and health practices in an organizational setting are communicated through managers, supervisors, bulletin board notices, memos, emails, handbooks and manuals, signs attached to safety equipment, etc. Such rules typically refer to a variety of employee behaviors. Read the following safety and health rules and regulations and write a justification for including them as safe practices within your organization.

Rules and Regulations	Justification
Using proper safety devices	
Using proper work procedures	
Following good housekeeping practices	
Complying with incident reporting procedures	
Wearing required safety clothing and equipment	
Avoiding carelessness and horseplay	
Providing job and safety instructions	
Conducting frequent safety and health audits	
Maintaining emergency preparedness	
Initiating emergency response	
Other:	
Other:	

housekeeping duties. Wiping oil, cleaning rust, painting equipment, adjusting low oil levels, repairing burned-out lights, eliminating jams from steel chips, lubricating wheels, changing and tightening bolts, and performing simple repairs are typical operator-centered functions.[4]

Table 3-11 distinguishes among three approaches to PM and offers examples from the airline industry.[5] Note that remedial maintenance and conditional maintenance occur only after a fault or problem has been detected in the system.

The authors go on to say, "...the type of maintenance control depends on the costs of a breakdown. The greater the cost in terms of money, time, liability, and customer goodwill, the greater the benefits from PM. That is, the benefits can easily justify the costs."[6]

Objectives of PM

The major objectives for PM include:

- Reduce downtime from all sources; make processes operable any time they are needed
- Reduce variation in performance by eliminating "special adjustments" or quick fixes (such as using chewing gum and bailing wire when setting up machinery), or keeping machines running efficiently
- Extend the life of equipment
- Prevent major equipment repairs[7]

While the wording of these objectives comes directly from the manufacturing arena, they may be applied to other types of human performance, as well. For example, reduced downtime is a worthwhile objective whether the worker is producing a widget or a weekly project sales report.

Implementing PM in the Workplace

Mechanical Associates Service, Inc., a firm that specializes in PM of air conditioning and mechanical systems, suggests using the following questions to guide the PM process:

1. Do you perform scheduled PM?
2. Do you have a firm, budgetable cost for annual maintenance?
3. Do you have a source for fast, reliable, emergency service?
4. Do you have specialized, in-house maintenance personnel?
5. Do you monitor and record maintenance tasks?
6. Do you stock tools, supplies, and replacement parts?[8]

This list of questions may also be applied to PM of "soft" processes such as software design and development, project management, snow removal, training, etc. The advice to the PT practitioner in PM should be to aim for zero failure, zero trouble, and zero waste. Guidelines for PM are proactive when they focus on the following issues:

- Maintaining normal machine conditions through
  - frequent inspections, regular cleaning, tightening of screws, nuts, and bolts
  - observing correct operating procedures
- Determining abnormal production conditions in a timely manner by using a twofold inspection process
  - using the five senses
  - using sophisticated diagnostic equipment
- Developing and implementing countermeasures to reinstitute normal machine efficiency by
  - frequently asking why and why not
  - establishing new standards for PM (see Job Aid 3-9).[9]

TABLE 3-11: Three Approaches to Preventive Maintenance (PM)

Approach	Timing	Example
1. Preventive Maintenance	Fault check performed before a breakdown occurs	An airline dismantles its jet engines every 1,000 hours to check breakdown faults
2. Remedial Maintenance	Complete overhaul, replacement, or equipment repair	Airline operations policy suggests lavatory or kitchen repair only after equipment breakdown
3. Conditional Maintenance	Overhaul or repair in response to an inspection	Airline tires are inspected every 24 hours and changed as needed.

Based on Robbins and Coulter, 1999, p. 600.

TABLE 3-12: Personnel Responsibilities for Zero Production Failures	
Production Personnel	**Maintenance Personnel**
1. Learn routine housekeeping and maintenance procedures (oiling, belt tightening, etc.) 2. Learn proper operating procedures 3. Pay attention to signs of early machine deterioration by careful and frequent observation	1. Assist production workers with self-maintenance activities 2. Restore equipment through inspection, disassembly, and readjustment 3. Determine weaknesses in machine design and specify corrective action 4. Focus on operator-centered maintenance by increasing maintenance skills

Based on Suzaki, 1987, p. 123.

JOB AID 3-9: The Five Whys of Preventive Maintenance

Directions: One aspect of preventive maintenance (PM) is making sure that problems that happen once do not recur. One way to help prevent recurring problems is to make "asking why" a persistent, ongoing strategy for PM. Taiichi Ohno of Toyota suggests asking why five times to capture the true cause of a problem. Follow the example below and use the Five Whys Template to guide you through the PM questioning process.

Example:	
Problem:	Malfunction of digital controller for NC machine
1. Why?	**Response:** Defective printed circuit board
2. Why?	**Response:** Lack of cooling
3. Why?	**Response:** Lack of air
4. Why?	**Response:** Lack of pressure
5. Why?	**Response:** Dust on filter
Solution:	Clean filter every month
Problem:	
1. Why?	**Response:**
2. Why?	**Response:**
3. Why?	**Response:**
4. Why?	**Response:**
5. Why?	**Response:**
Solution:	

Based on Suzaki, K. (1987). The new manufacturing challenge: Techniques for continuous improvement. New York: The Free Press, p. 116.
ISPI © 2001. Permission granted for unlimited duplication for noncommercial use.

Looking at these issues from another perspective, the PT practitioner should encourage collaborative relationships between production personnel and maintenance personnel (see Table 3-12).

Case Study 3-3: The GRASP Program at Ford Motor Company

Situation

In the 1990s Ford Motor Company introduced Guidelines, Responsibilities, and Safe Practices (GRASP), a company-sponsored health and safety program for hourly and salaried workers. The rationale for initiating the program was based on the combined direct and indirect costs of injuries—well over one-third of a billion dollars—and the strong conviction that, "With the advances of health and safety research and technology, today we have the ability to design health and safety into the methods, processes, and construction of every aspect of the workplace."[1]

Intervention

GRASP is a proactive program. Figure 3-8 illustrates the central logic of the GRASP process—the consequences of system failures in health and safety, the causes of those consequences, and the preventive strategies that the GRASP process employs to prevent the causes from occurring.[2]

"The GRASP process, with its attention to hazard recognition and control, (is designed to) encourage all employees to think in terms of process, engineering, and manufacturing design solutions when dealing with unsafe conditions."[3]

GRASP includes videos, manuals, employee training, an area safety checklist for supervisors, and an individual safety checklist for all employees. GRASP also identifies roles and responsibilities for managers, section supervisors, and unit supervisors.[4] Table 3-13 outlines these roles and responsibilities.

GRASP has been refined since its inception; however, it continues to use a combination of preventive strategies:
• Hazard recognition

FIGURE 3-8: GRASP Pyramid

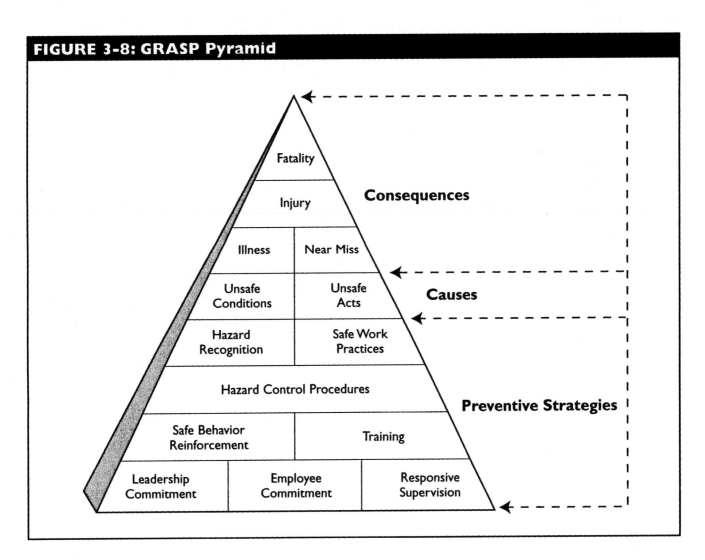

TABLE 3-13: GRASP Roles and Responsibilities

Managers	Section Supervisors	Unit Supervisors
• Develop policy in accordance with company policy • Support health and safety attitudes through positive action • Give supervisors authority and responsibility	• Role modeling • Identify and correct unsafe working conditions and behaviors • Provide advice and training • Conduct health and safety audits • Know and utilize health and safety resources	• Manage safe work methods • Provide job and safety instruction • Maintain safe and efficient machinery and equipment • Conduct daily health and safety audits • Enforce health and safety regulations • Develop a program of safe behavior reinforcement

Based on Ford Motor Company, 1992, pp. 8–14.

- Safe work practices
- Hazard control procedures
- Safe behavior reinforcement
- Training
- Leadership commitment
- Employee commitment
- Responsive supervision[5]

Results

The GRASP program has had positive effects on the employer, the employee, and the organization (see Figure 3-9).

Lessons Learned

- Safe working environments do not just happen. They must be deliberately planned, focused, and carefully executed.
- GRASP's success is due largely to top-level commitment from president down to section supervisors and the workers themselves. Supervisors are instrumental in monitoring work for safe practices. Workers also must act safely on the job. Top management must be committed to safety. Their commitment is channeled downward in the organization.
- Using a combination of interventions and constantly monitoring the results are keys to insuring a safe and healthy workplace.

This case study was written by Joan Conway Dessinger, EdD, The Lake Group, and James L. Moseley, EdD, LPC, CHES, Wayne State University, in cooperation with the UAW-Ford National Joint Committee on Health and Safety (NJCHS). Used with permission of UAW-Ford National Joint Committee on Health and Safety.

FIGURE 3-9: Results of GRASP

For the Employer...
- There is a distinct reduction in work-related injuries because of GRASP
- Corporate and executive liability were reduced with an adequate safety program
- A positive safety record enhances the marketing process
- Rising costs are reduced when a champion and an organization support safety and accident-prevention programs

For the Employee...
- Public relations are improved when a safety program is initiated and maintained and this has a positive effect on recruiting and retaining good employees
- Morale and productivity are improved
- Employees are generally happy when their safety needs are met
- Positive employee images of organizational culture are supported and enhanced
- There is greater employee compliance for safety and well-being because of GRASP

For the Organization...
- GRASP is a UAW-Ford combined effort—Ford National Joint Committee on Health and Safety. Company and union are working together in a collaborative way for the safety and well-being of workplace employees.
- GRASP represents a win-win effort
- A safety program advances the company's community responsibility—"It's the right thing to do!"

Based on Ford Motor Company, 1992, pp. 3-19.

QUALITY IMPROVEMENT

Organizations have identified quality as a critical competitive factor. A standard dictionary definition of quality is "a degree of excellence, an attribute, an essential characteristic of something."[1] The business environment sees quality as "a measure of how closely a product conforms to predetermined standards and customer satisfaction."[2] Quality improvement is about conducting business right the first time, every time. Quality and efficiency (economical production of goods and/or services using minimal resources) are the chief goals of quality improvement. Three activities support world class competence in a global marketplace and each one implies commitment to continuous quality improvement:

1. Encourage continuous improvement
2. Empower continuous change
3. Enable continuous learning.

Approaches to Quality Improvement

The recognized gurus on achieving quality are W. Edwards Deming, Joseph M. Juran, and Philip B. Crosby. While their approaches to quality are different, their message is the same—quality first. Deming's approach is philosophical, Juran's is managerial, and Crosby's is motivational and based on organizational behavior theory.[3] The following thumbnail sketches of Deming's 14 Points and Seven Deadly Diseases,[4,5] Juran's Trilogy,[6] and Crosby's 14 Steps[7,8] provide useful frames of reference for PT practitioners to help organizations improve or develop quality improvement efforts. Deming focuses on general quality improvement principles and the reasons why quality programs fail (Figure 3-10); Juran creates a vision of how quality improvement happens (Figure 3-11), and Crosby focuses on preventing poor quality (Figure 3-12).

Organizations that buy into any or all of these approaches to quality improvement may feel more confident in selecting or designing a quality improvement performance intervention such as Total Quality Management (TQM), Continuous Improvement, or Value Engineering.

Total Quality Management (TQM)

TQM was introduced into United States' business arenas in the mid 1980s. Although it was originally adopted by Japan in the 1950s, the Malcolm Baldridge National

FIGURE 3-10: Deming's 14 Points and Seven Deadly Diseases	
Deming's 14 Points	**Deming's Seven Deadly Diseases**
1. Create constancy of purpose for improvement of product and services.	1. Lack of constancy of purpose.
2. Adopt a new philosophy to reject mistakes and negativism.	2. Emphasis on short-term profits.
3. Cease dependence on mass inspection; build in quality from the start.	3. Evaluation by performance, merit rating, or annual review of performance.
4. End the practice of awarding business on price alone.	4. Mobility of management.
5. Improve every process constantly and forever.	5. Running a company on visible figures alone.
6. Institute training.	6. Excessive medical costs.*
7. Institute leadership.	7. Excessive costs of warranty, fueled by lawyers that work on contingency fee.*
8. Drive out fear.	
9. Break down barriers between units and staff areas.	
10. Eliminate slogans, exhortations, and targets for the staff.	
11. Eliminate numerical quotas.	*Diseases 6 and 7 are pertinent only to the USA
12. Remove barriers that rob people of pride in workmanship.	
13. Institute a vigorous program of education and retraining.	
14. Take action to transform the organization.	

Based on Mescon, Bovee, and Thill, 1999, p. 169; Walton, 1986.

FIGURE 3-11: Juran's Quality Trilogy: Plan, Control, Improve

Quality Planning...
1. Determine who your customer is (internal and external).
2. Determine customer needs.
3. Develop products that respond to customer needs.
4. Develop processes that produce products that respond to customer needs.
5. Transfer plans to action.

Quality Control...
1. Evaluate actual quality performance.
2. Compare actual performance to goals (desired performance).
3. Act on the differences (gaps).

Quality Improvement...
1. Establish infrastucture for quality improvement.
2. Identify quality improvement projects.
3. Establish a project team to focus on each improvement project.
4. Provide the resources, motivation, and training needed by the teams.

Based on Juran, 1986, pp. 19–24.

FIGURE 3-12: Crosby's 14 Steps to Quality Improvement

1. Obtain management buy-in and involvement.
2. Use quality improvement teams.
3. Use quality measurement as a basis for identifying areas for improvement and taking action.
4. Measure the cost of quality, i.e., the cost of non-quality.
5. Assure total quality awareness by all organization members.
6. Seek opportunities for corrective actions.
7. Do it right the first time (zero defects).
8. Train and educate employees at all managerial levels.
9. Sponsor a "Zero Defect Day."
10. Establish secondary goals to support the primary goal of zero defects.
11. Identify and analyze problems that prevent error-free work and remove causes.
12. Recognize those who meet the goals.
13. Establish quality councils.
14. Repeat steps 1–13.

Based on Longest, Rakich, and Darr, 2000, pp. 417–419.

Quality Award has institutionalized TQM's presence in the United States' management world.[1] The literature suggests many quality-oriented expressions have become part of everyday business jargon: total quality management, total quality commitment, quality circles, continuous quality teams, quality control, quality councils, quality of work life, etc. As more and more companies strive to compete globally for market share, quality has become ingrained in work processes, and TQM currently is the preferred terminology of global businesses.[2]

Definition and Scope

TQM is a comprehensive strategic management perspective that builds quality into organization-wide policies and practices. It includes doing things right the first time, striving for continuous improvement, and addressing customer needs and satisfaction.[3] The goal of TQM is the highest quality that can be produced from three perspectives: product quality, service quality, and customer quality.[4] Table 3-14 defines and provides indicators for these perspectives.

Why Utilize TQM as an Intervention?

There are a variety of reasons for using TQM as a performance improvement intervention, but all the reasons have a profit motive in mind. Maintaining market share in the real world of global competition means providing quality services and products. To achieve this, managers must foster a quality-minded attitude among employees. Drafke and Kossen provide several justifications for using TQM as the intervention of choice for achieving profit in a global economy:

• Increase return on investment

- Survive and compete against intense competition from Pacific Rim countries
- Enhance company effectiveness in utilizing resources
- Improve customer satisfaction and awareness
- Enrich employee morale and quality of work life.[5]

Elements of TQM

When a company focuses its energies on improving the quality of its policies, practices, and management philosophies, the concepts of quality become ingrained within the organization. The term *company* refers to a broad spectrum of organizations and institutions involved in improving service and customer satisfaction including manufacturing, automotive, chemical, industrial, educational, health care, government, etc. The elements of TQM remain the same for all and are described in Table 3-15.[6]

Implementing TQM in the Workplace

Performance improvement practitioners have many tools or techniques at their disposal to help them transform a traditional organization to a TQM organization. The tools and techniques are designed to help perceive, collect, analyze, or understand relevant data. However, here is a word of caution:

> *The tools are not TQM. Tools and techniques are useful but not sufficient for TQM. When made the focus of TQM, tools and techniques can even prevent the organization from taking the additional steps needed for TQM. In this way, an overemphasis on tools, in the mistaken belief that the tools are TQM, can lead the organization in the opposite direction away from organizational commitment to quality.[7]*

Table 3-16 describes some of the tools that TQM practitioners use.[8,9,10]

Baldridge Quality Award

Companies that follow TQM principles are eligible for the Malcolm Baldridge National Quality Award, named for the former US Secretary of Commerce who was killed in a rodeo accident. The award was first issued in 1987 and recognizes companies who show extraordinary achievement in quality and performance excellence. Categories eligible for the Baldridge Award are manufacturing, service, small business, education, and health care systems. The companies are self-nominated and must complete extensive paperwork. Then, a team of quality experts scrutinizes them thoroughly. Companies applying for the Baldridge Award must prove that their customers provide benchmarks of quality, their employees are involved in the quality initiative, and their vision and mission are linked to long-term quality improvement. The team of quality experts uses the following seven criteria:

1. Customer satisfaction
2. Quality results
3. Human resource development and management
4. Management of process quality
5. Leadership
6. Information and analysis
7. Strategic quality planning.[11]

Companies that receive the Baldridge Award are often benchmarked and enjoy competing in the international arena. The Baldridge criteria, when incorporated into an organization, will improve leadership, strategic planning, customer and market forces, information and analysis, process management, and overall performance results.

ISO 9000

Organizations may not qualify for a Baldridge Award but may seek ISO 9000 certification. ISO 9000 is the standard of quality management and quality assurance set by

TABLE 3-14: Perspectives on Quality

Quality Perspective	Definition	Indicators
Product Quality	Achieving or exceeding production standards	• Number of defects • Recalls • Scrap • Meeting standards
Service Quality	Responding to customers' needs before, during, and after product or service is delivered	• Service response time • Backlogs • Customer satisfaction indices • Appropriateness of service
Customer Quality	Meeting or exceeding customer expectations	• Customer surveys • Tracking customer complaints

Based on Miller, 1992, p. 47.

TABLE 3-15: Essential Elements of TQM

Elements of TQM	Potential Outcomes
Supportive organizational culture	Values, attitudes, feelings, biases, prejudices that support high-performance workplace environment
Management commitment and leadership	Organizational sense of direction (mission and vision statements), which focuses on quality and is communicated from senior management down; a champion from upper management
Analysis of customer quality needs	Discovering, understanding, and satisfying the quality requirements and standards of customers
Benchmarking	Accurate information about how competitors handle similar quality concerns
Standards	Realistic goals and objectives that employees can meet
Strategies to close gaps	Decisions and action plans based on performance analysis aim to close the gap between what is and what should be
Training	Involve all employees in TQM concepts through training in team building, problem solving, statistical methods, etc.
Quality teams	Conduct weekly productive meetings Empower employees Identify, analyze, establish objectives for problem solving Focus on internal (people within an organization) and external (people who purchase goods/services) customers

Based on Drafke and Rossen, 1998, pp. 396–403.

TABLE 3-16: Some Tools from the TQM Practitioner's Toolkit

Note: Tools marked with an asterisk (*) are not "traditional" TQM tools; however, they are frequently included in a TQM practitioner's toolkit.

This tool...	Provides...	For the purpose of...
Affinity Diagram*	Simple characterization process linking factors with one another, for example, people, strategies, resources, etc.	Illustrating the relationships between causes and effects
Checksheet or Checklist*	List of items to verify, validate, or monitor; each item is preceded by a box that may be checked off upon completion of the monitoring task	Verifying, monitoring, or validating factors related to process, performance, or product; for example, verifying that all the criteria for completing a task successfully have been met
Control or Process Control Chart	Horizontal axis display of the variation in an ongoing process, for example, plotting the variable "time" against upper, average, and lower control limits	• Discovering how much variability is due to random variation and how much is due to unique events or individual performance • Determining whether a process is within statistical control • Determining whether to change the process or the specifications
Cross Impact Matrix*	A format for organizing consequences and related factors; consequences are recorded in vertical columns and related factors in horizontal columns	• Discovering relationship between factors and consequences • Analyzing impact or effect of a specific factor on a specific consequence

TABLE 3-16: Some Tools from the TQM Practitioner's Toolkit *Continued*

This tool...	Provides...	For the purpose of...
Decision Wheel*	Thinking tool for probable effects of actions taken: • A decision is recorded in the center "bubble" • A circle with four bubbles is drawn around the center bubble; each of the four bubbles is used to record the effects of the decision • A second circle with four bubbles is drawn around the first circle and each bubble is labeled with the effects of the first set of effects	• Showing probable effects of actions taken or decisions made • Showing both intended and unintended effects • Showing how one effect may cause another effect (often unanticipated)
Fishbone Diagram *(aka* Cause & Effect Diagram *or* Ishikawa Diagram*)*	Graphic presentation of root causes that also sorts causes and shows relationships	Identifying causes responsible for an existing effect (problem)
Five Whys	Process for surfacing real cause of a problem: 1. Ask question 2. Listen to and record response 3. Ask why? 4. Repeat steps 2 and 3 five times	Determining true or real cause of a problem
Flowchart	Diagram of steps in a process in sequential order	Thinking through processes before implementation or redesign
Force Field Analysis*	Process for identifying, analyzing, and graphically displaying the forces (what and who) that may drive or restrain a specific organizational change	• Analyzing and graphically representing forces pushing for and against a specific change • Determining which forces will have the most impact on successful change implementation • Developing an action plan
Histogram	Bar chart representing the spread of variable data over time	• Showing the natural distribution of data • Showing how results of a repeated event vary over time • Showing variability or deviations from standard or normal range and how much of a deviation exists
Pareto Chart	Vertical bar chart that highlights process factors in descending order of importance or frequency of occurrence	• Identifying basic cause of a problem • Prioritizing which problem to solve first, second, etc. • Monitoring progress
Plan, Do, Check, Act (PDCA) Cycle	Systematic process used to get jobs or projects completed	Analyzing, designing, developing, implementing, and evaluating continuous improvement processes
Scatter Diagram	Plotted points that show correlations between two variables by plotting points for the variables on an X (vertical) axis and a Y (horizontal) axis, for example, X=time and Y=cost	• Proving that a relationship exists between two variables • Indicating the strength of the relationship • Determining whether the relationship is positive or negative • Not used for proving that one variable causes another.

Based on Bonstingh, 1992, pp. 51–68; Rothwell, 1996, p. 177; Memory Jogger, 1998.

the International Organization for Standardization. The standards are increasingly in demand. More than 100 countries have adopted ISO 9000 standards as their national standards: "The standards do not certify the quality of a product or service. Rather, they attest that a company has fully documented its quality-control processes and consistently adheres to them. If that's done, quality products and services generally follow."[12]

ISO 9000 certification is a five-step process:
1. ISO assessment—an extensive review of the company's quality systems and procedures based on ISO standards
2. Preparation of a quality assurance and policy manual, which includes a compilation of the company's specific quality-oriented techniques and policies
3. Training of employees in ISO 9000 or related standards
4. Documentation of work instructions, especially new procedures
5. Registration audit—special registration audits the company's quality efforts. It begins with a thoroughly documented company self-audit and ends with a review by a team of quality experts.[13]

Advantages and Disadvantages of TQM as a Performance Improvement Intervention
PT practitioners should thoroughly understand and appreciate an organization's culture before suggesting that the organization engage in TQM activities. TQM operations may need to be tailored to fit the uniqueness of the organization and employees will need to be prepared for TQM.[14,15] Table 3-17 lists advantages and disadvantages of implementing TQM.[16,17]

TQM Lessons for the Performance Improvement Practitioner
Companies that have implemented the TQM process have learned many valuable lessons. For starters, PT practitioners should reflect on the following:

- Teams should work within a policy consistent with company goals.
- Teams should be composed of natural work units.
- Quality improvement is an ongoing process—a systematic way of doing business that is rigorous and endless.
- Training is essential to the success of TQM.
- Give employees the skills they need to analyze and solve problems; then, facilitate the analysis and problem solving process and follow up on their suggestions.
- As quality rises, so does productivity.
- Prioritize needs to avoid diluting resources.
- Encourage and reward individual employees and teams for their quality efforts.
- It is vital to have a high-level champion—first steps should be taken by top management.
- Evaluate the TQM process at regular intervals[18]

Continuous Improvement

Companies survive because they make an effort to improve their goods and services. Continuous improvement is a TQM practice that emphasizes an ongoing effort to improve both the productivity and the quality within an organization. Continuous improvement activities seek to learn what customers want so their needs may be better served. Moseley and Solomon[1] link confirmative evaluation to continuous improvement. Their confirmative evaluation accountability model is heavily grounded in quality principles, "infers continuous improvement, (and is) integrated into the goals, setting, operations, and culture of an organization."[2]

Definition and Scope

Chang refers to continuous improvement as "a systematic approach that can be used to help make incremental and 'breakthrough' improvements in processes that produce

TABLE 3-17: Advantages and Disadvantages of TQM as an Intervention	
Advantages	**Disadvantages**
Total paradigm shift	Organizational success not guaranteed
Improvement based on outcome and process	Results in the creation of commitments, programs, and policies with unknown goals and purposes
Change based on needs of customer, not the values of the providers	Costly in terms of monetary and personnel resources
Demands rigorous process flow and statistical process analysis, and ongoing evaluation	Time-consuming process
Emphasis in problem characterization is on the system rather than on individuals	Potential difficulty in obtaining buy-in from top down

Based on Harris, 1997, p. 11; McLaughlin and Kaluzny, 1990, pp. 7–14.

products and services for customers."[3] Its long-range focus addresses organizational well-being and is built upon solid foundational pillars that give customers a voice in issues that affect them.[4] "Continuous improvement means undertaking improvement projects that range from fixing things that fail to creating new processes, services, and products. It means solving a customer's immediate problem and it means preventing the same problem (or class of problems) from happening again."[5]

Implementing Continuous Improvement Interventions in the Workplace

Unless organizations view continuous improvement as a constant, uninterrupted process, employees, management, and others will not consider it to be a routine component of performance—integral to the organization's mission, values, and goals. The literature cites five general strategies for continuous improvement. Figure 3-13 illustrates how the strategies exist on a continuum from reactive to proactive.[6]

To inaugurate a successful continuous improvement effort, the PT practitioner must make a fundamental paradigm shift in behavioral and organizational culture beliefs. For three examples of paradigm shifts that support continuous improvement, see Table 3-18.[7]

When determining where to apply continuous improvement interventions, the PT practitioner should select

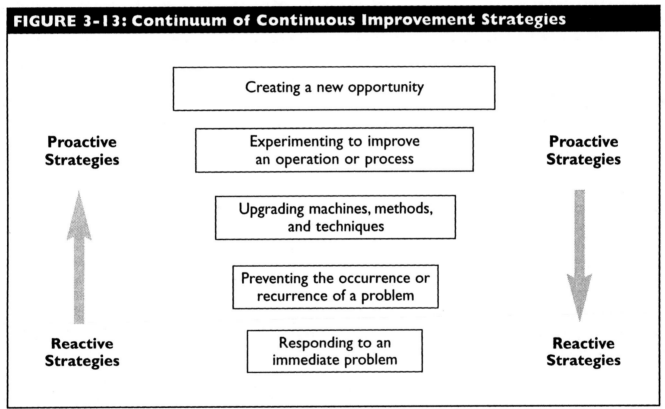

FIGURE 3-13: Continuum of Continuous Improvement Strategies

Creating a new opportunity

Experimenting to improve an operation or process

Upgrading machines, methods, and techniques

Preventing the occurrence or recurrence of a problem

Responding to an immediate problem

Proactive Strategies

Reactive Strategies

Based on Remich, 1999, pp. 1–2.

TABLE 3-18: Three Paradigm Shifts That Support Continuous Improvement

Shift from this...	To this...
Understanding of the content of one's job description	Understanding how the job contributes to the business process
Evaluating employees	Evaluating process improvement (value-added dimensions)
Rewarding employees who meet job standards	Rewarding employees who continuously improve work processes

Based on Chang, 1992.

processes and procedures that are critical to organizational outcomes or areas that represent deficiencies in customer satisfaction. For example:
- Problems or complaints generated by internal or external customers
- Areas representing high maintenance (personnel, money, etc.)
- Problems involving inadequate technological resources.[8]

A variety of organizing guidelines for continuous improvement exists in the literature on quality, including the following:
- Select a champion from top management to plan and communicate continuous improvement goals.
- Encourage total work force involvement; plan individual and team efforts.
- Emphasize skill and knowledge training in continuous improvement approaches that are applicable to the job.
- Hold employees accountable for performance; link quality indicators to customer requirements.
- Reward and recognize personnel who both talk and model continuous improvement at the various organizational levels.
- Evaluate the continuous improvement goals regularly and frequently (see Job Aid 3-10).[9]

The Six Sigma Approach to Quality Improvement
Companies like Motorola, Allied Signal, General Electric, Ford Motor Company, and Honeywell have implemented the Six Sigma approach to continuous improvement. Six Sigma is a systematic quality improvement process that is used on both the production and transactional sides of business to design, manufacture, and market goods and services that customers want to purchase and will continue to purchase.[10] Six Sigma principles require that "acceptable (product or service) variations fall within six standard deviations from the average…(so) Six Sigma measures changing statistical properties in a very precise and detailed manner."[11]

The PT practitioner may want to become involved on the people side of Six Sigma as a *Champion, Master Black Belt, Black Belt,* or *Green Belt.* At Honeywell International, the criteria for becoming a Six Sigma Plus Leader includes the following:
- Aptitude for learning
- Ability to lead
- Ability to mentor others
- Desire to continue to progress through the organization.[12]

Champions support Six Sigma project teams and help to institutionalize the process. The Black Belts are trained at

three different levels to use statistical and quality management techniques and tools, work in project teams, and implement a systematic process called DMAIC (Define, Measure, Analyze, Improve, and Control). This process is very similar to the process outlined in the HPT Model:
- *Define*—Identify product or service characteristics and performances that are critical to customer satisfaction; define the project scope, and map the process.
- *Measure*—Identify input variables; develop process measures and evaluate process performance.
- *Analyze*—Identify and validate sources of variation from performance objectives; prioritize the variables and determine root causes.
- *Improve*—Discover, generate, and validate process improvements and establish new procedures.
- *Control*—Institutionalize process improvements and implement ongoing process controls.[13,14]

Becoming involved in the successful implementation of Six Sigma throughout an organization requires a special mindset:
> While the heart and soul of Six Sigma lies in measurement and analysis, the process filters down to a series of simple concepts. To paraphrase the words of Dr. Mikel J. Harry, Six Sigma is based on the following ideas:
> - We don't know what we don't know
> - And, we won't know until we measure
> - And, we can't improve what we don't measure.[15]

Value Analysis/Value Engineering (VA/VE)

Value analysis/value engineering (VA/VE) has been around since the 1940s when General Electric developed the procedure as a way to analyze products. It has been part of the process used to target and manage costs before, during, and after production.[1] Traditionally, the focus of VA/VE is on product design; the outcomes deal with product value and cost. In the 1990s the focus includes the value chain, particularly the customer. VA/VE has become a way to help companies keep up with the trends and meet the challenges of a global market. If cost and/or customer satisfaction surface as concerns during performance analysis, then the PT practitioner should consider VA/VE as a possible intervention.

Definition and Scope

VA/VE is a formal and systematic procedure designed to analyze products to improve value and/or cut costs. Properly implemented, VA/VE can develop and continuously improve quality products, satisfy the customer, and insure low costs.

The procedure is generally associated with the job of product design engineers. Although the procedure does

JOB AID 3-10: Selecting Continuous Improvement Strategies

Directions: Continuous improvement strategies exist on a continuum from reactive to proactive. Review Figure 3-13, then use the form below to:
1. Describe the current situation (one sentence).
2. Select the current need and the category of strategy (responding, preventing, etc.) that best address the need.
3. Brainstorm specific strategies to improve the current situation. (For example, if "responding" is the most appropriate type of action, what can you do within your organization to respond to the immediate situation?)
4. Select the specific strategies that will work best for your organization.

The current situation is:	
If the need is to...	**Select this category/type of strategy**
Respond to an immediate situation	Responding (proactive or reactive) *Example:* Implement and monitor a process for timely and efficient handling of customer complaints
Prevent occurrence or re-occurrence of a problem	Preventing (proactive) *Example:* Inspect products for quality and refuse to approve substandard shipments
Upgrade machine, method, technique, etc.	Upgrading (proactive or reactive) *Example:* Replace an old workstation with an ergonomically sound workstation
Experiment to improve an operation or process	Experimenting (proactive or reactive) *Example:* Experiment with paint pigmentation to generate new and refined colors
Create a new opportunity	Creating (proactive or reactive) *Example:* Create cross-functional work teams

Suggested Strategies:

☐

☐

☐

☐

☐

involve brainstorming and group analysis, traditionally VA/VE has been "a function of specialists, not workers."[2]

While improving product design was the original objective of VA/VE, there is a direct tie to current manufacturing concerns such as cost cutting, just-in-time purchasing (stockless production), and leaner supplier relations. "…Value engineering strives to reduce the cost of a product while retaining the original specifications intact. It may also strive to increase the functional utility of the product while retaining the cost base."[3] In the global marketplace, companies are changing the focus of VA/VE from a single emphasis on consistent and sustainable cost reduction, to involving the complete value chain (all stakeholders) in the VA/VE process to achieve maximum customer satisfaction (see Figure 3-14).

Value-chain or stakeholder expectations are on the rise. Table 3-19 illustrates stakeholder expectations in the auto industry.

Benefits of VA/VE
"The kind of value engineering which reviews parts and production just to niggle a penny here or there may lead

to a great many changes without much overall impact, but value engineering built into the design process from the beginning has more benefit."[4] VA/VE can lead to cut costs, improved quality, and reduced resource requirements, and the process itself is a benefit for all the value chain members who participate.

From a management perspective, there are several benefits to integrating VA/VE into the entire product design process. For example, the VA/VE process encourages the following:

- Setting and prioritizing clear goals to focus the product design process, for example, continuous improvement of product, increase in customer satisfaction, low-cost production, etc.
- Keeping the design simple to reduce parts proliferation and decrease the number of setups during production
- Completing the design on time to avoid market and/or technology changes

VA/VE also provides a systematic way to manage communication when design teams are large or when links in the value chain (product designers, suppliers, manufacturers, etc.) are separated by time and space. In one instance, the product was a second-floor restaurant. The design called

FIGURE 3-14: VA/VE—Changing Emphasis, 1940s to Present

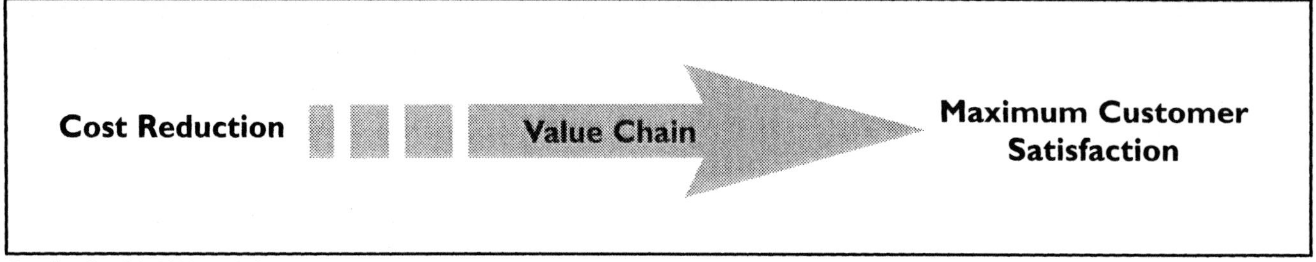

Cost Reduction → Value Chain → Maximum Customer Satisfaction

Based on Remich, 1999, pp. 1–2.

TABLE 3-19: Value-Chain (Stakeholder) Expectations in the Auto Industry

Stakeholder	Expectation
Customers	• Better quality • More added value • Lower operating costs
Dealers	• Better reliability and serviceability of key parts • On-time delivery • Customer satisfaction
Suppliers	• Provide more added value • Close partnership • Longer-term business relationship
Manufacturing and Assembly Plants	• Fewer "things gone wrong" • Reduced build times • Less complexity
Engineering	• Become industry leaders • Dream dreams and see visions

for two pulpers, one in the kitchen and one in the dish room. During the design process the kitchen pulper was removed to cut costs, but no one informed the food service director. Shortly after the kitchen became operational, water began leaking down to the first floor because the staff was dumping garbage and grease down the drain. Communication between the design team and the director would have saved time, money, and aggravation.

Another benefit of VA/VE is that the process encourages partnering between designers, suppliers, users, and other stakeholders both before and after resources are expended. A customer who manufactures treadmills asked an identification product maker to cut costs on an existing group of display panel overlays. The product maker views VA/VE as "a successful long-term business strategy" that includes collaborating with the customer.[5] The product maker worked closely with the customer to redesign the panels and the partnership resulted in a customer saving of more than $20,000 annually. In this instance VA/VE led to cut costs, improved quality, reduced resource requirements, and created a happy customer.

In summary, implementing VA/VE leads to a number of continuous improvement opportunities:
- Better win-win partnering relationship for all stakeholders
- Longer-term business perspective
- Affordable cost targets that ensure viability
- Sharing of target achievement responsibility and benefits with customers and suppliers

Implementing VA/VE

Perhaps the best way to illustrate the implementation of VA/VE is to review an example from the construction industry:

> Today's construction industry, like so many businesses, is being transformed almost on a daily basis. The era of traditional design, specify, bid, and construct is rapidly being updated and enhanced to meet today's time and financial constraints. The role of the architect as the master builder and orchestrator of the design team is being replaced by a team of specialists for almost every step of the design and building process…all part of the team at the project's inception…Construction costs, project scope, and design fees are packaged as a lump sum (for) one-stop shopping…Once distinct words describing individual processes—"design" and "build"—have merged into a single concept, (the) construction process.[6]

Today's construction process functions like this:
1. The full design team meets with the client to establish project requirements and preliminary budgets. The output is a project plan that meets current needs and minimizes future cost increases.

2. Lighting, power, heating, and cooling loads are calculated to determine equipment requirements and locations. Identifying major equipment early in the project provides a clear basis for cost comparisons when equipment is bid, and also simplifies the next step in the process.
3. Coordination between mechanical, electrical, structural, and architectural components is established to avoid conflict between major openings, structural supports, ceiling clearances, and system conflicts.
4. Design specifications are prepared to define scope, design conditions, and requirements for equipment and installation.

Following this process ensures a common basis for all bidders to ensure that bids are consistent with design intent and a chance for contractors to maintain a level of design and installation flexibility within the guidelines of the design intent. VA/VE procedures are used to control costs before design rather than after bids are received.

Cost-reduction opportunities may come from production, design, material specifications, negotiation, or overhead. Achievement of ongoing cost reductions and customer satisfaction depends on management team support that initiates and sustains a cultural change that could involve any or all of the following strategies:
- Tearing down functional and organizational chimneys and encouraging partnering
- Providing an environment supportive to cross-functional teams
- Fostering continuous learning and improvement
- Empowering team members
- Rewarding teams, not just individuals
- Championing commitment to customer value

The VA/VE process is complicated and requires knowledge and experience with a variety of tools and techniques. Job Aid 3-11 provides guidelines for implementing VA/VE.

Case Study 3-4: Quality Improvement Initiative at Mount Clemens General Hospital

Situation

Mount Clemens General Hospital is a 288-bed, acute-care osteopathic hospital, located in Macomb County, one of the three counties that makes up the Metropolitan Statistical Area of Southeast Michigan. In November 1989, this organization began examining the quality philosophies of Total Quality Management (TQM). Once the organization determined that it would embrace the concepts of TQM, the Chief Executive Officer (CEO) and senior leadership, with the Quality/Resource Management area, identified four organizational cultural values:
- Respect for Individuals

JOB AID 3-11: Guidelines for Implementing a Successful Value Analysis/Value Engineering (VA/VE) Intervention

Directions: Include all the core elements in the VA/VE process
- Cost-reduction process that is consistent and sustainable
- System to track and follow up on all cost-reduction proposals
- Shared responsibility and benefits between value chain members

Identify and select or design the tools and techniques you will need to identify, analyze, and graphically display the relationships between suppliers, manufacturer, distributor, and other costs
- Gap, cause, product, qualitative, and quantitative analysis techniques and tools
- Graphic display tools such as models, flowcharts, fishbone or pareto diagrams, histograms, pie charts, etc.
- Benchmarking data-collection techniques and tools such as library searches, acquiring professional and trade association data, use of internal and external experts, questionnaires and surveys, etc.
- Team-based analysis tools such as brainstorming, focus groups, nominal group technique, consensus decision making, etc.

Follow the VA/VE process illustrated in the overview below:

VA/VE Process Flow Overview	
1. Conduct a gap analysis focusing on the product and customer satisfaction; determine the cause of the gap	**Desired State vs Actual State...** Gap? Cause?
2. Develop a product proposal to meet the needs of all stakeholders	**Product Proposal**
3. Develop a business proposal, which includes a profit model; focus on the total cost to show how cost reduction may increase or decrease other costs.	**Business Proposal Profit Model** Target Price -Target Profit Target Cost
4. Verify compatibility between product and business proposal; make trade-offs if necessary	**Product Proposal** ◄ Compatible? ► **Business Proposal**
5. Establish target(s)	1.~~~~ 2.~~~~ 3.~~~~
6. Develop a plan for achieving the target(s)	How ~~~~~~~ What ~~~~~~ Where ~~~~~~ When ~~~~~~ Why ~~~~~~~
7. Implement and evaluate the plan	**PIE Formula:** **Plan + Implement + Evaluate = Success**

- Open Communications
- Teamwork
- Continuous Improvement.

The identification of cultural values provided the internal "safety" for performance improvement.

Under the CEO's leadership, the organization embraced a blend of Deming, Crosby, and Juran quality improvement principles. The CEO's vision continued to guide the organization until his retirement in 1998. His legacy of performance improvement is still embedded within the organization. An example of this application of TQM is the performance analysis and improvement activity that a team from the Nursing, Quality, and Risk Management disciplines initiated. This team identified a need for a fall-prevention program in January 1997. The organization's fall rate of 1.1% was below reported rates of 3.4% within the State of Michigan; the nursing management staff from the main medical/surgical areas wanted to demonstrate quality improvement.

Intervention

To address quality improvement within the general medical/surgical nursing care sites, the actual incidents of patient falls were evaluated as to severity of the falls. Then the actual number of falls was plotted on a process control run chart by month, using an 18-month measurement scale. Once the team identified that the patient falls were occurring due to a lack of process, they held several meetings to strategize the outcome needed, based on a Fishbone diagram. These meetings enabled the team to identify best practices in preventing slip and fall accidents.

The nursing professionals focused on improving the patient's initial assessment based upon the Hendrich/Nyhuis Fall Risk Model.[1] This scale uses Risk Factors/Risk Points (see Table 3-20)

assessed by the caregiver within 8 hours of admission and every 24 hours. Once the assessment is made and the Total Risk Score is determined, patients identified as "High Risk" or "Extremely High Risk" receive a red dot in their chart, as well as on their armband, in order to increase awareness. The only physical change to the patient was the replacement of the current patient slippers with non-skid patient "booties."

Results

Reducing serious patient injuries through a defined fall risk-prevention program required open communication between the staff of the general medical/surgical floors. It also required monthly and quarterly feedback as to actual data that were being monitored. The forums for this communication were both monthly staff meetings and quarterly Nursing Quality Assessment-Improvement dialogue between the Vice President of Clinical Services (nursing) and the nursing management staff. Graphic presentations (control charts) of the patient incidents (falls) were plotted monthly, enabling each medical/surgical nursing unit staff to identify with success.

The success of enabling staff and management to improve the process within the framework of the organization's cultural values is demonstrated by an overall mean fall rate decrease of greater than 25% from March 1997 through 1998. During 1999, the mean fall rate for serious injuries decreased to 0.5%, as compared to 1.1% in the 12-month period prior to implementation of the fall prevention program. All patient care areas now show a reduction in their mean fall rate since the introduction of the fall-prevention program.

Lessons Learned

Lessons learned during the 18-month period following the introduction of the fall-prevention program are:

TABLE 3-20: Fall Risk Assessment Using Risk Factor/Risk Point Analysis

Risk Factor	Risk Points	Patient Score
Recent history of falls (not slip/trip)	+7	
Depression	+4	
Confusion/disorientation	+3	
Altered elimination (incontinence, nocturia, frequency)	+3	
Dizziness/vertigo	+3	
Primary cancer diagnosis	+3	
Non-adaptive mobility/generalized weakness	+2	
Risk Score Key: 0–2 Normal/Low Risk / 3–6 High Risk / 7+ Extremely High Risk	**Total Risk Score:** _____	

Based on Holmberg, Case Study 3–4.

- Frequent (monthly/quarterly) review of objectives related to this aspect of patient care focuses the caregivers on the goal of reducing serious patient fall episodes.
- Identification of the patient-care process specific to serious patient falls highlights physical communication parameters, which allows caregivers to focus awareness on identified high-risk patients.
- Problem solving, supported by identified organizational cultural values, facilitates process improvement and increases positive outcomes for the patient.
- Respect for individual value enhances dialogue and supports objectives set.

- As a cultural value, open communication enhances the removal of barriers to performance improvement.
- Teamwork can be enhanced through encouraging each member of a staff to participate in an identified, objectively defined goal and to share measurement parameters frequently.
- Visual and verbal feedback ensure continuous improvement.

This case study was written by Lee Holmberg, MA, CPHQ (Certified Professional in Healthcare Quality), Mount Clemens General Hospital. Used with permission.

CHAPTER

PERSONAL DEVELOPMENT

"MUST YOU ALWAYS BE THE CENTER OF ATTENTION?"

PERSONAL DEVELOPMENT INTERVENTIONS

Personal development focuses on enhancing the individual through organizational opportunities and self-initiative. It enables individuals to take control of their current job situation and career future. Often, the organization provides the structure and processes so that employees can make accurate, positive decisions and improve their own performance. Individuals are responsible for self-assessment, setting their own direction, and motivating themselves to take advantage of opportunities. Personal development includes feedback, coaching, mentoring, emotional intelligence, and career development (see Table 4-1).

Feedback

Definition and Scope

Feedback is a powerful intervention and an integral part of overall individual development. Feedback means informing people about how others perceive their actions and communications. It is one way of helping employees determine if they are on track in meeting their personal goals and expectations. Some people are comfortable providing feedback and do so frequently; however, most people are reluctant because they fear hurting a co-worker's feelings. It is usually up to each employee to solicit feedback by approaching others with questions, such as:

- What should I do?
- How would you handle this situation?
- What do you think?
- How would you rate this issue on a scale of 1 to 5?[1]

Receiving Feedback

Feedback may not always be positive and can cause an employee to want to deny, dispute, or debate what is being said. However, it is important to listen to what is being said and not interrupt. Table 4-2 illustrates best practices relative to receiving feedback.

After receiving feedback, employees must convert the feedback into an action or proposal for self-improvement. This is an important step in personal growth. Successful problem solving and decision making on a personal basis may also be seen as indicative of leadership potential.[2]

Requesting Feedback

To receive feedback, employees must often ask for the information. Feedback can help in monitoring everyday work events. It can boost self-confidence and help in developing career goals and new job skills.

Kirkland and Manoogian provide the following recommendations for selecting a person to give feedback:

- "It should be a person whose opinion you respect and who will encourage you to improve your effectiveness, someone with credibility and integrity."
- "It should be someone who has a different work style and whose feedback will provide opinions and points of view that are new."
- "It should be someone with whom you must interact in order for you both to be successful."
- "It should be someone with whom you have worked long enough to have had opportunities to observe you in a variety of settings."[3]

TABLE 4-1: Personal Development Interventions From Enhanced HPT Model

- Feedback
- Coaching
- Mentoring
- Emotional Intelligence
- Career Development

TABLE 4-2: Guidelines for Receiving Feedback

- Ask for clarification or verification of information that is not completely understood.
- Remain objective about what is being said.
- Decide whether the feedback is valid.
- Provide an appropriate response, which could include a thank you or explanation, or take appropriate action.

Based on Lucas, 1994.

Giving Feedback

Coaches, managers, and supervisors are responsible for giving feedback. Although employees may solicit feedback on a decision or action, feedback should focus on the behavior or issue and not on the personality. Feedback should be timely, concise, and pertinent to the behavior or issue.[4] For example, it is seldom helpful to inform an employee that his or her report is "bad" and needs fixing. Employees need detailed comments regarding specific sections with suggestions of different ways to approach that report section.

In the book *Masterful Coaching,* Robert Hargrove discusses guidelines for providing feedback that makes a difference.[5] Table 4-3 describes effective feedback, which is part of the coaching process.

Implementing 360° Feedback in the Workplace

360° feedback represents a growing trend in organizations to change the way performance feedback and performance appraisals are provided to individuals. 360° feedback is a multi-source assessment that taps the collective wisdom of those who work with an individual including supervisors, peers, direct reports, and internal and external customers. Organizations using this approach indicate that multi-rater measures seem more reliable, valid, and credible to employees receiving the feedback than the traditional single-source feedback provided solely by one's supervisor. The 360° feedback approach is based on the premise that the collective intelligence of many raters is more likely to provide a clearer picture of specific behaviors and skills from which an individual can structure a meaningful personal plan for growth. When implementing a 360° feedback process, it is important to establish guidelines that ensure the overall improvement in effectiveness of the organization. Table 4-4 lists guidelines for establishing and evaluating existing 360° feedback performance management systems (see Job Aid 4-1).

TABLE 4-3: Effective Feedback

- Speak with honesty and good intent.
- Show where there is a problem and connect it to how people think and act.
- Make judgments and assessments and provide witnessable events as examples.
- Focus on what is missing or opportunities, not on what is wrong.
- Praise people for who they are, not just for their accomplishments.
- Present feedback in a manner that is perceived as an opportunity and not a threat.

TABLE 4-4: Guidelines for 360° Feedback Processes

- Align individual or team behaviors described in the assessment items with the organizational vision.
- Provide fair and accurate performance measures as assessment items.
- Focus on competency-based rewards for performance improvement as a result of the 360° feedback.
- Support a commitment to continuous learning and self-improvement.
- Use the 360° feedback process as a communication tool to reinforce other organizational initiatives such as quality, team empowerment, and customer service.

JOB AID 4-1: The Ten Commandments of Feedback*

Excellent feedback preserves an individual's dignity and integrity while allowing for improvement in his or her behavior. In *The Gentle Art of Feedback* Bob Wood and Andrew Scott offer these suggestions for giving feedback.

1. Offer feedback on observed behavior, not on perceived attitudes.
2. Offer a description of what you saw and how you felt, rather than a judgment.
3. Focus on behavior that can be changed.
4. Choose those aspects of job performance that are most important and limit comments to those.
5. Ask questions rather than make statements.
6. Set the ground rules in advance.
7. Comment on the things that an employee did well, as well as areas for improvement.
8. Relate all your feedback to specific items of behavior; don't make statements about general feelings or impressions.
9. Observe personal limits; don't give too much feedback at once.
10. Before offering any feedback, consider its value to the employee.

*Based on Wood, B., and Scott, A. (1989, April). The gentle art of feedback. Personnel Management, 26 (4), 48–51. Cited in Coaching and feedback. ASTD Info-Line, 1990 (6). Alexandria, VA: American Society for Training and Development. ISPI © 2001. Permission granted for unlimited duplication for noncommercial use.

Coaching

Definition and Scope

Coaching is an intervention designed to help employees gain competencies and overcome barriers to improving current job performance. It involves one-on-one suggestions relative to observable workplace situations, and usually is given by a supervisor or manager. It can be formal and planned or spontaneous and "on the spot" when the situation calls for immediacy. Coaching builds on the assumption that most employees are eager to do well, please their managers, and achieve an improved position in the organization. Supervisors, managers, or other internal or external people can serve as coaches.

In addition to acting as a role model for higher performance, a coach is responsible for:
- Clarifying expectations associated with the job as well as objectives tied to the mission of the organization
- Providing the training opportunities and resources employees need to improve performance
- Creating a culture or situation that motivates the employees to improve
- Providing feedback and praising employee successes.[1]

Coaching requires good communication and listening skills so that the coach is aware of what is going on and gets the necessary information. Coaches must also have the ability to praise a job well done and provide corrective feedback.

Coaching Process

Coaching, like any intervention, requires a systematic approach if it is to be efficient and effective. Many coaching models are available. In the book *Coaching Skills*, Robert Lucas presents an eight-step process.[2] Although his process focuses on supervisors as coaches, the process is applicable for any coaching situation. Table 4-5 lists steps in the coaching process.

A coach should carefully document interactions with an employee to ensure a record is available for future coaching opportunities or for management to review for job promotions.

Implementing Coaching Interventions in the Workplace

Currently, coaching is not pervasive in the workplace; yet every manager and supervisor ought to be a coach to all their employees. Coaching behavior needs to be designated through performance appraisal items that are evaluated through a multi-rater process. In addition, coaching behaviors need to be rewarded as part of employees' annual compensation review process. Expectations and evaluation of results need to be explicit and documented. In order to accomplish this, several performance support measures may be needed, such as training on feedback and coaching, job aids, role modeling by senior management, and on-the-job support by next-level management. In short, the organization must remain vigilant in supporting employees' needs and encouraging employees' efforts.

TABLE 4-5: Steps in the Coaching Process

1. *Establish reasonable goals with the employee.* Goals should be realistic and attainable in terms of the employee's skills and abilities. Success indicators might be revenue or reduced costs, quality, quantity, or timeliness.

2. *Collect performance data.* Gather large amounts of data regarding an employee's performance to ensure a thorough analysis of performance. Use external or internal customer surveys, performance appraisals, self-assessments, and interviews with peers, employees, and other supervisors.

3. *Analyze performance.* Analyze performance information to determine performance gaps. Consider the factors, such as knowledge and skill level and changes in the workplace, which may contribute to the gap.

4. *Review and modify performance goals, as needed.* Based on the gaps between actual and desired performance, redefine goals with the employee. Use this discussion time to provide feedback on personal observations and to get feedback from the employee.

5. *Identify developmental resources.* Discuss the training, educational, and mentoring opportunities for employees.

6. *Develop an action plan.* Work with the employees to develop a plan based on the goals and resources defined. The plan should reflect commitment on both sides.

7. *Implement strategies.* Ensure the employee has the tools and supplies, information, and support required to accomplish the goals.

8. *Evaluate performance.* Schedule follow-up sessions to discuss progress, respond to a request for additional support, or redefine goals based on feedback and discussion.

Based on Lucas, 1994.

Coaches as Team Facilitators

Besides interacting directly with individuals, coaches have other responsibilities. A coach is often called on to provide facilitation when supporting a team. The coach's role with the team is to get all team members involved in problem discussion and resolution. A team coach is responsible for keeping the discussion on track, helping the team apply problem solving tools, and working with the team to resolve differences and reach consensus.[3]

Coaches as Teachers—Masterful Coaching

Another process that deserves mention is the masterful coaching process developed by Robert Hargrove. This approach, which is based on Peter Senge's learning organization, calls on coaches to be teachers. Hargrove suggests that coaches should encourage the collective intelligences and abilities of employees to develop a new frame of reference for continued learning and growth.[4] In addition to the skills and abilities required of an effective coach, a masterful coach models intense discipline, as well as a passion, for learning.

Executive Coaching

Executive coaches periodically meet privately with organizational leaders to discuss and work on their personal learning and developmental issues.[5] The intent is to create positive behavior change and enhance skills and knowledge. This can be a difficult endeavor if there is a lack of executive commitment to the coaching process or when there is a poor match between the executive and the coach. Executive coaching works best if the following elements are present: accountability, integration with other systems, top management modeling, and confidentiality. Executives need varying levels of coaching (see Table 4-6) depending on their leadership abilities and the nature of their responsibilities.

To get the greatest payback value from executive coaching, it may be necessary to focus efforts on employees with "mission critical" high-value job assignments.[6] The organization needs to screen and match coaches carefully with leaders in terms of industry experience, executive-level experience, and coaching techniques. As use of executive coaching increases, the need to set objectives and evaluate results is more important.

Skeptics ask: "Why does an executive need a coach?" A coach can be a valuable sounding board in today's hectic business environment. Barry Mabry, Ernst & Young partner, explains,

> *"I've wrestled with this." He's a corporate finance partner in New Orleans. He has been with Ernst 27 years. He's successful; he's happy. His recent performance review was quite flattering. "Perhaps it's for the same reason that Tiger Woods needs a coach or Peter Sampras needs a coach," says Mabry. Tiger Woods would say, "I know how to play golf." But his coach is probably the most important person in his life (see Job Aid 4-2).[7]*

TABLE 4-6: Issues Covered in Executive Coaching

Level One (Highest)

- Improving and managing interpersonal relationships with boss and senior management
- Listening, being more personal, warm, and open
- Implementing layoffs and sensitive culture changes
- Relations with external customers, clients, partners, or community
- Varying voice tone intensity (especially for women)

Level Two

- Improving interpersonal relationships with teams and peers
- Meeting management skills
- Personal style behaviors
- Appearance
- Influencing team building; upward communication; dealing with difficult employees

Level Three

- Learning the language of others, "hot buttons" (e.g. loyalty) so others can "hear"
- Planning layoffs and sensitive culture changes
- Planning performance reviews, goal setting
- Career planning
- Presentation skills
- Transitions, entry, process improvement
- 360° feedback
- Validation of strengths
- Developmental action planning

Level Four (Lowest)

- Assessing staff needs for areas of responsibility
- Setting priorities
- Writing skills

Adapted from Hall, Otazo, and Hollenbeck, 1999, p. 43.

JOB AID 4-2: Assessing Coaching Skills

Directions: Use this job aid to assess your coaching strengths and areas for improvement. Rate yourself on each statement. Reflect on situations when you exhibited that behavior. Jot down ideas for your own personal performance improvement based on your reflection. Be your own *coach*.

	Yes	No
1. I provide frequent, timely, and specific feedback.		
2. I ask open-ended questions and listen to the responses.		
3. I never assume what motivates an employee. I ask.		
4. I applaud employee successes.		
5. I work with employees to develop measurable and attainable goals.		
6. I provide the resources employees need to succeed.		
7. I take time to discuss new ideas and initiatives with employees.		
8. I solicit and follow up on employee suggestions.		
9. I encourage creative problem solving.		
10. I encourage open and honest communication.		

Mentoring

Definition and Scope

Mentoring is a one-on-one relationship between a more-experienced employee (mentor) and a less-experienced employee (mentee). Mentoring and coaching are often confused. Although mentoring uses many of the same techniques as coaching, mentoring goes beyond teaching an employee how to do a job well. When mentoring, a mentor shares personal experiences, wisdom, and political savvy to enable top performers to take on tasks beyond those designated by their job descriptions.

As a result of today's labor market and expectations of clients and customers, the workplace has changed. Good employees need to be encouraged and developed. Gone is the "survival of the fittest" mentality, which more or less allowed nature to take its course in eliminating unsuitable employees. Instead, mentors guide a complex emotional transformation designed to help the mentee develop skills and capabilites for future success.[1] Also gone are the old boys' networks that picked their proteges from the "scrubs," or entry-level ranks.

> *Mentoring is a powerful, dynamic process—for both employees and organizations. To share wisdom is to share life experience. No matter which methodology is used, mentoring has the potential to elevate corporate dialogue from the mundane to the truly transformational.*[2]

Mentoring has been effective in overcoming hurdles resulting from the increased multicultural dimensions of the work force, particularly assisting in the success of people with racial or gender differences.[3] In addition, the field of information technology (IT) is so short of qualified workers it has turned to mentoring high school and college students, through summer and part-time jobs, as they prepare for IT careers.[4]

The mentor plays four key roles in an organization:
- *Role model*—practice the values that the organization endorses
- *Coach*—clarify the organization's culture and political structure so mentees can correctly direct their efforts
- *Broker*—help the mentee establish the contacts needed to succeed
- *Advocate*—recommend and support the mentee for projects and task groups

Table 4-7 illustrates the reasons for establishing mentoring, which include faster learning curves, increased loyalty, improved communication and sense of "team," reduced turnover time when new recruits are brought into the organization, faster dissemination of corporate information, and increased innovation.[5]

Mentor and Mentee Relationship

The relationship between the mentor and the mentee is key to the success of the mentoring process. Management's failure to provide its support will make mentoring very difficult. In addition to organizational support, mentoring requires that the right people are involved in the process. Coaching uses both external and internal resources, often supervisors or managers. Mentoring, on the other hand, relies on the internal expertise of those who are capable of getting the resources or assignments necessary for the mentee's development.

Phyllis Stone describes the characteristics to look for when selecting a mentor (see Table 4-8).

Not every employee is suitable to be mentored. They need to confide and discuss difficult situations honestly. They need to appreciate the wisdom offered without defensiveness. They need to be open to learning. According to Stone, an employee should demonstrate the characteristics listed in Table 4-9 to be considered as a mentee.

TABLE 4-7: Why We Mentor

Mentoring is a tool to accomplish the following goals:
- Attract and retain high performers.
- Upgrade employee skills and knowledge.
- Promote diversity of thought and style.
- Develop leadership talent.
- Preserve institutional memory.
- Create inclusion.
- Develop a line of succession.
- Foster a collaborative environment.
- Ease the transition to new assignments.
- Strengthen corporate competitive advantage.

Kaye and Scheef, 2000, p. 2.

TABLE 4-8: Selection Characteristics for Mentors

- Possesses strong interpersonal skills
- Has contacts and influence inside and outside the company
- Recognizes others' accomplishments
- Has excellent supervisory skills
- Knows his or her field
- Willing to be available to mentee
- Accepts risks that come with mentoring

Based on Stone, 1999, p. 97.

Implementing Mentoring Interventions in the Workplace

A mentor's primary role is that of an "advisor" providing meaningful, honest, and timely feedback.

Mentoring can be a valuable retention tool and a critical element in employee development. Effective mentoring, however, usually requires the development of a personal relationship between the mentor and the mentee. Good mentors become emotionally committed to their mentees' success. As a result, their relationship cannot be strictly professional.[6]

Mentoring programs should go "hand in glove" with career development. This enables the mentor and mentee to set direction, define advancement opportunities, and prepare for the future.[7]

It has long been recognized that people do what they are rewarded for. As a result, it is essential to plan for and provide higher wages for increasing skill levels of mentees. It is also important to compensate mentors for their contribution to the development of others (see Job Aid 4-3).

Emotional Intelligence

Definition and Scope

Emotional intelligence (EI) is "the ability to motivate oneself and persist in the face of frustrations; to control impulse and delay gratification; to regulate one's moods and keep distress from swamping the ability to think; to empathize and to hope."[1] Emotional intelligence is

the ability to skillfully do two things. First, the high EI person recognizes and deals with inner feelings and thoughts in an effective and complete way. In the workplace, the emotionally intelligent boss will be motivated, productive, and stable…Second, EI means the ability to understand one's own impact on others, how to deal with other people's feelings. The leader who is high in this skill knows how to harness emotional reactions toward a positive goal. She or he can inspire others.[2]

Emotional intelligence is critical to the success of organizations. In fact, there is substantial evidence that EI is more important than job-specific (technical) skills and knowledge or IQ. According to Goleman, 75% to 96% of job success is not related to IQ.[3] David McClelland and Lyle Spencer Jr. have conducted many studies of achievement and job success. For example, in a study of diplomats in the United States' State Department,

McClelland found that the stars [sic: high achievers] scored much higher than mediocre diplomats at accurately discerning the speaker's emotions. This

TABLE 4-9: Selection Characteristics for Mentees
• Track record of success
• Noticeable intelligence and initiative in previous jobs
• Loyalty to organization
• Desire to achieve results
• Willingness to take on challenge and responsibility
• Responsible for own career management and growth

Based on Stone, 1999, pp. 98–99.

translated into an ability to read emotional messages in people with backgrounds vastly different from their own, even when they couldn't understand the language being spoken—competence crucial not only for diplomats but throughout today's work world for capitalizing on diversity.[4]

Background

Because emotional intelligence is often discounted and poorly understood, it is necessary to be aware of the studies and scholars that led to claiming the criticality of emotional intelligence. The importance of emotional intelligence was first described by Jack Mayer, psychology professor at University of New Hampshire, along with Yale psychologist Peter Salovey.[5] According to Mayer, emotional intelligence is "a group of mental abilities which help you recognize and understand your own feelings and others. Ultimately, EI leads to the ability to regulate your feelings."[6]

The complexity of intelligence has been discussed for many years. As early as 1955, J.P. Guilford wrote about the structure of the intellect and in 1967, Guilford defined the multi-factor theory of intelligence, which was a structure-of-intellect model involving 120 factors. Later, Gardner proposed seven independent forms of competence: linguistic, logical-mathematical, spatial, musical, bodily-kinesthetic, interpersonal, and intrapersonal. Gardner's Multiple Intelligences Theory provides a useful framework for understanding the role of emotional issues related to interpersonal and intrapersonal competencies. In addition, recent behavioral studies link self-regulation, self-motivation, and self-assessment to achievement and success.[7]

Emotional Competence Framework

Daniel Goleman, Harvard-trained psychologist and former science editor of the *New York Times*, created the Emotional Competence Framework (see Table 4-10).

According to Goleman:

The more the leader exhibits competencies like initiative, nurture of others, team leadership, self-confidence, drive

JOB AID 4-3: **What Mentors Do**

Directions: Following is a list of things that mentors do. Use this list to determine if you would be a good mentor. As appropriate for each one, check "Others have done this for me" or "I've done this for others" or both.

	Others have done this for me	I've done this for others
Set high expectations of performance		
Offer challenging ideas		
Help build self-confidence		
Encourage professional behavior		
Offer friendship		
Confront negative behaviors and attitudes		
Listen to personal problems		
Teach by example		
Provide growth experiences		
Offer quotable quotes		
Explain how the organization works		
Coach mentees		
Stand by mentees in critical situations		
Offer wise counsel		
Encourage winning behavior		
Inspire their mentees		
Offer encouragement		
Assist with mentees' careers		

Based on Shea, G.F. (1992). Mentoring. Menlo Park, CA: Crisp Publications. ISPI © 2001. Permission granted for unlimited duplication for noncommercial use.

TABLE 4-10: Goleman's Emotional Competence Framework	
Personal Competence	**Social Competence**
How we manage ourselves	*How we handle relationships*
Self-Awareness: Knowing one's internal states, preferences, resources, and intuitions—emotional awareness, accurate self-assessment, and self-confidence	*Empathy:* Awareness of others' feelings, needs, and concerns—understanding others, developing others, service orientation, leveraging diversity, and political awareness
Self-Regulation: Managing one's internal states, impulses, and resources—self-control, trustworthiness, conscientiousness, adaptability, and innovation	*Social Skills:* Adeptness eliciting desirable responses in others—influence, communication, conflict management, leadership, change catalyst, building bonds, collaboration, cooperation, and team capabilities
Motivation: Emotional tendencies that guide or facilitate reaching goals—achievement, drive, commitment, initiative, and optimism	

Based on Goleman, 1995, pp. 26–27.

to achieve, and empathy, the more positive the climate. The more inspired people are, the more loyal they are. It's an organization where the best people stay, because they love what they do. And, the more an organization has that climate, the better its business performance, as measured by profit growth, net operating income, growth in sales, growth in earnings, attaining business goals.[8]

On the other hand, businesses without EI suffer for their indifference and insensitivity.

The price organisations [sic] have paid for the emotion-less approach can be counted in lost profit, deeply suspicious relationships, intense competitiveness at the cost of co-operative success, disappearing loyalty and mounting, frustrated anger that is acted out instead of worked out. All cut into valuable available resources.[9]

EI relates to individual productivity.

Emotional intelligence matters in surprising places such as computer programming, where the top 10 percent of performers exceeded average performers in producing effective programs by 320 percent, and the superstars at the 1 percent level produced an amazing 1,272 percent more than average. Assessments of these top performers revealed that they were better at such things as teamwork, staying late to finish a project, and sharing shortcuts with co-workers. In short, the best performers didn't compete, they collaborated.[10]

Implementing EI Interventions in the Workplace

EI interventions may be discouraged or adopted reluctantly within an organization because they do not jibe with mental paradigms and past experiences of many individuals.

Therefore, strong and consistent executive sanction will be necessary for significant efforts to occur. Initiatives will need to be justified and supported with examples from other organizations. PT practitioners may need to begin with web searches to secure examples that will be meaningful to senior management and to employees. PT practitioners can expect resistance by people who are unfamiliar with EI concepts, or find acquiring personal and social competence skills difficult, or anticipate that changes due to increased EI would threaten their current job status or well-being.

Valued Aspect of Intellectual Capital

Organizations need to realize the importance of EI as value-added intellectual capital, which is their human resource. This can be conveyed through workgroup meetings using materials (print or other media) to support management's message. Management will need to serve as role models, which may mean intensive training to hone their own skills. Management and supervisory training should include defining emotional intelligence and preparing non-exempt employees to apply EI skills. Dealing with emotions and developing sensitivity to others will be foreign to many industries, especially to some manual labor-intensive industries, such as factories.

Cultural Alignment

Applying EI will mean an entire change of culture in many workplaces. Following these strategies can help realign the culture to support EI.

- *Survey Culture:* Begin planning EI interventions by assessing the emotional climate of the workplace. Add questions relative to *Goleman's Emotional Competence Framework* (see Table 4-10) to annual culture surveys.
- *Individual assessment* can occur through the 360° feedback process. Again, questions can be added to

evaluate employees' self-awareness and sensitivity to the feelings of others.

- Management should *role model* positive EI. The rewards for wise application of EI should be obvious to others in the workgroup.
- *Communication* pieces, such as newsletters, should carry articles about the topic. In addition, general articles written about other subjects should cite factors of EI whenever they apply.

Training and Development Alignment

In addition, current efforts relative to interpersonal skill development should be re-assessed to ensure alignment with *Goleman's Competence Framework*. For example, courses in stress management may be reacting to symptoms that cause tension and fatigue and not addressing causes, which may be lack of EI. In addition, problem resolution and conflict management may focus on the situation and facts (content) of the problem without addressing the emotional consequences (feelings) related to the problem.

For the legions of soft-skills trainers who've long been stigmatized as training lightweights, Goleman's research is like manna from heaven. Finally, there is hard data to confirm what they've known all along: Personality and character count on the job. Not only that, but there's also solid research to prove that the skills that contribute to emotional intelligence can be taught. Unlike IQ, which is a person's intellectual potential that is fixed at birth, patterns of emotional intelligence (or "EQ") can be developed over time (see Job Aid 4-4).[11]

Career Development

Definition and Scope

Career development involves planning, acquiring, and maintaining a career.[1] During the 1950s and 60s, career development was basically a one-time occurrence. Workers tended to stay in the same job until they retired. Today, society and its workers are mobile, and career development has evolved into an ongoing process. As an intervention, establishing career development processes formalizes support for positive career management, enables the organization to forecast job needs, and helps employees match their own development efforts with future organizational needs.

Careers are increasingly self-managed. There are more options, but individuals need to understand their social and economic goals; critically and honestly assess their own values, skills, and abilities; and manage their own developmental options. This involves considerable self-research about possibilities for careers and for development experiences to attain personal career goals.[2]

Four basic questions need to be answered: Where do I want to be? Where am I now? How am I going to get there? How will I know when I have arrived?

The career development model (see Table 4-11) developed by Richard Knowdell, a noted expert, focuses on four stages of career development.

Career Coaches

There are three functions in the career development process: employee, manager, and human resources. In his model, Knowdell describes managers as career coaches, employees as career drivers, and human resources as the support system for career development. A coach manager assumes the roles of a guide, teacher, information provider, and assessor. As the career driver, Table 4-12 describes the employee's responsibilities.

According to Knowdell, Human Resources' role has changed from that of coach to providing resources such as training, orientation programs, administering tuition reimbursement, and conducting career development workshops.

TABLE 4-11: Four Stages of Career Development

Assessment	What are my skills, interests, and values?
Exploration	What are my options?
Goal setting and planning	Which is the best option for me? For my career goal?
Strategy	How will I reach my goal?

Based on Knowdell, 1996.

TABLE 4-12: Employee Roles in Career Coaching Situations

Self-assess own current knowledge, skills, and abilities

Explore options available to reach own career development goals

Define a career focus

Develop a strategy plan to manage own career

Based on Knowdell, 1996.

JOB AID 4-4: Emotional Intelligence Descriptor

Component	Description	Hallmarks
Self-Awareness	• Ability to recognize and understand personal moods and emotions • Drives their effect on others	• Self-confidence • Realistic self-assessment • Self-deprecating sense of humor
Self-Regulation	• Ability to control or redirect disruptive impulses and moods • Propensity to suspend judgment and to think before acting	• Trustworthiness • Integrity • Comfort with ambiguity • Openness to change
Motivation	• Passion to work for reasons that go beyond money and status • Propensity to pursue goals with energy and persistence	• Strong drive to achieve • Optimism even in the face of failure • Organizational commitment
Empathy	• Ability to understand the emotional makeup of other people • Skilled in treating people according to their emotional reactions	• Expertise in building and retaining talent • Cross-cultural sensitivity • Service to clients and customers
Social Skills	• Proficiency in managing relationships and building networks • Ability to find common ground and establish rapport	• Effectiveness in leading change • Persuasiveness • Expertise building and leading teams

Place a check next to any items that apply to you.
Prioritize by circling no more than three items you would like to improve immediately.

☐ Overly harsh with criticism   ☐ Expects too much from others
☐ Manipulative   ☐ Autocratic
☐ Insensitive   ☐ Outdated ideas and goals
☐ Unethical   ☐ Resists change
☐ Untrustworthy   ☐ Procrastinator

Identify someone to seek out for feedback on your checked and circled items.

Name:

Think about your behaviors. Jot down notes while you receive feedback and discuss possible improvement plans.

Based on Miller, M. (1999, July). Emotional intelligence helps managers succeed. Credit Union 65 (7), 25–26.
ISPI © 2001. Permission granted for unlimited duplication for noncommercial use.

Team-based Career Coaching

A team leader or coach can also play an important role in helping team members to manage their career growth. A team leader supports team members by:

- Preparing them to excel at their current jobs
- Preparing them to keep up with the technology so they are prepared as the job evolves into the future
- Championing members for temporary assignments on other projects or on cross-functional teams
- Encouraging them to seek out and move to new job assignments
- Encouraging them to get the education they need
- Helping them to build skills that will make them more valuable.[3]

Implementing Career Development Interventions in the Workplace

Career development and career planning are necessary to stay current with expected work force labor needs. Ensuring that skills, knowledge, and personal values are aligned with the ever-changing career market is not an easy job. Some organizations sponsor formal career planning in which employees can or must participate. However, employees should not assume their needs are fully met with these developmental plans. *It is the responsibility of individual employees to set their own career direction, drive their own career, and control their own job future.*[4]

Career Counseling

Some human resources organizations provide career counselors. They are a good resource to help formalize a career plan. Other resources available to help in career management are listed below.

- *Career assessments* help employees learn more about lifestyles, personal values, and career interests.[5] The following assessments provide career guidance.

Career Anchors, by E.H. Schein
University Associates Psychological Assessment Resources, Inc.
Pfeiffer/Jossey Bass Publishers
350 Sansome Street
San Francisco, CA 94104
Phone: 415-433-1740
Fax: 415-433-0499

Strong Interest Inventory, by E.K. Strong, Jr.
Consulting Psychologists Press, Inc.
3803 E. Bayshore Road
Palo Alto, CA 94303
Phone: 800-624-1765

Career Value Card Sort, by R. Knowdell
Career Research and Testing, Inc.
P.O. Box 611930
San Jose, CA 95161
Phone: 800-888-4945 or 408-441-9100
Fax: 408-441-9101

- *Personal style inventories*, such as Myers-Briggs Type Indicator, help employees learn more about their own problem solving and decision making styles, etc.[6]

Myers Briggs Type Indicator, by I. Myers and C. Briggs
Consulting Pyschologists Press, Inc.
3803 E. Bayshore Road
Palo Alto, CA 94303
800-624-1765

- *Professional organizations*, such as the International Society for Performance Improvement (ISPI) and the American Society for Training and Development (ASTD). These associations provide opportunities to network and keep up to date on the latest technologies in a given field.

- *Professional journals* help keep current on employment-related trends.

- *Cross-functional teams* within the organization help individuals expand their skills and knowledge into other professional areas.

Career Planning

Developing career plans help employees evaluate who they are, where they want to be in their future work setting, and what they need to do to get there.[7] Career plans should be reviewed with managers or career coaches frequently to ensure accuracy and access to the latest information.

Career development plans should include:
- Specific objectives
- Action steps identifying how the objectives will be met
- Timelines for meeting the objectives
- Process for ongoing evaluation of goals, action plans, job satisfaction, and business trends (see Job Aid 4-5).

Note: This chapter was written in collaboration with Judy Gohl, MA, Beyond Expectations, Inc. (BEI).

JOB AID 4-5: Career Development System Planner

Directions: Use the following system planner to guide your thinking about career development.

Assess
What are the desired outcomes? 1. 2. 3.
What is the senior management philosophy toward career development?
Who would be the sponsor?

What programs currently exist? Underline them.

Apprenticeship programs	Annual developmental plans	Training and employee development
Career assessment	Mentoring	Supervisory training
Career counseling	New employee orientation	Executive education
360° feedback	Succession planning	Job rotation
Job posting	Pre-retirement seminars	Skills banks

Design
Identify potential new program needs and target audience.

Target audience:	*New Program:*
Target audience:	*New Program:*
Target audience:	*New Program:*

Evaluation
How will the outcomes be evaluated? *Formative:* *Summative:* *Confirmative:* *Meta:*

Constraints
What are the anticipated problems or constraints? *Resources:* *Sponsorship:* *Operational/productivity reductions:* *Resistance to new programs:*

ISPI © 2001. Permission granted for unlimited duplication for noncommercial use.

Case Study 4-1: Mentoring: Ford Motor Engineering

The Ford Motor Company Ford Technical Education Program (FTEP), which has been in existence for approximately two years, grew out of the Ford Design Institute's objective to become the world's leading consumer company providing excellence in automotive products and services. To meet this objective, Ford realized that it required a work force capable of providing unmatched technical competence. As a result, Ford engineers are required to certify in the FTEP tools and methodologies key to its core engineering processes.

FTEP is a global process comprised of a series of steps leading to qualification. These include:
1. Identify business processes.
2. Identify the capability needed to support business processes.
3. Complete the Application of Prior Experience and Learning (APEL) test to determine which FTEP tools and methodologies one qualifies in.
4. Identify a personal training plan.
5. Complete the identified training programs (instructor-led and/or computer-based).
6. Complete the online post-test (if engineer fails, course must be repeated).
7. Apply methodologies in the workplace (a recommended three-month period).
8. Test to become FTEP-qualified (if engineer fails, repeat application and retake APEL). Engineers may take the APEL at any time to determine if they qualify in a FTEP tool or methodology.

Situation

Much time and energy was spent to develop the FTEP tools and methodologies that could effectively address the technical challenges that Ford faced. Engineers become FTEP certified by successfully completing a series of training programs, which focus on the consistent use of FTEP tools and methodologies. During the FTEP planning process, Ford management astutely recognized the need to provide ongoing support to engineers once they completed training and were certified to apply the methodologies in the actual work environment. To address this need, Ford initiated the role of Application Engineer as a unique feature in the FTEP process. Engineers qualify for this role by successfully completing the FTEP courses, demonstrating mastery in the application of FTEP methodologies, and expressing interest in working as a mentor with teams.

Description of Role

The role of an Application Engineer is that of an advisor rather than a facilitator. A team in need of application engineering services can go to the Ford intranet to locate the names, location, and contact numbers of certified engineers. The champion and team leader, not the Application Engineer, is responsible for driving the methodologies applied by a team as they problem solve. The team leader is the facilitator.

The Application Engineer's role is to remain in the background as an observer as a team proceeds through experimental runs, discusses findings, and documents results. The Application Engineer could best be described as a mentor who is there to answer questions, provide examples from experience, and advise a team on process and application results. The mentor reviews applications of FTEP methodologies for consistency and correctness. However, the mentor is not responsible for driving process by telling teams how to run an experiment or how to interpret results.

The Application Engineer documents observations and makes note of a team's findings and applications. These notes are processed online to provide a resource for other engineering teams.

Lessons Learned

Although the FTEP program is only two years old, the Application Engineers have compiled a formidable list of experiences to serve as a basis for ongoing continuous improvement and growth in the FTEP program. Among the lessons learned are the following:

- Not enough teams are taking advantage of the expertise and support the Application Engineers provide, which indicates a need for increased company support and promotion of the Application Engineer role.
- FTEP training is often approached as a means of filling required personal training hours rather than as "training" for a specific application or team to which one is assigned or will be assigned at the completion of the training.
- Application needs to be in the major timeline to fulfill team needs. Frequently, too much time elapses between completion of the FTEP training program and team application of the FTEP tools and methods.
- Roles and responsibilities of FTEP team leaders and Application Engineers need to be more clearly defined to eliminate confusion to team members.
- Computer-based training followed by a four-hour facilitated debrief session has proven to be a successful medium for FTEP training.

Case Study written by Judy Gohl, MA, Beyond Expectations, Inc., in cooperation with Sherry Orandi, MEd, Ford Motor Company—July, 1999.

CHAPTER
5

HUMAN RESOURCE DEVELOPMENT

"HE'S A GREAT WORKER...UNTIL HIBERNATION TIME."

HUMAN RESOURCE DEVELOPMENT INTERVENTIONS

Human resources (HR) refers to the people part of organizations. During the 1990s, the HR model included three sets of competencies for HR specialists:

- Knowledge of the business
- World-class delivery of HR practices
- Management of change processes.[1]

The forecast for the 21st century is that HR specialists and PT practitioners will join together to improve the people part of organizations and that both groups will need the set of competencies listed above as well as knowledge of the basics of performance improvement (PI).[2]

This chapter describes the HR-based interventions that help to improve individual and organizational performance. PT practitioners and HR specialists may partner to implement these interventions (see Table 5-1).

The purpose of this chapter is to:

- Expand the knowledge base and competency of HR specialists and PT practitioners
- Help focus human resources management (HRM) on PI issues
- Suggest ways to enhance the role of PT practitioners as strategic partners in the effort to "deliver high-quality HR practices."[3]

First, however, it is crucial to clarify the terminology (and acronyms) used in this chapter so that the reader and the authors will *talk the same talk*. Figure 5-1 reflects the authors' perspective as it defines and shows the relationships among the major concepts and acronyms. In addition, the organization of this chapter requires some clarification. Readers who are familiar with the companion book, *Fundamentals of Performance Technology*,[4] will note that the authors have changed this category of interventions from HRD interventions to HR interventions (see Table 5-1). HR refers to the overall system that deals with the people resources for an organization. The term *human resources development* emerged during the 1960s and 1970s when there was a movement toward more employee involvement.[5] It is the part of HR that designs and implements long-term strategies to "…ensure that organizational members have the competencies to meet current and future job demands."[6] HRM is the core business function of HR.

The authors also have divided HR interventions into three sub-categories:

1. *Human Resource Management (HRM)*—the interventions in this sub-category (staffing, compensation, retirement planning, health and wellness, and employee development) reflect the core business functions of HR.
2. *Individual Growth*—these interventions (motivation systems, performance appraisals, competency testing, assessment centers, and literacy) focus on the

TABLE 5-1: HR Interventions From Enhanced HPT Model

Human Resource Management (HRM)
- Staffing
- Compensation
- Retirement Planning
- Health and Wellness
- Employee Development

Individual Growth
- Motivation (Incentives and Rewards)
- Performance Appraisals
- Competency Testing
- Assessment Centers
- Literacy

Organizational Growth
- Succession Planning
- Career Pathing
- Leadership Development
- Executive Development
- Management Development
- Supervisory Development

organizational need to encourage and retain high-performance employees.

3. *Organizational Growth*—the interventions in this sub-category (succession planning, career pathing, leadership development, executive development, management development, and supervisory development) address the organizational need for long-term success.

The list of interventions in Table 5-1 is also slightly different from the companion book. For example, the authors added employee development to the list of HRM interventions, changed "selection and staffing" to "staffing," and changed "compensation and benefits" to "compensation." These changes reflect the functions of HRM discussed in the next section of this chapter.

FIGURE 5-1: Here a P, There an H, Everywhere a P or H

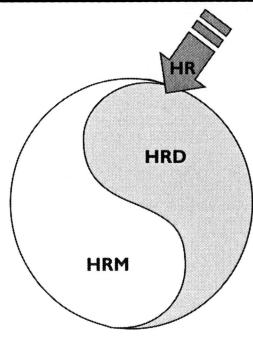

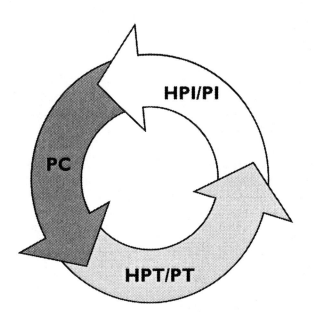

Human Resources (HR)
- An organization's people assets
- The business area that plans, acquires, motivates, and retains people assets

Human Resource Management (HRM)
- Business area that strategically plans and executes HR functions
- Planning and implementation of staffing, employee development, motivation, and maintenance activities

Human Resource Development (HRD)
- HRM function that develops, maintains, and updates people competencies
- Practice of enhancing employee knowledge, skills, abilities, attitudes

(Human) Performance Improvement (HPI/PI)
- Goal or benefits of the changes that result from the use of performance technology
- Outcome of the HPT/PT process

(Human) Performance Technology (HPT/PT)
- Process and tools to improve or enhance individual, group, and organizational performance
- Systems approach to PI: analyze performance problems and causes; select or design interventions; implement interventions and manage change; evaluate process and outcomes

Performance Consulting (PC)
- Service or practice of making performance technology work in a particular environment
- Systems thinking applied to solving HRD/performance problems

Van Tiem, Dessinger, and Moseley, 2000, pp. 2, 207–209; Langdon, Whiteside, and McKenna, 1999, pp. 1–5; Rosenberg, 1998, pp. 6–7.

HUMAN RESOURCE MANAGEMENT

Human resource management (HRM) is both a core function of HR and "a strategic partner in formulating the company's strategies, as well as in executing those strategies through HR activities."[1] Table 5-2 looks at HRM as a core business function; Table 5-3 describes the roles, goals, and deliverables of HRM as a strategic partner.

Staffing

Staffing is a critical HRM function. Peter Drucker, the eminent management guru, says: "No other decisions are so long lasting in their consequences or so difficult to unmake. And yet, by and large, executives make poor promotion and staffing decisions."[1] As more and more emphasis is placed on the human side of competitiveness and managing human capital, selecting the right person for the right job is crucial if the organization is going to prosper and maintain its competitive edge. Both the organization and the individual benefit from a carefully conceived staffing process.

Definition and Scope

Staffing is the HRM function that anticipates and fills open positions. It includes three major processes—

strategic personnel planning, recruitment, and selection.

- *Strategic personnel* planning links *human resource planning efforts to the company's strategic direction... It is a process by which an organization ensures that it has the right number and kinds of people, at the right place, at the right time, capable of effectively and efficiently completing those tasks that will help the organization achieve its overall objective.*[2]
  Two integral activities make up the strategic personnel planning process: forecasting and planning. Forecasting predicts personnel requirements (demand) and the potential availability of internal and external candidates to meet those requirements (supply). Planning discovers the best strategies for hiring, training, and preparing candidates for future job openings.[3] Strategic personnel planning relies heavily on job analysis.
- *Recruitment* is the process used to "attract a pool of viable job applicants."[4] Recruitment involves communicating information in a way that attracts the most qualified applicants and discourages less qualified applicants from applying for the position.[5]
- *Selection* is a highly visible part of the staffing function, the process that screens the applicants and selects the best candidate for the position. Selection activities include reviewing applications and resumes,

TABLE 5-2: Four Human Resource Management (HRM) Core Business Functions

Function	Goal	Activities
1. Staffing	Locate competent employees to meet business needs and get them into the organization	• Strategic HR planning • Recruitment • Selection
2. Employee Development	Develop competent, adapted employees with up-to-date skills	• Employee orientation • Training • Organization development • Career development
3. Motivation	Encourage competent, adapted employees with up-to-date skills to attain high performance levels	• Job design • Compensation and benefits • Rewards and incentives
4. Maintenance	Retain competent, adapted employees with up-to-date skills and high performance levels	• Safety and health • Ergonomics • Communication • Employee relations

Based on DeCenzo and Robbins, 1999, pp. 12–19.

interviewing and screening candidates, and making the final offer. Selection is an exercise in prediction because HRM personnel must predict which applicants have success potential.[6] It is a continuous exercise because turnover inevitably occurs and a waiting list of qualified applicants must be readily available. [7]

Environmental Factors

Environmental factors such as type of organization, organizational hierarchy, speed of decision making, etc., have an effect on the quality and effectiveness of the staffing process and outcomes. Table 5-4 describes six environmental factors and how they may impact staffing.

TABLE 5-3: HRM as a Strategic Partner

"Human resource departments can, should, and must find ways to accomplish necessary transaction work (for example, payroll) while focusing aggressively on work that executes strategy, increases employee contributions, and transforms organizations" *(Ulrich, 1997, pp. 232–233).*

Roles	Goals	Deliverables
Business Partner	Help to move strategic planning from the conference room to the marketplace	Executable strategies that meet business needs
Administrative Expert	Improve the efficiency of both HR functions and the entire organization	Administrative efficiencies that reduce costs while maintaining quality
Employee Champion	Represent employees to management; increase employee contributions and commitment	Increased employee contributions and commitment
Change Agent	Shape processes and culture that together improve an organization's capacity for continuous transformation	Increased organizational capacity for change

Based on Ulrich, 1998, pp. 124–129; Ulrich, 1997, pp. 37, 232–233.

TABLE 5-4: Environmental Factors That Affect Staffing and Selection

Environmental Factor	Effect on Staffing and Selection
1. Type of Organization	Effect varies for different types of organizations: • Private—profit-oriented focus; employees screened to achieve profit goals • Governmental—civil service focus; employees screened through competitive examination • Not-for-Profit—altruistic focus; employees qualified and dedicated; salaries generally non-competitive
2. Organizational Hierarchy	Selection process varies according to level of employment. For example, hiring a physician requires a different background check than hiring a unit clerk.
3. Speed of Decision Making	How long it traditionally takes to make a selection decision may be of critical importance. For example, when the program administrator and the secretary quit on the same day, it becomes a matter of urgency to fill the positions.
4. Applicant Pool	Selection is successful if there are enough applicants available to make a best choice selection. Expansion and contraction of the labor market influence the availability of qualified applicants. Internal factors that control the external image of the organization also affect the size of the applicant pool.
5. Probationary Period	This is the monitoring and evaluating component; usually 60–90 days. Careful selection usually insures successful completion of this process.
6. Legal Considerations	HR personnel need to understand the relationship between the selection process and legal issues related to discrimination, and other issues.

Based on Mondy, Noe, and Premeaux, 1999, pp. 209–211.

Outcomes

The outcomes of the staffing function have a critical impact on the organization in three areas: performance, bottom line, and legal implications.

- *Performance:* "Most managers recognize employee selection as one of their most difficult and most important business decisions."[8] The organization reaps substantial benefits by hiring the top performers. The result is the availability of competent people to shepherd organizational goals. Because organizations today have access to the same technology, the availability of competent people will make the real difference. An organization's unique advantage is grounded in its human resource system.[9]
- *Bottom line:* Recruitment, screening, selection, and hiring are costly processes by themselves, and become even more costly when they are impacted by or have an impact on other HRM functions such as compensation and employee training and development. For example, if the compensation package is not equal to or is greater than the organization's primary competition, it is difficult both to attract and to retain the best candidates.[10] Second, if, as a result of the selection process, the new hire is overqualified, underqualified, or does not walk the talk, HRM may need to increase personal development efforts, training, coaching, and/or mentoring, at additional cost to the organization.
- *Legal implications:* There are legal implications attached to poor or incompetent selection. Legislation, executive orders, and court orders influence the selection process. For example, Equal Employment Opportunity (EEO) legislation, guidelines, and court decisions require organizations to evaluate the effectiveness of their employee selection procedures and guard against unfair discrimination toward minorities, women, the older worker, or the physically challenged. Courts also hold employers liable for hiring workers with criminal records without checking or providing appropriate safeguard measures.[11]

Implementing Staffing Interventions in the Workplace

Figure 5-2 illustrates the processes and activities that make up the staffing function.

Each step in the staffing function offers a unique opportunity for PT practitioners to use their special competencies to develop a strategic partnership with HRM.

1. Analyze Jobs

Job analysis is a formal way of evaluating job requirements by looking at the job itself and at the kind of person needed to complete the job successfully. The outputs of job analysis are a job description (list of job duties and tasks) and job specifications (list of skills, aptitudes, education, and experiences that the worker needs to complete the job successfully). "Potential uses for job analysis are found in every major personnel function."[12] In the case of the staffing function, HRM uses data from job analysis for strategic human resource planning, describing position vacancies, and developing a profile of the successful candidate. The PT practitioner often conducts the job analysis and may use a job analysis survey to gather information from one or more employees and supervisors. For a more complete discussion of job analysis, see Chapter 3, including Job Aid 3-1: Job Analysis Survey.

2. Conduct Strategic Human Resource Planning

Strategic personnel planning is critical to the ongoing success of an organization.

> *Although recruiting is frequently perceived as the initial step in the staffing function, there are a number of prerequisites. Specifically, before the first job candidate is sought, HRM must embark on strategic human resource planning. This area alone has probably fostered the most change in human resource departments during the past 15 years. We can no longer hire individuals haphazardly. We must have a well-defined reason for needing individuals who possess specific skills, knowledge, and abilities that are directly likened to specific jobs required in the organization.... Not until the mission and strategy of the organization have been fully developed can human resource managers begin to determine the human resource needs.[13]*

As a partner in strategic personnel planning the PT practitioner may:

- Conduct job analysis, performance analysis (organizational, environmental, gap), and cause analysis, then guide HRM in the use of the resulting data for strategic planning
- Help keep HRM abreast of key industry trends that may impact the staffing function and beyond
- Suggest strategic planning activities for data gathering, goal setting, problem solving, decision making, and consensus building
- Train HRM and management to implement the activities
- Design job aids, forms, checklists, and other performance tools to support the activities
- Facilitate strategic planning sessions.

3. Recruit Applicants

Recruitment involves advertising the position or job to potential internal and/or external applicants. The goal is to secure a viable group of applicants who have relevant experience and potential job fit. There are a variety of sources that an organization may tap to locate potential candidates (see Table 5-5).

FIGURE 5-2: Staffing: Step Up to Peak Performance

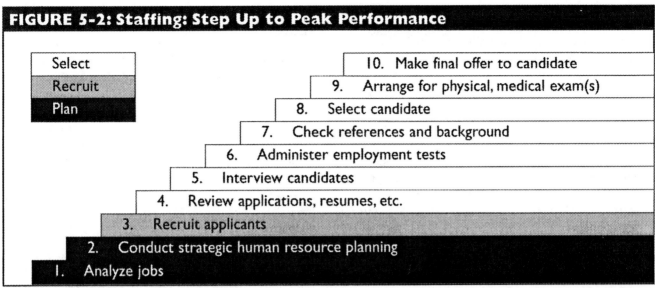

| Select |
| Recruit |
| Plan |

10. Make final offer to candidate
9. Arrange for physical, medical exam(s)
8. Select candidate
7. Check references and background
6. Administer employment tests
5. Interview candidates
4. Review applications, resumes, etc.
3. Recruit applicants
2. Conduct strategic human resource planning
1. Analyze jobs

Based on DeCenzo and Robbins, 1999, pp. 12–13; 169–174.

TABLE 5-5: Sources of Job Candidates

Source	Discussion of Best Practices
Internal Sources	Be aware of the positive and negative implications: • Employees known for their high performance, skills, and commitment may select similar candidates • Reliance on internal sources may lead to nepotism, inbreeding, and discontent
Advertising	Match the media to the job position and potential applicant pool: • Use newspapers for blue collar positions • Use professional/trade publications for white collar positions
Employment Agencies	Select the agency based on its potential applicant pool and experience: • Select type of agency (government, non-profit, private for-profit) based on its potential applicant pool • Verify agency's past success in filling similar positions—same or similar industry
Executive Recruiters or Head Hunters	Use recruiters to help fill executive or technical positions based on their experience and success rate
Walk-Ins	If walk-ins are encouraged, then… • Post a help-wanted sign outside of the job location or the building housing HR • Post notices on employee and retail bulletin boards
Older Workers	Don't forget *gray power:* • Contact American Association of Retired Persons (AARP) • Check your organization's retirement ranks • Contact firms that specialize in providing experienced consultants for specific industries
Internet	Use the power of the web: • Post position listings online—job opening services, professional organization bulletin boards, etc. • Use your organization's web site to post positions, interactive applications, and/or instructions for submitting online resumes.

Based on Dessler, 1998, pp. 297–298.

HRM may decide to keep recruitment activities in-house or outsource part or all recruitment activities. In either case, the PT practitioner may help HRM evaluate an existing recruitment program, design a new program, or select and evaluate potential vendors. In addition, the PT practitioner may provide job analysis data (job descriptions and job specifications) to use in writing job ads.

4. Review Applications, Resumes, etc.

Application forms and resumes give HRM quick and systematic access to an applicant's basic historical information. They also provide the following:

- Indications of whether the applicant meets minimum requirements
- Basis for interview questions
- Source of background and reference checks.[14]

The PT practitioner may help HRM evaluate existing job application forms or design new forms. Application forms vary from organization to organization and even from job to job; however, there are elements that are common to most applications. Figure 5-3 lists the common elements of a job application in the form of a checklist.

The PT practitioner may also use knowledge of human and organizational behavior to help HRM match an applicant's knowledge, skills, abilities, personality, and preferences to both job specifications and organizational business needs.

FIGURE 5-3: Checklist of Common Elements for a Job Application Form

Fill-in sections:

- ☐ Name
- ☐ Address
- ☐ Telephone Number (fax, email)
- ☐ Military Service (if applicable)
- ☐ Education
- ☐ Employment History

Preprinted statements that must be signed by the applicant:

- ☐ Certification that everything on the form is true. (Untrue statements could result in dismissal of the applicant.)
- ☐ Statement that the applicant understands that the position is employment at will, and that the employer or the employee can terminate employment at any time for any reason or no reason. (Do not include if this statement is prohibited by state law.)
- ☐ Permission for the potential employer to check the applicant's references.

Based on Mondy, Noe, and Premeaux, 1999, pp. 213–216.

---

5. Interview Candidates

Interviews are the most popular type of selection tool and also "serve as public relations tools for the organization."[15] Interviews may be structured or unstructured:

- *Structured interviews:* the interviewer asks every candidate the same questions and can compare candidates based on how they answer the questions.[16]
- *Unstructured interviews:* the interviewer selects which questions to ask a particular candidate. Questions are both probing and open ended.

Behavioral interviewing, which has been around since the 1980s, is one type of structured interview that focuses on matching job specifications with applicant skills, experiences, and qualifications.

> *This approach to screening candidates was designed to reveal pre-existing behaviors that would either be strengths or weaknesses in a specific position…By asking a question like, "Tell me about a time when you were asked to do an assignment that fell outside your normal duties," an interviewer can detect proficiency, deficiency, and aptitude for behaviors such as customer service, working in a team environment, and problem solving…Perhaps the best quality about behavioral interviewing is that it can be used as a tie breaker when a decision has to be made about two candidates with similar skills.[17]*

Hiring the wrong person is a costly mistake; not hiring a candidate based on diversity or other issues can also be costly in terms of legal fees. Behavioral interviewing helps to ensure that the final selection is both cost effective and legal.

FIGURE 5-4: Improving the Legal Implications of the Interview Process

1. Base interview questions and ratings on job analysis.
2. Select interviewers who represent diversity in race, sex, age, and national origin.
3. Train interviewers to ask appropriate questions. For example, it is illegal to ask an applicant's age, marital status, number of children, etc.
4. Design and use structured interviews.
5. Train interviewers to take notes and document, in writing, the rationale behind their hiring recommendations.
6. Monitor hiring recommendations for adverse impact. The monitoring process is especially important when group interviewers are inconsistent in their recommendations.

Based on Legal and Effective Interviewing: A Desk Reference, 1996, pp. 5–7; Harris, 1997, p. 143.

In the area of interviewing, the PT practitioner can provide training or job aids to:

- Navigate HRM and the organization through the many diversity and legal issues and concerns that surround interviewing job applicants. For example, the Society for Human Resource Management (SHRM) developed job aids that fit into a popular planner and include the following topics: interviewing questions to ask and not ask, interviewing dos and don'ts, topics to avoid, and interviewing people with disabilities.[18] Also, Figure 5-4 lists six actions that could improve the legal implications of the interview process.
- Develop interview questions that are based on job analysis data (job descriptions, job specifications) and use behavioral terms.
- Validate interview questions to make sure that they are structured to prevent bias. For example, the research findings in Figure 5-5 may be helpful in recognizing and reducing the effect of bias in interviews.

6. Administer Employment Tests

The selection process uses a variety of employment tests. Individuals differ in qualities related to job performance, so "the key in employment testing is to use a test that accurately predicts job performance."[19]

Table 5-6 identifies and describes the type of employment tests frequently used to supplement the selection process.

FIGURE 5-5: Research Findings on Bias in Interviews

- Prior knowledge about the applicant will bias the interviewer's evaluation.
- Interviewers tend to hold a stereotype of what represents a good applicant.
- Interviewers tend to favor applicants who share their own attitudes.
- The order in which applicants are interviewed will influence evaluations.
- The order in which information is elicited during the interview will influence evaluations.
- Negative information is given unduly high weight.
- Interviewers often make a decision concerning the applicant's suitability within the first four or five minutes of the interview.
- Interviewers forget much of the interview's content within minutes after the interview is concluded.
- Interviews are most valid in determining an applicant's intelligence, level of motivation, and interpersonal skills.
- A *cold* interviewer (one who is extremely formal and serious) can have a devastating effect on the verbal and nonverbal behaviors of applicants with low self-esteem.

Based on Robbins and Caulter, 1999, p. 351.

TABLE 5-6: Employment Test Categories and Functions

Test Category	Function
Cognitive Aptitude Tests	Determine general reasoning ability, memory, vocabulary, verbal fluency, and numerical ability
Psychomotor Tests	Measure strength, coordination, and dexterity
Job Knowledge Tests— Commercial and In-house	Measure knowledge of the duties of the job for which the applicant is applying (commercial tests are validated)
Simulations	Tests requiring the identification of a set of tasks that represent a particular job
Vocational Interest Tests	Indicators of the occupation in which a person is most interested and most likely to enjoy satisfaction
Personality Tests	Measures of personality traits such as sociability, adjustment, and energy; often used to identify motivated, flexible, team-committed people

Based on Mondy, Noe, and Premeaux, 1999, pp. 223–224.

Employment tests range from the simple to the complex. They may measure aptitudes, abilities, job knowledge, vocational interests, and personality. More sophisticated organizations seek a comprehensive view of the candidate by using a variety of tools, such as tests, simulations, role plays, and group interviews over a one- to four-day period.[20] (See the section on assessment centers beginning on p. 173.)

Three other tests are graphology tests, polygraph tests, and honesty tests.
- *Graphology tests* analyze handwriting to discover individual traits such as energy, enthusiasm, spontaneity, balance, and control. Ford Motor Company, General Electric (GE), and the CIA confer with graphologists to supplement their selection activities.[21] However, there is little evidence to support graphology as a valid selection tool.
- *Polygraph tests* are lie detector tests that verify application information. Organizations often use polygraph tests to screen applicants for jobs requiring security clearance. Polygraphs are considered valid instruments when administered by competent, highly trained individuals.[22,23]
- *Honesty testing* may also refer to paper and pencil tests that assess an individual's pattern of response in situations that test honesty and integrity. For example, an honesty test might ask: Have you ever made a long distance personal phone call on company time? Have you ever taken paper clips or pencils from your organization for personal use? Honesty testing is popular in the banking, retail, hospitality, and other industries where there are many temptations for an employee to be less than honest.[24]

Job Aid 5-1 is a guide to consulting with HRM about employment testing. The PT practitioner, especially one with a background in evaluation, is an invaluable resource when it comes to determining valid, fair, and equitable guidelines for establishing and administering an employment-testing program.

7. Check References and Background
Personal reference checks and background investigations provide additional insight into the selection process. Investigations are important "to verify the accuracy of factual information previously provided by the applicant, and to uncover damaging background information such as criminal records and suspended driver's licenses."[25]

The reference check or background investigation may take many forms:
- Verification of applicant's current position and salary
- Verification with current and previous supervisors

of applicant's motivation, technical competence, and ability to work with others
- Verification from commercial credit-rating companies of applicant's credit standing, indebtedness, reputation, character, and lifestyle
- Verification of applicant's work history and skills.[26]

The PT practitioner can play a crucial role in the verification process by helping HRM establish guidelines, design and develop verification forms, and train staff to ask the right questions, judge evasive answers, and determine legitimate references.

8. Select Final Candidate
The PT practitioner may help to design, document, or validate policies and procedures for making the selection.

The person whose qualifications most closely conform to the requirements of the open position and the organization should be selected...[from] those still in the running after reference checks, selection tests, background investigations, and interview information have been evaluated.[27]

9. Arrange for Physical, Medical Exams
After a preliminary or conditional offer of employment is made to and accepted by the successful candidate, the next step may involve a physical examination or other medical tests. The purpose of these tests is to determine whether or not the candidate is capable of performing the work required. "It also provides a baseline against which subsequent medical examinations can be compared and interpreted. The latter objective is particularly important in determinations of work-caused disabilities under workers' compensation law."[28]

The term *other medical tests* may include AIDS testing, drug and alcohol (substance abuse) testing, and genetic screening.
- Employment law now protects AIDS victims, and many companies are beginning to develop corporate policies to address the impact of the disease on the organization.
- Drug and alcohol abuse at work is a serious problem. Both alcohol and drugs affect the quality and quantity of employee output and impact employee morale. Urine sampling is the test of preference for drug and alcohol dependency. An organization may reject a candidate who fails a substance abuse test.
- Genetic screening identifies individuals who are hypersensitive to harmful pollutants in the workplace. It is then possible to screen these people out of chemically dangerous jobs.[29]

The PT practitioner may help HRM analyze, design, document, or monitor policies and procedures for the smooth and orderly functioning of a medical and physical testing program that is in compliance with federal guidelines. The PT practitioner may also conduct training programs on compliance, or provide performance support tools to help HRM identify current federal guidelines.

10. Make Final Offer to Candidate

Once a candidate successfully completes all the steps in the selection process, the organization notifies both the successful and unsuccessful candidates. Unnecessary delay may cause the organization to lose a prime candidate and also to lose the future goodwill of the unsuccessful candidates.[30,31]

As a strategic partner in the staffing function, the PT practitioner may:

- Analyze jobs and write job specifications that make it easier to screen and weed out unqualified individuals
- Understand the relationship between usefulness and legality
- Develop or document policies and procedures for notifying successful and unsuccessful candidates
- Design and develop forms and other performance support tools
- Train HRM staff to implement policies and procedures.

JOB AID 5-1: How to Review Current Employment Testing Policies and Procedures

Directions: As a PT practitioner, you are asked to help HR improve performance in terms of matching applicants to jobs. Use the questions in the first column to conduct a performance analysis, gap analysis, and cause analysis.
Based on the answers to the questions, use columns two and three to guide you in taking follow-up action and suggesting possible interventions.

Questions to Ask	Actions to Take	Suggestions to Make
1. Does the organization currently use employment testing?	• Find out why the organization is/is not using employment testing (Cause Analysis)	• Evaluate current program • Design, develop, implement, evaluate an employment testing program
2. If the organization currently uses employment testing, what are the policies and procedures for testing?	• Review current policies and procedures • Benchmark against best practices	• Document policies and procedures • Update policies/procedures to match current/future needs.
3. Does the organization have hiring and promotion standards?	• Determine whether the standards are current, accurate, defensible • Determine whether employment tests match current standards	• Develop standards • Update or revise standards • Redesign current tests to match standards
4. Have employment tests been validated to determine whether they address the business needs and requirements of the organization?	• Analyze employment test goals and business needs/requirements • Determine *goodness of fit*	• Initiate a validation program • Use a certified industrial or organizational psychologist or psychometrician to interpret and validate the tests currently in use • Improve current validation process
5. Do HR personnel maintain accurate and legible test records, especially when an applicant is rejected?	• Review current records • Review incidences of legal action based on selection policies or procedures	• Develop record-keeping forms • Establish record-keeping policies and procedures
6. Does HR maintain proper testing conditions, for example, do all applicants take the tests under the same conditions?	• Visit and evaluate testing location(s)—privacy, comfort, ADA standards, noise, lighting, etc. • Review complaints from past applicants	• Make physical adjustments to existing test locations to bring them to ADA standards • Set up an assessment center

Based on Mondy, R.W., Noe, R.M., and Premeaux, S.R. (1999). Human resource management *(7th ed.). Upper Saddle River, NJ: Prentice Hall, Inc., pp. 230–231.*
ISPI © 2001. Permission granted for unlimited duplication for noncommercial use.

Compensation

In order to attract and retain employees with *the right stuff,* organizations must develop and maintain a reward system made up of compensation and noncompensation components. Research over the past 70 years shows that "the organization's reward system is highly related to job satisfaction."[1]

This section will focus on the compensation dimension of the reward system: pay and fringe benefits. Compensation is a major function of HRM because it represents a tangible reward for employee service, as well as a source of recognition and livelihood. Fringe benefits are part of compensation and are also valued as the cost of medical care and retirement escalates, and the stresses of modern work life increase the need for time away from the job. In terms of job satisfaction, however, a good percentage of today's work force seems more concerned with noncompensation issues such as quality of work life and the psychological rewards associated with employment. For a discussion of the noncompensation dimensions of the reward system see "Motivation Systems" in the "Individual Growth" section of this chapter.

Definition and Scope

A compensation system includes "…all rewards that can be classified as monetary payments and in-kind payments (goods and services)."[2] The term *compensation* generally refers to pay for work and performance; the term *benefits* refers to all financial rewards that generally are not paid directly to an employee. Benefits are a central rather than a peripheral part of the organization's pay structure. Table 5-7 describes the dimensions of a compensation system.

"The compensation system results from the allocation, conversion, and transfer of a portion of the income of an organization to its employees for their monetary and in-kind claims on goods and services."[3] Allocation involves assessing employee contributions in order to distribute rewards fairly and equitably.[4] The manner in which compensation is allocated by management sends a clear message of priorities to employees: "Research has found that satisfaction is enhanced by the use of pay systems believed to be fair—with respect to both the level of compensation received, and the mechanisms used to determine that pay."[5]

Compensation is either direct or indirect:
- *Direct compensation* encompasses an employer's base wage and salary including traditional and state-based pay plans and performance-based pay including stock options, bonuses, merit, and incentives.
- *Indirect compensation,* on the other hand, is the benefit package provided by the employer. Federal and state

governments mandate protection programs such as social security, unemployment compensation, Medicare, and disability. Private protection programs such as pensions, savings; supplemental unemployment insurance; health care benefits (medical, dental, optical, prescription drugs; paid disability leave), and life cycle benefits (child care, elder care, life style changes) are all indirect compensation or benefits.[6]

In order to attract graduating college seniors in high-demand fields, employers often dangle job benefits or perks.[7] Here are some examples:
- Signing bonus ranging from $2,000 to $15,000 for business majors
- Gym memberships or on-site recreation rooms
- Dinner if working late
- Tickets to movies, sporting events, shows
- Computer hardware and software discounts
- Paid week off between Christmas and New Year's Day
- On-site dry cleaning service.

The common goals of a compensation policy include, but are not limited to, these components:
- Rewarding employees for past performance
- Remaining competitive and earning market share in the labor force
- Maintaining a just and equitable salary among employees
- Overseeing the budget and maintaining appropriate balance for all constituents
- Attracting and retaining new employees.[8]

Implementing Compensation Interventions in the Workplace

The outputs of job/task analysis become key inputs to the process of designing a fair compensation system (see Figure 5-6).

The relationship between job/task analysis and compensation system design puts PT practitioners in a unique position to assist with the system design process. PT practitioners can:
- Conduct job analysis and develop the job descriptions, and job specifications that HRM needs to design an equitable compensation system. As an analyst, PT practitioners are trained to break jobs or tasks into component parts, identify relationships between the parts, and compare jobs and tasks to performance requirements.[9]
- Identify and document knowledge, skill, aptitude, ability, and attitude requirements. "The most important factor influencing the rate of pay of an employee is the kind of job the person performs. In classifying or differentiating jobs for pay purposes, no one single

TABLE 5-7: Dimensions of a Compensation System

Dimension	Examples
1. Pay for work and performance	• Hourly pay • Salary • Base pay • Commissions • Bonuses
2. Pay for time not worked	• Holidays • Vacation • Sick days • Personal business days
3. Loss-of-job income continuation	• Unemployment insurance • Supplemental unemployment benefits • Severance pay
4. Disability income continuation	• Social Security • Workers' compensation • Short- and long-term disability
5. Deferred income	• Pension plans • Savings plans • Stock plans
6. Spouse (family) income continuation	• Life insurance • Pension plans • Social Security • Workers' compensation
7. Health, accident, and liability protection	• Various group insurance plans
8. Income equivalent payments (perks)	• Use of a company car or credit card • Paid expenses related to participation in a professional organization • Subsidized child care or adult day care services

Based on Henderson, 2000, pp. 17–22.

FIGURE 5-6: Relationship of Job/Task Analysis to Compensation System Design

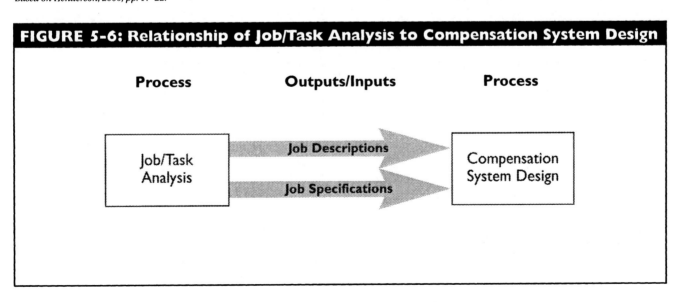

factor carries greater significance than the knowledge and skills required of the job holder."[10]

- Play a pivotal role in determining and updating competencies. Competencies are the basic units of knowledge and skills employees must acquire or demonstrate to perform the work. Pay rates and competency requirements often go hand in hand.
- PT practitioners should also be proactive in keeping management abreast of performance-related issues such as knowledge management, outsourcing, rightsizing, new learning technologies, industry reports of expenditures on training, compensation practices, work practices, performance management practices, and the like.[11]

The bottom line for PT practitioners is understanding the various elements that make up the world of pay and compensation and how these elements interact with performance technology (see Job Aid 5-2).

Retirement Planning

Although retirement is an American institution, many employees see it as a bittersweet experience. For some employees, it is a time for relaxation and enjoyment away from work force problems. For others, retirement itself is traumatic, as the once-busy employee is at the end of the line and has nothing to do. Issues of identity and self-worth become problematic for many retirees.[1]

Employers view retirement as a labor management device. In today's economic milieu of cost-cutting activity, retirement reduces labor and replaces older workers with younger ones.[2]

Definition and Scope

Retirement is a life event—a time of transition and change. It has multiple meanings based largely on individual perceptions:

- The termination of and formal withdrawal from a regular job under the provisions of a statutory pension system
- A demographic category
- An economic condition
- A developmental phase in the human lifespan
- The transition to old age
- A lifestyle dominated by leisure pursuits or, at least, by economically nonproductive activity[3]
- The absence of ideas about what to do with oneself.[4]

There are societal and individual impacts associated with retirement. For society, retirement is viewed as a social institution with rules of exit from the labor force based on age or length of service. Industrial societies like the United States direct about 10% of gross domestic product to public social security retirement pensions; another 20%–30% of

stocks, bonds, and government securities are held by employee pension programs.[5]

For individuals, "retirement is a transition to a life stage that does not require employment."[6] People retire for a variety of reasons. Chief among them are a person's financial status and health status.

The optimal retirement age is the age at which an older worker decides that he or she has sufficient income from pensions, Social Security, and personal assets to provide the desired level of compensation in retirement.[7]

Poor health also influences a person's ability to perform in the workplace. Tasks cannot be carried out efficiently and the efforts involved in waking, dressing, commuting, and doing work are laborious in themselves.[8]

Secondary reasons in framing retirement decisions involve attitudes such as the following:

- Retirement is like being put out to pasture
- Retirement will result in loss of status, friends, co-workers, challenges, etc.
- Family commitments and relationships will change (impacts on women, men, and couples)
- Life will/will not lose meaning after retirement.[9]

Adjusting to retirement is usually not problematic as long as the retirees:

- Have adequate retirement income
- Have role models to follow, with coaching and mentoring opportunities in place
- View retirement as a life transition
- Perceive themselves as competent, worthy, and productive individuals after retirement.[10]

A novel way of approaching retirement incorporates the financial, vocational, social, and spiritual needs of retirees. Wasik calls it "personal ecology," and feels that knowing how the retiree relates with self, family, and society will generate a truly successful retirement.[11] Table 5-8 compares the new values of retirement with traditional values.

Implementing Retirement Planning Interventions in the Workplace

Retirement planning is a broader performance improvement intervention than just helping people ease themselves into a new life style. Retirement itself is part of other performance interventions such as career pathing, rewards and incentives, compensation and benefits, succession planning, and so on.

PT practitioners have the analysis, planning, and organizational skills and tools needed to help an organization develop strategies that will assist employees with

JOB AID 5-2: Analyzing a Compensation System: What's Happening?

Directions: PT practitioners analyze existing systems to determine the actual state of performance (what's happening). This job aid will guide the PT practitioner through the analysis process. As an individual or a group:
1. Review the eight dimensions of a compensation system.
2. For each dimension find examples within the organization you are analyzing.
3. Rank the current effectiveness of *each* example: 7 = high; 1= low.
   Note: To rank the examples you will need to determine the organizational standard for effectiveness, for example, degree to which it meets business and/or employee needs.
4. If this is a group activity, discuss the results (*Optional:* reach consensus)

Compensation System Dimension	Examples from This Organization	Rank 1-7
1. Pay for work and performance *Examples:* Hourly pay, salary, base pay, commissions, bonuses	a b c d e	
2. Pay for time not worked *Examples:* Holidays, vacation, sick days, personal business days	a b c d e	
3. Loss-of-job income continuation *Examples:* Unemployment insurance, supplemental unemployment benefits, severance pay	a b c d e	
4. Disability income continuation *Examples:* Social Security, workers' compensation, short- and long-term disability	a b c d e	
5. Deferred income *Examples:* Pension, savings, and stock plans	a b c d e	
6. Spouse/family income continuation *Examples:* Life insurance, pension plans, Social Security, workers' compensation	a b c d e	
7. Income equivalent payments (perks) *Examples:* Use of company car or credit card; paid expenses for participation in professional organization; subsidized child care services	a b c d e	
8. Health, accident, liability protection *Examples:* : Subsidized group insurance plans	a b c d e	

Based on Henderson, R.I. (2000). Compensation management in a knowledge-based world (8ᵗʰ ed.). Upper Saddle River, NJ: Prentice Hall, Inc., pp. 17–22.
ISPI © 2001. *Permission granted for unlimited duplication for noncommercial use.*

TABLE 5-8: New Prosperity Values Versus Traditional Retirement Values	
New Prosperity Values	**Traditional Retirement Values**
Seeking balance through personal ecology	Leaving the work force cold turkey
Continuous education/re-education	I know too much already
Continuous spiritual/emotional growth	I've been to church
Re-entering/restoring community neighborhood	I'm getting out of this
Chance to pursue passions	Chance to play golf
Intellectual challenges	I'm not paid to think anymore
A quest every day	Everyday is a vacation

Based on Wasik, 2000, p. 8.

retirement planning issues and ease the transition into retirement for both the employee and the organization. For example, a PT practitioner might select, design, or even facilitate the following interventions based on an up-front needs assessment and analysis:

- Provide workers with information and training programs related to "finances, housing, relocation, family relations, attitude adjustment, and legal affairs"[12]
- Use retired volunteers to speak about life after retirement and how to manage change and leisure opportunities
- Provide time to examine the realities of life after work. For example, according to reports, Polaroid permits up to six months unpaid leave for employees who wish to test their retirement adjustment concerns.[13]

PT practitioners are trained to act as catalysts for change between employer and employee. In the role of change catalyst they may help select vendors to provide group sessions on overcoming resistance to retirement, or help reduce information overload by analyzing and transforming official policies and procedures into easy-to-understand educational materials or job aids.[14] Finally, PT practitioners may use analysis and data-collection skills and their knowledge of human and organizational behavior to help HRM strategic planners explore issues such as using retirement to cut work force costs or hire "new blood" (see Job Aid 5-3).

Health and Wellness

Employee health and wellness programs are making a difference in corporate America. Organizations have discovered that employees who are physically fit generally have higher morale, positive job attitudes, productive performance episodes, lower absenteeism, and overall enjoy better health and enhanced well-being.[1]

Definition and Scope

Health and wellness programs are company-sponsored initiatives that focus on health promotion, health protection, and health prevention. The emphasis in health promotion is on lifestyle changes, while health protection puts the emphasis on prolonging life and health prevention emphasizes preventing disease. Wellness programs focus on the employee's total physical and mental condition.[2]

Employee assistance programs help employees whose on-the-job performance is suffering because of physical, social, mental, and/or emotional problems. Employee assistance programs have traditionally focused on treatment of problems; wellness focuses on prevention. Wellness programs run the gamut from simple and inexpensive initiatives, such as nutrition programs or programs to make people aware of the dangers of second-hand smoke, to comprehensive and costly efforts, such as providing employee health screening and state-of-the art, on-site physical fitness and recreation facilities.[3]

Wellness programs are investments in employees. The programs provide three distinct services:

1. Help employees identify potential health risks through health appraisals.
2. Educate employees about health risks including sedentary life style, tobacco use, improper diet, occupational/environmental exposures, fatigue, and stress.
3. Encourage employees to make life style changes through physical exercise, proper nutrition, and health monitoring.[4]

Arnold Coleman, the CEO of Healthy Outlook Worldwide, a health fitness consulting firm, states, "If I can save companies 5% to 20% a year in medical costs, they'll listen. In the end you have a well company and that's where the word 'wellness' comes from."[5]

JOB AID 5-3: Issues to Consider When Planning for Retirement

Directions: Planning for retirement includes thinking about and/or acting on many of the issues listed below. Ask potential retirees to code each issue according to the scale in the second column, and explain their responses. This will provide information on individual needs as well as work force trends. For example, John needs to examine his financial situation before he retires, or 50% of the plant's workers have not thought about retirement goals.

Issues to consider when planning retirement	Where I stand on this issue
1. Retirement goals *Comments:*	☐ 5 I have acted on this issue ☐ 4 I have thought a lot about this ☐ 3 I have given this issue some thought ☐ 2 I have not thought about this issue ☐ 1 This issue does not concern me
2. Legal affairs *Comments:*	☐ 5 I have acted on this issue ☐ 4 I have thought a lot about this ☐ 3 I have given this issue some thought ☐ 2 I have not thought about this issue ☐ 1 This issue does not concern me
3. Health and wellness *Comments:*	☐ 5 I have acted on this issue ☐ 4 I have thought a lot about this ☐ 3 I have given this issue some thought ☐ 2 I have not thought about this issue ☐ 1 This issue does not concern me
4. Financial issues *Comments:*	☐ 5 I have acted on this issue ☐ 4 I have thought a lot about this ☐ 3 I have given this issue some thought ☐ 2 I have not thought about this issue ☐ 1 This issue does not concern me
5. Retirement housing *Comments:*	☐ 5 I have acted on this issue ☐ 4 I have thought a lot about this ☐ 3 I have given this issue some thought ☐ 2 I have not thought about this issue ☐ 1 This issue does not concern me
6. Leisure activities *Comments:*	☐ 5 I have acted on this issue ☐ 4 I have thought a lot about this ☐ 3 I have given this issue some thought ☐ 2 I have not thought about this issue ☐ 1 This issue does not concern me
7. Working after retirement *Comments:*	☐ 5 I have acted on this issue ☐ 4 I have thought a lot about this ☐ 3 I have given this issue some thought ☐ 2 I have not thought about this issue ☐ 1 This issue does not concern me
8. Volunteering after retirement *Comments:*	☐ 5 I have acted on this issue ☐ 4 I have thought a lot about this ☐ 3 I have given this issue some thought ☐ 2 I have not thought about this issue ☐ 1 This issue does not concern me

Alive and Well in the Workplace

Success stories on wellness in the workplace are easy to find. Here are just a few:

- Union Pacific Railroad's wellness program helps employees lower their risk of hypertension, high cholesterol-related problems, and obesity.[6]
- For every dollar spent on employee wellness, the Adolph Coors Company receives a $6 return on investment. This is reflected in reduced sick leave and increased productivity.[7]
- General Motors Corporation in Detroit offers yoga and tai chi at its Renaissance Center. Lunchtime meditation classes are planned. An all-encompassing fitness center is on the drawing board.[8]
- Northern Telecom's wellness program includes a fitness center, weight management classes, and a variety of physical education courses. Employee cost is $10 per month. Seventy percent of the firm's employees participate.[9]
- Steelcase tests workers for all healthy behaviors from seat belt use to cholesterol and obesity. A $20 million savings is expected over 10 years.[10]
- Eli Lilly, a pharmaceutical giant, gives employees a $50 bonus for each year's participation in the wellness program. The company extends its wellness offerings with an occupational medicine component. Together they provide physical exams, mammography screening, breast health education, flu shots, and psychological counseling.[11]
- The Gale Group, Farmington Hills, Michigan, offers $250 reimbursement for wellness activities including golf leagues, acupuncture, and massage therapy services. In addition to reducing health care costs, the reimbursement is a selling point in recruiting new employees.[12]
- Marriott International, Bethesda, Maryland, was cited as one of the 10 healthiest companies for women. Fifty percent of the staff is female. Wellness programs for corporate employees include massages, blood pressure and cholesterol checks, and learning low-fat cooking.[13]

Health and wellness programs should be an integral part of the corporate culture. They are an extension of the benefits package afforded an employee and are linked to recruitment and retention issues. Successful health and wellness programs include awareness or education, support, and follow-up activities.

Implementing Health and Wellness Interventions in the Workplace

Health and wellness programs can be implemented at three different levels. Table 5-9 describes the value, function, and typical activities for each level.

Another approach to implementation is to design health and wellness programs based on the core components of worksite wellness:

- Input—Generate a constructive wellness policy with input from many voices.
- Assessment—Conduct wellness screening and health risk appraisal assessments.
- Partnering—Join with communities to establish relationships and encourage resource sharing.
- Intervention—Provide health improvement strategies.
- Follow-up—Include follow-up counseling on a regular basis.
- Programs—Organize plant-wide or organization-wide wellness initiatives and programs.
- Evaluation—Conduct ongoing evaluation of wellness programs, products, and the related reduction in employees' health risks.
- Outreach—Involve employees and employees' family members in wellness events.[14]

A wellness program is essentially an employee and organizational development program. The PT practitioner can work with HRM personnel, occupational health professionals, safety directors, management information services technicians, union representatives, and frontline employees to support employee wellness. Together, they can generate the core components of the organization's wellness program, for example:

- Conduct needs assessments to help employees and organizations become aware of personal and corporate health and fitness needs
- Design, develop, and implement program activities that meet the explicit needs of the employees
- Evaluate to determine the value and worth of the efforts.[15]

Many successful organizations begin their health and wellness programs by starting small. For example, an organization might:

- Begin at Level I (see Table 5-9) and provide basic health information and screening rather than laying the foundation for a corporate wellness center. Level I has immediate educational value.
- Involve employees in planning and implementing programs.
- Assess the health, fitness, and recreation interests of the employees through surveys.
- Schedule events around the workday and before and after work.
- Study what other companies have done to develop effective programs.
- Partner with the local hospital or health agency for opportunities.[16]

TABLE 5-9: Implementing Health and Wellness Programs at Level I, II, or III

Level	Value	Function	Typical Activities
Level I	Educational	Activities designed to educate and instruct; no direct attempt to modify behavior	• Newsletter announcements related to health and wellness activities • Posters of good health practices • Health classes • Health screening, etc.
Level II	Educational and personal	Activities designed to modify by changing or altering behavior	• Physical fitness classes • Smoking cessation programs • Nutrition counseling programs • Stress reduction programs, etc.
Level III	Educational, personal, and organizational	Activities designed to create an organizational environment that both encourages and helps employees maintain healthy, energized life styles.	• Sentara Health Care—*Health Edge Program* helps high- and low-risk employees earn financial credits toward health coverage by participating in fitness, wellness, and risk-reduction activities. • Dow Chemical—*Backs in Action Program* encourages exercise, dieting, and ergonomics. • The Senior Services of Seattle/King County, Northshore Center—*Senior Wellness Project* includes these programs: exercise, health screening, disability/fall reduction, prevention of functional limitations to reduce health care use, living with a chronic illness, and mentorship program providing follow-up calls, companionship, and links to professional staff.

Based on O'Donnell, 1986, pp. 6–9. Activities based on Archstone Foundation Award for Excellence in Program Innovation, *1999, pp. 1–2.*

Corporate culture is willing to expend monies on better health for employees, "but truly exceptional wellness programs—the kind that change lives and transform corporate cultures—are the results of clear vision, insightful analysis, careful planning and admirable execution."[17] The Wellness Councils of America help employers create exemplary health promotion programs. They identify seven critical benchmarks that separate excellent wellness programs from mediocre ones. The best programs are presented with the Gold Well Workplace Award, the Wellness Council's highest distinction. Table 5-10 lists the critical benchmarks.

The PT practitioner plays a pivotal role when evaluating wellness programs, adding the technical skills of evaluation to the expertise provided by those who are the program's subject matter experts. The following easy and low-cost strategies may be helpful in determining the merits of a wellness program:

1. Solicit feedback from participants:
   • Devise a standard feedback form that can be modified
   • Ask standardized questions that are based on the program's objectives
   • Answer these and similar questions:

   — How important was this activity in helping you make a health behavior change?
   — How did you feel about (a specific aspect of the program)?
   — Which of the following statements best reflects where you are in terms of behavior change (no need to change, thinking about change, working toward change, made the change)?

2. Conduct Surveys:
   • Ask participants about their health status; discuss risk factors
   • Survey entire population or a random sample.

3. Monitor key productivity indicators—absenteeism, turnover, etc.

4. Conduct follow-up evaluation:
   • Use survey instruments, phone interviews, observations.
   • Allow six months to one year for behavior change programs—timing is important (see Job Aid 5-4).[18]

Employee Development

The employee development process begins after the candidate has accepted the final offer and continues throughout the employee's life with the organization. It

159

TABLE 5-10: Critical Benchmarks for Health and Wellness Programs

Critical Benchmark	Description
1. Exemplary senior-level support	Benefits from the efforts of a dynamic champion: • Visionary leadership • Compelling communication patterns • Monetary resources • Ability to model healthy behaviors
2. Cohesive organizational wellness team	Capitalizes on collective intelligence of strategic players—ability to create programs that are diverse and have broad appeal
3. Data to drive the wellness initiative	Commitment to gathering and examining multiple sources of data that identify organizational and individual health issues and concerns
4. Carefully crafted operating plan	Focuses on business needs and how a proposed initiative will impact business outcomes: • Link goals and objectives to aggressive timelines • Provide detailed budgetary data and evaluation plans
5. Multiple delivery channels	Uses multiple delivery channels including personal/social counseling, Internet resources, self-study materials, and home-based options
6. Supportive and healthy environment	Organization's benefits, policies, and practices must work in tandem to support healthy behaviors and behavior change
7. Consistent evaluation of outcomes	Evaluation component is continual and ongoing: • Measures program participation, satisfaction levels, and progress in behavior change • Monitors absenteeism, turnover, morale • Calculates cost effectiveness and cost savings

Based on Hunnicutt, 2000, pp. 36–40.

takes time for employees to adjust to their new jobs and their new organizations. It takes even more time for them to be productive. HRM plays a crucial role in shaping new employees so they can be fully productive within a short time. Employee development includes four related areas: employee training, employee development, career development, and organization development.[1] Table 5-11 provides an overview of employee development components, purpose, focus, and interventions.

Employee development and career development are employee centered. Employee training promotes competency on the job; and organization development is geared to system-wide changes. This section focuses on employee development.

Definition and Scope

Employee development "involves acquiring knowledge, skills, and attitudes [through] employer-sponsored learning opportunities, including (1) traditional instruction, (2) newer technology-oriented formats, (3) informally by means of mentoring, coaching, or on-the-job training, and (4) by team participation."[2] Employee training and employee development are similar in the methods used to

influence learning; however, their time frames differ. Employee training focuses on current job skills, employee development, on future job opportunities in the organization. The outcome of helping employees learn is the same for both.[3]

Employee development is more concerned with education than with job-specific training. The focus is on understanding and interpreting knowledge and on the employee's personal growth. A caveat worth remembering is that all employees, regardless of their position in the organization, can be developed.[4]

Although it is critical for individuals to be trained in specific skills related to managing—like planning, organizing, leading, controlling, and decision making—time has taught us that these skills are needed by nonmanagerial employees as well. The use of work teams, reductions in supervisory roles, allowing workers to participate in setting the goals of their jobs, and a greater emphasis on quality and customers have changed the way developing employees is viewed...[5]

There are a variety of employee development interventions available. Table 5-12 lists three on-the-job

TABLE 5-11: Employee Development Overview

Components	Focus and Purpose	Interventions
Employee Training	• Focus on skills and knowledge • Introduce new employees to the organization • Help employees acquire, maintain, or improve current job skills	• Employee orientation • Just-in-time training • On-the-job training • Coaching and mentoring • Job aids
Employee Development	• Focus on education • Plan for future business needs • Enhance employee's ability to understand and interpret knowledge	• Orientation handbook • Traditional or technology-based instruction • Corporate university • Job rotation • Team/committee assignments • Seminars • Simulations • Experiential learning (survival training, etc.)
Career Development	• Focus on long-term career effectiveness and success • Assist employees in advancing their work lives • Provide information and assessment to realize career goals	• Challenging job assignments (job rotation/enrichment) • Career counseling • Career workshops • Career pathing • Continuing education and training • Professional associations
Organization Development	• Focus on system-wide organizational changes • Change attitudes and values of employees • Help employees adapt to change (unfreeze status quo, change, refreeze)	• Feedback activities (surveys, etc.) • Team building activities • Third-party interventions (change management, conflict resolution, etc.)

Based on DeCenzo and Robbins, 1999, pp. 13–14, 218–270; Van Tiem, Moseley, and Dessinger, 2000, pp. 138–144, 208.

TABLE 5-12: Selected Employee Development Interventions: On and Off the Job

On-the-Job Interventions	Off-the-Job Interventions
Job Rotation • Moving employees in an organization to expand knowledge, skills, abilities • Broadening exposure to operations • Reducing boredom and stimulating new ideas • Turning a specialist into a generalist **Assistant-to Positions** • Apprenticeship programs • Working under a seasoned and experienced person in different areas **Committee Assignment** • Sharing in decision making • Learning by watching others • Investigating specific organizational problems	**Courses and seminars** • Acquiring knowledge and developing conceptual and analytical abilities • Interactive technologies • Distance learning • Telecommunications • Satellite conferencing **Simulations** • Training on actual work experiences • Case studies • Decision games • Role plays **Outdoor Training** (white-water rafting, mountain climbing, surviving a week in the wilderness, etc.) • Experiential learning • Working together • Gelling as a team • Reacting to difficulties

Based on DeCenzo and Robbins, 1999, pp. 234–236; Schermerhorn, Hunt, and Osborn, 2000, pp. 132–133.

interventions and three off-the-job interventions for employee development.

Implementing Employee Development Interventions in the Workplace

Employee development is the responsibility of both the employer and the employee. In order to remain competitive, organizations are promoting the integration of learning and working; for example, many organizations "promote continuous learning by crafting a learning organization."[6] Such organizations are skilled at five main activities:

1. Systematic problem solving
2. Experimentation with new approaches
3. Learning from the experiences of others
4. Learning from best practices
5. Transferring knowledge quickly and efficiently throughout the organization.[7]

Another employer approach to employee development is aligning training and employee development with business strategy through a department structure known as a corporate university.[8] Corporate universities provide state-of-the-art learning environments for their employees and for members of their customer chain.[9]

Employees can select a variety of options to support their own development in the workplace. Some examples follow.

- Join a professional organization that supports work efforts—a pivotal way to influence the profession and to network with colleagues
- Read books, periodicals, and journals—an excellent means of keeping current in one's field
- Attend conferences, workshops and seminars— helps to keep employees current and broadens their perspective.

At times, organizations may sponsor some or all of the activities listed above and may even offer continuing education credits or tuition.[10] When organizations fail to provide development programs, employees need to take responsibility. Failure to do so may render the employee obsolete. Here are some self-development suggestions that employees may find useful:

- Create a personal mission statement. Indicate a business goal and the role that leads to that goal. Remain flexible and fluid—think outside the box.
- Assume responsibility for personal direction and growth. Do not rely entirely on the organization in terms of career paths. Positions and departments can be eliminated.
- Choose enhancement over advancement. With right sizing, mergers, acquisitions, and joint ventures a reality, there are fewer opportunities for advancement. Broadening or enhancing skills in the short run often leads to advancement in the long run.

- Interview people in the positions that reflect personal career goals and seek suggestions on how to proceed. Gain valuable insight from experiences and networking.
- Set realistic goals. Personal goals should be both reasonable and achievable. Evaluate the goals quarterly.
- Make self-investment a priority. Self-investment is a personal responsibility that requires commitment and action.[11]

The PT practitioner can help HRM plan and design self-development support programs, orientation programs and materials, personal growth and development plans, or employee development programs that will meet the needs of the organization and the employees to continually change, grow, and improve (see Job Aid 5-5).

Case Study 5-1: Employee Development at Opus One Restaurant

Situation

Opus One is a privately owned fine dining establishment. It was opened in Detroit in 1987 by a highly skilled restaurateur and a new management team. The owners methodically assessed the Detroit business climate, expressway traffic patterns, and competition prior to concept development and opening. The restaurant, kitchen, loading dock, and parking designs were driven by the restaurant's conceptual framework. Hands-on wait staff orientation was immediately institutionalized as a key element in the restaurant's management.

The expanded range of services, which includes turnkey event planning, combined with increasingly sophisticated customers has dictated the need for more targeted staff training. In order to earn and retain Opus' present Five Star status, its owners focus on exceeding customer expectations for fine dining experiences. They are known to their staff for articulating the values/philosophy, "We are only as good as the last meal we served."

Intervention

The owners of this restaurant clearly identified standards of excellence required to build and expand their high-end customer base. These standards were initially translated to consistent orientation and new-hire training. Increasing demands by customers and staff turnover in a very competitive market made it evident that:

- Strong staff-selection methods were critical
- Ongoing training was imperative to continuously maintain and exceed standards of service
- Performance and conditions of employment had to be clearly linked in order for training to be effective.

JOB AID 5-4: Wellness Level Reality Check

Directions: The first step in developing a wellness program is to conduct a gap analysis,* and the first step in a gap analysis is to find out what is going on in the organization right now.

1. Review Table 5-9: Implementing Health and Wellness Programs at Level I, II, or III.
2. Review existing documents and record the information on the form below.
3. Use the form as a guide for interviews, discussions, focus groups, surveys, etc.
4. Adapt the form to help you discover the desired state for each level of wellness and the gaps that exist at each level between the actual and desired state.
5. Then you will be ready to begin a cause analysis!

Level I: Educational Value
Is the organization currently trying to educate employees about health and wellness issues? If yes, what educational activities are in place to accomplish this?

Level II: Educational and Personal Value
Is the organization currently trying to change or alter wellness-related behavior? If yes, what activities are in place to accomplish this?

Level III: Educational, Personal, and Organizational Value
Is the organization trying to create an organizational environment that both encourages and helps employees maintain healthy and energized lifestyles? If yes, what activities are in place to accomplish this?

For more information on gap and cause analyses see Van Tiem, D., Moseley, J.L., and Dessinger, J.C. (2000). Fundamentals of performance technology: A guide to improving people, process, and performance. Silver Spring, MD: International Society for Performance Improvement. pp. 38–41; 46–50.
Based on O'Donnell, M.P. (1986). Definition of health promotion: Part II—Levels of programs. American Journal of Health Promotion, 1 (2), 6–9.
ISPI © 2001. Permission granted for unlimited duplication for noncommercial use.

In 1996, obligatory continuous education was developed and implemented for Opus One wait staff. As a condition of employment, the following multi-pronged program was instituted.

During the interview process:
- A pre-employment test is administered. This written test includes key foundational business elements associated with food, beverage, and customer service requirements.
- If the applicant scores 70% or above, he or she is interviewed for employment. If he or she is hired, it is for a probationary period based on the specific, measurable criteria listed below.

During the probation period training:
- A formal orientation is completed
- The new hire is teamed with an exemplary performer as a support server who models appropriate behaviors. At no time during this period is the new hire given final responsibility for meeting customer needs.
- Attendance and mastery of four targeted training sessions are required. Each class spans six weeks (one session per week).

During full tenure of employment:
- Attendance and mastery of regularly scheduled targeted training sessions are required
- Training includes both lecture and hands-on elements
- Sessions include in-depth training on specific foods and food preparations, menu preparation and tastings; wine service, history, tastings; distilled spirits and beer history and tastings. Team expectations, market trends and restaurant marketing programs, Opus One's history and the history of its building are also key components of training sessions. Sales techniques are included in all food and beverage training.
- 85% demonstrable mastery of content is a condition of employment. If this criterion is not met, employment is terminated.
- No opportunities are given to retest for mastery, unless 50% of the class fails. In this case, Opus' management assumes responsibility for ineffective delivery and repeats the session for wait staff.

Results

During Opus One's 12 years of operation, it has maintained wait staff turnover at a level of 30%. This is well below the industry standard of 180%. The clearly identified requirement for excellence and mastery separates those individuals. It has been recognized consistently by both local and national sources as a Five Star establishment for both food and service. Awards received include repeated receipt of the *Wine Spectator* Award,

The DiRona Award, La Chaine des Rotisseurs Award for Excellence, State of Michigan Recognition for Excellence, Detroit Restaurant of the Year, *Gourmet* Magazine's Award for Top Restaurant for Business Dining in Michigan, and inclusion in *The Zagat Guide*.

Carefully calculated expansion of services includes one-stop dinner theatre packages (accompanied by shuttle services), FAX Food lunches, extensive off-site turnkey event planning/catering, Frequent Customer Programs, and Opus Money promotions, to name a few. These services are run by staff who are required to adhere to the restaurant's underlying standards of excellence and who are continuously trained and tested for mastery.

Lessons Learned

Several staffing and training lessons learned during 12 years of operation focus on how to implement training effectively and continuously:
- Link training directly to business goals
- Stress hands-on training
- Make training objectives quantifiable
- Ensure that training content is clearly mastered
- Build training into the fiber of the organization as a condition of employment

This case study was written by Maria Kokas, MS, EdS, and James Kokas, BA, owners of Opus One. Used with permission.

TABLE 5-13: Seven Principles of Employee Recognition— "Encouraging the Heart"

Set clear standards

Expect the best

Pay attention

Personalize recognition

Tell the story

Celebrate together

Set the example

Based on Kouzes and Posner, 1999.

INDIVIDUAL GROWTH

Organizations encourage the development of individual employees to provide a fulfilling work environment and also to maintain a competitive work force. Individual growth can be fostered by a number of interventions. This section discusses motivation, performance appraisals, competency testing and assessment centers, and literacy as key interventions for encouraging and promoting employee growth (see Table 5-13). It is essential that employees stay energized, enthusiastic, and committed to job excellence and career enhancement. Individuals are responsible for their own competitiveness and productivity. Individual growth relies on motivation based on feedback from performance appraisals, and is often supported by findings of assessment centers. Universal minimum literacy standards may be based on ASTD/Department of Labor studies[1,2] and other international organizations.

Motivation

Definition and Scope

"Motivation is the fuel for performance. Without motivation, performance suffers."[1] Motivation is the human energy to grow, to change, to survive, to advance, or to act in a certain manner or to do something.

People are motivated differently. Humans are complex creatures with a variety of needs. Studies by theorists such as Maslow, Herzberg, Vroom, and McClelland indicate that in addition to physical needs such as water, food, shelter, and air, humans also have emotional and psychological needs, such as wanting to achieve and be accepted by others. In addition, people are motivated differently at different times depending on desires, the situation, culture, and the possibility of attainment.[2,3]

Self-perception has a great impact on motivation. Three elements of self-perception (traits, competencies, and values) are inter-related. They energize, direct, and sustain organizational and individual behavior.[4] *Traits* are permanent patterns of behavior that define the essential character of individuals, such as dependable, conservative, ambitious, or lazy. *Competencies* are the skills, abilities, talents, and knowledge possessed by the individual. *Values* are the "concepts and beliefs about desirable end states or behaviors that transcend specific situations, guide

selections, or evaluation of behavior and events, and are ordered by relative importance."[5]

Kouzes and Posner, best-selling authors and management experts, contend that most people think that money is the ultimate motivator.[6] In truth, being appreciated is far more compelling. Building self-confidence is essential to positively influencing high performance in others. The phrase "encouraging the heart" motivates by building self-confidence through setting high expectations, linking rewards and performance, using a variety of rewards, making people feel like heroes, and allowing employees to do their best (see Table 5-13). Appreciation mobilizes people to excel.

Work can be very meaningful because it enables humans to accomplish goals, receive financial remuneration, permits social interaction, and influences social status.[7] As an intervention, managers, team leaders, or coaches need to determine how to motivate others to achieve desired performance.[8] Knowing employees or team members well is an important first step. This can be achieved by establishing a shared vision, communicating frequently and openly, and maintaining a positive work environment.[9] Motivation is not management's sole responsibility. It is essential for employees to share responsibility for motivation and realize the powers within themselves through self-motivation.[10]

Examples of work motivators include:
- Recognizing employees as useful and valuable contributors
- Promoting constructive social relationships
- Designing creative and challenging jobs
- Providing appropriate resources to perform the job
- Involving employees in organizational decision making processes
- Providing supportive leadership, management, and supervision.

Rewards

Rewards can be powerful motivators and significant interventions for improving employee performance and satisfaction. Rewards may be as simple as a weekly allowance for a child who completes chores or as complex as the pay, promotion, and fringe-benefit programs

TABLE 5-14: Motivational Significance	
Factor	**Effectiveness**
Availability	Rewards must be available as well as desired.
Timeliness	Separating the reward from the intended performance reduces motivational impact.
Performance contingency	Rewards should be linked to performance.
Durability	Intrinsic rewards, such as pride and job satisfaction, tend to last longer than extrinsic rewards, such as a pay increase or bonus.
Equity	Rewards must be perceived as fair and equal to what others receive for the same performance.

Based on Cummings and Worley, 1993.

associated with businesses. However simple or complex the reward is, it will only be effective in motivating improvement if goals and expectations are realistic, if individuals understand what is expected of them, and if they have the necessary skills and resources to be successful.[11] The ability of a reward to motivate performance depends on several factors covered in Table 5-14.

The fact that individuals often perceive something secret about a reward or how it is administered can nullify the meaning of the reward and decrease the intended value. Ideally, potential recipients should be included in designing the reward process. Realistically, this is not always possible. However, communication during the development process can help alleviate claims of secrecy and have a positive impact on motivation.

Incentives

Incentives are rewards that are linked directly to a job or task. Examples of incentives include sales commissions, bonuses, and profit-sharing programs. Incentives are effective motivators because they reinforce organizational goals by linking performance to the bottom line of an organization. Although they can increase productivity and lower production costs, organizations must ensure that the incentives do not sacrifice long-term organizational goals while attempting to meet short-term objectives.[12]

Implementing Motivational Incentive Interventions in the Workplace

PT practitioners are well suited to implement reward initiatives, such as building self-confidence. Often, more complex incentives are integrated into pay systems. HR compensation experts should be part of developing individual and group incentive plans (see Compensation section in this chapter). It can be difficult to maintain a fair incentive system because of differences in labor

markets and organizational needs related to various jobs, even within the same organization.[13] Based on desired results, compensation plans can include many factors, such as:

- Pay for performance (individual)
- Pay for knowledge (individual)
- Gain-sharing (Cost-Savings) plans (group)
- Profit-sharing plans (group)

Pay for Performance

Productivity is a typical measure used in pay-for-performance plans. For example, sales commissions reward accounts or goods sold. If the sales person does not make a sale, there is no payment for the effort. Workers who make goods such as clothing, or workers who engage in finite labor, such as plumbers installing sinks and toilets, farm workers picking a quantity of crops, or automotive mechanics repairing engines, can be paid on a work-completed basis. Automotive repair manuals define the typical amount of time needed to repair a transmission or replace brakes. Automotive technicians are paid the typical amount. If the job goes well, the technicians may finish early. If they run into trouble, the job may take longer than expected. In either case, the technicians' compensation is the same.

It is not unusual for sales incentives to be based on cash or items of value ("buck 'em with bucks") approach. However, Sanchez cautions that sales incentives can become disincentives when the incentive structure changes.[14] Sales incentive plans should also have "trophy value." In other words, they should have high visibility and extensive promotion. Quick personal notes of encouragement and congratulations reinforce the motivational value. Newsletter coverage and personal attention individualize their advantage. In short, although sales incentives frequently rely on tangibles, they are reinforced by intangible appreciation and personalized gestures.

Pay for Knowledge

The impetus for pay for knowledge is the need for workers with specialized skills and for a more flexible work force. Although acquiring certificates, licenses, or degrees does not guarantee workmanship or application of skills, it does represent accomplishment of minimum standards of knowledge and/or skills. In addition, they are helpful in legal cases in which it is prudent to verify that employees have a particular skill or knowledge.

According to the *Wall Street Journal,* approximately five percent to eight percent of companies in the United States use pay for knowledge.[15] Maintenance and skilled trades are often paid based on completion of apprenticeships and other skill-development programs. Information technology workers can be paid based on programming knowledge, network or systems skills, or problem solving abilities as measured through external testing and certification programs. In addition, teachers are frequently paid for degree completion and medical/allied health personnel are paid for completion of licensing tests and board certifications.

Competency- or skill-based pay systems are challenging to establish because it is difficult to arrive at consensus regarding definitions of competencies, methods of linking competencies to pay, employee populations to be covered, and the objectives for linking competencies to pay.[16]

Profit-Sharing Plans

Group incentives are an opportunity to demonstrate appreciation for employees' contributions to the organization.[17] Profit sharing focuses on profitability as a method of determining funds to be shared. The money can be distributed immediately or deferred until retirement or death. Profit sharing plans are simple to understand and are usually based on one of three performance measures:

- *Operating Margin* (total sales and revenues less total costs and expenses divided by total sales and revenues—example: American Airlines)
- *Operating Return on Assets* (operating income divided by average total assets—example: General Motors)
- *Earnings per Share* (income available to common stockholders divided by average number of common shares outstanding—example: Winn Dixie stores).[18]

JOB AID 5-5: Employee Development: Who Is Responsible for Success?

This instrument has multiple uses:
1. Identify current employee development activities; identify who is responsible for the success of each activity—the organization or the individual employee—and explain your perception of the current situation.
2. Identify current activities and who is responsible, and explain why you *agree* or *disagree* with the current situation.
3. Identify potential employee development activities, suggest who *should be* responsible for success, and justify the suggestions.

Directions: List the current employee development activities and assign responsibility by checking ORG for organization or IND for individual employee. Use the *Why?* column to explain your perception of the current situation, agree or disagree with the current situation, or justify suggestions for future employee development interventions.

Employee Development Activity	Responsible?		Why?
	ORG	IND	

JOB AID 5-6: Ranking Workplace Motivators

Create and retain a synergistic mind-set and employee enthusiasm by adopting and enhancing several of these powerful motivators. Rate your organization relative to motivators.

Directions: Review the motivational description. For each description:
1. Indicate how the motivator is manifested in your organization by citing a concrete example.
2. Rank the importance of the motivator in your organization (7 is high; 1 is low). Discuss your ranking with other team or workgroup members.

Motivator	Description	Example and Rank
Economic Rewards	Money is an important motivator. Compensation can be augmented by special achievement incentives, spot bonuses, and cash-equivalent rewards.	
Promotions	Social and psychological meaning (recognition and sense of accomplishment) outweighs additional money and perquisites.	
Formal Psychic Rewards	High-visibility recognition and other rewards of social significance are remembered for years.	
Informal Psychic Rewards	Positive feedback from managers, peers, and others has a profound impact on motivation. It makes people feel appreciated for what they do and who they are, and for their unique abilities, skills, and knowledge.	
Opportunity to Grow	Organizations form a win-win partnership with employees to maintain a talented work force.	
Leadership	By presenting a clear purpose, a vision worth striving for, and providing encouragement, leaders imbue people with hope, enthusiasm, and determination.	
Goals	Goals energize people, inspire exceptional effort, provide a clear sense of what is expected, and offer challenge.	
Challenging and Stimulating Work	The nature of work as a source of motivation varies with personality. The work is as important a motivator as money.	
Autonomy	Freedom to act, to make decisions, to work independently, is most valued by people. It is crucial to self-worth, strongly influences the decision of people to join and stay with an organization.	
Fun	Many workplaces are woefully devoid of smiles and laughter, yet humor brightens the day and infuses spirit into the culture.	

Based on Stern, G., and Borcia, Y. (2000, June) Motivation strategy, Executive Excellence, 17, 6, 18–20.
ISPI © 2001. Permission granted for unlimited duplication for noncommercial use.

JOB AID 5-7: How Motivating Is Your Organization?

Directions: Use this job aid to identify ways your organization motivates employees. Check (+) if motivation occurs and check (−) if improvement is needed.

+	−	Rules and Regulations
		The organization has clearly defined vision, mission, goals, and objectives.
		Performance criteria are clearly defined and communicated to all employees.
		Resources are provided to help employees attain their goals and objectives.
		Rewards and recognition are a part of the culture.
		A support network is in place so employees know where to go for assistance when needed.
		Whenever possible, the organization takes advantage of employee expertise by including them in meetings, discussions, and other fact-finding initiatives.
		Timely information sharing, including lessons learned, occurs at all levels of the organization.
		Communication is open and encouraged.
		The organization has a conflict resolution model available to all employees.
		The organization celebrates the successes of its team and employees.
		The organization supports personal growth with training opportunities and tuition reimbursement.

Gain-Sharing (Cost-Savings) Plans

Group plans encourage employees to work together to accomplish goals and are usually based on net profits or cost savings. Gain-sharing allows for targeting rewards to encourage selected behaviors and to share the value of the improvements. These plans begin by establishing current productivity standards and methods of measurement. Then formulas are created to determine sharing splits between management, workers, and stockholders. To be effective, plans must be perceived as fair by all parties, and they need to be easy to administer (see Job Aids 5-6 and 5-7).

Performance Appraisals

Definition and Scope

Performance appraisal is an important intervention linking goal setting and rewards. The purpose of a performance appraisal is to provide feedback on an individual's performance in order to encourage improvement. Many individuals would probably indicate that they have had a negative experience with the performance appraisal process. In fact, 90% of performance appraisal systems are judged ineffective.[1] This can be attributed to the fact that the majority of people view performance appraisals as subjective and lacking validity.[2]

Behavioral Anchored Scales

One effective way to reduce dissatisfaction is to use behavioral descriptors for ratings. Specific behaviors (desirable and undesirable) are used as descriptors for both extremes of the scale. This approach clarifies expectations and provides specifics for self-measurement and action planning throughout the year. It is also viewed as more objective.[3]

Benefits of Appraisals

Organizations continue to rely on performance appraisals to provide formal, documented feedback to individuals. Usually, they are also the basis of annual compensation changes. Table 5-15 illustrates their value to employees and to organizations.

TABLE 5-15: Benefits of Performance Appraisals

Individuals	Organizations
Focuses on goals, not personality	Provides legal documentation
Recognizes employee contributions	Assists in decisions regarding promotability, staffing, compensation, and training
Identifies educational and developmental needs	Fosters feedback and dialogue between manager and employee
Supports career planning process	Often initiates coaching
Basis of compensation determination	Creates need for face-to-face discussion

Based on Nelson, 2000, pp. 39–42.

Performance Improvement

It is essential to plan for performance improvement for each employee as part of the performance appraisal process. There is no one formula for every department, no one approach for all. There should be a clear connection between the organizational core needs and each individual's values and interests. Ideally, improvement plans tap into the individual's unique passions and career goals.

Organizations can take several steps to capitalize on employee assets:
- Encourage mobility by assuming new job assignments
- Provide employees with honest, objective feedback
- Inspire individuals to explore and try new ideas
- Share key information
- Support a mentoring program
- Supply relevant, cost-effective career development opportunities
- Ensure that understanding cultural differences is an integral part of organizational activities.[4]

Performance Management

Some organizations use performance appraisals for other human resources purposes, such as staffing and turnover planning, compensation, or career development. All organizations using performance appraisals create the process to document objectives for each employee and to provide feedback regarding success in meeting the objectives. Because the process is defined, structured, and ubiquitous, organizations may use the appraisal process to assist in compensation, staffing, career development, and other decisions.[5]

Priscilla King, human resources director for information systems and services at General Motors, distinguishes between two types of organizations. Traditional organizations believe that people adapt to the organization. They may plan for a 10% turnover annually in order to bring in new ideas. In that case, the employee is often on her or his own for personal development. King points to General Motors as an example of a proactive human resource department that is committed to getting the best

performance out of employees. HR, management, and employees work together to encourage talent; however, the ultimate responsibility for development is the individual employee.[6]

American Productivity and Quality Center (APQC) and Linkage studied "best practice" in performance appraisals. They noted that companies have found rigorous assessment of talent can lead to cutting out people who do not add sufficient value to the intellectual capital.[7] APQC is a well-respected organization that has helped companies make impressive improvements in quality and productivity. APQC suggests using performance management to transform an organization from a "best-effort" culture into a tough-minded, results-driven one. The organization asserts "that performance appraisal is the best tool available for muscle-building an organization."[8]

> *Organizations with world-class performance-management systems do things that the also-rans don't. They insist that all managers maintain consistent, demanding standards for everyone—and they keep raising those standards.*[9]

APQC and Linkage developed best practice guidelines for performance management (see Table 5-16).

Legal Issues

Although there are no laws directly connected with performance appraisals, the Civil Rights Act of 1964 is the basis for many legal actions regarding the treatment of protected groups. Performance appraisals, often considered subjective supervisory ratings that are the basis of personnel decisions, can be used in these cases.[10] It is critical that validity be established before initiating a performance appraisal process and continuously tracked after implementation. The performance measures should be clearly observable and job related. Ratings should be specific, not vague.

Performance appraisal systems need to be checked to ensure that they are not biased against a *protected group* (such as race, ethnic background, gender, sexual orientation,

TABLE 5-16: APQC/Linkage Best Practice Guidelines for Performance Management

Get Tough	Leadership Darwinism—Find the best; cull the rest. Weed out using a succeed-or-get-out process.
Cut to the Core	Determine attributes necessary to the core of the organization's success, such as accountability, customer focus, results orientation, and ethics/integrity.
Seek Mastery	Create descriptive–narrative portraits of desired behavior. Compare actual behavior to desired.
Check for Frequency	Determine how frequently the employee behaved like a "master."
Realize That Objectivity Is a Myth	Recognize that it is impossible to keep emotion and personal prejudices out of the process. Tolerate complexity.

Based on Grote, 2000, pp. 14–20.

or age). It is not necessary to intend to discriminate. However, the results or outcomes should not differentiate, such as for promotion, transfer, or dismissal, in a way that causes a disproportionate situation relative to a protected group. Disproportionate numbers can be considered *prima facie* evidence of discrimination.

Implementing Performance Appraisal Interventions in the Workplace

PT practitioners play vital roles, creating the performance appraisal process, tracking annual feedback meetings, and coaching managers regarding follow-up to improvement plans. PT practitioners can manage an intervention project from drafting behavior-oriented descriptors and rating scales to developing feedback forms and tracking systems. It is essential to ensure that managers have coaching and feedback skills and that the process ensures follow-up. These activities are aligned with the HPT model. However, when planning the compensation or staffing aspects of performance appraisals, PT practitioners need to team up with experts in the appropriate HR fields.

Designing an Appraisal System
When designing or redesigning an appraisal process, it is necessary to be mindful of common concerns:
- Managers can't assess employees' performance accurately
- Formal evaluations demotivate more than they motivate
- Reviews don't improve a company's performance.[11]

These concerns may be due to poor design of the performance appraisal process, failure to communicate the process, inconsistency in delivery, and unwillingness by supervisors to confront poor performance. When designing or changing a performance appraisal process, ensure that these factors are properly addressed by taking the following steps.

1. Involve the right people to guarantee all organizational and strategic issues are addressed.

2. Diagnose the current appraisal situation. When changing a performance appraisal process, examine the strengths and weaknesses of the existing process.
3. Define the purpose and objectives of the new process.
4. Design the process, including who will give appraisals, how performance will be measured, and how often feedback will be provided.
5. Pilot the process to diagnose flaws before organization-wide launch.
6. Evaluate and monitor the process.[12]

Evaluating Performance Appraisal Processes
It is important to evaluate the effectiveness of performance appraisal systems. Ted Farris, University of North Texas, recommends the following criteria in Table 5-17.

Interactive Appraisal Meetings
The performance appraisal meeting is an opportunity for a manager and employee to set goals and objectives for the next year. Managers should carefully prepare for performance appraisal meetings. The basis for the meeting is the job description, which explains what the individual is expected to do and the skills required. In addition, managers should solicit comments from others in the organization. Employees should complete a self-evaluation. Managers should particularly look for personal improvement indicators and accomplishments toward career goals. It is important to recognize where the individual has improved and where more improvement may be required.[13]

Although it is impossible to predict actual questions that may come up during the appraisal meeting, it is good practice to anticipate possible questions and be prepared to provide answers or direction. When setting goals and objectives for the next year, review the employee's career path to determine what objectives are appropriate and what resources are available to help the employee meet the objectives. Plan a follow-up meeting in two or three months to evaluate progress (see Job Aid 5-8).[14]

TABLE 5-17: Criteria for Evaluating Effectiveness of Performance Appraisal Processes

Validity	Does the measure track true customer requirements or real productivity?
Coverage	Does it track all relevant factors?
Comparability	Can it be compared across time or in different locations?
Completeness	Does it track all important sources that yield an output?
Usefulness	Does it guide action?
Cost-effectiveness	Are the tradeoffs between the cost of measurement and the potential benefits acceptable?

Taken from HR Focus, 2000, p. 7.

JOB AID 5-8: Performance Appraisal System Checklist

Directions: Creating and maintaining performance appraisal systems require vigilance, careful development, and continuous evaluation to ensure integrity. Performance appraisal systems need to cover the following categories. Use the job aid as a checklist to determine whether the necessary factors have been considered.

Research and Strategy
- ☐ Benchmarking studies determined *best practices* and analyzed key characteristics.
- ☐ Performance appraisal system based on research.
- ☐ Validity studies had sufficient rigor.
- ☐ Legal aspects thoroughly checked; disproportionate impact studies are sufficient and ongoing.
- ☐ Aligned with organization goals and core competencies.

Support and Design/Development Participation
- ☐ Top management supports process.
- ☐ All levels of workers were involved in process design and development.
- ☐ Employee participation also involved broad representation of job classifications and departments.

Preparation
- ☐ Managers trained to be reliable raters.
- ☐ Employees trained to receive feedback and in career self-management.
- ☐ Monitoring system is robust.
- ☐ Continuous improvement and redesign process in place.

Performance Appraisal Characteristics
- ☐ Provides sufficient honest, helpful, and constructive feedback.
- ☐ Encourages employee development.
- ☐ Consistent among and between departments and units.
- ☐ Incorporates best practice.
- ☐ Sufficient consequences for reluctant users.
- ☐ Adequate reward for conscientious users.

Based on Berke (1990). How to conduct a performance appraisal. ASTD Info-Line, Issue 9005. Alexandria, VA: American Society for Training and Development. ISPI © 2001. Permission granted for unlimited duplication for noncommercial use.

Competency Testing and Assessment Centers

Definition and Scope

Accurately determining the skills, knowledge, and abilities of employees can be critical. Regulated industries, such as hospitals, pharmaceutical producers, or power plants, need to ensure that their employees are prepared and capable to handle their assignments. Organizations, in general, use testing to determine readiness for new assignments or to confirm knowledge of machine operation or software and network systems. Testing should be carefully constructed and planned for so that employees are treated fairly.

Competency Testing

Competency tests provide direct evidence of an individual's ability and skill to perform a job. The activities in a competency test are representative of the job tasks and equipment that are actually part of the job. Two types of tests, referred to as work samples, are used in competency testing. The first, the verbal work sample, is used to determine the competency of candidates seeking positions as managers or customer service representatives. The second and most commonly used test is the motor work sample. It is used to determine the competency of candidates for skilled trade and clerical positions. Blueprint reading is an example of a motor work sample.

To ensure validity, it is critical that the appropriate job tasks are selected and properly ordered for the work sample. Organizations must carefully consider the time allowed for completion of the task, the directions provided, and the administrative plan that accompanies the work sample.

Standardized competency testing has its limitations. Today's jobs are complex, making it difficult to define specific job-related tasks. In addition, descriptions of the skills and knowledge may differ from one organization to another. Cost is also a factor in competency testing. Custom testing involves the purchase of equipment and materials, job analysis to identify representative job tasks, development of test instructions, and the time required for staff and facilities, which add substantial costs to the overall process.[1]

Assessment Centers

As an intervention, "an assessment center is a tool for making personnel decisions, including selection, promotion, transfer, or career development."[2] Assessment centers are used to evaluate individuals in terms of the knowledge, skills, and abilities relevant to organizational effectiveness. When used for job selection, the goal is to identify individuals who demonstrate the behaviors necessary to perform the dimensions of a specific job.

When used for career development, emphasis is on determining what the individual does well and where improvement is required. Candidates complete the assessment center in multiples.[3]

Assessment centers are based on simulation technology. According to Jaffee, Frank, and Mulligan, the US Office of Strategic Services began using simulations for evaluation purposes during World War II.[4] In 1958, Michigan Bell Telephone established the first operational assessment center for selecting first-line supervisors. In the 1960s, IBM, General Electric, Standard Oil of Ohio, and agencies of government established centers. By the 1990s, more than 2,000 organizations used assessment centers.

Assessment centers use a structured approach to ensure credibility, fairness, and consistency. Assessment center development begins with a job analysis to identify the activities or dimensions of a specific job for which behaviors can be measured with situational exercises or tests. Among the job-related behaviors frequently measured are adaptability, oral communication, decisiveness, stress tolerance, and tenacity. Exercises vary depending on the job for which a candidate is being assessed. Examples of situational exercises include:

- Interview simulations—One-on-one role plays between candidates
- Oral presentations—Short extemporaneous speech on a subject provided by the administrator (tests candidates' ability to think quickly on their feet)
- Leaderless group discussions—Candidates discuss an assigned topic and prepare a written report (tests leadership and team skills)
- Assigned-leader group discussion—Leader and task assigned. Candidates rotate leader during the exercise (tests leadership and management skills).[5]

Implementing Assessment Centers in the Workplace

PT practitioners can play many roles in establishing and maintaining assessment centers. However, if they are not qualified in psychometrics, a psychologist should be involved to ensure that measurements, decisions, and feedback are valid and reliable. PT practitioners possess strengths in job analysis, writing objectives, describing behaviors, and developing assessment activities. They are also good at program and individual evaluation and can ensure that the objectives of the center are met.

Establishing an Assessment Center

It is essential to design the center carefully due to the complexity of the context, the need for valid and reliable measures that are legally defensible, and the accuracy necessary to make personnel decisions based on simulations and tests. Table 5-18 documents the steps in designing centers.

TABLE 5-18: Designing an Assessment Center

Determine core/critical functions	Understand culture and customer expectations. It is critical that the center is organization specific, not generic.
Review and update job descriptions	Take a rational and reflective look to determine if updating is needed.
Conduct job analysis	Note differences between job descriptions and actual behaviors; eliminate differences.
Meet with representative candidates	Determine current skills and gap areas.
Develop assessment activities	Design simulations and exercises. Create a mix of activities that measure objectives.
Identify psychological tests	Use generic psychometric tests to supplement activities and validate findings. They serve as "non-prejudiced" indicators.
Evaluate performance	Prepare assessors to evaluate activities consistently and to rate participants against clearly defined standards.
Rank candidates	Determine weights for each assessment to rank candidates based on organizational priorities.
Compile narrative report	Determine reporting structure to candidates and to management.
Debrief candidates	Design method to inform candidates of strengths and weaknesses and to mutually determine a developmental program.
Pilot and revise process	Based on first set of candidates, determine and implement improvements.
Establish system for tracking results	Maintain records comparing results with career progress to ensure validity and reliability.

Based on Cosner and Baumgart, 2000, pp. 1–5; Wilson, 1999, pp. 10–12.

Assessors

The certified assessors who conduct the assessment center exercises and activities are usually managers within the organization. They must be a minimum of one level above the position candidates are testing for and must be familiar with the job. Assessor training is critical because although managers may be knowledgeable about job behaviors, they may not be skilled at observing and recording the behaviors.[6]

Half as many assessors as candidates are typically involved in the center. Their responsibility is to observe and evaluate candidate behaviors as they complete the simulation exercises. At the conclusion of the assessment, the assessors meet to discuss their observations, come to a consensus, and develop an overall rating for each candidate.

Validity

Validity is the ability of a test to achieve its aim and objectives. Validity is established through the accumulation of evidence that an assessment procedure measures what it is supposed to and contributes data to decisions.[7] In an assessment center, this results in a large accumulation of information because many types of evidence are used for multiple techniques and for a variety of different purposes.[8]

Ratings

Dimension ratings and overall ratings comprise the most meaningful results that come out of an assessment center. Dimension ratings indicate the strengths and weaknesses of an individual in the core competencies identified for his or her job function, e.g., first-line supervisor or master technician. These ratings are particularly important for compiling individual development plans, building a training curriculum, and developing managerial skills.

Overall ratings are typically used to determine the qualifications of an individual for selection or promotion. The overall ratings represent a combination of the dimension ratings. The weight or value assigned to each dimension is assigned by an assessor based on available information. Overall assessment ratings could take many forms, including the probability of success or the probability of promotion.[9]

Feedback

Promotion or selection programs, diagnostic programs, and training programs require different procedures for providing feedback to management and participants. In all cases, it is critical that the feedback is timely and matches the assessment purposes. Individuals have the right by law to know the results of any assessment or evaluation that will affect their status in an organization (see Job Aid 5-9).[10]

Literacy

Definition and Scope

Literacy has a variety of definitions. The traditional approach is to consider literacy as competence in reading, writing, and mathematics necessary to function fully as a citizen, parent, and semi-skilled worker. For many, it is an individual's ability to effectively articulate one's thoughts, ideas, and concerns verbally as well as in writing.

Others view personal literacy as a key factor in independence and personal growth. In this case, literacy involves self-analysis and self-understanding, understanding what is required for success, and how to communicate with others.

Work force planning experts[1,2] define basic workplace skills as:

- *Foundation:* Knowing how to learn
- *Competence:* Reading, writing, and computation
- *Communication:* Listening and oral communication
- *Adaptability:* Creative thinking and problem solving
- *Personal Management:* Self-esteem, goal setting/motivation, and personal/career development
- *Group Effectiveness:* Interpersonal skills, negotiation, and teamwork
- *Influence:* Organizational effectiveness and leadership.

Organizations that engage in global operations and international communications will need a skill set that spans cultures and respects diversity. A landmark study of CEOs from 28 countries identified four major categories of global literacy.[3]
- *Personal Literacy:* Understanding and valuing yourself
- *Social Literacy:* Engaging and challenging others
- *Business Literacy:* Focusing and mobilizing your organization
- *Cultural Literacy:* Valuing and leveraging cultural differences

Impact on the Workplace

Literacy, as a worldwide initiative, has had a tremendous impact on incomes and mortality rates.[4] In addition, literacy and basic skill competence have had a substantial impact on the workplace. The basic "three Rs" (reading,

JOB AID 5-9: Assessment Center Design Planner

Directions: Begin by conducting extensive studies involving analysis of the job and performance appraisal and other evaluation results, plus focus groups of job incumbents, managers, and direct reports, studies of "best practices," and other assessments of performance expectations. With assistance of an expert in assessment center design and validation, determine potential skills to be measured and methods of measurement. This planner is a sample of generic skills and typical methods. Each organization is unique and the planner will need to be adapted to suit each organization.

	Problem Solving Analysis	Discussion and Interview	In-Basket Exercise	Task Direction Exercise	Leaderless Group Discussion
Decision Making					
Leadership					
Perception (Identifies key elements)					
Adaptability					
Decisiveness					
Interpersonal Relations					
Oral Communications					
Written Communications					
Other					

Based on Jaffee, C.L., Frank, F.D., and Mulligan, C.P. (1990). Assessing potential. In W.R. Tracey (ed.), Human resources management and development handbook. *New York: AMACOM. ISPI © 2001. Permission granted for unlimited duplication for noncommercial use.*

writing, and arithmetic) are now joined by computer skills. These fundamental skills influence quality, safety, and productivity. They enable people to assume greater independence, responsibility, and empowerment.

Frequently, literacy skills are taken for granted. Too often, employers do not want to finance skill development in the basics. On the other hand, employees often try to hide their difficulties due to embarrassment. However, lack of these skills can lead to accidents, unfortunate incidents, and conflict.

Implementing Literacy Interventions in the Workplace

PT practitioners can be involved in implementing the full range of literacy interventions. They can analyze jobs to determine what literacies are needed. They can design customized learning activities or search for ready-made materials. They can establish and manage skill centers focused on improving workplace performance.

In larger organizations, particularly with large numbers of unskilled or semi-skilled workers, skills centers are often established to help employees develop literacy skills necessary for the workplace and personal life. Skills centers often use technology to help people in a convenient, individualized manner.[5] GED preparation (Tests of General Educational Development), occupational reading and vocabulary, writing, English as a Second Language (ESL), and vocational mathematics are common topics covered.[6] Placement and progress are frequently measured through standardized tests, such as McGraw-Hill's Tests of Adult Basic Education.

Small organizations, on the other hand, usually use local school districts or community colleges, through tuition assistance, to develop basic workplace and personal life skills.

Every worker can continue to grow and develop new skills. Gone is the notion that "you can't teach an old dog new tricks." Organizations can encourage individual growth through motivational strategies and incentives, by creating development plans as part of the annual planning process, or possibly by establishing standardized assessment centers to provide feedback and recommendations. However, in the end, it is the responsibility of each individual to stay current, while the organization provides direction and rewards.

An example of company-sponsored literacy development is Ford Motor Company making available a home computer, color printer, and unlimited access to the Internet for $5 per month to every employee from the manufacturing floor to senior executives. Ford anticipates that the program will cost about $300 million. Ford also expects to reap

substantial financial benefits by making all employees computer literate.[7]

Knowdell lists some ways to increase literacy:
- Understand what motivates you
- Know what you want and determine how to get it
- Express your ideas and preferences
- Identify personal goals and the means to measure personal growth
- Build your communication skills (see Job aid 5-10).[8]

Case Study 5-2: Flint Ink—Performance Appraisal

Situation

Flint Ink Corporation is a $1.35 billion privately held business in Ann Arbor, Michigan. The company has 3,900 employees specializing in inks and pigments for printing, graphics arts, and industrial uses. It prides itself on its pigment-related chemical expertise and efficient manufacturing and distribution of high-quality ink products.

Flint Ink Corporation created a performance management system that measures, recognizes, and rewards what is important to the organization. They developed a performance process and tool to facilitate meaningful dialogue between supervisors and employees.

The company decided to overhaul the performance appraisal system because there was widespread dissatisfaction with the existing practices for identifying position scope, accountabilities, and performance measurements. Top management wanted a performance management system that could accommodate unprecedented growth because revenues had doubled in five years. Managers needed a pragmatic tool that was flexible enough to accommodate multiple cultures while emphasizing the core competencies: communication, teamwork, productivity, dependability, quality, and problem solving. Finally, there was generally a need for a value-added evaluation system that would support a cultural shift from a multi-domestic, privately held business to a professionally managed, integrated, and international organization.

Intervention

The new performance tool was extremely flexible and responsive to rapidly changing business conditions. The weighting system and key responsibilities may be modified annually, or more frequently, if circumstances change significantly. The new performance evaluation system provided Flint Ink managers with increased confidence in their abilities to conduct truly meaningful and highly interactive discussions on employee performance. In addition, the introduction of this new tool brought about a shared approach to culture change and a greater understanding of business goals and the standards of performance necessary to meet them.

JOB AID 5-10: Literacy Curriculum Planner

Many organizations need to offer a variety of learning experiences designed to develop literacy skills. It is important to meet the varying needs of the workplace, but it is also essential to meet the various learner preferences based on learning style and external responsibilities. Planning should include self-study, classes, and individualized learning facilitated by learning center staff, who serve as learning coaches.

Directions: Complete the matrix by identifying books, audiotapes, workbooks, videotapes, workplace and tuition-assisted academic classes, and other available resources. This list should be distributed to management with a cover letter explaining the importance of literacy development for all employees.

Skill Need	Self-Study	Classroom	Learning Center
Reading/Vocabulary			
English as 2nd Language			
Mathematics			
Writing/Grammar			
Computers			
Learning to Learn			
Listening			
Oral Communication			
Creativity			
Problem Solving			
Self-Esteem (Emotional Intelligence)			
Goal Setting/Motivation			
Personal/Career Development			
Interpersonal Skills			
Negotiation			
Teamwork			
Organizational Effectiveness			
Leadership			

Based on Carnevale, A.P., Gainer, L.J., and Meltzer, A.S. (1990). Workplace basics: Essential skills employers want. San Francisco, CA: Jossey-Bass.
ISPI © 2001. Permission granted for unlimited duplication for noncommercial use.

Characteristics

This flexible performance appraisal instrument has the following design qualities:

- A fold-open, user-friendly, four-page format for defining and measuring employee performance
- Core competency weighting that can be individually customized
- "Key responsibility" format that allows a manager to identify and weight critical elements of job performance annually
- Standards of performance that allow the appraised employee to develop customized measurements annually
- "Annual objectives" section that is linked closely to on-the-job behaviors, thereby creating an achievement orientation overlay
- Key sections for manager and employee comments

The revised performance appraisal process was Lotus Notes based to provide online convenience and continuous access to word processing and spreadsheet formats. This was an important factor for a multi-national company operating in many time zones. Web-based technologies enable instant updating or revising and thereby eliminate problems due to mail delivery delays.

Support and Buy-In

Flint Ink designed and implemented the new performance appraisal system carefully. A design and implementation team consisting of employees at various levels and six disciplines was assembled to create this state-of-the-art performance management tool. Several champions (important top executives) were gathered at the earliest stages of development to provide direction, credibility, and design assistance. Special presentations to the Executive Management Group solidified support and high visibility for the design team.

Employee Development

Before launch, training and employee orientation prepared workers and managers for the changes. A highly concise and pragmatic workshop was delivered to educate managers who write and conduct performance appraisals. In addition, an employee orientation program helped appraised employees understand Flint Ink's expectations and measurements. Finally, a videotape training tool was developed to aid managers at small or remote locations, because it was not possible to bring the managers' training and employee orientation to all locations.

Piloting

The company piloted the program at corporate, field, and research/development locations for six months. Participants were asked to complete surveys after using the Employee Development Plan to identify advantages derived and modifications needed. The new performance appraisal system was launched company-wide with concurrent announcements in the company publication and individual letters from managers to business units as implementation proceeded.

Results

The Employee Development Plan Program is effective because it allows managers to focus on strategically critical initiatives and the development of core competencies. Employees have responded favorably to the implementation of a shared approach to cultural change and self-generated standards of performance that support supervisory priorities.

Business Alignment

Under the new system, core competencies and key responsibilities are linked to business goals and are weighted according to their importance to individual jobs and supervisor priorities. Employees, with their supervisors, define key responsibilities and performance standards, thus creating buy-in to the priorities and behaviors that are important to the company and their jobs. Supervisors then determine the appropriate weights that are discussed with each employee at the start of the performance cycle. As a result of this process, employees and supervisors communicate regularly and develop a mutual understanding of performance goals and objectives. Feedback from employees indicates that the new system is viewed as a positive and fair method of assessing their efforts.

Measures of Success

The ultimate measures of effectiveness—profitability and return on shareholder equity—were impressive. Flint Ink continued to produce record sales and profitability. One significant advantage is that the Chief Operating Officer and his management team consistently use this program to manage results as well as develop the future leadership of the company.

The effectiveness as measured by employee satisfaction was very positive. Through a combination of personal interviews, focus groups, and follow up surveys, employee opinions were monitored and improvements made resulting in greater functionality for the Employee Development Plan Program.

Lessons Learned

- Performance appraisal can be a highly creative and flexible tool to identify, measure, and reward the most critical executives for performance excellence.
- Managers realize that Employee Development Plan Program helped to focus on Key Responsibilities (critical job duties) and Core Competencies, which dramatically increased their confidence to conduct truly meaningful, highly interactive discussions on employee performance.
- The ability to modify the entire Core Competencies weighting system and the Key Responsibilities annually provides a reliable degree of responsiveness to rapidly changing business conditions.
- Because employees now have personal responsibility for developing job standards that support key areas of focus, communication has increased dramatically, and performance has become more easily observed and measured.
- Employees have a dramatically higher level of confidence in the performance management process because they are actively involved.

Case study provided by Tom Emerson, Director of Employee Relations, Flint Ink, Ann Arbor, MI, on November 15, 1999. Used with permission.

ORGANIZATIONAL GROWTH

An organization is a collection of people working together to achieve a common purpose and a specific set of objectives. It is consciously and formally established.[1] For example, a sports team sets out to win games and make money; a social services group provides valuable services to people in need, and a business enterprise has four common purposes:

- Make a profit
- Provide goods and services
- Provide an income for employees
- Increase level of satisfaction for all constituents.[2]

Other types of organizations have similar goals and responsibilities that people oversee.

Successful organizations (those that are market driven and provide value-added features) share a common set of success drivers and are "capable of rapid response, flexible, adaptable, focused, lean and cost-oriented, quality-oriented, customer oriented, and innovation-oriented."[3] These characteristics must receive the buy in and support of the organization's personnel to be realized.

A company's organizational growth is only as strong as its investment in human capital. Organizations need people who are "adaptable, committed, motivated, skilled/reskilled, highly energetic, good performers in diverse employee groups, and good team players."[4] Just as these characteristics and functions make a major impact on the organization, the organization similarly makes an impact on its work force. The ever-changing workplace environment demands a work force that is highly educated and technically competent. Consciously planned efforts like succession planning, career pathing, and development of top-level officials are HR interventions that guarantee organizational growth.

Succession Planning

We live in a world of permanent change. Tomorrow's marketplace will be substantially different from today's. In view of projected trends and expected changes, organizations need to take a proactive stance in developing profiles of qualified individuals who can lead their organization now, if necessary, and at some later time.[1]

Definition and Scope

Succession planning ensures that qualified people will be available to assume managerial and executive positions once the positions become available.[2] It is a career development activity that some human resource personnel view as having a formal process and an informal one. "Formally, succession planning means examining development needs given a firm's strategic plans. Informally, it means high-level managers identifying and developing their own replacements."[3]

However it is viewed, succession planning is a process of:
- Identifying key individuals by their productivity and work ethics
- Developing these individuals through formal training, coaching, and mentoring
- Tracking this group through their job successes and creative dynamics, and their value-added leverage.

These individuals have high potential; they walk the talk and they make a difference.

Organizations use three judgmental techniques to forecast human resource supply and demand: replacement planning, succession planning, and succession development. Replacement planning uses replacement charts or tables such as the one in Job Aid 5-11 at the end of this section. Replacement charts or tables show current occupants of positions, names of potential replacements, vacancies, and types of positions that are urgently needed.[4]

Replacement table succession systems are confidential because potential candidates are not informed of their inclusion on the charts or tables. Incumbents complete yearly work histories that are summarized along with performance evaluations. These data are the focus of succession meetings. This type of succession planning emphasizes neither personal career development nor team development.[5] Succession planning is a management inventory—similar to replacement planning. However, it tends to enjoy longer life, offers greater flexibility, and is more developmental in nature.[6] In fact, high-potential candidates are informed about succession and are often offered mentoring programs to strengthen their own development. This type of succession planning is linked to HRM systems.[7]

Another type of succession planning is succession development, which is "the process of determining a comprehensive job profile of the key positions and then ensuring that key prospects are properly developed to match these qualifications."[8] The strength of this approach is that candidates participate in their own managerial and executive development. They often complete personal development plans. Objective and subjective approaches (360° feedback instruments, psychological assessments, assessment centers, etc.) help these chosen candidates to implement, track, and evaluate their personal development plans.[9]

It is much easier for large organizations to have a succession plan in place because they can access an extensive upper management applicant pool. The candidates for a succession plan must have intellectual acumen, interpersonal skills, technical knowledge, appropriate educational credentials, and motivation. While characteristics may be similar, it is more difficult for small companies to have a plan in place.

In small companies succession planning is crucial because the sudden departure or illness of a key player can set the business floundering...(Small business owners) should consider whether they want to keep the business in the family, recruit an outside manager to run it, sell it to a key executive, or put it on the market.[10]

Failure to plan for an orderly business succession, whether in a large or small organization, can result in monetary

TABLE 5-19: Steps to Successful Succession Planning

Steps	Procedures
1. Job Profile/ Job Analysis	• Identify required competencies based on organization's mission and its rank in the marketplace. • Conduct structured interviews with managers; obtain current and projected managerial competencies. • Identify critical success factors of high performers.
2. Managerial Competencies	• Define strategic competencies in Step 1 through focus groups or by asking managers to provide definitions and examples of the competencies. • Divide the competencies into functions: for example, technical, interpersonal, human relations, managerial, or supervisory. • Use a "Degree of Competence" rating scale from 1 ("Skill is not developed") to 5 ("Skill level indicates outstanding performance").
3. Assessment Approaches	• Select assessment approaches to measure competencies of high performers. • Gather information from supervisors, peers, and subordinates to provide frequent and ongoing feedback. • Create or purchase validated instruments. • Use assessment centers to measure critical skills.
4. Administration	• Once the assessment method is decided, design a succession-development administration system. • Include database management and tracking. • Include replacement tables, succession analysis, development, and implementation.
5. Assessment and Analysis	• Conduct the assessment process with high performers. • Focus on candidates' strengths and areas of development. • Finalize replacement charts. • Discuss candidates' strategic competencies.
6. Feedback and Implementation	• Use results of assessment process to provide valuable feedback to potential candidates. • Assist candidates in preparing personal development plans that are consistent with individual and organizational goals. • Provide on-the-job experiences and external training.
7. Monitor and Evaluate	• Build a tracking mechanism into the succession system. • Evaluate development plans.

Based on Nowack, 1994, pp. 51–54.

losses, organizational downsizing, and even the potential loss of the business itself.[11]

Implementing Succession Planning Interventions in the Workplace

The suggestions in Table 5-19 will help the performance specialist inaugurate a succession plan that is linked with HRD systems and with the different features of the three approaches.

In succession planning, as in shoes, one size does not fit all. Any plan is exclusive to an organization and is modeled after the organization's mission, values, unique issues and business needs, and the human capital the organization can attract, train, and retain. Effective succession planning is integral to continuous improvement. The PT practitioner is adept at all seven of the steps to successful succession illustrated in Table 5-19, and may help an organization develop a succession plan by:

1. Analyzing and profiling jobs and positions
2. Defining and writing managerial competencies
3. Assessing managerial competencies
4. Designing and providing oversight for related database management and tracking systems
5. Analyzing and assessing performance
6. Designing and implementing feedback and implementation plans
7. Monitoring and evaluating processes and outcomes.

The PT practitioner may serve as the gatekeeper while the organization's succession plan is generated and as a change catalyst when the plan is implemented, helping to revise the plan as the organization undergoes transformation. The PT practitioner is trained to identify and stay focused on an organization's mission and goals. One way to do this is to help the organization link succession planning to key business needs and continuous improvement efforts.[12,13]

Career Pathing

If an organization is poised to maintain a competitive edge, it must invest in the career advancement of its personnel. Companies provide a variety of career development services to employees ranging from job postings, job analysis, skill inventories, and career resource centers to career paths.[1]

Definition and Scope

A career path is a realistic, sequential, and "flexible line of progression through which an employee typically moves during employment."[2] For example, a career path in a K–12 school setting may include the positions of teacher,

counselor, department head, assistant principal, principal, central office administrator, and superintendent.[3]

Career pathing becomes increasingly important as the available number of paths up the corporate management ladder begins to decrease due to downsizing and an abundance of middle-aged employees jockeying for one or two positions held by people very similar to themselves in age.[4]

Career path data should be developed for each job based on:
- Thorough job analysis (job descriptions and job specifications)
- Accurate historical trends and future projections
- Similarities to other jobs within comparable job categories and families.[5]

Career paths communicate potential job advancement.

To be realistic, career paths must specify the qualifications necessary to proceed to the next step and the minimum length of time employees must spend at each step to obtain the necessary experience. This information could be generated by computer.[6]

Career pathing data:
- Show relationship to other jobs with the organization
- Identify a variety of career alternatives, usually displayed in chart form
- List qualifications (education and experience) for a career change[7]
- Identify "training needs and employee development options other than promotion: lateral moves, downward moves, and moves to other departments "[8]

Current literature favors four types of career paths that organizations use—traditional, network, lateral skill, and dual-career. Table 5-20 shows the differences among the types of career paths an individual may choose.

Implementing Career Path Interventions in the Workplace

There are multiple approaches to implementing career paths within an organization. The following suggestions will help ensure the effectiveness of a career pathing program.
- Thoroughly analyze paths previously followed by top performers; note trends in the business in order to establish job markers and job transitions.
- Identify both entry and exit points into the career path; flow chart career paths.
- Identify potential time on task before advancement.
- Identify required education, specialized skills, certifications, licenses, etc.

JOB AID 5-11: Replacement Tables—A Tool for Succession Planning

Replacement tables (see the example below) are one of the tools that succession planners use. Replacement tables show position titles, current occupants of the positions, predicted replacement needs (urgency), and the names and promotion potential of possible replacements.

Directions: Review the example, then complete the blank form for high-profile managers in your organization. Adjust the chart as needed to represent the specific organizational unit.

Legend:

Replacement Need	Potential for Promotion
A Need now	1. Qualified now
B Need within one year	2. Qualified within six months
C Need within 2–5 years	3. Qualified in one year
D No anticipated need	4. Qualification uncertain but best available

Example:

Chief Executive Officer	B
J. Mosel	
J. Smith	1
S. Roberts	1
S. Myer	2

Personnel Director	A
T. Desy	
F. Sway	4
G. Soski	2
A. Turrin	3

Chief Financial Officer	C
J. Wilks	
S. Mann	3
G. Sway	3
B. Turneson	2

Compensation Director	D
N. Nowacki	
S. Recruit	1
J. Moses	3
K. Kim	3

Comptroller	B
L. Frezzar	
M. Friday	2
B. Balance	3
S. Rhine	1

Organizational Unit:

_____

Date: _____

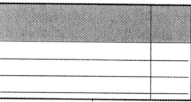

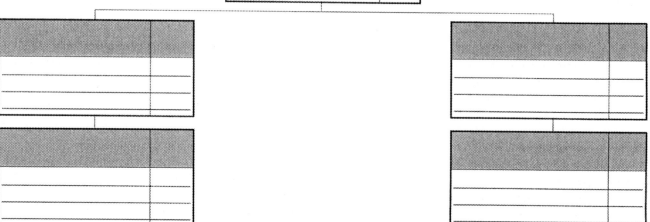

Based on Frottler, M.D., Hernandez, S.R., and Joiner, C.L. (1998). Essentials of human resource management in health services organizations. *Albany, NY: Delmar Publishers, p. 149. ISPI © 2001. Permission granted for unlimited duplication for noncommercial use.*

TABLE 5-20: Four Types of Career Paths

Traditional	**Definition:** Job progression upward from one job to the next
	Features: • Employee moves step by step to gain experience and preparation • Straightforward move, clearly laid out; job sequence known to employee • Movement based on tenure • Flawed approach for today's business due to mergers, acquisitions, joint ventures (see Chapter 8); erosion of loyalty and job security
Network	**Definition:** Job progression with both vertical and horizontal avenues for advancement
	Features: • Identifies vertical job sequence and horizontal job opportunities • Capitalizes on education and broad avenues of experience • Represents opportunities for employee development • Increases employee loyalty
Lateral Skill	**Definition:** Job progression that allows for lateral movement
	Features: • Employees can become revitalized and find new challenges, opportunities, and creative endeavors • Neither compensation nor benefits is associated here • Promotions are not involved • Employees become value-added commodities because they learn different jobs
Dual Career	**Definition:** A method of rewarding technical and professional personnel who want to continue to contribute but who choose not to be elevated to the managerial ranks
	Features: • Provides for progression in special areas—sales, marketing, finance, HRM, engineering, etc. • Personnel rewarded for specialized knowledge and personal contributions as individual and team members • Compensations comparable to what managers in other areas receive • Retention rates high • Helps organization make smooth transitions from within

Based on Mondy, Noe, and Premeaux, 1999, pp. 317–318.

- Remain focused on the organization's business needs; business needs determine work force personnel—number, kind, background, experience, etc.
- Keep abreast of changes in job content, work demands, cultural changes, managerial and supervisory needs, and diversity interests.
- Encourage training and employee development at each of the four pathing levels; continuous improvement is pivotal for retaining a competent work force.
- Encourage frequent feedback to employees at various levels and types of jobs; coaching, counseling, and mentoring are necessary.

- Suggest mechanisms for helping people cope and adjust to change in the work force.
- Use career pathing to guide career discussions.
- Periodically review and evaluate the jobs on the career pathing cycle.[9]

PT practitioners may use their unique perspective to help HRM implement the suggestions listed above. PT practitioners also need to stay current on changes in the global career landscape and help to develop career paths "within the context of human resource planning and strategic planning activities" (see Job Aid 5-12).[10]

JOB AID 5-12: Career Path Alternatives: Making a Choice

Career paths are lines of advancement for employees within an organization. There are four types of career paths: traditional, network, lateral skill, and dual career (see Table 5-20). The purpose of this job aid is to (a) help document the process for moving along each type of career path alternative that leads toward a specific job, and (b) select the best career path for the employee.

Directions: 1. Fill in the job title and specifications.
2. Check the career path alternatives that are available in this organization to reach the specific job.
3. Use the second column to list the steps for moving along each of the available career paths.
4. Use the third column to indicate the best career path for you/the employee to follow and the reason for making the selection. Reasons may include time, education, and training requirements versus experience, etc.

Job Title: _____

Job Specifications: _____

_____

Career path alternatives	Steps to take for each *available* path	Best choice? Why? (Select *one* and explain why in the appropriate box below.)
Traditional		
Network		
Lateral Skill		
Dual Career		

Based on Mondy, R.W., Noe, R.M., and Premeaux, S.R. (1999). Human resource management *(7th ed.). Upper Saddle River, NJ: Prentice Hall.*
ISPI © 2001. Permission granted for unlimited duplication for noncommercial use.

Leadership Development

Leadership is complex and elusive. The annals of history record leadership personified in Christ, Socrates, Plato, Charlemagne, kings, queens, presidents, dictators, popes, and CEOs. Most people would agree that, within organizations, leadership is neither understanding financial ratio analysis nor the ability to analyze balance sheets. Rather, it is the ability to manage the human capital side of the equation that makes the leadership process a powerful and compelling influence within organizations.[1]

Leadership and management are confusing terms. They are "two distinctive and complementary systems of action. Each has its own function and characteristic activities. Both are necessary for success in an increasingly complex and volatile business environment."[2] Good management controls complexity. It brings order and consistency to the workplace by looking at organizational structures and

monitoring results. Leadership produces change. It is about creating vision and aligning people to embrace the vision in practice.[3] "Leadership is one of the most highly valued management abilities."[4] Figure 5-7 portrays the synergistic relationships between leadership development and executive, management, and supervisory development.

Executives, supervisors, and managers exhibit leadership qualities that help them fulfill the duties of their jobs yet are so unique that they need pointed and specific leadership development. The following section highlights leadership development; subsequent sections will address executive, management, and supervisory development.

Definition and Scope

"Leadership is the process through which an individual attempts to intentionally influence another individual or a group in order to accomplish a goal."[5] In this definition,

FIGURE 5-7: The Synergy of Leadership

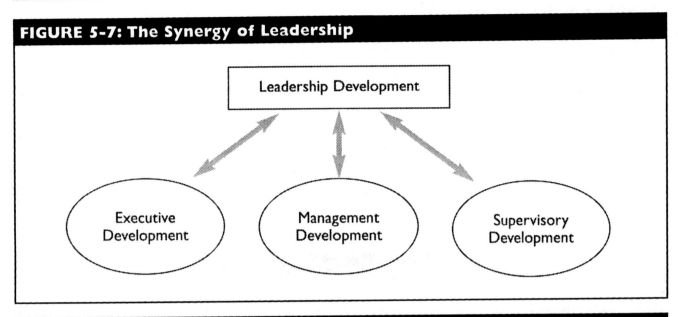

FIGURE 5-8: The Essence of Leadership

Based on Daft, 1999, p. 6.

process implies action over time and leadership means doing. The centrix or core element of leadership is person-directed and only an individual leads. The leader consciously, not accidentally, influences followers to think differently, feel passionately, act responsibly; the leader is change-directed. Finally, leadership is accomplished in order to fulfill a goal.[6] Figure 5-8 illustrates the basic elements or essence of leadership as a multi-dimensional process.

Traditional theories of leadership—trait, behavioral, and contingency theories—continue to enjoy rich discussion in HRD circles. Other leadership theories are gaining popularity, and the leaders they describe exhibit super-hero qualities. For example, neocharismatic theories are popular because John Q. Public relates to the charismatic leader who builds a special leader-follower relationship based on faith, loyalty, pride, and trust. In addition, there are theories that explain the transformational leader

who inspires followers to succeed; the transactional leader, who directs tasks and rewards to help others meet their organizational goals, and the visionary leader who generates and articulates an attractive vision of the future. Table 5-21 summarizes the four major leadership theories.

Organizations today are also focusing on the type of leader who opts for results. This type of leadership is linked to emotional intelligence (EI). Goleman defines EI as "the ability to manage ourselves and our relationships effectively…[it] consists of four fundamental capabilities: self-awareness, self-management, social awareness, and social skill. Each capability, in turn, is composed of specific sets of competencies."[7] Successful leaders use different styles of leadership (recurring patterns of behavior) based on their perception of how the components of EI relate to their current organizational environment. Table 5-22 identifies Goleman's six styles or recurring patterns of leadership behavior and presents phrases that

185

TABLE 5-21: Leadership Theories

Theory	Focus
Trait Theories	Focus on personal characteristics—social, physical, intellectual, personality traits
Behavioral Theories	Focus on specific leader behaviors—leaders differentiated from nonleaders
Contingency Theories	Focus on match between leader behavior and situation in which leader functions
Neocharismatic Theories	Focus on inspirational relationship between leader and follower; leader seen as visionary, empowering, and an ethical human being

Based on Robbins, 2001, pp. 314–332.

TABLE 5-22: Leaders Speak Out...

If a leader says...	The leadership style is...
"Do what I tell you."	Coercive
"Come with me."	Authoritative
"People come first."	Affiliative
"What do you think?"	Democratic
"Do as I do, now."	Pacesetting
"Try this."	Coaching

Based on Goleman, 2000, pp. 82–83.

explain the styles. (For more information, see Emotional Intelligence in Chapter 4.)

What factors are related to leadership effectiveness? What makes one leader successful and another not? The answers to these questions are found in research on leadership. It is not the purpose of this section to give an exhaustive overview of leadership research. The reader is encouraged to peruse any recent book on organizational behavior or any of the specialized leadership books for specific details.

The new language of leadership addresses seven trends for the 21st century that will have an impact on leadership roles, styles, strategies, and theories:

1. *Thinking in the future tense:* Leaders will chart the path to the future by recognizing emerging patterns and trends. They see something different.
2. *Loss of control:* Leaders will influence performance by modeling behaviors. Control that comes with traditional authority systems will be phased out with each new cohort of employees.
3. *Mass customizing:* Products, services, and markets will respond to speed, specificity, and economy of effort, the foundational steps of this trend.
4. *Information-based networks:* Information-based and managed networks will allow groups within organizations to communicate and collaborate instantly.

5. *Servant leadership:* Future leaders will be servants of the organization. As risk takers and change agents, they will track progress by how employees think and value themselves, their work, and their communities.
6. *Knowledge-based work:* Knowledge power unlike position power will drive the organization's tasks. Dialogue among workers will be paramount in self-directed team-driven settings.
7. *Changing the corporate culture:* Old values, norms, and traditional ways of doing things will give way to new values and vision. Neocharismatic leadership approaches will be valued. Leaders will walk the talk and carry their message with commitment and integrity.[8]

Implementing Leadership Development Interventions in the Workplace

The thrust of traditional leadership development programs has been on individuals and the competencies they need for success. Today, new radical remedies constitute successful leadership development; therefore, the PT practitioner must be adept at helping organizations to:

- *Begin with clearly defined and articulated objectives and outcomes and focus on business needs and desired outcomes.* This makes leaders more likely to support targeted business goals and sustain their support.
- *Center leadership development activities within an organizational context.* Too often a leadership

development program is focused on a brilliant leader, a visionary, a champion or some other superhero title. Quality, service, cost, speed, and information needs drive organizations today. Effective leadership cannot be separated from the organization's drivers, mission, culture, norms, and communication patterns. Leadership and organizational awareness are inextricably linked.

- *Begin at the top.* Employees are interested in what the top brass do. An individual leader cannot affect the change that is needed to transform an organization. However, the leadership team in the corporate boardroom can make substantial difference.

- *Start with results, finish with attributes.* Let the clearly defined and articulated business needs and outcomes of the organization guide the process. Strive for balance in outcomes among customers, clients, employees, and organization. Leaders need to produce results that affect the bottom line and guarantee a substantial market share. By evaluating leaders on the outcomes they produce, the linkage between results and attributes becomes clear.

- *Maintain a tally of results.* Leaders need to be motivated. Keeping score of their successes as they achieve their outcomes is a viable way to measure their progress.

JOB AID 5-13: How Do Individual Managers Approach Leadership?

Use this instrument as an individual and/or group activity to determine the alignment of an organization's leaders in terms of their individual approaches to leadership.

Directions: The respondents will read each statement, check their level of agreement from 5=Strongly Agree to 1=Strongly Disagree, and explain why they selected the response. After everyone has completed the instrument, the facilitator may ask the group to share and discuss their responses. The facilitator may also tally the responses for each statement to determine how closely aligned the leaders are in their approach to leadership.

	5 Strongly Agree	4 Agree	3 Not Sure	2 Disagree	1 Strongly Disagree
Nature Approach: People are born with leadership traits or develop them very early in life. *I selected this response because:*					
Nurture Approach: Traits provide the foundation upon which abilities and behavior develop. *I selected this response because:*					
Charismatic Approach: Traits, abilities, behaviors, situation are important, but visionary, inspirational, and empowering qualities are primary. *I selected this response because:*					
Situational Approach: Traits, abilities, behaviors, are important, but situational characteristics are primary. *I selected this response because:*					

- *Couple competencies with results.* Leaders' competencies need to be linked with the organization's results. By identifying areas of strength and weakness organizations can help leaders generate a realistic self-development plan.
- *Alter learning methodologies.* Lectures, case studies, simulations, role plays, and a variety of team building experiential activities are traditional ways to enhance leadership development. Internet, intranet, satellite, and other technologies will greatly expand the realm of possibilities when it comes to providing learning experiences. Timing on role plays and simulations will become critical—time is money. Action learning projects (see Action Learning in Chapter 2) will encourage people to take a stand and implement their recommendations. Engaging in storytelling about heros and heroines within the organization is becoming a popular learning methodology.
- *Change leadership development from an event into a process that lasts an entire career.* Leadership programs should not be one-time occurrences clothed in the one-day seminar, the three-day workshop, or the all-week retreat. In our need for information and knowledge management, leadership development is a continuous, ongoing process. To remain competitive, organizations will need to plan in detail what leaders as well as employees need to do differently, customize skill building to individual needs, and then measure outcomes to validate accomplishments.
- *Create accountability.* Leadership is about change and keeping the organization competitive. If results are measured, leaders become accountable for the organization's outcomes.
- *Assist leaders in seeing the big picture without being overwhelmed by details.* PT practitioners can help transform complexity into simplicity. A 25-page report can become a one-page executive summary; a five-page memo can transform into a one-screen email. The big picture is necessary to see a balanced approach in addressing employee, customer, and stakeholder needs. Details can come later.
- *Create opportunities for people to make frequent mistakes.* Help leaders prepare for realistic, pressure cooker situations. Allow them to broil, boil, and steam. Let them learn from their mistakes.
- *Prepare everyone in the organization to lead.* Organizations need to develop strong leadership in all their employees if they are to be high-performing organizations. Leadership and human capital are everyone's responsibility (see Job Aid 5-13).[9]

Executive Development

Leadership development manifests itself in many ways. A major focus is aimed at the development of executives— those men and women who are champions, visionaries, and pacesetters; who command large and impressive salaries and enjoy attractive incentives and perquisites (perks).

Definition and Scope

"Executive leaders are top managers who must create a vision that embraces organizational learning principles, create a new culture, and provide support to local line leaders. These individuals are also the transformational leaders who teach, guide, and continually reinforce the organizational vision."[1] (Refer to the section on Leadership Development in this chapter.) In short, they are the CEOs, CFOs, CIOs, CKMs, presidents and vice presidents of the organization. "The authority officially vested in the board of directors is assigned to a chief executive officer, who... is personally accountable to the board and to the owners for the organization's performance."[2] The term *executive* also refers to "a top-level manager who reports directly to a corporation's chief executive officer or the head of a major division."[3]

Meister, writing about CEOs as the driving force behind an organization's learning culture, assigns the following roles to the chief executive:
- Visionary—present a clear direction
- Sponsor—encourage, champion, and provide resources for new initiatives
- Governor—control functions and provide directions for evaluating effectiveness
- Subject Matter Expert—expert in, and "thought leader" for, the company's business
- Faculty—teaches by example or through more direct means
- Learner—serves as a model for lifelong learning
- Chief Marketing Agent—promotes the organization through speeches, interviews, annual reports, etc.[4]

The term *executive development* refers to the systematic development of an organization's executives through either specific skill programs or managerial skill programs. It is the primary lever that creates and accomplishes an organization's vision, values, strategies, and business needs. Its mission is to provide the foundation for the strategic development of the organization.[5]

Based on her extensive work with Aetna Life and Casualty and with Providian, Wertz cites four sources of executive development (see Table 5-23).

Despite the many opportunities and channels for executive development, some executives fail. According to a study by the Center for Creative Leadership in Greensboro, North Carolina, more than one-third of new executives fail at their new jobs because they don't understand cultural and political differences. Failure is defined as leaving

TABLE 5-23: Executive Development Sources

Sources	Examples
1. Executive development policies	• Policies that transform employees' thought processes • Policies that encourage CEOs to attend executive development programs which focus on business needs and core development issues • Policies for individual assessment routines • Development planning policies
2. Executive forums, curricula, and learning institutes	• Learning that is task oriented • Learning linked to business problems, opportunities, threats • Learning linked to processes • Learning linked to benchmarks • Mandatory learning programs, training packages, on-the-job experiences
3. Executive development support systems	• Information for strategic level decisions, e.g., five-year operating plans, trend analysis, etc.
4. Links to HR systems	• All activities for executive development integrated with HRM functions

Based on Wertz, 1996, pp. 623–635.

the job in less than five years. The cost of replacing an executive at the top levels can be as much as 150% of annual salary.[6]

Implementing Executive Development Interventions in the Workplace

PT practitioners can help an organization generate an executive development plan or program in several areas, including the following:
• Link development to the vision, values, and strategies of the organization.
• Integrate all systems used to develop executives and the organization.
• Establish executive competencies linked to the organization's core capabilities.
• Match educational activities for executives with the development needs of the organization.
• Provide appropriate coaching and feedback.
• Monitor executive development progress.
• Establish a database for recording change markers.[7]

In addition, here are some guidelines for designing effective executive development programs:
• Blend experience, training, and education; do not rely solely on classroom-based methodologies.
• Couple real-time interaction with real-life business issues and trends.
• Focus on continuous learning and knowledge creation for organizations and individuals.
• Help establish a pool of qualified leaders.
• Contribute to both individual talent and corporate talent (see Job Aid 5-14).[8]

Management Development

This section highlights strategies for management development interventions. Leadership and management are distinctive yet complementary terms, each with its own functions and activities.[1] Leaders create change while managers control complexity and produce short-term results.[2] Table 5-24 reviews the distinctions between leaders and managers.

Definition and Scope

Managerial decision making directly influences the organization's climate, survival, prosperity, and, ultimately, bottom-line results. It can make or break an organization.

TABLE 5-24: Leadership Versus Management

Leadership
• Establishing direction
• Aligning people
• Motivating and inspiring

Management
• Planning and budgeting
• Organizing and staffing
• Controlling and problem solving

Based on Kotter, 1996, p. 26.

Managers must keep their knowledge, skills, and ways of thinking updated in their respective fields. The need for continuous improvement and for adding new strengths to existing strengths is paramount in organizations today.[3]

Management development refers to "learning experiences provided by an organization for the purpose of upgrading skills and knowledge required in current and future managerial positions."[4]

Learning experiences that foster management development fall into five broad skill-based categories:

1. *Interpersonal Skills:* These skills aim at communicating with others, motivating them, leading them and working cooperatively with them.
2. *Technical Skills:* These skills focus on facility in using methods, processes, procedures, practices, and techniques, in short, the mechanics of a particular job or discipline.

JOB AID 5-14: Measuring PT Practitioner Competencies in Executive Development

Directions: How competent are you when it comes to helping your organization design, develop, evaluate, or maintain an executive development program? Use the instrument below to measure your competencies in executive development against an established set of standards.

- Respond to each question by checking *Yes* or *No* as appropriate.
- For each Yes answer, state why you feel each standard is important in terms of your role as an internal or external PT practitioner assisting an organization's executive development efforts.

Competency	Yes	No	This competency is important to my role because...
1. Do you believe that individuals and organizations are capable of significant change?			
2. Do you inspire confidence and trust in your work with top-level CEOs when helping them develop and implement large-scale interventions focusing on the organization's priorities?			
3. Do you have a working knowledge of the system's perspective on the change?			
4. Do you have the fortitude to work on all parts of the system simultaneously?			
5. Do you possess solid influence skills and polished communication abilities?			
6. Are you willing to experiment and innovate when carrying out development responsibilities?			
7. Do you possess skill in building educational programs?			
8. Do you possess skills in assessing individuals?			
9. Are you skilled in monitoring individual progress?			
10. Are you adept at providing consistent, frequent, and competent feedback?			
11. Are you an effective mentor and an understanding coach?			

Based on Wertz, L.H. (1996). Executive development. In Craig, R.L. (Ed.), The ASTD training and development handbook: A guide to human resource development *(4th ed.) pp. 634–635. New York, NY: McGraw-Hill. ISPI © 2001. Permission granted for unlimited duplication for noncommercial use.*

3. *Administrative Skills:* These skills help manage the organization through information gathering, data analysis, planning, organizing, and effective time managing.
4. *Conceptual Skills:* These skills enhance the ability to see the entire picture with all its inter-relatedness and synergy. Strength in this area helps managers view the organization as a business system.
5. *Decision Making Skills:* These skills identify a decision situation. They consist of problem identification and definition, seeking alternatives, and implementing and evaluating the best alternative.[5,6]

Organizations use a variety of management development programs to educate their current and potential managers:

- *Corporate universities:* These are company schools. Notable ones are Motorola University, McDonalds' Hamburger University, and the ones at Disney and Sears.
- *University-based programs:* Organizations partner with universities to train their managers (and executives) in business savvy. The Ivy League schools as well as other research-oriented and comprehensive universities offer such programs. Many of these programs are field-based and cohort-specific.
- *Professional organizations:* Groups such as the International Society for Performance Improvement (ISPI), the American Management Association (AMA), the American Society for Training and Development (ASTD), and the Society for Human Resource Management (SHRM) offer programs and self-instructional modules in numerous specialty areas and disciplines.
- *In-house programs:* These programs are often designed and developed by PT practitioners and a team of manager advisers. The programs are knowledge and skill specific.[7] Table 5-25 cites frequently mentioned reasons for conducting management development.

The methodologies and strategies used to train managers are as varied as the management development programs themselves. Perhaps the most popular methodology is the case study where managers do in-depth analysis and problem solving of real-life organizations. The emphasis is not on achieving correct answers as much as it is on seeking alternatives for organizational change. Role plays, simulations, games, experiential learning, action learning, and on-line learning are other favorites.[8]

Implementing Management Development Interventions in the Workplace

PT practitioners who are involved in designing management development programs should use sound performance improvement design principles such as the following:

- Link management development with the organization's strategic plan.
- Conduct a thorough needs assessment focusing on both current and future skill categories.
- Establish specific program objectives and performance objectives for all programs.
- Secure the involvement and commitment of senior management in all phases of the process.
- Provide a variety of formal and on-the-job training opportunities that are organization-specific.
- Ensure that managers are motivated to participate by providing appropriate and meaningful incentives.
- Evaluate the programs formatively, summatively, and confirmatively.
- Remain flexible and open-minded in analyzing, designing, developing, implementing, and evaluating proactive approaches and programs.
- Accept change as reality and deal with resistance as a growth process.[9]

Management development must be linked to the organization's mission, vision, goals, and structure for accomplishing business needs. Research suggests three desired linkages between an organization's structure and strategy and its management development offerings, as illustrated in Figure 5-9.

TABLE 5-25: Inside or Out: Reasons for Conducting Management Development	
Inside the Organization...	**Outside the Organization...**
• Training that is based on organizational needs • Reduction in costs • Current and consistent quality materials • Internal control of curriculum content and instructors • Foster organizational culture and teamwork • Timeliness	• Fresh and original perspective • New viewpoints and networking potential • Exposure to experts and research • Broader vision • Benchmarking potential—discovering industry's best practices

Based on Mondy, Noe, and Premeaux, 1999, pp. 274–275.

191

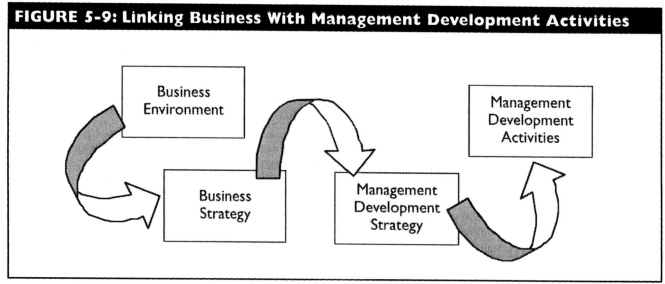

FIGURE 5-9: Linking Business With Management Development Activities

Based on Seibert, Hall, and Kram, 1995, pp. 549–567.

There are four channels to address the linkages in Figure 5-9:
- Begin by moving out and up to business strategy. Think business objectives and business issues as a starting point for approaching management behaviors and competencies.
- Put job experience before classroom activities, not vice versa.
- Be opportunistic. Avoid rigid programs in favor of those that adapt to an organization's changing needs.
- Provide support for experienced-based learning. Create a culture for individuals to take control of their own management development.[10]

PT practitioners need to view management development programs as management development systems that are interrelated and synergistic. Such systems share the characteristics reflected in Job Aid 5-15.

Supervisory Development

A supervisor's job has changed dramatically over the years. This is particularly true because of a diverse work force, the demands of technological change, the global economy, mission-critical policies, procedures, and practices, and the need to guide teams into islands of excellence. This section will offer insights and challenges surrounding the supervisor's job, role, and development need.

Definition and Scope

Organizations are often divided into four distinct categories: top management, middle managers, supervisors, and operative employees:
- *Top management* is vision, mission, goal, and objective driven. They develop the policies, procedures, and practices of the organization.

- *Middle managers* execute and may generate departmental goals.
- *Supervisors,* as part of the organization's management team, oversee the work of operative employees. They are the only managers who do not manage other groups of managers.
- *Operative employees* work on specific job tasks and physically produce an organization's goods and services.[1]

It is estimated that about 4 million people in the United States oversee skilled and semi-skilled workers in all industries. People in supervisory positions have titles such as assistant manager, department head, foreman, or team leader.[2]

The expectations of supervisors are changing as management science becomes clothed in solid action research. It was not uncommon a few years ago to observe supervisors who forcefully made decisions, bossed employees, told them what to do, and disciplined them when they were errant. Today, supervisors are described as trainers, advisors, mentors, facilitators, coaches, leaders, or behavioral specialists. For the most part, supervisors enjoy a multi-faceted role.[3]

Nonetheless, the supervisor's role will become increasingly important to organizations in the future for many reasons:
- Organizations implement programs to reduce costs and foster performance and productivity. These programs often focus on the work of operative employees. Supervisors oversee the change efforts of these programs and the personnel who are affected.
- Organizations are right sizing, and "lean and mean" is their theme. Supervisors have more people reporting to them. In fact, support unit tasks like scheduling and quality control among others will become the supervisor's responsibilities. In short, supervisors will play an expanded role.

- Organizations will value training for future employees who do not possess the skills to keep the organization in a competitive mode. Supervisors will identify employee deficiencies and, perhaps, work with the PT professional to design, develop, and coordinate training experiences.[4]

Supervisors are involved in multiple tasks. Table 5-26 reveals the results of a task identification survey of more than 650 supervisors.

The variety of supervisory tasks requires a set of critical competencies that are conceptual, interpersonal, technical, and political. Table 5-27 suggests the competencies required for successful supervisory performance.

In addition to these critical competencies, research shows other dimensions of a supervisor's job: "…administrative skills, ability to develop a plan for achieving goals, ability to deal with the manager to whom one reports, communications ability, capacity for dealing with people outside the unit and the company, and the ability to deal with employees reporting directly to the supervisor."[5] Still other competencies include facilitating, team building, working with self-managed teams, emotional resilience, social skills, and skills in trusting behaviors.[6]

Implementing Supervisory Development Interventions

Individuals planning effective, cutting-edge supervisory development programs need to keep the key supervisory

JOB AID 5-15: Evaluating a Management Development System

Directions: Read the following characteristics of effective management development programs. Check *Yes* or *No* to indicate whether the organization supports each characteristic. If you respond No to any of the characteristics, discuss why and what you might do to change the situation. You may also use this checklist to review your management development practices.

Characteristics of Effective Management Development Systems	Yes	No
1. Management development links with the organization's strategic plan.		
2. The organization conducts a formal needs assessment before embarking on a management development program.		
3. The organization establishes program objectives and performance objectives for management development programs up front.		
4. Senior management is involved and committed during all phases of management development.		
5. Participants have a variety of training opportunities that are specific to the organization's needs.		
6. The organization encourages motivation from the participants by providing meaningful and exciting programs.		
7. The organization evaluates management development programs.		
8. The organization remains proactive, flexible, and open-minded in all phases of management development.		
9. The organization accepts change as reality and deals with resistance as a growth process.		
10. The people who plan management development programs put job experience before classroom activities and let the experience guide the process.		
11. The people who plan management development programs never lose sight of the specific target population.		
12. The organization supports self-motivation with consistent and timely feedback.		

Based on Kotter, J.P. (1990, May-June). Leading change. Boston, MA: Harvard Business School Press, p. 26.
ISPI © 2001. Permission granted for unlimited duplication for noncommercial use.

TABLE 5-26: Essential Supervisory Tasks

Task	Pivotal Concern
1. Motivation	Foster employee change and performance improvement
2. Feedback	Offer continuous feedback to employees
3. Dispute Resolution	Resolve performance problems with individuals and groups
4. Alignment	Align goals with work requirements
5. Communication	Improve communication among employees
6. Gate Keeper	Keep employees current about work procedures and assignments
7. Career Assessment	Record employees' training and skills and encourage their advancement in and out of the organization

Based on Kraut, 1989, p. 287.

TABLE 5-27: Critical Competencies of Successful Supervisors

1. Conceptual	Ability to analyze and diagnose complex situations
2. Interpersonal	Ability to work with people in understanding, communicating, and motivating
3. Technical	Ability to capitalize on specialized knowledge and expertise
4. Political	Ability to establish a power base and establish connections

Based on Katz, 1974, pp. 90–102.

tasks and competencies in mind. Organizations use a variety of workplace policies and practices to improve performance. The ASTD *State of the Industry Report* highlights the interconnected system of policies and practices that PT professionals can tap to guide course content, program planning and design, program management, and evaluation.[7]

The literature suggests focused guidelines to follow for effective supervisory development. A viable program should:
- Emerge from a well-thought-out strategic plan for development
- Recognize and allow for the ambiguity, real or perceived, in the supervisory role, positioned as it is at the interface between management and employees
- Provide a sound conceptual foundation of essential management knowledge, skills, and attitudes upon which to build specific competencies
- Base the remainder of its content upon rigorously verified and precisely defined competency needs
- Allow for flexibility in the program's implementation, while maintaining consistency and continuity

- Introduce new development methods or techniques only after pretesting or otherwise verifying their suitability and effectiveness
- Guard against the inclusion of a course or subject matter that does not clearly meet an established competency need
- Establish standards of participant assimilation and/or improvement that, while challenging, are demonstrably within the range of attainment for the particular supervisory population
- Articulate and correspond with the organization's goals, policies, and prescribed relationships—as well as with the organization's beliefs and cultural norms
- Provide for measurement and evaluation of the effectiveness of each element of the program, especially in terms of improved supervisory performance.[8]

Supervisors—like executives and upper-level managers—learn best from reality-oriented practice and concrete examples. A balanced approach to method choice is essential. Table 5-28 offers structured guidance on selecting methods for supervisory development.

TABLE 5-28: Supervisory Development: How to Do It

To meet this objective...	Select from these methods...
Expand Knowledge	Lecture, discussion, case studies, observations, films, learning technologies, etc.
Reinforce skills	Role plays, demonstrations, job rotation, supervised practice, problem solving techniques, games, simulations, etc.
Change attitudes	Role plays, demonstrations, case studies, focus groups, conferences, videos, etc.
Develop ways of thinking	Case studies, observation, critical problem solving, case study analysis, etc.

Based on Bittel and Newstrom, 1996, p. 665.

The PT practitioner should work cooperatively with HRM to plan and design supervisor development because it is "a unique form of improvement activity, distinctive from the broader areas of management and executive development."[9]

The collaborative efforts of HR and PT practitioners should be based on the following:

- Ability to recognize qualifications and aspirations of supervisors participating in improvement activities
- Knowledge of core and key competencies of supervisors in various work assignments
- Sensitivity and empathy to roles and relationships imposed upon supervisors by the organization
- Realization that supervision is a continuously evolving role
- Flexibility, open-mindedness, and thinking outside the box (see Job Aid 5-16).[10]

Case Study 5-3: Management and Supervisory Development at Frank's Nursery and Crafts

Situation

Frank's Nursery & Crafts, Inc. is a lawn and garden and home décor retail chain. This 258-store, 15-state chain is the largest lawn and garden retailer in the United States. After multiple organizational shifts during the past decade, the chain was purchased by a private investment group in 1997. All organized training and personnel development programs had been terminated five years before this purchase. New processes and tools had to be developed and implemented at every level of the company. When the primary target audience for interventions was identified, the greatest challenge was determined: to institutionalize organizational development implementation systems.

Intervention

An extensive six-week needs analysis was conducted prior to the development of any programs. Results with recommenda-tions were presented to the company's management team. Although needs were clearly identified within all levels of the organization, it was determined that store managers should be the primary target audience for scheduled interventions. Organizational needs and development programs were aligned and prioritized. Feedback from the field organization and store managers clearly indicated the need for ongoing training support within districts. A budget was approved with certain restrictions placed on the development of program support systems.

In response to the organizational needs, budget restrictions, and the requirement that this support system be internally supported, a Training Managers' Network was conceptualized. Establishment of this network was delayed until a firm foundation for its roll-out and maintenance was clearly defined and then designed. This was accomplished by close coordination of key organizational groups:

- Store Operations worked closely with the newly formed Training and Development Department to identify exemplary managers.
- The Field Organization validated Store Operations' information.
- Exemplary managers were invited to join a Training Managers' Network.
- A three-day network development workshop was conducted with a select group of these managers.
- Managers who exhibited leadership qualities within this group were interviewed for the position of Field Training Manager. This position required a unique combination of expert-level store management communication skills coupled with strong analytical skills. Once this position was filled, the Training Managers' Network was rolled out. Subsequent network meetings/workshops were driven by operational needs and New Program Development. Network managers were each charged with the coordination and facilitation of store manager team meetings within their districts.

Results

Over the course of six months, newly researched and developed operations procedures were introduced to all Frank's store managers via the Training Managers' Network. Consistent training

JOB AID 5-16: Supervisory Roles and Functions

This tool challenges you to test your knowledge about supervisory roles and functions.

Directions: Respond to each question as clearly and briefly as possible. Share the questions with another colleague in your organization and compare your responses. What new insights were gained? What areas do you need to explore further to become more competent in implementing supervisory development as a performance improvement intervention?

1.   **Describe how technology is changing the supervisor's job.**
2.   **Explain how globalization affects supervisors.**
3.   **Describe why supervisors must be able to "thrive on chaos."**
4.   **Explain why the supervisor's role is considered ambiguous.**
5.   **Explain how a supervisor can reduce cost.**
6.   **List actions a supervisor can take to maximize employee motivation.**
7.   **Describe the essential elements of a supervisory development program.**
8.   **Which topics or courses would be included in a supervisory development program?**
9.   **How is a supervisory development program evaluated?**

Based on Robbins, S.P., and DeCenzo, D.A. (1998). Supervision today (2nd ed.) p. 601. Upper Saddle River, NJ: Prentice Hall.
ISPI © 2001. Permission granted for unlimited duplication for noncommercial use.

was delivered throughout the organization during specified, limited periods of time. All materials developed for training store managers (to deliver to their teams) were designed as models for Store Managers to use for training in their stores. Modeled behaviors, adult learning concepts, and operations requirements were clearly identified in all program elements. Encouraging a continuous flow of information to and from store managers to the Training Department has had multiple positive effects. It has provided the Training Department with critical operations information, accelerated review cycles and pilot testing of new programs, and has greatly contributed to continuous program improvement/validation cycles.

Lessons Learned

Lessons learned during the first six months of the Training Managers' Network include:

- Early buy-in to process development encourages multiple champions to help institutionalize new systems.
- Development of trust in a previously unstable environment is a tedious process.
- Regular meaningful feedback to and from program participants accelerates expansion and development efforts.
- Extensive interaction among strong and weak performers is critical for the development of an effective community of practice. A pending proposal to Frank's upper management suggests the initiation of monthly conference calls with groups of training store managers.

This case study was written by Maria Kokas, MS, EdS, Director of Training and Development, Frank's Nursery and Crafts, Inc. Used with permission.

CHAPTER

6

ORGANIZATIONAL COMMUNICATION

"I TOLD YOU TO GET THE OXYGEN!"

ORGANIZATIONAL COMMUNICATION INTERVENTIONS

Communication is "the transfer of meaning between sender and receiver."[1] Organizational or business communication "fosters connections between different components within an organization, among separate organizations, and between organizations and the larger culture in which they operate."[2] Whether organizational communication takes place within an organization (intraorganizational communication) or between an organization and its external stakeholders (interorganizational communication), "communication actually creates, defines, and sustains culture in the corporation, the nation, and the world."[3]

Understanding is the key element of all communication, including organizational communication. The basic communication model in Figure 6-1 illustrates the flow of communication from sender to receiver:

- The *sender* and *receiver* may be individuals or groups. The sender is responsible for encoding and distributing the message; the receiver is responsible for decoding the message and providing feedback.
- *Channels* may be oral (face to face, telephone, video conferences, teleconferences) or written (faxes, emails, memos, letters, electronic bulletin boards, reports, schedules, flyers, etc.). The sender, receiver, or an external source (organizational policy, availability of technology, geographic distance, etc.) may be respon-

sible for selecting the channel. Channels have postitive and negative effects on performance. On the positive side, they can integrate diverse areas of an organization and facilitate information dissemination and discussion; on the negative side, they can restrict access to information, manipulate information, and control the results of discussions.[4]

- *Noise* is anything that filters, blocks, or distorts the message. Noise may be a factor of the channel (lost faxes, video transmission problems, unavailability), the sender (incomplete information, unclear wording), the environment (unfavorable organizational climate, time constraints), or the receiver (lack of experience, personal resistance to message or sender). In order for understanding to occur, the receiver must receive and interpret the message as the sender intended it.
- *Feedback* confirms the success or failure of the communication and is vital to dialogue or discussion.

Understanding occurs when the sender produces a clear message, the channel is free of noise, and the receiver is able to interpret the message exactly as intended and respond appropriately (feedback).

One email circulating through cyberspace lists signs that prove you worked during the 90s, including the following: "You know you worked during the 90s if...Communication

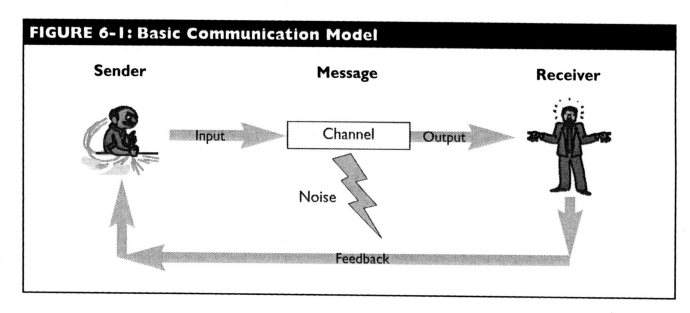

FIGURE 6-1: Basic Communication Model

Sender — Input — Channel — Output — Receiver

Message

Noise

Feedback

is something your section is having problems with."[5] A communication problem is often perceived as the cause of a performance problem; however, unless the PT practitioner has conducted a thorough cause analysis this may or may not be the situation.

> *The assumption underlying a communication intervention is that the practitioner believes current organizational performance to be related to a communication issue of some kind, such as information flow, cross-functional cooperation, or conveyance of organizational values...Communication is invariably cited by organizational members as a generic area in need of improvement, so the practitioner should use methods to determine whether a specific communication concern is involved. A true communication need is indicated when it can be determined that a change in information flow or availability or in communication style or an increase in awareness or enthusiasm for an idea will affect behavior even when the actual content of a message is not substantially changed.*[6]

This chapter will identify what to look for when analyzing communication problems and will describe the organizational communication interventions listed in the enhanced HPT Model (see Table 6-1).

Communication Networks

Communication networks provide the infrastructure for both communication and collaboration. "Knowing the communication relationships (networks) in an organization helps you know what normally happens in the organization (officially and unofficially), what is possible in the organization, and how information is processed."[1]

Definition and Scope

Communication networks have been variously defined as:
- *"patterns of communication interactions* (who communicates with whom and within what limits)"[2,3]
- "a series of *decision centers connected by channels*"[4]

TABLE 6-1: Organizational Communication Interventions From Enhanced HPT Model

- Communication Networks
- Information Systems
- Suggestion Systems
- Grievance Systems
- Conflict Resolution

- "a comprehensive and unlimited *range of communication relationships*."[5]

Whether they define communication networks as *patterns, channels,* or *relationships,* communication experts generally agree that "...lines of communication between people can greatly influence their job performance and satisfaction."[6]

In order to improve an organization's communication network, the PT practitioner must first discover the four attributes of the existing communication networks: level, structure, pattern, and flow or direction.

Communication Network Levels
Communication networks exist at three different levels:
- Organization-wide communication networks
- Individual networks that people use to get things done in an organization (information, support, mentoring)
- Group networks (teams, departments).[7]

It is not unusual for all three levels to co-exist in an organization, either officially or unofficially.

Communication Network Structures
The structure of communication networks is either formal or informal. Formal communication networks exist for the purpose of communicating rules, procedures, policies, etc. There are four different types of formal networks:
- *Regulative*—disseminate policies, practices, and procedures
- *Innovative*—focus on making the organization flexible and adaptive to changing demands and environments
- *Informative-instructive*—provide the training function and furthers organizational adaptability, morale, conformity, and institutionalization
- *Integrative*—close to informal networks because they focus on employee morale (employee grapevine, reward systems, etc.)[8]

Informal communication networks "...result from the interpersonal relationship of organization members... (and) co-exist with the formal flows established by management."[9] Informal communication networks are frequently referred to as grapevines. Communication received through the grapevine is often perceived as rumors and it is often difficult to separate fiction from fact. There are four types of grapevines:
- *Single strand*—each person tells one other person
- *Gossip*—one person tells everyone
- *Probability*—each person randomly tells others
- *Cluster*—some people tell selected others (this is the most typical)[10]

Grapevines are valuable as communication resources. "Management must pay heed to the grapevine and

TABLE 6-2: Communication Network Patterns

Pattern	Description	Benefits/Barriers
Chain	Each person communicates with one or two others **Variation:** • One person is the central link and communication flows down to that person from management and up to that person from staff • Communication flows horizontally with or without a central person	• Faster with less chance for distortion than circle • Limited, linear communication • May not have a central member/leader • Peers communicate with peers in horizontal variation • End members only communicate with one person
Y	Communication flows from the three ends of the Y to the point where all three lines intersect **Variation:** • Upside down Y-communication flows from two staff members to a superior who then reports to his or her superior	• Central member/leader can communicate with everyone • Works best for simple tasks • All members do not talk to each other
Wheel or X	Communication flows between the individuals at the tips of the wheel spokes and the person in the center	• Central member/leader • Works best for simple tasks • Members around the wheel do not communicate with each other
Circle	Each member communicates with two others in the network	• Each member equal • No central member/leader • Each member communicates directly with only two others • Must complete circle to be effective • Slow, with high level of distortion
All-channel or Pinwheel	All members communicate with each other **Variation:** • Central member/leader	• Every member communicates with every member • Central member/leader is highly participatory • Can process large amounts of information • Can handle complex tasks • Provides maximum amount of feedback • May be slow due to high level of participation • Distortion may be high due to large number of channels

Based on Longest, Rakich, and Darr, 2000, pp. 812–815.

actively get involved in using it to supplement the organization's formal chain of communication...This of course requires the creation of a trust relationship between management and the employees."[11]

Communication Network Patterns

"A predictable pattern of communication relationships facilitates coordinated activity within an organization... and can also help employees make accurate predictions that help smooth day-to-day operations."[12] There are five common networking patterns within organizations: chain, Y, wheel or X, circle, and all-channel or pinwheel. Table 6-2 illustrates and describes these structures.

All of the patterns in Table 6-2, with the exception of the circle, are either centralized or decentralized. In a centralized network, information must flow through a specific member of the network to reach others. If the network is decentralized, information flows freely without going through a central person. "Research has shown that these differences in communication networks are responsible for determining how effectively groups will perform various jobs...centralized networks are faster and more accurate on simple tasks, whereas decentralized networks are faster and more accurate on complex tasks."[13]

Communication Network Flow

Organizations need to plan for communication to flow downward, upward, horizontally, and diagonally. "Unhindered downward and upward communication are insufficient for effective organizational performance. In complex (organizations), especially those subject to abrupt demands for action and reaction, horizontal flow must also occur."[14] Diagonal flow is also important, even though it breaks all the rules by cutting across departments and work levels. Diagonal flow is becoming an expediter of just-in-time products and services.

An organizational chart is one indication of how formal communication flows; however, "organizational charts... do not tell the whole story regarding communication within an organization."[15] Office layout also offers significant insights into the flow of both formal and informal communication within an organization. For example, proximity of supervisors to employees, the location of support staff, the use of modular rather than permanent walls, and office sharing arrangements have an impact on communication flow. A communication audit helps to determine the real flow of communication.[16,17] Table 6-3 illustrates and describes the vertical (upward or downward), horizontal, and diagonal flow of communication networks.

TABLE 6-3: Flow of Communication Networks

Description	Purpose	Examples
Formal, vertical flow from higher to lower levels	Provide employees with specific information to facilitate performance	• Job instructions • Rationale for job/duties • Data required to perform job • Performance feedback • Ideological information (goals, mission, etc.)
Formal, vertical flow from lower to higher levels	Receive information from employees to: • facilitate decision making • reveal problems • reveal morale level • encourage employee involvement	• Suggestion systems • Grievance systems • Requests for supplies or support • Feedback on attitudes and feelings
Formal or informal flow between peers at same level	• Coordinate efforts • Build support • Share information • Facilitate problem solving • Facilitate immediate action	• Meetings • Conversations • Written communication • Social events • Committees and task forces
Cuts across functions, departments, or levels	Save time and effort when members cannot communicate through usual vertical or horizontal channels	• Verbal or written cross-functional communications (for example, health and safety alerts, new product information, survey results, etc.) • Cross-functional teams

Based on Gibson and Hodgetts, 1986, pp. 210–217; Longest, Rakich, and Darr, 2000, pp. 812–817.

Communication network flow may also "...set boundaries on what is possible in an organization. The flattened communication structure...makes it possible for everyone to talk to the company president. The 'tall' hierarchical structure of communication...discourages such direct contact."[18]

Implementing Communication Network Interventions in the Workplace

Organizations frequently call in the PT practitioner to solve a problem that involves their communication network. First, the PT practitioner should conduct a communication audit or analysis, which includes the elements of communication, the attributes of communication networks, and the organization's management style and climate.

> ...the structure of networks tells only part of the story. Management style and organizational climate also play a part in how and how well communication works within an organization. The styles of people occupying any given spot in the network influences how communication works within an organization... Organizational climate moderates the relationship between management style and the strategies managers use to exercise their influence.[19]

Once analysis is completed, the PT practitioner should select an appropriate intervention based on the analysis findings and the desired outcome:
- System interventions—change the direction (flow), amount, frequency, availability, and/or usability of exchanged information
- Interactive interventions—influence direct or indirect communication patterns
- Message campaign intervention—create unifying themes that direct performance.[20]

For example, to improve the general quality of an organization's communication networks try implementing "conversation as a core business practice."[21] Before implementation, however, ask questions to help discover how well an organization appreciates the value of conversation and how to improve the quality of conversation throughout the organization. For example, ask people to recall a really good conversation they had and what made it memorable, or ask for input on how to create a physical environment that supports good conversation (see Job Aid 6-1).

Information Systems

Advances in telecommunications and computer technology "have dramatically altered the way people do their jobs and the way organizations are managed."[1] Cellular phones and computers, voice mail and email, pagers, and fax machines are the norm rather than the exception.

With satellite technology, the sky is literally the limit when it comes to getting the message from sender to receiver, anywhere, anytime. Today's communication technology calls for an information system that will bring order out of overload: "...[a] software or paper-based system to collect, manipulate, store, and retrieve information related to requirements for business, human resources, materials resources, and management."[2]

Definition and Scope

An information system is "...a set of people, data, technology, and organizational procedures that work together to retrieve, process, store, and disseminate information to support decision making and control."[3] Information systems rely on information technology to keep them alive and effective. Information technology is a broad term that refers to any process, practice, or system that turns data into information. People distill the information via study or research, augment it by judgment and experience, and turn the information into informed decisions.[4] Figure 6-2 illustrates the components of an information system.

People at different levels of an organization require different information based on the type of decisions they must make. Table 6-4 summarizes the information needs at various levels of an organization.

Three basic types of information systems aid in the decision making process:
- *Pure information systems* provide a common database of information that is shared by and may be tailored to various levels within the organization. They are often called management information systems (MIS) and are frequently used as a continuous improvement tool to monitor and control daily or routine operations (also called red flag management or management by exception).[5]
- *Decision support systems* support the *process of decision making*. These systems go beyond providing information; they allow people to change how the information is structured and organized, look at alternatives, compare internal and external data, set up if-then scenarios, etc. "Decision support systems assist ...decision making by combining data, sophisticated analytical models, and user-friendly software into a single powerful system that can support semistructured or unstructured decision making."[6]
- *Transaction processing systems* provide detailed information about short-term or daily activities for operational decision making.[7]

Other Information Support Systems
"Electronic performance support systems (EPSS)—linking training, information systems, computer applications,

JOB AID 6-1: Analyze Network Attributes

Purpose: Use this job aid to help identify the attributes of the current communication network, determine whether the attributes support the organization's business needs, and select the appropriate type of performance change.

Directions:
1. Check all the communication levels, structures, patterns, and flows that apply to the current communication network.
2. Check the extent to which the whole attribute (level, structure, etc.) supports the organization's business needs.
3. Check the type of performance change that should take place.

1. What are attributes of current network?	2. Does this attribute support organization's business needs?	3. What type of performance change should take place?
Level ☐ Entire organization ☐ Individual ☐ Group ☐ Combination	☐ Always ☐ Usually ☐ Sometimes ☐ Rarely ☐ Never ☐ Don't Know	**If always or usually:** ☐ Maintain existing level ☐ Improve existing level **If sometimes or never:** ☐ Improve existing level ☐ Establish new level ☐ Extinguish existing level **If don't know:** ☐ Find out!
Structure ☐ Formal ☐ Informal ☐ Combination	☐ Always ☐ Usually ☐ Sometimes ☐ Rarely ☐ Never ☐ Don't Know	**If always or usually:** ☐ Maintain existing structure ☐ Improve existing structure **If sometimes or never:** ☐ Improve existing structure ☐ Establish new structure ☐ Extinguish existing structure **If don't know:** ☐ Find out!
Flow ☐ Vertical ☐ Horizontal ☐ Diagonal ☐ Combination	☐ Always ☐ Usually ☐ Sometimes ☐ Rarely ☐ Never ☐ Don't Know	**If always or usually:** ☐ Maintain existing flow ☐ Improve existing flow **If sometimes or never:** ☐ Improve existing flow ☐ Establish new flow ☐ Extinguish existing flow **If don't know:** ☐ Find out!
Pattern ☐ Chain ☐ Wheel ☐ Y ☐ Circle ☐ X or Pinwheel ☐ Centralized ☐ Decentralized	☐ Always ☐ Usually ☐ Sometimes ☐ Rarely ☐ Never ☐ Don't Know	**If always or usually:** ☐ Maintain existing pattern ☐ Improve existing pattern **If sometimes or never:** ☐ Improve existing pattern ☐ Establish new pattern ☐ Extinguish existing pattern **If don't know:** ☐ Find out!

Based on Gibson, J.W., and Hodgetts, R.M. (1986). Organizational communication: A managerial perspective. Orlando, FL: Academic Press College Division, pp. 228–233; Greenberg, J., and Baron, R.A. (1995). (5th ed.) Behavior in organizations. Englewood Cliffs, NJ: Prentice Hall. pp. 346–352; and Langdon, D.G., Whiteside, K.S., and McKenna, M.M. (1999). Intervention resource guide. San Francisco, CA: Jossey-Bass/Pfeiffer, p. 20.

FIGURE 6-2: Information System Components

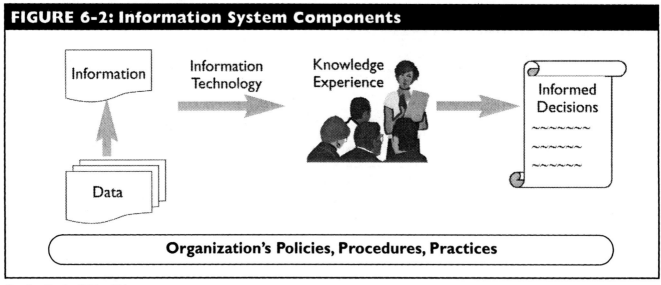

Information

Information Technology

Knowledge Experience

Informed Decisions

Data

Organization's Policies, Procedures, Practices

Based on Dessler, 1998, p. 614.

TABLE 6-4: Information Needs at Various Levels of an Organization

At this level...	People need information to help them...
Top or executive managers	Engage in long-range strategic planning: • Merger, acquisition, and joint ventures decisions • New factory locations • New product planning
Middle managers	Make intermediate-range decisions: • Budget analysis • Short-term forecasts • Variance analysis
First-line managers	Make short-term operational decisions: • Accounts receivable • Inventory control • Cash management
Work group or individual workers	Make immediate or daily work decisions: • Just-in-time supply needs • Emergency maintenance • Employee scheduling

Based on Dessler, 1998, p. 617.

and so on—will have a significant impact on the design and operation of an organization, and on human performance."[8] Expert systems and artificial intelligence are two examples of EPSS for decision making.

• *Expert systems* are information systems in which computer programs store facts and rules to replicate the abilities and decisions of true, human experts. The characteristics of an expert system include the ability to handle problems with missing or incomplete information, use both quantitative and qualitative data, assess probability or risk, and explain how it arrived at its conclusion.[9]

• *Artificial intelligence* is an information system that uses the computer's ability to accomplish tasks in a manner that is considered intelligent and is characterized by making decisions based on past *lessons learned*.[10]

At the work group level, there are a number of support systems, including email, bulletin boards, videoconferencing, group decision making systems, collaborative writing systems, group scheduling systems, and workflow automation systems.[11] Even telecommuting is a type of information support system. Telecommuters substitute "telecommunications and computers for the commute to a central office."[12]

Computer networks such as *local area networks* (LANs), *wide area networks* (WANs), and *distributed networks* are systems that support all levels of an organization:

- LANs use the organization's own computer and telecommunication systems to cover a limited distance. For example, they may link computers to a server so that people in the same or nearby buildings use a central printer or fax machine, or communicate with each other using three- to five-digit telephone extension numbers.
- WANs are "networks that serve microcomputers over larger, geographic areas, spanning distances that can cover a few miles or circle the globe."[13] WANs may use a common carrier or their own telecommunication system. More sophisticated companies are purchasing satellites or satellite time to increase the range of their "internal" communication system to include national or global distance learning, teleconferencing, Internet interfaces, etc.
- Distributed networks use small local computers to collect, store, and process information and send reports to various levels of management as needed.

The largest information superhighway in the world— the Internet—is fast becoming the information support system of choice for many organizations. The Internet offers low-cost or free access to the world. Many organizations develop their own intranets to link geographically dispersed departments and services. Customers love the Internet because they can research product information, track orders, even interact with real customer service representatives using video and telecommunication technologies. For example, at Lands End™, a retail catalog ordering company, if online customers cannot find the merchandise they want, they call a customer service representative. Then, the representative's *talking head* appears on the computer screen, and the representative locates and displays the merchandise.

Implementing Information System Interventions in the Workplace

Implementing information system interventions to improve performance is difficult because technology is changing so rapidly and because the changes will almost surely involve multiple interventions at multiple levels in the organization. The major success factor for any information system is a good management system that links all aspects of the system—people, data, technology, organizational procedures—to current and future business needs. Once again, the PT practitioner has an opportunity to shine by using performance technology techniques and tools to help management and information system staff design, develop, implement, and evaluate an effective and human information management system.

...the most useful way to understand technology and people within a system is to understand their relationship to the larger whole they serve. It's not enough to know how technology works. It's not enough to know what makes people tick. It's not enough to understand sales, manufacturing, and cost accounting. To make a system hum, you need feedback from customers, suppliers, regulators, local communities—outsiders who make demands for service, products, compliance support.[14]

Organizations that wish to maintain a competitive edge will need to remain adaptable and flexible in a constantly changing environment. As a result, analysis integrated with design will become an "ongoing activity of increasing importance."[15] PT practitioners are adept at acquiring, analyzing, and using information to improve human performance and system performance. They know how to uncover, collect, and organize the information needs of organizations, groups, and individuals; how to focus system design and evaluation on assessed needs; how to "use information as a driver (of performance improvement)."[16]

They must also know when to use information technology and how to use it wisely and well.[17] For example, the PT practitioner may suggest using an expert system despite its complexity and cost because the practitioner knows that the situation meets the selection criteria:
- The task is highly complex and time consuming.
- Human expertise is scarce or expensive.
- The outcomes have a high payoff value.
- The problem may be represented symbolically.
- The decision requires heuristics (contextual judgment) rather than pure logical deduction.[18]

PT practitioners also need to know how to enhance their own performance by developing a personal information system. A few suggestions appear below.
- Online surveys, discussion groups, or focus groups provide access to a geographically dispersed target audience and make it easy to store responses.
- Listservs, bulletin boards, and professional organization chat rooms make it possible to share information and resources with colleagues worldwide.
- Specially designed commercial software supports analysis, design, development, evaluation, and project management tasks.
- Videoconferencing, teleconferencing, pagers with text displays, and even fax machines make it possible to communicate with clients and resources at a distance.
- Electronic white boards, notebook computers with active matrix displays plus built-in audio and video capabilities, portable projection equipment, all enhance the ability of the PT practitioner to make presentations or facilitate training sessions.

207

Finally, PT practitioners must remain up to date on new and improved information technology. For example, they need to know that multiparticipant decision making (MDM) technology is available to help reduce communication barriers or noise, regulate decision processes, and generally enhance the interaction and flow of communication among the various members.[19] This technology may include a special room equipped with networked computers and electronic whiteboard, teleconferencing, video, and audio technology. (See the case study beginning on p. 218 and Job Aid 6-2.)

Suggestion Systems

Most proactive organizations rely on the suggestions of their employees to improve products, processes, and services. In fact, suggestion teams exist to minimize costs and/or increase productivity. Individuals and teams that raise the bar with positive results are often rewarded. This section will look more closely at suggestion systems and how they may be used to improve performance.

Definition and Scope

A suggestion system is a form of an employee recognition program that rewards employees or teams of employees for their ideas and contributions. It solicits, evaluates, implements, and rewards suggestions. Suggestions systems are mechanisms for ensuring upward communication in organizations by rewarding employees for sharing their creative thinking. Suggestion systems are often the intervention of choice when the organization wants to:

* Tap the reservoir of ideas and creative thinking of employees and teams
* Encourage upward communication
* Implement an organizational change initiative.

Suggestion systems may be implemented successfully in a variety of diverse organizational settings ranging from health care facilities, institutions of higher learning, government agencies to private-sector companies.[1]

In the United States, industries solicit an average of less than one-half of a suggestion per employee per year, whereas nine suggestions per employee per year are average in Japan.[2] In addressing world-class suggestion systems in total quality management (TQM) organizations, 40 ideas per person per year are generated and over 80% of the suggestions are used (see Table 6-5). Many of these quality management organizations educate employees on business improvement goals and then encourage brainstorming to realize the goals.[3]

Formal and Informal Systems

There are formal and informal suggestion systems. Formal systems are planned, implemented, and become

TABLE 6-5: Comparison of Average Number of Suggestions per Employee per Year
United States ....<.5
Japan...9
World-Class Suggestion Systems in TQM Organizations......................................40

Based on Bell, 1997, pp. 22–26; Savageau, 1996, pp. 16–18.

part of the organization's fabric. They usually require written input and include standards for feedback and for recognizing employees whose suggestion are implemented. Informal systems are loosely established and range from grapevine discussions to mottoes such as "We value your ideas." Informal systems welcome oral or written suggestions and do not have set standards for feedback and recognition.

Benefits and Barriers

Suggestion systems often result in lower costs, increased revenues, improved efficiency, and greater quality because they have an impact on performance in several ways, including:

* Serving as a mechanism for upward communication in the organization
* Serving as a motivational tool by helping employees with decision making skills
* Empowering employees by integrating the mission and vision of the organization with the personal goals of the employee
* Providing rewards to sustain employee involvement and interest
* Providing feedback that encourages the employee to try again, even when a suggestion is rejected.[4]

However, despite the merits of suggestion systems, some have failed due to some of the following factors:
* Inability to plan and communicate effectively
* Informality of implementation
* Poorly advertised, as in the case of the suggestion box looking more like a garbage receptacle than a mechanism for generating useful feedback
* Too many qualifiers or an institutional atmosphere that is too intimidating for employees or teams to contribute written ideas
* Lack of feedback from management.

Feedback is a major success factor. People who make suggestions have a right to positive or negative feedback.

JOB AID 6-2: Identify the Components of an Information System

Every organization has an information system—a system based on paper, computer hardware and software, telecommunications, or a combination of information technologies that collect, manipulate, store, and retrieve information to help people make decisions related to business needs. Every information system is made up of people, data, technology, and the organization itself (see Figure 6-2).

Directions: Use the questions in the first column to identify the components of a current information system. Use the questions in the second column to plan a new information system or revise an existing system.

Current Information System	New or Revised Information System
People: Identify stakeholders by name and position.	
1. Who champions the system? 2. Who manages the system? 3. Who selects or designs the technical elements of the system? 4. Who maintains the technical elements of the system? 5. Who collects data for the system? 6. Who inputs data into the system? 7. Who manipulates data in the system? 8. Who may retrieve data from the system?	1. Who will champion the system? 2. Who will manage the system? 3. Who will select or design the technical elements of the system? 4. Who will maintain the technical elements of the system? 5. Who will collect data for the system? 6. Who will input data into the system? 7. Who will manipulate data in the system? 8. Who will be able to retrieve data from the system?
Data: Identify the data needs of each level (see Table 6-4).	
1. What data are available to top management? 2. What data do top management need? 3. What data are available to middle management? 4. What data do middle management need? 5. What data are available to line managers? 6. What data do line managers need? 7. What data are available to work groups and workers? 8. What data do work groups and workers need?	1. What data will top management need? 2. Will the new system provide these data? 3. What data will middle management need? 4. Will the new system provide these data? 5. What data will first line managers need? 6. Will the new system provide these data? 7. What data will work groups and workers need? 8. Will the new system provide these data?
Technology: Identify all the information technology elements of the system.	
1. What paper-based information, computer-based (hardware and software), and telecommunications-based information technologies are included in this system? 2. What are the technical parameters of the system for collecting, storing, manipulating, and retrieving data? 3. What is the cost-benefit ratio for each information technology in this system? 4. How user friendly is each information technology in this system?	1. What paper-based information, computer-based (hardware and software), and telecommunications-based information technologies will be included in this system? 2. What will be the technical parameters of the system for collecting, storing, manipulating, and retrieving data? 3. What will be the cost-benefit ratio for each information technology in this system? 4. Will each information technology in this system be user friendly?
Organization: Identify policies, practices, procedures.	
1. Does the organization support the information system (time, money, resources, commitment)? 2. Does the organization have written policies related to managing the system and collecting, storing, manipulating, and retrieving data? 3. What are the organization's expectations in terms of input, process, output, and outcome? 4. Does the organization document procedures related to managing the system and collecting, storing, manipulating, and retrieving data?	1. Will the organization support the information system (time, money, resources, commitment)? 2. Will the organization write policies related to managing the system and collecting, storing, manipulating, and retrieving data? 3. What will the organization expect in terms of input, process, output, and outcome? 4. Will the organization document procedures related to managing the system and collecting, storing, manipulating, and retrieving data?

Based on Dessler, G. (1998). Human resources management (7th ed.). Upper Saddle River, NJ: Prentice Hall, Inc.; Hutchison, C.S., and Stein, F.S. (1997). A whole new world of interventions: The performance technologist as integrating generalist. Performance Improvement, 36(10), 28–35.

"Numerous firms provide not only explanations in writing to the employee, but also face-to-face discussions of the reasons for the rejection or acceptance of ideas."[5] A suggestion system that goes unacknowledged by management is soon viewed as a sham.

Tangible or intangible rewards are other success factors. In a formal system, the reward for a suggestion is often monetary. Companies offer cash rewards for cost-saving suggestions. In addition to monetary rewards, companies also offer vacation time, gift certificates, dining options, coveted parking spaces, certificates, family picnics, and other non-monetary incentives. Informal systems may or may not provide tangible rewards or incentives.

Implementing Suggestion System Interventions in the Workplace

The PT practitioner may suggest implementing a new suggestion system or improving an existing system as one way to open the lines of communication between the organization and employees. The PT practitioner may also make the following suggestions to help ensure that the suggestion system is uniquely structured to match the goals and values of the organization it will support:

- Initiate a formal suggestion system committee with representatives from all stakeholder groups.
- Analyze the specific benefits and barriers of a suggestion system.
- Ask who, what, when, where, why, and how questions. For example: Who may or may not submit suggestions? Who will evaluate the suggestions—individuals or teams?
- Establish a procedural format for submitting, evaluating, providing feedback, and implementing suggestions. For example, accepted suggestions need to be implemented immediately, with credit given to the originator.
- Establish an incentive program that matches the organizational goals and values. The value of the rewards should be commensurate with the suggestion's benefit to the organization.[6]
- Develop a marketing and advertising plan for the initial implementation and ongoing maintenance of the suggestion system.[7]

As the suggestions are implemented, the PT practitioner may keep the implementation targeted to business needs; provide performance support such as job aids and checklists; document policies, practices, and procedures; evaluate processes, outcomes, and impact; and help determine the cost-benefit ratio of implementation (see Job Aid 6-3).

JOB AID 6-3: Plan a Suggestion System

Use this job aid to gather information, document the planning process, make decisions regarding system structure, format, incentives, feedback, communication, etc., and evaluate the outcomes.

Directions: Fill in the information for all the sections. Revise the questions or add new ones as needed to adapt this job aid to a specific situation.

---

1. **Structure the Suggestion System**

   Why is the suggestion system needed?

   How will a suggestion system contribute to upward communication within the organization?

   What will the suggestion system look like (submission, evaluation, feedback, implementation, maintenance)?

   Who is responsible for implementing and maintaining the suggestion system?

   When will the suggestion system be inaugurated within the organization?

   Where are the strategic locations for the system?

JOB AID 6-3: Plan a Suggestion System *Continued*

2. Gather Input From Stakeholders

Which population is being targeted?

Which stakeholders have input?

Who else might be beneficial contributors?

3. Procedural Format

How will the suggestion system be used?

Are written suggestions required? ☐ Yes ☐ No

How is feedback given for rejection or acceptance of ideas?

4. Nature of Incentives

Will the rewards be ☐ monetary ☐ non-monetary ☐ both?

If the rewards are non-monetary, what type of incentives will be included?

Will the incentives be commensurate with the benefit of the suggestion to the company? ☐ Yes ☐ No
If yes, how will the benefit be established?

5. Driving Forces

Who champions the establishment of a suggestion system?

What communication barriers are the forces behind the suggestion system?

6. Communicate the Message

How is the suggestion system marketed throughout the organization?

How is the suggestion system advertised throughout the organization?

How is the suggestion system integrated within the organization?

Grievance Systems

It is common for employees to lodge formal complaints against their employers when employees feel that their wages, hours of employment, conditions of employment, and/or work practices have been compromised. Organizations set grievance systems in place to investigate these problems and assist in resolution. Grievance systems thus become potential performance improvement interventions.

Definition and Scope

A grievance system is a formal process for submitting, evaluating, and providing feedback related to employee grievances. A grievance is an employee's dissatisfaction or feeling of personal injustice relating to employment. Unions encourage filing grievances for the following reasons:

- Terms of the contract may be violated
- Evidence that the union is fulfilling its legal obligation to represent clients in a fair manner
- Political reasons, such as the need to seem tough with management[1]

Grievances affect contracts and organizational administration, and may focus on wages, hours, or other conditions of employment. Disciplinary actions against an employee or issues related to seniority, promotions, transfers, layoffs, absenteeism, insubordination, overtime, vacations, job evaluations, or plant rules are sources of grievances.[2]

Generally, grievance systems are found in a unionized organization, although they may also operate in a non-union environment. For example, an ombudsperson may facilitate the grievance resolution and represent the worker to management.

Formal Grievance Procedures

In unionized organizations, collective bargaining contracts contain a grievance procedure, which specifies step-by-step processes, time limits, and specific rules for filing grievances.[3] Basically, the employee presents a grievance orally to a supervisor and a union steward, an advocate dedicated to representing an employee's case to management. Unresolved grievances proceed through an appeal process.

Unionized employees have specific steps to follow in filing a grievance. Time limits are generally set for resolving the grievance. Each time a procedure fails to resolve a grievance, the next step becomes more time consuming and more formal.[4] A five-step process for filing a grievance follows:

1. Present grievance to supervisor and union steward.
2. If unresolved, forward grievance to plant manager and union grievance committee.
3. If unresolved, refer grievance up the company and union hierarchy.
4. If unresolved, submit grievance to arbitration.
5. If unresolved, arbitrator makes a decision.[5]

Benefits of Grievance Procedures

Union grievance procedures are beneficial to both management and employees. In resolving sources of conflict, the grievance procedure serves three separate groups:

- Employers and unions—interpreting and adjusting the agreement
- Employees—protecting contractual rights and channeling appeal processes
- Society—maintaining industrial satisfaction and reducing legal disputes[6]

Grievance procedures are charters for organizational justice. They protect employees from arbitrary management decisions. They assist management in settling conflicts quickly and efficiently so work stoppages are prevented. Grievance procedures are viewed by management as upward communication channels to monitor and fix sources of employee dissatisfaction.[7]

Implementing Grievance System Interventions in the Workplace

PT practitioners need to know what constitutes effective grievance procedures so they may help managers and staff design or implement appropriate procedures. Constructive grievance procedures depend on the ability to recognize, diagnose, and correct causes of employee dissatisfaction. It is important to develop the proper environment before grievances occur.[8] For example, Table 6-6 lists some critical guidelines for supervisors who are handling grievances.

When organizations adopt proper procedures of just cause and fairness, the grievance rate is significantly lowered in discipline grievances.[9] "Employers must ensure that the employee is adequately warned of the consequences, that the rule involved is related to an operation of the company, that a thorough investigation is undertaken, and that the penalty is reasonable."[10] In areas unrelated to discipline, organizations can avoid grievance situations by educating supervisors and managers about labor relations and about collective bargaining.[11]

When an organization must deal with grievances, it is vital that a pre-planned grievance system is available. Table 6-7 lists the keys to effective grievance systems and ways the PT practitioner plays a vital role in designing and implementing the systems (see Job Aid 6-4).

TABLE 6-6: Handling Grievances: Tips for Supervisors

Do...	Don't...
• Investigate and handle each and every case as though it may eventually result in an arbitration hearing. • Talk with the employee about his or her grievance. Give the employee a good and full hearing. • Require the union to identify specific contractual provisions allegedly violated. • Comply with the contractual time limits of the company for handling the grievance. • Determine whether there were any witnesses. • Examine the employee's personnel record. • Fully examine prior grievance records. • Treat the union representatives as equals. • Hold grievance discussions privately. • Fully inform your own supervisor of grievance matters.	• Discuss the case with the union steward alone. The grievant should definitely be there. • Make arrangements with an individual employee that are inconsistent with the labor agreement. • Hold back the remedy if the company is wrong. • Admit to the binding effect of a past practice. • Relinquish to the union your rights as a manager. • Settle grievances on the basis of what is "fair." Instead, stick to the labor agreement, which should be the only standard. • Bargain over items not covered by the contract. • Treat as subject to arbitration claims demanding the discipline or discharge of managers. • Give long, written grievance answers. • Trade a grievance settlement for a grievance withdrawal, or try to make up for a bad decision in one grievance by bending over backward in another. • Deny grievances on the premise that your "hands have been tied by management." • Agree to informal amendments in the contract.

Based on Baer, 1970.

TABLE 6-7: Implementing Effective Grievance Systems

Keys to Effective Implementation	How the PT Practitioner Can Help
Maintain an effective, fair grievance procedure that is supported by labor and management.	• Suggest techniques and activities for gaining support • Facilitate group activities aimed at gaining and maintaining support
Frequently review the efficacy of the grievance procedure.	• Design evaluation plan, criteria, process • Develop evaluation instruments • Evaluate process and outcomes
Handle grievances promptly.	• Develop process flowcharts for handling grievances • Suggest time management techniques
Make sure that procedures and forms for airing grievances are user friendly.	• Analyze existing forms • Design new forms or repurpose existing forms • Pilot forms with users
Make sure that both employees and supervisors are totally familiar with procedures, forms, and general format of the grievance procedures.	• Design and develop training programs • Design and develop information packets or job aids
Provide avenues of appeal from supervisor ruling.	• Suggest appeal process flow chart • Facilitate review of process to determine effectiveness
Keep channels of communication open by developing an organizational climate that fosters productivity and quality.	• Be alert to potential links with other types of interventions, for example, communication networks, job analysis and work design, organizational development interventions, etc. • Conduct organizational and environmental analysis

Based on Baer, 1970.

JOB AID 6-4: Grievance Procedure Review

Part I: Review the typical steps involved in filing a grievance. Use the steps as a guideline for completing Part 2.

Part 2: Use the following format to document the existing grievance procedures in your organization and make suggestions for modification.

Directions:
1. The employee presents the grievance orally and informally to the immediate supervisor in the presence of the union steward.
2. A meeting occurs between the plant manager, the human resource manager, or a grievance committee.
3. The grievance is written, dated, and signed by the employee and the union steward.
4. The written grievance states the events as the employee perceives them.
5. The written grievance cites the contract provision that was allegedly violated.
6. The written grievance cites the desired settlement.
7. The organization's top labor representatives and high union officials are involved.
8. The grievance goes to arbitration.

Organization's Grievance Procedure	Suggested Modifications
1.	1.
2.	2.
3.	3.
4.	4.
5.	5.
6.	6.
7.	7.
8.	8.

Conflict Resolution

Conflict is a natural condition—neither good nor bad. Yet, to most people conflict implies hostility, friction, and argument. When conflict exists in an environment that allows and encourages communication and collaboration, it may prove beneficial both to individuals and to their organization. Learning to manage conflict is critical in the ongoing process of improving how an organization adapts to and takes advantage of change.

> *Conflict in organizations is inevitable. However, the extent to which conflict has detrimental or beneficial effects depends on how effectively it is managed... When conflict is managed effectively, it can enhance individual organization members' willingness and ability to contribute their best efforts and to integrate their contributions effectively with each other. When conflict is managed poorly, organizational members are often blocked in their efforts to contribute, and colleagues can become enemies.[1]*

Definition and Scope

"Conflict is the process of expressing dissatisfaction, disagreement, or unmet expectations with any organizational interchange."[2] It takes two to conflict—a minimum of two parties with individual goals that are in opposition. "As we commonly use the word, the connotation of conflict covers a broad spectrum of interactive behavior, usually carrying negative connotations."[3] Figure 6-3 portrays Beck's view of conflict as continuum that moves from a minor difference of opinion to all-out war. The range of responses to conflict is usually determined by where people are on the continuum, for example, people in the difference-disagreement stage of conflict often try to discuss, educate, and, finally, negotiate.

Conflict may exist at three different levels; individual, organization, or society.[4] It may be task oriented or people oriented:

> *The former concerns the substance of the work that needs to be done, such as ideas or procedures. The latter occurs in connection with such things as struggles for leadership, unequal workloads, and personality differences. They can take place simultaneously (or) any episode can contain elements of both...[5]*

Positive and Negative Views of Conflict

The view of conflict as a totally negative experience is slowly changing:

> *Conflict theories remained relatively unchanged through the 1950s. Theorists were still equating conflict with negative outcomes, hurt feelings, and dysfunctional confrontation...Modern theorists still acknowledge the drawbacks of conflict but recognize that some positive outcomes are possible.[6]*

Some positive benefits of conflict follow:
- Prevents stagnation
- Encourages debate and change
- Stimulates interest, curiosity, and creative thinking
- Provides a means to air problems and resolve problems
- Produces alternative solutions
- Opens the possibility of a win-win solution[7,8]

Even Beck sheds a more positive light on his continuum (see Figure 6-3) by adding a range of responses to his conflict continuum. On the left side, the individuals themselves may handle conflict resolution. In the center, it is still possible for the individuals to negotiate a win-win solution. However, the right side of the spectrum usually requires third-party intervention or mediation.[9]

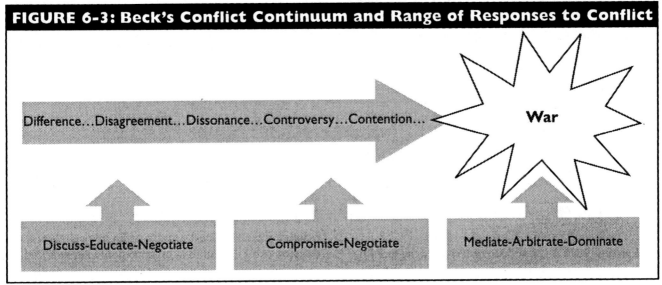

FIGURE 6-3: Beck's Conflict Continuum and Range of Responses to Conflict

Difference...Disagreement...Dissonance...Controversy...Contention... War

Discuss-Educate-Negotiate   Compromise-Negotiate   Mediate-Arbitrate-Dominate

Based on Beck, 1999, pp. 280–283.

On the other hand, conflict is still perceived as negative—a win-lose or lose-lose situation, or, at best, a situation involving dominance and compromise. Some of the negative outcomes of unmanaged or mismanaged conflict include disputes, competition, sabotage, inefficiency, lack of productivity, low morale, distrust, suspicion, resistance, withholding knowledge, rebellion, and boredom.[10,11]

"For conflict to produce positive results, however, it must be brought out and dealt with quickly, lest it erupt into warfare among the parties to the detriment of the organization."[12] In other words, the challenge is "to cultivate conflict without distress" to the organization, the work environment, the work, or the worker.[13]

Implementing Conflict Resolution Interventions in the Workplace

Several trends have intensified the need for implementing sound conflict resolution practices to improve organizational performance. These trends include increases in:
* Diversity of the work force
* Need for frequent and quick change to keep up with the marketplace
* Use of participatory management
* Reliance on cross-functional teams[14]

Implementation of conflict resolution requires a supportive communication environment, an environment that:
* Focuses on practical ways to accomplish what needs to be accomplished within the context of organizational goals (emphasis on problem solving)
* Recognizes that each participant has valid concerns
* Encourages clarification of the position and goals of each participant to each participant
* Fosters empathy; treats all participants with genuine concern
* Accepts insights from all participants and recognizes that past solutions do not necessarily fit current situations
* Allows spontaneity; works with the process as it unfolds without preconceived solutions[15]

Conflict Resolution Strategies

The need to implement conflict and collaboration interventions may arise from incidents as diverse as failing to reach consensus on a new product name to actual physical violence on the shop floor. To help implement successful conflict resolution, the PT practitioner should be familiar with various styles that managers traditionally use to deal with conflict.

Back in the 1960s, Blake and Mouton created the building blocks for today's view of how manager's handle conflict.

They labeled the strategies as forcing, withdrawing, smoothing, compromising, and problem solving.[16] Today, the literature suggests that managers tend to use five conflict-handling strategies: accommodate, avoid, compromise, compete, or collaborate.[17]

Two techniques can help manage and resolve conflict: negotiation and mediation.[18] For maximum success, both negotiation and mediation require trained professionals who are experienced in conflict resolution.

Negotiation

"Negotiation is not a result but a process; the deal concludes when the parties shake hands."[19] Currently, negotiation is the major tool used to manage conflict in organizations. Effective negotiations accomplish the following:
* Serve the interests of the parties involved rather than the self-interest of the negotiator
* Generate a mutually satisfying outcome
* Maintain or enhance the parties' ongoing relationship and ability to work with each other in the future.[20]

It is difficult for a negotiator to meet all three criteria. However, to increase the level of effectiveness, the negotiator may:
* Adapt his or her level of cooperation to the other party's level of cooperation
* Choose between the direct outcomes of the negotiation and the relationship on the basis of their relative importance in a given situation
* Choose situations in which it is possible to establish a mutually collaborative approach
* Listen and give weight to all issues, assuming that the parties' issues are not mutually exclusive[21]

Mediation

Mediation is familiar to organizations in which the employees are unionized. Whether the mediation is formal (management-union bargaining) or informal (a manager resolving a conflict between two employees), the process involves a third party who objectively reviews both sides of the conflict and brings the parties to a resolution that they can each accept. "The role of the mediator is that of the judge at ringside, not at the middle of the fight."[22] If mediation fails, the problem may go to arbitration where an arbitrator makes a final decision on the outcome.

Collaboration

Viewing conflict as a problem solving activity "opens the door to working with the other party rather than against him/her."[23] Working together creates an environment of collaboration. "The best conditions for managing conflict constructively are found in organizations characterized by trust, collaboration, and an integrative cycle of mutual problem solving."[24] The keys to collaboration include a willingness to share needs, goals, and information; explore creative alternatives; downplay emotions; and apply creative problem solving techniques. On the one hand, collaboration is not always easy to achieve; on the other hand, the rewards of working together are worth the effort:

In the majority of conflicts, at least one of the participants is not a collaborator by instinct. However, in most workplace and personal conflicts, collaboration is the most productive style...other styles will not produce as positive an outcome (see Job Aid 6-5).[25]

JOB AID 6-5: Develop a Macro View of a Conflict Management System

Directions: Use this job aid to produce a macro or "big picture" view of a current conflict management system or to design goals and objectives for a new program. Approach this as an individual or group activity with all stakeholders included.

1. Identify current organizational stakeholders	
2. Identify stakeholder assumptions	
a. Conflict is inevitable within this organization.	☐ Agree ☐ Disagree
b. Conflict is neither good nor bad.	☐ Agree ☐ Disagree
c. Collective/stakeholder participation in creating conflict processes is essential.	☐ Agree ☐ Disagree
d. The process of conflict is fluid and organic, not linear.	☐ Agree ☐ Disagree
e. Organizations are constantly changing and evolving.	☐ Agree ☐ Disagree
f. Managing change is related to managing conflict.	☐ Agree ☐ Disagree
3. Identify focus of conflict management.	
a. Focus is on work/production.	☐ Agree ☐ Disagree
b. Focus is on worker/performance.	☐ Agree ☐ Disagree
c. Focus is on work environment.	☐ Agree ☐ Disagree
4. Identify how most managers prefer to handle conflict.	
a. Accommodate	☐ Agree ☐ Disagree
b. Avoid	☐ Agree ☐ Disagree
c. Compromise	☐ Agree ☐ Disagree
d. Compete	☐ Agree ☐ Disagree
e. Collaborate	☐ Agree ☐ Disagree
5. Identify current organizational response to conflict.	
a. Negotiation	☐ Agree ☐ Disagree
b. Mediation (arbitration)	☐ Agree ☐ Disagree
c. Collaboration	☐ Agree ☐ Disagree
6. Identify major sources of conflict within the organization.	☐ Agree ☐ Disagree

Based on Costantino, C.A., and Merchant, C.S. (1996). Designing conflict management systems. *San Francisco, CA: Jossey-Bass.*

Case Study 6-1: The Role of an Information System in a Non-Profit Organization

Situation

This case takes place in a large, urban, non-profit cancer institute, which is referred to in this case study as the Institute. More than 1,000 individuals are employed by the Institute, which has 15 regional offices and is integrated with a nationally recognized Carnegie Research medical school and six hospitals. The Institute's senior management maintains a strong commitment to promoting effective internal communication through both non-technologically supported and technologically supported means.

The primary expectations of the Institute with regard to its information system are:
* Provide fast and accurate information dissemination
* Promote teamwork
* Improve the overall efficiency of departmental and interdepartmental business processes

This case study will describe the current interventions, the results realized from these interventions, and the lessons learned. At the end of the case study is a job aid for summarizing technological interventions for internal organizational communication and the functions they provide.

Interventions

The Institute relies on three primary information technologies for fast and accurate information dissemination: email, the World Wide Web (web), and an intranet. Information technologies for teamwork support and business process improvement include a calendar, ad hoc groupware, network file servers, threaded discussions, video conferencing, PDF files, and database-backed web applications.

Information Dissemination

Email is the most common method of information dissemination due to its ease of use, the simplicity of setup and support by an Information Systems (IS) department, and the relatively low costs involved in implementing this technology. The ability to attach external documents to email greatly increases its usefulness. Common document types attached to email include word processing, spreadsheet, PDF files, images, and multimedia presentations. The Institute takes attachments one step further by sending audio-visual files in email to provide personal *telemedicine* to patients.

The Institute finds that email is best suited to disseminating specific information to a specific number of recipients. In addition, it is used for impromptu messages that the sender wants the recipient to be made aware of as soon as possible. Lastly, employee access to email is also far more common than access to update content on corporate web pages.

Web

While email can be used to send information to large numbers of recipients, web pages are better suited for this purpose for several reasons:
* First, sending email to a large number of recipients uses a tremendous amount of immediate network bandwidth that can slow down or even crash an organization's email system or network. Web pages circumvent this by allowing employees to access the information anytime, anywhere. The anywhere characteristic is important to organizations with mobile employees who require more flexible access to information than email software, which requires configuration. The Institute is presently developing a web-based email interface to resolve this issue.
* Second, web pages provide a central repository for information and employees can easily access the information on a repeated basis as well as perform searches through large volumes of current and historical information. Access to current, real-time information is a key feature of the web. The Institute has several clinical and administrative software applications currently accessible through a web browser. This allows employees to receive and enter information directly into the Institute's corporate databases. Network file servers combine several of the advantages and disadvantages of email and web pages. While they do not provide access to the real-time information that web pages offer, they are as easy to use as email and act as a central repository for receiving and entering information.

Intranet

Web pages containing information for internal communication are located in an intranet, which implies that technical security restrictions are in place to prevent non-employees, or unauthorized users, from accessing the web pages. The Institute uses its intranet for a number of information dissemination purposes. Internal job postings and news releases are placed on the intranet for the employees to access. Important presentations by the Institute's senior management, medical grand rounds, community outreach events, public relations special events, and television segments are also recorded to digital video so employees may view them at their discretion using web-based streaming software. The advent of streaming technology has made this a practical solution by virtually eliminating the download time required to view audio-video files, which typically have large file sizes. Presentations can also be streamed real-time, although the Institute does not consider this necessary. Real-time streaming also places greater stress on the network and requires a more sophisticated technology configuration.

Teamwork Support

A number of information technology applications are available to support decision making and teamwork within the organization: calendar applications, groupware, network file servers, and web-based applications.

A web-based calendar is available to disseminate organization-wide and departmental information. Calendars are used to post such information as physician on-call and floor coverage, meeting dates/times, and training schedules. The Institute also uses network-based calendars, which were implemented before web-based calendars were available. Network calendars are used for conference room scheduling and by individuals who want a personal electronic calendar to keep track of appointments and meetings.

Team- or groupware software packages are specifically designed to support communication, coordination, and collaboration among groups of employees often separated by distance. While the Institute has not adopted a fully integrated, comprehensive information technology to support teamwork, it has implemented ad-hoc technologies to provide a higher degree of collaboration among employees, teams, and external contacts than the traditional email and telephone technologies.

Network file servers provide a shared storage repository for files that employees wish to share. Once available on a file server, files may be accessed and edited by several individuals for collaboration on projects. Commonly shared files include spreadsheet and word processing documents, as well as small database applications. Specific file servers, or subdirectories within them, can be made accessible to particular users or departments, and the files can be given either "read" or "read-write" access. Network files have the added benefit of being backed up more frequently.

While numerous web-based interventions are available for team communication, the Institute currently uses only intranet-secured threaded discussions that allow team members to engage in two-way, ongoing, asynchronous communication. Although threaded discussions are not suitable for real-time communication and collaboration among team members, the hierarchical manner in which messages are posted and stored and access to all previous messages provides an excellent forum for ongoing project communications between team members. In the future, the Institute may consider the following web-based technologies: whiteboards, project management software, synchronous chat rooms, and listservs for team-wide email messaging.

The Institute recently built a state-of-the-art video conferencing room to allow executives and physicians to communicate with other health care facilities and government agencies. The room has seating for 25 individuals in a U-shaped table configuration with voice-activated speakers at each seat. At the front of the room is a 50-inch drop-down screen, accompanied by premium speakers and a personal computer with Internet access, a digital video disc (DVD) drive, and multimedia and presentation software. Located on the ceiling is a motion- and sound-sensitive camera that can follow speakers during a meeting or presentation. In addition to the video conferencing room, the Institute has been slowly providing desktop computer-based web cams to its employees for audio-visual, person-to-person communication and collaboration.

Business Process Improvement

The web provides a powerful means for organizations to improve their business processes through workflow automation over a centralized, platform-independent technology. For several years, the Institute has been using its intranet for business process improvement and, with the release of more mature software, is continuing to place a high priority on development of these projects. Using the web for business process improvement can provide substantial cost savings by:

- Reducing the time required to complete tasks
- Providing a single, user-friendly interface to decentralized and geographically dispersed data and information systems
- Disseminating timely information stored in its corporate databases
- Reducing organizational paper flow and file storage

The Institute currently uses two web-based technologies to promote business process improvement: PDF files and database-backed web applications. Web sites and the web pages within them are created and delivered in HTML (hypertext markup language). The purpose of HTML, or hypertext, is to allow the delivery of content over the web with embedded images and "hyperlinks" that allow the web site visitor to navigate both within and between documents on the web to view information.

However, HTML is not well suited to present documents with complex formatting that include numerous tables, charts, images, and photographs. To reduce paper flow and storage, the Institute has made most organizational forms available over the web in Adobe PDF (portable document format). PDF has become the universal format for delivering documents over the web that are not easily presented in HTML. The following documents are examples of items that are currently available in PDF format over the Institute's website:

- Request forms for time off, tuition reimbursement, expense reimbursement, travel reimbursement, direct pay, supplies, purchase orders, building services, petty cash, and business cards
- Employee recognition forms
- Performance evaluation forms
- Volunteer application and employment application
- User and technical documentation
- Grant applications
- Organizational chart
- Employee handbook containing benefits information and company policies

The second business process improvement intervention, database-backed web applications, is one of the more ambitious information systems and technology undertakings. While the up-front development time and cost for this intervention is typically far greater than many other interventions, the long-term time and cost savings associated with it, in most cases, justifies the outlay of resources. The Institute currently has three database-backed web applications in production that provide for business process improvement. Each of these applications has eliminated file storage redundancy, facilitated faster and more efficient updates of information, allowed for easier searching and reporting of the information, and made the information more accessible to the individuals in need of the information. The Institute is currently investigating the use of wireless devices such as personal digital assistants and notebooks to provide even more convenient access to corporate databases and information.

Results

While substantial work lies ahead for The Institute to fully exploit its information systems infrastructure as an information dissemination, teamwork support, and process improvement tool, employees and management generally agree that the results so far have been very positive. Of the information systems and technology implemented to date, those listed below have proven to be the most beneficial.

- Network file servers to disseminate and share information.
- Intranet to disseminate internal organizational communication, news, and organizational forms.
- Database-backed web applications to disseminate information and improve business processes.
- Online employee directory to disseminate information and facilitate teamwork.
- Video conferencing room to facilitate teamwork and research collaboration.

Based on these results, the Institute concluded the following regarding the progress of using information systems and information technology for internal communication:

- Meeting information dissemination goals is clearly the most successful accomplishment, with a wide variety of technologies in place to meet the complex and diverse internal communication needs of the Institute.
- Process improvement and work flow automation projects undertaken to date have been very successful, but significant opportunities still exist within the Institute for the implementation of similar systems.
- The following business processes are in need of automation through database-backed web applications: the human resource process of receiving, recording, managing, and reporting vacation time, sick time, and employment opportunities; the public relations process of managing and publishing press releases; and the purchasing process of requesting equipment and supplies.
- The Institute needs a searchable knowledge base of best internal practices.

Lessons Learned

The Institute adopts and implements new information systems and technology for internal communication as soon as possible, and has learned many lessons through their evolution and institutionalization within the Institute. At a macro-level, several important planning and management issues are now known:

- Clearly identify goals for the project at the outset to determine the type of organizational communication and information systems best suited for implementation. In their quest to exploit information systems for organizational communication, the Institute identified the following goals: (1) speed information dissemination, (2) assist change management efforts, (3) promote employee morale and retention, (4) provide seamless integration of previously decentralized information systems, (5) improve productivity, (6) reduce the effort required to maintain an Intranet by replacing static HTML pages with a database-backed, template-driven web site, (7) facilitate teamwork and research collaboration, and (8) reduce paperwork and file storage.
- Establish a return-on-investment (ROI) goal and use metrics to evaluate both project progress and results. The Institute plans to include this goal in the future.
- During the project planning stage, identify the type of internal communication required by the organization (vertical, horizontal, etc.). Also consider whether the information needs to be sent and received real-time (synchronously) or not (asynchronously). These considerations will also dictate the type of information system and technology necessary to achieve the desired communication goals (see Job Aid 6-6 on p. 221).
- Choose and enforce the appropriate source of information dissemination to ensure the credibility and consistency of the information. Email distribution lists, which allow an employee to send email to a large number of recipients, are an excellent example to highlight the importance of this issue. Like most companies, The Institute has an email alias called staff@companyname.org, which can be used to send an email to all employees. The ability to use this alias should be restricted to a few key individuals, such as the communication department and top executives. Before enforcing this policy, the Institute had several cases of inappropriate use of the alias for personal purposes.
- Obtain buy-in from the human resource department to accept responsibility for maintaining a centralized electronic directory of employees names, email addresses, and security permissions for the intranet. The Institute uses LDAP (Lightweight Directory Access Protocol) to accomplish this, but without human resource buy-in the process of maintaining the directory is a very cumbersome process.
- The most significant technological lesson learned has been the need for the seamless integration of the Institute's information systems. In this large organization, numerous information systems exist that were implemented over many

years, as new technology became available. Consequently, several of these systems are unable to communicate with one another and substantial inefficiencies and losses in productivity occur. Planning for the seamless integration of these many information systems, that is, their ability to communicate and interact with one another, will yield enormous benefits: (1) reductions in end-user training needs, (2) more efficient utilization of technical staff, (3) increased productivity, (4) reduced data and information corruption, (4) faster and better analysis of data and information, and (5) an overall increase in the ROI in information systems and technology.

This case study was written by David Maier, MS, ABD, Information Technology Consultant and Adjunct Assistant Professor. David has worked in the health care industry for six years implementing information systems for business process improvement and internal and external communication. Used with permission.

JOB AID 6-6: Summary of Information Technologies

This job aid provides information to help you select the most appropriate technology for your organizational needs.

Technology	Synchronous/ Asynchronous	Information Dissemination	Work Flow Automation	Teamwork	Anytime, Anywhere	Difficulty of Support	Implementation Cost
Email	Asynchronous	X		X		Low	Low
Web-based Email	Asynchronous	X		X	X	Low	Low
Listserv	Asynchronous	X		X		Low	Low
File Server	Asynchronous			X		Low	Low
Web Pages	Asynchronous	X		X	X	Low	Low
Adobe PDF Files	Asynchronous	X				Low	Low
Threaded Discussions	Asynchronous	X		X	X	Low	Low
Message (White) Board	Asynchronous	X		X	X	Low	Low
Network Calendar	Asynchronous	X		X		Low	Low
Web Calendar	Asynchronous	X		X	X	Low	Low
Online Project Management	Asynchronous	X		X	X	Low	Medium
Directory Services	Asynchronous			X		Medium	Low
Web Chat	Synchronous			X	X	Medium	Medium
Video Conferencing	Synchronous			X		Medium	Medium
Online Databases	Hybrid	X	X	X	X	Medium	Medium
Wireless Intranet Access	Hybrid	X	X	X	X	High	High
Video Streaming	Asynchronous	X		X	X	Medium	Medium
Video Streaming	Synchronous				X	High	High
Internal Portal	Asynchronous	X	X	X	X	High	High

CHAPTER

7

ORGANIZATIONAL DESIGN AND DEVELOPMENT

IN THE LAND OF INTELLIGENCE,
THE SMART KIDS ARE THE BULLIES.

ORGANIZATIONAL DESIGN AND DEVELOPMENT

Organizational design and development means adapting organizations to increase people's contribution or improve the work environment. It is not unusual for organizations to focus on profitability, productivity, service to customers, market share, or shareholder value. However, they frequently lose sight that it is people who accomplish goals and meet targets. It is essential for organizations to continuously improve process and outcomes, but these achievements come through people's leadership and commitment.

Empowerment means enabling people to work to their highest levels by believing in them and establishing processes and systems that support their efforts. Empowerment is based on team building, problem solving, and decision making.

Pro-active organizational design and development interventions provide direction that may create radical change, which can be stressful even if the change is warranted. Before implementation, senior management should thoroughly consider interventions. Change efforts need strong commitment by senior-level champions who are prepared to see the change process through successfully. Change planning needs to involve participative cross-functional and cross-level approaches. Organizational pro-action includes strategic planning, operations management, environmental scanning, benchmarking, and reegineering, realignment, and restructuring.

Finally, organizations need to treasure a positive culture that celebrates diversity. Organizations can benefit from a variety of ideas. Expectations of the community are changing and it is essential for organizations to act with integrity. Spirituality in the workplace recognizes social responsibility to the environment, to local citizens, the wider community, and to workers. Companies are recognizing the value of spirituality and are even including success stories in their brand advertising campaigns. Organizational values interventions help people succeed by supporting the "right" decisions, maximizing the significance of employee, supplier, customer, and client, encouraging workers to think globally, and treating people with respect and trust. Organizational values include culture, diversity, globalization, ethics, and spirituality (see Table 7-1).

EMPOWERMENT

Empowerment provides three important interventions that support the work life of employees: team strategies, problem solving, and decision making. During the Industrial Era, managers told workers frequently to "check their brains at the door, and use only their brawn (manual labor) in the workplace." In that context, management was responsible for the brains (problem solving and decision making) and workers for the muscle and the physical effort. Although this brains-and-brawn mentality is not entirely eradicated, it is commonly recognized that the people who perform a task are the ones best suited to think through the issues and resolve the problems. Workers should be empowered to think, overcome obstacles, and resolve problems.

Empowerment interventions encourage all employees to do their best to continuously improve the workplace by identifying situations that create challenges and looking for better ways of doing things. Just as the Ritz-Carlton corporation does, Tom Peters challenges organizations to change employees into "Michelangelos"… The Ritz-Carlton has "Michelangelos of Parking," "Michelangelos of House-keeping," "Michelangelos of Accounts Receivable." Employees should exert energy, take ownership, and share responsibility and authority to make things better. Employees should be encouraged to take initiative and to look for improvement opportunities.[1]

Most employees enjoy working in groups and have much to contribute due to their knowledge, skills, experience, and commitment or motivation. Yet work groups or teams are not always functional.

TABLE 7-1: Organizational Design and Development Interventions From Enhanced HPT Model

Empowerment
- Team Strategies
- Problem Solving
- Decision Making

Organizational Pro-Action
- Strategic Planning
- Operations Management
- Environmental Scanning
- Benchmarking
- Reengineering, Realigning, Restructuring

Organizational Values
- Culture
- Diversity
- Globalization
- Ethics
- Spirituality in the Workplace

Frequently, previous experiences with authoritarian work structures or rigid organizational culture can discourage employees. They must unlearn or remove old personal attitudes and organizational obstacles. The transition is difficult for employees who previously worked in situations where problem resolution was discouraged. Often, they resist looking for opportunities to solve problems. In addition, formerly hierarchical managers find it a challenge to share responsibility and authority. They, too, resist changes.

Team Strategies

Definition and Scope

In this information era, teams are necessary to effectively create and maximize workplace information. Jobs are interdependent and decisions require input from many people. As a result, team participation leads to greater commitment to common goals and action plans. As an intervention, teams enable employees to work together in a creative manner.

A team is a group of people working together as a cohesive unit to accomplish a common goal. Some employees may be assigned to more than one team. For example, an employee might lead a task group to revise policies and procedures, while at the same time serve as a member of a team developing a workshop to address leadership gaps.

The need for performance improvement is increasing. Managing performance and any changes that are required is complex.

The rapid, far-reaching, and continuing changes of recent years have brought about a situation where understanding the psychology of individuals and teams is of prime importance in work settings. Organizational structures have shifted radically to the point where individual managers and professionals have far greater autonomy, responsibility and accountability. Organizations seek to reduce central control and to "empower" individual employees. Those employees combine in teams that are frequently cross-functional and project-based rather than hierarchical in their construction...The capacity of people to cope with the scale and speed of these changes has become a major issue.[1]

Bringing a group of people together to accomplish a common objective does not automatically make any group an effective team. In *Team Fitness*, Meg Hartzler and Jane Henry present a model for effective teams that includes four main areas of activity:
- Identify *customer focus* including an understanding of the requirements and expectations of the team as related to customer focus
- Set *team direction* as defined by a team vision, mission, goal, and objectives
- Understand *oneself*, *other teams members*, *team dynamics*, and *organizational culture* as they impact team performance
- Establish *team accountability*, based on a sharing of values and beliefs, planning, and agreement as to how the team will work together.[2]

Team Empowerment

Empowerment provides the opportunity, means, and authority required to effectively make work-related decisions. Empowerment stems from the participative management philosophy of the 1960s that aimed at getting employees involved in the decision making process. The 1960s practice was neither a success nor a failure, primarily because managers did not understand their role. They were unsure whether it meant conducting more meetings, providing more motivation, or just being friendlier to employees.[3]

The concept of empowerment evolved out of this earlier confusion surrounding participative management. For a team to be empowered, it requires direction (goals and measurements); knowledge (information, skills, and training); resources (tools, materials, facilities, and money); and support (coaching, feedback, approval, and encouragement).[4]

Value of Team

Effective teams add immense value to organizations. Workplace teams have increased dramatically due to two movements in the late 1900s: British socio-technical systems design and Japanese lean production systems.[5] Teams effectively tackle diverse issues, such as health and safety, learning on the job, and product quality and liability.

Socio-technical systems encourage open dialogue and trust between stakeholders such as workers, managers, executives, unions, customers, and suppliers, which promise improved problem solving. Enhanced production systems, such as the Japanese lean production system, use less of everything compared to mass production:

> ...half the human effort in the factory, half the manu-facturing space, half of the investment in tools, half the engineering hours to develop a new product in half the time. Also, it requires keeping far less than half the needed inventory on site, results in many fewer defects, and produces a greater and ever growing variety of products.[6]

Teams have been part of reducing the complexity of orga-nizations and have shifted much of the workplace control to the front-line. The focus is on taking responsibility, adding value, continuously improving, and being client driven. Other benefits include enhancing knowledge and skills and reducing stress and psychosomatic symptoms caused by work, such as stomach pains, headaches, and sleeping difficulties.[7]

Implementing Team Strategy Interventions in the Workplace

Team Development
Teams are established through the selection and assignment of team members to achieve a common goal. Some factors to consider when making team assignments are job skills, experience, social and communication skills, and desire to be a team member. However, no matter what the makeup of the team, teams go through four stages of development that may differ in length and intensity depending on the dynamics of the selected team members and the situation.[8]

Forming stage—Team members get acquainted with each other and with the concept of working as a team. Members begin to define the guidelines for how they will work together and to determine a vision and mission that aligns with customer focus. When working with a newly formed team, find a time and place for the team to meet and start the bonding process by having members talk about themselves so the team can begin to identify common traits. Ensure the members understand the purpose of the team and are involved in defining the vision and mission of the team. Employees will need knowledge and skills in interacting with others, problem solving, making decisions, and taking action.[9]

Storming stage—Often described as the most difficult, this stage is characterized by conflict and confusion among members over how to react when issues arise. Leaders may emerge but may not be accepted readily by other team members. Because team members have not been together long enough to establish trust and confidence in each other, confusion reigns. The need for an established problem solving process becomes clear. Leadership emerges as the "voice of common sense," providing information and assuring the team that conflict is typical. Continual focus on the team's mission and goals helps resolve conflicts.[10]

Norming stage—Diminished conflict comes with the acceptance of each person's individual differences, under-standing and endorsing ground rules, and agreeing on the roles and responsibilities. Leadership is shared when members become more comfortable expressing personal views that others may not always agree with. Information sharing and the willingness of team members to work through their differences energize the team.

Teams should become more self-directed at this stage. All members should participate and become more confident in their team roles. Managers and team coaches should observe and listen as team members interact and provide meaningful feedback as needed to help the team maintain its focus.[11]

Performing stage—Maturity of the team is marked by strong team identity and loyalty. Problem solving and implementation of team decisions are now part of the team's established practices. Spirit is strong. Managers and team coaches should continue to listen to, encourage, and support the team. They should also recognize and reinforce team successes.

Team development does not end when the team reaches the performing stage; it is an on-going process. Situations such as a member transferring into or out of the team may cause the team to go back to an earlier stage to make the adjustment.[12]

Team Effectiveness
Teams need proficiency in the following skills to work effectively: teambuilding and team formation, conflict resolution, interpersonal communications, leadership, meeting management, coaching and counseling, and change management.

Many factors influence team effectiveness. Colin Coulson-Thomas studied 100 United Kingdom organizations with combined annual revenues of 150 billion pounds and employing more than one million people.[13] His report, *Harnessing the Potential of Groups*, discusses enablers of more effective group work and teamwork. Coulson-Thomas (see Table 7-2) lists teamwork and project manage- ment as important skills. Table 7-2 also indicates organizational factors that are equal to and, in some cases, more important than skills.[14] Some of the key organizational factors are clear and measurable objectives, personal commitment, management attitudes, account-ability, empowerment, and overcoming departmental barriers. Although skills are important, organizational factors probably have greater influence on the effectiveness of teams.

To achieve fitness in these areas, a team should have guidance and support from a manager or champion and be self-directed, with all members willing to share leadership responsibilities. How can employees know when a team is fit? Hartzler and Henry identify common characteristics shared by effective or fit teams:

- Capitalization on member strengths to produce team results
- Member investment in team success and accountability for output
- Observable spirit and energy
- Demonstration of member trust and collaboration
- Candid discussion of issues that could impact team performance
- Focus on the team goal[15]

Team Sponsor

Typically, teams work on problems or projects. Sometimes their job is to resolve issues and determine solutions. At other times, teams are expected to complete a project composed of many tasks. Frequently, teams are cross-functional—employees from many departments are brought together to achieve a goal. It is critical that there is a clear mandate and someone in management, known as the sponsor, who supports the team. It is not unusual for cross-functional teams to come from different units or departments with differing commitments to the team's goals and time frames. Often, the team sponsor must resolve these varying expectations.

Team sponsors approve the team's vision, mission, goals, and monitor progress. The sponsor can serve in a role of coach to help clarify organizational issues or assist in resolving internal or external misunderstandings.

Team Challenges

Being on a work team is similar to participating on a sports team.[16] Each member brings talents, skills, knowledge, and capabilities. Frequently, team members are assigned based on their unique qualities, which leads to significant diversity within the group. These personal differences can lead to conflict and challenge progress and results. One of the hardest things to learn is sensitivity

TABLE 7-2: Survey Results: Ranking Enablers of More Effective Groupwork and Teamwork (in order of "very important" responses)

Enablers	% of Organizations that Ranked Enablers "Very Important"
Clear and measurable objectives	71%
Personal commitment	66%
Management attitudes	63%
Teamworking skills	54%
Accountability	49%
Empowerment	48%
Overcoming departmental barriers	41%
Roles and responsibilities	37%
Project management skills	36%
Supporting software, e.g., groupware	36%
Supporting hardware, e.g., network connectivity	34%
Management processes	33%
Tackling vested interests	30%
Role model behaviour	29%

Coulson-Thomas, 1993, as cited in Coulson-Thomas, 1997, p. 230.

TABLE 7-3: Critical Issues for Establishing Ground Rules

Factor	Criteria
Policy	Acknowledging and valuing differences of opinion
Definitions	Member roles and responsibilities
Specifications	Quality for the work produced by the team
Plan	How the team will communicate

Chang, 1994.

to what is good for the team. Individuals need to focus on the team and not expect people to recognize and reward their individual contributions. Teams gradually learn to trust each other and work for the good of the entire group.

Another difficult issue is allocating work and determining a fair amount to assign to each individual. Because each team member usually has other work duties, different members may be able to accomplish different workloads. Team members frequently come from different managers or supervisors, each with different attitudes and commitments toward the team's goals. As a result, each team member can only do as much as his or her manager or supervisor will allow. In addition, due to unexpected problems, it may be necessary for team members to back each other up and accomplish tasks that originally were assigned to someone else. Clearly, roles, responsibilities, and allocation of tasks are complex issues.

Team Conflict

Conflict is a given as a team works toward its goal. The objective of a team should be to work through conflict effectively. Not all conflict needs to be resolved. Sometimes it is better to manage it to keep it as a positive force. Conflict can be one of the most powerful parts of teams because it recognizes diversity.

Establishing ground rules is an important step toward dealing with conflict. Chang (see Table 7-3) states that ground rules should address the important criteria.[17]

When team members take sides or attack a person's ideas before the individual is finished speaking, it usually indicates that a team is in substantial conflict. Resolving or minimizing conflict is never easy and requires time, thought, and patience. However, it can also provide an opportunity to build team understanding and acceptance of differences. In its forming stages, a team should adopt a conflict resolution model so it is prepared to deal with issues that may arise. Chang suggests the five steps in his conflict resolution model (see Table 7-4).[18]

TABLE 7-4: Chang's Model for Conflict Resolution

1. Acknowledge that the conflict exists
2. Identify the "real" conflict
3. Hear all the points of view
4. Explore ways to meet the objectives together
5. Gain agreement and responsibility for a solution

Chang, 1994.

PT practitioners possess critical skills in facilitation, team formation, team effectiveness, and project management. These team skills can be particularly helpful in writing ground rules, recognizing and alleviating conflict, or assisting teams with roles and responsibilities. In addition, PT practitioners can assist team leaders with issues of authority, because team leaders often do not have direct responsibility for team members' assignments or evaluations (see Job Aids 7-1 and 7-2).

Problem Solving

Definition and Scope

Problem solving and decision making interventions are outcomes of empowered teams and empowered individuals. As an intervention, problem solving focuses on understanding the problem and its causes. Decision making, as an intervention, generates potential solutions and then evaluates the options based on ethical, financial, organizational, and other factors. In general, employees who will be affected by any workplace decision should be represented or participate in any problem solving or decision making process.

Rational Problem Solving

Traditionally, rational problem solving involves a structured, linear approach. Facts are identified, causes examined, potential solutions defined, alternatives evaluated, and actions described. Although the solutions developed

JOB AID 7-1: Team Fitness Evaluator

Directions: Take a minute to review your team's fitness by responding to the following items.

---

1. **Who is/are your team's customer(s)?**

2. **Is the team empowered? How do you know?**

3. **Are team meetings comfortable and enjoyable? Are team discussions open and respectful?**

4. **What process does the team use to arrive at consensus decisions?**

5. **How does the team ensure that work and effort are allocated fairly? Does everyone do his or her fair share?**

6. **What does the team do to keep members motivated?**

7. **How does the team communicate among members? With others outside the team?**

JOB AID 7-2: Enabling Effective Teams: What Team Members Can Do

Directions: Use this job aid as a discussion tool and as a team-building activity.

Be honest with each other	• Communicate candidly. Act with integrity. Be sincere. • Tell the truth—lies and exaggerations breed distrust. • Be trustworthy—effective teamwork absolutely requires trust.
Communicate openly	• Openly share information, feelings, concerns, and reactions. • Share negatives as well as positives. Learn to say, "Does anyone know how to…" Give negative feedback in a constructive manner. • Be willing to confront issues. • Include everyone—on a team of collaborators, there can be no outsiders, secret-keepers, or conspirators.
Create and use a team shared space	• Maintain a central copy of your team's "stuff": minutes of meetings, records of discussions and decisions, interim work results, and in-process and complete deliverable products. Store in a team room, a database, or even a notebook. • Make the central copy shared and sharable—all team members must be able to add and annotate, review and revise, and use the team's material. • Remember that the shared space contains the work of the team, not the work of any one individual!
Empower each other	• Jointly agree on goals, work out the strategy, and plan the team's approach. • Use each other's resourcefulness. • Allow risk taking—do not criticize failure. • Empower your team members to give you negative as well as positive feedback. Accept constructive criticism. • If something goes wrong, don't point fingers. Accept that mistakes happen; learn from them and move on.
Empower yourself	• Take personal responsibility to accomplish team goals, to produce team products, and for the actions of the team as a whole. • Commit your time and energy to the collective effort. • Take risks. Volunteer to take on and "stretch assignments." State your opinions openly. Take the risk that someone might disagree with you. Trust your team members to support your efforts. • Remember that team members cannot be empowered by external sources; they must empower themselves.
Respect each other	• Listen objectively to fellow team members; treat each other's views and opinions seriously. • Focus on the task to be performed, not the person performing it; on issues, not positions; on results, not political/territorial issues. • Don't gossip—gossip kills respect. • Be sensitive to the needs of your team members. Show concern for their struggles. Be sensitive to their preferences.
Review, reflect on, revise team processes	• Monitor, evaluate, and work to improve the effectiveness of your collaborative development, decision making, giving and receiving feedback, and meetings. • Take responsibility to facilitate team process.

Unger, J. (1997, May). Enabling effective teams. ISPI Technologist (Michigan Chapter ISPI newsletter).

are often useful, they may not be the optimal solutions. Zachary explains that "Rational problem solving is effective for routine problems with a clear set of standards to assess the appropriateness of the final solution."[1]

Creative Problem Solving

Creative problem solving emphasizes new ways of looking at the problem. There is an intentional commitment to avoid "mental sets" or automatic patterns of assumptions and relationships.[2] Highly entertaining and engaging puzzles, jokes, games, and simulations can be used to break down stereotypes and conventional thinking. Breakthrough thinking involves finding new clues, avoiding old traps, and eliminating predispositions. Ordinary people can make dazzling breakthroughs by removing barriers to creativity, such as previous experiences, assumptions, judgments, and patterns of thinking.[3] In fact, potentially useful information is often inhibited by prior learning of interfering material.[4]

It is important to use discipline and rigor even when using creative problem solving. For example, Dr. Edwin Land's invention of instant photography required unconventional thinking. Photographers normally developed film in darkrooms using chemicals. In order to develop pictures within the camera casing, Dr. Land had to visualize and devise a new photo finishing process. In a similar manner, 3M Corporation is noted for encouraging creative problem solving, leading to new products or extensions of existing products. They have a structured approach that encourages taking risks and trying out new ideas.

Altier recommends three steps for increasing creativity:
1. Forget the relationships we believe connect the pieces of a situation.
2. Look at the pieces without the relationships.
3. Rearrange the relationships and pieces in a different way.[5]

Predicting Problems

Anticipating problems and predicting the effects of the problems have been especially important to manufacturing and industry. In order to improve quality, Failure Mode Effects Analysis (FMEA) is a process that predicts potential failures, and attempts to determine the risks of failure and take appropriate actions. Additionally, Anticipatory Failure Determination (AFD) attempts to deal with root causes. AFD views failures as an intended consequence, and devises ways to ensure that, hypothetically, the failure happens reliably. At this point, the problem solving team fully understands and can predict the failure. "Invariably the real cause of the problem becomes obvious from the results of the studies" (see Table 7-5).[6]

Implementing Problem Solving in the Workplace

Data Gathering

Teams have been particularly successful at solving workplace problems. Team problem solving requires gathering ideas and prioritizing them so the team can reach a meaningful decision.

Among the methods that are most common and easiest to use for gathering data are the following:
- *Brainstorming*—Allows each team member to express ideas on a topic; all ideas are accepted and recorded; comments, criticisms, and discussion of ideas are held until the brainstorming session ends.
- *Brain writing*—A good alternative for team members who may have problems expressing themselves verbally or are uncomfortable with the speed of brainstorming. Each team member receives a paper divided into 21 squares; members record ideas in three squares, place paper in center of table, and take another member's paper from the center pool to record three ideas on it. Activity continues until all squares are filled on each member's paper.
- *Affinity diagram*—Team members write ideas for a specified topic on separate slips of paper; slips are spread on table or posted on a wall and can be moved to create groupings. Team discusses patterns and meanings from the patterns.

Prioritizing

Prioritizing ideas can be achieved using techniques such as the Nominal Group Technique and multi-voting. The Nominal Group Technique gives team members an equal voice in selecting the ideas the team will focus on. Multi-voting involves a series of votes that enable team members to reduce the ideas the team generated to a manageable number for further discussion.[7] The key to effective problem solving is not allowing teams to get so bogged down in the process that they fail to reach a timely decision on an issue.

TABLE 7-5: Steps in Anticipatory Failure Determination (AFD)

1. Formulate the original problem.
2. Identify the "success scenario."
3. Localize the failure.
4. Search for solutions.
5. Spell out available resources. Use them to produce the wanted effect. Look for contradictions.
6. Formulate hypotheses and tests for verifying them.

Clarke, 2000, p. 80.

Problem solving is often a group effort because each person brings unique ideas and experiences related to a given problem. Effective team problem solving usually depends on several factors, including:

- Willingness and ability to listen
- Belief that conflict is vital to good decisions
- Willingness to encourage and support team members
- Self-discipline to avoid extraneous and repetitive discussion
- Refusal to use power as a problem solving tool
- Ego strength and confidence to accept member challenges.[8]

Problem Solving Stages
Problem solving is usually structured to proceed in stages. The actual step-by-step approach can be varied to meet the needs of the particular situation. Table 7-6 lists the common steps in problem solving (see Job Aid 7-3).

Decision Making

Empowering employees through teams or by encouraging continuous improvement through problem solving *enables people to aim for the best they can be and seek the best workplace they can have.* Decision making, as an intervention, involves placing values on ideas or options and determining resulting actions. It requires encouraging risk and change. Many organizations and individuals are reluctant to verbalize values or personal ideas; they prefer "tacit" or unstated inferences.

Definition and Scope

Decision making is the act of making judgments and drawing conclusions. There are three primary approaches: rational-choice, intuitive, and experiential (see Table 7-7).[1]

Ethical Dilemmas
Deciding requires people to place value on options and make judgments, which can lead to ethical dilemmas. Ethical decisions are not determined by a single moral standard, but they are influenced by gender, age, moral philosophy, education, work experience, organizational culture, stated and unstated codes of ethics, awareness and knowledge of the situation, rewards and sanctions, and opinions of significant others (such as co-workers or peers).[2] For example, one study found that younger males make more utilitarian decisions and older males make more legalistic choices. Women tend to be more interested in fairness and justice.[3]

Executive Decisions
Executives have long believed that decisions are their privilege. They are accustomed to creating directives, defining strategies, and expecting implementation from others. Although decisive executives are necessary in many situations, greater participation within the work force can lead to increased quality of decisions and provide for smoother implementation.

TABLE 7-6: Seven-Step Approach to Problem Solving

1. Explore the problem issues and define the problem.
2. Gather information and intelligence on the situation and causes.
3. Choose criteria for judging the information and determine their relative importance.
4. Explore *ideal* solution and generate possible *realistic* options.
5. Evaluate the realistic options and choose.
6. Implement the choice and evaluate the decision.
7. Adjust implementation based on evaluation.

Team Decisions
In most cases, team decision making is more productive than individual decision making. The benefits associated with team decision making include:

- Concerns and self-interests are surfaced
- Understanding and support is increased
- Strong commitment to the decision emerges
- Awareness and empathy for the decision making process is created.[4]

Teams can make decisions using a number of methods including majority vote, unanimity, minority rules, autocracy, and consensus (see Job Aid 7-4). No matter which approach a team uses, certain criteria (see Table 7-8) need to be in place if the decision making process is to be effective.

Consensus Decision Making
Consensus decision making does not mean that everyone has to agree with an accepted decision, or that it has to be everyone's first choice. What is required is that all team members are able to live with the decision, are willing to play an active role in its implementation, and feel they have been heard and understood by other team members.[5]

Deborah Harrington-Mackin suggests consensus decision making be used when:

- A solution to one problem may create other problems.
- A number of alternatives and courses of action should be considered.
- The issue being resolved is important and the unity gained is worth the time.
- The process to reach a decision is as important as the decision itself.
- Team synergy is a priority.
- Delay caused by the process of reaching consensus will prevent a team from jumping to a conclusion.[6]

Implementing Consensus Decision Making in the Workplace

When working toward consensus, a team should ensure that the environment is conducive to success by developing team building skills, encouraging risk taking, maintaining motivation and interest, and encouraging positive attitudes (see Table 7-9).

TABLE 7-7: Three Decision Making Approaches

Rational-Choice	Intuitive	Experiential

• Deconstruct, analyze, study, make decision trees to play options from different perspectives and to account for varying probabilities.
 	
• Use when faced with tough decisions, such as buying a house, picking a site for a new factory, or making a job choice.
 	
• *Advantage*—keeps people from hasty decisions, helps identify missing pieces of information.
 	
• *Drawbacks*—time consuming, deliberation on complexity of problem, options, and consequences delays decisions. Often objectives are not that clear and specific objectives are necessary for this approach.
	• Relies on experiences and inner wisdom. Based on preferences.
	
	• Use for fast decision making or when there is insufficient evidence for thorough analysis. Good when there is a margin for error.
	
	• *Advantage*—"At its best, intuition means relying on our experience without having to analyze everything—that is, when you spot a pattern that makes you worry, perhaps you can't analyze what exactly triggered your concern, but you need to pay attention to it. Studies of brain activity show that people have an awareness of the right answer even before they consciously realize it. Studies of skilled chess players show that the first option they think of is usually a good one, and often the best." (p. 18)
	
	• *Drawbacks*—If there is little experience, this method will not work.
		• Experience results in the ability to:
		  – Size up situations quickly
		  – Recognize typical ways of reacting to problems
		  – Mentally game out an option to see if it will work
		  – Focus on the most relevant data elements
		  – Form expectancies
		  – Detect anomalies and problems
		  – Figure out plausible explanations for unusual events
		
		• Use when decider recognizes the dynamics of the situation. Especially good for situations where there is a need for a quick "recognize/react" strategy. However, experience helps people recognize the dangers as similar to previous situations. Skilled decision makers don't act on the first thought that pops into their head. Use for sports, emotional situations, and times when it is necessary to "think on your feet."
		
		• *Advantage*—Under pressure or in competition, provides for agility based on similar situations and minimizes surprises.
		
		• *Drawbacks*—May keep people in "rut" using outdated strategies, rather than trying new methods.

Based on Klein and Weick, 2000.

TABLE 7-8: Criteria for Effective Team Decision Making

• A clearly defined issue or problem
• Agreement on who is responsible for the decision
• Appropriate team size (representatives from essential constituent areas)
• A method for determining the best choice
• Clarity about the team's authority to recommend or decide
• Agreement on procedures and methods to be used for decision making
• Honest commitment from the organization to carry out the decision.

Based on Harrington-Mackin, 1994, pp. 108–109.

TABLE 7-9: Guidelines Conducive to Consensus Decision Making

• Do not employ win-lose techniques, such as voting.

• Look to alternatives that are next most acceptable as ways to break a stalemate.

• Don't encourage members to give in to keep harmony.

• Ensure that the correct attitudes and behaviors required for effective decision making are present, including an ability to distinguish fact from opinion; low level of competitiveness, ability to identify and name feelings, ability to express ideas verbally, and a low level of defensiveness.

Based on Harrington-Mackin, 1994, pp. 111–112.

JOB AID 7-3: Problem Solving Worksheet

Directions: Use this job aid to follow the seven steps to problem solving.

1. Describe problem.	The problem is...
2. Define desired state and current state, and delineate gap.	Desired state: Current state: Gap:
3. Analyze information and equipment, individual capacities, and motivation to determine causes.	Information and equipment: Individual Capacities: Motivation:
4. Brainstorm and prioritize possible solutions.	Rank results:
5. Select and plan solution to alleviate problem and minimize cause.	Action plan:
6. Implement plan (timeline, steps, responsibilities, measurable outcomes).	Timeline: Steps: Responsibilities: Measurable outcomes:
7. Evaluate solution (measure outcomes and determine return on investment).	Measure outcomes: Determine return on investment:

Risk taking should be encouraged when groups are working toward consensus. As teams brainstorm ideas and gather facts, they should be encouraged to be creative and resourceful and consider options that may have substantial benefit but may involve considerable unknowns. Safe, easy solutions may not always be the best choice. Team members, sponsors, and management should support unique solutions, as long as the ideas are well considered. Fault finding and failure avoidance can make teams leery of trying what they consider the optimum solution. The notion "We don't do things like that here" can prevent teams from making breakthrough decisions.

Reaching team consensus requires sensitivity to timing and commitment to hard work. A team leader needs to recognize when a team is getting frustrated or bogged down in the process. Calling a break for a few days or a week is acceptable and may help team members to better evaluate alternatives when they return as a group.[7]

Decision making improves with skill building and experience. The following techniques lead to proficient decision making:[8]

- Define decision requirements.
- Obtain feedback about the decisions made.
- Make up scenarios and use them.
- Observe how to manage uncertainty.
- Take advantage of people who have expertise.

PT practitioners can play key roles in changing the decision making dynamics of an organization. Due to its systematic and thorough approach, the HPT Model relies on careful and honest decision making throughout. Decision making improvements often mean changes in organizational culture, such as viewing employees as partners with valuable information and insight. PT practitioners can help establish a culture that encourages risk taking, innovation, and creativity.

The Empowerment section of this chapter was written in collaboration with Judy Gohl, MA, Beyond Expectations, Inc.

JOB AID 7-4: Decision Making Approaches

Directions: Select and implement the most appropriate decision making processes, based on available resources and organizational culture.

Multi-Voting	1. Brainstorm ideas without commenting on any of them. 2. When ideas are completely recorded, group discusses them in systematic manner. Proposer explains idea and other participants add to idea or comment about idea. 3. After ideas are clearly understood and all possibilities explored, group rates ideas. 4. Colored markers or self-adhesive dots are usually used for voting to indicate preferences. Each participant is allowed an agreed-upon number of "dots" or "marks." 5. "Dots" or "marks" are calculated and the group preferences are determined by the highest number of votes.
Force-Field Analysis + | − → ← → ← → ←	1. Create columns to represent alternatives (usually two). 2. Label the columns, such as "pro and con," or "advantages and constraints." 3. List factors in appropriate columns. 4. Consider and discuss factors. 5. Make decision based on what seems to be the optimum column.
Fishbone (Ishakawa) Diagram Equipment People Methods Materials → Effect	1. Draw single line in center and draw 4–6 lines from center like fish bones. 2. Write desired outcome at fish's head. 3. Write major causes currently preventing desired outcome at end of each fishbone. 4. Write problems relative to each cause like "mini-bones." 5. Discuss problems thoroughly to understand the issues.
Weighted Matrix	1. Draw a matrix with rows for each category of importance and columns for each decision factor plus one for weights. For example, rows for each critical job skill and columns for each final job candidate. 2. Prioritize each category (row) and assign weight to reflect importance. Put weights in *Weights* column. 3. Score each column and multiply score by importance (weight). 4. Add up weighted scores to make final decision (such as new hire).

Based on Cassidy, M.F. (1999, June). Group decision making. ASTD InfoLine Issue 9906. Alexandria, VA: American Society for Training and Development; Van Tiem, D., Moseley, J.L., and Dessinger, J.C. (2000). Fundamentals of performance technology: A guide to improving people, process, and performance. Silver Spring, MD: International Society for Performance Improvement. ISPI © 2001. Permission granted for unlimited duplication for noncommercial use.

Case Study 7-1: Problem Solving: Mott Community College

Situation

Historical Context

Mott Community College (MCC), established in 1923, is located in Flint, Michigan. Flint was home of the famous UAW 1937 sit-down strike at a General Motors facility, which lead to dramatically increased bargaining strength for unions. At the college, six local bargaining units are represented by three international unions: Michigan Education/National Education Association (MEA/NEA), Service Employee International Union (SEIU), and the United Auto Workers (UAW).[a] The community college is located in the "heart of GM-UAW country." Labor contracts at Mott College evolved similar to those of nearby General Motors facilities. Negotiations, grievances, and day-to-day problem solving resembled the hard-line, confrontational style made famous by "our UAW neighbors."

By the mid-1990s, employee morale had reached an all-time low. The college had a mature staff with high seniority. The unions had developed contracts that were steeped in tradition. Unfair labor petitions, grievances, and arbitrations were nearing one per member for the non-faculty bargaining groups. Nearly half of the labor agreements had been expired for a year or more, with the balance of the contracts ready to expire soon. Contract bargaining was difficult. Tempers were short. Gains for either side were almost non-existent. Communication seemed like a method of placing blame and sharing frustration, not for information sharing, problem solving, or seeking resolutions. In short, the ultimate goal was winning.

Evolving Context

The three unions (MEA/NEA, SEIU, and UAW) recognized that the most effective way for them to advocate for their members was to have a stronger leadership role at the college. Led by the presidents of the Supervisors/Management-UAW unit and Professional Technical (Pro-Tech)-MEA unit, unions began a dialog with one another to discuss common problems, issues, options, and opinions. As their relationship began to solidify, the unions approached the college administration about creating a labor-management partnership. Initially, the idea was met with distrust, disinterest, and resistance. However, the Pro-Tech-MEA unit persuaded the new Human Resources (HR) director that holding the existing 40 grievances in abeyance for one last attempt to resolve them had merit. At that time, the 40 grievances were ready to move into arbitration. Both labor and management understood that each issue would move forward to arbitration if or when an impasse was reached on that issue. To place the problem in perspective, at that time, arbitrations were lasting about three years with an average annual cost of $25,000–$35,000 for each side (union and management).

Intervention

Pro-Tech Grievance Resolutions

Several factors helped the joint process of developing a productive partnership. First, the preferred bargaining style of both the new HR director and the Pro-Tech president (a registered nurse) was non-confrontational. Second, the labor contract violations had occurred before the new director was hired, which allowed him to look objectively at the issues. Third, resolution would revolve around the concept of what was fair and equitable while not creating additional issues for the union membership, the college management, or other units. Fourth, weekly meetings occurred for 9 months and resulted in a resolution of 38 of the 40 grievances, thus saving thousands of dollars for both the union and the college.

Successful resolution of the Pro-Tech grievances resulted in a more solid working relationship, trust, and a tentative working "style." However, both sides understood that the relationship was "like pieces of sandpaper placed face to face," that any movement had to have clear signals and agreement to prevent damage to the partnership.

Joint Union Partnership

During this same time, the unions continued to meet frequently and were in the process of building their own partnership. Where there once had been distrust and miniature kingdoms, the unions were moving toward unity. Real communication occurred more frequently. A commitment was made to first serve their own membership and, if possible, do no harm to the other units in the process. Critical thinking about short or long-term impact to other units was a new behavior. Conflicts became further apart and less confrontational as solutions developed that would work for both (or multiple) sides. Working in unity gave strength to the unions when dealing with management. Union morale improved.

Win-Win Collaborative Bargaining Training

Managers' beliefs about creating a union-management partnership ranged from those who strongly opposed the concept of sharing power or authority, to a middle group who were willing to learn about the process, to ones who didn't care as long as they didn't have to change or participate. The HR director had a difficult "sell" ahead of him, but he was willing to lead the way once the MCC Board of Trustees professed a willingness to underwrite the cost and support the effort. The MEA provided a meeting location and the college provided the money for a trainer to begin the discovery of what Win-Win or collaborative Bargaining was all about. (This bargaining approach is also known as Interest-Based Bargaining.)

During several full days of bargaining training, the group used the DISC Personal Profile System®[b] to profile each member, allowing them to learn about one another. They learned that each person has a particular style with a predictable set of "buttons," or sensitivities, that should never be pushed and a set that had to be in place to move forward. The group learned to recognize each other's "buttons" and what efforts were needed to result in forward progress.

Win-Win Collaborative Bargaining Guidelines

The larger groups separated into specific bargaining groups to discuss and design a set of guidelines, called ground rules, to use for meetings or bargaining. The rules were unique to each group but were similar in content. The guidelines established rules for every conceivable occasion, spelling out how to determine priorities, bring issues forward, state or restate problems, reach consensus, distribute information, set meeting dates, and more. No issue was too minor to have a rule, for example, no gum chewing or note passing.

Bargaining Changes

The heart of the change centered around learning about each other's profile (DISC), developing very solid, precise ground rules for meetings prior to looking at any issue, and then using a structured problem solving approach to the issues. Both sides actively worked together to restate the issues brought to the table as problems. The approach created a mentality of "our" problem and eliminated "sides." In other words, *the problem statement could not have a solution attached to it.* Once the solution was eliminated, both sides frequently found that the issue was not what was originally thought. Finding the real problem was difficult and time consuming but well worth both the trouble and time. Both sides brainstormed ideas, placed the ideas in priority order, and then consensus was used to determine solutions. Once the difficult work of defining the problem occurred, each group found it was usually easy to come to a swift, long-term resolution that met both management and union needs. In addition, the solutions were usually better than either side initially expected.

Initial Bargaining Process

The bargaining trainer attended the first couple of bargaining sessions as a facilitator to ensure that the rules were followed and the groups stayed within the guidelines without resorting to old ways or hostility. Using the problem solving method, problems were resolved with significant gains on both sides.

Results

Recognition and Awards

Currently, bargaining gains continue to be positive. Each labor unit meets monthly to resolve issues instead of stockpiling problems for years and then trying to reach resolution at a table in anger. There have been three awards and one finalist designation because of this problem solving effort. Since the ProTech MEA unit had more gains in the first year of Win-Win Collaborative Problem Solving than in all the other years added together, the unit was presented the 1998 Michigan Education Pacesetter Award in recognition of that success.

The Win-Win Collaborative Bargaining approach worked so well that the National Education Association, together with UAW and Saturn, presented the National Partnership Award to the college and all of its unions, represented by the MEA, SEIU, and UAW in 1998. In 1999, MCC and unions were finalists for the University of Florida's Futurist Award. In September 1999, the Arbor Award for Excellence was presented by the Arbor Consulting Group (an HR firm) together with Eastern Michigan University.

Extending the Success

Along with all the recognition and awards was an increased determination to continue to improve skills, utilize strengths, and continue on the tenuous path of partnering that has helped us attain so many of our goals.

Problem solving training was offered to all MCC employees in order to continue this forward momentum. Learning to recognize each other's strengths and needs supports the ability to use quality problem solving at the lowest levels, both at work and at home. It provides an educated and thoughtful response to customers, students, and each other that resolves the problems and issues without the anger and frustration the same issue would have generated previously.

Other Benefits

Building on this problem solving initiative, current diversity efforts focus on the way people think, believe, and interact. Giving value to each person's style creates a level of comfort that increases productivity while limiting adversarial posturing and positioning.

Lessons Learned

There are many valuable lessons that were learned from this win-win collaborative problem solving approach.
- Change is possible.
- Quality of life can be improved regardless of the age or position of the company if at least one leader on each side will take a leadership role. When others follow their lead, positive change increases exponentially.
- Trust is a byproduct of effective partnership but is not essential to begin the process.
- Creating very detailed ground rules before dealing with issues sets the expectations for communication, ethics, respect, progress, measuring of goals, and more, while limiting the behaviors of the past that prevented progress.
- Learning what makes people "tick" and understanding each other better helps to move the collaborative process forward. It prevents inadvertent hurt feelings and "stepping on other people's toes."
- Developing collaborative problem solving skills in all employees places problem solving at the lowest level of the company and increases morale and productivity.

- Partnerships can develop on several levels within differing groups at the same time.
- When it's working right, you can't tell the sides apart.
- It is better to be at the water's edge watching the ripples of partnership grow and touch each other than to be in the water throwing stones at each other.

Endnotes

[a] Michigan law allows managers to be members of an organized union. MCC mid-managers are affiliated with the UAW.

[b] DISC Personal Profile System® is a tool that assesses four behavioral characteristics: dominance, influence, steadiness, and conscientiousness. The DISC profile system was developed by Carlson Learning Company.

Case study written by Clella Banks RN, President Pro-Tech unit, MEA/NEA, in cooperation with Dr. Joyce Toet, President Supervisory/Management, UAW, and Mark Kennedy, Executive Director of Human Resources. Used with permission.

"Players" and their original titles are as follows; please contact them for further information:

- *Clella "Kelly" Banks RN, President, Professional-Technical Unit, MEA/NEA*
  kbanks@email.mcc.edu
- *Joyce Toet, EdD, President, Supervisory Management Unit, UAW*
  jtoet@email.mcc.edu
- *Steven Robinson, President Faculty Unit, MEA/NEA*
  srobinso@email.mcc.edu
- *Terry Travis, Chair Maintenance & Operations Unit, SEIU*
  ttravis@email.mcc.edu
- *Sandy Hill, Chair-Secretarial/Clerical Unit, SEIU*
  shill@email.mcc.edu
- *Mark Kennedy, Executive Director Human Resources*
  mkennedy@email.mcc.edu
- *MaryAnn Cockman, MEA Uniserv Director*
  mcockman@mea.org

ORGANIZATIONAL PRO-ACTION

Pro-action means thinking ahead, planning for the future with creativity and commitment, and understanding the economic, political, and social climate sufficiently to inspire employee confidence. Pro-active, up-front preparation within organizations *helps employees succeed* because wise planning enables employees to thoroughly understand the organization and anticipate problems, obstacles, and challenging situations. Careful planning and execution *helps employees believe* in their own future and see how each worker fits into the total operation.

When PT practitioners reflect on their performance analysis and cause analysis findings, it is not unusual to determine that current decisions are reactive to crises and actions are taken in haste to alleviate problems. Clearly, it would be better to anticipate situations and craft vision statements, plans, and policies that set direction and assist in decision making. Strategic planning, operations management, environmental scanning, benchmarking and reengineering, realignment and restructuring are all forward-focused processes. They require data, anticipatory thinking, and thorough understanding of the current organization and its capability to move into the future. They are used to establish functional systems and processes within an organization. However, just having a well-planned system in place is not enough; it is management's responsibility to communicate its intentions and to make clear its decisions. With well-crafted systems and parameters in place, employees are more likely to succeed because they will have the understanding necessary to

implement correct actions and, ultimately, the motivation to become pro-active, as well.

Strategic Planning

Definition and Scope

Strategic planning creates the blueprint for an organization. It documents goals and performance objectives based on internal capabilities and competencies and external environmental conditions. It is not a panacea. Effective strategic planning requires wisdom and mature judgment. The company vision should be used as a guide through all levels of management to all employees. Viewing the organization as a system and sharing the strategic plan are critical to establishing realistic, organization-wide, tangible implementation plans.

Strategic planning, as an intervention, provides direction, focus, and the organizational target. Without a clear, well-accepted plan, an organization seems "rudderless." Competitive winds come up and the organization sways to the pressure of each gust. Employees often express the frustration of frequent changes as "flavor of the month," "program of the year," or "brainchild" of a high-potential executive on the move.

Strategic plans are long term, often five to ten years in advance. "Strategic" means they focus on broader issues. They do not document implementation, but set the stage for later implementation details, which are part of operations management.[1] Strategic plans should be linked year to year to provide continuity and have sufficiently broad involvement to deter single-issue programs or "bandwagons." Employees acquire confidence in senior management decisions because the strategic plan offers guidance and parameters. Performance improves when employees have confidence and believe in the future of the organization.

Non-Profit Planning

Although strategic planning was initially associated with business and industry, non-profits are increasingly using formal or informal planning processes. This is caused by increased demand for non-profit services (due to cuts in public services) coupled with decreased support (such as less government subsidy, tax law changes, and donor skepticism).[2] As non-profits mature in their strategic planning processes, one difference emerges. Organizations with smaller planning groups tend to use mathematical modeling and quantitative tools, while larger planning groups use more qualitative methods. It may be that smaller groups do not have the depth of experience and so they compensate with quantitative methods.[3]

Employee Involvement

Many organizations today realize the importance of involving employees in planning and integrating their feedback and perspective, because the employees will actually carry out the strategic plan. Managers as sole decision makers are fading and employee input is more systematically integrated into the strategic planning process. Employees are critical to making the plan work and helpful in recommending issues that should be addressed. In addition, employees who understand the strategic plan are more likely to understand their role and contribution within the organization, leading to a sense of ownership and fuller participation.

Implementing Strategic Planning in the Workplace

Strategic planning is a process of thoroughly understanding the organization, anticipating future directions, and defining possible consequences and barriers relative to accomplishing the predicted direction. Strategic planning begins by assigning a team composed of executives, representatives from senior management, and selected employees from operational and support functions. The team defines their actual process, timeframes, and communications plan for the strategic planning activities. Data gathering is critical and typically involves:

* *SWOT analysis (Strengths, Weaknesses, Opportunities, Threats)*—determine the organization's current state (strengths and weaknesses), future possibilities (opportunities), and barriers (threats) to accomplishing the possibilities (see Table 8-4).

* *Core competencies*—determine the unique qualities that distinguish the organization and set it apart from other organizations. They can be product features (such as miniaturization for Sony or engines for Honda), service (distribution for Wal-Mart), or quality (manufacturing excellence for Toyota).[4]
* *Internal scan*—thoroughly understand the organization's culture, intellectual capital, resources, and capabilities.
* *External scan*—research present conditions and speculate (using trend analysis) about future directions for the competition, customer requirements and expectations, government regulations and legislation, demographics, etc.

After the comprehensive analysis, strategic planning involves refining or recommitting to a vision and mission, building possible scenarios, and determining actions to accomplish the preferred scenarios. Scenarios are descriptions of situations that optimize the findings from the analysis and maximize the core competencies of the organization. Scenarios need strong consensus by the strategic planning team and also by a wider group of decision makers to craft a consensus scenario that is do-able and broadly supported in the organization. Action planning is the operational management function that results in the implementation of the strategic plan.

For example, General Motors Corporation (GM) has adopted a strategy of forming partnerships rather than mergers or acquisitions. GM will be able to focus its financial resources on innovative products and services rather than work through issues of culture and marketplace. The commitment is to cooperation instead of control. The goal is to "realize synergies faster than in a full buyout, if that option had even been available."[5]

Planners

Planners and the planning process are not always respected and valued.[6] Planners are often viewed as remote, "ivory tower" intellectual types. They lack experience in operation and execution. Strategic planners should not stifle progress or limit creativity, risk taking, and willingness to meet customer, client, or constituent expectations. Planners identify trend indicators and make assumptions about future events. However, in the end, an organization must not be bogged down when unanticipated factors surface.

Bryson's Ten-Step Strategic Planning Process (see Table 7-10) is an example of strategic planning. The sub-items explain and augment the 10 steps.[7]

PT practitioners can support strategic planning by using their expertise in systematic and systemic thinking. The HPT Model and the strategic planning model are

TABLE 7-10: Ten-Step Strategic Planning Process

1. Initiate and agree upon a strategic planning process.
- ☐ How will the plan be identified?
- ☐ Who will be responsible for outlining the plan?
- ☐ How will data/input from all levels of management and employees be gathered?

2. Identify organizational mandates.
- ☐ What are the time and budget constraints?
- ☐ Which locations will be affected by this plan?
- ☐ What priorities were set by the organization?

3. Clarify organizational mission and values.
- ☐ Is the mission of the organization to be the biggest? To have the most diverse product line? To expand globally? To be voted the best place to work?
- ☐ Does the organization value loyalty? Is dedication rewarded? Is achievement recognized?

4. Assess the organization's external and internal environments to identify strengths, weaknesses, opportunities, and threats.
- ☐ Develop standard questionnaire format for all employees to complete and submit.
- ☐ Review and brainstorm at regularly held team, department, or cross-functional team meetings.
- ☐ Identify associations, chambers of commerce, and local business bureaus for further information. Create standard questionnaire for gathering information from these sources. Get sufficient information to understand competitors' strengths and weaknesses and potential future direction (Porter, 1980).

5. Identify the strategic issues facing the organization.
- ☐ Is the organizational goal to increase sales, increase or decrease products offered, increase productivity, combat increased competition?
- ☐ Is there high turnover that must be addressed?
- ☐ Are the directors of the organization in agreement on the critical issues?

6. Formulate strategies to manage these issues.
- ☐ Identify current and future situation scenarios.
- ☐ Identify training or recruiting process to reduce turnover, evaluate position descriptions, and/or build in measurable objectives.
- ☐ Discrepancies at the head of an organization filter down through all levels. It is critical that upper management agrees on the objectives.

7. Review and adopt the strategic plan or plans.
- ☐ Set up regular team meetings to review, create timelines, compare and chart progress.
- ☐ Have a champion.
- ☐ Report progress.

8. Establish an effective organizational vision.
- ☐ Where does the company want to be in one year, in five years?
- ☐ What are the core competencies and primary objectives of the organization?
- ☐ Where do the directors visualize the organization going? Do the employees "see" where they fit in?

9. Develop an effective implementation process.
- ☐ Establish regular meetings to review.
- ☐ Maintain timelines and chart progress.
- ☐ Create storyboards to help visualize status.

10. Reassess strategies and the strategic planning process.
- ☐ How was the planning process?
- ☐ Create an open forum for everyone to give input regarding ways to improve or reassess strategic plans. Evaluation should be an ongoing component of the strategic planning process.

Based on Bryson, 1995.

JOB AID 7-5: Strategic Planning Preparation

Directions: Strategic planning is a detailed process involving many steps. This job aid is designed to help employees think through the actual planning cycle. Please note responses in the space provided.

1. Building the responsible team	• Who is responsible for implementing the strategic plan? • Are all of the key individuals with the appropriate skills included in the planning process? ....☐ Yes ☐ No • Who else might be a beneficial contributor to the strategic planning team?
2. Starting the process	• Has the current situation been evaluated? ....☐ Yes ☐ No • Have the long-term goals been defined? ....☐ Yes ☐ No • Does management, as well as all employees, understand the scope of this long-term project? ....☐ Yes ☐ No • How will employees be informed of the organization's strategic plan?
3. Implementing the plan	• Has the team set the strategic planning goals and desired outcomes? ....☐ Yes ☐ No • Have the specific milestones been determined and has a timeline been set? ....☐ Yes ☐ No • What is the concrete plan for implementing the strategy? • Have additional individuals been called to assist in implementing the plan? If yes, who? ....☐ Yes ☐ No
4. Evaluating the results	• What has the team integrated into the plan that will make it easy to track and maintain? • How will employees develop ownership of the strategic plan? • How will employees become empowered to contribute to and respect the organization's strategic plan? • Does the strategy match the evolution in the respective industry? ....☐ Yes ☐ No

TABLE 7-11: Operations Process			
	Input	**Throughput**	**Output**
Automotive	Steel, rubber, glass	Stamping, casting	Vehicle
Publisher	Manuscript, paper	Printing, binding	Book
Accounting	Invoices, receipts	Deposits, withdrawals	Annual report
Non-Profit Agency	Qualified clients	Services, referrals	Alleviated problems

both structured variations of systems thinking. Many of the techniques discussed in the companion book, *Fundamentals of Performance Technology*, can be used to support the strategic planning process (see Job Aid 7-5).

Operations Management

Definition and Scope

Operations management is the direction, coordination, and control of the inputs ("raw materials"), throughputs (what is done to the raw materials), and outputs (what is produced). Table 7-11 illustrates the operations process in several industries. The operations function is the lifeblood of the organization.

Effective operations management facilitates performance improvement and provides a safe and well-organized workplace with quality supplies and adequate tools. Employees then have the resources they need to do their jobs well and succeed. The organization benefits because daily functions are in control, allowing for more flexibility to adapt when situations change. Operations planning includes contingency planning, which assumes that something is likely to go wrong and prepares to address adverse conditions. In contrast, when an organization has poor operations management, unexpected events create chaos and fear.

Timeframes
Operations management takes the long-term strategic plan and adds implementation details, using medium- and short-term planning (see Table 7-12).

TABLE 7-12: Operations Management Planning Timeframes	
Type of Planning	**Timeframes**
Long-term planning . . . . .1 to 5 years	
Medium-term planning . . . . .3 to 18 months	
Short-term planning . . . . .1 to 60 days	

In reality, the actual time frames are not that distinct. There are usually overlap and variances due to the nature of the input (raw materials) and the complexity of the throughput (processes).

Implementing Operations Management in the Workplace

Operations management staff begins by creating an annual business or operations plan based on forecasts. Sales or marketing staff attempts to anticipate future sales volume and product array based on talking with customers and doing market research. Production control and engineering departments try to match production capacity with anticipated needs. The finance department estimates costs and sales revenue and creates a budget to support the business plan. Ideally, information systems link all parts of the organization through effective networks and software to control the implementation of the plan and create daily and summary reports to monitor progress.

Detailed Planning
Operations management refers to the actual processes fulfilled by the organization, the lifeblood, the reason for being. Operations (direct) activities refer to healing for hospitals, providing books (information) for libraries, educating students for universities, or providing energy for electric utilities. Support functions (indirect) refer to those organizational units and activities that enable the direct operational activities to occur. For example:

- X-rays and physical therapy enable healing to occur after surgery.
- Inter-library loans allow libraries to provide books for special requests.
- Academic counseling allows students to create an academic program and select appropriate courses for degrees.
- Utility repair personnel restore energy to homes and businesses after storms.

Operations plans include the following implementation sub-plans.[1] The questions in Table 7-13 are examples of typical considerations in each sub-plan.

TABLE 7-13: Operations Management Implementation Planning

1. Operations Plan
- ☐ Will sufficient inventory be available to meet the needs of the strategic plan?
- ☐ Are the organizational processes robust enough to meet unexpected situations?
- ☐ Are management and supervision skilled in interpersonal and technical areas?

2. Information Systems Plan
- ☐ Are the available hardware and software robust enough to link all resources, operations, and support functions?
- ☐ Are information-related needs and problems able to be solved in a reasonable time frame?
- ☐ Do employees use and value available information and participate willingly in knowledge capture and knowledge management efforts?

3. Financial Plan
- ☐ Do reports track meaningful data and illustrate all (or most) indicators required?
- ☐ Is intellectual capital valued and measured?
- ☐ Do financial analysts serve as advisors to functional departments?

4. Quality or Continuous Improvement Plan
- ☐ Is the continuous improvement process sanctioned and endorsed by senior management?
- ☐ Is interdepartmental problem solving encouraged to deal with the side effects of any problem solving solution?
- ☐ Is the use of newer technologies encouraged with sufficient resources?

5. Human Resources Plan
- ☐ Will any organizational areas be restructured? Realigned? Reengineered?
- ☐ Are there any anticipated knowledge and skill deficiencies where training is needed?

6. Communications Plan
- ☐ Do supplier communication channels provide for "partnerships" and cooperation?
- ☐ Do employees believe they are well informed and able to understand organizational direction?

7. Maintenance Plan (if applicable)
- ☐ Is routine maintenance effective in minimizing downtime and cost? (Merli, 1991)
- ☐ Are predictive and preventive maintenance dominant rather than fixing broken or malfunctioning equipment?

8. Research and Development
- ☐ Are research activities in line with the strategic plan and market research?
- ☐ Do research activities take advantage of the latest technology?

9. Other
- ☐ Do any anticipated legislation or regulations affect the organization?
- ☐ Is the organization in compliance with regulations (especially environmental and safety), labor laws, and legislation?
- ☐ Are any public relations opportunities anticipated and planned for?

Based on Viale, 1995.

"Soft Issues"

It is not unusual for organizations to minimize the importance of "soft issues," such as culture and ethics, information flow, and core competencies. These factors are critical to organizational efficiency and the ability to compete.[2] For example, safety used to focus on engineering, education, and enforcement. However, safety experts now realize that other critical building blocks of safety include culture, organizational strategy, performance leadership, and organizational behavior.[3] In addition, inter-organizational processes that cross departments and functions need to ensure compatible and productive linkages.[4]

PT practitioners can play vital roles in most aspects of operations management because it is so practical and action oriented. The HPT Model fits well with operations management thinking. Data taken from the strategic plan can be expanded through analysis to explain the gaps and to understand the causes. Interventions are designed at the operational sub-planning phase. PT practitioners may need to work with experts in various sub-planning areas, such as finance, maintenance, quality, or human resources (see Job Aid 7-6).

Environmental Scanning

Definition and Scope

Although evaluating the internal organization and external environment are part of the strategic planning process,

environmental scanning should also be an ongoing activity. Analyzing the environment contributes to understanding which factors threaten the organization and what opportunities can be observed and maximized. Examples of important information include pending legislation and regulations, customer requirements, political passions and priorities, competitor changes, demographic fluctuations, organizational culture, employee values, and "think tank" reports.

Environmental scanning involves observing, assessing, and documenting anticipated trends in economic data, political events, technical developments, and structural changes in similar organizations. "Changes in the environment can come from almost anywhere, anytime."[1]

Internal Scan

Organizational scanning helps people understand the inner aspects of an organization. The investigation should be thorough and balanced, looking at several levels including organizational, people, and work levels. For each level, it is essential to investigate conditions, processes, and outcomes. Donald Tosti and Stephanie Jackson illustrate the parameters of organizational scans in Table 7-14.

Implementing Environmental Scanning in the Workplace

As an intervention, environmental scanning can empower every employee to be observant and suggest changes that could have a positive effect on the organization. Employees

TABLE 7-14: Tosti and Jackson's Parameters of Organizational Scan

	Conditions	Process	Outcomes
Organizational Level	*Strategy, Structure* Mission, strategy External business drivers Functional grouping Budget/decision authority	*Systems* Degree of centralization Consistency of operations Flexibility	*Organizational Results* Satisfaction of investors Satisfaction of societal stakeholders Measures of success Goal alignment with mission

People Level	*Climate Practices*
	 Company values, individual
	   values
	 Management/leadership
	   practices
	 Team norms
	 Ethics, integrity
		Performance Requirements
		 Skills, knowledge
		 Job aids/references
		 Selection
		 Conference
			Motivation, Feedback
			 Satisfaction of employees
			 Frequency, timing, form
			 Rewards and recognition
			 Expectations

Work Level	*Environmental, Resources* Physical environment Tools, materials, information Support personnel/services Accessibility of resources Work load demands	*Methods* Allocation of functions Processes, procedures Work flow Duplication/gaps	*Products, Services* Satisfaction of customers Productivity levels Standards/criteria Quality of product delivery

Tosti and Jackson, 1997, p. 24.

JOB AID 7-6: Operations Management Worksheet

Directions: Create one worksheet for each sub-plan.

- Operations Plan
- Information Systems Plan
- Financial Plan
- Quality or Continuous Improvement Plan
- Human Resources Plan

- Communications Plan
- Maintenance Plan (if applies)
- Research and Development
- Information Systems
- Other

Question	Responses
What are the strategic goals related to this sub-plan?	
What is the current reality relative to the strategic goals?	
What is the ideal situation if the strategic goals were fully realized?	
What are the major objectives needed to pursue these strategic goals?	
What are the barriers?	
What specific action steps are needed to achieve the goals?	

Based on Napier, R., Sidle, C., and Sanaghan, P. (1998). *High impact tools and activities for strategic planning. New York: McGraw-Hill.*

JOB AID 7-7: Environmental Scanning Preparation

Directions: Jump start your environmental scan by completing the following items.

1. Preparation	• Has an employee-led team with the necessary evaluation skills been identified?..☐ Yes ☐ No • Before officially beginning, has a preliminary brainstorm analysis been performed that covers organizational strengths, weaknesses, opportunities, and threats? ....☐ Yes ☐ No

2. Data Collection	• Will the following trends, both internal and external, be addressed?
	
	  1. Political..☐ Yes ☐ No
	  2. Economic..☐ Yes ☐ No
	  3. Societal..☐ Yes ☐ No
	  4. Technological..☐ Yes ☐ No
	  5. Educational ....☐ Yes ☐ No
	  6. Physical...☐ Yes ☐ No
	  7. Competitive ....☐ Yes ☐ No
	
	• What data gathering methods will be used?
	  — External
	
	  — Internal

3. Communication	• How are individuals and teams in the organization made aware of the process and how will their input be solicited? • How will external individuals be invited to participate and informed of results?

JOB AID 7-8: Questions for an Organizational Scan

Directions: The following questions provide structure to an organizational scan. They can also be used as an internal environmental scan.

Conditions, Organizational Level: Strategy, Structure

1. Is the change compatible with the organization's mission and strategic direction? If so, is that clear to people who carry out the change?
2. Will the change help (or at least not hinder) the organization in addressing external business drivers or pressures on the organization?
3. Does the organization's current division into units or functions support the proposed change? Do functions have outputs of recognized value? Will groups that need to work closely together find it easy to do?
4. Will people have the budget or decision making authority they need to implement the change and meet their goals and responsibilities?

Conditions, People Level: Climate, Practices

1. Is the change compatible with current organizational values and with what the organization considers important about the way it conducts business? Are those values generally consistent across organizational groups affected by the change?
2. Is there typically a match between what the organization states as values and the kind of behavior that is actually recognized and rewarded?
3. Do current management and leadership practices support the change?
4. Do current team norms about work behavior support the change?
5. Is the change compatible with people's beliefs about integrity and ethical behavior?

Conditions, Work Level: Environment, Resources

1. Does the current physical environment support the change?
2. Do people have the equipment, tools, materials, and information they need to make the change work?
3. Are support services or personnel necessary to make the change work available?
4. Are the resources people will need to make the change work easily accessible to them?
5. Will the overall workload be manageable, given the change effort?

Process, Organization Level: Systems

1. Are the current systems (information, rewards, etc.) centralized or decentralized in a way that supports the change?
2. Does the degree of consistency or variability of operations from one area to another support the change?
3. Do organizational systems currently have the degree of flexibility required to support the change?

Process, People Level: Performance Requirements

1. Do the people who will make the change happen have the skills, knowledge, and experience to make it work?
2. Are on-the-job references or job aids available to support the change, if needed?
3. Are people currently selected for qualities that match the requirements of the roles they will need to fill?
4. Do people have the confidence they need to try the change and make it work?

Process, Work Level: Methods

1. Is the current assignment of job functions or tasks appropriate to support the change?
2. Are work procedures or processes currently supportive of the change?
3. Is the current workflow designed to support change efficiently and effectively?
4. Is the work design generally free of duplications of effort or gaps that could interfere with the change?

Outcomes, Organizational Level: Organizational Results

1. Are the goals in units involved in or related to the change consistent and compatible with the change's requirements and the results expected?
2. Are organizational measurements in place that will allow people to determine the success of the change? Are those measurements clearly tied to organizational success?
3. Will the change contribute to increasing or maintaining satisfaction of shareholders, owners, or others who have a stake in the organization's performance?

Outcomes, People Level: Motivation, Feedback

1. Is the way in which people now get feedback about their work compatible with the change, frequent enough, timed appropriately, and in usable form?
2. Are people currently rewarded and recognized for behavior that is compatible with or supports the change?
3. Are current expectations about work and work behavior compatible with what the change will require?
4. Will the change contribute to increasing or maintaining employee satisfaction?

Outcomes, Work Level: Products, Services

1. Are current productivity levels sufficient to meet the requirements of the change?
2. Are work standards or criteria currently compatible with those the change requires?
3. Will the change contribute to increasing or maintaining customer satisfaction?
4. Are current time requirements or allowances for completing work compatible with the change?
5. Is the predictability of the workload compatible with the requirements of change?

Tosti, D., and Jackson, S.D. (1997). The organizational scan. Performance Improvement, 36 (10), p. 25.

should be encouraged to think about the current organization and what the organization could be and to acquire data to support their ideas. Encouraging pro-active responses to the environment shortens the change process because employees expect to adapt and stay current. Participation and involvement are powerful factors in positive change.

Environmental scanning has external and internal aspects. In environmental scanning, PT practitioners should explore the following internal categories:

- Technology
  - Is state-of-the-art technology available?
  - Is it critical to have the latest technology in order to succeed?
  - What alternatives will function well enough to perform?
- Relationships
  - What is the relationship between directors and managers?
  - Is communication between managers and employees functional?
  - Do the employees understand the objectives set by the directors?
- Resources
  - Are human resources being utilized to the fullest?
  - Is the right person in the right position or would changes increase performance or productivity?
- Political roles
  - Are decision makers listening to others or dictating?
  - Are open forums available for dialogue and exchange of ideas?
- Structure
  - Is the organizational structure efficient and does it flow naturally?
  - What changes, big or small, would help the flow of information and contribute to a solid organizational structure?

External categories should be evaluated as well, such as:

1. Forces and trends
   - Political: War, peace, military conflicts, elections, referendums, voting
   - Economic: Stable, unstable, growing, declining, inflation, recession, depression
   - Social: Environment, status, support systems
   - Technological: E-commerce, reaching audience through new technological means, networking, databases and information sharing
   - Demographic
     - Who is your target audience, client, or customer?
     - Is the profile of your target group changing? Market studies are available through organizations and chamber of commerce resources.
2. Key resource controllers: Look to marketing and public relations departments, if available, for information on

external sources. Define who will collect and maintain information in an easily accessible database.
3. Actual and potential competitors or collaborators
   - What organizations have the same products and target markets?
   - Where would collaboration or diversification be beneficial?
   - Would a joint venture situation bring the most efficiency or performance to the organization?
   - Would outsourcing bring improved performance results (see Job Aids 7-7 and 7-8)?

Benchmarking

Definition and Scope

Benchmarking is a tool for setting goals and defining methods for achieving the goals based on the success or failure of other organizations. In other words, it is a systematic process of comparing an organization to other organizations for the purpose of learning better methods and determining best practices.[1] Best practices serve as models for creating or adapting procedures within the benchmarking organization, to meet or exceed the best practices identified from the outside organization.[2]

Employee Involvement

Benchmarking, as an intervention, involves active searching for improvement possibilities. It is based on reality and allows employees to actually observe possible approaches. Participation and involvement enhance buy-in for change. Broad involvement of employee groups reduces resistance and minimizes unintended side effects due to the failure to anticipate consequences of a planned change. It is very difficult to make massive paradigm shifts and take full advantage of the possibilities uncovered in benchmarking. Organizational readiness for a "paradigm shift" would be necessary to accomplish dramatic results.[3]

Benefits

One of the major values of benchmarking is sharing.[4] Benchmarking can benefit organizations in a wide variety of ways, such as:

- Strategy formulation
- Organizational development
- Improved training
- Lower costs, making improvements easier
- Opportunities for people to learn about new ways of working together
- Improved internal communications.[5]

Commonalities in Best Practice Organizations

The Defense Evaluation and Research Agency (DERA), a US government-owned research and technology organization, studied the process of benchmarking. DERA found that best practice organizations have certain commonalties (see Table 7-15).

TABLE 7-15: Commonalities in Best Practice Organizations

Commonalities	Description
Company-wide management systems	• Integral part of the business, helping them achieve goals. • Senior management clearly state their requirements. • Progress toward goals is measured and monitored. • Quality expertise is key in designing the system. • Senior management buy-in and involvement are at very high levels.
Processes	• Connected to business goals • Communicated and managed
History	• Small, simple, well-integrated organizations have an advantage. • If previous systems were old, complex, and discrete, they may have created barriers.
Local control	• Size and complexity of organization has great bearing on communication and change. • Local control is an advantage.

Based on Morling and Tanner, 2000, pp. 425–426.

Implementing Benchmarking Interventions in the Workplace

Steps
Benchmarking begins by defining the problem to be compared with other organizations in order to examine best practices. Problem definition involves thoroughly understanding the present situation and determining what the situation would be if the problem were solved. It is also necessary to understand the impact of the problem on the organization.

The benchmarking team next researches organizations that face similar circumstances and learns how they cope with the circumstances. Frequently, benchmarking involves looking throughout the same industry and into other industries that face similar circumstances. Often, the approach used to cope in other industries provides insight and can change the benchmarker's paradigm about the situation.

Next, the benchmarking team communicates with selected organizations and eventually visits partner organizations to view actual workplace solutions to the selected problem. Finally, following research, observation, and information sharing, the team determines best practice and applies lessons learned from the partner organization to the troublesome situation. Action steps are created to solve the problem.

Reciprocity
Because benchmarking involves sharing processes and organizational practices with similar or competitive organizations, there is great sensitivity regarding use of the information, which may be viewed as organizational secrets or competitive advantage. It is important to establish clarity to protect individuals involved in the sharing. Normally, reciprocity is expected. Because of the need to share information that would normally be private, it is essential that there is strong sanction and support from senior management. The American Productivity and Quality Center (APQC) developed the Benchmarking Code of Conduct. This Code summarizes the guidelines and ethics for the benchmarking partners. It includes these nine principles: legality, exchange, confidentiality, use, contact, preparation, completion, understanding, and action.

Code of Conduct
In addition to the Code of Conduct, APQC suggests that before contacting benchmarking partners, an organization should do the following:

1. *Determine details on what will be benchmarked.*
   - Does the team want to know how other organizations collect data, implement performance improvement, or improve process flow?
   - Define what will be the focus of the research before embarking on the process of gathering information.
2. *Identify key performance variables.*
   - Know ahead of time and collect information on what the team feels are key performance variables.
   - Be open to new input, but it is a good idea to have a clear picture of what the team feels is appropriate.
   - How is performance measured and observed?
3. *Complete a self-assessment of one's own organization.*
   - Perform the benchmarking assessment on one's own organization. This will help refine the procedure and methods of data collection and help focus or narrow the desired information.

After the benchmarking partner has been contacted, use the following guidelines for further action:

1. Have the questionnaire and interview prepared and available in advance if requested.
2. Identify the purpose of the study and clarify the intended application of data received.
3. Confirm an atmosphere of sharing, and a willingness to provide requested information and disclose information gathered as a partner.
   - Confirm the confidentiality and application of the information.
   - Express the value the second party's information will bring.
4. Create specific times to meet with the partners and maintain all schedules and meeting arrangements.
5. Have a project management tool available, including timeline, responsible individuals, tasks, and objectives.

Senior Management Support

Management should actively support benchmarking. Senior management can increase effectiveness by standardizing the processes and forms. Benchmarking teams should be cross-functional with support (indirect) departments included. It is also beneficial to benchmark the way successful organizations have minimized resistance and implemented their process so as not to reinvent procedures that work.

PT practitioners can be major contributors to benchmarking projects. The HPT Model fits well with the systematic benchmarking approach. PT practitioners are accustomed to gathering data and then implementing actions based on the findings. Benchmarking has disciplined processes based on the APQC Code of Conduct. PT practitioners are accustomed to managing performance improvement projects and can assume major responsibilities on benchmarking efforts (see Job Aid 7-9).

Reengineering, Realigning, Restructuring

Definition and Scope

Reengineering, realigning, and restructuring are management processes that should be integrated into strategic planning as performance improvement initiatives. They focus on increasing efficiencies, implementing lessons learned, streamlining process flow, and creating an organizational foundation on which to grow and prosper.

JOB AID 7-9: Benchmarking Planner

Directions: Complete the following questionnaire as a "reality check" while planning the benchmarking project.

- Have the parameters of the benchmark study been determined? .... ☐ Yes ☐ No

- Has a champion been identified? .... ☐ Yes ☐ No

- Have key performance variables been identified? .... ☐ Yes ☐ No

- Has a self-assessment been completed to understand the current situation within the organization? .... ☐ Yes ☐ No

- Have high-performing organizations been identified? .... ☐ Yes ☐ No

- Have partnership sharing opportunities (such as benchmarking networks) been investigated? .... ☐ Yes ☐ No

- Has the benchmarking questionnaire been developed? .... ☐ Yes ☐ No

- Have standardized guidelines for the interview been developed? .... ☐ Yes ☐ No

- Are existing benchmarking strategies available for adaptation or will it be necessary to create a unique strategy for the organization? .... ☐ Yes ☐ No

- Is it understood what is confidential and what should be discussed only in the context of the benchmark study and not with external sources? .... ☐ Yes ☐ No

Reengineering

Reengineering is a "radical redesign of an organization's processes to achieve performance breakthroughs."[1] It is a systematic approach used to dramatically change the processes, technology, structure, and infrastructure of an organization in order to eliminate non-value-added work and to improve delivery of quality products and services.[2] Hammer and Champy state that

Business reengineering isn't about fixing anything. Business reengineering means starting all over, starting from scratch...It means forgetting how work was done in the age of the mass market and deciding how it can best be done now.[3]

Hammer and Champy's intent was to enrich jobs.

Reengineering requires a thorough understanding of the existing processes, defining each step using flow charting, which must incorporate the "principles and practices of organizational development and change management."[4] The reengineering team looks for ways to do the tasks radically better by trying new methods. Brainstorming and research focus on innovation and creativity. Nothing is "sacred," everything can change. Videotaping is often used to ensure total understanding of what actually occurs. Targets may seem unreachable in the beginning of the process, but through creativity the targets are usually achievable. Linking reengineering and total quality management (TQM) integrates proven methods and strategies for changing the work environment.[5] (See Chapter 3 for more information on TQM.)

Realigning

Realigning is focusing the organization on its core competencies. Core competencies are single elements or groups of elements within an organization that are deemed successful and efficient, and merit organizational focus. If an organization has diversified too much, realignment is necessary to get back on track.[6] To make the transition back to an efficient organization, management must communicate its intentions openly with the organization so that no one is surprised. Employees have the opportunity to increase their own performance during periods of realignment, but they need adequate warning. If direction is not given or communication is blocked, performance will likely decrease.

Realigning focuses on re-purposing around core competencies. After core competencies are determined, the organization defines non-core competencies, which are often support functions, such as training. Organizations are likely to out-source non-core functions to suppliers who specialize in them. For example, one of the first areas to outsource is usually payroll. Companies specialize in efficient check preparation and report generation. By outsourcing non-core functions, the organization can focus on core competencies.

Realigning can also mean adjusting the size and capacity of the work force to better meet organizational goals. Organizations can benchmark externally or internally between facilities and determine internal best practices. Organizations can take advantage of the internal lessons to improve efficiencies.[7]

Restructuring

Restructuring reorganizes the units or departments, usually resulting in a new organizational chart and new responsibilities, and may involve new reporting relationships. It is partially caused by market factors, such as foreign competition, and demand for increased profitability. Workflow may be restructured in order to accommodate the market requirements. This will impact many areas including:

- Existing teams
- Individual performance
- Training requirements
- Quality measures
- Financial allocations

For example, is the purchasing department commodity based or platform oriented? Are efforts being duplicated because the existing structure does not allow for streamlining? In order to restructure, it is necessary to document the process flow and analyze the means of improving efficiencies.

Implementing Reengineering, Restructuring, and Realignment Interventions in the Workplace

Communication and Participation

Communication is essential to successful change. Business process reengineering

can be successfully carried out only when both the direction for change and the benefits gained from them are clearly explained. This will contribute either to reducing employees' resistance to changes or to converting their complaints into positive attitudes. Therefore, it is necessary to analyze employees' expected reactions in advance.[8]

Reengineering, restructuring, and realignment affect employees on a daily basis, usually changing their processes, procedures, departmental configuration, and often the culture of their work group. Because the nature of the intended change is so personal and individual, it is essential to prepare employees adequately for any type of management change. If employees are informed, management intervenes in a timely manner, and employees are included in the decision making process, the likelihood of success is much greater.[9]

As interventions, reengineering, restructuring, and realignment can make the workplace more efficient and can correct imbalances in work assignments. The three approaches can also increase workload and stress. Participation by employees in the planned changes can increase the likelihood of positive results and minimize negative consequences.

Transformation and Change

Realigning, restructuring, and reengineering require change. "Change does not come easy."[10] Cameron "found that as many as three quarters of all reengineering, TQM, strategic planning, and downsizing efforts have failed or created problems serious enough to threaten the survival of the organization."[11]

People must step outside known patterns of behavior—they must surrender their present selves and put themselves in jeopardy by becoming part of an emergent system. This process usually requires the surrender of personal control, the toleration of uncertainty, and the development of a new culture at the collective level and a new self at the individual level...Traditional change strategies are not likely to be effective.[12]

One of the major reasons is that senior management—the leadership of the organization—does not change its behavior. Leaders make plans for changes in others, but do not change themselves.

Implementation Steps

Effective implementation of reengineering, realignment, or restructuring can be initiated by the following steps as identified by Langdon, Whiteside, and McKenna:

1. Identify the project and scope.
   Will it focus on one department or the entire organization? What are the budgetary and time guidelines?

JOB AID 7-10: Reengineering, Realigning, Restructuring

Directions: As you embark on the change process, use this checklist as a job aid to ensure you stay on the desired path.

Reengineering
- ☐ Identify the organization's *current business processes*, department by department.
- ☐ Evaluate the *process flow* and *chain of command* within the organization.
- ☐ Confirm that each *process step* is controllable and repeatable.
- ☐ Prepare standard *interview* questions for employees and management, to be administered initially during the development and information-gathering stages and then again upon completion of the implementation.
- ☐ Review *structure and foundation of organization*. How can it be improved? How can employees within the system work more efficiently?

Realigning
- ☐ Review the organization's *current alignment* to business objectives. Is everyone working toward a common goal? Is everyone aware of the objectives? Does everyone know how their work makes a difference and contributes to the whole?
- ☐ Create and develop *revised process for alignment to business objectives*. Give employees guidelines for keeping the objectives apparent.
- ☐ Evaluate *advantages and disadvantages* of major change in the organization.
- ☐ Identify main reason, incentive, or desired outcomes for *implementing change*.

Restructuring
- ☐ *Document and analyze* the structure of the organization.
- ☐ Confirm that each process step is *controllable and repeatable*.
- ☐ *Document* everything!
- ☐ Review and improve the performance of your processes *through measurement and feedback*.

Applicable to all change management strategies
- ☐ Integrate *employee input* into management change practice.
- ☐ Allow *opportunities for feedback* from all employees in the organization.
- ☐ Provide employees with *relevant information* as part of the change process and prior to management implementation of change so that they can provide input and also prepare to adapt the change into on-the-job performance.
- ☐ Communicate process of reengineering, realignment, or restructuring to the organization.

2. Create the vision, values and goals.
   Where does the organization want to be? Is there management buy-in?
3. Evaluate and redesign the flow of current business operations.
   Where is the process flow held up?
   Where can barriers be reduced or eliminated?
4. Conduct proof-of-concept.
   Project the reengineering concept into the future.
   How does it look and what areas might be improved?
5. Plan the implementation.
   Document the steps for implementing the plan and carrying it through.
6. Obtain approval for implementation.
   Does management agree with the means of implementing? Do they have recommendations or suggestions?
7. Implement! Follow the plan step by step.
8. Make the transition to a continuous improvement environment.[13]

PT practitioners can be vital contributors in realignment, restructuring, or reengineering efforts. The HPT Model provides a systematic and systemic structure for substantial change efforts. The field of PT provides guidance in analysis, change planning, and implementation. PT also stresses the need for evaluation to ensure that the effort is on the right course and to provide data for mid-change corrections, if needed (see Job Aid 7-10).

The Pro-Action section of this chapter was written in collaboration with Margaret Korosec, MA.

Case Study 7-2: Restructuring Mann+Hummel Automotive

Situation

Mann+Hummel (M+H) is an automotive tier-one supplier of plastic injection-molded engine components. With a small team in 1996, the company established a North American presence supported by the headquarters in Germany. Once established, the company needed to acquire a local manufacturing facility. In December 1997, M+H acquired Geiger Technic (Geiger), which provided the foundation on which to bring the German technology to the US The product lines of Geiger complemented the technology and products that would be introduced by M+H.

In addition to the challenges of manufacturing, sales, and quality, the other real challenges were integrating two cultures, German and American, as well as integrating Mann+Hummel with Geiger. Without the foresight, insight, and leadership of Jim Riordan, the North American president, the process of finding balance, increased performance, and other leaders from within

would likely have taken much more time. His leadership was and continues to be key in the restructuring process.

Intervention

In order to focus the restructuring process of the newly joined companies, organizational goals were established at an offsite meeting with representatives from all departments providing input and feedback. This was a vital exchange of information because natural work groups were given the opportunity to interact with other departments. Everyone gained insight into the issues others faced. Ultimately, the real issues of communication and collaboration surfaced.

Part of this process was to define the vision of the organization and get buy-in from all directors, managers, and employees. Individuals were empowered to take responsibility for their portion of the change, by giving them the authority to initiate and implement changes in their areas.

Results

Listening and understanding issues within other departments were key to recognizing the overall system. It also helped strengthen the bond between individuals and departments in which finger pointing had previously been the norm.

Giving authority and empowering individuals to do what they felt was right in the context of the restructuring allowed for natural leaders to surface. The process was initiated slowly and some management changes were necessary to truly give the authority to those whose leadership warranted it.

Lessons Learned

Lessons learned during the first year and a half of the merger of M+H with Geiger are:
- Continuously review the status of the organizational system and focus on the goals, keeping both individuals and departments on track.
- Have flexibility and patience to let the natural leaders surface.
- Individuals are responsible for change and their own contribution and impact.
- Cross-functional dialogue allows for learning and provides opportunities for understanding the overall organization.
- Organizational change affects all levels of management and employees.
- Maintaining communication through team-based or company-wide meetings and other electronic media and publications is necessary to keep everyone informed.
- Recognizing achievement and rewarding individual contribution motivates.

Mann+Hummel case study written by Margaret Korosec, MA, in collaboration with Kathy Strah, Human Resources Manager at Mann+Hummel. August 1999.

ORGANIZATIONAL VALUES

Organizational values are the "stuff we all live by," our organizational energy, the reason for the organization to exist. Companies have profit motives in order to remain vital and functioning, but they also need wholesome values to accomplish those same goals. Unfortunately, when an organization goes through difficult times or needs to make tough decisions, organizational values are often sacrificed. Organizational values create the organization's vision of the world:

- How people are treated; how information is communicated and shared
- How employees act and create
- How they function as teams and make decisions
- How people respond to mistakes and failures
- How individuals take risk, learn, and grow.

In other words, business values and people values are the organizational anchors.[1]

Organizational values include culture, diversity, globalization, ethics, and spirituality in the workplace. In order for employees to succeed in their positions, organizations must be aware of how these factors affect employees. Organizational values interventions help people succeed by supporting the "right" decisions; maximizing the significance of employee, supplier, customer, and client; encouraging workers to think globally; and treating people with respect and trust.

Culture

Definition and Scope

Organizational culture refers to collective human behaviors, such as decision making, speech, writing, and actions based on mutual acceptance of values, myths, heroes, rites and rituals, symbols, and artifacts.[1]

- *Values* (organizational and individual) are the basic concepts and beliefs, the heart of culture. They are evidenced in standards, such as "if you do this, this will happen."
- *Heroes* are the role models, the visionaries, the memorable people who "made it." Representative organizational heroes include Thomas Edison as an inventor, Jack Welsh as an Information-Era chief executive officer, Alfred Sloan as a crafter of corpora-

tion structure, Andrew Carnegie as a philanthropist, and Henry Ford as an expert in assembly line manufacturing and work design.
- *Rites and rituals* refer to the methods of celebrating successes, holidays, and customs relative to daily organization life, such as how employees drink coffee (in groups at tables or individually at their own desks).
- *Symbols* are the posters, awards and plaques, lobby pictures and decorations, and organizational logo.
- *Artifacts* include the annual report, newsletters, brochures, and "giveaways," such as coffee mugs and ball-point pens.[2]

Culture is pervasive; it virtually shapes and controls employee behavior. Most of culture is unwritten and often is not discussed, except informally among close friends and colleagues. Management needs to be sensitive to the power of culture in planning and decision making. Culture can be changed, but managers must plan the change and anticipate some resistance.

Power of Culture

The importance of culture is often underestimated by Western organizations, which tend to focus on efficiency, process, and productivity. However, Okio Morita, former chair of the Sony Corporation, recently commented that "culture may impact products, services, and operations by only 10%, but this is the most important 10%. This 10% determines success or failure."[3]

The power of culture often goes unrecognized when senior executives create mergers or make acquisitions. This can be the most difficult part of a merger or acquisition and often the cause of failure. Each organizational culture needs to be defined and then decisions should be made about which cultural aspects will be encouraged and which will not. Divestitures also need extensive planning so that there is not a vacuum when the division becomes independent.

Balanced Culture

Healthy cultures promote a balance of emphasis on productivity, profits, and people.[4] There should be respect and understanding of the reason the organization exists (such as manufacturing, banking, service, or education). However, there should also be an understanding that organizations accomplish their mission and goals through people.

According to Deal and Kennedy in their landmark book *Corporate Cultures: The Rites and Rituals of Corporate Life,* "Values form the bedrock of any corporate culture."[5]

> *If employees know what their company stands for, if they know what standards they are to uphold, then they are much more likely to make decisions that will support those standards. They are also likely to feel as if they are an important part of the organization. They are motivated because life in the company has meaning for them.*[6]

Culture and Ethics

Experts in international marketing management state that culture is a critical aspect of ethics and is essential for effective business relations. "As more and more firms operate globally, an understanding of the effects of cultural differences on ethical decision making becomes increasingly important for avoiding potential business pitfalls and for designing effective international marketing management programs."[7]

Culture of Imagination and Innovation

For years, organizations have been improving quality, reducing costs, speeding delivery, and eliminating waste. These efforts have improved product, customer satisfaction, and profits. However, organizations are finding less and less to improve as they get better and better. The next arena for competitive advantage will be the ability to innovate quickly and efficiently. Gary Hamel, a leading strategic thinker, believes the world is entering the "age of imagination" when he says:

> *To fully realize the promise of our new age, each of us must become a dreamer, as well as a doer. In the age of progress, dreams were often little more than fantasies. Today, as never before, they are doorways to new realities. Our collective selves—our organizations—must also learn to dream. In many organizations, there has been a massive failure of collective imagination. How else can one account for the fact that so many organizations have been caught flat-footed by the future?*[8]

Implementing Culture Interventions in the Workplace

Culture and Change

In order to implement change, management needs consensus and strong commitment regarding the need for change and the process to be used. Employees often realize that resistance can lead management to "back down" and eventually to abandon the initiative. Employees

often refer to this pattern as "flavor of the month" or the "latest bandwagon." It is very easy to create a culture of resistance to change inadvertently by not anticipating the entire change process and then planning for resistance and contingencies before beginning the change effort.

Adopting a philosophy of continuous improvement and the capacity to deal with consistent change are critical competitive advantages. A culture that supports change begins with a strong senior management commitment to making change visible. The attitude of management is critical. Change planning requires an interdisciplinary and collaborative approach because no one person or department alone can make change succeed. Management stimulates change by its own actions and encourages employees to see their part in the improvement of the organization. Employee involvement and information sharing are critical to implementing changes.[9]

One example of a major change is the new emphasis on the extended enterprise, which includes customers, suppliers, and strategic partners. There will be less emphasis on research and development (R&D), and more emphasis on innovation through outsourcing. Each part of the enterprise will bring new ideas, based on their experience and expertise. Each company will not need to invest in a full range of research activity. Ideas will be shared and innovations will require collaboration to increase value and capture competitive advantage. Production facilities will specialize and more suppliers will create parts or sub-assemblies based on their strengths. Some people fear those who may "steal ideas"; however, the potential rewards seem to outweigh the risks.[10]

Management's Role

Culture is often defined in value words, such as trust, openness, respect, customer focus, and responsibility. When organizations use their words, they need to back up their statements with consistent actions. When employees observe hollow and self-serving statements from upper management, resentment occurs. "It isn't what we say we're like, it's what we actually do that makes a difference."[11] For example, chief executive officers (CEO), believing in the critical importance of learning, have effectively driven learning cultures in a number of organizations.[12] Jack Welsh, General Electric, has conducted management training sessions for years. Michael Dell of Dell Computer created a corporate university, called Dell Learning, to accomplish the following:

- Align learning with key business initiatives
- Make learning directly available to everyone who needs it
- Create clarity around competencies required for continued success
- Provide consistency, where needed, through a global curricula.[13]

Management has a strong bearing on the success of culture change efforts, such as TQM. Two out of every three TQM implementations fail. The waste of operational dollars, potential customer benefits, and opportunity costs is phenomenal.[14] Successful TQM implementations have cultures conducive to long-term commitment (three or more years) supported by innovative ways of thinking and customer satisfaction as the company's primary goal. These cultures have strong support from top management. On the other hand, cultures that do not favor TQM methodologies use leadership strategies that emphasize short-term (quarterly) productivity goals. Managers who emphasize structure, details, and daily routine are at a disadvantage.[15] (See Chapter 3 for more information on TQM.)

Creating a Positive Culture

It is easy to underestimate the power of culture to make or break a change effort. Change planners can get caught up in work processes, information systems, corporate structures, and business strategies. They can overlook how people feel and believe, their fears and anxieties, their dreams and ambitions, their hopes and expectations.[16] Management can foster desirable beliefs about the future of the organization by connecting experiences employees have in their work groups with the larger organization. People are looking for consistency between the mission and goals, the organizational message, and their daily experiences.[17]

Culture can be beneficial and support a positive work environment.[18] Because culture affects everyone, employees need to actively participate to feel responsible and proud of their organization.

Milcare, a Grand Rapids, Michigan, company known for innovation in health care furniture, offers these 10 guidelines for effective participation.[19]
1. Participation is a right and responsibility.
2. Everyone must be "literate" on business realities.
3. Participation is neither paternalistic nor permissive.
4. Everyone must accept "problem ownership."
5. Management is open to competent influence.
6. Participation is the means to become more competitive.
7. Decisions are made at the most appropriate level.
8. Employees have access to all the necessary resources.
9. Everyone must adhere to a system of accountability and commitment.
10. Participation is a process that is managed and continually renewed.

Cultural Barriers

Just as there are factors that positively affect culture, there are six common causes, or "silent killers," that discourage employees and foster a negative culture. It may be difficult to establish that a "silent killer" (see Table 7-16) exists because organizations and people tend to be defensive and resist diagnosis to determine causes of problems.

Cultural Surveys

Organizations have found that surveys provide data that help determine gaps and identify causes of organizational problems. In addition, surveys identify strong areas within the organization. This allows the organization to enhance its strengths and take corrective action to improve weaknesses. Standardized cultural tests exist. Representative tests are listed.

Organizational Readiness Inventory (ORI): Diagnosing Your Organization's Ability to Adapt to the Future. Moseley, J.L., and Swiatkowski, D.J. Published in *The 2000 Annual: Volume 2, Consulting.* San Francisco: Jossey-Bass/Pfeiffer.

Organizational Culture Inventory (OCI), Cooke, R.A. and Lafferty, J.C. (1994).
Human Synergistics International
39819 Plymouth Road C-8020
Plymouth, MI 48170-8020
Phone: 800-622-7584
Fax: 734-459-5557
Email: info@humansyn.com

PT Role in Culture

PT practitioners are familiar with cultural issues because culture is an important component of the HPT Model. PT practitioners are capable of assessing the culture and identifying strengths and weaknesses. Their background in change management provides the experiences necessary to lead or support any cultural improvement initiatives (see Job Aid 7-11).

Diversity

Definition and Scope

Organizations are becoming increasingly diverse. Therefore, it is important that employees understand and respect diversity. Diversity represents workplace differences based

TABLE 7-16: Cultural "Silent Killers"

1. Unclear strategic direction and priorities
2. Ineffective management team
3. Leadership that is too top-down or too laissez-faire
4. Ineffective vertical communication
5. Lack of coordination and integration
6. Lack of down-the-line leadership development

Based on Eisenstat and Dixon, 2000, pp. 52–54.

JOB AID 7-11: Cultural Analysis

Directions: Complete the questionnaire with input from various levels of the organization.

1. **What are the organization's stated values and standards? Are they beneficial and healthy?**
2. **What are the unstated values and standards? Are they beneficial and healthy?**
3. **Who are the heroes? Are legends or stories about them helpful?**
4. **What are the rituals or rites? Formal and informal?**
5. **Are the internal and external communications positive and healthy? Do the formal communication pieces have any influence? Does the grapevine control people's emotions, fears, and behavior?**
6. **List healthy aspects of the culture.**
7. **List detrimental aspects of the culture.**
8. **Identify factors for potential improvement. How pervasive and strong are these factors in the current culture? Describe ideal improvements.**

on gender, ethnic background, economic background, societal background, age, disability, religion, cultural heritage, and family situation.

Primary categories, known as "protected" by the US Equal Employment Opportunity Laws and Executive Orders, are age, disabilities, gender, religion, and ethnic background. Diversity categories are also covered by Civil Rights Acts, Age Discrimination in Employment Act (ADEA), Americans with Disabilities Act (ADA), Pregnancy Discrimination Act, Vietnam-Era Veterans Readjustment Act, and other legislation and executive orders.[1] The laws are administered by the Equal Employment Opportunity Commission (EEOC) and Office of Federal Contract Compliance Programs (OFCCP). All organizations with 20 or more employees must keep records that can be requested by either the EEOC or the OFCCP. EEOC has enforcement authority to initiate litigation and to intervene in private litigation.[2]

An organization's diversity policies and practices are usually associated with one of three paradigms: discrimination-and-fairness paradigm, access-and-legitimacy paradigm, and learning-and-effectiveness paradigm.[3] Discrimination-and-fairness focuses on avoidance of problems through meeting target numbers and compliance to laws and executive orders. This approach denies different points of view.

Not only does the discrimination-and-fairness paradigm insist that everyone is the same, but, with its emphasis on equal treatment, it puts pressure on employees to make sure that important differences do not count.[4]

Access-and-legitimacy tries to optimize differences, but it tends to compartmentalize people. For example, minorities may be assigned marketing roles to focus on the minority group of which they are a part. For example, Hispanics are assigned to the Hispanic marketing area. Sales staff are matched with similar customers. There is little opportunity in the organization beyond their own diversity areas, such as their own ethnic identity. This policy limits inclusion and opportunity. The learning-and-effectiveness paradigm takes advantage of differences, which may lead to rethinking work processes. By incorporating employees' varying perspectives, organizations may redefine markets, products, strategies, missions, and business practices. Creativity and innovation can be unleashed because different people can have different assumptions.

Valuing Differences
Although there are laws defining protection, organizations have also found that it is good business to be sensitive to differences in people and to understand and respect those

differences. Organizations have found that managing diversity makes strategic sense because customers and suppliers are diverse and represent substantial differences.[5] For example, customers of phone companies are very diverse. Phone companies learn a great deal about customer's differences by learning about employee differences. In addition, the US work force has increased representation of women, minorities, immigrants, and disabled people. Finally, attention to differences helps companies compete in a global marketplace.

Consequently, a general commitment to respecting differences is very helpful in supporting positive day-to-day operations. The
benefits of demographic diversity are more likely to emerge in organizations that, through their culture, make organizational membership salient and encourage people to categorize one another as having the organization's interests in common, rather than those that emphasize individualism and distinctiveness among members.[6]

Increasingly, organizations are emphasizing actual workplace productivity and issues of recruiting and retaining a diverse work force. Managers and employees are learning to respect differences and not expect conformity in dress, opinions, and work styles.

Diversity as an Asset
Diversity can also be viewed as an organizational asset that should be used to the fullest. Maximizing the unique perspectives of individual employees from diverse backgrounds is a tremendous, potentially untapped resource. For example, research indicates that gender diversity on teams increases their functioning.[7] Teams with almost equal representation of males and females rated themselves highest in team functioning. Diversity interventions are activities or initiatives that promote positive respect and sensitivity toward the value of differences in people.[8] Minorities want and expect inclusion, encouragement, and opportunity.[9] "Building an inclusive organization requires a serious commitment to fundamental change in the structures, behaviors, operating procedures, human resource systems, formal and informal reward systems, leadership practices, competency requirements, and culture of the organization."[10]

Implementing Diversity Interventions in the Workplace

Management's Responsibility
Senior executive attitudes and actions have a significant influence on employees' opinions of diversity efforts. These attitudes filter into the approach that employees take in dealing with diverse issues. Minorities experience

subtle discriminatory actions that have a great influence on all employees. *Fortune* magazine reported a survey of minority executives and found that 59% observed a double standard in the delegation of assignments, 45% had personally been a target of racial or cultural jokes, and 44% held back anger for fear of being seen as having "a chip on their shoulder."[11]

Senior management needs to establish specific goals and change behaviors and decision making processes to deal with diversity issues with credibility.

> *Effective supervisors or managers have always been aware of personality, educational background, and past work experience as variables influencing individual behavior. But race, ethnicity, age, gender, sexual orientation, or disability have not been properly recognized as important factors in explaining behavior.[12]*

Community Programs
Companies are establishing programs in high schools to prepare students for rewarding careers. Cisco sponsors a curriculum to prepare teens for jobs in networking fields with full credentials. Hyatt Corporation established a culinary professional school in a predominantly Hispanic high school in Chicago.[13]

Audits, Litigation, and Mediation
Lawsuit settlements have successfully changed the social fabric of many organizations. For example, manufacturing workplaces were difficult for women, because of harassment. Today, there are more opportunities for advancement and inclusion. Other organizations discriminated against certain races or people with various gender preferences. Again, there is greater acceptance demonstrated by diversity at the executive level. Diversity interventions usually begin with ensuring legal compliance through postings, reports, plans, and audits. Broader issues of valuing differences and maximizing the potential of each person's unique contribution can provide important organizational advantage.

Posting
Employers, employment agencies, and labor organizations covered by the Act are required to post EEOC-prepared notices summarizing the requirements of Civil Rights Act of 1964 (Title VII), the ADEA, the Equal Pay Act, the ADA, and the Civil Rights Act of 1991.

Reports
Employers with 100 or more employees must file the Employer Information Report (Standard Form 100, also known as EEO-1) annually with EEOC. The report breaks down the work force in specified job categories by race, sex, and national origin. Similar forms are required from unions, political jurisdictions, educational institutions,

school districts, and joint labor-management committees that sponsor apprenticeship programs. These forms are used to determine whether unlawful employment practices have been committed, such as insufficient recruitment initiatives for protected groups.[14]

Compliance
Two types of parity are considered. Employment parity is related to the overall proportion of minorities and women employed by an organization relative to the relevant labor market. Occupational parity looks at employment practices based on job categories in relation to women and minorities.

Affirmative Action Plans
An affirmative action plan (AAP) is a written document outlining specific goals and timetables for remedying past discriminatory practices or documenting fair employment practices. All federal contractors or subcontractors with contracts over $50,000 and 50 or more employees are required to develop and implement written affirmative action plans, which are monitored by the OFCCP. Approximately 225,000 companies in the United States are expected to fill out the plans.[15] In addition, all US government agencies prepare affirmative action plans.

AAPs usually contain three sections: analysis of data, narrative, and adverse impact. In addition, specifics of the AAP are sometimes determined by court rulings or mediation agreement when discrimination is found.[16] These plans are often information intensive and involve statistical tests to determine such factors as adverse impact. (Adverse impact means that the employment practices are adversely affecting the employment opportunities of women and minorities.) Software is available that uses data from many company sources (such as payroll or benefits) and from many software applications (such as Access or Oracle) to create a large database. The software then processes the data and creates reports. The software can statistically test the data and prepare adverse impact tables and reports.[17]

Policies
Most organizations have specific policies, usually part of employee manuals, stating that they are against discrimination and harassment. The policies usually define and describe:
1. Inappropriate behaviors, including examples of undesirable situations.
2. Complaint procedure to be taken when an undesirable situation occurs.
3. Investigation process, including who will investigate.
4. Hearing process, including who will hear the complaint and what happens if the evidence is sufficient.
5. Appeals process if any party believes the decision is unreasonable.

6. Punitive measures, including discipline for the discriminator and sanctions and/or compensation for the victim.
7. Record keeping, including the file system for complaints and the entire process.
8. Time schedule for each step in the process.
9. Confidentiality, including decision on whether victim's names will be disclosed.
10. Publicity to inform and educate employees.
11. Follow-up on all actions to determine implementation.
12. Review policy annually and revise, if necessary.[18]

It is critical that organizations maintain up-to-date employee manuals. In addition, the manual must be legally sound. Specialized software based on expert systems prompts manual writers through hundreds of questions related to a wide range of topics. The software contains legal text and practical explanations of topics, such as "at will" employment relationships, discrimination policies, or disabilities procedures. It is wise to have an attorney review software-based manuals written in house for legal soundness.[19]

Accommodation
Adjustments may be needed for learning disabled, vision or hearing challenged, motion or mobility challenged, and emotional challenged.[20] Most accommodations are not expensive, but they are often ingenious. Few cases will be won in court for refusing to make an accommodation. An easily forgotten issue is the need to accommodate people with disabilities when they attend training classes.

Diversity Training
Diversity training facilitates learning to appreciate differences, to understand the reasons for differences, and to value differences within the organization.[21] Diversity training should not be a one-time "fix-it," but rather an ongoing process of addressing stereotypes and discriminatory behavior.[22] There is frequently training for managers on the laws, their responsibility related to compliance, affirmative action, and valuing diversity. Companies often underestimate the importance of training in affirmative action. Organizations may think that a written anti-discrimination policy is sufficient. However, the US Court of Appeals for the 10th Circuit ruled that the policy must be followed up with an aggressive education program to shield the company from punitive damages, such as those stemming from an alleged violation of the ADA.[23]

Many public and private companies provide diversity training. Federal and state agencies help companies in their jurisdiction comply with federal and state civil rights law. For example, in Michigan the Department of Civil Rights—Problem Resolution Process Department provides training for Michigan employees. Other states are likely to have agencies that assist with compliance related to state law. John Golaszewski can help readers identify the correct state agency in other states.

John Golaszewski, Team Coordinator
Problem Resolution Process
State of Michigan
Department of Civil Rights
State of Michigan Plaza Building
1200 Sixth Avenue
Detroit, MI 48226
Phone: 313-256-2649
Fax: 313-256-2427
E-mail: golaszewskij@state.mi.us

Three traditional types of diversity training exist: affirmative action, valuing differences, and managing diversity. Gardenswartz and Rowe developed a table to compare the three types (see Table 7-17).

Diversity training is evolving beyond traditional training to address more specific business and organizational requirements. Figure 7-1 explains the relationship of the various types of training. Organizations usually begin by ensuring that affirmative action and executive orders are in conformance. Disputes or court orders may require substantial efforts around conformance issues.

Organizations are moving on to efforts that actually provide great potential for benefit to people and business metrics. Valuing differences is necessary to understand the potential brought to the workplace by each individual. People are encouraged to speak freely and all employees are treated with dignity and respect. Effective management skills enable organizations to encourage unique contributions rather than preferring a consistent and customary approach. People learn to listen with greater openness and to create synergy from the possibilities presented by diversity. On-the-job application focuses on business requirements and helps define and describe strategies for reaching objectives that draw upon the potentials of the various styles for contributing.[24]

In addition, there is a tremendous concern about recruiting and retaining a talented work force. Recognizing the positive impact of cultural diversity and fostering diverse contributions can be powerful staffing and selection strategies.

In order to understand themselves better with regard to diversity issues, trainees often benefit from personal profile assessments that enable people to:
- Recognize the reality of individual uniqueness
- Identify personal opinions and feelings about work force diversity
- Increase both personal and workplace productivity

TABLE 7-17: Comparing Affirmative Action, Valuing Differences, and Managing Diversity

Affirmative Action	Valuing Differences	Managing Diversity
Quantitative. Emphasis is on achieving equality of opportunity in the work environment through the changing of organizational demographics. Progress is monitored by statistical reports and analysis.	*Qualitative.* Emphasis is on the appreciation of differences and the creation of an environment in which everyone feels valued and accepted. Progress is monitored by organizational surveys focused on attitudes and perceptions.	*Behavioral.* Emphasis is on building specific skills and creating policies that get the best from every employee. Efforts are monitored by progress toward achieving goals and objectives.
Legally driven. Written plans and statistical goals for specific groups are utilized. Reports are mandated by EEO laws and consent decrees.	*Ethically driven.* Moral and ethical imperatives drive this culture change.	*Strategically driven.* Behaviors and policies are seen as contributing to the organizational goals and objectives, such as profit and productivity, and are tied to rewards and results.
Remedial. Specific target groups benefit as past wrongs are remedied. Previously excluded groups have an advantage.	*Idealistic.* Everyone benefits. Everyone feels valued and accepted in an inclusive environment.	*Pragmatic.* The organization benefits: morale, profits, and productivity increase.
Assimilation model. Model assumes that groups brought into system will adapt to existing organizational norms.	*Diversity model.* Model assumes that groups will retain their own characteristics and shape the organization as well as be shaped by it, creating a common set of values.	*Synergy model.* Model assumes that diverse groups will create new ways to work together effectively in a pluralistic environment.
Opens doors. Efforts affect hiring and promotion decisions in the organization.	*Opens attitudes, minds, and the culture.* Efforts affect attitudes of employees.	*Opens the system.* Efforts affect managerial practices and policies.
Resistance. Resistance is due to perceived limits to autonomy in decision making and perceived fears of reverse discrimination.	*Resistance.* Resistance is due to a fear of change, discomfort with differences, and a desire to return to the "good old days."	*Resistance.* Resistance is due to denial of demographic realities, of the need for alternative approaches, and of the benefits of change. It also arises from the difficulty of learning new skills, altering existing systems, and finding the time to work toward synergistic solutions.

Adapted from Gardenswartz and Rowe, 1993, in Galagan, 1993, p. 32.

FIGURE 7-1: Evolution of Diversity

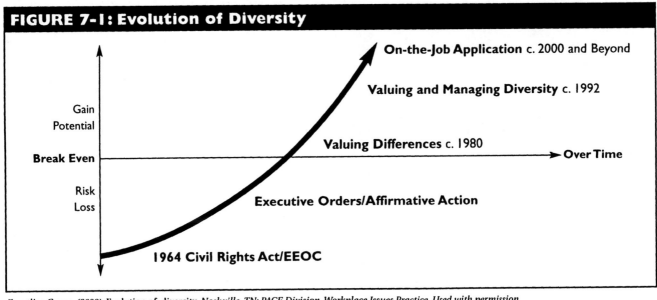

Frontline Group. (2000). Evolution of diversity. Nashville, TN: PACE Division, Workplace Issues Practice. Used with permission.

JOB AID 7-12: Diversity Organizational Assessment

Directions: Use the questions to determine your organization's "diversity quotient."

1. Are the *leaders of the organization* informed and supportive of cultural and diversity issues?	☐ **Always** ☐ **Sometimes** ☐ **Never** ☐ **Not sure**	
2. Has *input from all employees* been integrated into diversity planning?	☐ **Always** ☐ **Sometimes** ☐ **Never** ☐ **Not sure**	
3. Does the diversity planning integrate the *core strategic objectives* of the overall organization?	☐ **Always** ☐ **Sometimes** ☐ **Never** ☐ **Not sure**	
4. Is diversity viewed as an *advantage* and *essential* to good organizational operations?	☐ **Always** ☐ **Sometimes** ☐ **Never** ☐ **Not sure**	
5. Is a *self-assessment* used to help employees identify stereotypes and possible areas of personal challenge?	☐ **Always** ☐ **Sometimes** ☐ **Never** ☐ **Not sure**	
6. Does the diversity *training* build on the success of current diversity situations and cover major issues of all "protected" categories?	☐ **Always** ☐ **Sometimes** ☐ **Never** ☐ **Not sure**	
7. Is there a *steering committee* set up to facilitate open dialogues and discussion groups within the departments?	☐ **Always** ☐ **Sometimes** ☐ **Never** ☐ **Not sure**	
8. Are members of *management role models* for diversity and culturally sensitive issues?	☐ **Always** ☐ **Sometimes** ☐ **Never** ☐ **Not sure**	
9. Are employees given scenarios or examples of *sensitive situations* to discuss and resolve so that they recognize diversity issues?	☐ **Always** ☐ **Sometimes** ☐ **Never** ☐ **Not sure**	

List the names of people who will serve as diversity resources, such as coaches or mentors for problem situations:

- Expand personal appreciation of differences
- Identify potential areas of conflict, and gain insights to achieve positive resolution

Discovering Diversity Profile is an assessment tool that is simple to administer and use.

Carlson Learning Company, Performax Systems International,® *Discovering Diversity Profile*™
Mendez-Russell, A., Wilderson, F., and Tolbert, A.S., 1994.

In addition, many companies sponsor training for minorities and women on business savvy and job effectiveness. These courses discuss topics that mentors and coaches often cover. In the actual workplace, it is not unusual for white males to receive advice that is not shared with women and minorities. The training attempts to overcome that lack of informal advice.

Few PT practitioners realize that the EEOC, in *Facts about Religious Discrimination* (January, 1994 EEOC-FS/E-3),[25] has guidelines about "new age" training programs. It is wise to be cautious and flexible regarding requests for accommodation because the standard for determining religious beliefs is influenced by the employee's own value system. If there is a question regarding the need for accommodation, it is best to phone the nearest EEOC office for clarification.

Mandatory "new age" training programs designed to improve employee motivation, cooperation or produtivity through meditation, yoga, biofeedback or other practices, may conflict with the non-discriminatory provisions of Title VII [of the Civil Rights Act of 1964]. Employers must accommodate any employee who gives notice that these programs are inconsistent with the employee's religious beliefs, whether or not the employer believes there is a religious basis for the employee's objection.[26]

Consider these factors (see Table 7-18) when creating, designing and defining a diversity intervention.

PT practitioners can lead diversity initiatives, often based on AAPs. They can create teams and determine interventions. They can track accomplishments against goals and expected outcomes. Diversity requires sensitivity to people issues and the capacity to understand data and the impact of information on planning and reporting (see Job Aid 7-12).

Globalization

Definition and Scope

Today, organizations are faced with the reality that success in the home market does not necessarily equate to success in the global marketplace. "Globalization constitutes a fundamentally new state of affairs."[1] In other words, what works in one environment does not necessarily work in another. Successful international organizations need to understand and anticipate global issues.

Globalization means respecting others and linking aspects of culture, language, customs, and traditions between home-based and international units. This approach impacts the organization's activities, such as the negotiation process and contract agreements, and levels of individual interaction and performance.

As a performance improvement intervention, globalization requires learning about and respecting customs, etiquette, workplace expectations, and the heritage of people with whom an employee directly or indirectly interacts. Anticipating and understanding the reasoning behind cultural differences helps employees view the diversity in a positive light.[2]

TABLE 7-18: Issues Related to Diversity Interventions or Programs

☐ Are self-assessments used to help employees identify stereotypes and potential areas of conflict that may hamper productivity and positive work relationships?

☐ Is respect for others addressed?

☐ Are effective listening techniques addressed?

☐ Are participants given the opportunity to suspend judgment and eliminate bias?

☐ Are participants given the chance to interact in a role-play environment?

☐ Are differences rewarded or acknowledged?

☐ Are cultural events planned throughout the year to give various opportunities to experience cultural differences?

Based on Mendez-Russell, Wilderson, and Tolbert, 1994.

Rosenzweig states the following:

As a result of rapid foreign investment, many multi national firms now have work forces that are spread across continents and countries, and that include an increasingly complex blend of cultures and nationalities. Their challenge is to capture the benefits of a diverse work force while also forging necessary consistency around the world.

In order to make diversity the strength of a global organization, all employees must be aware of and "buy-into" the globalization goals and objectives of the organization.[3]

Cultural Awareness

There is much more to global cultural awareness than learning etiquette and workplace "do's and don'ts." Phillip Hoffman, director of training and staff development for General Motors China, in Shanghai, believes the process begins by a person understanding his or her own culture thoroughly.[4] Learning about the differences in cultural heritage helps people understand the reason behind a certain behavior, expectation, or belief. It is particularly helpful in developing non-verbal sensitivities.

Global Adjustment

Global adjustment considerations are complex because they revolve around content and context. For example, expatriates face personal issues regarding selecting dentists and doctors and also business issues related to hiring, training, and coaching local employees. *Content* applies to the actual qualifications of the medical professional or governmental control and interference in company matters. *Context* refers to the subtle factors such as the doctor's sensitivity toward childhood fears or government officials expecting "special appreciation and gratuities" in order to process an application promptly.[5]

Implementing Global Interventions in the Workplace

Consistent Global Culture

Employees of multinational companies need to believe they are part of a unified organization. Cultural, economic, and political differences make that a challenge requiring

creativity and the willingness to try "unexpected solutions." To add to the challenge, frequently organizations purchase existing companies, through mergers or acquisitions, in order to gain presence in a particular location. This cross-organization, cross-cultural situation calls for merging various cultures with various processes and procedures into one functioning organization. Chapter 8 contains more information on mergers, acquisitions, and joint ventures.

"Globalization of HR Practices Benchmarking Study" found that companies commonly take certain actions to develop a consistent culture (see Table 7-19).

Global Leadership Requirements

In order to achieve global business success, the leadership must be viewed as a critical resource. The following global leadership characteristics are important.

- A set of context-specific abilities and core competencies
- General leadership characteristics
- Physical stamina to handle the constant travel, jet lag, and stress of working in different languages and across different cultures
- A sense of adventure and desire to see and experience new things
- Ability to understand people
- Integrity
- Capacity to deal with uncertainty and manage tensions
- Organizational savvy
- Intimate knowledge of the firm's capabilities and their own ability to mobilize resources to capture market opportunities[6]

Essential Competencies for Successful International HRD Assignments

Many different capabilities are necessary for people assigned to cross-cultural, global jobs, including the following:

- Knowledge of one's own culture (cultural awareness)
- Knowledge and appreciation of other cultures
- Global perspective and mindset
- Respect for the values and practices of other cultures
- Cultural flexibility, adjustment, and resiliency
- Ability to acculturate learning programs and events

TABLE 7-19: Creating a Consistent Global Culture

Organizational Mission	Create an organizational mission based on input from individuals or teams from all offices and locations
Management Education	Provide management education in all locations and offices about how the company wants to conduct business
Common Systems	Establish common systems (accounting, distribution, marketing, IS, and so forth) used in all locations and offices

Based on Globalization of HR Practices Benchmarking Study, *Development Dimensions International, 2000; Wellins and Rioux, 2000, p. 85.*

- Communication skills
- Cultural empathy
- Patience and a sense of humor
- Commitment to continuous learning[7]

Planning and Preparation

The following factors should be considered when developing interventions to help people succeed in a global environment. Organizations need to expect detailed planning and extensive preparation for multi-national interactions.

Foreign Assignments

Effective employee preparation on how to succeed in foreign environments includes, but is not limited to:

- Daily life—gather information from overseas partner, compile list of banks, markets, stores and shops, provide how-to for opening bank account, etc.
- Expectations—without being stereotypical, what can be expected from the foreign community? What is fair to assume one will be confronted with?
- Basic if not intensive language preparation—at minimum, an expatriate should be armed with basic phrases of daily interaction. An easy reference manual geared toward the area would be most helpful.

Headquarters-based Environments

Effective preparation to help home-based employees succeed when doing business with different cultures, includes the following:

- Culturally dependent negotiation factors
  - Create resource for culturally dependent factors in the negotiating process.
  - Provide list of common approaches to bargaining, bartering, reaching agreement, etc.
- Customs and mores
  - How should someone approach business negotiations? What are the unspoken rules of doing business in the subject country?
- Performance expectations of home office and foreign partner, subsidiary, or client
  - What are the specific expectations of the expatriate or employee dealing with foreign clients? What is the timeframe for such expectations?
    - > What resources are available to assist individuals in their process?
    - > What ramifications are expected if performance expectations are not met?
- Understanding and respect for foreign counterpart
  - Culture training and appreciation will assist the employee.
  - Interface with partners or clients in the US will help ease the transition and improve performance once in the foreign country.

An organization my face organizational challenges in the following areas:

Policy and procedures
- Document differences, if available.
- Specify which policies are applicable to the employee, often regardless of location.
- Note resources available for employee.

Organizational goals
- Document organizational goals of home office versus the foreign office. What are the differences, and how do those differences influence the performance requirements of the organization? Which system will be applicable to individual reviews?

Legal processes
- What legal entities are available for reference and what factors may need to be addressed in a foreign country?
- Clarify areas in which Human Resources will be of assistance and areas in which the employees must fend for themselves.
- Gather required information for registering in the foreign country, work permits from the embassy, and foreign company internal documentation.
- Maintain close contact with the foreign entity for updates and changes.

Products or services offered
- Where will differences in the market influence the products or services offered?
- How can the differences be compensated? What areas of the business have flexibility to be different and which must remain constant across borders?
- Identify where this information is collected and maintained—perhaps within the marketing division or other departments.

Market conditions and economic environment
- What influences must be considered when evaluating differences? Which factors are risks and which are assets that can be utilized?
- Document information and chart conditions and environment for valuable historical perspective.

Re-entry

It is important to prepare an expatriate for re-entry.[8] If an employee has been an expatriate for an extended period of time, effective re-entry upon return to the original country occurs in stages.[9]

- *Orientation*—"Going home" can be viewed with excitement and high expectations. However, a careful assessment of professional gain leveraging the global experience will maximize re-entry job assignment. Regret and readiness lead to mixed emotions.
- *Trepidation*—Eagerness wanes due to challenges in saying "good-bye" to friends and customs. Home country may seem unfamiliar as new skills and routines need to be established to re-enter successfully.

- *Frustration*—Irritation and resentment may result from "disillusionment" regarding readjustment. There is career anxiety during reconnection with home culture.
- *Acclimation and re-assimilation*—New appreciation of cultural differences and sense of normalcy follows transition.

PT practitioners can participate in the globalization efforts of their organization by using the HPT Model to help analyze issues or activities in various locations, determine internal best practices, and help document common practices. They can also help with the implementation by using their skills in change management and process consulting (see Job Aid 7-13).

Ethics

Definition and Scope

The concept of ethics has many sources, such as religion, philosophy, societal demands, or moral principle. In general, ethics means realizing what is right and wrong and then doing what is right. Each person's values are unique, based on individual background and experience; thus, when discussing the ethics of an organization, it is important to establish guidelines for the organization that everyone is aware of, willing to follow, and committed to enforcing. Although ethics applies to all employees, it is often believed to primarily be associated with executive-level responsibility and "white collar crime."

There is abundant evidence that people and organizations do care. A recent Bentley College survey of the Fortune 500 industrial and service companies found that almost 75 percent had codes of ethics. In addition, 35 percent were providing employee training on ethics, 14 percent had ethics committees and 6 percent had ethics omsbudsmen. Public opinion polls, however, reflect real concerns about the integrity of those in business. A Gallup poll taken the same time as the Bentley survey mentioned above found that half of those interviewed believed business values were

JOB AID 7-13: Globalization Readiness

Use these questions to determine your organization's global readiness.
Directions: Select "yes" or "no" based on whether the organization is "mostly yes" or "primarily no."

1. Do organizational leaders realize that respecting diversity requires multiple perspectives within global organizations? ☐ Yes ☐ No

2. Are the *strategic goals* of the organization in line with succeeding globally? ☐ Yes ☐ No

3. Do specific *policies or procedures* support globalization? ☐ Yes ☐ No

4. Do *individual departments* have the freedom to state their own terms for succeeding in a global organization? ☐ Yes ☐ No

5. Is globalized *joint problem solving and collaboration* encouraged? ☐ Yes ☐ No

6. Is *constructive dialogue* encouraged on a frequent basis to keep informed as well as to resolve issues? ☐ Yes ☐ No

7. Are the leaders of the organization role models for successful interaction while conducting business in a *global organization?* ☐ Yes ☐ No

8. Do the employees have the *tools* they need to succeed in a global organization? ☐ Yes ☐ No

9. Does the organization have *champions* of globalization throughout the various divisions and units? ☐ Yes ☐ No
   Names, Unit, Contact Phone:

declining. In a Harris survey conducted that same year, only 18 percent expressed "great confidence" in the leaders of major companies. This was down from 27 percent in the early 1970s and 55 percent in 1966.[1]

Ethical Dilemmas

Ethics is an issue that applies to each employee, while ethically oriented policies, procedures, and customs are usually established or encouraged by management. Although ethical dilemmas can occur in any department, the following ethical scenarios serve as illustrations from purchasing, human resources/labor laws, finance, and copyrights/legal.

The scenarios in Job Aid 7-14 are only examples of issues that any employee can face. Are employees encouraged to speak up if they believe they have been asked to do something that may be wrong? What would be the consequences of their initiative to speak up? There is a tremendous need to rethink ethics issues because individuals' perspectives change over time due to maturity and experiences.[2]

Stages of Ethical Thinking

There are four stages of ethical thinking, adapted by Shea, based on Kohlberg and Dewey.[3]

1. Obey orders to avoid punishment
2. Conform to group norms, a "law and order" mentality
3. Principled responsibility, a universal morality approach
4. Personal integrity, based on integration of thought and feeling (creative, caring, and sensitive)

Six Perspectives

As everyone knows there are vast differences in people. In fact, there are extraordinary differences in perspectives about any ethical issue. In order to understand other people's perspectives on a given situation, it is good to think through the six perspectives listed in Table 7-20. After describing a problem in terms of each perspective, it is possible to begin trying to define possible common ground among the perspectives. This kind of intense thinking is necessary because what is right or correct to one person may not seem right or correct to someone else.

TABLE 7-20: Six Ethical Perspectives

Categorical Imperative	Emphasizes the importance of rules and equal respect for individuals. "Rules should be enforceable and universalized. Judges implement laws, rather than derive them from absolutes. Fairness and treating others as free people are key to this philosophical position."
Utilitarian	"Emphasizes doing what works for and/or benefits the greatest number of people. This perspective may go so far as to risk harm to an individual or individuals for the sake of saving or maximizing benefits to a greater number...Little time should be spent on ways that particular decisions have been reached. Rather, the emphasis is on identifying an uncomplicated way to manage day-to-day living."
Divine Imperative	"Based on assumption that there is an absolute set of right behaviors. Knowing these right behaviors leads to good decisions. These may be learned from religious texts, meditation, or conscience. Desirable behaviors can be experienced or described, and should be emulated. A Divine Being clarifies right behavior. When one is attentive, he or she will do what is right, ethical, and good."
Golden Mean	"Midpoint between extremes. An individual...finds the middle ground, serves a peacemaker role, and emphasizes fairness and respect for others. This position is not hard-edged; rather, it is tolerant of many perspectives and seeks to identify the greatest balance among positions."
Hedonism	"Emphasizes the value of self, with self-reliance, self-preservation, and self-determination as key...does not look to forces, laws, or structures outside of the self. Rather, independence, decisiveness, [pleasure], and absence of pain are primary."
Veil of Ignorance	"People should make decisions about roles, obligations, and rights [based on self-interest] without any knowledge of what role they, themselves, would play. This 'veil of ignorance' ensures that the structure created will serve everyone fairly."

Based on Roehl, Murphy, and Burns, 2000, p. 10.

JOB AID 7-14: Ethical Dilemmas in the Workplace

Directions: Read each scenario and decide what is the correct approach for your organization or for an appropriate organization with which you are familiar. Share and discuss the results with your work group.

Department	Scenario	What would you do?	Whom would you contact?
Purchasing	Purchasing decides not to conduct a fair bidding process but rather to predetermine awards and use the actual bidding as a "showcase" (a sham) to justify a decision.		
Purchasing	Buyers accept substantial gifts of money, dinners, entertainment, or vacations to overlook errors or quality flaws.		
Staffing—HR	Recruiters ask inappropriate questions during pre-employment interviews about family status or family planning intentions, forcing interviewees to believe that if they resist answering the question they will not be seriously considered for the position.		
Restructuring—HR	Downsizing plans favor certain age groups and discriminate against protected employees.		
Compensation	Hourly workers falsified timesheets, often to cover "legitimate" needs, such as dentist appointments		
Finance	Finance department keeps two sets of books to disguise certain practices.		
Finance	Accounts receivable insists on payment terms from customers that the organization would not be willing to pay out to its own suppliers.		
Legal	Employees are encouraged to photocopy materials that are protected by copyright because the organization believes it lacks sufficient funds to pay the copyright holder for use of the materials.		
Any department	People watch and do nothing while one employee is singled out and treated unfairly or subjected to a form of harassment.		

Implementing Ethics Interventions in the Workplace

Ethics is difficult to deal with because employees are at different stages in their personal thinking and because solving ethical problems usually involves admitting that current practices and customs may not be desirable or correct. Ethics also may place employees in situations in which they must confront people and relationships that they depend on for essential needs, such as paychecks.

Pre-thinking helps people act quickly when the actual situation arises. In order to be prepared to do the right thing, employees should think through the questions in Table 7-21. The questions should guide employees' thinking when decisions are needed.

Ethical Parameters and Policies

In order to cope with the complexity and subtlety of ethics issues, it is necessary to first establish and document the parameters in which an organization will work. Additionally, depending on the size of the organization, it may be necessary to develop an overall ethics policy for the organization and then separate policies for individual departments. It is important to ensure that the organizational message is consistent. For example, Lockheed-Martin has ethics training integrated into a board game, which may send a confusing message that ethics is not taken seriously. Andrew McIlvaine states, "Clearly, ethics are desperately needed. But to be effective, an ethics program must become an ingrained part of the company culture rather than an event destined to be forgotten, or worse yet, laughed at."[4]

Ethics and Organizational Culture

Integrating ethics into the organizational culture is essential to confronting ethical dilemmas confidently. "Managing ethics in the workplace holds tremendous benefit for leaders and managers, benefits both moral and practical. This is particularly true today when it is critical to understand and manage highly diverse values in the workplace."[5]

The following potential steps are listed below:
1. Integrate ethical questions into change process activities. Provide "what if" scenarios to help employees better understand the impact of their actions.
2. Discuss ethical dilemmas at team or communication meetings.
3. Scan newspapers and applicable journals for issues pertaining to ethics in other organizations. Use their situations as lessons learned.
4. Provide questionnaires periodically to keep employees aware of the impact their decisions may have.

Benefits of Ethics Management

In his *Complete Guide to Ethics Management: An Ethics Toolkit for Managers*, Carter McNamara lists many benefits of managing ethics in the workplace that go beyond the moral benefits to the organization. Among the benefits are the following:
- Attention to business ethics has substantially improved society.
- Ethics programs help maintain a moral course in turbulent times.
- Ethics programs cultivate strong teamwork and productivity.
- Ethics programs support employee growth and meaning.
- Ethics programs are an insurance policy—they help ensure that policies are legal.
- Ethics programs help avoid criminal acts "of omission" and can lower fines.
- Ethics programs help manage values associated with quality management, strategic planning, and diversity management.
- Ethics programs promote a strong public image.[6]

TABLE 7-21: Thinking Through Ethical Issues

1. Is the ethically oriented problem defined accurately?

2. How would someone on "the other side of the fence" define the problem?

3. How did the problem occur in the first place (its history)?

4. What was the original intention of the ethically questionable procedure or practice?

5. How does the original intention compare with the current probable results?

6. Whom could the questionable practice, procedure, or decision injure?

7. What would be the consequences of discussing the practice, procedure, or decision with management, senior executives, society, or the press?

8. What is the potential for misunderstanding?

9. What is the symbolic potential?

Based on Nash, cited in Nierenberg, 1987, pp. 33–34.

JOB AID 7-15: Ethics Assessment

Directions: Select "yes" or "no" based on whether the organization is "mostly yes" or "primarily no." Use this job aid for discussion with your work group.

1. Does the organization recognize that ethics should be viewed as a learning process? ....☐ Yes ☐ No

2. Is it clear that the goal in establishing an ethics program is to support preferred behaviors in the workplace? ....☐ Yes ☐ No

3. Does the organization believe that eliminating ethical dilemmas by means of an ethics program is the best way of avoiding ethical issues?..☐ Yes ☐ No

4. Does the organization have ethics policies? Are the ethics policies known throughout the organization? ....☐ Yes ☐ No

5. Is ethics management integrated into other management practices? ....☐ Yes ☐ No

6. Have cross-functional teams been involved when developing and implementing the ethics management program? ....☐ Yes ☐ No

7. Does the organization operate under a policy of forgiveness or is there retribution if something goes wrong? ....☐ Yes ☐ No

8. Does upper management support the ethics policy? ....☐ Yes ☐ No

9. Is there an ethics management committee? ....☐ Yes ☐ No

   Names, departments, contact phones:

10. Is there a specific individual that employees can go to in the event there is an ethical issue to discuss?...☐ Yes ☐ No

   Name, department, contact phone:

10a. If yes, are you certain every employee knows to whom to go? ....☐ Yes ☐ No

11. Does the ethics policy incorporate all aspects of your organization, i.e., international subsidiaries, examples of real situations, current joint ventures or business arrangements?............☐ Yes ☐ No

Information summarized from McNamara, C. (1998). Complete guide to ethics management: An ethics toolkit for managers. Located at http://www.mapnp.org/library/ethics/ethxgde.htm. *ISPI ©2001. Permission granted for unlimited duplication for noncommercial use.*

Attention to ethics in the workplace is the right thing to do. Performance technology as a profession has defined ethics in relation to PT practice (see Chapter 9 on Skills and Knowledge Needed). These documents and articles can be helpful when working on other organizational initiatives. PT practitioners can benchmark policies or write scenarios that help define policies. PT practitioners can be integral to ethics policy development and management (see Job Aid 7-15).

Spirituality in the Workplace

Definition and Scope

Spirituality in the workplace has become an increasingly important issue as individuals search for deeper meaning in their lives and fulfillment in their jobs.[1] Spirituality means "the basic feeling of being connected with one's complete self, others, and the entire universe."[2] "Interconnectedness" is important. Employees desire jobs that enable them to "deploy more of their full creativity, emotions, and intelligence. They want organizations to harness their full potential. Spirituality often leads to a deeper sense of life's meaning."[3]

Success, in terms of spirituality, is more than material abundance. It "also includes good health, energy and enthusiasm for life, fulfilling relationships, creative freedom, emotional and psychological stability, a sense of well-being, and peace of mind."[4]

People often look beyond their job description for inspiration. "People reach into their hearts and their life aspirations to find the energy they need. That is where renewal energies brew; that is how organizations are enlivened over and over again into future generations."[5]

Common Good

Spirituality means striving for the common good of individual employees and for the common good of the organization. Whirlpool Corporation defines "common good" in its shared values statement as:

We will serve responsibly as members of the communities in which we live and work, respecting cultural distinctions throughout the world. We will preserve the environment, prudently utilize natural resources and maintain all property we are privileged to use.[6]

According to Richard Barrett, individuals care about:
- Finding meaning in the workplace
- Making a difference while accomplishing their job responsibilities and tasks
- Providing service through work[7]

Barrett states that, "organizations are living entities that share motivations similar to those of individuals. Every organization has a distinct personality, which is called corporate culture." Organizations, like individuals, go through stages of meeting human needs (see Figure 7-2). Some stages focus on self-interests, such as physical survival or emotional self-esteem. As organizations mature, they can go through a transformation, resulting in a commitment to the common good of the organization, the community, and society as a whole.[8]

In fulfilling the human needs of spirituality, organizations promote the common good by:

- Improving the organization as a workplace
- Improving the community by employing citizens and providing wages, benefits; purchasing supplies and services; and creating a learning environment for employees to acquire new skills and knowledge
- Improving society through use of the products and services of the organization; through donations, grants, and foundation awards; by encouraging and allowing employees to volunteer during work time; and generally by being a good corporate citizen.

Trends Leading to Spirituality

Several workplace trends (see Table 7-22) move toward people seeking meaning, purpose, and a sense of community in the workplace.

Workplace Examples

Spiritual aspects of the workplace are increasing. For example, enrollments in motivational training programs have escalated as employees try to find the balance between themselves and their contribution at work. Companies are encouraging employees to tutor during company time. Organizations are sending employees to clean up rivers, paint houses for welfare moms, and rake leaves for senior citizens. One of the biggest challenges is creating meaningful work for each worker, while another is establishing community action worker programs.

FIGURE 7-2: Organizational Personality Development

Self-Interest	Transformation	Common Good
Physical Survival Emotional Self-Esteem		Organization Community Society as a whole

Based on Barrett, 1998, p. 66

TABLE 7-22: Societal Trends Leading to Workplace Spirituality

- Down sizing, reengineering, and layoffs have demoralized the work force.
- Decline in neighborhoods, churches, civic groups, and extended families as principal places of getting connected.
- Eastern (Asian) philosophies stress meditation and values such as loyalty, finding spiritual center, and finding acceptance.
- As baby boomers move closer to "life's greatest uncertainty—death" there is growing interest in contemplating life's meaning.
- Pressures of global competition encourage organizations to foster creativity and innovation, which are difficult in a stressful organization.

Based on Ashnos and Duchon, 2000, pp. 134–135.

Total Quality Management (TQM) and People Orientation

It is widely recognized that Japan has considerable experience and success with TQM, which has a strong people orientation. In fact, to a large extent TQM's people orientation has been influenced by the Asian culture, such as Confucianism.[9] For example, one of W. Edwards Deming's principles for transformation is "Drive out fear."[10] Deming, a world famous quality consultant to Japan, believed it is important to put people at ease and value their contribution.

The Confucian approach means to design the workplace to bring out the best in people.[11] Thurley summarizes seven crucial ideas in Japanese management for managing people in Table 7-23.

Implementing Spirituality Interventions in the Workplace

Encouraging Employees

Management can be vigilant in encouraging the common good for all employees. If an employee is not performing up to the standard of what is required or expected, the manager should keep in mind the following factors:

- Is the employee challenged in his or her work?
- Can a point in time be determined when motivation and productivity improved or fell? What factors affected this change?
- Are incentives and recognition designed to increase motivation and satisfaction on the job?
- Is the employee given an opportunity to contribute to the larger scope of organizational objectives or changes?
- Does the employee have leadership qualities that can be brought forth through coaching and training? Is this what the employee desires?
- Is strength of character encouraged? Are employees recognized for their judgment? Responsibility? Compassion? Mental toughness? Cooperation? Flexibility? Self-confidence?[12]

By knowing that their work is important, employees can feel increased responsibility for their role in contributing to the organization. It is the organization's responsibility to share information regarding its current status and future plans so that everyone has the opportunity to contribute or give input.[13]

Meaningful Work

Some employees have special requests relative to providing a meaningful and fulfilling workplace. Managers should consider these factors:

- Does the employee need time during to day to meditate or pray? What are the pros and cons of meeting their needs? Can a mutually beneficial compromise be reached?
- Does an employee require a flexible schedule to meet family obligations?
- What are the ramifications of implementing a company-wide flextime schedule—what type of impact would that have?
- Have the benefits to the organization and the employees by having on-site day care or other assistance to working parents been evaluated?

Based on Barrett, organizational spirituality begins by focusing on internal connectedness. It begins with a positive culture that supports employee fulfillment. Employees are encouraged to be productive through creativity, innovation, and positive problem solving. There is an internal cohesion, trust, and encouragement of risk taking. Work should be viewed as fun.

- Does alignment exist between employee's personal motivation and the organization's vision and mission? Are cross-functional teams for problem solving encouraged?
- Do employees feel connected with each other and the organization? Are exit interviews and culture surveys taken seriously? Are the results acted upon?
- Is failure viewed as lessons learned? Are people encouraged to continue to innovate?
- Is workplace safety a primary issue? Is worker well-being viewed as important?
- Is creating meaning an important aspect of the learning community?[14]

TABLE 7-23: Japanese Philosophy for Managing People

All employees should have a sense of belonging to the company and feel collective responsibility for its success.

All employees should be educated to perform multiple skills in a wide variety of roles and functions.

All employees should have potential for development and they should be given autonomy to do their work.

All employees should have a sense of job security so that they can give their maximum effort to solve working problems.

All employees should be motivated to stimulate their loyalty and develop their skills through a life career.

Management should be governed by a corporate philosophy with sufficient flexibility to fit the changing environment.

Management should pursue the Tao of people-based management that recognizes the importance of daily interaction with all employees and a shared identity with them in solving work problems.

Thurley, 1990, as cited in Mak, 2000, p. 538.

Community Consciousness

Organizations can next move to community consciousness, a level of external connectedness. For example, organizations encourage employees to be concerned about nature. PG&E Corporation, a public utility, found that ospreys, nesting on the top of their utility distribution poles, were at risk from electrical currents. Employees built safer platforms for the birds in many locations. The birds felt comfortable enough with PG&E platforms to return the next year for nesting.[15]

Organizations often begin by creating partnerships between suppliers, themselves, and customers. They create strategic alliances that embrace communities and become aware of their role as good global citizens.

- Does the organization support the local economy by collaborating with local businesses and voluntarily improving the environment and the local community?
- Does the organization go beyond the letter of the law in being a good citizen?
- Does the organization conduct external social and environmental audits?

Humanity and the Planet

Eventually, organizations may commit to service to humanity and the planet. This stage recognizes "the interconnectedness of all life and the need for both individuals and institutions to take responsibility for the welfare of the whole."[16]

- Does the organization promote social activism and human rights?
- Is philanthropy an integral part of the corporate strategy?
- Does the organization enjoy respect and goodwill from the society at large? Is it socially responsible?[17]

For example, Ford Motor Company has become a society-sensitive company, taking an interest in social responsibility and environmental issues. In its *2000 Annual Report to Stockholders,* Ford admitted that the Explorer sports utility vehicle (SUV) "fouls the air more than cars," thus contributing to global warming. SUVs also can be a menace to smaller vehicles on the road. Ford pledged to engineer breakthroughs to make SUVs clean and safe.[18] A *Fortune* magazine advertisement explained that Ford Motor Company partnered with Conservation International to create a walkway that helps preserve part of the Brazilian Atlantic rain forest and lets visitors experience this rich ecosystem.[19] Another *Fortune* advertisement stated "When fires in Mexico destroyed 490,000 acres of forest and 870,000 acres of grassland, Ford Motor Company, our dealers, and the government of Mexico joined together to plant more than 3 million trees in an effort to bring the ecosystem back into balance."[20] Bill Ford, Chair of Ford Motor Company, believes, "A good company delivers excellent products and services, a great one delivers excellent products and services and strives to make the world a better place."[21] Obviously, Ford Motor Company is creating an image of a company concerned for the common good and for society.

Policies and Programs

Supporting spirituality in the workplace means giving responsibility, gaining trust, and working collaboratively. It is not necessarily any particular intervention, but rather the atmosphere of respect and a commitment to worker and societal well-being.[22] Because each situation and combination of circumstances is unique, an organization must weigh the advantages and disadvantages before proceeding with any new spirituality-oriented program or policy. Audits, such as exit interviews and culture surveys, can indicate progress or success in spirituality. It is essential to solicit input from employees as to how they feel about workplace, community, and societal spirituality —whatever that specifically means to them. Nurturing spirituality requires ongoing attention and frequent feedback. It is a gradual organizational maturation. Once trust is established and respect is present, special teams can be established to collaborate with management and the rewards of emphasizing spirituality will be apparent.

Performance technology is a people-oriented profession.[23] As a result, PT practitioners are inclined to support spirituality by helping management and employees implement their people- and community-oriented ideas. PT practitioners usually have substantial skills in project management that can be used for the common good. In addition, PT practitioners can play a key leadership role in defining outcomes for socially responsible projects and identifying behaviors and tasks to accomplish the outcomes.[24] PT is in a unique position to help organizations make a significant impact on society (see Job Aid 7-16).

The Organizational Values section of this chapter was written in collaboration with Margaret Korosec, MA.

Case Study 7-3: Culture—Interior Systems Contract Group

Situation

Billie Jo Wanink is president and co-owner of a $17 million contract furniture business in Royal Oak, Michigan. Although small, Interior Systems Contract Group (ISCG) has "a big commitment" to people and their work environment. ISCG's core purpose is "to create desirable environments for living and working." Desirability is integrated into the work environment because Wanink believes that employees should want to come to work, not feel obliged to work.

JOB AID 7-16: Spirituality Assessment

Spirituality means healthy work environments, fulfilling relationships, creative freedom, emotional and psychological stability, a sense of well being, and peace of mind.

Directions: Complete the questionnaire with input from several levels of the organization. Use the results to discuss how your organization meets the human need for spirituality in the workplace.

1. How does the organization express spirituality in the workplace? Individually? Organizationally?
2. Do you think that current employees would like a recognized policy regarding spirituality? Explain.
3. What systems are in place to recognize employees with improved performance?
4. Does the organization support families with children or dependent elders by having appropriate policies?...☐ Yes ☐ No If yes, how?
5. Has the organization performed a cost/benefit analysis on a spirituality program?.........................☐ Yes ☐ No If yes, what was the outcome?
6. Are there opportunities available for meaningful work within your organization?.........................☐ Yes ☐ No Why or why not?
7. Do you feel employees have the freedom to say whether they would like to investigate having a community action program? ....☐ Yes ☐ No
8. Are internal job postings and other employee well-being programs accessible to all employees?.............☐ Yes ☐ No Why or why not?
9. Is this organization respected by the news media and the public for social responsibility and community involvement?...☐ Yes ☐ No

Spirituality definition based on Chopra, D. (1994). The seven spiritual laws of success: A practical guide to the fulfillment of your dreams. *San Rafael, CA: Amber-Allen Publishing and New World Library, p. 2. ISPI © 2001. Permission granted for unlimited duplication for noncommercial use.*

ISCG's desirable environment has been recognized widely. For example, the company was selected as one of the "Top Ten Best Places to Work in Southeast Michigan–1999." In 1993, Wanink was selected "Woman Business Owner of the Year" by the National Association of Women Business Owners. Since 1993, ISCG has been included in *Crain's Detroit Business* newspaper as one of the "Top 25 Woman-Owned Businesses" in Michigan.

Intervention

Wanink and ISCG believe that culture provides a competitive advantage. ISCG is a great place to work because of its growth, its mission and values, and its commitment to customers and employees. The business has a clear balance between business success and people success. Business growth provides opportunities to make substantial commissions and to advance within the organization.

Culture begins with the physical workplace. ISCG uses optimum interior systems in their own workplace so that designers, sales staff, and project leaders can work to their optimum capacity. The attractive surroundings also serve as office space models, sparking ideas for customers when they attend meetings at ISCG.

Wanink encourages openness, feedback, and self-improvement. Employees are included in decision making; their ideas are valued. The doors between management and employees are open. She also opens her books to employees and encourages feedback and suggestions. Informal feedback is welcome at any time and semi-annual performance appraisals include extensive feedback from clients, peers, and management. In addition, employees are appreciated through their substantial benefits, including a flexible "cafeteria-style" benefits plan and a 401(k) pension plan with matching funds tied to the profit-sharing program.

Training and orientation are vital so that people have fresh ideas. ISCG sponsors between 25 and 40 hours of training per year. All employees attend internal and external workshops annually to ensure personal growth opportunities for all employees. Between 25 and 40 hours are spent orienting new employees. In addition, newly promoted employees are provided 8 to 24 hours of coaching, mentoring, and training for their new positions.

Finally, ISCG has been honored for promoting a balance of work and family life.[25] Gregory Jones, a first-grade volunteer "room parent" stated, "Here, it's take care of the family first. Work will come second. That's very impressive."

Results

ISCG has grown substantially since its inception in 1976. In 1998, revenue was $17 million with an annual growth rate of approximately 19%. Revenues were projected to be $20 million in 2000. This growth provides opportunities for sizable sales commissions, substantial profit sharing, and opportunities for advancement within the organization.

ISCG benefits from a stable workforce. Due to employee satisfaction, turnover rates are low, with hourly and salaried supervisory/management less than 5% and salaried non-supervisory turnover less than 10%.

ISCG and Billie Jo Wanink have been recognized with many awards. Since 1998, *Crain's Detroit Business* has recognized ISGC as one of the Top 25 Woman-owned Businesses. In addition, the company has won the following awards:

- 1994 *Woman Business Owner of the Year* by National Association of Women Business Owners
- 1998, 68th among the Michigan Private 100
- 1998 *Today's Workplace of Tomorrow* by Women's Economic Club
- 1998 *Working Woman's Top 500 Women-Owned Companies in America*
- 1999 *Top 10 Best Places to Work* in Southeast Michigan
- 1999 *Michigan's Private 100 Fastest Growing Companies*

Lessons Learned

- Attractive surroundings are important. Good lighting allows people to communicate effectively and an open workstation environment promotes teamwork. It is also important to have places for people to come together as groups.
- Openness and feedback are critical to a dynamic organization. Management should encourage suggestions and reward good ideas. Employees should be consulted frequently through formal 360° feedback and informal discussions. Financial information should be available to employees.
- People appreciate a balance of work and family life. They also like benefits such as flexible "cafeteria-style" benefits, pension programs linked to profit sharing, training, and mentoring.

Case study was written by Darlene Van Tiem, PhD, based on an interview with Billie Jo Wanink on November 23, 1999, various newspaper articles about the company and their awards, and Crain's Detroit Business—The Best Places to Work.

CHAPTER

8

FINANCIAL SYSTEMS

"A REMOTE CONTROL WOULD HAVE BEEN CHEAPER."

FINANCIAL SYSTEMS

Organizations face business challenges daily. One major challenge is an efficient and effective financial system that affects the organization's purchasing power, shareholder value, and opportunities for future growth. To be a key decision maker, the PT practitioner must assume a proactive role in the organization's financial planning. While it is true that the PT practitioner may not be directly responsible for orchestrating the organization's financial systems, he or she must be ready to use wise financial judgment when implementing interventions and be involved in communicating the organization's financial picture to employees, clients, stakeholders, and other audiences. The financial picture is key in determining business needs, performance needs, learning needs and work environment needs. There are many ways to acquire the knowledge, skills, attitudes, and ways of thinking associated with financial decisions and to communicate them in useful, practical, and non-technical ways. This chapter looks at typical financial systems interventions that determine bottom-line results (see Table 8-1).

Open Book Management

The top-down style of management, with its chain-of-command principles popularized by Frederick Taylor and Henri Fayol, is no longer in vogue. The new buzz-words in corporate boardrooms and learning/teaching organizations are total quality management, continuous quality improvement, outsourcing, self-directed teams, empowerment, "walking the talk," and "raising the bar."

TABLE 8-1: Financial Systems Interventions From Enhanced HPT Model

- Open Book Management
- Profit Versus Cost Centers
- Financial Forecasting
- Capital Investment and Spending
- Cash Flow Analysis and Cash Flow Forecast
- Mergers, Acquisitions, and Joint Ventures

Employees are no longer cogs in machines. They are now viewed as responsible and accountable employees—people who can think and understand why they are solving problems, cutting costs, and reducing defects. In some organizations, even the nomenclature changes from employees to associates, from managers to coaches, from trainers to analysts and intervention specialists, and from organization development consultants to change managers and evaluators.[1,2] There is a comprehensive rethinking of management with a business logic perspective. Called open book management, it "may well become the business paradigm that finally helps fulfill the promise of the total quality and process reengineering movements."[3]

Definition and Scope

Open book management is "a way of running a company that gets everyone to focus on helping the business make money."[4] It is both a process and a system "in which a company fully shares its financial status with its employees, who then become active participants in a coordinated effort to optimize future financial performance."[5] Organizations that adopt open book policies present key financial documents, income and cash flow statements, balance sheets, inventory flow methods, ratio analysis, and so forth to their employees for thoughtful review, discussion, advice, and corrective action.[6] Employees are motivated "to reach the financial targets that trigger their profit-based bonuses."[7] As an intervention, open book management improves team functioning and provides information to help employees understand issues and make better decisions.

A high-performance workplace is linked to increased productivity and long-term financial performance.[8] For open book management to be successful, the organization must be open and aligned. Table 8-2 captures characteristics of both open organizations and fundamental alignments.

Successful open book management enjoys these characteristics:
- Sharing financial information with employees, thus helping them track the financial pulse and business acumen of the organization.

TABLE 8-2: Characteristics of Open Organizations and Fundamental Alignment

Open Organization Characteristics	Fundamental Alignment Characteristics
• Employees understand organization success factors. • Employees understand roles and responsibilities in achieving financial and operational goals and objectives. • Employees are involved in goal setting. • Employees are active learners in problem solving, decision making, and delegating. • Employees share rewards and successes.	• Strategic element (process path) • Marketing element (forecasting path) • Business process element (customer, product, and quality paths) • Human resource (people element and culture paths) • Leadership/governance element (organization path)

Based on McCoy, 1996, pp. 17–47.

- Educating employees in the art and science of financial information by helping them use financial data and showing them how they can make a difference.
- Changing the fundamental relationships in the organization by creating a climate where people act as owners.
- Having fun in practicing open book management as a prime indicator of the organization's success.[9]

Although open book management takes many forms and is often practiced differently, elements common to most forms are open books, empowerment, profit sharing, highly participative management, planning and decision making, and weekly alignment meetings.[10]

Implementing Open Book Management Interventions in the Workplace

Full-scale open book management includes three phases. Each phase, if done thoughtfully, usually takes a full year to implement. Table 8-3 highlights the approaches.

The PT practitioner plays a crucial role in orchestrating open book management by:
- Reinforcing the purpose of open book management with employees
- Suggesting reading materials on various aspects of business in general and of accounting and finance in particular
- Leading discussions on appropriate business topics, e.g., team development, empowerment issues, problem solving, decision making, delegating, and so on
- Developing business literacy training with lots of interactive exercises and providing constructive feedback for coaching and mentoring
- Monitoring the process to encourage employees to use the information and data gathered in their daily work

- Helping employees design, develop, and implement motivating games
- Evaluating the entire process to see that employees remain focused and have fun (see Job Aid 8-1).

Profit Versus Cost Centers

Introduction

Organizations are structured according to lines of responsibility for achieving their goals, monitoring their performance, and increasing their productivity. These lines of responsibility are grouped in hierarchal order. Some organizations, such as hospitals, group their centers by function, for example, pediatrics, family practice, internal medicine, emergency room, pathology labs, and so forth. Other organizations, such as retail chains, group their centers by geography, for example, east, west, north, south regions of the state. Still others organize by product. For example, a manufacturing firm may sell televisions, exercise equipment, furnaces, and precision tools, and may have an established unit for each product.[1] Locations where costs occur and where costs are assigned are called responsibility centers. They are sub-units of the larger organization that have budgetary responsibility. Two of the various kinds of responsibility centers are profit (revenue) centers and cost centers.[2]

Definition and Scope

A profit (revenue) center is charged with controlling costs and generating revenue. It enjoys both an expense budget and a revenue budget. It is successful when it meets the goals embedded in its revenue budget.[3]

Examples of profit (revenue) centers are in-hospital laboratories, in-hospital pharmacies, luggage and fine china retail store outlets (part of a chain), hospital cafeteria, and cafeterias on military bases that service enlisted men, officers, and civilians. Some training departments are obliged to generate revenue by selling some form of product or services to external or internal customers. "Training organizations usually have three products they can sell externally: training programs, training facilities, and training expertise."[4] An organization's revenue centers, through its revenue production, must cover costs of all cost centers and of all profit (revenue) centers.[5]

A cost center is charged with managing costs. It has neither revenue budget nor obligation to earn revenues for the organization. It is a center that has "overhead." In other words, it is an organizational unit that contributes costs without offsetting the costs with revenue.[6] Typical cost centers in organizations are administrative units, human resource departments, housekeeping services, maintenance and repair, and clerical and office pools. "Being a cost center does not make a unit any less important than any other unit in the organization."[7] Cost centers need to be lean, efficient, effective, and flexible. To remain successful

TABLE 8-3: Phases and Methodologies to Full-Scale Open Book Management

Phases	Time Frame	Contribution
Introducing the Concept	Year 1	• Scoreboards — Used to post and keep track of key business needs numbers, e.g., profitability, revenue growth, clients serviced, etc. — Used to get employees thinking about numbers without overwhelming them. • Reading and Discussion Groups — Read primers of useful information on managerial accounting, financial management, and business savvy. — Discuss practical financial applications for non-financial managers. • Business Literacy Training — Show how wealth is created through an organization's products and services. — Use interactive exercises showing how organization events affect the balance sheet and income statement. • Business Games — Used as educational experiences to motivate and encourage buy-in. — Used to attack a visible organization weakness, usually a critical number. — Used to quantify a goal or department or unit objective. — Indicates a time frame to achieve goal. — Defines payoffs in achieving the goal. — Goals are specified in percentage improvement. — Payoffs are gift certificates, cash bonuses, etc.
Company-Wide Bonus Plan	Year 2	• Four-fold purpose: — Educate employees in organization's critical numbers. — Fix weaknesses. — Increase stock value. — Provide short-term motivational rewards. • Characteristics: — Include all employees. — Have goals based on critical numbers. — Have quarterly payouts. — Have a rising bonus pool. — Have a duration of one fiscal year.
The Great Game of Business— Full-Blown Open Book Management	Year 3	• Components — Involve employees in full financials. — Have weekly meetings to discuss scoreboards to keep numbers visible. — Keep employee bonus plan tied to scoreboards. — Develop annual plan and 3- to 5-year strategic plan. — Develop a vision and mission—provide a single beat.

Based on Burlingham, 1999, pp. 2–4.

JOB AID 8-1: Financial Education for All Employees

Directions: There are many elements involved in creating an open-management organization. Think about your organization and then respond to the following questions. You may also choose to discuss this information with a colleague.

Question	Responses
How does your organization make a profit?	
How does your organization generate cash?	
What is the source of your organization's revenue?	
What costs and expenses are associated with your organization's business?	
How does your organization use the following financial ratios as indicators of performance (profitability, efficiency, solvency, liquidity)? • Liquidity ratios (measure the organization's ability to meet maturing short-term obligations)	
• Leverage ratios (measure extent to which the organization has been financed by debt)	
• Activity ratios (measure how effectively the organization is using its resources)	
• Profitability ratios (measure management's overall effectiveness as shown by returns generated on sales and investment)	
• Growth ratios (measure organization's ability to maintain its economic position in the growth of the economy and industry)	

Based on Cox, R.A.K., Stout, R.G., and Vetter, D.E. (1995). Financial administration and control. *Cambridge, MA: Blackwell Publishers, Inc.; McCoy, T.J. (1996).* Creating an open book organization...where employees think and act like business partners. *New York: AMACOM.*

JOB AID 8-2: An Organization's Responsibility Centers

Directions: Conduct an in-depth study of your organization to find its responsibility centers. Identify those organizational units that fit within each. Then answer the question.

Responsibility Centers	
Cost Centers	**Organizational Units**
	• _____
	• _____
	• _____
	• _____
	• _____
	• _____
Profit (Revenue) Centers	**Organizational Units**
	• _____
	• _____
	• _____
	• _____
	• _____
	• _____

How would a training or performance department repurpose itself from a cost center to a profit (revenue) center? Consider:

What: _____

_____

Who: _____

_____

When: _____

_____

Where: _____

_____

Why: _____

_____

How: _____

_____

and maintain market share, organizations need to reduce costs and increase their revenue holdings. Profit versus cost centers as an intervention determines the best mode of service delivery relative to financial factors.

Implementing Profit (Revenue) Versus Cost Center Interventions in the Workplace

Is a training or performance department a cost or a profit (revenue) center? Most organizations see training as "overhead" expense; therefore, it is a cost center. However, a training or performance department can position itself to generate revenue by selling the products or services developed for internal use to external clients. A department can "sell or license programs, …sublease training classroom space, …contract out experienced training staff to external clients."[8] The PT practitioner should conduct a SWOT analysis prior to offsetting training costs with revenue (see Table 8-4).

A training or performance department "that is managed as a profitable revenue center commands greater credibility in any organization as a productive business partner rather than as simple overhead."[9] Ford Motor Company runs its Ford Training and Development Center as a profit center. Units are "charged back" course fees through the internal accounting system. Ford also actively trains suppliers on a course fee basis. This tends to make training departments more accountable because units have to pay for their training. Great emphasis is placed on value for the training dollar. General Motors and General Physics share similar practices.

It takes persistence, the wisdom of Solomon, the patience of Job, and honed business acumen to generate revenue from a training or performance department. PT practi-tioners who venture into this financial arena may find these suggestions helpful:

- Determine whether the training or performance department is positioned as a cost center or a profit (revenue) center.
- Discuss the advantages and disadvantages of both as financial responsibility centers.
- Take a position. If the organization has overhead and it is not contributing revenue, it is a cost center. Be prepared for the negative enthusiasm associated with simple overhead concerns. If, on the other hand, the department wishes to convert to a revenue center, it must have product or service to sell internally and/or externally (such as to suppliers).
- Develop a business plan that includes answers to these questions:
  — What products or services are involved?
  — Where is the business and why?
  — Who is the competition?
  — How will the products and services be marketed and advertised?
- Work with finance personnel to pinpoint these activities:
  — Budgeting matters
  — Establishing accounts
  — Handling support resources such as information systems, marketing, etc.
  — Processing invoices
  — Collecting delinquent accounts[10]
- Keep an open mind. It takes times to establish a business mindset and build a business enterprise (see Job Aid 8-2).

Financial Forecasting

From one day to another, people holding leadership positions (executives, managers, supervisors) make countless decisions without knowing their ramifications.

TABLE 8-4: Training or Performance Department's SWOT Analysis for Increasing Revenues From Training			
Strengths	**Weaknesses**	**Opportunities**	**Threats**
• Pro-active • Selling training programs • Selling training facilities • Selling training expertise • Business mindset • Making training or per-formance department more accountable	• Diminished profit level with expenses in: — production — sales — services — marketing — advertising • Business expertise may be unavailable	• Find value in external market • Convert a support function to a business enterprise • Increase revenues	• Increase in revenue may decrease product quality • Contracting experienced training personnel strains loyalty • Time factor

Based on Waagen, 2000, p. 9.

Nordstrom orders shoes without knowing what sales will be. Sears Auto orders new equipment without knowing the demand for transmissions, spark plugs, tires, and so forth, and in capital investments, interest rates and profits are unknown. Leadership personnel are charged with reducing this uncertainty and making more solid estimates of future business happenings. This is the essence of forecasting.[1]

Definition and Scope

Forecasts attempt to predict future trends, events, and outcomes. They are educated assumptions and visions of how variables will change the future. Financial forecasting deals with the business side of the organization—profit, interest, supply, demand, "technological innovation, cultural changes, new products, improved services, stronger competitors, shifts in government priorities, changing social values, unstable economic conditions, and unforeseen events."[2]

Types of Forecasts

Although any component within an organization can be forecasted, most organizations forecast future revenues and new technological advances. Simply stated, *revenue forecasting* is predicting revenues. Data for revenue forecasts come from historical revenue figures with adjustments made on changes in demography, economics, marketing and social patterns. For example, a university's income from tuition and state funding will influence the entire fabric of the institution from curricular offerings, staffing needs and salary increases, to planned giving, new construction, renovation and repair, and so forth.[3]

Another forecasting type is *technological forecasting,* which predicts technological changes and their economic feasibility. Organizations that can forecast new technologies and convert their production areas to accommodate them are leaders in business enterprise.[4]

Forecasting techniques can be classified into two categories—qualitative and quantitative. *Qualitative forecasting* uses expert judgment and opinions to predict the future. When the need for precise data is limited, difficult to obtain, or when resources are non-existent, qualitative methods are used.[5,6] Table 8-5 explains the qualitative techniques.

By contrast, *quantitative forecasting* techniques use mathematical and statistical rules and analyses of data banks to predict the future. These techniques are often prepared and interpreted by specially trained staff or by external consultants.[7] Table 8-6 highlights quantitative forecasting techniques.

Implementing Financial Forecasting Interventions in the Workplace

Financial forecasting as an intervention means that organizations improve decision making based upon solid prediction data. Financial forecasting is essential to every component of the business enterprise. Consider supply and demand and how they affect human resource planning. If the planning process is miscalculated, organizations may not have the necessary employees to keep up with demand, resulting in lost revenue and client dissatisfaction. On the other hand, if too many employees are hired and trained, the organization may need to lay off personnel.[8]

TABLE 8-5: Qualitative Forecasting Techniques

Techniques	Description	Practical Application
Jury of Executive Opinion	Combines opinions with statistical models and results in a group estimate	Polling the organization's marketing division to predict next year's competitive environment
Salesforce Composite	Combines and analyzes salesforce estimates at regional level with district and national levels to research an overall forecast	Predicting next year's sales and marketing of a popular cosmetic
Customer Market Survey	Combines input from customers about future purchases	Surveying major drug companies to determine types and quantities of products
Delphi	Combines data from selected experts in different places; precisely structured questions and repeated cycles of the process coverage to consensus	Predicting roles and responsibilities of PT practitioners by surveying in cyclic fashion 8–10 experts until general consensus is reached

Based on Robbins and Coulter, 1999, p. 272; Render and Stair, Jr., 1997, pp. 175–176.

TABLE 8-6: Quantitative Forecasting Techniques

Techniques	Description	Practical Application
Time Series Analysis	Uses evenly spaced data points (weekly, monthly, quarterly, etc.) to predict with historical data; considers trends, seasonality, cycles, and random variations	Predicting next month's sales of farm equipment based on two years of previous sales records
Regression Models	Predicts on the basis of dependent and independent variables	Predicting product sales based on advertising budget, price charged, competitor prices, etc.
Economic Indicators	Uses economic indicators, e.g., supply, demand, etc., to predict the future economy	Using surplus financing to stop inflation
Econometric Models	Uses regression equations to simulate the economy	Predicting change in personal computer sales as a result of tax law requirements
Substitution Effect	Uses a mathematical formula to predict how a new product replaces an old one	Predicting the effect of sub-zero refrigerators on the sale of conventional refrigerators

Based on Robbins and Coulter, 1999, p. 272; Render and Stair, Jr., 1997, pp. 176–196.

Consider the demand for products influenced by trends, seasonality, cycles, and random variations.[9] Consider customer market surveys and how they influence future purchasing plans.

Forecasting is one of the most important and complex tools a PT practitioner can master because every organization needs to conduct financial forecasts. Eight steps to forecasting are reported in the literature. They "present a systematic way of initiating, designing, and implementing a forecasting system."[10] The authors have added a ninth step.

In conjunction with other organization personnel from all cost and revenue centers, the PT practitioner, should:
1. Determine the use of the forecast—what objective is the organization trying to obtain?
2. Select the item or quantities that are to be forecasted.
3. Determine the time horizon of the forecast—is it 1–30 days (short term), one month to one year (medium term), or more than one year (long term)?
4. Select the forecasting model or techniques.
5. Gather the data needed to make the forecast.
6. Validate the forecasting model or technique.
7. Make the forecast.
8. Implement the results.[11]
9. Evaluate the results based on a clearly defined set of criteria established and agreed upon beforehand.

Bateman and Snell, in citing research of Peterson and Makridakis, give practical advice for using forecasts of all kinds:

- Use multiple forecasts and perhaps average their predictions.
- Remember that accuracy decreases the farther into the future you are trying to predict.
- Forecasts are no better than the data used to construct them.
- Use simple forecasts when possible.
- Important events often are surprises and represent a departure from predictions.[12,13,14]

There are many ways to predict the future. Large organizations use varieties of the qualitative and quantitative techniques discussed in Tables 8-5 and 8-6. Smaller organizations use more subjective methods like intuition and experience. No one particular strategy or technique is perfect under all the circumstances and demands imposed upon the organization by its internal and external clientele. Approaches must be monitored and controlled so that forecasting does not get out of hand.[15] The PT practitioner plays a crucial role in the planning, gathering data, and monitoring processes of financial forecasting (see Job Aid 8-3).

Capital Investment and Spending

Countries, organizations, businesses, and individuals become wealthy if they possess more of the following factors of production than their competitors:
- Natural resources (land, water, minerals, etc.)
- Human resources (people with desired knowledge and/or skills who produce goods and services)
- Entrepreneurs (people who take risks in creating and operating businesses)

JOB AID 8-3: Financial Forecasting: Significance and Rationale

Directions: Financial forecasting predicts future trends, events, and outcomes by dealing with the business side of the organization. Review the following list of items related to the business enterprise. Then with a colleague or peer from your organization:

        1. Discuss the item's significance in financial forecasting.
        2. State your rationale for using the item in financial forecasting.

Trends, Events, Outcome	Significance	Rationale
• Profit		
• Interest		
• Supply		
• Demand		
• Technological Innovations		
• Cultural Changes		
• New Products		
• Improved Services		
• Stronger Competitors		
• Shifts in Government Priorities		
• Changing Social Values		
• Unstable Economic Conditions		
• Unforeseen Events		
• Other _____ _____ _____		

Based on David, F.R. (1999). Strategic management: Concepts and cases, (7th ed.). Upper Saddle River, NJ: Prentice Hall.
ISPI © 2001. Permission granted for unlimited duplication for noncommercial use.

- Capital (resources like facilities, equipment, money, hardware, software, etc. to produce goods and services).[1]

This section highlights the capital investment and spending factor of production.

Definition and Scope

"Capital investment and spending refers to commitment or use of money and other assets made in anticipation of greater financial returns in the future and usually involves large sums of money."[2] It is "money paid to acquire something of permanent value in a business."[3,4] It is also a process that helps management identify opportunities and analyze alternatives before an action plan is realized. An effective capital management system may take different forms and vary by size of the organization, proportion of opportunity, kind and amount of structure, procedures, practices, and terminology. However, any sound capital investment and spending process that seeks to maximize value and minimize risk includes the steps noted in Table 8-7. Improved understanding and involvement in capital investment and spending can enhance the PT practitioner's respect within the organization.

The financial analyst, in deciding whether to pursue an investment, has to decide on the value potential for the stakeholders. The investment returns must exceed the costs. Determining which costs and benefits are relevant to the investment must be noted. Invested capital has a cost and the company has to pay for its use.[5] The PT practitioner plays an important role in capital spending

that relates to designing, building, and equipping training centers and in purchasing technology-based training systems. Like other things in the world of finance, advantages and disadvantages are associated with capital investment and spending. Table 8-8 captures them.

Implementing Capital Investment and Spending Interventions in the Workplace

Overseeing the entire capital investment and spending practices of an organization resides with the accountants and the financial team. The PT practitioner can assist in the focusing phases of capital investment and spending and in monitoring, implementing, and evaluating the procedures (see Table 8-7). Beyond this, the following guidance is helpful:

- Know how the organization internally defines capital, and how this definition or categorization is reflected on balance sheets and profit and loss sheets.
- Understand and be able to articulate the larger concepts under which capital investment and spending decisions are made.
- Interview individuals who serve as investment advisors for corporations and organizations to learn more about industry-specific criteria, parameters, and challenges.
- Read *The Wall Street Journal, Baron's,* and other financial dailies and/or quarterlies to increase business acumen and innovative capital investment and spending practices and solutions.
- Volunteer your services with an organization that is having problems with a capital investment and spending issue.[6]

TABLE 8-7: Solid Capital Investment and Spending Phases and Procedures	
Phases	**Methods/Procedures**
Phase One: Plan • Comparison of investment and spending practices to the organization's strategic goals and objectives	• Identify strategic goal and objectives • Establish performance measurements • Align goal and objectives to practices
Phase Two: Assess • Assessment of risk in decision making regarding alternatives	• Seek input from management • Use financial tools and models
Phase Three: Decide • Determination of cost, return on investment, and/or performance data to decide outcome of capital investment and spending decisions	• Provide progress reports • Conduct performance audits • Chart activity analysis
Phase Four: Evaluate • Evaluation and comparison of capital investment and spending to alternatives	• Use a multiple decision making process that includes financial and non-financial attributes and full disclosure of validated assumptions • Use management information and tracking system

Based on Grossman, 1977; Trigergis, 1995; Anderson-Claiborne, 2000, p. 5.

TABLE 8-8: Capital Investment and Spending Advantages and Disadvantages

Advantages	Disadvantages
• Highly influenced by positive tax policies	• Highly influenced by negative tax policies, tight credit markets, and inflation
• Challenges the organization to operate, increase productivity, grow, and prosper	• Requires careful analysis of future business trends and potential profit margins
• Opportunities to hasten adoption of new technologies	• Expensive and requires high initial debt funding
• Used as a benchmark to examine current state of an organization's investment and spending	• Excludes discussion on capital budgeting, cost management, accounting, and operational procedures—all extensions of capital investment and spending

Based on Anderson-Claiborne, 2000, pp. 2–3; Deku, 1999, p. 2.

JOB AID 8-4: The Disciplines of Fiscal Management

Directions: The PT practitioner is often challenged in the world of fiscal management. Review the two disciplines of fiscal management below. Then:

1. Determine your awareness level of each area on a scale from 5 to 1 (5 = Excellent Awareness and 1 = Little or No Awareness).
2. Generate a personal action plan to become more sophisticated in the discipline.

Disciplines	Awareness Level (Check a response)				
Accounting:					
Financial Accounting	☐ 5	☐ 4	☐ 3	☐ 2	☐ 1
Tax Accounting	☐ 5	☐ 4	☐ 3	☐ 2	☐ 1
Managerial Accounting	☐ 5	☐ 4	☐ 3	☐ 2	☐ 1
Auditing	☐ 5	☐ 4	☐ 3	☐ 2	☐ 1
Financial Management:					
Capital Budgeting	☐ 5	☐ 4	☐ 3	☐ 2	☐ 1
Financing	☐ 5	☐ 4	☐ 3	☐ 2	☐ 1
Working Capital Management	☐ 5	☐ 4	☐ 3	☐ 2	☐ 1
Financial Planning	☐ 5	☐ 4	☐ 3	☐ 2	☐ 1

Personal Action Plan:

_____

_____

_____

- Increase personal awareness levels of managerial accounting, financial management, and economics.
- Discuss with colleagues the capital investment and spending prospectus uses of recognized investment banking firms (see Job Aid 8-4).[7]

Contributions to this section were made by Susan Anderson-Claiborne, MBA, ABD, First Vice President, Manager, Credit Training & Administration Group, Comerica Bank, Detroit, MI, and Becky Deku, MEd, Instructional Systems Designer, Raytheon Systems Company, Troy, MI. Used with permission.

Cash Flow Analysis and Cash Flow Forecast

The PT practitioner should have a basic understanding of four major financial statements: balance sheet, income statement, statement of stockholders' equity, statement of cash flows (see description in Table 8-9). Each is useful in specific ways and important in understanding the organization's short- and long-term financial picture. Table 8-9 describes them. This section looks at the statement of cash flows, which provides information about an organization's cash receipts, cash payments, operating, investing, and financing activities during a point in time. It zeros in on cash flow analysis and cash flow forecast.

Definition and Scope

Cash flow analysis is a financial tool or process used by businesses and banks to determine the various sources and uses of an organization's cash, and to make accurate projections of cash inflows and outflows for forecasting purposes. It allows the organization to analyze the effectiveness of its financial controls, and makes corrections in marketing, production, purchasing, financing, and other areas to improve stability and long-term profitability.

Cash flow analysis takes several forms. The accounting statement of cash flows is one of four general purpose financial statements required by Generally Accepted Accounting Principles (GAAP). This statement is prepared along with the balance sheet, income statement, and stockholders' equity statement when the organization closes its books, and services to reconcile the beginning-of-period cash balance with the end-of-period cash balance (see Table 8-9). It is historical in nature, and shows the sources and uses of the organization's cash. It can be used to evaluate the financing, cash generating, and spending activities of an organization, and is used as a measure of management's ability and expertise.

Preparation of a formal Accounting Statement of Cash Flows can be done in one of two ways: the direct method or the indirect method. The Financial Accounting Standards Board (FASB) prefers the direct method because it is easier to understand.[1] However, most organizations prefer to use the indirect method because it is easier to prepare. The Statement of Cash Flows includes three sections: Operating Activities, Investing Activities, and Financing Activities. Each of these sections involves sources and uses of cash. The statement also:

- Identifies the organization's ability to generate cash flows from operations
- Highlights the organization's need for external financing
- Illustrates the reasons for the differences between net income and net cash flow from operations
- Shows the effects of cash and non-cash investing and financing transactions
- Explains changes in cash and cash equivalents by listing those activities that increase and decrease cash. Each activity is segregated by the three sections noted above.[2]

The difference between the direct and indirect methods of statement preparation is in the Operating Activities Section. In the direct method, actual cash receipts and payments from customers and to suppliers are combined

TABLE 8-9: Major Financial Statements

Name of Statement	Usefulness
Balance Sheet	Shows how management invests resources in assets and how assets are financed by liabilities and owners' equity
Income Statement	Shows all the revenues and costs with net income resulting as revenues minus costs
Statement of Stockholders' Equity	Shows changes in the status of the ownership of an organization
Statement of Cash Flow	Shows sources of all funds the organization acquired and how the funds were used.

Based on Needles, Jr., Anderson, and Caldwell, 1990, pp. 732–733; Cox, Stout, and Vetter, 1995, pp. 12–32.

with taxes and interest paid to arrive at net cash used or provided by operating activities. This must be reconciled to net income from the income statement using a separate schedule. The indirect method is a one-step process that begins with net income and works back to net cash flows. It does not require the reconciling schedule.[3]

Increased competence in cash flow analysis and forecasting can be a powerful companion intervention to support open book management. It improves the ability of employees to understand the significance of data. It also improves the ability to participate in forecasting.

A cash flow forecast is a forecasting tool used by organizations and banks considering loan applications to analyze cash inflow and outflow cycles. It is an essential tool because an organization must identify its financial cycles and ensure that adequate cash is available at all times to support its activities. During periods when cash outflows exceed cash inflows, short-term financing must be available to the organization. When the production-to-receivables-to-cash cycle is completed, short-term financing can be paid down.[4]

The cash flow forecast uses basic economic assumptions and forecasts of sales and production (in a manufacturing environment) to arrive at a schedule of the organization's cash cycle. Cash outflows often exceed cash inflows, especially early in the business cycle, and it is at these times that organizations require short-term external sources of financing. A cash flow forecast provides the firm with a schedule of when the short-term financing is required throughout the year, and in what dollar amounts.[5]

The cash flow forecast generally includes these components:
- Sales and production forecast
- General economic trends
- Forecast of credit sales as a percentage of total sales
- Schedule of average days to payment on credit sales
- Schedule of purchases to support sales or production schedules
- Schedule of salaries, benefits, and tax payments
- Schedule of interest and dividend payments
- Schedule of other general and administrative expense payments.[6,7]

There are strengths and limitations of the Accounting Statement of Cash Flows and the Cash Flow Forecast. These are summarized in Table 8-10.

Implementing Cash Flow Analysis in the Workplace

Because this is the realm of managerial accounting and financial management, the PT practitioner may not be directly involved in preparation of cash flow analysis. However, the PT practitioner must become more proficient in understanding business needs. The business needs of an organization drive the performance needs, which drive the learning needs. PT practitioners analyze and use accounting reports provided by the finance department, monitor spending, and plan budgets based on data. They then can use their understanding of cash flow to help set tuitions, determine compensation for vendors and consultants, and make decisions relative to cost versus profit centers. There are many resources available that are primers of useful information for non-financial managers.

Two practical guides, one on accounting basics and another on financial applications, are noted in the references to this section.[8,9] In addition to reading the financial literature, the PT practitioner should:
- Become familiar with accounting and finance basics by enrolling in introductory courses to refresh previous course content in these areas.

TABLE 8-10: Strengths and Limitations of Cash Flow Analysis

Managers	Strengths	Limitations
Accounting Statements of Cash Flows	• Based on Generally Accepted Accounting Principles (GAAP) • Accepted by United States government, banks, investment firms • Based on historical data	• Based on historical data • No allowance for prediction of needs or analysis of future trends • Difficult for non-financial personnel to understand and use
Cash Flow Forecast	• Based on known information • Allows organization to plan for cash needs well into the future • Prevents financial difficulty and even bankruptcy	• Not prepared from audited financial statements • Relies on a large number of independent forecasts • Loses accuracy the more futuristic the projection

Based on Witucki, 2000, p. 4.

- Benchmark successful organizations to observe their cash flow analysis and forecasting activities.
- Prepare a cash flow statement from data in the annual report of a familiar organization and compare it to the PT department's schedule in the annual report.
- Prepare a simple cash flow forecast using the PT department's income and expenditure information.
- Prepare solutions to case studies on cash flow analysis from accounting and finance books.
- Compare cash flow benefits or disadvantages that should be considered in adopting a profit versus cost center approach.
- Seek information on the topic from a local certified public accountant or a certified management accountant or a bank loan officer.
- Ask questions of your organization's accountants and financial managers to gain a better understanding of cash flow analysis (see Job Aid 8-5).[10]

Alan P. Witucki, MM, MBA, EdS, CMA, Training Specialist, DaimlerChrysler Corporation, Auburn Hills, MI, is the chief contributor to the Cash Flow Analysis and Cash Flow Forecast section. Used with permission.

Mergers, Acquisitions, and Joint Ventures

Organizations evolve over time. Today's organizations will be significantly different two years from now. Organizations purchase new businesses with new products and clients; sell off old businesses that no longer address market share; merge with existing businesses to form new organizations with new policies, processes, products, and personnel; implement growth strategies for greater productivity. In the popular movie *Pretty Woman*, Richard Gere earns millions by buying undervalued companies and selling them off in pieces. The world of mergers, acquisitions, and joint ventures is planned with long-range goals, finances, and performance in mind.[1]

Definition and Scope

Mergers occur when two or more separate organizations of equal or similar size combine operations to become one new organization through an exchange of stocks.[2,3] "A classic example is the 1988 merger of Nabisco, Inc., a producer of cookies and other baked goods famous for brands such as Fig Newtons and Oreos, with R.J. Reynolds, Inc., a major producer of tobacco products, to become RJR Nabisco."[4]

Acquisitions occur when large organizations purchase (acquire) smaller ones, usually with more than 50% of the voting stock, and assume control of the organization's property and liabilities.[5,6]

Over the last several years, Johnson & Johnson, a health care products company, has acquired several companies that manufacture and market dental products, oral contraceptives, wound care products, prescription drugs, hospital products, over-the-counter drugs, diapers, feminine hygiene products, and infant products.[7]

A joint venture occurs when two or more organizations join forces for a common purpose, "such as to develop a new technology, enter new markets, generate new products, or meet customer demands quickly."[8] It is a way to generate productivity. The classic joint venture in the auto industry is between Mazda and Ford and their combined efforts in 1991 to produce the first global car, the Ford Escort.[9]

A substantial body of literature describes mergers and acquisitions and, to a lesser degree, joint ventures. Each strategy or alliance involves changes in the organization's assets and activities. For purposes of this discussion, the three terms are treated collectively.

Rationale

Organizations engage in mergers, acquisitions, and joint ventures for these reasons:
- Provide improved capacity utilization
- Make better use of existing sales force
- Reduce managerial staff
- Gain economies of scale
- Smooth out seasonal trends in sales
- Gain access to new suppliers, distributors, customers, products, and creditors
- Gain new technology
- Reduce tax obligations
- Experience synergism in being privately and publicly held[10]
- Commit to long-term success[11]

The productivity of these strategies is "fueled by organizations' drive for market share, efficiency, and pricing power as well as by globalization, the need for greater economies of scale, reduced regulation and antitrust concerns, and the stock market rewarding...activity with higher stock prices."[12]

Most attempts at mergers, acquisitions, and joint ventures are amicable. However, there are hostile takeovers in which an outside organization buys enough stock in another organization to take control of it against the wishes of the board or the corporate officers.[13] The trend in alliances today is influenced by long-term productivity and growth. "Instead of using debt to take over and dismantle a company for a quick profit, corporate buyers are using cash and stock to selectively acquire businesses that will enhance their position in the marketplace."[14]

JOB AID 8-5: Cash Flow Analysis and Forecasting Template

Directions: The cash flow analysis and forecasting job aid is similar to an Excel 97 spreadsheet. Follow the instructions on the spreadsheet. Enter basic economic assumptions and forecasts for sales volumes, salaries, cash payments, and other expenses in the appropriate areas. The spreadsheet performs the required calculations for the borrowing portion of the forecast. The case study at the end of this chapter has a completed template.

Schedule of Cash Collections and Accounts Receivable
Enter data in the shaded boxes. Other cells contain formulas for automatic calculations.

	Prior Year 4th Quarter	Current Year 1st Quarter	2nd Quarter	3rd Quarter	4th Quarter
Receivables at start of period..........		$ –	$ –	$ –	$ –
Sales..........	$ –		$	$	$
Collections..........					
Sales in current period (80%)..........	–	–	–	–	–
Sales in prior period (20%)..........	–	–	–	–	–
Total Collections..........	$ –	$ –	$ –	$ –	$ –
Receivables at end of period (1)..........	$ –	$ –	$ –	$ –	$ –

Cash Forecast

	Current Year 1st Quarter	2nd Quarter	3rd Quarter	4th Quarter
Sources of Cash				
Collections on Accounts Receivable..........	$ –	$ –	$ –	$ –
Other..........	$ –	$ –	$ –	$ –
Total Sources..........	$ –	$ –	$ –	$ –
Uses of Cash				
Payments on Accounts Payable..........	$ –	$ –	$ –	$ –
Labor, Administrative, and Other Expenses..........	$	$	$	$ –
Capital Expenditures..........	$ –	$ –	$ –	$ –
Taxes, Interest, and Divdends..........	$	$	$	$ –
Other..........	$	$	$	$ –
Total Uses..........	$ –	$ –	$ –	$ –

Receivables at start of first quarter = ending receivables from fourth quarter of prior year.

Short-Term Financing Requirements

	Prior Year 4th Quarter			
Cash at start of period..........	$ 5.0	$ 5.0	$ 5.0	$ 5.0
Change in cash balance (sources less uses)..........	(41.5)	(15.0)	(26.0)	(35.0)
Cash available for operations (2)..........	(36.5)	(10.0)	(31.0)	(40.0)
Ending cash balance (minimum $5.0) (3)..........	$ 5.0	$ 5.0	$ 5.0	$ 9.5
Cumulative short-term financing required (4)..........	$ 0.0	$ 41.5	$ 56.5	$ 30.5	$ 0.0

(1) Ending Accounts Receivable = beginning accounts receivable + sales – collections
(2) Cash at start of period + change in cash balance
(3) Ending cash balance = Cash available for operations – prior quarter cumulative short-term financing OR the required $5.0 minimum
(4) Cumulative short-term financing required = prior quarter cumulative short-term financing balance—cash available for operations + ending cash balance

This job aid was written by Alan P. Witucki, MM, MBA, EdS, CMA, Training Specialist, DaimlerChrysler Corporation, Auburn Hills, MI. Used with permission. ISPI ©2001. Permission granted for unlimited duplication for noncommercial use.

Implementing Mergers, Acquisitions, and Joint Ventures Interventions in the Workplace

According to a recent survey conducted by Clemente, Greenspan & Company of Glen Rock, New Jersey, and reported in the training literature, HR personnel are asking for greater up-front planning and implementation roles in these alliances, in particular, in mergers and acquisitions. Interesting results from this US survey reveal these findings:

- Lack of sufficient technical knowledge and other corporate growth activities to support strategy development (81%)
- Specific training (83%) and education (80%) needed in these alliance strategies.

- Training related to employee communication regarding alliances (58%)
- Help in understanding basic strategic planning (57%)[15]

Mergers, acquisitions, and joint ventures are all about people and, when they are given the opportunity, HR personnel rise to the challenge of managing human capital. Bramson recounts her experiences in HR when Shaw's Supermarkets were acquired by Star Markets in 1999 for approximately $500 million.[16] HR personnel joined forces and integrated, both operationally and culturally, the following initiatives:

- Identification of organizational structure and managerial levels

JOB AID 8-6: Strategic Alliances

Directions: Indicate the strengths and limitations associated with mergers, acquisitions, and joint ventures. Share your ideas with colleagues to see if your views and theirs are similar. Discuss reasons for the differences. Then, individually or collectively, answer the question that follows.

Alliances	Strengths	Limitations
Mergers		
Acquisitions		
Joint Ventures		

Speculate on how employees feel about being involved in these alliances regarding:

- loss of knowledge of the organization
- loss of control
- loss of friends
- loss of physical location
- loss of organizational synergy
- loss of cultural compatibility
- other concerns

- Analysis of critical players and resources
- Retention of essential personnel and separation of non-essential ones
- Establishment of a rewards strategy for the combined organization
- Development and integration of a synergistic communication system
- Payroll benefits plan integration
- Ability to do the above with speed, accuracy, and efficiency[17]

Only in rare situations is the PT practitioner directly involved in mergers, acquisitions, and joint ventures. The practitioner, however, plays a pivotal role in working with the organization's personnel who are displaced by these alliances, however friendly or hostile. Specifically, the PT practitioner can:

- Anticipate the changing organizational environment by conducting a thorough performance analysis including an organizational and environmental analysis and a culture audit.
- Recognize channels of organizational change efforts by focusing on:
  — organizational mindset about change
  — change process
  — structures for managing change
  — personal response to change
  — communication networks
  — environmental factors and conditions
  — financial boundaries
  — client demands
- Suggest interventions to alleviate concerns.
- Monitor those people who are resistant to change efforts and provide appropriate support for them as they live through the mergers, acquisitions, and joint ventures. Focus on resistance, control, politics.
- Provide occupational and career suggestions and guidance for employees involved in friendly deals, e.g., executives whose careers come to an end, employees who are laid off, spouses and children whose lives are uprooted, etc.
- Provide mental health suggestions and stress management sessions for employees involved in hostile takeovers.
- Identify public relations issues, especially for communities whose factories, small companies, and support businesses become empty.
- Design, integrate, or adapt processes such as an integrated billing system or a parts inventory system.
- Redesign similar jobs if they are going to be combined.
- Support the efforts of leadership, human resources, labor relations, and similar groups as they address the issues before them.
- Serve as the beacon for resolving ethical issues and dilemmas imposed by the alliances.
- Think "outside the box" while being attentive to opportunities and challenges that lie ahead for the new organization, its processes, products, and services (see Job Aid 8-6).

Case Study 8-1: The Stratford Tool and Die Company

The Stratford Tool and Die Company manufactures precision machined fittings for sale to plumbing wholesalers. Products are sold on cash and trade credit terms, with terms of net 45 days. Stratford's controller wants to support the aggressive sales improvement program forecast by the vice president of marketing.

Stratford currently has excess plant capacity, so the controller knows that expenditures for additional plant expansion will not be required. He also knows that the firm's sales are highest in the third and fourth quarters of the year, and lower in the first two quarters. However, to meet demand for Stratford's high-quality products, the wholesalers like to build up inventory early in the year.

The following data are available to the controller:
- Sales Forecast ($ in millions)

Prior Year 4th Qtr	Current Year 1st Qtr	2nd Qtr	3rd Qtr	4th Qtr
$75	$87.5	$78.5	$116	$131

- 80% of all sales are cash. 20% are trade credit.
- Accounts Receivable balance at the beginning of the year was $30 million
- Forecast of future expenditures are as follows ($ in millions):

	1st Qtr	2nd Qtr	3rd Qtr	4th Qtr
Payments on Accounts Payable	$ 60.0	$ 60.0	$ 55.0	$ 50.0
Labor, Administrative	30.0	30.0	30.0	30.0
Capital Expenditures	$ 32.5	$ 1.3	$ 5.5	$ 8.0
Taxes, Interest, and Dividends	4.0	4.0	4.5	5.0
Total Expenditures	$126.5	$ 95.3	$ 95.0	$ 93.0

- Stratford expects to sell a used machine tool for $12.5 million in the third quarter.

Create a cash budget and schedule of short-term financing requirements for Stratford using the above information. A blank template is provided to help you fill in the numbers. It is followed by the case study solution.

Schedule of Cash Collection and Accounts Receivable: Template

Enter data in the shaded boxes. Other cells contain formulas for automatic calculations.

	Prior Year 4th Quarter	Current Year 1st Quarter	2nd Quarter	3rd Quarter	4th Quarter
Receivables at start of period		$ –	$ –	$ –	$ –
Sales	$ –		$	$	$
Collections					
Sales in current period (80%)		–	–	–	–
Sales in prior period (20%)		–	–	–	–
Total Collections	$ –	$ –	$ –	$ –	$ –
Receivables at end of period (1)	$ –	$ –	$ –	$ –	$ –

Cash Forecast

	Current Year 1st Quarter	2nd Quarter	3rd Quarter	4th Quarter
Sources of Cash				
Collections on Accounts Receivable	$ –	$ –	$ –	$ –
Other	$ –	$ –	$ –	$ –
Total Sources	$ –	$ –	$ –	$ –
Uses of Cash				
Payments on Accounts Payable	$ –	$ –	$ –	$ –
Labor, Administrative, and Other Expenses	$ –	$ –	$ –	$ –
Capital Expenditures	$ –	$ –	$ –	$ –
Taxes, Interest, and Divdends	$ –	$ –	$ –	$ –
Other	$ –	$ –	$ –	$ –
Total Uses	$ –	$ –	$ –	$ –

Short-Term Financing Requirements

	1st Quarter	2nd Quarter	3rd Quarter	4th Quarter
Cash at start of period	$ 5.0	–	–	–
Change in cash balance (sources less uses)	–	–	–	–
Cash available for operations (2)	–	–	–	–
Ending cash balance (minimum $5.0) (3)	$ 5.0	$ 5.0	$ 5.0	$ 9.5
Cumulative short-term financing required (4)	$ –	$ –	$ –	$ –

(1) Ending Accounts Receivable = beginning accounts receivable + sales – collections
(2) Cash at start of period + change in cash balance
(3) Ending cash balance = Cash available for operations – prior quarter cumulative short-term financing OR the required $5.0 minimum
(4) Cumulative short-term financing required = prior quarter cumulative short-term financing balance – cash available for operations + ending cash balance

This template was written by Alan P. Witucki, MM, MBA, EdS, CMA, Training Specialist, DaimlerChrysler Corporation, Auburn Hills, MI. Used with permission.

Stratford Tool and Die Company: Case Study Solution

Schedule of Cash Collections and Accounts Receivable

	Prior Year 4th Quarter	Current Year 1st Quarter	2nd Quarter	3rd Quarter	4th Quarter
Receivables at start of period		$ 30.0	$ 32.5	$ 30.7	$ 38.2
Sales	$ 75.0	87.5	78.5	116.0	131.0
Collections					
Sales in current period (80%)		70.0	62.8	92.8	104.8
Sales in prior period (20%)		$ 15.0	$ 17.5	$ 15.7	$ 23.2
Total Collections		$ 85.0	$ 80.3	$ 108.5	$ 128.0
Receivables at end of period (1)		$ 32.0	$ 30.7	$ 38.2	$ 41.2

Cash Forecast

	Current Year 1st Quarter	2nd Quarter	3rd Quarter	4th Quarter
Sources of Cash				
Collections on Accounts Receivable	$ 85.0	$ 80.3	$ 108.5	$ 128.0
Other	$ —	$ —	$ 12.5	$ —
Total Sources	$ 85.0	$ 80.3	$ 121.0	$ 128.0
Uses of Cash				
Payments on Accounts Payable	$ 60.0	$ 60.0	$ 55.0	$ 50.0
Labor, Administrative, and Other Expenses	$ 30.0	$ 30.0	$ 30.0	$ 30.0
Capital Expenditures	$ —	$ —	$ —	$ —
Taxes, Interest, and Divdends	$ 32.5	$ 1.3	$ 5.5	$ 8.0
Other	$ 4.0	$ 4.0	$ 4.5	$ 5.0
Total Uses	$ 126.5	$ 95.3	$ 95.0	$ 93.0

Short-Term Financing Requirements

	Prior Year 4th Quarter			
Cash at start of period	$ 5.0	$ 5.0	$ 5.0	$ 5.0
Change in cash balance (sources less uses)	(41.5)	(15.0)	26.0	35.0
Cash available for operations (2)	(36.5)	(10.0)	31.0	40.0
Ending cash balance (minimum $5.0) (3)	$ 5.0	$ 5.0	$ 5.0	$ 9.5
Cumulative short-term financing required (4)	$ 0.0	$ 41.5	$ 56.5	$ 30.5	$ 0.0

(1) *Ending Accounts Receivable = beginning accounts receivable + sales – collections*
(2) *Cash at start of period + change in cash balance*
(3) *Ending cash balance = Cash available for operations – prior quarter cumulative short-term financing OR the required $5.0 minimum*
(4) *Cumulative short-term financing required = prior quarter cumulative short-term financing balance – cash available for operations + ending cash balance*

This case study was written by Alan P. Witucki, MM, MBA, EdS, CMA, Training Specialist, DaimlerChrysler Corporation, Auburn Hills, MI. Used with permission.

CHAPTER

9

IMPLEMENTING INTERVENTIONS IN THE WORKPLACE

ALTHOUGH HE KEPT WELL FED, MORRIS
DIDN'T HOLD ONTO FRIENDS FOR VERY LONG.

IMPLEMENTING INTERVENTIONS IN THE WORKPLACE

"What is good for General Motors is good for the country, and vice versa."[1]

—Charles Wilson, former Secretary of Defense

Most PT practitioners have heard that quote from Charles Wilson, Secretary of Defense in President Eisenhower's Cabinet. In the 1950s, the idea that General Motors offered great jobs, great cars, and sound investments to shareholders was viewed as positive both to the country and to the company. Although good products, jobs, and investments are worthy criteria for judging the value of an organization, few would support a public statement like that today.

The public now expects organizations to add value to the community, to consider their environmental and societal impact, the labor market potential, and the expectations of many external and internal customers. Organizations have responsibilities to governmental agencies, such as the Occupational Safety and Health Administration and Equal Employment Opportunity Commission. They have expectations from civic groups, such as churches and city councils. In general, they are expected to provide great products, useful jobs, and to be "good citizens."

Peter Drucker, respected management guru, challenges us in the HRD and PT profession to adapt to the changing world. Global demographics have changed, and we need to adjust our profession.[2,3] In order to reach this new reality, Roger Kaufman, noted PT and strategic planning expert, suggests that PT practitioners "Focus first and foremost on Mega-societal value added... Link everything your organization uses, does, produces, and delivers to external client and societal value added."[4]

Kaufman developed the Organizational Elements Model (OEM) (see Table 9-1) to describe the type of planning and results that are expected at each level in an integrated PT approach. In order to be successful PT practitioners, it is necessary to align the external and internal elements.[5]

Arbor Consulting Mega Case Study as Example of Intervention Implementation and Change

Arbor Consulting Group's mega case study (see page 301) is designed to be a comprehensive illustration of the implementation of various interventions. In addition, it is designed to demonstrate the use of selected job aids from the chapters of this book. The case study serves as an example of implementing several interventions simultaneously. Although it is much easier to implement interventions one at a time, it may not always be feasible or wise. By working on one intervention solution at a time, it may take too long for results to be evident. This delay can lead to loss of confidence and commitment to performance improvement.

The HPT Model, as described in Chapter 1 and also in the companion book, *Fundamentals of Performance Technology,*

TABLE 9-1: Organizational Elements Model (OEM)

Organizational Element	Type of Planning to Which Element is Related	Name of Type of Result
Mega	Mega-Societal	Outcome
Macro	Macro-Organizational	Output
Micro	Micro-Individual or Small Group	Product
Process	Efficiency	Process, Means, Activities
Input	Resources	Inputs

Kaufman, 2000, p. 26.

defines four aspects of intervention implementation and change: change management; process consulting; employee development; and communication/networking and alliance building.[6] Arbor Consulting used all four aspects to successfully realign the organization after dissolving the partnership.

Change Management—Strategic Planning

Change management is illustrated by Arbor Consulting Group's strategic planning process. Internal leaders (president, vice president, and senior consultant) spearheaded the effort to create a direction and set of plans for operational and infrastructure upgrades that redefined services and revised the marketing approach and materials.

Process Consulting—Realignment

Arbor Consulting Group realigned its major internal processes. Because the company does process consulting for businesses, this effort was handled internally, which demanded many hours that were not billed to clients. The realignment resulted in improvements in the computer and information infrastructure (i.e., networked computer system and shared directory system) and required new business procedures and practices.

Employee Development—Realignment and Team Evaluation (Learning Organization)

Arbor Consulting Group is an example of an active learning organization. Development of skills and knowledge were part of two interventions. Realignment required learning new computer skills and software. Employees supported each other as they adapted to these new computer systems.

In addition, Arbor Consulting Group's teams use collaboration and team problem solving to help each other acquire new skills and capabilities. Team evaluation provides a helpful description of ways to support team effectiveness and growth.

Communication, Networks, and Alliances—Culture Analysis

Arbor Consulting Group has strong internal communications, including clearly stated values that are widely respected by the employees. Also, unstated values are recognized and accepted. Company rituals provide networking and camaraderie. The close-knit cooperative culture promotes alliances between individuals to support each other's projects.

Arbor Consulting Mega Case Study as Example of Performance Domains and Outcomes

Ed Holton, a noted PT guru, stresses the importance of whole system improvement. In the PT profession, it is critical to avoid "quick fixes" and faddish improvement projects. It is essential to focus on domains of performance and to account for outcomes, such as market share, customers, quality, cost, time, and product features.[7] Mission, process, sub-systems, and individuals are essential domains of performance improvement. Arbor Consulting Group, since realignment, dealt with a full range of domains resulting in impressive outcomes (see Table 9-2).

Arbor Consulting Group's Outcomes

Increased Revenue
Arbor's effort to better define its services and use a more targeted marketing approach was successful and led to

TABLE 9-2: Holton's Domains and Drivers Applied to Arbor Consulting Group

Domain	Intervention	Outcome
Mission	Strategic Planning	• Increased revenue • Established a national practice • Increased percentage of work for Fortune 500 corporations • Developed reputation of excellence • Established major awards program
Process	Realignment	• Increased retention of employees
Sub-systems	Team Evaluation	• Enhanced reputation as employer of choice • Increased involvement in professional organizations
Individual	Culture (Heroes and Rituals)	• Received awards for organization culture • Invited to speaking engagements

Holton, 1999, p. 33.

increased revenues. Particularly noteworthy is a five-fold increase in federal contractor compliance work.

Established a National Practice
Fortune 100 companies with multiple sites across the country outsourced their affirmative action plan preparation processes to Arbor. Arbor currently has clients nationwide from California to Massachusetts and Minnesota to Texas.

Increased Retention of Employees
The employees who were with Arbor during its realignment have remained with the organization, and turnover of staff has been minimal. Arbor participates in cooperative education and internship programs, and turnover of these individuals is not included in Arbor's retention rate. Only two consultants have left over a five-year period, and both chose to leave the work force to stay home with small children, rather than leaving for new employment opportunities.

Increased Percentage of Work for Fortune 500 and Other Prestigious Organizations
More focused services and marketing efforts led to Arbor being contacted by high-quality clients interested in long-term relationships. Arbor completed work for the W.K. Kellogg Foundation, Mayo Clinic, Monsanto, Transamerica, Blue Cross Blue Shield, Masco, and others. Presently, 75% of Arbor's work is for Fortune 500 or other prestigious organizations. The remaining 25% includes work for smaller, high-tech, or entrepreneurial organizations.

Developed a Reputation for Excellence
Satisfied clients recommend Arbor's services to others and speak on behalf of Arbor to potential clients. Using no paid advertisements, Arbor's integrity and quality of services has led to countless referrals and inquiries. In fact, 100% of Arbor's business was built by referrals.

Invited to Speaking Engagements
Since realignment, Arbor has addressed over 50 professional organizations and industry groups seeking information on trends in human resources, retention, hiring, employment law compliance, sexual harassment, and organization culture and change. Part of Arbor's expertise in these areas is based on the fact that it has been successful managing these issues in its own firm.

Enhanced Reputation as Employer of Choice
Arbor's enhanced reputation as an employer of choice has led to a doubling in calls by job seekers wanting to work at Arbor. Even in this tight labor market, people continue to seek Arbor out as an employer.

Increased Involvement in Professional Organizations
Arbor staff pursued and attained leadership positions in professional organizations and industry groups at local, regional, and national levels. Presently, the following positions in the Society for Human Resource Management (SHRM) are held by Arbor staff: Chapter President of the Greater Ann Arbor Society for Human Resource Management, SHRM Area III Diversity Chair, and National Human Resource Development Committee Member.

Established Major Awards Program to Recognize Organizations for HR Excellence
Since realignment, Arbor initiated a partnership with Eastern Michigan University's Master of Science in Human Resources and Organization Development program to award companies and HR practitioners for best practices in human resources. The Arbor Awards for Excellence program began in 1996, and 46 organizations have been recognized to date.

Knowledge, Skills, and Competencies Needed

The final section of the book looks at the vast array of knowledge, skills, and competencies possible for an informed and prepared PT practitioner. The role of ethics in the profession of performance technology challenges practitioners to decide what will be their areas of expertise and skill. Self-assessment to understand current competencies and striving to develop further skills takes honesty and determination. This section can serve as a guidepost for our future practice.

USING A BUSINESS SETBACK TO REALIGN FOR SUCCESS: THE ARBOR CONSULTING GROUP, INC.

This comprehensive case study is designed to illustrate the application of the HPT Model and to describe the implementation of selected interventions by using job aids from the previous sections. *Note: Job aids from previous chapters are indicated with the original job aid number in brackets [ ].* The case study recognizes the complexity of business and performance issues and demonstrates use of the HPT Model. The intention is to make the value of job aids clear while defining the nature of the selected interventions.

Scenario

The Arbor Consulting Group, Inc., a national human resources management consulting firm, experienced a business setback in 1993, when the two managing partners split the operation's revenue base and one partner left to form a separate consulting practice. Upon the dissolution, the partners agreed each would continue to work in the same general field, yet target different markets. While approximately 50% of its revenues left with the departing partner, The Arbor Consulting Group retained all Michigan employees and associated business expenses.

Background

The Arbor Consulting Group, Inc., headquartered in Plymouth, Michigan, was founded in 1983 by Joan E. Moore. In 1984, Moore invited two partners to join the business to expand the service offerings to its developing client base. Over the next several years, the business grew rapidly and Arbor continued to increase its staff size and established an East Coast office. Early on in the partnership, one of the newer partners left the organization, deciding to continue to pursue corporate interests. In 1993, the two remaining partners dissolved the partnership, with Ms. Moore retaining all Michigan staff and ongoing operating expenses. This case study examines the process Arbor underwent to realign its business after these events.

Arbor is a woman-owned, human resources consulting firm that provides services centered around employment

law compliance, employee relations assessments, HR audits and organization diagnostic work, especially during mergers and acquisitions, and other related services. In 1983, when Arbor was established, the business of human resources management was neither well established nor recognized as a profession, at the level it is today. With vision and skill, Arbor forged relationships and conducted consulting assignments in this field before terms like reengineering, TQM, quality circles, and team building were well known. Today, the main challenge in the industry is higher levels of competition from non-traditional sources, such as accounting and law firms, compensation/ benefit firms, and insurance organizations. The high-quality, boutique consulting firms, such as Arbor, now compete for clients with large, international conglomerates.

Since its realignment, Arbor has continued to develop and has become an award-winning company. In 1998, Arbor received the Women's Economic Club Tribute Award for Organization Vision and Culture. This award was presented to only six organizations, including Chrysler Corporation and Valassis Communications, whose leading-edge practices demonstrate true quality of life and innovation for the 21st century. Arbor was recognized as a highly successful business with a visionary workplace characterized by high levels of trust and teamwork, a constant sharing of ideas and information, open and honest communication, and the freedom to fail. Although the Arbor workplace has taken many years to develop and will constantly evolve, it is a living example of a successful human resource management approach. The Arbor workplace and its culture have resulted in high levels of employee retention and satisfaction, while producing high-quality, nationally recognized work.

In another accomplishment, The Arbor Consulting Group was named to the US Department of Labor's Working Women Count Honor Roll and received recognition from the Secretary of Labor, as did many Fortune 500 companies. This award underscores Arbor's commitment and active work to create policies and programs that support working women and their families. Through this award, information about Arbor's policies and workplace programs have been made available to others around the country who want to help make work better for families.

HPT Model—Performance and Cause Analyses

Moore, the remaining partner and current president, decided that the partnership split was an opportunity to reassess Arbor's business strategy and conduct a performance gap and cause analysis between the state of the organization in the past and her desired vision for Arbor in the future. As part of the HR consulting work it conducts for clients, Arbor often assesses gaps between present and desired organization structures and cultures. It was this work with clients that provided a model for Arbor's internal assessment of what was working, what was not, why not, and what to do about it. One core finding from the analysis was that, like many developing businesses, especially with multiple partners, Arbor was not tightly focused on a core set of services. It was decided that a realignment of the business might provide an opportunity for Arbor to define itself in a more focused and directed method.

The Realignment Worksheet (see Job Aid 9-1 [7-10]) is the type of tool Arbor used to examine the issues identified by the gap and cause analysis, and helped Arbor decide whether realignment was indeed the best intervention. Implementing realignment required three other interventions: (1) strategic planning, (2) team building and evaluation, and (3) culture analysis and development. Arbor Consulting Group used tools similar to the job aids in this book to assist in their implementation.

Realignment of The Arbor Consulting Group

Arbor identified the following issues while considering and planning for its realignment to new business objectives related to Job Aid 9-1 [7-10], Reengineering, realigning, and restructuring.

Current Alignment Issues

During the time of the partnership, business objectives differed by partner and the staff did not operate as a unified whole. There was a tendency to accept projects in diverse areas of human resources, versus focusing on a core set of services. This was particularly difficult because each partner had different objectives for the business and was interested in doing work in different HR consulting areas. As a result, Arbor was being pulled in different directions, an approach that was stressful for the partners and the staff. After one partner left the business, Arbor

had an opportunity to refocus and strategically realign its services, concentrating on the core set of practice areas the team was best suited to provide.

Revised Plan for Alignment to Business Objectives

Arbor's plan for realignment included: communicating the vision for the organization, defining its mission and setting business objectives, defining the consulting services Arbor would and would not provide, creating a plan to market the organization to potential clients, and creating a culture and infrastructure that supported the new vision, values, work and the ways in which employees would need to interact.

As it developed a plan for realignment, Arbor applied what it knew about organization change and development, and followed its own advice given to clients in the midst of change. Arbor knew that in order to be successful, it needed leadership commitment; availability of key individuals; a willingness to experiment; clear and consistent communication; buy-in and participation in the process; openness to feedback, even if negative; and an environment of trust.

It was critical that Arbor's leadership be highly committed to the realignment process. While the workload continued following the partnership split, employees also were asked to make themselves available for meetings about the realignment effort. The situation called for the business to take risks in order to experiment with new services, and a more refined focus, and leadership was willing to experiment. It was possible to send clear and consistent messages about the realignment because all employees would be present during realignment meetings. The process of realignment would be the leadership's opportunity to model behaviors it desired in its new culture, such as participation and buy-in, continuous communication and feedback, and trust.

To meet its new business objectives, Arbor needed to update its infrastructure and make it easier for employees to have access to all resources and information in the office. As a small office, it was important that everyone know how to handle clerical functions, use the filing system appropriately, and save time by not interrupting fellow employees for help locating a file or record. To that end, Arbor decided to update and network its computer system to meet recent advances in technology and position itself for the future. For an organization of its size in the 1980s, Arbor was ahead of its time with a networked system and a shared file directory. A very systematic directory system also was developed and all manual files were subsequently realigned for a total organized system.

JOB AID 9-1 [7-10]: Reengineering, Realigning, Restructuring With Arbor Consulting Group—Issues and Examples

As you embark on the change process, use this checklist as a job aid to ensure that you stay on the desired path.

Realigning	Some of the issues were:
1. Review the organization's *current alignment* or lack thereof to business objectives. — Is everyone working toward a common goal? — Is everyone aware of the objectives? — Does everyone know how his or her work makes a difference and contributes to the whole?	• Arbor was not focused on a core set of services • Objectives differed by partner • Teamwork fluctuated • Employee groups operated independently • Employees were unclear as to the value they added to the organization
2. Create and develop *revised plan for alignment to business objectives.* Give employees guidelines for keeping the objectives apparent.	• Applied own advice • Focused on internal issues • Developed business objectives • Established an infrastructure to meet objectives • Reinforced objectives through culture change
3. Evaluate *advantages and disadvantages* of major change in the organization.	• Consultants working on realignment had less time for revenue-producing work • Realignment meetings had teambuilding effects • Changes to infrastructure had short-term negative effects on productivity, but long-term advantages
4. Identify main reason, incentive, or desired outcomes for *implementing change.*	• To define the organization's mission and strategically analyze the consulting services Arbor would offer • To achieve the new vision for the organization that would be successful
Applicable to all change management strategies:	
5. Integrate *employee input* into management change practice.	• Employees were part of the process, included in brainstorming and strategic planning sessions
6. Allow *opportunities for feedback* from all employees in the organization.	• Employees helped to define the new organization culture and how they wanted to work in the future • Collected feedback through regular meetings and discussions
7. Provide employees with *relevant information* as part of the change process and prior to management implementation of change so that they can provide input and also prepare to adapt the change into on-the-job performance.	• Plans were shared with employees • Positive and negative effects of changes were encountered. Sought training and involved all employees
8. Communicate process of reengineering, realignment, or restructuring to the organization.	• Held in-house meetings • Documented file system and shared directory system • Created new marketing brochure and materials

Advantages and Disadvantages

Including all employees in realignment meetings created some disadvantages for Arbor. Consultants bill clients by the hour. When employees are meeting on internal issues they are not billable and, therefore, the amount of time available for billable client projects was reduced. In addition, defining a mission, a desired culture, and realigning the business operations to the new mission was an extensive project. It involved researching the costs and benefits of the ideas being exchanged, environmental scanning about the HR consulting market, and mental fortitude to deal with large-scale changes.

On the other hand, including employees in the realignment process was an advantage because employees enjoyed a clear picture of the mission and vision for Arbor's future. The sessions had a teambuilding effect, and employees reaffirmed their commitment to helping Arbor achieve its goals.

The changes to the infrastructure (i.e., networked computer system and shared directory system) were seen as a future advantage, with short-term negative effects. Working with a computer consultant to define desired capabilities, building the shared directory system, and creating the new file system was labor intensive, and it took time for employees to learn and adapt to the changes. While all employees received training on the new computer system and software packages, each had a different learning curve and was temporarily slowed and frustrated by the changes.

Implementing Change Issues

Communicating the president's vision for the organization was not difficult. Employees were motivated and inspired by her leadership, and believed that the organization could achieve the desired outcome.

In order to define the organization, Moore used information she collected from ongoing scanning of the environment to identify the HR consulting services available in the local and national markets, and to learn how to differentiate Arbor from the competition. In addition, the skill sets of current employees were analyzed to refine the types of consulting services offered and how best to staff new projects.

Implementing a new marketing approach also was viewed as an investment, as it was a labor-intensive process with no immediate, direct return. Initial goals were to create a new tri-fold brochure, revise all supporting marketing materials, and have Moore increase her exposure in professional organizations.

The changes that most affected the staff included the new culture and establishment of a new infrastructure. Analyzing the organization's culture gave employees a clear picture of what was and was not working for them in terms of culture. Based on their past experiences and Moore's desired goals for the organization's culture, Arbor staff defined core values and came to understand how to work together as a team. Arbor used tools like the Culture Analysis (Job Aid 9-4 [7-11]) and Team Fitness Evaluator (see Job Aid 9-3 [7-1]) to define and measure its progress toward its desired culture.

Employee Input Issues

Throughout the realignment process, Arbor demonstrated its commitment to developing a culture in which open communication was sought and welcomed. Employees were included in meetings and were asked to verbalize their concerns and suggestions about the changes to the organization. The behavior necessary to make the company successful was true teamwork and trust. As a result of needing to work this way, the team saw clearly that a new culture and organization was emerging.

Opportunities for Feedback Issues

Employees had opportunities to provide feedback at all times during realignment. Staff meetings and lunches were held frequently and the team modeled aspects of the desired culture by seeking diverse opinions and ideas. Decisions affecting employees were made by consensus, whenever possible, to make sure buy-in to the changes was achieved.

Relevant Information Issues

Information was shared with employees as it became available. All staff received training for the new computer system and software packages, and everyone shared the tips and short-cuts they discovered so organizational learning could proceed quickly. Because everyone was learning together, a great deal of communication occurred as problems were encountered. All employees were called for mini-meetings or asked to participate in lunch meetings to discuss issues and solve problems as a team.

Communication Issues

The realignment process was completed through group meetings of all employees; therefore, communication about what was happening was shared openly. To communicate the logic of the centralized filing system and shared directory computer system, models of the systems were documented in table form to guide employees trying to locate information. The key words and descriptions of the

JOB AID 9-2 [7-5]: Strategic Planning Preparation

Directions: Please note responses in the space provided.

1. Building the responsible team	• Who is responsible for implementing the strategic plan? • Are all of the key individuals with the appropriate skills included in the planning process? .... ☐ Yes ☐ No • Who else might be a beneficial contributor to the strategic planning team?
2. Starting the process	• Has the current situation been evaluated? .... ☐ Yes ☐ No • Have the long-term goals been defined? .... ☐ Yes ☐ No • Does management, as well as all employees, understand the scope of this long-term project? .... ☐ Yes ☐ No • How will employees be informed of the organization's strategic plan? • Has the team set the strategic planning goals and desired outcomes? .... ☐ Yes ☐ No • Have the specific milestones been determined and timeline set? .... ☐ Yes ☐ No
3. Implementing the plan	• What is the concrete plan for implementing the strategy? • Have additional individuals been called to assist in implementing the plan? .... ☐ Yes ☐ No
4. Evaluating the results	• What has the team integrated into the plan that will make it easy to track and maintain the strategic plan? • How will management integrate employees into having ownership for following the strategic plan? • How will employees become empowered to contribute to and respect the organization's strategic plan? • Does the strategy deal with a structural evolution in the respective industry? .... ☐ Yes ☐ No

color-coded filing system were shared, as well. As a result of building a network, employees could access each other's documents on line. This called for continuous communication about where to save documents based on the shared understanding of the directory system.

In addition, Arbor's new marketing plan was communicated through a tri-fold brochure and revised marketing folders. Employees contributed to the development of the new marketing materials as part of the realignment plan (see Job Aid 9-2 [7-5]).

Strategic Planning at The Arbor Consulting Group

1. Building the Responsible Team

- Who is responsible for implementing the strategic plan?
    Three key employees, including the president, the vice president and a senior consultant.
- Are all of the key individuals with the appropriate skills included in the planning process?
    Yes. These individuals brought business leadership, operations and infrastructure expertise, and marketing and organization diagnostic skills to the team.
- Who else might be a beneficial contributor to the strategic planning team?
    A presidential advisory board comprised of presidents from other small organizations, professional colleagues, and the organization's accountant and financial advisor were consulted about the realignment plan.

2. Starting the Process

- Has the current situation been evaluated?
    Yes. Arbor used the same type of strategic analysis used to diagnose client organizations to identify what was working, what was not, why not, and what to do about it.
- Have the long-term goals been defined?
    Yes. Arbor's goals were to retain the current staff; increase operational efficiency by building and improving the infrastructure; and expand the consulting business to a national audience.
- Does management, as well as all employees, understand the scope of this long term project?
    Yes. Although these were large, ambitious changes, all involved understood the importance of accomplishing them, both for the short- and long-term success of the business.
- How will employees be informed of the organization's strategic plan for realignment?
    Team meetings and ongoing working sessions with all staff were planned and held on a regular basis.

- Has the team set the strategic planning goals and desired outcomes?
    Yes. Detailed plans were created and individual team members took on various leadership roles during the realignment. For example, the vice president took the lead on operational and infrastructure upgrades and improvements; the president and senior consultant took responsibility for redefining consulting services, the marketing approach and associated marketing materials.
- Have the specific milestones been determined and timeline set?
    Yes. A Gantt chart listing the major activities of the realignment plan with timelines for task completion was distributed and used to track the realignment process. Major tasks were entered into Arbor's online project management software where they were tracked and reviewed for completion on a regular basis.

3. Implementing the Plan

- What is the concrete plan for implementing the strategy?
    Arbor created a multi-faceted realignment strategy that touched many aspects of the business. The responsibility for implementing the plan was shared among three key members of the organization. The implementation was managed by holding regular all-staff meetings; scheduling changes during anticipated down time, whenever possible; providing computer and software training for staff; and modeling desired behaviors for the new culture.
- Have additional individuals been called to assist in implementing the plan?
    The realignment plans were implemented by both internal and external experts. A computer consultant was hired to work with the vice president to build the network and shared directory. Computer and software training also was provided by an outside vendor. A graphics consultant was contracted to design the look of the new marketing materials, with the president and senior consultant providing the content.

4. Long-Term Goals

- What has the team integrated into the plan that will make it easy to track and maintain the strategic plan?
    Realignment meetings were scheduled frequently to update staff on the progress of the changes and any adjustments to the Gantt chart or timeline. Fortunately, Arbor staff uses this type of project management approach on client projects and has a high level of respect for deadlines and the completion of tasks.

- How will management integrate employees into having ownership for following the strategic plan?

    Employees already were invested in the success of the realignment, because failure meant possibly losing the business as they knew it. There were points along the way, once some changes were implemented, when the organization had to secure additional employee buy-in. For instance, there was resistance to the use of new software programs. It took time for some employees to see that leadership was serious about requiring all employees to use the software. Buy-in was slow, but came along once leadership modeled behavior by using the software on a regular basis.

- How will employees become empowered to contribute to and respect the organization's strategic realignment plan?

    The structure and size of the business allowed all employees to be involved in the planning and implementation of the organization's realignment. Employees were empowered to offer their opinions and ideas along the way, and their contributions were valued by the organizational leaders.

- Does the strategy deal with a structural evolution in the respective industry?

    Arbor's realignment was based on data gathered from ongoing environmental scanning and knowledge of the industry at the time. Scanning the environment for trends and changes always has been a continuous process for Arbor. Arbor continues to evolve based on the external market and the needs of its clients.

Team Evaluation of The Arbor Consulting Group

Implementing the plan for realignment required a high level of teamwork from the entire work force that had been used to operating on a more independent basis. The realignment process itself provided Arbor's leadership with an opportunity to model desired team behaviors and to demonstrate commitment to the organization's new culture based on teamwork, respect, and trust. During realignment, it made more business sense for the organization to remain focused on the items in the plan that would most quickly lead to efficiency and bottom-line payoff. Improving the level of teamwork in the organization developed naturally through implementation and the conscious effort of the leadership to model effective team behaviors.

The Team Fitness Evaluator job aid (Job Aid 9-3 [7-1]) was used after realignment to illustrate how far Arbor's work force had developed.

Team's Customers

Arbor's customers include past, present, and potential clients. Arbor considers customers to include contacts from local professional associations; HR professionals who participate in Arbor-sponsored events such as HR Roundtable meetings; and HR and business vendors with whom Arbor has had dealings. In addition, consultants treat each other as internal customers. Client work is conducted in teams of two to three consultants, where collaboration is critical to making projects a success. When working on client projects, there is regular communication about progress and a commitment to deliver work products for editing and review when promised, so workloads can be managed accordingly.

Team Empowerment

The Arbor team is empowered. Due to the size and flexibility of the organization, it is possible to make change happen instantaneously. For example, clients have called with emergency needs, and the organization is able to respond and mobilize to start an assignment immediately. Internally, the members of the organization have been a part of, and have made decisions about, changes to the organization in the span of a 15-minute meeting. For example, after hiring new staff, there was a need to add office space and furniture. An action plan regarding phone lines, office equipment, furniture and decor was created in a matter of one or two lunch discussions.

Team Meetings

In addition to working as business colleagues, Arbor team members like and respect each other on a personal level and they have fun together. Often the meetings held during lunch begin on a social level and transition to a discussion of business issues. When difficult situations must be discussed, there may be moments of discomfort, but the staff is able to get beyond them due to the high level of trust held for each other and the knowledge that staff members will use their best judgment when handling difficult situations.

Team Consensus

The team does not use consensus for all decision making. It simply is not appropriate for all business decisions to be made by the team, although often the team's input and feedback is sought. When a decision is to be made by consensus, the team openly discusses the issue and everyone has an opportunity to voice his or her ideas and concerns. There are no assigned roles during the meeting; however, someone will try to bring the discussion to a

JOB AID 9-3 [7-1]: Team Fitness Evaluator

Directions: Take a minute to review your team's fitness by responding to the following items.

1. **Who is/are your team's customer(s)?**
2. **Is the team empowered? How do you know?**
3. **Are team meetings comfortable and enjoyable? Are team discussions open and respectful?**
4. **What process does the team use to arrive at consensus decisions?**
5. **How does the team ensure that work and effort are allocated fairly? Does everyone do his or her fair share?**
6. **What does the team do to keep members motivated?**
7. **How does the team communicate among members? With others outside the team?**

close. Often, there tends to be a common direction to the discussion, and the team members agree that they have reached consensus. If it appears consensus is not possible, the team will take a break and revisit the topic at a later date. Arbor has learned that it needs information and a logical argument in order for the team to reach consensus.

Work Allocation

Arbor allocates its work based on who has the skills needed for projects and the time available to work on them. Moore carries a larger burden of the workload because she is involved in most client projects and is the lead person in running the operation. Fairness comes into play when those who have down time or less billable work focus their efforts on marketing or operations. The team takes a longer view of fairness by understanding that workloads fluctuate and that staff will continue to contribute to the organization in ways beyond client work. In addition, an automated "to do" program allows the team to fully communicate status and track progress on projects, business issues, and marketing efforts. This system is used by all, with no restrictions, so that each staff member knows the progress of every person's activities.

Team Motivation

Arbor has the traditional profit-sharing plan for employees. However, there are other ways the organization motivates its members. Arbor acknowledges and celebrates milestones, such as the completion of a major project, an employee anniversary, or getting through a difficult situation. The culture itself is in many ways a motivator for employees. It is rare to have a workplace in which there are few internal conflicts and such a strong feeling of camaraderie.

As discussed in the forthcoming Culture Analysis, employees laugh, share their burdens, and support each other on personal and professional levels. The treat basket and wellness programs are other employee motivators. The treat basket is a basket of small, wrapped gifts such as funny Post-it notes or fancy toiletries, which employees use to recognize each other's accomplishments. When an employee observes that a co-worker has creatively solved a problem, successfully completed a tough assignment, or done anything excellent that deserves recognition by the whole team, the co-worker is nominated to receive a treat from the treat basket. All employees gather to learn why the person was nominated and watch as the nominated employee selects a gift from the treat basket. Everyone celebrates the employee's accomplishment and the gift is passed around for all to see. The treat basket provides Arbor with an easy and instantaneous way to recognize and motivate employees.

The wellness program is an exercise program in which employees agree to exercise for a minimum of 30 minutes per day, three times per week, for a reward at the end of the month. The monthly rewards are set by the team and vary from month to month. In addition, the work itself is a fundamental motivator for the team.

Team Communication

To maintain a collaborative work environment, Arbor implemented the following communication strategies. Employees use open-door policies for immediate access to another perspective or instant feedback to an idea; MSMail is used to communicate and share ideas without interrupting each other; Arbor's conference room is designed for collaborative working; and group lunches are a format to discuss issues and gain everyone's input. There is only one rule about communicating with each other: Employees must treat each other with respect and civility.

Forms of external communication depend on the circumstances and with whom the employees need to communicate. Phone calls, conference calls, faxes, email messages, and mailings are common forms of communication with clients. When networking or marketing services to a prospective client, Arbor usually meets face to face with representatives of that organization. Marketing mailings are used to maintain ongoing contact with potential clients, often informing them of trends, changes in relevant regulations, or other issues which may add value to their businesses. Arbor believes strongly in providing value through its marketing efforts.

Cultural Analysis of The Arbor Consulting Group

The Cultural Analysis job aid (see Job Aid 9-4 [7-11]) illustrates the realignment of Arbor's organizational culture to its new business objectives. The questions in the job aid point out the desired cultural factors which, at the time of the partnership split, were just emerging. After many years of working on its culture, Arbor's culture has evolved and become central to the way the organization operates. In 1998, Arbor received a Special Tribute Award for Vision and Culture as part of the "Today's Workplace of Tomorrow Awards" sponsored by the Women's Economic Club of Detroit. The answers to the Cultural Analysis Job Aid are based on Arbor's award-winning, post-realignment culture.

Stated Values

The following values were adopted to keep Arbor focused on its central mission:
• Add value at all times and exceed expectations.

JOB AID 9-4 [7-11]: Cultural Analysis

Directions: Complete the questionnaire with input from several employees.

1. **What are the stated values and standards? Are they beneficial and healthy?**
2. **What are the unstated values and standards? Are they beneficial and healthy?**
3. **Who are the heroes? Are legends or stories about them helpful?**
4. **What are the rituals or rites? Formal and informal?**
5. **Are the communication media positive and healthy? Do the formal communication pieces have any influence? Does the grapevine control people's emotions, fears, and behavior?**
6. **List healthy aspects of the culture.**
7. **List detrimental aspects of the culture.**
8. **Identify factors for potential improvement. How pervasive and strong are these factors in the current culture? Describe ideal improvements.**

- Uphold Arbor's image as the gold standard of consulting firms.
- Refrain from participating in negative discussions regarding a client or competitor.
- Each client will be given an appropriate amount of attention to complete the assignment in a timely and cost-effective manner (no special favors based on the size of the project).
- "That's not my job" is not an acceptable response in Arbor's culture. Everyone is expected to perform tasks at all levels, and all work is valued.
- Temper expectations about what Arbor can, cannot, will, and will not do. It is acceptable to say no to an inappropriate request.
- Maintain a sense of humor.
- Do not point fingers. Solve the problem.
- Consultants will work in the best interest of clients' organizations, not in the interest of individual agendas (i.e., delivering the hard news even if it means a potential fallout in the relationship with that client).
- Make every attempt to deliver work on time, within budget, and at the highest quality.
- Do not be afraid to ask for help.
- Continuous improvement and sharing of lessons learned are critical to Arbor remaining highly competitive in the marketplace and responsive to clients and their needs.
- Constant and extensive communication is expected so there are no surprises.
- Exceptional performance will be recognized with customized rewards, personalized recognition for accomplishments, and incentive pay.
- The extremely high expectations of employees are necessary in order to provide the high-quality services and complex work products demanded by Arbor's clientele.
- Arbor's management dismisses the widely held belief that the amount of hours worked directly correlates to an employees' ability to be responsible for important work. Arbor accepts employees who integrate home and work life, and employs high-level employees who work a reduced schedule. The only requirement is to be responsible to make sure the work is done, as promised, within appropriate time frames.
- Employees are expected to totally support each other, be reliable sounding boards for each other, and contradict and challenge ideas to make them better.

Unstated Values

- "Walk the talk"—Arbor is a living example of the advice it shares with clients. It walks its own talk through the organization's willingness to change its workplace to better accommodate the needs of the organization, employees, and clients. This means

Arbor is committed to taking actions that are in line with its stated values, which is the message shared in Arbor's client work, and is believed to be the foundation of organization success. Through the actions of its leadership and the changes made based on employee suggestions, Arbor reinforces its cultural values.

- Holistic approach—In its client work, Arbor advocates taking a holistic approach, or considering all sides of an issue. Applying the same logic to its staff, Arbor treats employees as whole persons, recognizing their life outside of work. Arbor management understands the difficulty of maintaining a career with a busy personal life, and welcomes discussion about family obligations and their impact on work. Many times, employees help one another with family/work life needs, such as rearranging schedules to accommodate unforeseen emergencies at home.
- A village approach—Arbor uses the phrase, "a village approach" to describe its family-like atmosphere, which includes the families of each employee. On many occasions, the skills and connections of the spouses and family members of Arbor staff have been offered to help the organization and fellow co-workers complete specific tasks. For example, spouses have repaired and moved furniture in the office, a family has helped an employee relocate twice, co-workers pet-sit for each other, and teenage children have been emergency babysitters for co-workers' young children.
- Freedom to fail—There is no humiliating punishment for making a mistake at Arbor. Instead, employees are recognized for their success and mistakes are treated as opportunities for learning. This approach encourages employees to take initiative by allowing them to present ideas and projects in draft form. Internal work is often routed for proofing and feedback while in the rough, conceptual stage. This is a simple, yet unique practice that works at Arbor because there is no penalty associated with launching new ideas and being creative, which means sometimes failing. Arbor leadership strongly believes that trying out ideas internally reaps benefits and helps to avoid failing externally with clients.

Heroes

Heroes are the people who have played large roles in the realignment of the organization because they are responsible for what Arbor has become today. For instance, Moore is the visionary risk-taker; vice president Terri Luter is responsible for the development of the infrastructure. There are many stories about the lengths to which Arbor has gone to service client needs, and these stories are shared, and the message reinforced, on a regular basis. The stories about Arbor's heroes are helpful in conveying the culture during the indoctrination of new employees.

Arbor uses the stories to reinforce what is important and appreciated about its culture.

Rituals

Lunch

Arbor has learned that getting out of the office setting into a different location for lunch is a good mental break for the staff, and the relaxed environment promotes creativity and discussion. Lunch, therefore, has become an important part of the Arbor culture. On any given day, at about 11:15, the conversation about lunch begins. (Who's going?, Where do you want to go?, What do we need to talk about?, Does anyone have errands they need to run?, etc.) Often, lunch becomes a working session, because it may be the only time everyone is able to get together to discuss a project or brainstorm to solve a problem.

Shopping

Shopping is sometimes included in the lunch plans—busy people trying to balance work and family obligations have little time for running errands that have to be done during business hours. This is hard to manage because everyone is so busy with work, but periodically Arbor tacks on a half hour segment to lunch and tells everyone to run errands for 30 minutes. Arbor also is looking into using a dry cleaning pick up and delivery service to the office to help ease work/life stress. Giving employees the freedom to complete personal errands during lunch boosts employee productivity for the rest of the day, because employees can focus on work and stop thinking about when they will have time to finish personal tasks.

Birthday Celebrations

Arbor celebrates birthdays with a staff lunch at the restaurant of the birthday person's choice, and cake is served in the afternoon. Rather than sing, it is an Arbor tradition to hum "Happy Birthday" to the birthday person.

Treats

Watching co-workers select a treat from the treat basket has become a ritual. To recognize the individual, the entire office gathers as the person opens the gift and to learn what the person has accomplished, discovered, or solved in order to be nominated for a treat.

Holiday Celebration

Arbor's holiday celebration was designed with the needs of its work force in mind. Rather than a large office party, the entire office participates in a holiday lunch and a half-day of holiday shopping. Employees plan for this outing weeks in advance, since it is sometimes the only opportunity for employees to do holiday shopping during business hours when the stores are less crowded. Feedback about Arbor's holiday event is that employees

appreciate the opportunity to have fun together and have the time to attend to personal needs during business hours. This is preferred over a traditional office celebration.

Communication Media

Formal communication takes place via group email messages or during monthly staff lunches. Informal communication takes place daily over email or as employees see each other in the office, but it tends to be on a one-on-one basis.

Confidential discussions are held on occasion between employees, or in small groups. These conversations are useful for clarifying issues and working through problems in a more efficient manner than meeting with the whole office.

Healthy Aspects

Treating everyone like equal contributors and valuing everyone's input is a healthy aspect of the culture. Employees are treated with respect and trust and are allowed to use their best judgment. In addition, there is a lot of laughter in the office. The culture encourages humor and using it appropriately with one another to briefly escape the seriousness of the client work. Arbor also attempts to build fun into its environment by customizing its celebrations to meet the needs and interests of its staff.

Detrimental Aspects

The on-time, on-budget, high-value way in which Arbor works and its core mission to stay true to the fundamentals of HR sometimes have been detrimental to winning projects. At times, potential clients want the fast, cheap, and easy solution to very complex and difficult problems that have emerged over long periods of time. The fast, cheap, easy approach is not in line with Arbor's business values or the way in which it provides consulting services, because the organization knows these "magic wand" approaches do not work.

A factor that can be detrimental to Arbor internally is its commitment to having open communication. At times, the leadership has business information that would be inappropriate to share with employees, or to share before further details are gathered. It is difficult not to share information openly, because this behavior is counter to what has been developed as an essential part of Arbor's culture. Furthermore, internal communication can be detrimental to the business because it takes time that may otherwise be spent on billable work. However, Arbor believes, in the long run, greater value is added by sharing information with employees.

Another detrimental factor is the high level of expectations Arbor has for its employees. People have to be willing to be life-long learners to work at Arbor and to work very hard and be extremely organized to make best use of their time. This makes it difficult to find people who will work well in Arbor's culture. It is for that reason that Arbor continually screens HR professionals for skills and potential fit. The employees who fit well have remained with the organization for several years.

Factors for Improvement

Arbor continues to work on balancing the time it takes to maintain its culture with the ongoing demands of its business. To reinforce the critical function culture plays in a successful business, Arbor has nominated itself for certain awards. These awards have had criteria that did not require many financial or people resources as so many awards do, but were tied to culture and long-term business strategies for success. Winning these awards has served to underscore how far the organization has developed in terms of its culture and its approach to business.

HPT Model—Intervention Implementation and Change

Since its realignment, Arbor has made a concentrated effort to build a national reputation and client base, and currently serves clients from California to Connecticut and Minnesota to Texas. Arbor successfully expanded its business and increased revenues beyond its own expectations.

Another indicator of success includes the organization's culture and the awards it has received for having a work-place of the future. In addition to being placed on the Department of Labor's Working Women Count Honor Roll, Arbor has been recognized for its vision and culture.

Success also is indicated by the number of people who approach the organization about employment opportunities. This interest is viewed as an indicator of the positive image Arbor has built in the marketplace.

Today, Arbor's vision is that it is considered by its present and future clients to be a highly respected, national HR management consulting practice, with a reputation for excellence. The organization has worked very hard to achieve this vision, which is closely linked to strong underlying principles and practices that have guided the business since its realignment. Research out of the Saratoga Institute validates the fact that most financially and organizationally successful businesses are guided by similar human asset management practices.[1] The practices followed at Arbor include: a constant focus on

adding value; flexibility coupled with dedication to the long-term core strategy; a strong linkage between culture and systems; constant and extensive communication; partnering with clients and with other experts to provide better service; a high level of collaboration; innovation and risk taking; and a passion for improvement.

HPT Model—Evaluation

The evaluation of Arbor's realignment is a continuous process. The organization decided to use a formative approach, or continuous improvement, to remaining highly competitive in the marketplace and responsive to client needs. Arbor continues to ask what is working, what is not, why not, and what to do about it. In being open to new ideas garnered through its client work and through the continuous scanning of business trends and information, Arbor positions itself to constantly improve.

The underlying culture of trust allows Arbor to be a learning organization, where continuous improvement is required. As discussed earlier, Arbor's culture is one where information is shared constantly. This includes sharing "learnings" with one another to speed the development of all members and prevent the duplication of wasted effort. Particularly important is that Arbor defines "learnings" to include an assessment of what could be done differently in every important situation, and incorporates that knowledge into planning. After client meetings, presentations, or other major events, staff members debrief to discuss and document what went well and what needs to be changed to improve performance and results next time.

Arbor's environmental scanning also is considered to be essential to continuous improvement. Ideas on workplace/business trends and information of merit are incorporated to improve internal productivity and the workplace environment. Examples include the introduction of more "fun" activities at Arbor as a way to increase productivity. This idea was detailed in *Inc.* magazine and has led to a better understanding of the benefits of a "work hard, play hard" environment. Arbor has incorporated impromptu walks around the block, afternoon breaks, and time for personal errands during the day as stress relievers, which have a highly positive impact on productivity.

External resources such as trade journals, catalogues, and newspapers are circulated in the office as stimulus for creative thought. Employees pay special attention to finding the latest approach to client work and any practices with which the organization might experiment. Even entertainment magazines and catalogues, when circulated for reading pleasure on personal time, often become the basis of discussions on trends and lead to new ideas.

Future

In the future, Arbor will continue to reinvent itself and target its marketing efforts accordingly. Exciting challenges that lie ahead include creating a website and further refining marketing efforts and consulting services to respond to the changing business landscape, such as providing compliance and HR due diligence support during mergers and acquisitions.

Case study written by Mim Munzel, BS, SPHR, The Arbor Consulting Group, Inc. Used with permission.

The Profession of Performance Technology (PT)

Knowledge, Skills, and Competencies Needed—A Word to the Wise

By this point in this book, it is clear that PT interventions are wide ranging and involve almost anything that can have an impact on performance. PT practitioners can focus on various levels in the workplace. They can concentrate on grass-roots worker problems, such as job design or safety engineering, or broader, organizational issues, including strategic planning, globalization, or spirituality in the workplace.

Each individual PT practitioner needs to work ethically within his or her own range of expertise. It is imperative for PT practitioners to recognize their own knowledge, capabilities, and strengths and bring in colleagues with suitable expertise, as needed. It is necessary to monitor performance improvement efforts to ensure that competent individuals are assisting and supporting the implementation of the interventions. This is easy to say—but not necessarily easy to do. It is difficult to be totally honest in self-assessment and it is often difficult to recommend to a client that they include another professional in their performance improvement effort.

PT practitioners need to be clear regarding what is professional competence relative to a given intervention or strategy. Critical and honest self-assessment is essential to engage in ethical practice. Then, it is necessary to involve appropriate practitioners in projects that require knowledge, skills, or competencies that the PT practitioner does not possess.

Ethics and Professional Standards

Many people dislike discussing ethics, believing that ethics and standards are about as useful as an umbrella is to a fish. However, competencies and ethics are linked and are necessary to define adequate and best practices. Competencies define the major activities of the PT practice and also the knowledge, skills, and abilities necessary. Ethics defines the "how-to or how-much" of the activity, skill, knowledge, or ability.

There has been substantial discussion on competencies in recent years, led by William Rothwell and Patricia McLagan. Rothwell identified the performance improvement (PI) aspects of human resources development (HRD) and instructional systems design (ISD) and also defined PI knowledge, skills, and competencies.[1] McLagan defined the knowledge, skills, and competencies necessary to practice in the field of HRD.[2]

The Academy of Human Resources Development (AHRD) published Standards on Ethics and Integrity to guide HRD practitioners. The interdisciplinary field of HRD focuses on systematic training and development, career development, and organizational development to improve processes and enhance the learning and performance of individuals, organizations, communities, and society.[3]

Although the field of HRD has a much narrower practice area than PT, the goals of process and PI are similar. Therefore, it is very common for experts and leaders to practice in both fields. There is much intermingling of ideas and beliefs.

Table 9-3 documents some of the primary principles of AHRD (1999–2000). Because PT includes systematic training, career development, and organizational development, AHRD standards are helpful and appropriate for PT practitioners.

In general, HRD and PT practitioners need to engage in honest self-assessment, be knowledgeable of research and best practices, participate in ongoing structured learning experiences and other self-learning, and honor their own boundaries of competence. It is essential to act with integrity and social responsibility.

Code of Professional Conduct

Based on the AHRD Ethics Standards, Watkins, Leigh, and Kaufman[4] developed a preliminary code of professional conduct for performance technologists. The professional code begins with one objective (see Table 9-4).

Clearly, good practice of PT involves adequate knowledge of research and best practice, personal skill building with structured experience, and ongoing professional education. In addition, it requires integrity and a commitment to clients and to society.

Intervention Competence

Reflecting on the extensive list of possible interventions covered in this book, it is difficult to determine the amount of knowledge, skills, and abilities an individual must possess before using the job title "Performance Improvement Specialist" or "Performance Technologist."

The challenge of the job lies in crafting appropriate recommendations to eliminate or minimize performance problems. PT practitioners who are unfamiliar with the extensive possibilities for performance improvement are likely to approach intervention selection and design too narrowly. There is an old saying that is likely to apply—"To a carpenter, every squeaky floorboard can be quieted with a nail." PT practitioners need sufficient knowledge, skills, and abilities to recognize the most appropriate

TABLE 9-3: Highlights of AHRD Principles

Competence	Ensure high standards recognizing personal boundaries of a particular competency and limitations of expertise.
	Provide only services for which qualified by education, training, and supervised or other appropriate professional experience.
	Maintain knowledge of relevant research and professional information related to services rendered and participate in ongoing education, including consultation with experts.
Integrity	Be honest, fair, and respectful of others.
Professional Responsibility	Uphold professional standards of conduct, clarify their professional roles and obligations, accept appropriate responsibility for behavior, and adapt methods to the needs of different populations.
Respect for People's Rights and Dignity	Respect the fundamental rights, dignity, and worth of all people to privacy, confidentiality, self-determination, and autonomy, mindful of legal and other obligations.
Concern for Others' Welfare	Contribute to the welfare of those with whom the practitioner interacts professionally.
Social Responsibility	Minimize adverse affects on individuals, groups, organizations, society, and the environment. Strive to advance human welfare, human development, and sustainable future.

AHRD, 1999–2000, p. ii.

TABLE 9-4: Objective of Professional Conduct

The objective of my work as a professional is

(a) to provide organizations and individuals with the skills, knowledge, abilities, and attitude necessary to create opportunities for achieving desired and required individual, organizational, and societal results;

(b) to assist in the generation of new and valid knowledge that will lead to the attainment of results that meet the performance criteria demanded by individuals, organizations, and society;

(c) to acquire the knowledge through systematic and valid research methods without jeopardizing the success of my client, my client's clients, or society; and

(d) to produce the results required by my client.

Watkins, Leigh, and Kaufman, 2000, p. 17–21.

intervention possibilities. They also need sufficient competence to design and implement any intervention for which they are responsible. It can be tough to "bow out" and invite another colleague to implement a performance solution.

Hutchison and Stein discussed the huge potential of interventions, referring to the situation as the "whole new world of interventions" (see Table 9-5). Recognizing the vastness of the options, they recommend that performance technologists:
1. Think systematically, addressing performance gaps with integrated intervention solutions. The impact needs to be recognized, addressed, and planned for.
2. Be generalists, rather than specialists, in one area of practice. Generalists "are able to integrate a number of interventions in ways that have a greater impact than that of the sum of the individual specialties."
3. Have a broad range of specialties within their repertoire.[4]

Hutchison and Stein recommend a rigorous self-knowledge approach. It is the responsibility of performance technologists to honestly measure themselves against the AHRD Ethics and Personal Specialties standards and determine their own competencies. PT practitioners need to main-tain competence in the fields in which they practice and be knowledgeable in related areas, as well.

Performance Technology as a Profession— A Word to the Wise

Performance technology is a profession covering a vast range of activities and options. Selection, design, and implementation of interventions are just part of the entire HPT process. This vastness requires disciplined self-assessment to ensure sufficient proficiency to practice as a PT professional. It demands constant vigilance through ongoing education to maintain expertise relative to the latest research and best practices. Performance technology, as a profession, needs colleagues with commitment to people, community, and society—people who are positive and willing to do the "right thing." It is not easy, but it is exciting; the work is interesting and challenging, and the rewards can be thrilling. PT practitioners must use wisdom and good judgment in pursuit of best practice.

In the end, as the Scottish philosopher Francis Hutchison stated, PT practitioners need to believe that "wisdom denotes the pursuing of the best ends by the best means."[5]

TABLE 9-5: Hutchison and Stein's Performance Technologist Personal Specialties Repertoire

Expert	Expert in 15 to 25 interventions across 10 or more categories
Design	Able to custom design a solution for any set of conditions that would stand up to the scrutiny of other experts
	Able to design and implement a number of solutions within each intervention area
Working Knowledge	Knowledge of 45 to 75 interventions across 15 or more intervention categories
Basic Principles	Know basic research and principles of half of the interventions and be able to recognize expertise in them
Network of Experts	Have contacts with experts in all intervention areas

Hutchison and Stein, 1997, pp. 28–35.

APPENDIX

INTERVENTION SELECTION TOOL

"USING DYNAMITE AS A BATON HAS
DRAMATICALLY IMPROVED THEIR TIME."

INTERVENTION SELECTION PROCESS

Definition and Scope

Performance improvement is complex because it involves many uncertainties, such as individual human behavior, collective organizational behavior, and the dynamics of the internal and external environment. Almost anything can influence behavior: workspace design, supervision, communication, financial systems, motivation, strategic and operational planning, or skills and knowledge. In turn, an infinite range of performance improvement activities exists. Creativity and "out-of-the box" thinking can lead to intervention solutions that match the culture and objectives of the organization.

Interventions are improvement activities designed to correct or minimize problems in the workplace. Usually there is a diagnosis phase, which can be formal or informal, to determine and gain consensus regarding the workplace problems.

Intervention selection is one of the core capabilities of successful PT practitioners. Using sound selection methods is actually more important than simply getting the right "answer." Group involvement and group commitment to the ultimate decision will minimize conflict and resistance later during implementation. PT practitioners normally facilitate this selection process because they have experience and expertise in performance improvement. The selection team and the PT practitioner collaborate to identify the best interventions.

There is no easy method for selecting possible interventions or solutions to performance problems. However, the techniques and tools described here are designed to simplify and structure the tasks, but the overall process is still complex. Consequently, the intervention selection process is divided into three phases to keep the tasks manageable: Preliminary, Survey, and Selection.

This tool does not cover the entirety of possible interventions; however, it does contain many of the most common interventions. They are divided into clusters to demonstrate the relationship between interventions: Performance Support Systems, Job Analysis and Work Design, Personal Development, Human Resource Development, Organi-zational Communication, Organizational Design and Development, and Financial Systems.

HPT Model

Intervention selection is part of a larger methodology called performance technology (PT). "PT is the systematic process of linking business goals and strategies with the work force responsible for achieving the goals" (Van Tiem, Moseley, and Dessinger, 2000, p. 2). PT systematically analyzes performance problems and their underlying causes, identifies and implements solutions, and evaluates results. The HPT Model (see Figure A-1) illustrates the process. This assessment process and the intervention selection tool is part of Interventions Selection and Design.

Implementing the Intervention Selection Process

Successful implementation of performance interventions depends on strong support, carefully appointed team members, good decision making, and determined change-management leadership during both the selection and implementation phases. There is an old tale about an operations manager who needed help with a performance problem and so he brought in a wide range of consultants. The accounting expert recommended an accounting intervention to solve the problem. The product engineering expert recommended product redesign. The process improvement specialist recommended a process change. The PT practitioner, who did not come in with a bias for any particular solution, proposed a structured process, using the HPT Model, for validating the problem, deter-mining the root cause, and identifying a range of potential solutions prior to making a selection decision (St. Clair, 2000). This performance intervention selection process structures, reinforces, and depends on collaboration and openness to new ideas.

Champion

The strong support of a champion is essential for the success of interventions. The champion should have a fairly high level of function, such as a senior executive. Steady, consistent backing of the project is essential.

FIGURE A-1: HPT Model: Intervention Selection and Design Phase

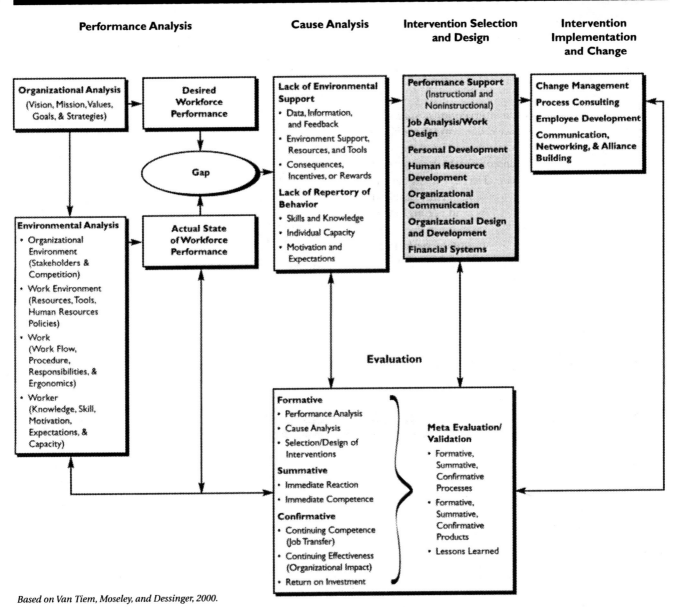

Based on Van Tiem, Moseley, and Dessinger, 2000.

If not, change efforts eventually fizzle and have minimal impact. The role of the champion is to:

- Set direction and establish authority and responsibility
- Lend credibility and clout
- Rally senior executives
- Alleviate concerns and resistance
- Maintain a high profile commitment to the change effort.
- Support the team through difficulties

Team

Interventions usually have a substantial impact on the affected organization. Therefore, it is essential to have broad acceptance and support for any improvement

activity. Creating a team to select potential interventions helps to ensure that there is a broad base of support. In addition, team members can provide different perspectives and ideas that can enrich the group's decisions.

The intervention selection process should be structured so that the ideas of every team member are valued and considered. It is equally important that the teams be cross-functional to ensure a diversity of experiences and ideas needed to harness the creative forces within the organization. Teams should include representatives from the departments involved in the problem. Some representatives should be enthusiastic and energetic supporters of change and some should be more reserved and tend to ask "tough questions." There should also be cross-departmental involvement from areas that provide or receive associated output and may be affected by the interventions.

Overview of Performance Intervention Selection Process

Selecting the most appropriate interventions for an organization is a complex process involving three phases. The essential goal of the selection process is to have strong employee and management consensus around the chosen interventions. People need to believe the selected interventions are likely to solve or alleviate the problems and improve organizational or individual performance.

The three phases and five major steps of the performance intervention selection process are mapped in Figure A-2.

Preliminary Phase: Performance and Cause Analysis

This phase sets the stage for selecting interventions. Intervention selection depends upon reliable performance (gap) and cause analyses. It is essential to have agreement on what the problems are and what causes the problems. If formal analyses already are completed, the intervention selection team needs to concur that the findings and recommendations are valid. Analysis data are a powerful resource for decision making. If no formal performance (gap) and cause analyses were conducted, the team needs to facilitate discussion and come to agreement about problems and causes before the intervention selection process. If there are multiple problems, it is necessary to rank the problems according to pre-selected criteria. (For example, which problem has the most impact on the bottom line? Which problem can be fixed in the shortest time/for the least expenditure of resources?) Usually the criteria can be developed from the results of the performance analysis, especially the organizational and environmental analyses.

Survey Phase

There are two parts to this phase. Both require creativity and a willingness to try new strategies.

Group
The group, with a team leader or PT practitioner, reads through the possible interventions listed on Job Aid A-1 and discusses possibilities.

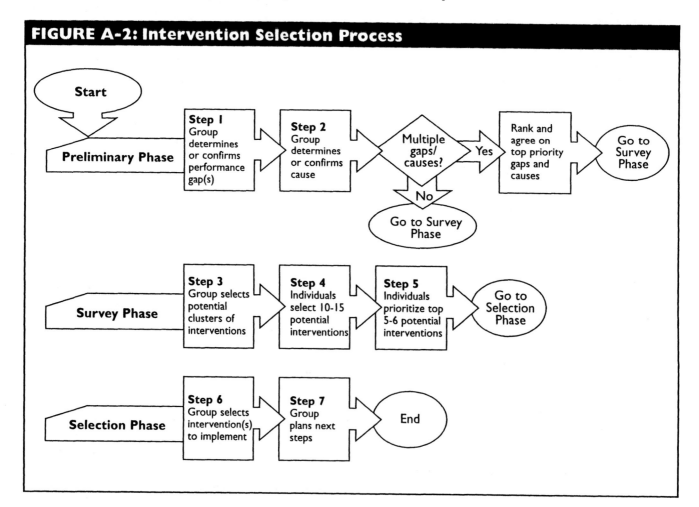

FIGURE A-2: Intervention Selection Process

Start

Preliminary Phase

Step 1 Group determines or confirms performance gap(s)

Step 2 Group determines or confirms cause

Multiple gaps/ causes? — Yes → Rank and agree on top priority gaps and causes → Go to Survey Phase

No → Go to Survey Phase

Survey Phase

Step 3 Group selects potential clusters of interventions

Step 4 Individuals select 10-15 potential interventions

Step 5 Individuals prioritize top 5-6 potential interventions

Go to Selection Phase

Selection Phase

Step 6 Group selects intervention(s) to implement

Step 7 Group plans next steps

End

Individual

Each team member reads the survey descriptors independently and reflects on a maximum of 10–15 possible remedies. Each team member relies on his or her own experience and judgment to select potential interventions and prioritize them according to pre-selected criteria.

Intervention Selection Phase

The final phase is team-based. The team uses brainstorming and multi-voting to select the intervention(s) that best resolves the performance problem. Then the team plans next steps (action planning) and sets a potential timetable.

Group acceptance and support is necessary in order to make changes in people, processes, or the organization. Group involvement assures that many ideas are included and that any decisions have collaboration and participation from diverse areas and levels of the organization. Diversity is critical for bringing all the potential issues to the discussion table before implementation. In addition, team decisions can serve as communication mechanisms so that the entire affected organization feels a sense of participation.

INTERVENTION SELECTION PROCESS PRELIMINARY PHASE: PERFORMANCE AND CAUSE ANALYSIS

Definition and Scope

The Intervention Selection Process helps manage and simplify the selection effort. Interventions need to be selected, planned, and implemented carefully. The purpose of the Preliminary Phase is to focus attention on the performance problem(s) and the cause(s), rather than symptoms, of the problem(s). Interventions based on symptoms may temporarily improve a situation but the underlying problem remains. In order to make headway and to be effective, it is necessary to select interventions that will alleviate or improve causes of poor performance and benefit both the worker and the organization.

Implementing the Preliminary Phase

During the preliminary phase, the team conducts performance and cause analyses or reviews and validates previous performance and cause analyses findings.

Note: In most cases, there is a great advantage to conducting a structured analysis of performance and causes prior to selecting interventions. *Fundamentals of Performance Technology: A Guide to Improving People, Process, and Performance* (Van Tiem, Moseley, and Dessinger, 2000) is a companion book that provides information about performance and cause analysis.

Step 1: Conduct and/or Validate Performance (Gap) Analysis

Step 2: Conduct and/or Validate Cause Analysis

It is necessary to have a good grasp of the problem and its causes before beginning to think about solutions. You have been chosen to be a part of an intervention selection team. As a group, you need to agree on the problems and their causes. Usually, a PT practitioner, analyst, or consultant would facilitate the process of defining the problems and causes. In other cases, quality teams or performance improvement teams identify and define the problems. Then, using quality or group-process tools the teams determine the causes of the problems.

If your organization or team has completed formal performance and causes analyses, the team needs to understand the analysis findings and prioritize the recommendations. If a formal analysis did not occur, the team needs to facilitate a discussion of performance problems and causes in order to identify and gain consensus about the problem.

Performance (gap) analysis and cause analysis are phases of the HPT Model (see Figure A-3). They are important first steps. Without a clear consensus on the problem and its cause, it is difficult to agree on solutions or their imple-mentation. It is too easy to put energy into efforts that miss the mark. These failed attempts cause discouragement in the work force and lead to loss of credibility and trust for senior management and the improvement team.

FIGURE A-3: HPT Model: Performance and Cause Analysis Phases

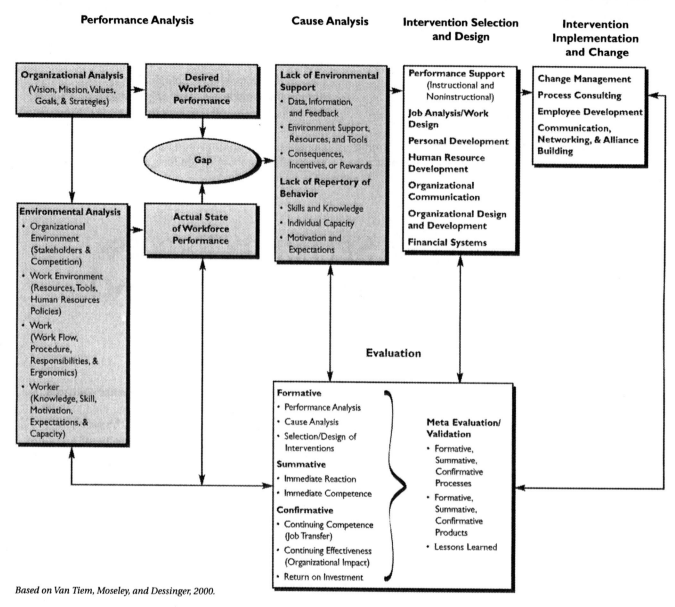

Based on Van Tiem, Moseley, and Dessinger, 2000.

During these phases it is essential to pay attention to causes, rather than symptoms, of performance problems. Interventions based on symptoms may temporarily improve a situation but the underlying problem remains. In order to make headway and to be effective, it is necessary to focus attention on the most important causes and select interventions that will alleviate or improve causes to benefit workplace performance.

To illustrate the relationship between performance, cause, and intervention selection, consider the situation of employees who are reluctant to use new customized software (see Table A-1). The software was designed to make their jobs easier and to improve accuracy. There is plenty of work, so there is no fear of job loss to technology

and automation. Even after training, employees still prefer the old system.

In other words, one single performance problem (software resistance) can have three main causes ("glitches," learning time, and forgetting steps) and at least six possible interventions as solutions (continuous improvement, suggestions systems, feedback, rewards, job aid, and coaching). Usually organizations will choose several interventions to resolve the many aspects of the problem. The interventions are carefully "blended" or integrated so that the plan fits each solution together. Not all interventions need to begin at the same time; the "blended" solutions can be phased in. Intervention selection means matching potential solutions with causes and prioritizing to determine where to start (see Job Aid A-1).

TABLE A-1: HPT Model Applied to Common Workplace Problem	
Performance Gap	Although employees attended training, they are resisting using new software, preferring the previous (legacy) systems.
Causes	1) There are a few software *"glitches"* and employees do not know how to overcome them 2) New software system *takes longer* to use at first and managers push for speed. 3) Employees *can't remember* all the steps and using the documentation is awkward on their desks.
Potential Interventions (clustered related to three causes)	1) *Continuous Improvement*—to remove "glitches" *Suggestion Systems*—to communicate problem "glitches" 2) *Feedback*—Managers stress the importance of using new software, such as for generating reports *Reward*—Token of appreciation for efforts to use new software 3) *Job Aid*—Small spiral notebook containing key steps only *Coach*—readily available resource person to help employees with initial usage

JOB AID A-1: Performance Problems (Gap) and Causes

Formal Analysis: If a formal analysis was conducted, in the space below paraphrase the problems and causes that were identified. Writing about the problems in your own words will give you a chance to validate the problem in your own mind. Be sure to discuss any concerns with the intervention selection team.

No Formal Analysis: If no formal analysis was conducted, use the space below to record what you believe is currently wrong in the organization. Use data, if possible, to describe the problems and causes related to this performance improvement effort. Your intervention selection team will meet to discuss each team member's opinions about problems and causes and come to consensus on the performance problem and causes.

Performance Problems (Gap)

Example: Although employees attended training, they are resisting using new software, preferring the previous (legacy) systems.

Probable Causes

Example: There are a few software "glitches" and employees do not know how to overcome them.

INTERVENTION SELECTION PROCESS: SURVEY PHASE

Definition and Scope

The intervention selection process began by rethinking the performance problems and causes. Now it is time to identify a maximum of 10–15 possible interventions and rank or prioritize these interventions.

The interventions are divided into clusters based on the chapters of this book. The categories are part of the HPT Model: Intervention Selection and Design Phase, described briefly in Chapter 2. A more complete performance gap and cause analysis description can be found in the companion book, *Fundamentals of Performance Technology*. The intervention categories are:
• Performance Support (Instructional and Non-Instructional)
• Job Analysis/Work Design
• Personal Development
• Human Resource Development
• Organizational Communication
• Organizational Design and Development
• Financial Systems

Implementing the Survey Phase

The survey phase should be completed as a facilitated group activity or privately on a individual basis. In either case, there should not be any external influence on the process.

Step 3: Identify Possible Interventions (Part of Survey)

Group Process
With your PT practitioner or team leader, your team may be able to chose the most likely categories (such as financial systems or personal development) to focus on by using Job Aid A-2. When in doubt, it is best not to eliminate any potential categories as an opportunity for performance improvement. Thinking creatively at this point may provide the greatest opportunity for successful results.

After the possible categories are selected, make sure that everyone on the team understands the meaning of each intervention in the category. Some interventions are familiar and others are less common. Definitions for each intervention are in the glossary and there is further information in the book chapters. The next step is to rank the organization's *degree of implementation of the intervention* using the ranking scale.

Individual Process
Each participant reads the assessment items for the selected categories based on Job Aid A-2 and uses the Intervention Selection Survey to select 10–15 potential interventions within the categories. Finally, participants rank and prioritize the interventions (see Job Aid A-3). The outcome of the individual activity is a prioritized list of approximately six interventions that the group can work with during Step 3.

Performance Intervention Survey

The purpose of this tool is to help groups or individuals select possible interventions that meet the needs of their organization and improve performance.

Best Practice
Each intervention in the survey is described by a best-practice statement. *The best-practice statements are by no means the entirety of possible best practices.* However, the statement represents common practice.

Read each best practice statement as a description of your organization. Caution: Although the statement represents good practice, it *does not represent the only possible good practice.*

Best Practice Implementation
Below each best practice statement are qualifying descriptions ranging from less than desirable to desirable implementation of the best practice. The qualifiers represent a continuum of examples of good and poor practices. Again, they are by no means the only examples of desirable and undesirable implementation.

Do your best to rate your organization based on your personal opinions and judgment. Decide which implementation description best characterizes or represents your organization. Circle the appropriate rating number.

JOB AID A-2: Intervention Selector

Directions: Based on the cause analysis and performance (gap) analysis, select approximately 10-15 interventions that might improve the situation. Place a check next to each intervention to be considered. Complete the rest of the intervention selection process to prioritize and plan the implementation.

Performance Support Systems
Instructional Performance Support Systems
- ☐ Knowledge Management
- ☐ Learning Organization
- ☐ Corporate Universities
- ☐ Action Learning
- ☐ Education and Training
- ☐ Self-Directed Learning
- ☐ Technical and Non-Technical Training
- ☐ Just-in-Time Training
- ☐ On-the-Job Training
- ☐ Interactive Learning Technologies
- ☐ Enterprise Training
- ☐ Classroom Learning
- ☐ Distance/Distributed Learning
- ☐ Computer-Based Learning
- ☐ Online/e-learning
- ☐ Games and Simulations

Non-Instructional Performance Support Systems
- ☐ Job Aids
- ☐ Electronic Performance Support Systems (EPSS)
- ☐ Documentation and Standards

Job Analysis/Work Design
Job Analysis
- ☐ Job Descriptions
- ☐ Job Specifications

Work Design
- ☐ Job Design
- ☐ Job Enlargement
- ☐ Job Rotation
- ☐ Job Enrichment

Human Factors
- ☐ Ergonomics
- ☐ Safety Engineering
- ☐ Preventive Maintenance (PM)

Quality Improvement
- ☐ Total Quality Management (TQM)
- ☐ Continuous Improvement
- ☐ Value Analysis/Value Engineering (VA/VE)

Personal Development
- ☐ Feedback
- ☐ Coaching
- ☐ Mentoring
- ☐ Emotional Intelligence
- ☐ Career Development

Human Resource Development
Human Resource Management (HRM)
- ☐ Staffing
- ☐ Compensation

- ☐ Retirement Planning
- ☐ Health and Wellness
- ☐ Employee Development

Individual Growth
- ☐ Motivation (Incentives and Rewards)
- ☐ Performance Appraisals
- ☐ Competency Testing
- ☐ Assessment Centers
- ☐ Literacy

Organizational Growth
- ☐ Succession Planning
- ☐ Career Pathing
- ☐ Leadership Development
- ☐ Executive Development
- ☐ Management Development
- ☐ Supervisory Development

Organizational Communication
- ☐ Communication Networks
- ☐ Information Systems
- ☐ Suggestion Systems
- ☐ Grievance Systems
- ☐ Conflict Resolution

Organizational Design and Development
Empowerment
- ☐ Team Strategies
- ☐ Problem Solving
- ☐ Decision Making

Organizational Pro-Action
- ☐ Strategic Planning
- ☐ Operations Management
- ☐ Environmental Scanning
- ☐ Benchmarking
- ☐ Reengineering, Realigning, Restructuring

Organizational Values
- ☐ Culture
- ☐ Diversity
- ☐ Globalization
- ☐ Ethics
- ☐ Spirituality in the Workplace

Financial Systems
- ☐ Open Book Management
- ☐ Profit Versus Cost Center
- ☐ Financial Forecasting
- ☐ Capital Investment and Spending
- ☐ Cash Flow Analysis/Cash Flow Forecast
- ☐ Mergers, Acquisitions, and Joint Ventures

Other Interventions
- ☐

Think about your experiences and observations in the workplace. On the survey, place a star next to the boxes of approximately five or six interventions of the 10–15 interventions that you believe would be most helpful in alleviating the workplace problems and causes.

At the end of this survey, you will find directions for listing the five or six interventions and the associated description rating numbers into a priority table (see Job Aid A-3).

After the priority table is complete, you will be ready to participate in the group intervention selection session.

Your PT practitioner or team leader may request that you email your prioritized list before the team meeting. This would enable the PT practitioner or team leader to compile the rankings and the priorities.

JOB AID A-3: Intervention Priority Chart (Individual)

Directions: After reflection, select six interventions that you believe to be most critical to the organization and use this to rank each intervention from 6 (highest priority) to 1 (lowest priority). If you select fewer than six interventions, you should still begin with 6 and leave the lower numbers blank.

After you have prioritized intervention description rankings, add personal comments to assist you with the group phase of the selection process. Begin with your highest priority intervention on the first line. In the left column, write your description ranking from the survey form.

Priority (6-1)	Intervention and Personal Comments	Description Ranking
Example: 6	Coach—readily available resource person to help employees with initial usage	2
6		
5		
4		
3		
2		
1		

ISPI © 2001. Permission granted for unlimited duplication for noncommercial use.

INTERVENTION SELECTION PROCESS

Definition and Scope

Selecting successful performance interventions requires group involvement. The survey phase was primarily an individual effort; it is now necessary to come together as a group to make a final intervention(s) selection and determine next steps.

Implementing the Intervention Selection Phase

During Step 4 team members may brainstorm and discuss their own opinions and judgments about prioritizing the possible interventions selected in the survey phase. The group will gradually combine ideas and prioritize possibilities in order to identify the final solutions to implement. Multi-voting is effective for capturing the ideas of all participants.

The final part of the intervention selection process is to scope out action plans and reasonable timelines for implementation and change management (Step 5). Exact plans and timelines will be refined later during actual implementation planning. Substantial planning is important because interventions should be scoped out and managed the same as projects.

Step 4: Selecting the Intervention(s) to Implement

Several facilitated group processes are useful for making the final determination regarding which intervention(s) to implement: consensus building, brainstorming, and multi-voting.

Reconfirm Problems and Causes

Step 4 begins by reconfirming the problems and the causes. Many significant insights into the organization are gathered during the individual intervention survey phase that could change or otherwise impact the initial analyses. It is essential for all team members to reconfirm the problem and the causes. Consensus building techniques are useful here.

The PT practitioner or team leader will establish a context to support the team in making sound decisions. The group needs to think about the organizational culture and history of related change efforts. Interventions need to fit into the mission and goals of the organization and be planned in context with other initiatives.

Brainstorm

Following the discussion about the performance problem and causes, the final phase of intervention selection begins. The PT practitioner or team leader will facilitate a group discussion of the individual priority lists gathered during the survey phase. Using brainstorming techniques, each team member discusses his or her highest priority (sixth priority) intervention using a "round robin" format. Record all team ideas.

After the first round, each team member discusses his or her own intervention selection in the fifth position. This continues from the fourth position to the lowest. Although there may be substantial redundancy in the interventions discussed, each team member has a unique reason for making the selection. Therefore, each intervention needs to be discussed relative to the reason why each person selected it.

Multi-Voting

Each intervention selection team member should review his or her personal priorities based on the team discus-

sion. Your PT practitioner or team leader will establish the multi-voting process. For example, 3M Post-IT™ Notes or dots could be used so that the votes can be tallied quickly. In other words, each identified intervention should have the associated "stickies" or dots placed next to it. The "stickies" or dots become votes to tally.

At this point, it may be possible to see clear agreements. These should be confirmed through group decisions. If there are not clear indications, the team should discuss the voting results. A second voting may be needed to narrow down the top selections. This second vote should result in clear priorities so that action planning can begin.

Step 5: Action Planning With Potential Timeframes

It is not sufficient to simply select interventions. The team needs to describe what it had in mind. Using Job Aid A-4, the team also needs to provide ideas, steps, and examples for how to actually implement the interventions. This is not the time for complex and detailed planning. It is simply a method for capturing the team's discussions and the reasoning behind the decisions sufficiently so that people assigned to implementation will know the basis for the priorities.

In addition, the intervention selection team may create potential timetables that can be used by senior executives for endorsement and sanction. They can also be used to communicate intervention decisions to all employees so that everyone feels part of any change process.

Additional Resources

Michalski, W.J., with King, D.G. (1997). Tool navigator: The master guide for teams. Portland, OR: Productivity Press.
Martin, P. and Tate, K. (1997). Project management memory jogger. Salem, NH: Goal/QPC.
Team memory jogger. (1995). Salem, NH: Goal/QPC-Oriel Publication.
Bens, I. (1999). Facilitation at a glance. Salem, NH: Goal/QPC.
Problem solving memory jogger. (2000). Salem, NH: Goal/QPC.

References

St. Clair, B. (2000). Informal email notes on intervention selection. Louisville, KY: St. Clair and Associates, Inc.
Van Tiem, D.M., Moseley, J.L., and Dessinger, J.C. (2000). Fundamentals of performance technology: A guide to improving people, process, and performance. Silver Spring, MD: International Society for Performance Improvement.

JOB AID A-4: Intervention Action Planner

Intervention Title:	Project Sponsor:
PT Practitioner or Team Leader:	Preparer:

Intervention Purpose and Objectives:

Project Customers (Direct and Indirect):

Customer Expectations and Deliverables:

Possible Timetable and Anticipated Constraints:

Reviews and Approvals Required:

Estimated Budget Requirements:

INTERVENTION SELECTION SURVEY

Performance Support Systems (PSS)

Forward-thinking organizations integrate learning and doing with technology into PSS that help workers obtain the knowledge or skill they need to initiate new performance or improve existing performance. They support the performer on the job and just in time and may replace or enhance training.

Instructional Performance Support Systems (PSS)

Instructional PSS help workers initiate new performance or change their actual performance until that performance is equal to or better than desired performance. The PT practitioner may select or design an instructional PSS intervention when a gap exists between the current knowledge, skill, or attitude of a worker or group of workers and the job specifications. PSS integrate learning and doing with technology.

☐ Knowledge Management (KM)

Organization systematically identifies, captures, codifies, stores, transforms, disseminates, and shares knowledge and encourages people to use their collective knowledge and experience to foster business innovation (creativity) and competitive advantage.

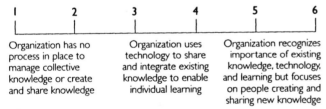

☐ Learning Organization

The entire organization values and supports continuous improvement and lifelong learning. Learning is aligned with business goals and is considered a competitive strategy and a broad, long-term intervention to achieve continuous improvement.

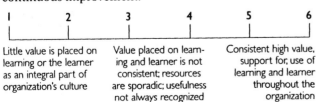

☐ Action Learning

The organization uses small groups to solve real, relevant, and challenging organizational problems and encourages learning by doing. Members of the group share, question, experience, reflect, make decisions, and take action on a single project basis or as an open group.

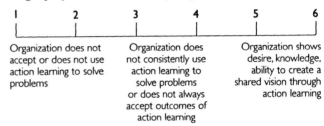

☐ Education and Training

The organization uses education and training to enhance and enable employee learning and development. The use of interactive learning technologies involves the learner and supports just-in-time and just-for-me learning. Emphasis on education and training helps organizations achieve goals of employee retention and competitive advantage.

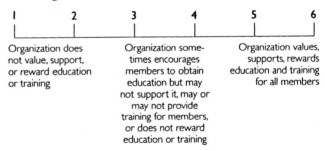

☐ Interactive Learning Technologies

Interactive learning technologies are used by the organization to encourage and support the active involvement of the learner with the content, the instructor, the technology, other learners, and the learning resources.

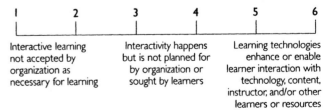

☐ Games and Simulations

The organizational culture supports experiential learning techniques to enhance problem solving and bring near reality into interactive learning.

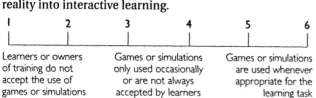

| | | | | | |
|1|2|3|4|5|6|

Learners or owners of training do not accept the use of games or simulations

Games or simulations only used occasionally or are not always accepted by learners or owners of training

Games or simulations are used whenever appropriate for the learning task

Non-Instructional Performance Support Systems (Non-Instructional PSS)

Non-instructional PSS integrate doing with technology, but may inherently or consciously include elements of learning and instruction. Non-instructional PSS use a variety of technologies—paper-, computer-, and video-based, to provide workers with just-in-time, just-enough information to perform a task.

☐ Job Aids

The organization uses performance support tools to provide just-in-time, on-the-job, and just-enough information, enabling a worker to perform a task efficiently and successfully without special training or reliance on memory.

| | | | | | |
|1|2|3|4|5|6|

Job aids are not used due to lack of knowledge or expertise

Job aids are infrequently used despite indications they would be useful

Job aids are accepted as an alternative to training, based on task and user analysis

☐ Electronic Performance Support Systems (EPSS)

Electronic (computer-mediated) technology is used to empower learners, enhance organizational learning, and enable knowledge management. Like a job aid, EPSS supports the concepts of just-in-time, on-the-job, just-enough, and just-for-me information.

| | | | | | |
|1|2|3|4|5|6|

Organization does not have resources, expertise, or desire to develop EPSS

EPSS resources and expertise available but not used due to lack of acceptance

EPSS are accepted and used; technology and expertise exist; task and user analysis drives decisions

☐ Documentation and Standards

Workers are informed of job expectations through well-designed documents. Outputs, outcomes, and performance are measured using clear, concise standards.

| | | | | | |
|1|2|3|4|5|6|

Organization does not see value of documentation or standards

Organization use of documentation is not systematic; not consistent in developing and following standards

Organization has a systematic process for developing user-friendly, accessible documentation; uses standards to guide and measure performance, outputs, outcomes

Job Analysis/Work Design

Job analysis is collecting information about duties, tasks, and responsibilities for specific jobs. Work design is a blueprint of job tasks structured to improve organizational efficiency and employee satisfaction.

Job Analysis

☐ Job Descriptions

The work of the job positions is so well portrayed that the duties are clear. The new employee understands the job if he or she reads the job description.

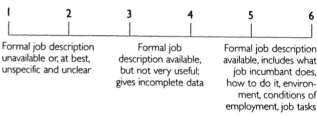

| | | | | | |
|1|2|3|4|5|6|

Formal job description unavailable or, at best, unspecific and unclear

Formal job description available, but not very useful; gives incomplete data

Formal job description available, includes what job incumbent does, how to do it, environment, conditions of employment, job tasks

☐ Job Specifications

Job descriptions are extended to include human traits and experiences required to perform the job as well as the kind of person to recruit.

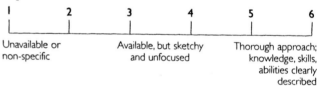

| | | | | | |
|1|2|3|4|5|6|

Unavailable or non-specific

Available, but sketchy and unfocused

Thorough approach; knowledge, skills, abilities clearly described

Work Design

☐ Job Enlargement

Organization encourages enlargement to offset high specialization, tedium and boredom associated with narrow job scope.

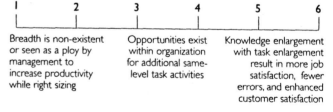

| | | | | | |
|1|2|3|4|5|6|

Breadth is non-existent or seen as a ploy by management to increase productivity while right sizing

Opportunities exist within organization for additional same-level task activities

Knowledge enlargement with task enlargement result in more job satisfaction, fewer errors, and enhanced customer satisfaction

☐ Job Rotation

As a lateral transfer process, this intervention exposes employees to a kaleidoscopic view of organizational life.

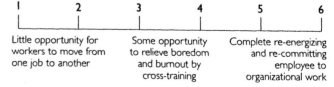

| | | | | | |
|1|2|3|4|5|6|

Little opportunity for workers to move from one job to another

Some opportunity to relieve boredom and burnout by cross-training

Complete re-energizing and re-committing employee to organizational work

☐ Job Enrichment

Organization increases job depth and empowers employees to be independent thinkers and responsible workers.

Little opportunity for redesigning jobs	Some opportunity for job redesign by adding tasks and responsibilities	Great opportunities for workers to experience feelings of responsibility, achievement, and growth

Human Factors

☐ Ergonomics

The organization fashions an appropriate fit between the machine and the work environment.

Little attention paid to creating ergonomically sound workplaces	Some attention paid to ergonomic issues in work practices and workstation design	Organization supports and encourages an appropriate balance between physical ergonomics and cognitive ergonomics

☐ Safety Engineering

Organization establishes systematic processes to make the work environment safer and healthier for employees.

Physical and psychological aspects of safety downplayed or ignored	Physical context and psychological context for promoting safety done sporadically	Organizations make concerted efforts to address safe and healthy work environments for employees; commitment to workers primary

☐ Preventive Maintenance (PM)

Organization establishes proactive processes for all systems and sub-systems before major problems occur.

No formal preventive maintenance program in place; organization operates in reactive mode	Limited proactive processes in motion; collaborative relationships among personnel diffused	Proactive approaches to preventive maintenance address zero failure, zero trouble, zero waste; benefits justify costs

Quality Improvement

☐ Total Quality Management (TQM)

Organization-wide policies and practices support a strategic management perspective of product, service, and customer quality.

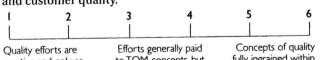

Quality efforts are reactive and only as much as absolutely necessary	Efforts generally paid to TQM concepts, but organization fails to involve all employees in process	Concepts of quality fully ingrained within organizational fabric; frequent use of TQM tools to solve problems

☐ Continuous Improvement

Organization establishes strategies for improvement to learn what customers want so their needs can be better served; it has long-range focus and is both internal and external.

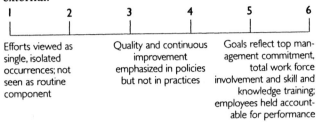

Efforts viewed as single, isolated occurrences; not seen as routine component	Quality and continuous improvement emphasized in policies but not in practices	Goals reflect top management commitment, total work force involvement and skill and knowledge training; employees held accountable for performance

☐ Value Engineering/Value Analysis

Organization develops systematic procedures and practices to analyze products by improving value and/or cutting costs. It is a proactive approach to meeting challenges of a global market.

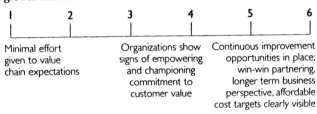

Minimal effort given to value chain expectations	Organizations show signs of empowering and championing commitment to customer value	Continuous improvement opportunities in place; win-win partnering, longer term business perspective, affordable cost targets clearly visible

Personal Development

Personal development interventions are planned work-related activities that are the employee's personal responsibility. Each individual assumes ownership of their success or failure. Personal development requires and enables individuals to take control of their own job situation. The organization provides the structure and processes so that employees can make accurate, positive decisions and improve their own performance.

☐ Feedback

Managers and co-workers freely provide suggestions and advice. Structured feedback, such as 360° feedback, is viewed as non-threatening and helpful.

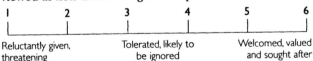

Reluctantly given, threatening	Tolerated, likely to be ignored	Welcomed, valued and sought after

☐ Coaching

Managers assist employees to improve performance by analyzing problems, offering suggestions, discussing errors and mistakes, and recommending organizational resources (such as training) to overcome problems.

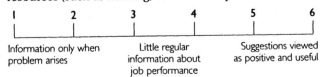

Information only when problem arises	Little regular information about job performance	Suggestions viewed as positive and useful

☐ Mentoring

Experienced employees help new hires or people with new job assignment to quickly adapt to new job requirements. Following the wise counsel of mentors leads to job advancement or better projects and assignments.

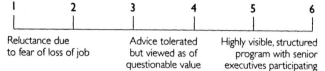

Reluctance due to fear of loss of job	Advice tolerated but viewed as of questionable value	Highly visible, structured program with senior executives participating	

☐ Emotional Intelligence

Self-management skills of self-awareness, self-regulation, motivation, empathy, and social adeptness are encouraged and modeled.

Autocratic, manipulative harsh work environment	Employee's well-being taken for granted	Open, caring culture self-confident managment, service orientation

☐ Career Development

Career opportunities are realistic, promotions from within are common, and preparation for job advancement is supported.

Most hiring is from outside	Job posting is policy, job transfers common	Future needs forecasted, developmental opportunities with resources available

Human Resource Development

Human resource (HR) development interventions are essential to human resource management and are shaped by the organization's mission and its ability to maintain market share.

Human Resource Management (HRM)

☐ Staffing

Organizations and individuals benefit from a carefully conceived staffing process that manages human capital.

Staffing process seen as complete once applicants are hired or promoted	Some attention paid to helping new employees achieve familiarity with policies, procedures, and endeavors	Total orientation of new employees to the organization and unit; efforts seen as ways to retain and maximize human resources

☐ Compensation

Compensation policies and practices reward employees with salary benefits for the job they perform within the organization.

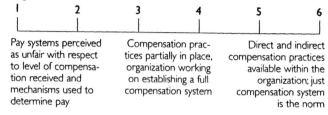

Pay systems perceived as unfair with respect to level of compensation received and mechanisms used to determine pay	Compensation practices partially in place, organization working on establishing a full compensation system	Direct and indirect compensation practices available within the organization; just compensation system is the norm

☐ Retirement Planning

Organization assists employees exit from the labor force. Planning process may be bittersweet.

Very little effort devoted to retirement preparation	Traditional retirement practices influence ongoing retirement planning	New prosperity values influence retirement planning

☐ Health and Wellness

Organization sponsors initiatives that focus on health promotion, health protection, and health prevention.

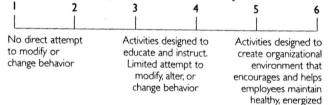

No direct attempt to modify or change behavior	Activities designed to educate and instruct. Limited attempt to modify, alter, or change behavior	Activities designed to create organizational environment that encourages and helps employees maintain healthy, energized lifestyles

☐ Employee Development

Both the organization and the individual play pivotal roles in the employee development process from the time the candidate accepts the offer through the employee's entire tenure.

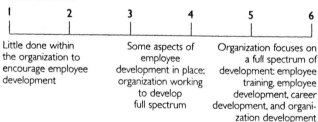

Little done within the organization to encourage employee development	Some aspects of employee development in place; organization working to develop full spectrum	Organization focuses on a full spectrum of development: employee training, employee development, career development, and organization development

Individual Growth

☐ Motivation Systems (Incentives and Rewards)

Employees are enthusiastic and energized to work effectively; organization demonstrates appreciation through rewards and incentives.

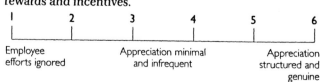

Employee efforts ignored	Appreciation minimal and infrequent	Appreciation structured and genuine

☐ Performance Appraisals

Performance appraisals are viewed as constructive, containing honest representation of employee efforts and helpful recommendations for improvement.

1	2	3	4	5	6

Create fear and resentment

Annual event to beendured but not beneficial

Healthy dialogue establishing workable objectives and plan consistent application

☐ Competency Testing and Assessment Centers

Competency testing determines appropriate skill levels and job readiness. Assessment centers identify good candidates for future job assignments.

1	2	3	4	5	6

Testing used for discipline or work force reduction

Testing not related to actual jobs

Testing identifies best candidates

☐ Literacy

Workplace basics include fundamentals (reading, writing, computation, and computers), knowing how to learn, communication, adaptability, personal management development, group effectiveness, and influencing others.

1	2	3	4	5	6

No developmental opportunities

On-the-Job Training (OJT) and tuition assistance

Development enhanced through coaching, mentoring, training, and special assignments

Organizational Growth

☐ Succession Planning

Systematic processes are used to identify employees for senior management positions.

1	2	3	4	5	6

No formal process in place for preparing high-level personnel

Planning is sporadic with minimum implementation

Experiential assignments, mentoring, training, and personnel development prepare people for high-level assignments

☐ Career Pathing

Organization effectively develops employees through a series of jobs and related assignments.

1	2	3	4	5	6

Systematic planning does not include development of people

Opportunities may be available but no systematic approach exists

Vertical and horizontal lines of opportunity in place

☐ Leadership Development

Organization provides opportunities for individuals to manage human capital by creating vision and aligning people.

1	2	3	4	5	6

Organization does little to encourage and develop specific leadership development

Opportunities exist for individuals to influence followers who think differently, feel passionately, and act responsibly

Formal leadership programs and training opportunities firmly in place; leadership development moves from an event into a process that lasts an entire career

☐ Executive Development

Opportunities for high-level strategic development prepare people for value-driven visionary implementation.

1	2	3	4	5	6

Executive development neither linked to vision, values, and strategies nor to organization's core capabilities

Some attention given to executive development but training in real-time interaction with real-life business issues and trends ignored

Prepares leaders to make wise decisions; the primary level that triggers an organization's vision, values, strategies, and business needs

☐ Management Development

A variety of formal and on-the-job training opportunities that are organization-specific are linked to the organization's mission, vision, goals, and structure for accomplishing business needs.

1	2	3	4	5	6

Little attention paid to interpersonal, technical, administrative, conceptual, and decision making skills

Some attention paid to organization's changing needs; individual reluctant to take control of personal management development

Wide range of management development activities exist incorporating corporate inventories, university-based programs, professional organizations, and in-house programs

☐ Supervisory Development

Experienced personnel interface between management and employees in a continuously evolving role based on sensitivity and empathy.

1	2	3	4	5	6

No formal program exists; decisions autocratic and manipulative

Reality-oriented practice and concrete examples used sporadically

Critical competencies which are conceptual, interpersonal, technical, and political in nature are identified; supervisor seen as trainer, adviser, mentor, facilitator

Organizational Communication

Organizational or business communication makes it possible to send and receive messages between different components within an organization, among separate organizations, and between organizations and society. Effective communication is essential for creating, maintaining, or improving the culture and performance of organizations.

☐ Communication Networks

Organization supports and encourages a communication system that allows messages to move from sender to receiver, informally and formally, enhancing job performance and job satisfaction.

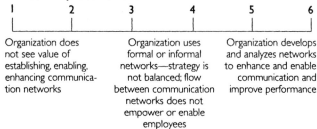

Organization does not see value of establishing, enabling, enhancing communication networks

Organization uses formal or informal networks—strategy is not balanced; flow between communication networks does not empower or enable employees

Organization develops and analyzes networks to enhance and enable communication and improve performance

☐ Information Systems

People, data, and technology work together to retrieve, process, store, and disseminate information, supporting informed decision making and sound organizational management.

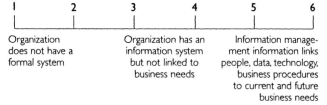

Organization does not have a formal system

Organization has an information system but not linked to business needs

Information management information links people, data, technology, business procedures to current and future business needs

☐ Suggestion Systems

Proactive organization relies on suggestions of employees to improve products, processes, and services.

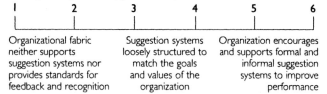

Organizational fabric neither supports suggestion systems nor provides standards for feedback and recognition

Suggestion systems loosely structured to match the goals and values of the organization

Organization encourages and supports formal and informal suggestion systems to improve performance

☐ Grievance Systems

Organizations set grievance systems in place to investigate complaints about wages, hours and conditions of employment, and/or work practices.

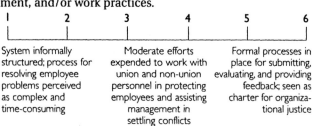

System informally structured; process for resolving employee problems perceived as complex and time-consuming

Moderate efforts expended to work with union and non-union personnel in protecting employees and assisting management in settling conflicts

Formal processes in place for submitting, evaluating, and providing feedback; seen as charter for organizational justice

☐ Conflict Resolution

Organizational culture allows individuals or groups to resolve differences of opinion amicably or through negotiation, mediation, or collaboration.

Organization fosters conflict among members (may be called *competition*)

Organization not consistent in resolving conflict or supporting collaboration

Organization develops and uses sound conflict resolution practices; encourages and rewards collaboration

Organizational Design and Development

Organizational design and development is a process that examines the operation and management of an organization and facilitates needed changes in an effort to improve efficiency and competitiveness.

Empowerment

☐ Teambuilding Strategies

Teams are empowered and supported throughout developmental stages by strong sanction and reliable sponsorship.

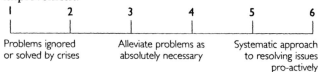

Teams have responsibility but inadequate authority

Teams assigned but outcomes ignored

Teams highly visible, efforts valued and rewarded

☐ Problem Solving

Systematic problem solving is a part of daily work life as evidenced by encouraging continuous performance improvement.

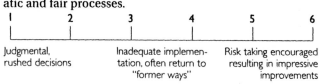

Problems ignored or solved by crises

Alleviate problems as absolutely necessary

Systematic approach to resolving issues pro-actively

☐ Decision Making

Decision making develops group support through systematic and fair processes.

Judgmental, rushed decisions

Inadequate implementation, often return to "former ways"

Risk taking encouraged resulting in impressive improvements

Organizational Pro-Action

☐ Strategic Planning

The organization's strategic plan provides direction, focus, and clear, well-accepted goals and targets.

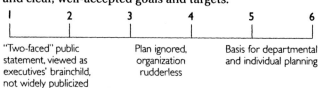

"Two-faced" public statement, viewed as executives' brainchild, not widely publicized

Plan ignored, organization rudderless

Basis for departmental and individual planning

☐ Operations Management

Based on realistic forecasts, operations management provides a safe and well-organized workplace with quality supplies and adequate tools.

1	2	3	4	5	6

Numbers driven, focused on "looking good" | Slip-shod, careless, not realistic | Processes linked into systems, pride in details and safety

☐ Environmental Scanning

Organization keenly aware of internal and external environmental threats and opportunities through on-going observations and data collection.

1	2	3	4	5	6

Ignores signs of change, doesn't use opinion polls and data | Too little, too late, "drags feet" acknowledging changing conditions | Continuous monitoring of employees, customers, competition, stakeholders, and markets

☐ Benchmarking

Organization systematically compares self to other organizations for purpose of learning better methods and determining best practices.

1	2	3	4	5	6

Committed to "our way of doing things" | Improvements make work easier for employees, but not to address opportunities | Keen awareness of competition and expectations of customers and stakeholders

☐ Reeingineering, Realigning, Restructuring

Radical workplace redesigns are used to increase efficiency, implement lessons learned, streamline processes, and create a foundation for positive organizational growth.

1	2	3	4	5	6

Hasty changes, reactionary | Changes not supported fully by executives | Strong champion, sufficient resources, patience, adequate time to succeed

Organizational Values

☐ Culture

Organizational culture is aligned with and generally supports the organization's mission, vision, and core values.

1	2	3	4	5	6

Not supportive | Generally supportive | Highly supportive

☐ Diversity

Organization respects and encourages unusual ideas, various points of view, and other differences, even if they are counter to senior management's views.

1	2	3	4	5	6

Discourages unusual ideas and differences | Tolerates unique ideas and differences | Encourages unique ideas and differences

☐ Globalization

Global strategies include appropriate implementation tools, such as multinational problem solving and collaboration.

1	2	3	4	5	6

Headquarter's "correctness" | Overseas "foreign" mentality | Collaborative partnership uniquely purposed

☐ Ethics

"Doing the right thing" is ingrained in the organizational culture.

1	2	3	4	5	6

Words and actions mismatch | Situation-by-situation approach | All levels adhere

☐ Spirituality in the Workplace

Community and societal responsibility and bringing out the best in each employee are valued and encouraged.

1	2	3	4	5	6

Isolated from community, competitive organizational values | Community involvement tolerated, but not encouraged | Highly visible encouragement

Financial Systems

Financial systems refer to the monetary affairs (income, reserves, expenses, and dividends) of an organization. They are usually summarized in an annual report that includes an income statement, balance sheet, cash flow statement, and explanatory notes.

☐ Open Book Management

Financial information is widely available to get employees to focus on helping the organization make money which increases productivity and long-term financial performance.

1	2	3	4	5	6

Organization neither open nor aligned; information restricted | Review, discussion, advice, and corrective position of financial information minimal | Complete sharing of financial information; employees make a difference

335

☐ Profit Versus Cost Center

The decision to create a profit or cost responsibility center is based on solid business practices.

1	2	3	4	5	6

Responsibility centers viewed as wasteful, ineffective, and non-productive

Solid business practices considered but not implemented with rigor

Centers perceived as lean, efficient, effective, flexible, and highly regarded

☐ Cash Flow Analysis

Systems are in place to anticipate various sources and uses of cash and to make accurate projections.

1	2	3	4	5	6

Negative corrective actions frequent and poorly planned

Positive and negative corrective actions selected but not optimized

Stability and long-term profitability viewed as positive indicators

☐ Financial Forecasting

Planning for the financial future of the organization includes traditional factors such as profits, interest, supply and demand, and non-traditional issues such as innovation, culture, new products and services, competitors, etc.

1	2	3	4	5	6

Limited to short-term financial measurables only

Medium range; some attention to demography, economics, marketing, social patterns

Prepares organizations for future trends, events outcomes, and customer satisfaction

☐ Mergers, Acquisitions, and Joint Ventures

Organizations are well-prepared to address short-term and long-term financial issues as well as organizational change efforts to effectively maintain competitive advantage.

1	2	3	4	5	6

Decisions made in haste, leading to financial and organizational problems

Financial aspects are successful but culture issues neglected

Up-front planning permits accommodating differences in culture, financials, products, services, and potentials for future growth

☐ Capital Investment and Spending

Prudent practices are used to identify opportunities and analyze alternatives for acquiring investments of permanent value.

1	2	3	4	5	6

Limited match with the strategic goals and objectives of the organization

Some attention to planning, assessing, deciding, evaluating to align with organizational goals

Processes maximize value and minimize risk

CITATIONS

Chapter 1: Systematic and Reproducible Solutions

Interventions as Solutions
1 Deterline and Rosenberg, 1992, p. 3
2 Stewart, Taylor, Petre, and Schlender, 1999
3 Deming, 1986
4 Stewart, Taylor, Petre, and Schlender, 1999
5 Stewart, Taylor, Petre, and Schlender, 1999
6 Gearson, 1999
7 Stewart, Taylor, Petre, and Schlender, 1999
8 Deterline and Rosenberg, 1992
9 Guralnik, 1980, p. 1460
10 Sanders and Ruggles, 2000, p. 32
11 Gilbert, 1978; Sanders and Ruggles, 2000, p. 32
12 Sanders and Ruggles, 2000, pp. 26–36
13 Van Tiem, Moseley, and Dessinger, 2000
14 Ulrich, 1997, pp. 23–48

HPT Model
1 Van Tiem, Moseley, and Dessinger, 2000, p. 2
2 Harkins, 1998, p. 74
3 Harkins, 1998, p. 75
4 Rosenberg, 1996, p. 6
5 Swanson, 1994, p. 151
6 Rossett, 1992, p. 105
7 Gordon, 1994, p. 34
8 Gilbert, 1978, p. 88
9 Van Tiem, Moseley, and Dessinger, 2000, p. 51
10 Donaldson and Scannell, 1986, p. 12
11 Spitzer, 1992, p. 121
12 Dormant, 2000, pp. 237–259
13 Van Tiem, Moseley, and Dessinger, 2000, p. 158
14 Chambers and Lacey, 1994, p. 167
15 Chambers and Lacey, 1994, p. 168
16 Chambers and Lacey, 1994, p. 177
17 Main, 2000, p. 459
18 Harkin, 1998, p. 75

Chapter 2: Performance Support Systems

Performance Support Systems (PSS)
1 Paul, 1999, p. 18
2 Paul, 1999, p. 18
3 Dublin, 1995, pp. 11–12
4 Villachica and Stone, 1999, pp. 443–444
5 Villachica and Stone, 1999, p. 444
6 Gerber, 1991, p. 23

Instructional PSS
1 Bruner, 1966, p. 1
2 Harless, 1993
3 Van Tiem, Moseley, and Dessinger, 2000, p. 67
4 Rothwell and Sanders, 1999

Knowledge Management
1 Barclay and Murray, 1997, pp. 1–2
2 Mcintosh, 2000, p. 1
3 Cowley-Durst, 1999, p. 23
4 Gordon, 1999, p. 32
5 Whiting, 1999, p. 2
6 Barclay and Murray, 1997, p. 1
7 *Stopwatches Ready?*, 2000, p. 5
8 Smith, 2000
9 Barclay and Murray, 1997, p. 5
10 Mcintosh, 2000, p. 1
11 Barclay and Murray, 1997, p. 3
12 Barclay and Murray, 1997, pp. 2–3
13 McElroy, 1999, pp. 86–88
14 Gordon, 1999, p. 33
15 Eight Things, 2000, p. 2
16 Fitter, 1999, p. 55
17 Whiting, 1999, p. 2
18 Charney, 1999, p. 96
19 Barclay and Murray, 1997, p. 13
20 Sveiby, 1999, p. 40
21 Gordon, pp. 33–34
22 Cowley-Durst, 1999, p. 23
23 Barclay and Murray, 1997, p. 1
24 Barth, 2000, p. 31
25 Fitter, 1999, p. 55
26 Shand, 1999, p. 32
27 Shand, 1999, p. 34

28 VanBuren, 1999, p. 72
29 VanBuren, 2000, p. 5
30 Cowley-Durst, 1999, p. 24
31 Rossett, 2000
32 Paul, 1999, p. 18
33 Fitter, 1999, p. 56
34 Paul, 1999, pp. 18–19
35 Paul, 1999, p. 22
36 Strassman, 1999, pp. 30–31
37 Barclay and Murray, 1997, p. 13
38 Barclay and Murray, 1997, p. 22
39 Barclay and Murray, 1997, p. 6
40 Barth, 2000, p. 31
41 Barclay and Murray, 1997, p. 28
42 Leon, 2000, p. 39
43 Leon, 2000, p. 41
44 Leon, 2000, p. 40
45 Barclay and Murray, 1997, pp. 28–29
46 Fitter, 1999, p. 60
47 Cohen and Becker, 1999, p. 46
48 Sveiby, 1999, p. 41
49 Shand, 1999, p. 39
50 Lee, Baek, and Schwen, 2000, p. 6

Learning Organization
1 Halprin, 1994, p. 3
2 McElroy, 1999, p. 88
3 Barclay and Murray, 1997, p. 2
4 Marsick and Watkins, 1995, p. 345
5 Greenwood, Wasson, and Giles, 1993, p. 7
6 Greenwood, Wasson, and Giles, 1993, p. 7
7 Halprin, 1994, p. 3
8 Zemke, 1999, p. 4
9 Greenwood, Wasson, and Giles, 1993, p. 8
10 Mumford, 1992, p. 143
11 Greenwood, Wasson, and Giles, 1993, p. 8
12 Mumford, 1992, p. 144
13 Kim, 1993, pp. 37–38
14 Peter Senge cited in Zemke, 1999, p. 46
15 Colins, 1999, p. 84
16 *The Corporate University Best-in-Class Report*, 1998, p. 6
17 Gordon, 1999, p. 3

[18] *The Corporate University Best-in-Class Report*, 1998, p. 6

[19] *The Corporate University Best-in-Class Report*, 1998, p. 6

[20] Kerker, 2000, p. 3

[21] Brandon Hall cited in Kerker, 2000, p. 1

[22] Peter Senge cited in Zemke, 1999, p. 49

[23] Peter Senge cited in Zemke, 1999, p. 41

[24] Peter Senge cited in Zemke, 1999, p. 42

[25] Halprin, 1994, p. 4

[26] Halprin, 1994, pp. 4–5

[27] Halprin, 1994, p. 5

[28] Gordon, 1999, p. 30

[29] Van Tiem, Moseley, and Dessinger, 2000, pp. 24–25

[30] Swanson, 1994, pp. 188–233

Action Learning

[1] Bierema, 1998, p. 93

[2] Peter Senge cited in Zemke, 1999, pp. 40; 46

[3] Marquardt, 1999b, p. 3

[4] Bierema, 1998, p. 87

[5] Marquardt, 1999b, pp. xii; 20

[6] Barker, 1998, pp. 9–22

[7] Revans, 1998, pp. 23–27

[8] Thiagi in Salopek and Kesting, 1999, p. 32

[9] Marquardt, 1999b, pp. 42–53

[10] Marquardt, 1999a, p. 2

[11] Marquardt, 1999a, p. 3

[12] Bierema, 1998, p. 87

[13] Marquardt, 1999b, pp. 44–46

[14] Marquardt, 1999a, p. 4

[15] Thiagi cited in Salopek and Kesting, 1999, pp. 32–33

[16] Bierema, 1998, p. 87

[17] Marquardt, 1999b, p. 44

[18] Glaser, 2000, p. 167

[19] Glaser, 2000, p. 172

[20] Silverman and Ernst, 1999, p. 259

[21] Silverman and Ernst, 1999, p. 259

[22] Marquardt, 1999b, p. xiii

[23] Bierema, 1998, pp. 88–92

[24] Dixon, 1998, p. 58

[25] Lanahan and Maldonado, 1998, p. 85

[26] Dilworth, 1998, p. 30

[27] Marquardt, 1999b, p. 4

[28] Marquardt, 1999b, p. 11

[29] Dilworth, 1998, pp. 35–37

[30] Dilworth, 1998, pp. 28; 42

[31] Yorks, O'Neil, Marsick, Lamm, Kaladny, and Nilson, 1998, p. 59

[32] Dilworth, 1998, pp. 38; 42–43

[33] Marquardt, 1998, p. 126

[34] Marquardt, 1998, pp. 118–127

[35] Yiu and Saner, 1998, p. 145

[36] Bierema, 1998, p. 87

[37] Dilworth, 1998, pp. 39

[38] Van Tiem, Moseley, and Dessinger, 2000, pp. 156–187

Education and Training

[1] Kerker, 2000, p. 2

[2] Jewell and Jewell, 1992, p. 211

[3] Jewell and Jewell, 1992, p. 211

[4] Jewell and Jewell, 1992, p. 226

[5] Brookfield, 1994, p. 25

[6] Caudron, 1999, pp. 28–29

[7] Ford, 1999, p. 2

[8] Caudron, 1999, p. 27

[9] Caudron, 1999, p. 28

[10] Caudron, 1999, p. 30

[11] VanBuren and King, 2000, p. 12

[12] *Webster's New Universal Unabridged Dictionary*, 1983, p. 576

[13] Banathy, 1991, p. 31

[14] Houle, 1996, p. 256

[15] Caffarella, 1994, p. 2

[16] Caffarella, 1994, p. 2

[17] Jewell and Jewell, 1992, p. 226

[18] Langdon, 1999, pp. 382–383

[19] Pepitone, 1995, p. 13

[20] VanBuren and King, 2000, pp. 9–10

[21] Kerker, 2000, p. 2

[22] Kerker, 2000, p. 5

[23] Dobbs, 1999, pp. 51–52

[24] Brady, 1999, p. 1

[25] *Industry Report*, 1999, p. 1

[26] Gayeski, 1999, p. 7

[27] Rothwell, 1996, p. 249

[28] Rothwell, 1996, p. 250

[29] Rothwell, 1996, p. 249

[30] Gordon, 1999, p. 35

[31] Stamps, 1999, p. 45

[32] Gordon, 1999, p. 36

[33] Pepitone, 1995, p. 13

[34] Barron, 1999a, p. 2

[35] Waugh, 1999, p. 3

[36] Waugh, 1999, p. 3

[37] Clark, 1994, p. 89

[38] Clark, 1994, pp. 90–91

[39] Clark, 1994, p. 121

[40] Clark, 1994, p. 42

[41] Clark, 1994, p. 148

[42] Clark, 1994, pp. 124–125

[43] Johnson, 1991, p. 9

[44] Waugh, 1999, p. 3

[45] Waugh, 1999, p. 3

[46] Winer, Rushby, and Vazquez-Abad, 1999, p. 889

[47] Winer, Rushby, and Vazquez-Abad, 1999, p. 889

[48] Winer, Rushby, and Vazquez-Abad, 1999, p. 889

[49] Brandenberg and Binder, 1999, p. 846

[50] Brandenberg and Binder, 1999, p. 846

[51] Dobbs, 2000, p. 58

[52] Waugh, 1999, p. 3

[53] VanBuren and King, 2000, p. 11

[54] Jacobs, 1999, p. 606

[55] Rothwell, 1996, p. 249

[56] Jacobs, 1999, p. 608

[57] Jacobs, 1999, p. 607

[58] Jacobs, 1999, p. 607

[59] Jacobs, 1999, pp. 606–607

[60] Ford, 1999, p. 26

[61] Charchian and Cohen, 2000, pp. 12–16

[62] Charchian and Cohen, 2000, pp. 12–13

Interactive Learning Technologies

[1] VanBuren and King, 2000, p. 11

[2] VanBuren and King, 2000, p. 11

[3] Vazquez-Abad and Winer, 1992, p. 676

[4] Wagner, 1999, pp. 642–643

[5] Vazquez-Abad and Winer, 1992, p. 676

[6] Stamps, 1999b, p. 42

[7] Stamps, 1999b, p. 42

[8] Stamps, 1999b, p. 43

[9] Stamps, 1999a, pp. 44–46

[10] VanBuren and King, 2000, p. 11

[11] Elliot Masie quoted in Kerker, 2000, p. 4

[12] Yelon, 1999, p. 485

[13] Yelon, 1999, pp. 486–487

[14] Murphy, 1997

[15] Wagner, 1999, p. 627

[16] Ely, 2000, p. 26

[17] Schreiber, 1999, p. 4

[18] Verduin and Clark, 1991, p. 8

[19] Wagner, 1999, p. 629

[20] Wagner, 1999, p. 626

[21] Wagner, 1999, p. 626

[22] Mantyla and Gividen, 1997, p. 5

[23] Vazquez-Abad and Winer, 1992, p. 676

[24] Vazquez-Abad and Winer, 1992, p. 676

[25] Strouppe, 1998, p. 19

[26] Strouppe, 1998, p. 21

[27] Dobbs, 2000, pp. 56–57

[28] Rosenberg, 2000, p. 35

[29] Rosenberg, 2000, p. 37

[30] Boettcher and Kumar, 2000, pp. 14–16

[31] Dobbs, 2000, p. 56

[32] Dobbs, 2000, p. 56

[33] Dobbs, 2000, p. 56

[34] Alec Hundnut cited in Kerker, 2000, p. 4

[35] Barron, 1999c

[36] Brandon Hall cited in *The New Corporate University Review*, 2000, p. 4

[37] Kerker, 2000, pp. 4–5

[38] Rosenberg, 2000, p. 35

[39] Rosenberg, 2000, p. 35

[40] Barron, 1999c

[41] Barron, 1999c

[42] Von Hoffman, 1998, p. 18

[43] Von Hoffman, 1998, p. 18

[44] Von Hoffman, 1998, p. 18

[45] Von Hoffman, 1998, p. 19

[46] Barron, 1999c

[47] Brandon Hall cited in *The New Corporate University Review*, 2000, pp. 1; 4

[48] Kuse and Keil, 2000

[49] Dessinger and Conley, 2001

[50] Sugrue, 2000, p. 1

Games and Simulations

[1] Browner and Preziosi, 1995, p. 176

[2] Browner and Preziosi, 1995, p. 177

[3] Thiagarajan, 1999b, p. 419

[4] *Thiagi Game Letter* cited in Salopek and Kesting, 1999, p. 29

[5] Nilson cited in Salopek and Kesting, 1999, p. 31

[6] Browner and Preziosi, 1995, p. 176

[7] Barron, 1999b, p. 16

[8] Whitcomb, 1999, p. 43

[9] Barron, 1999b, p. 12

[10] Kiser, 2000, p. 23

[11] Barron, 1999b, p. 17

[12] Barron, 1999b, pp. 16–17

[13] Kiser, 2000, p. 26

[14] Barron, 1999b, p. 16

[15] Browner and Preziosi, 1995, p. 176

[16] Thiagarajan, 1999b, pp. 419–420

[17] Browner and Preziosi, 1995, p. 177

[18] Carroll, 1994, p. 65

[19] Whitcomb, 1999, p. 43

[20] Carroll, 1994, p. 65

[21] Coleman and Shepherd, 1994, p. 3

[22] Coleman and Shepherd, 1994, pp. 8–9

[23] Whitcomb, 1999, p. 43

[24] Schwartz cited in Coleman and Shepherd, 1994, p. 9

[25] Carroll, 1994, p. 70

[26] Kirrane, 1990, p. 17

[27] Hueley, 1990, p. 17

[28] Kirrane, 1990, p. 17

[29] Browner and Preziosi, 1995, p. 178

[30] Thiagi cited in Salopek and Kesting, 1999, p. 29

[31] Browner and Preziosi, 1995, p. 178

[32] Thiagi cited in Salopek and Kesting, 1999, p. 30

[33] Based on Rees, 1992, p. 217–221

[34] Thiagarajan, 1999a, p. 247

[35] Thiagarajan, 1999a, pp. 248–257

[36] Nilson as cited in Salopek and Kesting, 1999, p. 29

[37] Browner and Preziosi, 1995, p. 178

[38] Browner and Preziosi, 1995, pp. 179–181

[39] David Merrill cited in Filipczak, 1997, p. 27

Case Study 2–1

[a] Jossi, 2000, p. 22

[b] Jossi, 2000, p. 22

[c] Jossi, 2000, p. 20

[d] Jossi, 2000, pp. 20–21

[e] Jossi, 2000, p. 22

[f] Jossi, 2000, p. 22

[g] Jossi, 2000, p. 22

Non-Instructional PSS

Job Aids

[1] Rossett and Gautier-Downes, 1991, p. 15

[2] Pipe, 1992, p. 363

[3] Rossett and Gautier-Downes, 1991, p. 4

[4] Rossett and Gautier-Downes, 1991, p. 54

[5] Rossett and Gautier-Downes, 1991, p. xi

[6] Rossett and Gautier-Downes, 1991, pp. 15–26

[7] Harless, 1986, p. 111

[8] Pipe, 1992, p. 354

[9] Pipe, 1992, p. 354

[10] Van Tiem, Moseley, and Dessinger, 2000, pp. 33–37

[10] Pipe, 1992, p. 363

Electronic Performance Support Systems (EPSS)

[1] Raybould, 1995, p. 21

[2] *Definition*, 2000, Online

[3] Gery, 1999, p. 142

[4] Winer, Rushby, and Vazquez-Abad, 1999, p. 879

[5] Raybould, 1995, p. 11

[6] Gery, 1995, p. 51

[7] Gery, 1999, p. 143

[8] Clark, 1992, p. 22

[9] Raybould, 1995, p. 11

[10] Laffey, 1995, p. 45

[11] Winer, Rushby, and Vazquez-Abad, 1999, p. 879

[12] Gery, 1999, p. 143

[13] Winer, Rushby, and Vazquez-Abad, 1999, p. 879

[14] Gery quoted in Villachica and Stone, 1999, p. 457

[15] Raybould, 1995, pp. 20–21

[16] Winer, Rushby, and Vazquez-Abad, 1999, p. 880

Documentation and Standards

[1] Rossett and Gautier-Downs, 1991, p. 4

[2] Hale, 1998, pp. 155–156

[3] Rummler and Brache, 1995, p. 168

[4] Westgaard, 1992, p. 592

[5] Westgaard, 1992, p. 600

[6] Gayeski, 1992, p. 437

[7] Horn, 1999, p. 357

[8] Carroll, 1992, p. 331

[9] Carroll, 1992, p. 332

[10] Carroll, 1992, p. 332

[11] Carroll, 1992, p. 337

[12] Carroll, 1992, p. 338

[13] Carroll, 1992, pp. 338–343

[14] Carroll, 1992, p. 344

[15] Carroll, 1992, p. 344

[16] Hackos, 2000, pp. 1–2

[17] Hale, 1998, p. 136

[18] Hale, 1998, p. 160

[19] Hale, 1998, p. 160

[20] Dean, 1998, p. 10

[21] Hale, 1998, p. 155

[22] Hale, 1998, pp. 32–33

Chapter 3: Job Analysis/Work Design

Job Analysis/Work Design

[1] Langdon, 1995, p. 12

[2] Shortell and Kaluzny, 1997, pp. 205–207

Job Analysis

[1] Mondy, Noe, and Premeaux, 1999, pp. 107–109
[2] Schuler and Huber, 1993, p. 153
[3] Rothwell, 1996, p. 33
[4] Mondy, Noe, and Premeaux, 1999, p. 107
[5] Van Tiem, Moseley, and Dessinger, 2000, Chapter 5
[6] Schuler and Huber, 1993, p. 153
[7] Gomez-Mejia, Balkin, and Cardy, 1998, p. 63
[8] Cascio, 1998, p. 131
[9] Gatewood and Feild, 1987
[10] Gomez-Mejia, Balkin, and Cardy, 1998
[11] Mondy, Noe, and Premeaux, 1999
[12] DeCenzo and Robbins, 1999
[13] Gomez-Mejia, Balkin, and Cardy, 1998
[14] DeCenzo and Robbins, 1999, p. 140

Job Descriptions

[1] Mondy, Noe, and Premeaux, 1999, p. 110
[2] Schuler and Huber, 1993, p. 158
[3] Mondy, Noe, and Premeaux, 1999, p. 115
[4] Dessler, 1997, pp. 97–99
[5] Schuler and Huber, 1993, p. 156

Job Specifications

[1] Mescon, Bovee, and Thill, 1999, p. 294
[2] Robbins and Coulter, 1999, p. 343
[3] Dessler, 1998, pp. 292–293
[4] *Otterbein College-Instructional Designer*, October 19, 1999, p. B66

Work Design

[1] Robbins and Coulter, 1999, p. 490
[2] Rothwell, 1996, p. 238
[3] Robbins and Coulter, 1999, p. 490
[4] DeSimone and Harris, 1998, p. 49
[5] Mondy, Noe, and Premeaux, 1999, p. 124
[6] Nahavandi and Malekzadeh, 1999, p. 199
[7] Schuler and Huber, 1993; pp. 568–569
[8] Schuler and Huber, 1993
[9] Campion, 1982
[10] Bateman and Snell, 1999, p. 40
[11] Herzberg, 1968, pp. 53–62
[12] Sherman, Bohlander, and Snell, 1996, pp. 142–144

[13] Bateman and Snell, 1999, p. 450
[14] Weisbord, 1987, p. 143
[15] Scarpello and Ledvinka, 1988, pp. 205–206
[16] Schuler and Huber, 1993, pp. 567–568

Job Enlargement

[1] Griffin, 1982
[2] Campion and McClelland, 1993, pp. 339–51
[3] Robbins and Coulter, 1999
[4] Gordon, 1999, pp. 437–438
[5] Campion and McClelland, 1993, pp. 239–251
[6] LaBar, 1995, p. 71
[7] Mink, 1996, pp. 36–42

Job Rotation

[1] Sherman, Bohlander, and Snell, 1996, p. 141
[2] Gomez-Mejia, Balkin, and Cardy, 1998, p. 60
[3] Sherman, Bohlander, and Snell, 1996, p. 141
[4] Ewald and Burnett, 1997, pp. 440–456

Job Enrichment

[1] Gordon, 1999
[2] Gomez-Mejia, Balkin, and Cardy, 1998
[3] Herzberg, 1968, pp. 53–62
[4] Sherman, Bohlander, and Snell, 1996, p. 142
[5] Sherman, Bohlander, and Snell, 1996, p. 142
[6] Lawler, 1986
[7] Sherman, Bohlander, and Snell, 1996, p. 142
[8] Hackman, 1973, pp. 57–71
[9] Reif and Tinnell, 1973, pp. 29–37

Human Factors

[1] Sherman, Bohlander, and Snell, 1996, p. 140
[2] Mondy, Noe, and Premeaux, 1999, p. 461
[3] Mondy, Noe, and Premeaux, 1999, pp. 468–469

Ergonomics

[1] Sherman, Bohlander, and Snell, 1996, p. 140
[2] Mondy, Noe, and Premeaux, 1999, p. 469

[3] Ostrom, 1993, p. 8
[4] Sherman, Bohlander, and Snell, 1996, p. 140
[5] *Ergonomics*, 1997, n.p.
[6] Ramsey, 1995
[7] *Tufts Ergonomic Alliance*, n.d., n.p.
[8] Langdon, Whiteside, and McKenna, 1999, pp. 82–83
[9] Kearny and Smith, 1999, p. 11
[10] Kearny and Smith, 1999, pp. 12–13
[11] Ostrom, 1993, pp. 8–11
[12] Hequet, 1995, p. 47
[13] Schuler and Huber, 1993, p. 671

Safety Engineering

[1] Schuler and Huber, 1993, pp. 660–669
[2] Mondy, Noe, and Premeaux, 1999, pp. 464–465
[3] Schuler and Huber, 1993, p. 660
[4] Sherman, Bohlander, and Snell, 1996
[5] US Department of Labor, Occupational Safety and Health Administration, 1980
[6] Ledvinka and Scarpello, 1991, p. 215
[7] Dessler, 1997, p. 622
[8] *Crain's Detroit Business*, January 10, 2000, p. 8
[9] Dessler, 1997, pp. 624–625
[10] Dessler, 1997, pp. 625–626
[11] Schuler and Huber, 1993, pp. 669–670

Preventive Maintenance (PM)

[1] Hall, 1983, p. 133
[2] Van Tiem, Moseley, and Dessinger, 2000, p. 210
[3] Ciampa, 1988, pp. 24–25
[4] Hall, 1983, p. 134
[5] Robbins and Coulter, 1999, p. 600
[6] Robbins and Coulter, 1999, p. 600
[7] Hall, 1983, pp. 133–134
[8] Mechanical Associates Service, Inc., Online
[9] Suzaki, 1987, p. 115

Case Study 3-3

[1] Ford Motor Company, 1992, p. 19
[2] Ford Motor Company, 1992, p. 16
[3] Ford Motor Company, 1992, p. 19
[4] Ford Motor Company, 1992, pp. 3; 16
[5] Ford Motor Company, 1992, p. 15

Quality Improvement

[1] *Webster's New Universal Unabridged Dictionary*, 1983, p. 1474

2 Mescon, Bovee, and Thill, 1999, p. G13

3 Lowe and Mazzeo, September 1986, p. 22

4 Mescon, Bovee, and Thill, 1999, p. 169

5 Walton, 1986

6 Juran, 1986, pp. 19–24

7 Rakich, Longest, and Darr, 1992, p. 95

8 Longest, Rakich, and Darr, 2000, pp. 417–419

Total Quality Management (TQM)
1 Harris, 1997, p. 346

2 Drafke and Kossen, 1998, pp. 395–396

3 Mescon, Bovee, and Thill, 1999, p. 168

4 Miller, 1992, p. 47

5 Drafke and Kossen, 1998

6 Drafke and Kossen, 1998, pp. 396–403

7 Sashkin and Kiser, 1993

8 Bonstingl, 1992, pp. 51–68

9 Rothwell, 1996, p. 177

10 *Memory Jogger*, 1998

11 Drafke and Kassen, 1998, p. 403

12 Meyer, 1998, p. 66

13 Dessler, 1997, p. 324

14 Jackson, 1998, pp. 348–349

15 McLaughlin and Kaluzny, 1990, pp. 7–14

16 Harris, 1997, p. 11

17 McLaughlin and Kaluzny, 1990, pp. 7–14

18 Dessler, 1993, pp. 322–323

Continuous Improvement
1 Moseley and Solomon, May/June 1997

2 Moseley and Solomon, May/June 1997, pp. 15–16

3 Chang, 1992

4 DeCenzo and Robbins, 1999

5 Kinlaw, 1992, p. 13

6 Kinlaw, 1992, p. 14

7 Chang, 1992

8 Chang, 1992, p. 9

9 Chang, 1992, p. 6

10 Hauser and Clausing, 1988, p. 63

11 Cappelli, 1998, p. 1

12 Green, 2000, p. 25

13 Dingwall, 1999, p. 1

14 Six Sigma, 1999, p. 1

15 Six Sigma, 1999, p. 2

Value Analysis/Value Engineering (VA/VE)
1 IFAC, October 25, 1999

2 Schonberger, 1982, p. 192

3 Hall, 1983, p. 183

4 Hall, 1983, p. 183

5 Remich, October, 1999, pp. 1–2

6 Zak, August, 1999, p. 1

Case Study 3-4
1 Hendrich and Nyhuis, et al., 1995, pp. 129–139

Chapter 4: Personal Development

Feedback
1 Lucas, 1994

2 Hathaway, 1990

3 Kirkland and Manoogian, 1998, pp. 7–8

4 Lucas, 1994

5 Hargrove, 1995

Coaching
1 Edwards and Ewen, 1996

2 Lucas, 1994

3 Stone, 1999

4 Hargrove 1995

5 Thach and Heinselman, 1999, pp. 36–39

6 Peterson and Hicks, 1999, pp. 7–8

7 Mabry in Morris, 2000, p. 151

Mentoring
1 Ibarra, 2000

2 Kaye and Scheef, 2000, p. 1

3 Tebo, 2000; Lengnick-Hall, 2000

4 Baron, 2000

5 Stone, 1999

6 Segal, 2000, p. 157

7 Kuo, 2000

Emotional Intelligence
1 Goleman, 1995, p. 34

2 Johnson, 1999, p. 10

3 Goleman, 1998; Goleman, 1995

4 Goleman, 1998, p. 19

5 Goleman, 1998, p. 18

6 Epstein, 1999

7 Epstein, 1999, p. 20; Guilford, 1955, p. 875

8 Shepard, Fasko, and Osborne, 1999

9 Goleman, 1995, pp. 26–27

10 *Executive Excellence*, 1999, p. 6

11 Morris, 1999, p. 8

Career Development
1 Caudron, 1999, p. 63

2 Caudron, 1999, p. 62

3 Knowdell, 1996

4 Lyon and Kirby, 2000

5 Deeprose, 1995

6 Van Tiem and West, 1997

7 Hagevik, 2000, p. 45

Chapter 5: Human Resource Development

Human Resource (HR) Interventions
1 Ulrich, Brockbank, and Yeung, 1989, p. 315

2 Burke, 1997, p. 71

3 Ulrich, Brockbank, and Yeung, 1989, p. 316

4 Van Tiem, Moseley, and Dessinger, 2000, p. 63

5 DeSimone and Harris, 1998, p. 5

6 DeSimone and Harris, 1998, p. 7

Human Resource Management
1 Dessler, 1998, p. 283

Staffing
1 Drucker, 1985, p. 22

2 DeCenzo and Robbins, 1999, p. 130

3 Dessler, 1998, pp. 296–297

4 Dessler, 1998, p. 297

5 DeCenzo and Robbins, 1999, pp. 156–157

6 Robbins and Coulter, 1999, p. 347

7 Sherman, Bohlander, and Snell, 1996, p. 191

8 Mondy, Noe, and Premeaux, 1999, p. 208

9 Buhler, 1996, p. 26

10 Mondy, Noe, and Premeaux, 1999, pp. 209–211

11 Dessler, 1997, pp. 168–169

12 Milkovich and Newman, 1993, p. 63

13 DeCenzo and Robbins, 1999, p. 12

14 Sherman, Bohlander, and Snell, 1996, p. 196

15 Schermerhorn, Hunt, and Osborn, 2000, p. 131

16 Bateman and Snell, 1999, p. 340

17 Robbins and Coulter, 1999, p. 351

18 *Interviewing* (1997) Society for Human Resource Management

19 DeCenzo and Robbins, 1999, p. 172

20 Schermerhorn, Hunt, and Osborn, 2000, pp. 131–132

[21] Sherman, Bohlander, and Snell, 1996, pp. 198–199

[22] DeCenzo and Robbins, 1999, pp. 199–200

[23] Sherman, Bohlander, and Snell, 1996, pp. 198–199

[24] DeCenzo and Robbins, 1999, pp. 199–200

[25] Dessler, 1997, pp. 184–185

[26] Dessler, 1997, pp. 184–185

[27] Mondy, Noe, and Premeaux, 1999, p. 238

[28] Sherman, Bohlander, and Snell, 1996, pp. 198–199

[29] Schuler and Huber, 1993, p. 251

[30] Mondy, Noe, and Premeaux, 1999, p. 238

[31] Schermerhorn, Hunt, and Osborn, 2000, p. 132

Compensation

[1] Greenberg and Baron, 1995, p. 175

[2] Henderson, 2000, p. 17

[3] Henderson, 2000, p. 17

[4] Schuler and Huber, 1993, p. 367

[5] Greenberg and Baron, 1995, p. 176

[6] Schuler and Huber, 1993, pp. 367–368

[7] Kozlowski, January 19, 2000, p. 4A

[8] Sherman, Bohlander, and Snell, 1996, pp. 344–345

[9] Carlisle, 1986, p. 5

[10] Henderson, 2000, p. 31

[11] McMurrer, VanBuren, and Woodwell, Jr., 2000, pp. 21–23

Retirement Planning

[1] Dessler, 1997, p. 406

[2] Atchley, 1996, p. 439

[3] Monk, 1994, p. 3

[4] Freedman, 1999, p. 53

[5] Atchley, 1996, pp. 437–438

[6] Atchley, 1996, p. 437

[7] Clark, 1994, p. 38

[8] Riekse and Holstege, 1996, p. 201

[9] Riekse and Holstege, 1996, pp. 201–203

[10] Atchley, 1996, p. 443

[11] Wasik, 2000, pp. 7–8

[12] Wasik, 2000, p. 8

[13] Mondy, Noe, and Premeaux, 1999, p. 602

[14] Crampton, Hodge, and Mishra, 1996, p. 247

Health and Wellness

[1] Maynard, 1997, pp. 9–10

[2] Robbins, 2001, p. 572

[3] Gomez-Mejia, Balkin, and Cardy, 1998, pp. 506–508

[4] Gomez-Mejia, Balkin, and Cardy, 1998, p. 508

[5] Pramik, 1999, pp. 10–11

[6] Greenberg and Baron, 2000, p. 242

[7] DeCenzo and Robbins, 1999, p. 446

[8] Palm, 2000, p. 14

[9] Harris, 1997 p. 381

[10] Tully, 1995, pp. 98–106

[11] Ziegler, 1998, pp. 29–31

[12] Palm, 2000, p. 14

[13] Chambliss, 1996, pp. 61–63; 73–74

[14] Heirich, Erfurt, and Foote, 1992, pp. 627–637

[15] Lawson, 1995, p. 18

[16] Epes, 1995, pp. 12–13

[17] Hunnicutt, 2000, p. 36

[18] Chapman, 1996, p. 7

Employee Development

[1] DeCenzo and Robbins, 1999, p. 14

[2] Van Tiem, Moseley, and Dessinger, 2000, p. 208

[3] DeCenzo and Robbins, 1999, pp. 227–228

[4] DeCenzo and Robbins, 1999, pp. 232–233

[5] DeCenzo and Robbins, 1999, p. 233

[6] Van Tiem, Moseley, and Dessinger, 2000, p. 138

[7] Garvin, 1993, p. 81

[8] Van Tiem, Moseley, and Dessinger, 2000, pp. 139–140

[9] Meister, 1998, p. 29

[10] Coleman, 1992, pp. 637–639

[11] Gomez-Mejia, Balkin, and Cardy, 1998, pp. 288–289

Individual Growth

[1] Carnevale, Gainer, and Meltzer, 1990

[2] Carnevale, Meltzer, and Gainer, 1990

Motivation (Incentives and Rewards)

[1] Green, 2000, p. 1

[2] Maslow, 1970

[3] Gordon, 1996

[4] Leonard, Beauvais, and Scholl, 1999, pp. 969–998

[5] Schwartz and Bilsky, 1990, cited in Leonard, Beauvais, and Scholl,

1999, p. 974

[6] Kouzes and Posner, 1999

[7] Vroom, 1964

[8] Rosenbaum, 1982

[9] Banks, 1997

[10] Waitley, 1979, pp. 87–101

[11] Cummings and Worley, 1993

[12] Cummings and Worley, 1993

[13] Pavlinski, 1999, p. 26

[14] Sanchez, 1999, p. 24

[15] *Wall Street Journal*, 1986, December 16 as cited in Milkovich and Newman, 1993, p. 348

[16] Cira and Benjamin, 1998, p. 22

[17] Rosen, 1991

[18] Milkovich and Newman, 1993, p. 372

Performance Appraisals

[1] Nelson, 2000, p. 39

[2] Cummings and Worley, 1993

[3] Cummings and Worley, 1993

[4] Fox, Byrne, and Rouault, 1999, pp. 38–40

[5] Hattersley, 1999, p. 2

[6] Hattersley, 1999, p. 2

[7] Grote, 2000, pp. 14–20

[8] Grote, 2000, p. 14

[9] Grote, 2000, p. 18

[10] Berke, 1990, p. 10

[11] Anonymous, 2000, p. 2

[12] Sachs, 1992

[13] Sachs, 1992

[14] Sachs, 1992

Competency Testing and Assessment Centers

[1] Gatewood and Feild, 1998

[2] Cosner and Baumgart, 2000, p. 2

[3] Thornton, 1992

[4] Jaffee, Frank, and Mulligan, 1990

[5] Cummings and Worley, 1993

[6] Cummings and Worley, 1993

[7] Cummings and Worley, 1993

[8] Thornton, 1992

[9] Thornton, 1992

[10] Thornton, 1992

Literacy

[1] Carnevale, Gainer, and Meltzer, 1990

[2] Carnevale, Meltzer, and Gainer, 1990

[3] Rosen, Digh, Singer, and Phillips, 2000

[4] Wagner, 2000, p. 14

[5] Sherry, August 1990, p. 411

[6] Cushieri, 1999

[7] Knowdell, 1996

[8] Knowdell, 1996

Organizational Growth

[1] Schermerhorn, 1999, p. 5

[2] Bateman and Snell, 1999, p. 15

[3] Schuler and Huber, 1993, p. 75

[4] Schuler and Huber, 1993, p. 76

Succession Planning

[1] Mondy, Noe, and Premeaux, 1999, pp. 154–155

[2] Schuler and Huber, 1993, p. 137

[3] Nowack, 1994, pp. 49–54

[4] Schuler and Huber, 1993, p. 137

[5] Nowack, 1994, p. 50

[6] Mondy, Noe, and Premeaux, 1999, pp. 154–156

[7] Nowack, 1994, pp. 50–51

[8] Mondy, Noe, and Premeaux, 1999, p. 156

[9] Gomez-Mejia, Balkin, and Cardy, 1998, p. 276

[10] Gomez-Mejia, Balkin, and Cardy, 1998, pp. 276–277

[11] Amundson, 1997, p. 1

[12] Hicks, 2000, pp. 79–80

[13] Frottler, Hernandez, and Joiner, 1998, p. 149

Career Pathing

[1] Gomez-Mejia, Balkin, and Cardy, 1998, pp. 278–281

[2] Mondy, Noe, and Premeaux, 1999, p. 315

[3] Van Tiem, Moseley, and Dessinger, 2000, p. 93

[4] Anthony, Perrewe, and Kacmar, 1996, p. 434

[5] Mondy, Noe, and Premeaux, 1999, pp. 315–316

[6] Gomez-Mejia, Balkin, and Cardy, 1998, p. 279

[7] Mondy, Noe, and Premeaux, 1999, p. 316

[8] Leibowitz, Farren, and Kaye, 1986, p. 140

[9] Cascio, 1998, pp. 170–171

[10] DeSimone and Harris, 1998, p. 374

Leadership Development

[1] Sheerer, 1998, p. 13

[2] Kotter, 1990, pp. 103–111

[3] Robbins, 2001, p. 313

[4] Shortell and Kalauzny, 1997, p. 103

[5] Shortell and Kalauzny, 1997, p. 103

[6] Shortell and Kalauzny, 1997, pp. 103–104

[7] Goleman, 2000, p. 80

[8] Coile, 1998, pp. 18–23

[9] Zenger, Ulrich, and Smallwood, 2000, pp. 22–27

Executive Development

[1] DeSimone and Harris, 1998, p. 467

[2] Bateman and Snell, 1999, p. 281

[3] Mondy, Noe, and Premeaux, 1999, p. 16

[4] Meister, 2000, pp. 54–58

[5] Wertz, 1996, pp. 622–623

[6] Roush, 2000, pp. 1; 45

[7] Wertz, 1996, p. 634

[8] Vicere, 1996, pp. 79–80

Management Development

[1] Kotter, J.P., 1990, pp. 103–111

[2] Kotter, J.P., 1996, p. 26

[3] Mondy, Noe, and Premeaux, 1999, p. 274

[4] Mondy, Noe, and Premeaux, 1999, p. 274

[5] Mescon, Bovee, and Thill, 1999, pp. 165–167

[6] Scarpello and Ledvinka, 1988, p. 515

[7] Mondy, Noe, and Premeaux, 1999, pp. 274–275

[8] Gomez-Mejia, Balkin, and Cardy, 1998, p. 285

[9] DeSimone and Harris, 1998, pp. 431–432

[10] Seibert, Hall, and Kram, 1995, pp. 549–567

Supervisory Development

[1] Robbins and DeCenzo, 1998, pp. 5–7

[2] Silvestri and Lukasiewicz, 1987, pp. 46–64

[3] Robbins and DeCenzo, 1998, pp. 11–15

[4] Crandall, 1988, pp. 24–31

[5] Bittel and Newstrom, 1996, p. 657

[6] Bittel and Newstrom, 1996, pp. 657–660

[7] McMurrer, VanBuren, and Woodwell, Jr., 2000, pp. 3–25

[8] Bittel and Newstrom, 1996, p. 656

[9] Bittel and Newstrom, 1996, p. 676

[10] Bittel and Newstrom, 1996, p. 676

Chapter 6: Organizational Communication

Organizational Communication Interventions

[1] Van Tiem Moseley, and Dessinger, 2000, p. 107

[2] Ewald and Burnett, 1997, p. 2

[3] Rakich, Longest, and Darr, 1996, p. 559

[4] Ewald and Burnett, 1997, p. 44

[5] *Signs You Worked During the 90s*, 2000, Online

[6] Svenson in Langdon, Whiteside, and McKenna, 1999, pp. 90–91

Communication Networks

[1] Ewald and Burnett, 1997, p. 41

[2] Greenberg and Baron, 1995, p. 347

[3] Gibson and Hodgetts, 1986, p. 228

[4] Scott, 1967, p. 165

[5] Ewald and Burnett, 1997, p. 41

[6] Greenberg and Baron, 1995, p. 349

[7] Gibson and Hodgetts, 1986, p. 228

[8] Gibson and Hodgetts, 1986, p. 229

[9] Longest, Rakich, and Darr, 2000, p. 814

[10] Longest, Rakich, and Darr, 2000, p. 815

[11] Gibson and Hodgetts, 1986, pp. 227–228

[12] Ewald and Burnett, 1997, p. 44

[13] Greenberg and Baron, 1995, p. 348

[14] Longest, Rakich, and Darr, 2000, p. 812

[15] Ewald and Burnett, 1997, p. 42

[16] Dessinger, 1996

[17] Watson, 1999

[18] Ewald and Burnett, 1997, p. 43

[19] Ewald and Burnett, 1997, p. 46

[20] Swenson in Langdon, Whiteside, and McKenna, 1999, p. 92

[21] Brown and Isaacs, 1997, p. 3

Information Systems

[1] Dessler, 1998, p. 614

[2] Hutchison and Stein, 1997, p. 28

[3] Dessler, 1998, p. 617

[4] Dessler, 1998, p. 614

[5] Beck, 1999, p. 325

[6] Dessler 1998, pp. 621–622

[7] Dessler, 1998, p. 619

[8] Rosenberg, Coscarelli, and Hutchison, 1999, p. 24

[9] Estes, 1999, pp. 159–160

[10] Dessler, 1998, pp. 623–624

[11] Dessler, 1998, pp. 629–630

[12] Dessler, 1998, p. 630

[13] Dessler, 1998, pp. 630–631

[14] Weisbord, 1987, p. 159

[15] Brandenburg and Binder, 1992, p. 666

[16] Rossett, 1999, pp. 87–115

[17] Kaufman, 1998, pp. 63–64

[18] Estes, 1999, p. 161

[19] Marakas, 1999, pp. 165–170

Suggestion Systems

[1] Nelson, 1994

[2] Bell, 1997, pp. 22–26

[3] Savageau, 1996, pp. 16–18

[4] Sherman, Bohlander, and Snell, 1996, p. 549

[5] Drafke and Kossen, 1998, p. 99

[6] Trunko, 1993. pp. 85–89

[7] Bell, 1997, pp. 22–26

Grievance Systems

[1] Davy and Bohlander, 1992, pp. 184–190

[2] Dessler, 1997, pp. 575–576

[3] Dessler, 1997, pp. 575–576

[4] Gomez-Mejia, Balkin, and Cardy, 1998, pp. 478–479

[5] Gordon, 1999, p. 283

[6] Schuler and Huber, 1993, p. 718

[7] Gomez-Mejia, Balkin, and Cardy, 1998, p. 479

[8] Dessler, 1997, pp. 575–576

[9] Schuler and Huber, 1993, p. 721

[10] Schuler and Huber, 1993, p. 721

[11] Schuler and Huber, 1993, p. 721

Conflict Resolution

[1] Allred, 1997, p. 27

[2] Costantino and Merchant, 1996, p. 5

[3] Beck, 1999, p. 280

[4] Beck, 1999, p. 281

[5] Sessa, 1994, p. 1

[6] Russo and Eckler, 1994, p. 3

[7] Beck, 1999, p. 282

[8] Russo and Eckler, 1994, p. 3

[9] Beck, 1999, p. 283

[10] Beck, 1999, p. 282

[11] Russo and Eckler, 1994, p. 3

[12] Beck, 1999, p. 295

[13] Sessa, 1994, p. 5

[14] Allred, 1997, p. 28

[15] Beck, 1999, p. 294

[16] Blake and Mouton, 1964

[17] Hiam, 1999

[18] Beck, 1999

[19] Beck, 1999, p. 295

[20] Allred, 1997, p. 28

[21] Allred 1997, pp. 44–45

[22] Weiss, in Beck, 1999, p. 295

[23] Russo and Eckler, 1994, p. 4

[24] Sashkin, 1989, p. 19

[25] Hiam, 1999, p. 9

Chapter 7: Organizational Design and Development

Empowerment

[1] Peters, 2000, pp. 3–6

Team Strategies

[1] Williams, 1998, p. xiii

[2] Hartzler and Henry, 1994, pp. 1–9

[3] Gordon, 1996

[4] Byham, 1988

[5] Hummels and de Leede 2000, p. 76

[6] Womack, Jones, and Roos, 1991, p. 13

[7] Hummels and de Leede, 2000, p. 81

[8] Lloyd, 1996

[9] Byham, 1988

[10] Lloyd, 1996

[11] Lloyd, 1996

[12] Lloyd, 1996

[13] Coulson-Thomas, 1997, pp. 226–233

[14] Coulson-Thomas, 1993, as cited in Coulson-Thomas, 1997, p. 230

[15] Hartzler and Henry, 1994, pp. 11–12

[16] Pritchett, 1992

[17] Chang, 1994

[18] Chang, 1994

Problem Solving

[1] Zachary, 2000, p. 24

[2] Abbott, Gold, and Rotella, 2000, p. 71

[3] Quay, 2000, p. 61

[4] Perfetto, Bransford, and Franks, 1983, as cited in Dominowski and Buyer, 2000, p. 268

[5] Cassidy, 1999; Van Tiem, Moseley, and Dessinger, 2000

[6] Clarke, 2000, p. 78

[7] Harrington-Mackin, 1994

[8] Cassidy, 1999; Van Tiem, Moseley, and Dessinger, 2000

Decision Making

[1] Klein and Weick, 2000

[2] Low, Ferrell, and Mansfield, 2000

[3] Libby and Agnello, 2000

[4] Harrington-Mackin, 1994, p. 95

[5] Deeprose, 1995

[6] Harrington-Mackin, 1994, p. 110

[7] Deeprose, 1995

[8] Klein and Weick, 2000, p. 16

Organizational Pro-Action

Strategic Planning

[1] Rigby, 1998

[2] Crittenden and Crittenden, 2000, p. 150

[3] Crittenden and Crittenden, 2000, p. 159

[4] Hamel and Prahalad, 1995

[5] Kurylko, 2000, p. 40

[6] Napier, Sidle, and Sanaghan, 1998

[7] Bryson, 1995

Operations Management

[1] Viale, 1995

[2] Rantakyro, 2000, p. 16

[3] Hansen, 2000, p. 26

[4] Roy and Seguin, 2000, p. 451

Environmental Scanning

[1] Spurge, Spivak, and Hamermesh, 1997, p. 239

Benchmarking

[1] Blinn, 1998

[2] Spendolini, 1992

[3] Dervitsiotis, 2000, pp. 641–647

[4] Althany, 1991, as cited in Simpson and Kondouli, 2000, p. 623

[5] Simpson and Kondouli, 2000, p. 623

Reengineering, Realigning, Restructuring

[1] Spurge, Spivak, and Hamermesh, 1997, p. 486

[2] Langdon, Whiteside, and McKenna, 1999

[3] Hammer and Champy, 1993, p. 2

[4] Moosbrucker and Loftin, 1998, p. 287

[5] Tonnessen, 2000, p. 773

[6] Hamel and Prahalad, 1994

[7] Anselmi and Sundararajan, 2000, pp. 28–34

[8] Hwang and Lee, 2000, p. 733

[9] DuBain, 1996

[10] Quinn, Spreitzer, and Brown, 2000, p. 147

[11] Cameron, 1997, cited in Quinn,

Spreitzer, and Brown, 2000, p. 147

[12] Quinn, Spreitzer, and Brown, 2000, p. 147

[13] Langdon, Whiteside, and McKenna, 1999, p. 325

Organizational Values
[1] Hunt, 1998, pp. 8–10

Culture
[1] Deal and Kennedy, 1982
[2] Kilmann, Saxton, Serpa, and Associates, 1985
[3] Marquart, 1999, p. 1
[4] Rosen, 1991
[5] Deal and Kennedy, 1982, p. 21
[6] Deal and Kennedy, 1982, p. 22
[7] Lu, Rose, and Blodgett, 1999, pp. 99–105
[8] Hamel, 2000, p. 11
[9] Allan, Sommerville, Kennedy, and Robertson, 2000, pp. 602–607
[10] Jonash and Sommerlatte, 1999; Dess and Picken, 1999
[11] Tosti and Jackson, 2000, p. 16
[12] Meister, 2000, p. 52
[13] Cone, 2000, p. 58
[14] Krumwiede and Lavelle, 2000, p. 9
[15] Krumwiede and Lavelle, 2000, pp. 9–17
[16] Green and Butkus, 1999
[17] Connors and Smith, 1999, p. 14–15
[18] Jaffe and Scott, 1998
[19] Rosen, 1991

Diversity
[1] Byars and Rue, 1994, pp. 24–38
[2] Byars and Rue, 1994, p. 52
[3] Thomas and Ely, 1996, pp. 79–90
[4] Thomas and Ely, 1996, p. 81
[5] Galagan, 1993
[6] Chatman, Polzer, Barsade, and Neale, 1998
[7] Alexander, Lichtenstein, Jinnett, D'Aunno, and Ullman, 1996, p. 49
[8] Karp and Sutton, 1993
[9] Mehta, 2000, p. 181
[10] Miller, 1998, p. 151
[11] Mehta, 2000, pp. 184–186
[12] Blank and Slipp, 1994, p. 7
[13] Tarpley, 2000, p. 196; LeBlanc, Vanderkam, and Vella-Zarb, 2000, pp. 190–200
[14] Byars and Rue, 1994, pp. 52–55
[15] Phone interview with Ben Nicholas, 2000

[16] Byars and Rue, 1994, p. 57
[17] Yocum and McKee, 1996
[18] Tally and Waller, 1992, p. 6
[19] Meade, 1998, pp. 44–46
[20] Thomas and Ely, 1996, p. 81
[21] Tracey, 1995
[22] Gardenschwartz and Rowe, 1994, pp. 5–6
[23] Van Duch, 1999, p. B1
[24] Engelmeier, 2000; Anand, 2000
[25] Office of Equal Employment Opportunity, 1994
[26] Office of Equal Employment Opportunity, 1994

Globalization
[1] Friedman, 1999, p. 19
[2] Sanchez, 2000, pp. 56–70
[3] Rosenzweig, 1998, pp. 646–647
[4] Kemper, 1998
[5] Grundling, 1999
[6] Thaler-Carter, 2000, p. 86
[7] Marquart, 1999, p. 6
[8] Payne and Mobley, 1993, p. 10
[9] Adapted from Grundling, 1999

Ethics
[1] Maddux and Maddux, 1989, p. i
[2] Hatcher and Aragon, 2000, pp. 179–185
[3] Shea, 1988, p. 27
[4] McIlvaine, 1998, pp. 30–34
[5] McNamara, 1998
[6] McNamara, 1998

Spirituality in the Workplace
[1] Cohen, 1997
[2] Mitroff and Denton, 1999, p. 83
[3] Scheinin, 1999, p. F1
[4] Chopra, 1994, p. 2
[5] Bellman, 2000, p. 68
[6] Whirlpool Shared Values, 2000, Online
[7] Barrett, 1998
[8] Barrett, 1998, p. 66
[9] Mak, 2000, p. 537
[10] Deming, 1986, p. 59
[11] Dore, 1987, as cited in Mak, 2000, p. 538
[12] Coates, 1999, p. 9
[13] Herman and Gioia, 1998
[14] Janov, 1995
[15] PG and E advertisement, *Fortune*, 2000, pp. 3–4
[16] Barrett, 1998, p. 70

[17] Amaewhule, 1997, p. 53
[18] *Newsweek*, 2000, p. 50
[19] *Fortune* C, 2000, p. 13
[20] *Fortune* B, 2000, p. 2
[21] *Fortune* A, 2000, p. 4
[22] Neal, 1997
[23] Van Tiem, Moseley, and Dessinger, 2000, pp. 9–10
[24] Hatcher, 2000, pp. 18–19
[25] Lienert, 1998

Chapter 8: Financial Systems

Open Book Management
[1] Case, 1995, p. 26, Online
[2] Rothwell, Hohne, and King, 2000
[3] Proudfit, 1999, p. 1, Online
[4] Case, 1995, p. 26, Online
[5] Proudfit, 1999, p. 1, Online
[6] Proudfit, 1999, p. 1, Online
[7] Proudfit, 1999, p. 1, Online
[8] McCoy, 1996, pp. 17–47
[9] Burlingham, 1999, pp. 2–3, Online
[10] Burlingham, 1999, p. 3, Online

Profit Versus Cost Centers
[1] Cox, Stout, and Vetter, 1995, pp. 45–46
[2] Mc Lean, 1997, p. 136
[3] Mc Lean, 1997, p. 136
[4] Waagen, 2000, p. 9
[5] Mc Lean, 1997, p. 136
[6] Waagen, 2000, p. 9
[7] Mc Lean, 1997, p. 136
[8] Waagen, 2000, p. 9
[9] Waagen, 2000, p. 9
[10] Waagen, 2000, p. 9

Financial Forecasting
[1] Render and Stair, Jr., 1997, p. 174
[2] David, 1999, p. 125
[3] Robbins and Coulter, 1999, pp. 270–271
[4] Robbins and Coulter, 1999, p. 271
[5] Schermerhorn, Jr., 1999, p. 147
[6] Robbins and Coulter, 1999, p. 271
[7] Schermerhorn, Jr., 1999, p. 147
[8] Mescon, Bovee, and Thill, 1999, p. 291
[9] Render and Stair, Jr., 1997, p. 178
[10] Render and Stair, Jr., 1997, p. 174
[11] Render and Stair, Jr., 1997, p. 174
[12] Bateman and Snell, 1999, p. 65
[13] Peterson, 1996, pp. 10–12

[14] Makridakis, 1996, pp. 435–437

[15] Render and Stair, Jr., 1997, p. 200

Capital Investment and Spending

[1] Mescon, Bovee, and Thill, 1999, p. 14

[2] Van Tiem, Moseley, and Dessinger, 2000, p. 207

[3] Mescon, Bovee, and Thill, 1999, p. 543

[4] Clark, and Gottfried, 1957, p. 62

[5] Van Tiem, Moseley, and Dessinger, 2000, p. 114

[6] Deku, 1999, pp. 1–2

[7] Anderson-Claiborne, 2000, p. 3

Cash Flow Analysis and Cash Flow Forecast

[1] Needles, Jr., Anderson, and Caldwell, 1990, pp. 334–336

[2] Witucki, 2000, p. 2

[3] Witucki, 2000, p. 2

[4] Witucki, 2000, p. 1

[5] Witucki, 2000, p. 3

[6] Needles, Jr., Anderson, and Caldwell, 1990, pp. 1109–1115

[7] Weston and Bringham, 1979, p. 155

[8] Jacquet and Miller, Jr., 1992

[9] Gill, 1990

[10] Witucki, 2000, pp. 4–5

Mergers, Acquisitions, and Joint Ventures

[1] Mescon, Bovee, and Thill, 1999, p. 116

[2] Van Tiem, Moseley, and Dessinger, 2000, p. 115

[3] David, 1999, p. 59

[4] Greenberg and Baron, 2000, p. 496

[5] Van Tiem, Moseley, and Dessinger, 2000, p. 115

[6] Mescon, Bovee, and Thill, 1999, p. 116

[7] Robbins and Coulter, 1999, p. 250

[8] Van Tiem, Moseley, and Dessinger, 2000, p. 209

[9] Anthony, Perrewe, and Kacmar, 1996, p. 424

[10] David, 1999, pp. 58–60

[11] Nahavandi and Malekzadeh, 1999, p. 64

[12] David, 1999, p. 60

[13] Mescon, Bovee, and Thill, 1999, p. 118

[14] Mescon, Bovee, and Thill, 1999, p. 118

[15] Salopek, 1999, p. 12

[16] Bramson, 2000, pp. 59–61

[17] Bramson, 2000, pp. 59–61

Chapter 9: Implementing Interventions in the Workplace

[1] Wilson, 1953

[2] Galagan, 1998, pp. 23–27

[3] Schlender, 1998, pp. 163–174

[4] Kaufman, 2000, pp. 25–26

[5] Langdon, 2000, p. 22

[6] Van Tiem, Moseley, and Dessinger, 2000; Rothwell, 1996

[7] Holton, 1999, p. 33

Using a Business Setback to Realign for Success: The Arbor Consulting Group, Inc.

[1] Fitz-Enz, cited in Ulrich, Losey, and Lake, 1997, pp. 217–228

The Profession of Performance Technology (PT)

Knowledge, Skills, and Competencies Needed—A Word to the Wise

[1] Rothwell, 1996

[2] McLagan, 1989

[3] AHRD, 1999–2000, p. ii

[4] Hutchison and Stein, 1997, pp. 28–35

[5] Frank, 1999, p. 929

Glossary of Terms

360° Feedback – A multi-source assessment that taps the collective wisdom of those who work with an individual, including supervisors, peers, direct reports, and internal and external customers.

Acquisitions – When larger organizations purchase (acquire) smaller ones, usually with more than 50% of the voting stock, and assume control of the organization's property and liabilities.

Action Learning – A small group process or program that integrates commitment, learning, and doing to solve real, relevant, and challenging organizational problems. Members of the group share, question, experience, reflect, make decisions, and take action on a single project basis or as an open group. Action learning builds opportunities for learning around real problems brought to the workplace by employees.

Assessment Centers – Use standardized selection as a tool for making personnel decisions, including selection, promotion, certification, and career development. They are used to evaluate knowledge, skills, and abilities necessary to perform a specific job. In career development, they are used to determine areas of strength and where improvement is needed.

Balance Sheet – Shows how management invests resources in assets and how assets are financed by liabilities and owners' equity.

Benchmarking – A systematic process of comparing an organization to other organizations to identify better methods and determine best practices. It helps define customer requirements, establish effective goals and objectives, develop true measures of productivity, and identify education and training needs for current and future employees.

Benefits – A central part of the organization's pay structure, consisting of the non-cash portion of a compensation program intended to improve the quality of work life for an organization's employees. They are rewards that generally are not paid directly to an employee.

Business Plan – The formal planning involved in starting a new business. A business plan views the entire picture and describes all the related elements.

Capital – Sources of long-term financing (investments and loans) available to an organization.

Capital Investment and Spending – Capital investment refers to commitment or use of money and other assets made in anticipation of greater financial returns in the future, usually involving large sums of money. Capital spending involves risk-return trade-off analysis in order to secure long-term financial advantage.

Career Assessment – Uses the results of standardized interest and personal style inventories to help an employee develop career goals, strategies, and a personal educational plan.

Career Development – An ongoing process involving planning, acquiring, and maintaining a career. It attempts to match the person's abilities and interests to the person's position and career plan with a focus on professional growth and enhancement of the work role.

Career Pathing – Communicates potential job advancement as employees move up the career ladder. A planned sequence of job assignments, usually involving growth-oriented tasks and experiences that employees assume in preparation for future job opportunities.

Case Studies – In-depth, print-based accounts of an event or situation presented in story form and designed to seek justifiable answers or solutions to problems. The length of case studies may vary from one page to several pages. Traditionally, they are learning tools rather than tools for implementing performance improvement. Participants analyze the case individually, then discuss and analyze it as a group.

Cash Flow Analysis – A financial tool or process used by businesses and banks to determine the various sources and uses of an organization's cash, and to make accurate projections of cash inflows and outflows for forecasting purposes.

Cash Flow Forecast – A tool used by organizations and banks considering loan applications to analyze cash inflow and outflow cycles.

Cause Analysis – The process of determining the root cause of past, present, and future performance gaps.

Change Management – Involves problem solving in a concerted effort to adapt to changing organizational needs.

Classroom Learning – Education or training delivered by a live instructor to a group of learners at a location separated from the actual work site.

Coaching –Assistance that managers give employees by evaluating and guiding on-the-job performance. Coaching helps employees gain competencies and overcome barriers to improving performance. It involves one-on-one suggestions related to observable workplace situations, usually by a supervisor or manager. It can be formal and planned, or spontaneous and provided on the spot, when the situation calls for it. Coaching builds on the assumption that most employees are eager to do well, please their managers, and achieve position in an organization.

Cognitive Ergonomics – The study of the impact of the physical/sensory environment on mental (cognitive) aspects of work processes.

Collaboration – Cooperating with others to achieve a desired output or outcome.

Communication – The transfer of meaning between sender and receiver.

Communication Networks – The patterns that form when messages move from sender to receiver. They illustrate the relationships and interactions between and among individuals and organizations. The networks are either formal or informal and flow in a variety of directions, for example, top down, bottom up, or horizontally. They influence job performance and job satisfaction.

Company – Refers to a broad spectrum of organizations and institutions involved in improving service and customer satisfaction, including manufacturing, automotive, chemical, industrial, educational, health care, government, etc.

Compensation – Pay for work and performance, including disability income; deferred income; health, accident, and liability protection; loss-of-job income; continuation of spouse's income when there is a loss due to an employee's relocation.

Competency Testing – Examines current job knowledge and skills necessary for present and future performance. Competency tests provide direct evidence of an

individual's ability and skill to perform a job. The activities in a competency test are representative of the job tasks and equipment that are actually part of the job.

Confirmative Evaluation – Provides information about the competence and effectiveness of employees in order to explain and confirm the value of the performance intervention over time.

Conflict – A natural condition that evolves when an individual, group, or organization holds and expresses opinions or ideas that do not match those of another individual, group, or organization. Conflict can range from a resolvable difference of opinion to all out war, depending on the degree of collaboration that is supported by the environment.

Conflict Resolution – Involves alleviating a disagreement between two or more people who share differing views.

Continuous Improvement – An ongoing, systematic process to assure, maintain, and improve processes, products, and services based on predetermined standards and customer satisfaction. The entire organization, including internal and external stakeholders, is committed to and involved in the process.

Corporate University – A strategic learning structure for developing and educating employees, customers, and suppliers in order to accomplish business goals and strategies.

Cost Center – A center charged with managing costs. It has neither revenue budget nor obligations to earn revenues.

Culture – A shared system of values, beliefs, and behaviors that characterizes a group or organization. Organizational culture refers to collective human behavior of employees (decision making, speech, writing, and actions) based on mutual acceptance of values, myths, heroes, symbols, and artifacts.

Culture Audit – An analysis procedure that focuses on workers, work processes, and workplace, and answers the question "How do we think about things or do things in our organization?"

Debriefing – The process of facilitating a discussion after a game, simulation, case study or other group activity to help participants share, question, reflect, and discover lessons learned.

Decision Making – Involves making choices, ideally based on structured problem solving.

Direct Compensation – Encompasses an employee's base wage and salary.

Distance Learning – A system for delivering instruction to learners who are separated by time and/or space. It is also known as distance education, distance training, and teletraining. Distance learning uses a variety of print (yes, print), computer, and telecommunication technologies.

Distributed Learning – A form of distance learning that adapts to and supports the expressed needs of the learner. While the terms distance learning and distributed learning often are used synonymously, there are operational distinctions between the two. For example, distributive learning has a just-in-time, just-for-me orientation.

Diversity – Represents differences in gender, ethnic, economic or societal background, age, disabilities, religion or cultural heritage, and family situation. These categories are known as "protected categories" in US Equal Employment Opportunity legislation and executive orders.

Documentation – Codes information, preserves it, and makes it accessible to the current and future work force. Organizations use documentation to codify and record progress, accomplishments, failures, lessons learned, policies, procedures, job specifications, standards, problems, and decisions.

Economies of Scale – The term used for the cost savings that result when goods and services are produced in large volume.

Education – A formal process for developing knowledge, skills, or attitudes. It is sometimes used as an umbrella term for any education or training experience, but most often, it refers to learning that takes place within the K–12 or higher education systems and may or may not be employer-supported. Education improves work performance in a focused direction beyond the employee's current job. The emphasis is on broad knowledge, understanding, comprehension, analysis, synthesis, and evaluation, and on transferring knowledge to future objectives, as well as immediate job-related applications.

Electronic Performance Support System (EPSS) – An electronic, computer-mediated infrastructure that empowers the user as performer and learner, enhances organizational learning, and enables knowledge management. EPSS uses software to integrate performance-based content, knowledge, learning, and structure into a user-friendly performance and learning support system. Job aids and computer-based training are subsets of EPSS. EPSS is a highly sophisticated job aid, with access to large databases of information designed to coach the learner through a question-and-answer format, and to be user friendly.

Emotional Intelligence (EI) – "The ability to motivate oneself and persist in the face of frustrations; to control impulse and delay gratification; to regulate one's moods and keep distress from swamping the ability to think; to empathize, and to hope" (Goleman, 1995, p. 34).

Employee Assistance Programs – Part of employee benefits that help employees whose on-the-job performance is suffering because of physical, social, mental, and/or emotional problems.

Employee Development – Process that begins after the candidate accepts the final offer of employment and continues throughout the employee's life with the organization. It involves acquiring knowledge, skills, and attitudes through employer-sponsored learning opportunities including traditional instruction; newer technology-oriented formats; informally by means of mentoring, coaching, on-the-job training; or by team participation.

Employee Selection – A selection process of choosing the right person for the job.

Employment Tests – Tests that measure abilities, job knowledge, vocational interests, personality, and other qualities.

Enterprise Training – Any system that delivers instruction that is critical to the entire organization and must be disseminated to a large number of people dispersed over a wide geographic area.

Environmental Analysis – The process used to identify and prioritize the realities that support actual performance: work, organization, and competitive environment.

Environmental Scanning – A strategic planning technique for monitoring trends in the external environment of an organization. It involves observing, assessing, and documenting economic situations, political events, technical developments, and structural changes in similar organizations or industries.

Environmental Support Analysis – Seeks to define causes related to information (data, information, and feedback), instrumentation (environmental support, resources, and tools), and motivation (consequences, incentives, and rewards).

Ergonomics – Involves the study and design of work stations, work practices, workflow, equipment, and tools to accommodate the physical and psychological capabilities and limitations of employees. The term ergonomics is used interchangeably with human factors.

Ethics – Defines good and bad standards of conduct. Standards are cultural and vary among countries, companies, incidents, and situations. Ethics is realizing what is right and wrong and then doing what is right. Each employee's values are unique, based on individual background and experience. Thus, when discussing the ethics of an organization, it is important to establish guidelines for the organization that everyone is aware of, willing to follow, and committed to enforcing.

Executive Development – The systematic development of an organization's executives either through specific skill programs or through managerial skill programs. It enhances senior management's ability to create vision, values, and business strategies.

Explicit Knowledge – Recorded information, for example, a written policy or procedure.

Feedback – Informing people about how others perceive personal actions and communications. It is one way of helping the employee determine if he or she is meeting personal goals and expectations.

Fidelity – The degree of distortion or accuracy achieved by a simulation technique. The three-dimensional, immersive systems used to train pilots are considered high fidelity. The goal is to use the level of fidelity required to assure learning transfer.

Financial Forecasting – Predicting future trends, events, and outcomes with business perspectives in mind, that is, profit, interest, supply, demand, and similar issues.

Financial Systems – Refer to the monetary affairs (income, reserves, expenses, and dividends) of an organization. They are usually summarized in an annual report that includes an income statement, balance sheet, cash flow statement, and explanatory notes.

Formal Suggestion System – Suggestions are planned and implemented and often require written input. They include standards for feedback and for recognizing emplyees whose suggestions are implemented.

Formative Evaluation – Conducted to improve the design of performance interventions. It begins during the performance and cause analysis stages, continues through the selection and design of interventions and, if a pilot stage is included in the intervention plan, may extend into early intervention implementation.

Games – Experiential learning activities for two or more participants that contain elements of competition and fun. Games are frequently used in connection with training teams to solve problems and make decisions. They may bring an element of familiarity to the training by emulating popular board games or TV game shows.

Gap Analysis – Describes the difference between current results and consequences and desired results and consequences. It is the last step in the performance analysis process.

Globalization – Respecting and linking facets of culture, language, religion, customs, and traditions among organizational units that have an impact on the organization's activities, such as the negotiation process, the contract agreement, levels of individual interaction, and performance. It is a means of achieving higher productivity and efficiency by identifying and focusing on an organization's efforts and resources in major world markets.

Graphology Test – Analyzes handwriting to discover individual traits.

Grievance System – A formal process for submitting, evaluating, and providing feedback related to employee grievances.

Health and Wellness Programs – Company-sponsored initiatives that focus on health promotion, health protection, and health prevention. They are designed to enhance employee morale and productivity, and reduce absentee rates and health care costs.

Honesty Testing – Assesses an individual's patterns of response in situations that test honesty and integrity.

Hostile Takeover – Outside group buys substantial stock in an organization to assume control against the wishes of the corporate directors.

Human Factors – see Ergonomics

Human Performance Technology (HPT) – Analyzes performance problems and their underlying causes, and describes exemplary performance and success indicators. HPT identifies or designs interventions, implements them, and evaluates the results. It is the systematic process of linking business goals and strategies with the work force responsible for achieving the goals.

Human Resource Development Interventions – Activities that are essential to human resource management and are shaped by the organization's mission and its ability to maintain market share.

Human Resource Management – A sub-category of human resources that refers to staffing, compensation, retirement planning, health and wellness, and employee development interventions.

Human Resources – The "people" part of organizations.

Hybrid Interactive Learning Technologies – The integration of delivery and support modes—CBT, WBT, and instructor-led classroom training—into one product or training bundle.

Hypermedia – A nonlinear, computer-based representation of information. It is a form of knowledge management that makes it easy for the learner to access and control large quantities of random but interrelated information using a variety of media. It links nodes of information by building relationships that make sense to the user. Learners actually learn to learn by using hypermedia.

Incentives – Link pay with a standard for performance, such as salary, differential pay, allowances, time off with pay, deferred income, loss-of-job coverage, or desirable working conditions, training, adequate equipment, and materials.

Income Statement – Shows all the revenues and costs with net income resulting as revenues minus costs.

Indirect Compensation – The benefit package provided by the employer.

Individual Growth – A sub-category of human resources that focuses on the organizational need to encourage and retain high-performance employees.

Informal Suggestion System – Loosely established suggestions that range from grapevine discussions to mottoes such as, "We value your ideas." They can be both oral and written and they do not have set standards for feedback and recognition.

Information System – Uses a variety of information technologies to turn data into information and eventually into knowledge. It is composed of people, data, and technology working together to retrieve, process, store, and disseminate information that will support informed decision making and business transactions.

Instructional Performance Support System (PSS) – Helps workers initiate new performance or changes their actual performance until that performance is equal to or better than desired performance. The PT practitioner may select or design an instructional PSS intervention when a gap exists between the current knowledge, skill, or attitude of a worker or group of workers and the job specifications. It is a function of knowledge management, learning organization, action learning, education and training, interactive learning technologies, games, and simulations.

Interactive Learning Technologies – Any technology-based learning applications that encourage and support the active involvement of the learner with the content, the instructor, the technology, other learners, and the learning resources.

Interface Design – The linkage between machinery and processes to ensure smooth, easy, user-friendly functionality.

Interventions – Conscious, deliberate, planned activities designed to improve human performance and solve workplace problems. They can be targeted at organizations, departments, work groups, and individuals.

Job Aids – Performance support tools that provide just-in-time, on-the-job, and just-enough information to enable a worker to perform a task efficiently and successfully without special training or reliance on memory. They may inform, support procedures, or support decisions.

Job Analysis – A formal way of evaluating job requirements by looking at the job itself and at the kind of person needed to complete the job successfully. Job analysis collects information about duties, tasks, and responsibilities for specific jobs. It identifies, lists, and describes the tasks (job description) and performances (job specifications) required for successful completion of the job.

Job Analysis Interventions – Include the analysis process itself, plus the outputs of the process: job descriptions and job specifications.

Job Description – A written statement documenting the tasks and functions of a job. It includes what is done on the job, how it is done, and under what conditions it is done.

Job Design – The process of putting tasks together to form complete jobs. Job designers must consider how tasks are performed, the relationship of the job to organizational work, and employee-related issues such as challenge and empowerment.

Job Enlargement – A work design option that increases the job scope by expanding a performer's job duties. For example, job enlargement may require a worker to perform traditionally unrelated tasks or may increase the knowledge requirement for a specific job.

Job Enrichment – A job design option that makes a job more rewarding and satisfying by adding tasks (horizontal job enrichment) or responsibilities (vertical job enrichment).

Job Rotation – A form of job enlargement that occurs when employees do numerous and entirely different jobs on a flexible, revolving schedule without disrupting the workflow. Job rotation usually involves cross training.

Job Specification – A list of the minimum qualifications that a person must possess in order to perform a specific job successfully.

Joint Ventures – When two or more organizations join forces for a common purpose, such as exploring new technologies, pursuing new markets, generating new products, etc.

Knowledge Management (KM) – A systematic and conscious effort to identify, capture, codify, store, transform, disseminate, and share knowledge so that people within an organization can use the organization's collective knowledge and experience to foster business innovation and competitive advantage.

Leadership Development – Prepares employees to cope with changes through prioritizing, overcoming obstacles and assumptions, and initiating action.

Learning Organization – Values and supports continuous improvement and lifelong learning for all members of the organization and aligns learning with the achievement of business goals. Learning is considered a competitive strategy and a broad, long-term intervention to achieve continuous improvement. Learning organization involves the belief and practice that individuals and teams can learn continuously and cooperatively to foster an organization's competitive advantage. Hallmarks of learning organizations are sharing the organizational vision, individual excellence, team learning, creating common mental models, and use of systematic thinking.

Learning Portals – Online services that offer on-demand points of entry into choices for learning. Members of the organization can go to find and/or buy education and training resources, or register for and participate in education or training curricula, courses, or classes.

Learning Technologies – Methods or media that are designed and used to present information to learners. The two major delivery systems for learning technologies are instructor-led classroom and distance learning. Both delivery systems use computer technologies and wired or wireless telecommunication technologies to enable and enhance learning.

Literacy – Includes a variety of definitions. The traditional approach is to consider literacy to be competence in reading, writing, and mathematics necessary to function fully as a citizen, parent, and semi-skilled worker. For many, it is the ability of an individual to effectively articulate one's thoughts, ideas, and concerns verbally as well as in writing. In general, literacy means a person's knowledge, especially the ability to read and write, which enables the person to function in society.

Management Development – Prepares managers to support the organization's mission, strategy, goals, and objectives. It fosters learning experiences that upgrade skills, knowledge, attitudes, and ways of thinking.

Mediation – A process that organizations use to resolve conflict. Mediation is formal, (management-union bargaining), or informal (a manager resolving a conflict between two employees). A third party or mediator objectively reviews both sides of the conflict and brings the parties to a mutually acceptable resolution.

Mentoring – The offering of experience, emotional support, and guidance by an experienced person to a less experienced person. Mentoring is a one-on-one relationship between a more experienced employee (mentor) and a less experienced employee (mentee). Mentoring and coaching are often confused. Although mentoring uses many of the same techniques as coaching, mentoring goes beyond teaching an employee how to do a job well. When mentoring, a mentor shares personal experiences, wisdom, and political savvy to enable top performers to take on tasks beyond those designated by their job descriptions.

Mergers – Two or more separate organizations of equal or similar size combine operations to become one new organization through an exchange of stocks.

Meta Evaluation – The process of evaluating formative, summative, and confirmative evaluation by literally zooming in on the evaluation processes, products, and outcomes to examine what happened and why.

Motivation – The human energy to grow, change, survive, and advance. It is inner drive, emotion, or incentive to act in a certain manner or do something.

Negotiation – A process that organizations use to resolve conflict. Successful negotiation serves the interests of all the parties involved,

generates a mutually satisfying outcome, and maintains or enhances current and future collaboration.

Networking – Establishing patterns of interpersonal communication interactions to facilitate the dissemination and collection of information.

Non-Instructional Performance Support System (PSS) – Stresses the integration of doing and technology but may inherently or consciously include elements of learning and instruction. Non-instructional PSS uses a variety of technologies from paper-based to computer-based to provide workers with just-in-time, just-enough information to perform a task.

Online Learning – A system for delivering instruction to learners using internet or intranet technology. It is also called web-based learning, web-based training, e-learning, or distance learning.

Open Book Management – Everyone in the organization helps the business make money. Financial status is fully shared and employees become active participants in financial performance.

Operations Management (Direct Functions) – The direction, coordination, and control of the inputs (raw materials), throughputs (what is done to the raw materials), and outputs (what is produced). The operations (direct functions) are the lifeblood of the organization.

Organization – A collection of people working together to achieve a common purpose and a specific set of objectives.

Organizational Analysis – Examines the organizational mission, vision, values, goals, and strategies.

Organizational Design and Development – A process that examines the operation and management of an organization and facilitates needed changes in an effort to improve efficiency and competitiveness.

Organizational Growth – A sub-

category of human resources that addresses the organizational need for long-term success.

Organizational or Business Communication – Refers to the transfer of information and knowledge among employees, suppliers, and customers for the purpose of accomplishing efficiency and effectiveness. Makes it possible to send and receive messages between different components within an organization, among separate organizations, and between organizations and society. Effective communication is essential for creating, maintaining, or improving the culture and performance of organizations.

Overhead – Organizational functions and activities that do not contribute revenue.

Performance Analysis – Identifies and clarifies the problem or performance gap by focusing on three areas: desired performance state, actual performance state, and the gap between desired and actual performance. It looks at three levels: organization, process, and job/performer and considers three variables: goals, design, and management.

Performance Appraisal – A structured process used by managers to provide feedback on an individual's performance to encourage improvement. Performance appraisals also provide information for salary decisions and promotions.

Performance Standards – Concise statements that serve as a gauge for measuring accomplishment. The organization, the industry, workers, and/or government or other regulatory agencies set the standard or criteria that are used to guide the performer and evaluate the performance outputs, and outcomes.

Performance Support Interventions – Affect the workplace, the work, and the worker through planned change efforts based on knowledge and skills transfer. They can be instructional (when the problem is a result of a lack of knowledge or skill) or non-instructional (to improve individual, group, or team performance, improve processes, products, and services, and guide business plans, deliverables, results, and success measures).

Performance Support Systems (PSS) – Integrate learning and doing and technology to help workers obtain the knowledge or skill they need to initiate new performance or improve existing performance. They support the performer on-the-job and just-in-time. PSS may replace or enhance training. See Instructional PSS and Non-Instructional PSS.

Performance Technology – The science and art of improving people, process, and performance.

Personal Development Interventions – Planned work-related activities that are the employee's personal responsibility. Each individual assumes ownership of success or failure. Personal development requires and enables individuals to take control of their own job situation. The organization provides the structure and processes so that employees can make accurate, positive decisions and improve their own performance.

Physical Ergonomics – The primary focus of ergonomics is the design or redesign of machines and tools to match the physical ability of the employee to use and react to the tools or machinery required for a job/task. Assessing and improving user friendliness and environmental factors, such as noise and lighting, fall within the scope of physical ergonomics.

Polygraph Tests – Lie detector tests that verify application information.

Preventive Maintenance (PM) – A manufacturing term for a proactive approach to equipment maintenance that focuses on repair and adjustment issues within a production system. However, the concept of PM may be applied to any operating system, including management systems, human resource development systems, information systems, etc.

Pro-Action – Thinking ahead, planning for the future with creativity and commitment, and understanding the economic, political, and social climate sufficiently to inspire employee confidence.

Problem Solving – The structured process of defining the problem, gathering data about the situation and causes, considering alternatives, making choices, implementing choices, evaluating the new situation, and making adjustments based on evaluation.

Process Consulting – Results in revising processes and often involves reengineering or restructuring an entire organization.

Profit (Revenue) Center – A center charged with controlling costs and generating revenues. It has an expense and a revenue budget.

Qualitative Forecasting – Refers to forecasting techniques that use expert judgment and opinions to predict the future.

Quality – A predetermined standard of excellence that may be applied to a product or service to measure how closely the product or service conforms to the standard and satisfies the customer. Related terms include total quality management (TQM), quality control, quality assurance, and quality improvement.

Quality Improvement – A continuous process that focuses on conducting business right the first time, every time, using predetermined quality standards as the guidelines.

Quantitative forecasting – Refers to forecasting techniques that use mathematical and statistical rules and analyses of past data to predict the future.

Realignment – Getting the organization focused on its core competencies.

Recruitment – Process of attracting a pool of viable job applicants and communicating with them.

Reengineering – The radical redesign of processes for the purpose of extensive (not gradual) performance improvements.

Repertory of Behavior Analysis – Examines people-oriented factors that cause performance problems related to information (skills and knowledge), instrumentation (individual capacity), and motivation (motivation and expectation).

Responsibility Center – Units, locations, or areas within an organization where costs occur and where costs are assigned.

Restructuring – Reorganizes the units or departments, usually resulting in a new organizational chart, new responsibilities, and may involve new reporting relationships. It is partially caused by market factors, such as foreign competition, and demand for increased profitability.

Retirement Planning – Helps employees prepare for legal issues, housing arrangements, and health and wellness following their working years.

Revenue Forecasting – Forecasts of future revenues based on historical revenue figures.

Rewards – Designed to change and reinforce behavior through techniques, such as public recognition, gift certificates, or vacations and travel based on meeting sales quotas.

Safety Engineering – A planned process to reduce the symptoms and costs of poor safety and health and make the work environment safer and healthier for employees. Safety engineering focuses on creating both a psychological and a physical context or environment that promotes safety and reduces accidents.

Scenario-Based Training – Uses real-life situations and formal role-playing by professionals (business theater facilitators or subject matter experts) who enact scripted, real-life situations to reinforce classroom learning. Trainees use lessons learned during class to debrief the scenarios and/or actually participate in segments of the scenario.

Selection – An exercise in predicting the best candidate for a job. It involves reviewing applications and resumes, interviewing and screening candidates, and making a final job offer.

Self-Directed Learning – Training designed to master material independently and at the employee's own pace.

Simulation Games – Experiential learning activities that combine the characteristics of a game and a simulation. There is a direct or indirect similarity between components of the game and the real world. An example is a game that emulates Chutes and Ladders™. They are also called game-based simulations.

Simulations – Highly interactive experiential learning activities that mirror reality and allow participants to manipulate equipment or situations to practice a task, for example, land a plane, troubleshoot electrical circuits, or decide how to handle a conflict between two employees. Simulations are useful when training requires a show and do approach and it is impossible to do it in the real world because of excessive costs or safety factors. They range in complexity from paper-based to computer-assisted simulations; from simple linear video to interactive video; from role plays to digital simulators.

Six Sigma – A systematic quality improvement process that is used on both the production and transactional sides of the business to design, manufacture, and market goods and services that customers may desire to purchase.

Spirituality – Involves striving for the common good for individual employees and common good for the organization.

Spirituality in the Workplace – Encourages organizations to recognize employee needs and promote

employee involvement.

Staffing – The human resource management function that anticipates and fills open positions in organizations.

Standards – The principles or criteria for consistent, ultimate, superior performance outcomes or for how individuals and organizations conduct themselves (ethics). See also Performance Standards.

Statement of Cash Flows – Shows sources of all funds the organization acquires and how the funds are used.

Statement of Stockholders' Equity – Shows changes in the status of the ownership of an organization.

Strategic Management – Supports the organizational vision through the day-to-day implementation of the strategic plan.

Strategic Planning – The process by which an organization envisions its future and develops the necessary goals and procedures to achieve that vision. Strategic planning creates the blueprint for an organization. It documents directional goals and performance objectives based on internal capabilities and competencies and external environmental conditions.

Structured Interviews – Candidates are asked the same questions and comparisons are made on how they answered the questions.

Succession Planning – A career development activity that identifies qualified individuals for managerial and executive positions when the positions are available.

Suggestion System – Employee recognition program that rewards employees or teams of employees for their ideas and contributions. It allows employees to increase workplace responsibility and accountability by offering ideas for improving products or services. Often, rewards are provided for suggestions that result in positive value to the organization. See Formal Suggestion System and Informal Suggestion System.

Summative Evaluation – Considers the usability and adequacy of the intervention and gathers information that will be useful to senior decision makers in the organization.

Supervisory Development – Prepares trainers, advisers, mentors, facilitators, coaches, leaders, behavioral specialists, etc. in critical competencies of a conceptual, interpersonal, technical, and political nature. Supervisory development enables front-line managers to establish work standards and enforce organizational policies and procedures primarily for non-management employees.

Support (Indirect) Functions – Those organizational functions that enable the direct operations to occur.

SWOT Analysis – An analysis tool highlighting strengths, weaknesses, opportunities, and threats to an entity.

Tacit Knowledge – Knowledge that resides in people's heads. It is also referred to as know-how, rules of thumb, or heuristics.

Team – A group of people working together as a cohesive unit to accomplish a common goal.

Teambuilding – Based on the philosophy that people work better and more creatively in groups than they do alone. It focuses on trust, collaboration, openness, and other interpersonal factors.

Technological Forecasting – Forecasts the future based on technological changes and economic feasibility.

Training – Instruction provided to employees by employers to establish, improve, maintain, or extinguish performance as it relates to business needs.

Unstructured Interview – The interviewer selects which questions to ask a particular candidate in a probing, open-ended fashion. It is non-directive and time consuming.

Value Chain – Composed of all the stakeholders (designers, suppliers, manufacturers, customers, etc.) who add value to or receive value from specific products or services.

Value Analysis/Value Engineering (VA/VE) – VA/VE is a formal and systematic procedure applied to the components of a job, unit, product, or service to determine and improve value and/or cut costs. Properly implemented, VA/VE can develop and continuously improve quality products, satisfy the customer, and ensure low costs.

Work – What the worker must do on the job.

Work Design – Creates a blueprint of job tasks structured to improve organizational efficiency and employee satisfaction. It focuses on how the job can be altered to fit a specific work environment and achieve maximum results.

Work Design Interventions – Include job design (rotation, enlargement, enrichment), human factors (ergonomics, safety engineering, PM), and quality improvement (TQM, continuous improvement, value analysis/value engineering).

Workplace Learning and Performance (WLP) – Refers to the integration of learning and other performance interventions to improve human performance and align it with individual and organizational needs.

REFERENCES

6 Sigma. (1999, September 20). Ford Motor Company Management System Communication. Available online: www.6sigma.ford.com/corporate/consumer.html.

Abbott, C., Gold, S.F., & Rotella, M. (2000). Archimedes' bathtub: The art and logic of breakthrough thinking. *Publisher's Weekly, 247,* (22).

Abernathy, D., & Ellis, R. (2000, May). An open-door discussion on learning portals. *Training and Development, 54* (5), 58–61.

Academy of Human Resource Development. (1999–2000). *Standards on ethics and integrity* (1st ed.). Baton Rouge, LA: Author.

Alexander, J.A., Lichtenstein, R., Jinnett, K., D'Auno, T.A., & Ullman, E. (1996). The effects of treatment team diversity and size on assessments of team functioning. *Hospital and Health Services Administration, 41* (1).

Allan, C., Sommerville, J., Kennedy, P., and Robertson, H. (2000). Driving for business excellence through environmental performance improvements. *Total Quality Management, 11* (4–6).

Allerton, H.J. (2000, August). News you can use: Hard drive. *Training and Development, 54* (8), 18–19.

Allred, K.G. (1997). Conflict management. In L.J. Bassi and D. Russ-Eft (Eds.), *What works: Training and development practices* (pp. 27–50). Alexandria, VA: American Society for Training and Development.

Alternatives to the annual performance review. (2000, February). *Harvard Management Update,* 5 (2).

Althany, D. (1991). Share and share alike. Industry Week, 240. Cited in Simpson, M., and Kondouli, D. (2000, July). A practical approach to benchmarking in three service industries. *Total Quality Management,* 11 (4–6).

Amaewhule, W. (1997). Industry focus: Oil companies, communities, and social responsibility, *Training and Development,* 51 (7).

Amundson, G.K. (1997, May 19) Form a business succession plan in seven steps. *Small Business Enterprise.* Available online: bizjournalscom/Louisville.

Anand, R. (2000, August 28). Phone Interview with Rohani Anand. Washington, DC: National Multicultural Institute.

Anderson-Claiborne, S. (2000). Capital investment and spending (Report No. 4). Detroit, MI: WSU College of Education, IT 7320.

Andrews, P.H. (1999). Ethics and organizational communication. *Management Communication Quarterly,* 12 (3).

Anselmi, F.J., & Sundararajan, S. (2000, June). Aligning workers and workloads. *IIE Solutions,* 32 (6).

Anthony, W.P., Perrewe, P.L., & Kacmar, K.M. (1996). *Strategic human resource management* (2nd ed.). Fort Worth, TX: The Dryden Press/Harcourt Brace College Publishers.

Archstone foundation award for excellence in program innovation. (1999). Long Beach, CA: Archstone Foundation and the Gerontological Health Section of the American Public Health Association.

Ashnos, D.P., & Duchon, D. (2000, June). Spirituality at work: A conceptualization and measure. *Journal of Management Inquiry,* 9 (2).

Atchley, R.A. (1996). Retirement. In *Encyclopedia of gerontology: Age, aging, and the aged:* Volume 2 (pp. 433–438). San Diego, CA: Academic Press.

Baer, W. (1970). *Grievance handling: 101 guides for supervisors.* New York: American Management Association.

Balanced scorecard collaborative. (1999). Available online: http://www.bscollaborative.com.

Banathy, B.H. (1991). *Systems design of education: A journey to create the future.* Englewood Cliffs, NJ: Educational Technology Publications.

Banks, L. (1997). *Motivation in the workplace.* West Des Moines, IA: American Media Publishing.

Barclay, R.O., & Murray, P.C. (1997). What is knowledge management? Available online: http://www.media-access.com/whatis.html.

Barker, A.E. (1998). Profile of action learning's principal pioneer—Reginald W. Revans. *Performance Improvement Quarterly,* 11 (1).

Baron, T. (2000, April 24). Need IT talent? Cultivate your own. *InformationWeek*, 783.

Barrett, R. (1998). *Liberating the corporate soul: Building a visionary organization*. Woburn, MA: Butterworth-Heinemann.

Barron, T. (1999a). Technical training heads to the web. *Technical Training*, 10 (6).

Barron, T. (1999b). Simulation gets real. *Technical Training*, 10 (6).

Barron, T. (1999c). Harnessing online learning. *Training and Development*, 53 (9). Available to subscribers online: http://www.astd.org.

Barth, S. (2000, June). Miles to go. *Knowledge Management*, 3 (6).

Bateman, T.S., & Snell, S.A. (1999). *Management: Building competitive advantage* (4th ed.). Boston, MA: Irwin, McGraw-Hill.

Bayrs, L.L., & Rue, L.W. (1994). *Human resource management* (4th ed.). Burr Ridge, IL: Irwin.

Beck, C.E. (1999). *Managerial communication: Bridging theory and practice*. Upper Saddle River, NJ: Prentice Hall.

Bell, R.F. (1997). Constructing an effective suggestion system. *IIE Solution*, 29 (2).

Bellman, G.J. (2000, May). The beauty of the organizational beast. *Training and Development*, 54 (5).

Berke, G.B. (1990, May). How to conduct a performance appraisal. *InfoLine* (issue 005). Alexandria, VA: American Society for Training and Development.

Bierema. L.L. (1998). Fitting action learning to corporate programs. *Performance Improvement Quarterly*, 11 (1).

Bittel, L.R., & Newstrom, J.W. (1996). Supervisor development. In R.L. Craig (Ed.), *The ASTD training and development handbook: A guide to human resource development* (p. 657). New York: McGraw-Hill.

Blank, R., & Slipp, S. (1994). *Voices of diversity: Real people talk about problems and solutions in a workplace where everyone is not alike*. New York: AMACOM.

Blinn, J.D. (1998). Benchmarking can help control cost of risk. In *National Underwriter: Property & Casualty/Risk Benefit Management Edition*. Chicago, IL: National Underwriters.

Boettcher, J., & Kumar, V. (2000, June). Distance education's digital plant. *Syllabus*, 13 (10).

Bond, M.A., & Pyle, J.L. (1998). The ecology of workplace diversity in organizational settings: Lessons from a case study. *Human Relations*, 51 (5).

Bonstingl, J.J. (1992). *Schools of quality: An introduction to total quality management in education*. Alexandria, VA: Association for Supervision and Curriculum Development.

Brady, T. Corporate training industry generates $8 billion in 1998. *Lifelong Learning*, 4 (10).

Bramson, R.N. (2000, October). HR's role in mergers and acquisitions. *Training and Development*, 54 (10).

Brandenburg, D.C., & Binder, C. (1992). Emerging trends in human performance interventions. In H.D. Stolovitch, & E.J. Keeps (Eds.), *Handbook of human performance technology: A comprehensive guide for analyzing and solving performance problems in organizations*. San Francisco: Jossey-Bass/Pfeiffer/ISPI.

Brandenburg, D.C., & Binder, C.V. (1999). Emerging trends in human performance interventions. In H.D. Stolovitch & E.J. Keeps (Eds.), *Handbook of human performance technology: Improving organizational performance worldwide*. (2nd ed., pp. 843–866). San Francisco: Jossey-Bass/Pfeiffer/ISPI.

Bridges, W.P. (1998). Work and occupations. *Change at Work*, 25 (4).

Brinkerhoff, R.O. (1987). *Achieving results from training*. San Francisco: Jossey Bass.

Brookfield, S.D. (1994). *Understanding and facilitating adult learning*. San Francisco: Jossey-Bass.

Brown, J., & Isaacs, D. (December 1996/January 1997). Conversation as a core business process. *The Systems Thinker*, 7 (10).

Browner, E.S., & Preziosi, R.C. (1995). Using experiential learning to improve quality. In J.W. Pfeiffer (Ed.), *The 1995 Annual: Volume 1, Training*. (pp. 169–174). San Francisco: Jossey-Bass/Pfeiffer.

Bruner, J.S. (1966). *Toward a theory of instruction*. Cambridge, MA: The Belknap Press of Harvard University Press.

Bryson, J.M. (1995). *Strategic planning for public and nonprofit organizations*. San Francisco: Jossey-Bass.

Buhler, P. (1996, May). Managing in the 90s. *Supervision*, 57.

Burke, W.W. (1997). What human resource practitioners need to know for the twenty-first century. *Human Resource Management*, 36 (1), 71–79.

Burlingham, B. (1999, September). Open-book management. Available online: www.fed.org/leading compmics/nov96/motiv.html.

357

Byars, L.L., & Rue, L.W. (1994). *Human resource management* (4th ed.). Burr Ridge, IL: Irwin Professional Publishing.

Byham, W.C. (1988). Zapp: *The lightning of empowerment.* New York: Ballantine Books.

Caffarella, R.S. (1994). *Planning programs for adult learners: A practical guide for educators, trainers, and staff developers.* San Francisco: Jossey-Bass.

Cameron, K.S. (1997). Techniques for making organizations effective: Some popular approaches. In *Enhancing Organizational Performance.* Washington, DC: National Academy Press. Cited in Quinn, R.E., Spreitzer, G.M., and Brown, M.V. (2000, June). Changing others through changing ourselves: The transformation of human systems. *Journal of Management Inquiry,* 9 (2).

Campbell, A. (1999). Tailored, not benchmarked: A fresh look at corporate planning. *Harvard Business Review,* 77 (2).

Campion, M., & McClelland, C. (1993). Follow-up and extension of the interdisciplinary costs and benefits of enlarged jobs. *Journal of Applied Psychology,* 78.

Campion, M.A. (1982). Development and field evaluation of an interdisciplinary measure of job design. Unpublished doctoral dissertation, North Carolina State University.

Cappelli, W. (1998, July 17). Six Sigma: The new wave in quality management. Available online: www.rlis.ford.com/giga/jul98/0799 81-WC98.html.

Carlisle, K.E. (1986). *Analyzing jobs and tasks.* Englewood Cliffs, NJ: Educational Technology Publications.

Carnavale, A.P., Gainer, L.J., & Meltzer, A.S. (1990). *Workplace basics: The skills employers want* (two-year research project sponsored jointly by the US Department of Labor and American Society for Training and Development, p. 358.

Carnavale, A.P., Meltzer, A.S., & Gainer, L.J. (1990). *Workplace basics: Essential skills employers want.* San Francisco: Jossey-Bass.

Carroll, J.M. (1992). Minimalist documentation. In H.D. Stolovitch & E.J. Keeps (Eds.), *Handbook of human performance technology: A comprehensive guide for analyzing and solving performance problems in organizations* (pp. 331–351). San Francisco: Jossey-Bass/ Pfeiffer/ISPI.

Carroll, J.S. (1994). Designing scenarios for human action. *Performance Improvement Quarterly,* 7 (3).

Cascio, W.F. (1998). *Applied psychology in human resource management* (5th ed.). Upper Saddle River, NJ: Prentice Hall.

Case, J. (1995, June). The open-book revolution. Available online: www.incmagazine.com/incmagazine/archives/06950261.html.

Cassidy, M.F. (1999, June). Group decision making. *InfoLine* (Issue 9906). Alexandria, VA: American Society for Training and Development.

Caudron, S. (1999). Free agent learner. *Training and Development,* 53 (8).

Caudron, S. (1999, July). The hard case for soft skills. *Workforce,* 78 (7).

CBT/McGraw-Hill. (1987). Tests of adult basic education (TABE). Monterey, CA.

Chambers, D.R., & Lacey, N.J. (1994). *Modern corporate finance.* New York: HarperCollins.

Chambliss, L (1996, June). The 10 healthiest companies for women. *Working Woman,* 61–63, 73–74.

Chang, R.Y. (1992). Continuous process improvement. *InfoLine* (Issue # 9210). Alexandria, VA: American Society for Training and Development.

Chang, R.Y. (1994). *Success through teamwork.* Irvine, CA: Richard Chang Associates.

Chapmen, L.S. (1996, September). Focusing on feedback: Three simple, low-cost ways to evaluate a wellness program. *Workplace Vitality,* 5 (8).

Charchian, R., & Cohen, S.L. (2000). It's your move: Playing a new game as a training professional. *Performance Improvement,* 39 (7).

Charney, M. (1999, June). KM from the ground up. *Knowledge Management,* 296 (6).

Chatman, J.A., Polzer, J.T., Barsade, S.G., & Neale, M.A. (1998). Being different yet feeling similar: The influence of demographic composition and organizational culture on work processes and outcomes. *Administrative Science Quarterly,* 43 (4).

Chopra, D. (1994). *The seven spiritual laws of success: A practical guide to the fulfillment of your dreams.* San Rafael, CA: Amber-Allen Publishing and New World Library.

Ciampa, D. (1988). *Manufacturing's new mandate: The tools for leadership.* New York: John Wiley & Sons.

Cira, D.J., & Benjamin, E.R. (1998, September/October). Competency-based pay: A concept in evolution. *Compensation and Benefits Review,* 30 (5).

Clark, D.T., & Gottfried, B.A. (1957). *University dictionary of business and finance.* New York: Thomas Y. Crowell Company.

Clark, R.C. (1992). EPSS-look before you leap: Some cautions about applications of electronic performance support systems. *Performance and Instruction,* 31 (5).

Clark, R.C. (1994). *Developing technical training: A structured approach for the development of classroom and computer-based instructional materials.* Phoenix, AZ: Performance Technology Press.

Clark, R.C., & Zuckerman, P. (1999). Multimedia learning systems: Design principles. In H.D. Stolovitch & E.J. Keeps (Eds.), *Handbook of human performance technology: Improving individual and organizational performance worldwide.* (2nd ed.) (pp. 564–588). San Francisco: Jossey-Bass Pfeiffer/ISPI.

Clark, R.L. (1994). The decision to retire: Economic factors and population trends. In A. Monk (Ed.), *The Columbia retirement handbook* (p. 38). New York: Columbia University Press.

Clarke, D.W., Sr. (2000, June 15). Inventive troubleshooting. *Machine Design,* 72 (12).

Coates, D.E. (1999). Strengths of character: A new dimension of human performance. *Performance Improvement,* 38 (4).

Cohen, A. (1997). The guiding light. *Sales and Marketing Management,* 149 (8).

Cohen, S.L., & Becker, N.K. (1999, September). Making and mining intellectual capital: Method or madness. *Training and Development,* 53 (9), 46–50.

Coile, R.C., Jr. (1998). *Millennium management: Better, faster, cheaper strategies for managing 21st century healthcare organizations.* Chicago: Health Administration Press.

Coleman, M.E. (1992). Developing skills and enhancing professional competence. In H.D. Stolovitch & E.J. Keeps (Eds.), *Handbook of human performance technology: A comprehensive guide for analyzing and solving performance problems in organizations* (pp. 637–639). San Francisco: Jossey-Bass/Pfeiffer/ISPI.

Coleman, M.E., & Shepherd, D.M. (1994, April 7). Creating scenarios: A performance technology tool for strategy development. Presented at the National Association for Performance and Instruction (NSPI) International Conference, Chicago, IL [Handout].

Collins, J. (1999). Viewpoint: the learning person. *Training,* 36 (3).

Cone, J. (2000). How Dell does it. *Training and Development,* 54 (6), 58–70.

Connors, R., & Smith, T. (1999). Work with beliefs. *Executive Excellence,* 16 (8).

Cook, J. (1998). Shifting direction. *Human Resource Executive,* 12 (10).

Cooke, R.A., & Lafferty, J.C. (1994). *Organizational culture inventory* (OCI). Plymouth, MI: Human Synergistics International.

Cosner, T.L., & Baumgart, W.C. (2000, June). An effective assessment center program: Essential components. *FBI Law Enforcement Bulletin,* 69 (6).

Costantino, C.A., & Merchant, C.S. (1996). *Designing conflict management systems.* San Francisco: Jossey Bass.

Coulson-Thomas, C. (1993). Harnessing the potential of groups (a survey conducted for Lotus Development, London, Adaptation Ltd.). As cited in C. Coulson-Thomas (1997). *The future of the organization: Achieving excellence through business transformation.* London: Kogan-Page.

Coulson-Thomas, C. (1997). *The future of the organization: Achieving excellence through business transformation.* London: Kogan-Page.

Cowley-Durst, B. (1999). Gathering knowledge for your knowledge management system. *Performance Improvement,* 38 (7).

Cox, R.A.K., Stout, R.G., & Vetter, D.E. (1995). *Financial administration and control.* Cambridge, MA: Blackwell Publishers Inc.

Crampton, S., Hodge, J., & Mishra, J. (1996, July). Transition-ready or not: The aging of America's work force. *Public Personnel Management,* 25, 247.

Crandall, R.E. (1998, November). First-line supervisors: Tomorrow's professionals. *Personnel,* 24–31.

Crittenden, W.F., & Crittenden, V.L. (2000, Summer). Relationships be-tween organizational characteristics and strategic planning processes in nonprofit organizations. *Journal of Managerial Issues,* 12 (2).

Cummings, T.G., & Worley, C.G. (1993). *Organizational development and change* (5th ed.). St. Paul: West Publishing Company.

Cushieri, R. (1999, September 20). Discussions with Rose Cushieri, coordinator for the learning center, Romulus engine plant, General Motors Corporation, Romulus, MI.

Daft, R.L. (1997). *Management* (4th ed.) Fort Worth, TX: The Dryden Press.

Daft, R.L. (1999) *Leadership: Theory and practice.* Forth Worth, TX: The Dryden Press/Harcourt Brace College Publishers.

Dale, E. (1967). *Organizations*. New York: American Management Association.

Davenport, T.H., & Prusak, L. (1997). *Working knowledge: How organizations manage what they know.* Boston, MA: Harvard Business School Press.

David, F.R. (1999). *Strategic management: Concepts and Cases* (7th ed.). Upper Saddle River, NJ: Prentice Hall.

Davy, J., & Bohlander, G. (1992). Recent findings and practices in grievance-arbitration procedures. *Labor Law Journal*, 44.

Deal, T.E., & Kennedy, A.A. (1982). *Corporate cultures: The rites and rituals of corporate life.* Reading, MA: Addison-Wesley Publishing.

Dean, P.J. (1998). Performance improvement interventions: Methods for organizational learning. In P. J. Dean & D.E. Ripley (Eds.), *Performance improvement interventions: Instructional design and training.* Silver Spring, MD: International Society for Performance Improvement.

DeCenzo, D.A., & Robbins, S.P. (1996). *Human resource management* (5th ed.). New York: John Wiley & Sons.

DeCenzo, D.A., & Robbins, S.P. (1999). *Human resource management* (6th ed.). New York: John Wiley & Sons.

Deeprose, D. (1995). *The team coach.* New York: AMACOM.

Deku, B. (1999). Capital investment and spending (Report No. 4). Detroit, MI: WSU College of Education, IT 7320.

Deming, W.E. (1986). *Out of the crisis.* Boston, MA: Massachusetts Institute of Technology, Center for Advanced Engineering Study.

Dervitsiotis, K.N. (2000, July). Benchmarking and business paradigm shifts. *Total Quality Management*, 11 (4–6).

DeSimone, R.L., & Harris, D.M. (1998). *Human resource development* (2nd ed.). Fort Worth, TX: The Dryden Press.

Dess, G.G., & Picken, J.D. (1999). *Beyond productivity: How leading companies achieve superior performance by leveraging their human capital.* New York: AMACOM.

Dessinger, J.C. (1996). *Communication audit.* St. Clair Shores, MI: The Lake Group, Inc.

Dessinger, J.C., Brown, K.G., Reesman, M.N., & Elliott, L.E. (1998). Measuring attitudes to assess training: The IDL Group looks at learning and transfer from satellite training. In D.A. Schreiber and Z.L. Berge (Eds.), *Distance training: How innovative organizations are using technology to maximize learning and meet business objectives.* San Francisco: Jossey-Bass.

Dessinger, J.C., & Conley, L. (2001). Beyond the sizzle: Sustaining distance training for Ford Motor Company dealerships. In Z.L. Berge (Ed.), *Sustaining distance training: Integrating learning technologies into the fabric of the enterprise.* San Francisco: Jossey-Bass.

Dessler, G. (1997). *Human resource management* (7th ed.). Upper Saddle River, NJ: Prentice Hall.

Dessler, G. (1998). *Management: Leading people and organizations in the 21st century.* Upper Saddle River, NJ: Prentice Hall.

Deterline, W.A., & Rosenberg, M.J. (1992). *Performance technology: Success stories.* Silver Spring, MD: International Society for Performance Improvement.

Dilworth, R.L. (1998). Action learning in a nutshell. *Performance Improvement Quarterly*, 11 (1).

Dingwall, R. (1999, December). Six Sigma: What is it? VS&P's Global Communicator, 4 (3), pp. 1–2. Available online: www.mso.ford.comfcsd/vsp/news/dec99news/six_sigma.html.

Dixon, N.M. (1998). Action learning: More than just a task force. *Performance Improvement Quarterly*, 11 (1).

Dobbs, K. (1999). Winning the retention game. *Training*, 36 (9).

Dobbs, K. (2000). Who's in charge of e-learning? *Training*, 37 (6).

Dobbs, M.F. (1998). Managing diversity: The department of energy initiative. *Public Personnel Management*, 27 (2).

Dominowski, R.L., & Buyer, L.S. (2000, Summer). Retention of problem solutions: The re-solution effect. *The American Journal of Psychology*, 113 (2).

Donaldson, L., & Scannell, E.E. (1986). *Human resource development. The new trainer's guide.* Reading, MA: Addison-Wesley.

Dore, R.P. (1987). Taking Japan seriously: A Confusian perspective on leading economic issues. London: The Athlone Press. As cited in Mak, W.M. (2000, July). The tao of people-based management. *Total Quality Management*, 11, 4–6.

Dormant, D. (1999). Implementing human performance technology in organizations. In H.D. Stolovich & E.J. Keeps, (Eds.), *Handbook of human performance technology: Improving individual and organizational performance worldwide* (2nd ed.), (pp. 237–259). San Francisco: Jossey-Bass/Pfeiffer/ISPI.

Drafke, M.W., & Kossen, S. (1998). *The human side of organizations* (7th ed.). Reading, MA: Addison-Wesley.

Drucker, P.F. (1985). Getting things done: How to make people decisions. *Harvard Business Review,* 63 (4).

DuBain, A.J. (1996). *Reengineering survival guide: Managing and succeeding in the changing workplace.* Cincinnati, OH: Thomson Executive Press.

Dublin, L.E. (1995, June 5). Session M 43: Performance support and the business revolution. Presented at ASTD International Conference and Exposition, Dallas, TX.

Edwards, M.R., & Ewen, A.J. (1996). *360 degree feedback.* New York: AMACOM.

Eight things that training and performance professionals must know about knowledge management. (2000). Bill Communications, Inc. Available online: http://www.lakewoodconferences. com/kmwp/closing.html.

Eisenstat, R.A., & Dixon, D.L. (2000, July/August). Building organizational fitness. *Health Forum Journal,* 43 (4).

Ely, D. (2000, June). Looking before we leap. *Syllabus,* 13 (10).

Engelmeier, S. (2000, August 24). Phone interview with Shirley Engelmeier. Nashville, TN: Frontline Group, PACE Division, Workplace Issues Practice.

Epes, E. (August, 1995). Start an employee wellness program. *Training and Development,* 49 (8).

Epstein, R. (1999, July/August). The key to our emotions. *Psychology Today,* 32 (4).

Ergonomics: Break the RMI habit. (1997). Virginia Beach, VA: Coastal Training Technologies Corp. n.p.

Estes, F. (1999). Expert systems. In D.G. Langdon, K.S. Whiteside, K.S., & M.M. McKenna (Eds.), *Intervention resource guide: 50 performance improvement tools* (pp. 158–165). San Francisco: Jossey-Bass/Pfeiffer.

Ewald, H.R., & Burnett, R.E. (1997). *Business communication.* Upper Saddle River, NJ: Prentice Hall.

Executive Intelligence. (1999, November). Interview with Don Goleman, *Intelligence at Work,* 16 (11), 6–7.

Facts about Religious Discrimination (EEOC–FS/E-3). (1994, January). US Equal Employment Opportunity commission.

Fisher, B. (1996, January/February). Reengineering your business process. *Journal of Systems Management,* 47 (1).

Fitter, F. (1999, June). The human factor. *Knowledge Management,* 2 (6).

Fitz-Enz, J. (1997). The truth about best practices: What they are and how to apply them. In Ulrich, D., Losey, M., & Lake, G. (Eds.), *Tomorrow's HR Management: 48 thought leaders call for change* (pp. 217–226). New York: John Wiley & Sons.

Flynn, G. (1998). The harsh reality of diversity programs. *Workforce,* 77 (12).

Ford, R. (1999). Traditional vs real-time training. *Performance Improvement,* 38 (1).

Forsyth, D.R. (1983). *An introduction to group dynamics.* Monterey, CA: Brooks/Cole.

Fortune A. (2000, April 17). Paid Ford Motor Company advertisement, 141 (8).

Fortune B. (2000, May 29). Paid Ford Motor Company advertisement, 141 (10).

Fortune C. (2000, July 24). Paid Ford Motor Company advertisement, 141 (14).

Fortune D. (2000, September 4). PG&E Corporation Advertisement, 142 (5).

Fox, D., Byrne, V., & Rouault, F. (1999, August). Performance improvement: What to keep in mind. *Training and Development,* 53 (8).

Frank, L.R. (1999). *Random House Webster's Quotationary.* New York: Random House.

Freedman, M. (1999). *Prime time: How baby boomers will revolutionize retirement and transform America.* New York: Public Affairs.

Friedman, T.L. (1999). *The lexus and the olive tree.* New York: Farrar, Straus and Giroux.

Frontline Group. (2000). Evolution of diversity. Nashville, TN: Author (PACE Division).

Frottler, M.D., Hernandez, S.R., & Joiner, C.L. (1998). *Essentials of human resource management in health services organizations.* Albany, NY: Delmar Publishers.

Galagan, P.A. (1993). Navigating the differences. *Training and Development,* 47 (4).

Galagan, P.A. (1997). Strategic planning is back. *Training and Development,* 51 (4).

Galagan, P.A. (1998). Peter Drucker. *Training and Development,* 52 (9).

Gardenswartz, L., & Rowe, A. (1993). Managing diversity: A complete desk reference and planning guide In P.A.Galagan (1993). Navigating the differences. *Training and Development,* 47 (4).

Gardenschwartz, L., & Rowe, A. (1994). *The managing diversity survival guide: A complete collection of checklists, activities, and tips.* Burr Ridge, IL: Irwin Professional Publishing.

Gardner, R.L. (1999). Benchmarking organizational culture: Organization culture as a primary factor in safety performance. *Professional Safety,* 44 (3).

Garvin, D. (1993, July-August) Building a learning organization. *Harvard Business Review,* 71 (4).

Gatewood, R.D., & Feild, H.S. (1987). *Human resource selection.* Chicago: The Dryden Press.

Gatewood, R.D., & Feild, H.S. (1998). *Human resource selection* (4th ed.). Fort Worth, TX: Dryden Press.

Gayeski, D.M. (1992). Video-based instruction. In H.D. Stolovitch & E.J. Keeps (Eds.), *Handbook of human performance technology: A comprehensive guide for analyzing and solving performance problems in organizations* (pp. 431–448). San Francisco: Jossey-Bass/Pfeiffer/ISPI.

Gayeski, D.M. (1999). Multimedia learning systems: Design principles. In H.D. Stolovitch & E.J. Keeps (Eds.), *Handbook of human performance technology: Improving individual and organizational performance worldwide* (2nd ed.) (pp. 589–605). San Francisco: Jossey-Bass/Pfeiffer/ ISPI.

Gearson, R.F. (1999). The people side of performance improvement. *Performance Improvement,* 38 (10).

General Motors and Whirlpool: Two approaches for developing performance benchmarks. (2000, June). *HR Focus,* 77 (6).

Gerber, B. (1991). HELP! The rise of performance support systems. *Training,* 28 (12).

Gery, G. (1989). Gloria Gery. *CBT Directions, II* (6).

Gery, G.J. (1991). *Electronic performance support systems.* Boston, MA: Weingarten.

Gery, G.J. (1995). Attributes and behaviors of performance-centered systems. *Performance Improvement Quarterly,* 8 (1).

Gery, G.J. (1999). Electronic performance support system (EPSS). In D.G. Langdon, K.S. Whiteside, & M.M. McKenna (Eds.), *Intervention resource guide: 50 performance improvement tools* (pp. 142–148). San Francisco: Jossey-Bass/Pfeiffer.

Gibson, J.L., Ivancevich, J.M., & Donnelly, J.H., Jr. (1994). *Organizations: Behavior, structure, processes.* Burr Ridge, IL: Richard D. Irwin, Inc.

Gibson, J.W., & Hodgetts, R.M. (1986). *Organizational communication: A managerial perspective.* Orlando, FL: Academic Press College Division.

Gilbert, T.F. (1978). *Human competence: Engineering worthy performance.* New York: McGraw-Hill.

Gill, J.O. (1990). *Understanding financial statements: A primer of useful information.* Menlo Park, CA: Crisp Publications, Inc.

Gilmartin, R.V. (1999). Diversity of competitive advantage at Merck. *Harvard Business Review,* 77 (1).

Glaser, D.R. (2000). The potent pause: How organizations and individuals learn from experience. In E. Biech (Ed.), *The 2000 annual: Volume 2, Consulting* (pp. 167–173). San Francisco: Jossey-Bass/Pfeiffer.

Goleman, D. (1995). *Emotional intelligence.* New York: Bantam Books.

Goleman, D. (1998). *Working with emotional intelligence.* New York: Bantam Books.

Goleman, D. (2000). Leadership that gets results. *Harvard Business Review,* 78 (2).

Gomez-Mejia, L.R., Balkin, D.B., & Cardy, R.L. (1998). *Managing human resources* (2nd ed.). Upper Saddle River, NJ: Prentice Hall.

Gordon, J. (1992). Performance technology: Blueprint for the learning organization. *Training,* 29 (5).

Gordon, J. (1999). Intellectual capital and you. *Training,* 36 (9).

Gordon, J.R. (1996). *Organizational behavior: A diagnostic approach* (5th ed.). Englewood Cliffs, NJ: Prentice Hall.

Gordon, J.R. (1999). *Organizational behavior: A diagnostic approach* (6th ed.). Upper Saddle River, NJ: Prentice Hall.

Gordon, S.E. (1994). *Systematic training program design.* Englewood Cliffs, NJ: Prentice Hall.

Green, R. (2000, December). Reshaping Six Sigma at Honeywell. *Quality Digest,* 20 (12).

Green, T. (2000). *Motivation management: Fueling performance by discovering what people believe about themselves and their organizations.* Palo Alto, CA: Davies-Black.

Green, T.B., & Butkus, R. (1999). *Motivation, beliefs, and organizational transformation.* Westport, CT: Quorum.

Greenberg, J., & Baron, R.A. (1995). *Behavior in organizations: Understanding and managing the human side of work* (5th ed.). Englewood Cliffs, NJ: Prentice Hall.

Greenberg, J., & Baron, R.A. (2000). *Behavior in organizations: Understanding and managing the human side of work* (7th ed.). Upper Saddle River, NJ: Prentice Hall.

Greenwood, T., Wasson, A., & Giles, R. (1993, April). The learning organization: Concepts, processes, and questions. *Performance and Instruction*, 32 (4), 7–11.

Griffin, R. (1982). *Task design: An integrative approach.* Glenview, IL: Scott Foresman.

Grossman, E.S. (1977). *A guide to the determinants of capital investment.* New York: The Conference Board, Inc.

Grote, D. (2000). The secrets of performance appraisal: Best practices from the masters. *Across the Board,* 37 (5).

Grundling, E. (1999). How to communicate globally. *Training and Development*, 53 (6).

Guilford, J.P. (1955). the structure of human intellect. *Science,* 122.

Guralink, D.B. (Ed.). (1980). *Webster's New World Dictionary of the American Language,* Second College Edition. Englewood Cliffs, NJ: Simon and Schuster.

Hackman, J.R., Oldham, G., Janson, R., & Purdy, K. (Fall,1975). A new strategy for job enrichment. *California Management Review*, 16.

Hackos, J. (2000). Six tips on how to build online documentation employees will use. *The Lakewood*

Report on Technology for Learning. Minneapolis, MN: Lakewood Publications.

Hagevik, S. (2000, April). Career satisfaction and the importance of asking questions. Journal of *Environmental Health,* 62 (8).

Hale, J. (1998). *The performance consultant's fieldbook: Tools and techniques for improving organizations and people.* San Francisco: Jossey-Bass/Pfeiffer.

Hall, D.T., Otazo, K.L., & Hollenbeck, G.P. (1999, Winter). Behind closed doors: What really happens in executive coaching. *Organizational Dynamics,* 27 (3).

Hall, R.W. (1983). *Zero inventories.* Homewood, IL: Dow Jones-Irwin.

Halprin, M. (1994, April 8). Promoting learning organizations: New opportunities for performance technologists. Presentation to National Society for Performance and Instruction (NSPI) International Conference [Handout].

Hamel, G. (2000). *Leading the revolution.* Boston, MA: Harvard Business School Press.

Hamel, G., & Prahalad, C.K. (1994). *Competing for the future: Breakthrough strategies for seizing control of your industry and creating the markets of tomorrow.* Boston, MA: Harvard Business School Press.

Hamel, G., & Prahalad, C.K. (1995). Thinking differently. *Business Quarterly,* 59 (4).

Hammer, M., & Champy, J. (1993). *Reengineering the corporation: A manifesto for business revolution.* New York: HarperBusiness

Hansen, L.L. (2000). The architecture of safety excellence. *Professional Safety,* 45 (5).

Hargrove, R. (1995). *Masterful coaching.* San Francisco: Jossey-Bass/Pfeiffer.

Harkins, P.J. (1998, October). Why employees stay—or go. *Work force.*

Harless, J. (1993, April). Presentation at the 1993 National Society for Performance and Instruction. Chicago, IL.

Harless, J.H. (1986). Guiding performance with job aids. *Introduction to Performance Technology.* International Society for Performance Improvement. Silver Spring, MD.

Harrington-Mackin, D. (1994). *The team building tool kit.* New York: AMACOM.

Harris, M. (1997). *Human resource management: A practical approach.* Fort Worth, TX: The Dryden Press.

Hartzler, M., & Henry, J.E. (1994). *Team fitness: A how-to manual for building a winning work team.* Milwaukee: ASQC Quality Press.

Hatcher, T. (2000, August). The social responsibility performance outcomes model: Building socially responsible companies through performance improvement outcomes. *Performance Improvement,* 39 (7).

Hatcher, T., & Aragon, S.R. (2000, Summer). A code of ethics and integrity for HRD research and practice. *Human Resources Development Quarterly,* 11 (2).

Hathaway, P. (1990). *Giving and receiving feedback.* Menlo Park: CA: Crisp Publications.

Hattersley, M.E. (1999, May). How to get the best out of performance reviews. *Harvard Management Communication Letter,* 2 (5).

Hauser, J.R., & Clausing, D. The house of quality. *Harvard Business Review*, 66 (3).

Heirich, M.A., Erfurt, J.C., & Foote, A. (1992). The core technology of worksite wellness. *Journal of Occupational Medicine*, 34 (6).

Henderson, R.I. (2000). *Compensation management in a knowledge-based world* (8th ed.). Upper Saddle River, NJ: Prentice Hall.

Hendrich, A., & Nyhuis, A., et al. (August, 1995). Hospital falls: Development of a predictive model for clinical practice. *Applied Nursing Research*, 6 (3).

Hequet, M. (May, 1995). Ergonomics. *Training*, 32 (5).

Herman, R.E., & Gioia, J.L. (1998). Making work meaningful: Secrets of the future-focused corporation. *The Futurist*, 32 (9).

Herzberg, F. (January/February 1968). One more time: How do you motivate employees? *Harvard Business Review*, 46 (2).

Hiam. A. (1999). Dealing with conflict instrument. Amherst, MA: HRD Press, Inc.

Hicks, S. (2000). Succession planning. *Training and Development*, 54 (3).

Holton, E.F. (1999). Performance domains and their boundaries. In R.J. Torraco (Ed.), *Performance improvement theory and practice*. Monograph in the advances in developing human resources series, #1. Baton Rouge, LA: Academy of Human Resources and San Francisco: Berrett-Koehler Communications.

Hopke, W.E. (Ed.) (1968). *Dictionary of personnel and guidance terms* (pp. 3, 6, 331). Chicago: J.G. Ferguson Publishing Co.

Horn, R.M. (1999). Structured writing. In D.G. Langdon, K.S. Whiteside, & M.M. McKenna (Eds.), *Intervention resource guide: 50 performance improvement tools* (pp. 357-364). San Francisco: Jossey-Bass/Pfeiffer.

Houle, C. (1996). *The design of education* (2nd ed.). San Francisco: Jossey-Bass.

Hummels, H., & de Leede, J. (2000, July). Teamwork and morality: Comparing lean production and sociotechnology, *Journal of Business Ethics*, 26 (1).

Hunnicutt, D. (2000). America's healthiest companies: Scaling the heights of good health. *Business & Health*, 18 (3).

Hunt, M. (1998). *DreamMakers: Putting vision and values to work*. Palo Alto, CA: Davies-Black

Hutchison, C.S., & Stein, F.S. (1997). A whole new world of interventions: The PT practitioner as integrating generalist. *Performance Improvement*, 36 (10), 28–35.

Hwang, G., & Lee, J. (2000, July). The process innovation in a competitive telecommunications market: A case study. *Total Quality Management*, 11 (4–6).

Ibarra, H. (2000, March/April). Making partner: A mentor's guide to the psychological journey. *Harvard Business Review*, 78 (2).

Industry report 1999: Introduction. *Training*, 36 (10).

International Federation of Accountants (IFAC). Target costing for effective cost management: Product cost planning at Toyota Australia, FMAC Study 10. Available online: http://www.ifac.org.

Interview with Dan Goleman: Intelligence at work. (1999, November). *Executive Excellence*, 16 (11).

Interviewing. (1997). Society for Human Resource Management (SHRM) (Franklin Planner insert). Salt Lake City, UT: Franklin-Covey.

Jackson, T. (February 27, 1998). A black belt in quality. *Financial Times*.

Jacobs, R.L. (1999). Structured on-the-job training. In H.D. Stolovitch & E.J. Keeps (Eds.), *Handbook of human performance technology: Improving individual and organizational performance worldwide* (2nd ed.) (pp. 606-625). San Francisco: Jossey-Bass/Pfeiffer/ISPI.

Jacquet, J.L., & Miller, W.C., Jr. (1990). *The accounting cycle: A primer for nonfinancial managers*. Menlo Park, CA: Crisp Publications, Inc.

Jaffe, D.T., & Scott, C.D. (1998). Reengineering in practice: Where are the people? Where is the learning? *The Journal of Applied Behavioral Science*, 34 (3).

Jaffe, D.T., & Scott, C.D. (1998). Values: The organization's cultural bedrock. *Perspectives on Business and Global Change*, 12 (1).

Jaffee, C.L., Frank, F.D., & Mulligan, C.P. (1990). Assessing potential. In W.R. Tracey (Ed.), *Human resources management and development handbook* (2nd ed.). New York: AMACOM.

Janov, J.E. (1995, May). Creating meaning: The heart of learning communities. *Training and Development*, 49 (5).

Jewell, S.F., & Jewell, D.O. (1992). Organization design. In H.D. Stolovitch & E.J. Keeps (Eds.), *Handbook of human performance* technology: A comprehensive guide for analyzing and solving performance problems in organizations (pp. 211–232). San Francisco: Jossey-Bass/Pfeiffer/ISPI.

Johnson, L. (1999). Emotional intelligence. *Executive Excellence*, 16, (8).

Johnson, S.D. (1991). Training technical troubleshooters. *Technical and Skills Training*, 2 (7).

Jonash, R.S., & Sommerlatte, T. (1999). *The innovation premium: How next-generation companies are achieving peak performance and profitability.* Cambridge, MA: Perseus Books.

Jossi, F. (2000). Under construction. *Inside Technology Training*, 4 (7).

Juran, J.M. (August, 1986). The quality trilogy. *Quality Progress*, 19.

Karp, H.B., & Sutton, N. (1993, July). Where diversity training goes wrong. *Training*, 47 (7).

Katz, R.L. (1974). Skills of an effective administrator. *Harvard Business Review*, 52 (5).

Kaufman, R. (1998). The internet as the ultimate technology and panacea. *Educational Technology*, 38 (1).

Kaufman, R. (2000, July-August). Thriving and not just surviving: New directions for tomorrow's performance-improvement managers. *Education Technology*, XL (4).

Kaye, B., & Scheef, D. (2000, April). Mentoring. *InfoLine* (Issue 0004). Alexandria, VA: American Society for Training and Development.

Kearny, L., & Smith, P. (January, 1999). Creating workplaces where people can think: Cognitive ergonomics. *Performance Improvement*, 38 (1).

Keller, J.M. (1999). Motivational systems. In H.D. Stolovitch & E.J. Keeps (Eds.), *Handbook of human performance technology: Improving individual and organizational performance worldwide* (2nd ed.) (pp. 373–394). San Francisco: Jossey-Bass Pfeiffer/ISPI.

Kemper, C.L. (1998, February). Global training's critical success factors. *Training and Development*, 52 (2).

Kerker, S. (2000, January-February). Letter from the publisher: A Lilliput strategy for corporate universities. *The New Corporate University Review*, 8 (1).

Key Concepts: Glossary. (2000) Available online: http://www.EPSS.com.

Kilmann, R.H., Saxton, M.J., Serpa, R., & Associates. (1985). *Gaining control of the corporate culture.* San Francisco: Jossey-Bass.

Kim, D.H. (1993, Fall). The link between individual and organizational learning. *Sloan Management Review*, 35.

Kinlaw, D.G. (1992). *Continuous improvement and measurement for total quality.* San Diego, CA: Pfeiffer & Co. and Homewood, IL: Business and Irwin.

Kirkland, K., & Manoogian, S. (1998). *Ongoing feedback: How to get it, how to use it.* Greensboro, NC: Center for Creative Leadership.

Kirrane, D. (1990). Four by four: The case method. *Training and Development*, 44 (3).

Kiser, K. (2000) Operation learning. *Inside Technology Training*, 4 (5).

Klein, G., & Weick, K.E. (2000, June). Decisions. *Across the Board*, 37 (6).

Knowdell, R. (1996). *Building a career development program.* Palo Alto, CA: Davies-Black.

Kogut, B. (1999). What makes a company global? (Book review of The Myth of the Global Corporation, 1998). *Harvard Business Review*, 77 (1).

Kotter, J.P. (1990, May-June). What leaders really do. *Harvard Business Review*, 68 (3).

Kotter, J.P. (1996). *Leading change.* Boston, MA: Harvard Business School Press.

Kouzes, J.M., & Posner, B.Z. (1999). *Encouraging the heart: A leader's guide to rewarding and recognizing others.* San Francisco: Jossey-Bass.

Kozlowski, K. (2000, January 19). Teachers' union chief calls for big raises. *The Detroit News*.

Kraut, A.J. (1989, November). The role of the manager: What's really important in different management jobs. *Academy of Management Executives*.

Krumwiede, D.W., & Lavelle, J.P. (2000, June). The effect of top-manager personality on a total quality management environment. *Engineering Management Journal*, 12 (2).

Kuo, K. (2000, March/April). The power of mentoring. *Educause Review*, 35 (2).

Kurylko, D.T. (2000, July 3). Wagoner says tie-ups beat takeovers. *Automotive News*, 74, 58–82.

Kuse & Keil. (2000). *Technology-based training: The art and science of design and delivery.* San Francisco: Jossey-Bass.

LaBar, G. (1995). IRS Accounts for Ergonomics. *Occupational Hazards*, 57 (4).

Laffey, J. (1995). Dynamism in electronic performance support systems. *Performance Improvement Quarterly*, 8 (1).

Lanahan, E.D., & Maldonado, L. (1998). Accelerated decision making via action learning at the Federal Deposit Insurance Corporation (FDIC). *Performance Improvement Quarterly*, 11 (1).

Langdon, D.G. (1995). *The new language of work*. Amherst, MA: HRD Press.

Langdon, D.G. (1999). Training. In D.G. Langdon, K.S. Whiteside, & M.M. McKenna (Eds.), *Intervention resource guide: 50 performance improvement tools* (pp. 381–386). San Francisco: Jossey-Bass/Pfeiffer.

Langdon, D.G. (2000, March). Aligning performance: The ultimate goal of our profession. *Performance Improvement*, 39 (3).

Langdon, D.G., Whiteside, K.S., & McKenna, M.M. (Eds.). (1999). *Intervention resource guide: 50 performance improvement tools*. San Francisco: Jossey-Bass/Pfeiffer.

Lawler, E. (1986). *High involvement management*. San Francisco: Jossey-Bass.

Lawson, R.W. (1995). Utilizing performance technology in the implementation of a wellness program. *Performance and Instruction*, 34 (3).

LeBlanc, E., Vanderkam, L., & Vella-Zarb, K. (2000, July 10). Companies for minorities. *Fortune*, 142 (2).

Ledvinka, J., & Scarpello, V.G. (1991). *Federal regulation and human resource management* (2nd ed.) p. 215. Boston, MA: PWS-Kent.

Lee, H.K., Baek, E.O., & Schwen, T.A. (2000, April 12). Session W 15:

Knowledge management in an academic environment. Presented at International Society for Performance Improvement Conference & Expo, Cincinnati, OH.

Legal and effective interviewing: A desk reference. (1996). Virginia Beach, VA: Coastal Video Communications Corp.

Leibowitz, Z.B., Farren, C., & Kaye, B.L. (1986). *Designing career development systems*. San Francisco: Jossey-Bass.

Lengnick-Hall, M.L. (2000, Spring). Book review in *Personnel Psychology*, 53, 1 (pp. 224–227) of Murrell, A.J., Crosby, F.J., & Ely, R.J. (1999). *Mentoring dilemmas: Developmental relationships within multicultural organizations*. Mahwah, NJ: Lawrence Erlbaum Associates.

Leon, M. (2000, June). New economy, new risks. *Knowledge Management*, 3 (6).

Leonard, N.H., Beauvais, L.L., & Scholl, R.W. (1999). Work motivation: The incorporation of self-concept-based processes. *Human Relations*, 52 (8).

Libby, B., & Agnello, V. (2000, August). Ethical decision making and the law. *Journal of Business Ethics*, 26 (3).

Lienert, A. (1998, November 10). Group honors area companies that balance work, family life. *The Detroit News*.

Lloyd, S.R. (1996). *Leading teams: The skills for success*. West Des Moines, IA: America Media Publishing.

Longest, B.B., Jr., Rakich, J.S., & Darr, K. (2000). *Managing health services organizations* (4th ed.). Baltimore, MD: Health Professions Press.

Low, T.W., Ferrell, L., & Mansfield, P. (2000, June). A review of empirical

studies assessing ethical decision making in business. *Journal of Business Ethics*, 25 (3).

Lowe, T.A., & Mazzeo, J.M. (September, 1986). Crosby, Deming, Juran: Three preachers, one religion. *Quality*, 25 (9).

Lu, L., Rose, G.M., & Blodgett, J.G. (1999). The effects of cultural dimensions on ethical decision making in marketing: An exploratory study. *Journal of Business Ethics*, 18 (1).

Lucas, R.W. (1994). *Coaching skills: A guide for supervisors*. New York: McGraw-Hill.

Lyon, D.W., & Kirby, E.G. (2000, April). The career planning essay. *Journal of Management Education*, 24 (2).

Maddux, D.J., & Maddux, R.B. (1989). *Ethics in business: A guide for managers*. Menlo Park, CA: Crisp Publications.

Main, R.E. (2000). Leveraging technology for performance improvement. In G.M Piskurich, P. Beckschi, and B. Hall (Eds.), *The ASTD handbook of training design and delivery: A comprehensive guide to creating and delivering training programs—Instructor-led, computer-based, or self-directed* (pp. 453–472). New York: McGraw-Hill.

Mak, W.M. (2000, July). The tao of people-based management. *Total Quality Management*, 11 (4–6).

Makridakis, S. (1996, September). Business forecasting for management: Strategic business forecasting. *International Journal of Forecasting*, 12 (3).

Mantyla, K., & Gividen, J.R. (1997). *Distance learning: A step-by-step guide for trainers*. Alexandria, VA: American Society for Training and Development.

Marakas, G.M. (1999). *Decision support systems in the 21st century.* Upper Saddle River, NJ: Prentice Hall.

Marquart, M. (1999). Successful global training. *InfoLine* (Issue 9913). Alexandria, VA: American Society for Training and Development.

Marquardt, M.J. (1998). Using action learning with multicultural groups. *Performance Improvement Quarterly,* 11 (1).

Marquardt, M.J. (1999a, May 26). Action learning in action: The key to building learning organizations. Presentation at American Society for Training and Development International Conference and Exposition. Atlanta, GA. Session W406 [Handout].

Marquardt, M.J. (1999b). *Action learning in action: Transforming problems and people for world-class organizational learning.* Palo Alto, CA: Davies-Black Publishing.

Marsick, V.J., & Watkins, K.E. (1995). The learning organization: An integrative vision for HRD. *Human Resource Development Quarterly,* 5 (4).

Masciarelli, J.P. (1998). Managing staff relationships. *HR Focus,* 75 (8).

Maslow, A.H. (1970). *Motivation and personality* (2nd ed.). New York: Harper & Row Publishers.

Maynard, R. (1997, January). A wellness program's bottom line benefits. *Nation's Business.*

Mc Lean, R.A. (1997). *Financial management in health care organizations.* Albany, NY: Delmar Publishers.

McCall, M.W., Jr., Lombardo, M.M., & Morrison, A.M. (1988). As cited in DeSimone, R.L. & Harris, D.M. (1998). *Human resource development* (2nd ed.) (p. 419). Fort Worth, TX: The Dryden Press.

McCoy, T.J. (1996). *Creating an open book organization...where employees think and act like business partners.* New York: AMACOM.

McElroy, M. (1999, October). The second generation of KM. *Knowledge Management,* 2 (10).

McIlvaine, A.R. (1998). Work ethics. *Human Resources Executive,* 12 (11).

Mcintosh, A. Position paper on knowledge asset management. Edinburgh, UK: Artificial Intelligence Applications Institute (AIAI). Available online: http://www.aiai.ed.ac.uk/~alm/kam.html.

McLagan, P.A. (1989). *Models for HRD practice.* Alexandria, VA: American Society for Training and Development.

McLaughlin, C.P., & Kaluzny, A.D. (Summer, 1990). Total quality management in health: making it work. *Health Care Management Review,* 15 (3).

McMurrer, D.P., VanBuren, M.E., & Woodwell, W.H., Jr. (2000). *The 2000 ASTD state of the industry report.* Alexandria, VA: The American Society for Training and Development.

McNamara, C. (1998). Complete guide to ethics management: An ethics toolkit for managers. Available online: http://www.mapnp.org/library/ethics/ethxgde.htm.

Meade, J. (1998, November). Helpers for employee manuals and incentive pay plans. *HR Magazine,* 43 (12).

Mechanical Associates Service, Inc. Available online: http://www.mechassoc.com/maipm.htm.

Mehta, S.N. (2000, July 10). What minority employees really want. *Fortune,* 142 (2).

Meister, J.C. (1998). *Corporate university* (Revised and updated edition). New York: McGraw-Hill.

Meister, J.C. (2000). The CEO-driven learning culture. *Training and Development,* 54 (6).

Mendez-Russell, A., Wilderson, F., & Tolbert, A.S. (1994). *Exploring differences in the workplace.* Minneapolis, MN: Carlson Learning Systems.

Merli, G. (1991). *Co-Makership: The new supply strategy for manufacturers.* Cambridge, MA: Productivity Press.

Mescon, M.H., Bovee, C.L., & Thill, J.V. (1999). *Business today* (9th ed.). Upper Saddle River, NJ: Prentice Hall.

Meyer, H.R. (March, 1998). Small firms flock to quality system. *Nation's Business,* 863.

Milkovich, G.T., & Newman, J.M. (1993). *Compensation* (4th ed.). Homewood, IL: Richard D. Irwin.

Miller, F.A. (1998). Strategic culture change: The door to achieving high performance and inclusion. *Public Personnel Management,* 27 (2).

Miller, M. (1999). Emotional intelligence helps managers succeed. *Credit Union,* 65 (7).

Miller, T.Q. (1992). A customer's definition of quality. *Journal of Business Strategy,* 131.

Mink, M. (1996). Ergonomic audits can prevent injuries. *Credit Union Executive,* 36 (3).

Mitroff, I.I., & Denton, E.A. (1999, Summer). A study of spirituality in the workplace. *Sloan Management Review,* 40 (4).

Mondy, R.W., Noe, R.M., & Premeaux, S.R. (1999). *Human resource management* (7th ed.). Upper Saddle River, NJ: Prentice Hall.

Monk, A. (1994). Retirement and aging: An introduction to the columbia retirement handbook. In Monk, A. (Ed.), *The Columbia Retirement Handbook* (p. 3). New York: Columbia University Press

Moosbruker, J.B., & Loftin, R.D. (1998). Business process redesign and organizational development: Enhancing success by removing the barriers. *The Journal of Applied Behavioral Science,* 34 (3).

Morling, P., & Tanner, S. (2000, July). Benchmarking a public service business management system, *Total Quality Management,* 11 (4–6).

Morris, B. (2000, February 21). So you're a player. Do you need a coach? *Fortune,* 141 (4).

Morris, L. (1999, November/ December). Are you emotionally intelligent? *The British Journal of Administrative Management,* 25 (4).

Moseley, J.L., & Solomon, D.L. (May/June, 1997). Confirmative evaluation: A new paradigm for continuous improvement. *Performance Improvement,* 36 (5).

Mumford, A. (1992). Individual and organizational learning: The pursuit of change. *Management Decision,* 30 (6).

Murphy, T.H. (1996). Verbal interaction in videoconference classes. Presented at the 12th Annual Conference on Distance Teaching and Learning. University of Wisconsin at Madison.

Nahavandi, A., & Malekzadeh, A.R. (1999). *Organizational behavior.* Upper Saddle River, NJ: Prentice Hall.

Napier, R., Sidle, C., & Sanaghan, P. (1998). *High impact tools and activities for strategic planning: Creative techniques for facilitating your organization's planning process.* New York: McGraw-Hill.

Nash, L.L. (1981, November-December). Ethics without sermons. *Harvard Business Review,* pp. 79–90. Cited in Nierenberg, G.I. (1987). *Workable ethics: What you need to succeed in business and life.* New York: Nierenberg and Zeif Publishers.

Neal, J.A. (1997). Spirituality in management education: A guide to resources. *Journal of Management Education,* 21 (1).

Needles, B.E., Jr., Anderson, H.R., & Caldwell, J.C. (1990). *Principles of accounting* (4th ed.). Boston, MA: Houghton Mifflin Company.

Nelson, B. (1994). *1001 ways to reward employees.* New York: Workman Publishing.

Nelson, B. (2000, May/June). Are performance appraisals obsolete? *Compensation and Benefits Review,* 32 (3).

Nicholas, B. (2000, August 15). Phone interview. Yocom and McKee Law Firm, specialists in affirmative action plans.

Nowack, K.M. (1994). The secrets of succession planning. *Training and Development,* 48 (11).

O'Donnell, M.P. (1986) Definition of health promotion: Part II: Levels of programs. *American Journal of Health Promotion,* 1 (2).

OSHA out to lunch. (2000, January 10). *Crain's Detroit Business,* 16 (2).

Ostrom, L.T. (1993). *Creating the ergonomically sound workplace.* San Francisco: Jossey Bass.

Oswald, S.L., & Mossholder, K.W., & Harris, S.G. (1997). Relations between strategic involvement and managers' perceptions of environment and competitive strengths. *Group & Organization Management,* 22(3).

Otterbein College, Westerville, Ohio. (October 15, 1999). Instructional designer. *The Chronicle of Higher Education Bulletin Board.*

Palm, K. (2000, April 24). Corporate wellness programs are no longer just a walk in the park. *Crain's Detroit Business,* 16 (17).

Paul, L.G. (1999, September). Thinking together. *Inside Technology Training,* 3 (8).

Pavlinski, K. (1999, April). Compensation design in college station: Skill- and competency-based pay. *Public Management,* 81 (4).

Payne, T., & Mobley, M. (1993, May). Valuing and managing diversity. *InfoLine* (Issue 9305). Alexandria, VA: American Society for Training and Development.

Pepitone, J.S. (1995). *Future training: A roadmap for restructuring the training function.* Dallas, TX: AddVantage Learning Press.

Peters, T. (2000, June). We are all Michelangelos. *Executive Excellence,* 17 (6).

Peterson, D.B., & Hicks, M.D. (1999, February). Strategic coaching: Five ways to get the most value. *HR Focus—Special Report on Training and Development.* New York: American Management Association.

Peterson, R.T. (1996, Summer). An analysis of contemporary forecasting in small business. *Journal of Business Forecasting Methods and Systems,* 15 (2).

Pfeiffer, J., & Sutton, R.I. (2000). *The knowing-doing gap: How smart companies turn knowledge into action*. Amherst, MA: Harvard Business School Press.

Pipe, P. (1992). Ergonomic performance aids. In H.D. Stolovitch & E.J. Keeps (Eds.), *Handbook of human performance technology: A comprehensive guide for analyzing and solving performance problems in organizations* (pp. 352–364). San Francisco: Jossey-Bass/Pfeiffer/ISPI.

Porter, M.E. (1980). *Competitive strategy: Techniques for analyzing industries and competitors*. New York: Free Press.

Porter, M.E. (1997). Creating advantages. *Executive Excellence, 14* (12).

Pramik, M. (1999, January 18). Wellness programs give businesses healthy bottom line. *Columbus Dispatch*.

Pritchett, P. (1992). *Teamwork: The team member handbook*. Dallas, TX: Pritchett & Associates, Inc.

Proudfit, C. (1999, September). The open book management opportunity. Available online: www.tsbj. com/editorial/02050914.htm.

Puterbaugh, G. (1990). CBT and performance support. *CBT Directions*, III (6).

Quay, J. (2000, May). The thinking manager's toolbox: Effective processes for problem solving and decision making. *Consulting to Management*, 11 (1).

Quinn, R.E., Spreitzer, G.M., & Brown, M.V. (2000, June). Changing others through changing ourselves: The transformation of human systems. *Journal of Management Inquiry*, 9, 2.

Rakich, J.S., Longest, B.B., Jr., & Darr, K. (1992). *Instructor's manual for managing health services organizations* (3rd ed.). Baltimore, MD: Health Professions Press.

Ramsey, R.D. (August, 1995). What supervisors should know about ergonomics. *Supervisor,* 56 (12).

Rantakyro, L. (2000, June). Strategic management in small metal job shops in Sweden and the US. *Engineering Management Journal*, 12 (2).

Raybould, B. (1995). Performance support engineering: An emerging development methodology for enabling organizational learning. *Performance Improvement Quarterly*, 8 (1).

Rees, F. (1992). From controlling to facilitating: How to LEAD. In J.W. Pfeiffer, (Ed.), *The 1992 annual: Volume 1, training* (pp. 213–222). San Francisco: Jossey-Bass/Pfeiffer.

Reif, W.E., & Tinnell, R.C. (1973, Autumn). A diagnostic approach to job enrichment. *MSU Business Topics*, 22–97.

Remich, N.C., Jr. (October, 1999). Steps cut costs. Business News Publishing Co. Available online: http:// www.proquest.com/pdqweb.

Render, B., & Stair, R.M., Jr. (1997). *Quantitative analysis for management* (6th ed.). Upper Saddle River, NJ: Prentice Hall.

Riekse, R.J., & Holstege, H. (1996). *Growing older in America*. New York: The McGraw-Hill Companies, Inc.

Rigby, D.K. (1998). What's today's special at the consultants' café? *Fortune*, 138 (5).

Robbins, S.P. (2001). *Organizational behavior* (9th ed.). Upper Saddle River, NJ: Prentice Hall.

Robbins, S.P., & Coulter, M. (1999). *Management* (6th ed.). Upper Saddle River, NJ: Prentice Hall.

Robbins, S.P., & DeCenzo, D.A. (1998). *Supervision today* (2nd ed.). Upper Saddle River, NJ: Prentice Hall.

Robinson, D.V. (1998, December). Behavioral interviewing at CIGNA. HR Focus, 75(12) Available online: http.://wwwproquestcom.

Roehl, J., Murphy, S., & Burns, S. (2000, May/June). Developing a model for ethical dialogue and decisionmaking. *Performance Improvement*, 39 (5).

Rosen, R., Digh, P., Singer, M., & Phillips, C. (2000). *Global literacies: Lessons on business leadership and national cultures*. New York: Simon & Schuster.

Rosen, R.H. (1991). *The healthy company: Eight strategies to develop people, productivity, and profits*. Los Angeles, CA: Jeremy P. Tarcher.

Rosenbaum, B.L. (1982). *How to motivate today's workers: Motivational models for managers and supervisors*. New York: McGraw-Hill.

Rosenberg, M.J. (1996). Human performance technology: Foundations for human performance improvement. In W.J. Rothwell (Ed.), *ASTD models for human performance improvement, roles, competencies and outputs* (pp. 5–10). Alexandria, VA: American Society for Training and Development.

Rosenberg, M.J. (1998, November-December). Tangled up in terms. *Performance Improvement*, 37 (9).

Rosenberg, M.J. (2000). Reinventing training. *Knowledge Management*, 3 (8).

Rosenberg, M., Coscarelli, W.C., & Hutchison, C.A. (1999). The origins and evolution of the field. In H.D. Stolovitch & E.J. Keeps (Eds.), *Handbook of human performance technology: Improving individual and organizational performance worldwide* (pp. 22–46). San Francisco: Jossey-Bass/Pfeiffer/ISPI.

Rosenzweig, P. (1998). Managing the new global workforce: Fostering diversity, forging consistency. *European Management Journal,* 16 (6).

Rossett, A. (1992). Analysis of human performance problems. In H.D. Stolovitch & E.J. Keeps (Eds.), *Handbook of human performance technology: Improving individual and organizational performance worldwide* (pp. 97–113). San Francisco: Jossey-Bass.

Rossett, A. (1999). *First things fast: A handbook for performance analysis.* San Francisco: Jossey-Bass/Pfeiffer.

Rossett, A. (2000, May). Knowledge management meets analysis. *Training and Development,* 53 (5).

Rossett, A., & Gautier-Downes, J. (1991). *A handbook of job aids.* San Diego, CA: Pfeiffer & Company.

Rothwell, W., Hohne, C.K., & King, S.B. (2000). *Human performance improvement: Building practitioner competence.* Houston, TX: Gulf Publishing, Inc.

Rothwell, W.J. (1996). *ASTD models for human performance improvement: Roles, competencies, and outputs.* Alexandria, VA: American Society for Training and Development.

Rothwell, W.J. (1996). *Beyond training and development: State-of-the-art strategies for enhancing human performance.* New York: AMACOM.

Rothwell, W.J., & Kazanas, H.C. (1994). *Improving on-the-job training: How to establish and operate a comprehensive OJT program.* San Francisco: Jossey-Bass.

Rothwell, W.J., & Sanders, E.S. (1999). ASTD models for workplace

learning and performance. Sunrise session presented at American Society for Training and Development International Conference and Expo, Orlando, FL.

Roush, M. (2000, May 15). Why executives fail: Not enough of the right info. *Crain's Detroit Business,* 16 (20).

Roy, C., & Seguin, F. (2000, June). The institutionalization of efficiency-oriented approaches for public service. *Public Productivity and Management Review,* 23 (4).

Russo, E., & Eckler, M.P. (1994). Mastering conflict. King of Prussia, PA: *Human Resource Development Quarterly.*

Sachs, R.T. (1992). *Productive performance appraisals.* New York: American Management Association.

Salopek, J.J. (1999, June). Good Scouts. *Training and Development,* 53 (6).

Salopek, J.J., & Kesting, B. (1999, February). Stop playing games. *Training and Development,* 53 (2).

Sanchez, C.M. (2000). Performance improvement in international environments: Designing individual performance interventions to fit national cultures. *Performance Improvement Quarterly,* 13 (2).

Sanchez, D. (1999, August). Putting motivation back in sales incentives. *Sales and Marketing Management,* 151 (8).

Sanders, E.S., & Ruggles, J.L. (2000, June). HPI soup: Too many cooks haven't spoiled the broth. *Training and Development,* 54 (6).

Sashkin, M., & Kiser, K.J. (1983). *Putting total quality management to work.* San Francisco: Berrett-Koehler Publishers.

Savageau, G. (1996). World class suggestion systems still work well. *The Journal for Quality and Participation,* 19 (2).

Scarpello, V.G., & Ledvinka, J. (1988). *Personnel/human resource management: Environments and functions.* Boston, MA: PWS-Kent Publishing Company.

Scheinin, R. (1999, October 10). Trauma focuses you: Conversations with Robert Grant. *Detroit Free Press.*

Schermerhorn, J.R., Jr. (1999). *Management* (6th ed.). New York: John Wiley & Sons.

Schermerhorn, J.R., Hunt, J.G., & Osborn, R.N. (2000). *Organizational behavior* (7th ed.). New York: John Wiley & Sons.

Schlender, B. (1998, September 28). Peter Drucker takes the long view. *Fortune,* 138 (6).

Schonberger, R.J. (1982). *Japanese manufacturing techniques: Nine hidden lessons in simplicity.* New York: The Free Press.

Schreiber, D.A. (1998). Organizational technology and its impact on distance training. In D.A. Schreiber & Z.L. Berge (Eds.), *Distance training: How innovative organizations are using technology to maximize learning and meet business objectives* (pp. 3–18). San Francisco: Jossey-Bass.

Schuler, R.S., & Huber, V.L. (1993). *Personnel and human resource management* (5th ed.). Minneapolis/St. Paul, MN: West Publishing Company.

Schultz, D., & Schultz, S.E. (1998). *Psychology and work today: An introduction to industrial and organizational psychology* (7th ed.). Upper Saddle River, NJ: Prentice Hall.

Schwartz, S.H., & Bilsky, W. (1990). Toward a theory of the universal content and structure of values: Extensions and cross-cultural replications. *Journal of Personality and Social Psychology,* 58, pp. 878–891. As cited in Leonard, N.H., Beauvais, L.L., & Scholl, R.W. (1999). Work motivation: The incorporation of self-concept-based processes. *Human Relations,* 52 (8).

Schwen, T., & Burton, C. (1999, March 25). Knowledge management at a global R&D organization—offering a KM primer to senior management: A case study. Session T48. Presented at International Society for Performance Improvement Conference. Long Beach, CA.

Scott, W.G. (1967). *Organization theory.* Homewood, IL: Richard D. Irwin, Inc.

Segal, J. (2000, March/April). Mirror-image mentoring. *HR Magazine,* 45 (3).

Seibert, K.W., Hall, D.T., & Kram, K. (1995). Strengthening the weak link in strategic executive development: Integrating individual development and global business strategy. *Human Resource Management,* 34.

Senge, P.M. (1990). *The fifth discipline.* New York: Currency Doubleday.

Sessa, V.J. (1994). Can conflict improve team effectiveness? *Issues & Observations,* 14 (4).

Shand, D. (1999). Return on knowledge. *Knowledge Management,* 2 (4).

Shea, G.F. (1988). *Practical ethics.* New York: American Management Association.

Shea, G.F. (1992). *Mentoring.* Menlo Park, CA: Crisp Publications.

Sheerer, J.L. (1998). Lessons in leadership: Keys to success from some of corporate America's best-known leaders. *Healthcare Executive,* 13 (2).

Shepard, R., Fasko, D., Jr., & Osborne, F.H. (1999, Summer). Intrapersonal intelligence: Affective factors in thinking. *Education,* 119 (4).

Sherman, A., Bohlander, G., & Snell, S. (1996). *Managing human resources* (10th ed.). Cincinnati, OH: South-Western College Publishing.

Sherry, P. (1990, August). Web-based training: Using technology to design adult learning experiences. *Technical Communication,* 46 (3).

Shortell, S.M., & Kaluzny, A.D. (1997). *Essentials of health care management.* Albany, NY: Delmar Publishers.

Signs you worked during the 90s. (2000, June 19). Online: Personal email message.

Silverman, L.L., & Ernst, L. (1999). SEDUCE: An effective approach to experiential learning. In E. Biech (Ed.), *The 1999 annual: Volume 1, training* (pp. 259–265). San Francisco: Jossey-Bass/Pfeiffer.

Silvestri, G.T., & Lukasiewicz, J.M. (1987, September). A look at occupational employment trends to the year 2000. *Monthly Labor Review.*

Simpson, M., & Kondouli, D. (2000, July). A practical approach to benchmarking in three service industries. *Total Quality Management,* 11 (4–6).

Skyrme, D. (1998). *Measuring the value of knowledge.* Business Intelligence LTD.

Smith, J.C. (2000, April). Knowledge management for performance improvement: Building "smarts" for small enterprises. Session W31. Presented at International Society for Performance Improvement Conference. Cincinnati, OH.

Spendolini, M.J. (1992). *The benchmarking book.* New York: AMACOM.

Spitzer, D.R. (May/June, 1989). Best performer analysis. *Performance and Instruction,* 28 (5).

Spitzer, D.R. (1992). The design and development of effective interventions. In H.P. Stolovitch & E.J. Keeps (Eds.), *Handbook of human performance technology: Improving individual and organizational performance worldwide* (pp. 114–129). San Francisco: Jossey-Bass.

Spurge, L., Spivak, K.M., & Hamermesh, R.G. (1997). *Knowledge exchange: Business encyclopedia.* Santa Monica, CA: Knowledge Exchange.

Stamps, D. (1999a). Enterprise training: This changes everything. *Training,* 36 (1).

Stamps, D. (1999b). Wired, wired world. *Training,* 36 (8).

Stern, G., & Borcia, Y. (2000, June). Motivation strategy. *Executive Excellence,* 17 (6).

Stewart, T.A., Taylor, A., Petre, P., & Schlender, B. (1999, November). Businessman of the century. *Fortune,* 140 (10).

Stolovitch, H., & Thiagarajan, S. (1980). *Frame games.* Englewood Cliffs, NJ: Educational Technology Publications.

Stone, F.M. (1999). *Coaching, counseling & mentoring.* New York: AMACOM.

Stopwatches ready? 60 seconds on KM. (2000, May 2). Online Learning News, 3 (6). Available online: http://www.lakewoodconferences.com.

Strassman, P. (1999, April). Manage knowledge capital. *Knowledge Management,* 2 (4).

Strouppe, J. R. (1998). Measuring interactivity. *Performance Improvement*, 37 (9).

Suzaki, K. (1987). *The new manufacturing challenge: Techniques for continuous improvement*. New York: The Free Press.

Sveiby, K-E. (1999, June). Distill human competence. *Knowledge Management*, 2 (6).

Swanson, R.A. (1994). *Analysis for improving performance: Tools for diagnosing organizations and documenting workplace expertise*. San Francisco: Berrett-Koehler Publishers.

Swenson, J. (1999). Communication. In D.G. Langdon, K.S. Whiteside, & M.M. McKenna, (Eds.), *Intervention resource guide: 50 performance improvement tools* (pp. 91–97). San Francisco: Jossey-Bass/Pfeiffer.

Tally, B.D., & Waller, M.L. (1992, February). Sexual harassment: What trainers need to know. *InfoLine* (Issue 9202). Alexandria, VA: American Society for Training and Development.

Tarpley, N. (2000, July 10). Hyatt gets cooking in high school. *Fortune*, 142 (2).

Tebo, M.G. (2000, March). Collecting good advice. *American Bar Association Journal*, 86.

Tersine, R., & Harvey, M. (1998). Global customerization of markets has arrived. *European Management Journal*, 16 (1).

Thach, L., & Heinselman, T. (1999, March). Executive coaching defined. *Training and Development*, 53 (3).

Thaler-Carter, R.E. (2000, May). Whither global leaders? *HR Magazine*, 45 (2).

The corporate university best-in-class report. (1998). Institute for Education Best Practices (IEBP) and American Productivity and Quality Center (APQC). Available online: http://www.apqc.org.

Thiagarajan, S. (1999a). How to design and guide debriefing. In E. Biech, (Ed.), *The 1999 annual: Volume 1, training* (pp. 247–257). San Francisco: Jossey-Bass/Pfeiffer.

Thiagarajan, S. (1999b). Small group activities. In H.D. Stolovitch and E.J. Keeps (Eds.), *Handbook of human performance technology: A comprehensive guide for analyzing and solving performance problems in organizations* (pp. 412–430). San Francisco: Jossey-Bass/Pfeiffer/ISPI.

Thomas, D.A., & Ely, R.J. (1996, September, October). Making differences matter: A new paradigm for managing diversity. *Harvard Business Review*, reprint #96510.

Thomas, D.C. (1999). Cultural diversity and work group effectiveness: An experimental study. *Journal of Cross-Cultural Psychology*, California, 30 (2).

Thornton, G.C. (1992). *Assessments centers in human resource management*. Reading, MA: Addison-Wesley.

Thurley, D. (1990). Foreword. In S. Mito (Ed.), The Honda book of management: A leadership philosophy for high industrial success (pp. viii-xvi). London: Kogan Page. As cited in Mak, W.M. (2000, July). The Tao of people-based management. *Total Quality Management*, 11, 4–6.

Tonnessen, T. (2000, July). Process improvement and the human factor. *Total Quality Management*, 11, 4–6.

Tosti, D., & Jackson, S.D. (1997, November/December). The orga-

nizational scan. *Performance Improvement*, 36 (10).

Tosti, D., & Jackson, S. (2000, May-June). Get the culture you need: Why understanding culture change is important to HPT. *News & Notes: The Newsletter of the International Society for Performance Improvement*.

Tracey, W.R. (1995). *Training employees with disabilities: Strategies to enhance learning & development for an expanding part of your workforce*. New York: AMACOM.

Trigergis, L. (1995). *Real options in capital investment: Models, strategies, and applications*. Westport, CT: Praeger Publishers.

Trunko, M.E. (1993). Open to suggestions. *HR Magazine*, 38 (2).

Tufts Ergonomic Alliance. *Work-place Ergonomic Safety*. [Brochure]. Boston, MA: Tufts Ergonomic Alliance.

Tully, S. (1995, June 12). America's healthiest companies. *Fortune*, 136 (11).

Tziner, A., Joanis, C., & Murphy, K. (2000, June). A comparison of three methods of performance appraisal with regard to goal properties, goal perception, and ratee satisfaction. *Group and Organization Management*, 25 (2).

UAW-Ford National Joint Committee on Health and Safety. (1992). Guidelines, responsibilities and safe practices (GRASP): A reference manual for salaried employees, research, engineering and technical development components. Dearborn, MI: Ford Motor Company.

Ulrich, D. (1997). *Human resource champions: The next agenda for adding value and delivering results*.

Boston, MA: Harvard Business School Press.

Ulrich, D. (1998, January-February). A new mandate for human resources. *Harvard Business Review,* 76 (1).

Ulrich, D., Brockbank, W., & Yeung, A. (1989). Beyond belief: A benchmark for human resources. *Human Resource Management,* 28 (3).

US Department of Labor, Occupational Safety and Health Administration. (1980). All about OSHA (revised). Washington, DC: Author.

US Equal Employment Opportunity Commission. (1994, January). Facts about religious discrimination (EEOC-FS/E-3). Washington, DC: Author.

Unger, J.A. (1997, May). Enabling effective teams. *ISPI Technologist* III (5). Allen Park, MI: International Society for Performance Improvement, Michigan Chapter.

Van Duch, D. (1999, September 27). Written bias policy alone is no defense. *National Law Journal,* 22 (5).

Van Tiem, D., & West, A.C. (1997). Career self-management: Employability for the new millennium. *Performance Improvement,* 36 (7).

Van Tiem, D.M., Moseley, J.L., & Dessinger, J.C. (2000a). *Fundamentals of performance improvement: A guide to improving people, process, and performance.* Silver Spring, MD: International Society for Performance Improvement.

VanBuren, M.E. (1999, May). A yardstick for knowledge management. *Training and Development,* 53 (5).

VanBuren, M.E., & King, S.B. (2000). *The 2000 ASTD international comparisons report: ASTD's annual accounting of worldwide patterns in employer-provided training.* Alexandria, VA: American Society for Training and Development.

Vasquez-Abad, J., & Winer, L.R. (1992). Emerging trends in instructional interventions. In H.D. Stolovitch & E.J. Keeps (Eds.), *Handbook of human performance technology: A comprehensive guide for analyzing and solving performance problems in organizations* (pp. 672–687). San Francisco: Jossey-Bass/Pfeiffer/ISPI.

Verduin, J.R., & Clark, T.A. (1991). *Distance education: The foundations of effective practice.* San Francisco: Jossey-Bass.

Viale, J.D. (1995). *Basics of manufacturing: Fundamental concepts for decision makers.* Menlo Park, CA: Crisp Publications, Inc.

Vicere, J. (1996). Cited in DeSimone, R.L. and Harris, D.M. (1998) *Human resource development* (2nd ed.) (p. 416). Forth Worth, TX: Dryden Press.

Villachica, S.W., & Stone, D.L. (1999). Performance support systems. In H.D. Stolovitch & E.J. Keeps (Eds.), *Handbook of human performance technology: Improving organizational performance worldwide* (2nd ed.) (pp. 441–463). San Francisco: Jossey-Bass/Pfeiffer/ISPI.

Von Hoffman, C. What kind of training is this anyway? *Inside Technology Training,* 2 (10).

Vroom, V.H. (1964). *Work and motivation.* New York: John Wiley & Sons.

Waagen, A.K. (2000). How to budget training. *InfoLine* (Issue 0007). Alexandria, VA: American Society for Training & Development.

Wagner, C.G. (2000, July/August). Global living standards improve. *The Futurist,* 34 (4).

Wagner, E.D. (1999). Beyond distance education: distributed learning systems. In H.D. Stolovitch & E.J. Keeps (Eds.), *Handbook of human performance technology: Improving individual and organizational performance worldwide* (2nd ed.) (pp. 626–648). San Francisco: Jossey-Bass/Pfeiffer/ISPI.

Wagner, S. (1999). Globalization drives training in Europe. *Training and Development,* 53 (2) 59.

Waitley, D. (1979). *The psychology of winning.* Chicago: Nightingale-Conant Corporation.

Walton, M. (1986). *The Deming management method.* New York: Perigee Books (Putman Publishing Group).

Wasik, J.F. (2000). The new retirement philosophy. *Aging Today,* XXI (2).

Watkins, R., Leigh, D., & Kaufman, R. (2000, April). A scientific dialogue: A performance accomplishment code of professional conduct. *Performance Improvement,* 38 (4).

Watson, T.R. (1999). *Corporate communication assessment.* Amherst, MA: HRD Press.

Waugh, D.A. (1999, Number 3). Global trends in training and development. *IFTDO NEWS.*

Webster's new universal unabridged dictionary. (1979). (2nd ed.). New York: Simon and Schuster.

Webster's new universal unabridged dictionary. (1983). (2nd ed.). Cleveland, OH: Dorset & Baber.

Weisbord, M.R. (1987). *Productive workplaces: Organizing and managing for dignity, meaning, and community.* San Francisco: Jossey-Bass.

Wellins, R., & Rioux, S. (2000, May). The growing pains of globalizing

HR. *Training and Development,* 54 (5).

Wertz, L.H. (1996). Executive development. In R.L. Craig (Ed.), The *ASTD training and development handbook: A guide to human resource development* (4th ed.) (pp. 622–635). New York: McGraw-Hill.

Westgaard, O. (1992). Standards and ethics for practitioners. In H.D. Stolovitch & E.J. Keeps (Eds.), *Handbook of human performance technology: A comprehensive guide for analyzing and solving performance problems in organizations* (pp. 576–601). San Francisco: Jossey-Bass/Pfeiffer/ISPI.

Weston, J.F., & Bringham, E.F. (1979). *Essentials of managerial finance.* Hinsdale, IL: The Dryden Press.

Wetzel, M. (2000). Virtual driving. *Inside Technical Training,* 4 (7).

Whirlpool shared values. (1998, May 12). Available online: http://www2.whirlpool.com/html/corp/story/corpvalues.htm.

Whitcomb, C. (1999, June). Scenario-based training at the FBI. *Training and Development,* 53 (6).

Whiting, R. (1999, November 22). Myths and realities: What's behind one of the most misunderstood IT strategies. Internet Week ONLINE News. Available online: http://www.informationweek.com/762/know2.htm.

Why Ford came clean. (2000, May 22). *Newsweek,* xxxvi (20).

Wiig, K.M. (1997). Integrating intellectual capital and knowledge management. *Long Range Planning,* 30 (3).

Williams, R.S. (1998). *Performance management: Perspectives on employee performance.* London: International Thomson Business Press.

Wilson, C. (1999, May/June). Tough choices. *The British Journal of Administrative Management.*

Wilson, C.E. (1953, January 23). Remarks to the press by Secretary of Defense, Charles E. Wilson, President Eisenhower's Cabinet.

Winer, L.R., Rushby, N., & Vasquez-Abad, J. (1999). Emerging trends in instructional interventions. In H.D. Stolovitch & E.J. Keeps (Eds.), *Handbook of human performance technology: Improving individual and organizational performance worldwide* (2nd ed.) (pp. 867–894). San Francisco: Jossey-Bass/Pfeiffer/ISPI.

Witucki, A.P. (2000). *Cash flow analysis.* (Report No. 4). Detroit, MI: WSU College of Education, IT 7320.

Womack, J.P., Jones, D.T., & Roos, D. (1991). *The machine that changed the world.* New York: Harper Perennial.

Wood, B., & Scott, A. (1989, April). The gentle art of feedback. *Personnel Management* 21(4), pp. 48–51. Cited in Coaching and feedback. *InfoLine* (June, 1990, Issue 006). Alexandria, VA: American Society for Training and Development.

Yelon, S.L. (1999). Live classroom instruction. In H.D. Stolovitch & E.J. Keeps (Eds.), *Handbook of human performance technology: Improving individual and organizational performance worldwide* (2nd ed.) (pp. 485–517). San Francisco: Jossey-Bass/Pfeiffer/ISPI.

Yiu, L., & Saner, R. (1998). Use of action learning as a vehicle for capacity building in China. *Performance Improvement Quarterly,* 11 (1).

Yocum, & McKee, P.C. (1996). *The complete AAP software information.* Self-published report. Golden, CO.

Yorks, L., O'Neil, J., Marsick, V.J., Lamm, S., Kaladny, R., & Nilson, G. (1998). Transfer of learning from an action reflection learning program. *Performance Improvement Quarterly,* 11 (1).

Zachary, M.K. (2000, June). Labor law for supervisors: Creative problem solving as a complement to rational problem solving. *Supervision,* 61 (6).

Zak. (August 1999). p. 1. Available online: http://proquest.umi.com.

Zemke, R. (1999, September). Why organizations still aren't learning. *Training,* 36 (9).

Zenger, J., Ulrich, D., & Smallwood, N. (2000, March). The new leadership development. *Training and Development,* 54 (3).

Ziegler, J. (1998, December). America's healthiest companies. *Business & Health,* 16 (12).

AUTHORS' BIOGRAPHIES

Darlene Van Tiem

Dr. Darlene Van Tiem is an assistant professor in the School of Education, the University of Michigan–Dearborn. From 1992 to 1996, Darlene was the training director in the Human Resources Department at Ameritech advertising services (yellow pages business unit). She was responsible for HR training (not sales or systems specific) for four states: Michigan, Ohio, Indiana, and Wisconsin. From 1986 to 1992, Darlene was with General Physics Corporation. She was curriculum manager for General Motors Technical Curriculum and program manager for materials management curriculum, which included training GM suppliers. She also was project manager for Ford Motor Company's Failure Mode Effects Analysis curriculum development. From 1978 to 1986, Darlene was on the faculty of Marygrove College as director of the Learning Skills Center.

She is active in the Michigan Chapter and a member of the International Society for Performance Improvement (ISPI). In the American Society for Training and Development (ASTD), she is a past-president of the Greater Detroit Chapter and a former director of the National Technical and Skills Professional Practice Area. She received the ASTD National Technical Trainer of the Year–1992 award and the 1993 National Excellence in Leadership award for her work with the automotive industry. She is the lead author of the companion book, *Fundamentals of Performance Technology: A Guide to Improving People, Process, and Performance.* Academic Credentials: BA, Albion College; MSA, Central Michigan University; MEd, Marygrove College; MA, Michigan State University; and PhD, Wayne State University.

James L. Moseley

Dr. James L. Moseley is an associate professor of Community Medicine in the School of Medicine, Wayne State University, Detroit. He returned to his faculty position after 22 years of administrative experience in medical education. Jim is a specialist in educational gerontology and teaches Gerontological Health Care, Designing Instruction for Older Learners, and Community/Public Health. He also enjoys full faculty graduate status in Wayne State's College of Education. He teaches Human Performance Technology and Program Evaluation there and he directs and serves on dissertation committees. Jim has received teaching awards and service awards from the University and from professional organizations. Before his university affiliation, he was a successful high school English teacher, a director of guidance, and principal of two different high schools. He served as President of the International Society of WORKSHOP WAY® EDUCATORS and as president of the Michigan Society of Gerontology.

Jim is a member of the local and international chapters of ISPI and he has published in the organization's journals and monographs. He is also a member of ASTD. He has conducted workshops at the conferences of both organizations and he has consulted in a variety of settings. Jim is a co-author for the companion book, *Fundamentals of Performance Technology: A Guide to Improving People, Process, and Performance.*Academic Credentials: AB, MA, University of Detroit; MSA, Central Michigan University; MSLS, MEd, EdS, and EdD, Wayne State University. In addition to his degrees, Jim holds numerous certifications and licenses.

Joan Conway Dessinger

Dr. Dessinger is president of The Lake Group, Inc., a performance improvement company that she founded in 1989. She specializes in performance analysis, program and product evaluation, and designing distance learning. Her clients include national and international organizations including Ford, GM, Proctor and Gamble.

Before becoming a performance consultant, Dr. Dessinger designed, implemented, and evaluated reading and writing workshop programs for adult learners at the adult basic education, high school completion, and college levels. She continues her interest in adult education by designing and teaching a graduate course in performance analysis for the Instructional Technology Department at Wayne State University. She also designed and teaches a course on health care education program administration for The University of Detroit–Mercy and Madonna University. Dr. Dessinger is active in ASTD and ISPI. Since 1980, she has made presentations and facilitated workshops for over 50 state, national and international conferences including conferences sponsored by Michigan Council on

Learning for Adults, Michigan Association for Adult and Continuing Education, American Association of Adult and Continuing Education, American Society for Training and Development, International Society for Performance Improvement, and the International Coalition on Technology in Education.

Dr. Dessinger and Dr. Moseley have co-authored several articles on the adult learner and evaluation. In 1998, they co-authored a chapter on the Dessinger-Moseley Evaluation Model for ISPI's *Performance Improvement Series.* Dr. Dessinger also co-authored a chapter on evaluating satellite training in *Distance Training,* and a chapter on satellite distance training for Ford Motor Company's dealerships in *Sustaining Distance Training,* both published by Jossey-Bass. Dr. Dessinger is a co-author for the companion book, *Fundamentals of Performance Technology: A Guide to Improving People, Process, and Performance.* Academic Credentials: BA, MEd, Marygrove College; EdD, Wayne State University.

INDEX

International Society for Performance Improvement

The **International Society for Performance Improvement (ISPI)** *is dedicated to improving individual, organizational and societal performance.* Founded in 1962, ISPI is the leading international association dedicated to improving productivity and performance in the workplace. ISPI represents more than 10,000 international and chapter members throughout the United States, Canada, and 40 other countries.

ISPI's mission is to develop and recognize the proficiency of our members and advocate the use of Human Performance Technology. This systematic approach to improving productivity and competence uses a set of methods and procedures—and a strategy for solving problems—for realizing opportunities related to the performance of people. It is a systematic combination of performance analysis, cause analysis, intervention selection, change management and evaluation that can be applied to individuals, small groups, and large organizations.

Experience ISPI...Experience Value!

Website:	**www.ispi.org**
Mail:	International Society for Performance Improvement 1400 Spring Street, Suite 260 Silver Spring, Maryland 20910 USA
Phone:	1.301.587.8570
Fax:	1.301.587.8573
E-mail:	info@ispi.org

Printed in the United States
58362LVS00001B/7-30